CW00591467

Icon	Control Panel Applet	Applet Function	Setting
	Multimedia	Configures multimedia devices including audio, video, and CD	System
	Network	Configures the network adapter, protocols, and services	System
	PC Card (PCMCIA)	Examines and configures PCMCIA cards	System
	Ports	Specifies the communications parameters for serial ports	System
	Printers	Installs and configures local and remote printers	System
	Regional Settings	Sets up local language settings (language, keyboard, currency, and so on)	User/System
	SCSI Adapters	Installs and configures SCSI adapters and IDE CD-ROMs	System
	Server	Reviews and manages the properties of the Server service	System
	Services	Controls NT system services	System
	Sounds	Associates sounds with events	User
	System	Reviews and manages system settings	System
	Tape Devices	Installs and configures tape backup devices	System
	Telephony	Controls and configures telephony functions	System
	UPS	Configures the Uninterruptible Power Supply	

Windows NT™ 4

Workstation

KINGSTON UPON HULL CITY LIBRARIES

2 7 MAR 2001

COMMERCIAL & TECHNICAL LIBRARY

Sean Mathias,
Eric D. Osborne, et al.

SAMS
PUBLISHING

201 West 103rd Street
Indianapolis, IN 46290

UNLEASHED

Copyright © 1996 by Sams Publishing

FIRST EDITION

All rights reserved. No part of this book shall be reproduced, stored in a retrieval system, or transmitted by any means, electronic, mechanical, photocopying, recording, or otherwise, without written permission from the publisher. No patent liability is assumed with respect to the use of the information contained herein. Although every precaution has been taken in the preparation of this book, the publisher and author assume no responsibility for errors or omissions. Neither is any liability assumed for damages resulting from the use of the information contained herein. For information, address Sams Publishing, 201 W. 103rd St., Indianapolis, IN 46290.

International Standard Book Number: 0-672-30972-6

Library of Congress Catalog Card Number: 96-69058

99 98 97 96   4 3 2 1

Interpretation of the printing code: the rightmost double-digit number is the year of the book's printing; the rightmost single-digit, the number of the book's printing. For example, a printing code of 96-1 shows that the first printing of the book occurred in 1996.

Composed in AGaramond and MCPdigital by Macmillan Computer Publishing

Printed in the United States of America

Trademarks

All terms mentioned in this book that are known to be trademarks or service marks have been appropriately capitalized. Sams Publishing cannot attest to the accuracy of this information. Use of a term in this book should not be regarded as affecting the validity of any trademark or service mark. Windows NT™ 4 is a trademark of Microsoft Corporation.

Publisher and President	*Richard K. Swadley*
Publishing Team Leader	*Dean Miller*
Managing Editor	*Cindy Morrow*
Director of Marketing	*John Pierce*
Assistant Marketing Managers	*Kristina Perry*
	Rachel Wolfe

Acquisitions Editor
Grace M. Buechlein

Development Editor
Brian-Kent Proffitt

Software Development Specialist
Cari Skaggs
Patty Brooks

Production Editor
Ryan Rader

Copy Editors
Kris Simmons
David Bradford
Mary Inderstrodt

Indexer
Ginny Bess

Technical Reviewer
Robert Bogue

Editorial Coordinator
Katie Wise

Technical Edit Coordinator
Lynette Quinn

Resource Coordinator
Deborah Frisby

Editorial Assistants
Carol Ackerman
Andi Richter
Rhonda Tinch-Mize

Cover Designer
Tim Amrhein

Book Designer
Gary Adair

Copy Writer
Peter Fuller

Production Team Supervisors
Brad Chinn
Charlotte Clapp

Production
Mona Brown, Michael Dietsch, Donna Martin, Gene Redding, Dana Rhodes, M. Anne Sipahimalani

005.4469 RT
B38 907 2979
HCT 3/01

Overview

Contents

Part V Networking Windows NT Workstation

16 Installing Windows NT Networking 417

17 Windows NT Network Protocols 429

Acknowledgments

Pouring out of your head all of your collective knowledge and experience in a subject as complex and dynamic as Windows NT and computer networking into a readable and understandable form is an arduous task indeed. I hope it has been successful and proves useful to the reader. I must first and foremost thank Grace Buechlein and Brian-Kent Proffitt of Sams Publishing for their patience, support, and help.

I must also thank those who shared their knowledge and expertise with me, as well as supported me in my endeavor to be the best Windows NT engineer: Frank "Rocky" McJannet and Eric Wheeler for teaching me how to use a computer and Windows 3.1; Jon LeVee for introducing me to Daytona and setting the ball in motion; Derek Vincent and R. David Parker for being gracious enough to share their enormous networking expertise with me; and lastly, to Elsa Skinner for loving and believing in me. Oh, and let's not forget my best friend, coffee!

—*Sean Mathias*

Dedication

To my son, Riley, and the forgotten ones, the systems administrators. Silence is golden.

—*Sean Mathias*

About the Authors

Lead Author

Sean Mathias is a Microsoft Certified Systems Engineer in Seattle, Washington. He has implemented Windows NT networks into critical care environments running real-time patient care monitoring systems. He lectures at learning institutions and seminars on occasion and is on the Board of Directors of the BackOffice Professionals Association (BOPA), a fledgling organization of professionals specializing in the Microsoft BackOffice server suite. Currently he is the Director of Network Services for Online Interactive, engineering a secure, redundant network for online commerce. On rare occurrences of spare time he enjoys golfing, hiking, and cycling.

Contributing Authors

Eric D. Osborne is a senior staff member with the Department of Computer and Information Science of Ohio State University in Columbus, Ohio. He is also the president of Micro Efficiencies, a Columbus, Ohio based consulting firm. Eric has an extensive background in UNIX, TCP/IP networking, telephony, and computer and network security. He was one of the primary architects of the NT/UNIX integration project recently completed by the CIS department at Ohio State. He has been involved in the design and administration of large distributed computing sites since 1984. He currently lives in Columbus with his two children.

Pablo Geralnik is Flash Creative Management Incorporated's network administrator for its Windows NT LAN that includes Windows NT Advanced Server, SQL Server, Exchange, and IIS. Before joining Flash, he was employed at Fein Property Management, Inc., in New York. Prior to that, he helped to administer a mixed DOS/VAX system at Bernstein & Belsky, CPA.

Pablo is a Microsoft Certified Professional in Networking with Microsoft Windows 3.1, implementing and supporting Microsoft Windows NT Server 3.51, implementing and supporting Microsoft Windows NT Workstation 3.51, and Mail for PC Networks v3.2–Enterprise. He is also a Novell Authorized CNE, as well as a Novell sysop on the Novell Netwire forums. In addition, he is an editor for *Networking Central*.

Thomas Lee is a computer consultant and educator living in the UK, and has been working with Windows NT since 1993. Educated at Carnegie Mellon University in the U.S., he worked on two successful operating systems projects (Comshare's Commander II and ICL's VME) before joining Andersen Consulting in 1981. Thomas founded PS Partnership, a Microsoft Solutions Provider, in 1987 and is today a partner. He is a Fellow of the British Computer Society, as well as a MCSE, MCT, and MVP. You can contact Thomas at tfl@psp.co.uk.

Patrick L. Lujan is president and CEO of Luhan Inc., which encompasses Luhan Computer Services and Luhan Software Company. His companies specialize in developing custom

32-bit, C/C++/MFC-based Windows 95 and Windows NT applications for their numerous clients and marketing of their own software products. No programming project is too small or too big for Luhan Inc. The rest of the time, Patrick enjoys the outdoors, movies, reading, and staying in top physical and mental shape. He can be reached by e-mail on the Internet at Luhan@nmhu.campus.mci.net or on CompuServe at 104033.366@compuserve.com.

Jefferson M. Mousseau (jeffm@io.org) was educated at the University of Toronto's Trinity College. Currently he lives in Toronto, Canada where he works for Clearnet Inc., a wireless PCS telecommunications company. There he takes care of network security, which includes firewalls, Cisco routers, and SecurID access servers. He is also in charge of Internet connectivity and enterprise messaging. He spends his spare time with his wife, Orie; his son, A.J.; his daughter, Sloane; and close friends, A.L., C.M., and L.B.

Tim Parker is an Ottawa-based consultant and technical writer. He has written more than 1,000 feature articles and 20 books, covering all aspects of the computer industry. Tim is the Technical Editor for *SCO World Magazine*, a columnist with *Canadian Computer Reseller*, the Editor of *UNIQUE: The UNIX Systems Information Source*, and a contributing editor to many magazines including *UNIX Review, HP Professional, Windows NT Systems, Dr. Dobb's, Web Techniques*, and *Advanced Systems Magazine*. As a consultant, Tim has worked with many large corporations and law enforcement organizations, including the US Navy, Royal Canadian Mounted Police, NorTel, Wang, IBM, and others. When not writing or consulting, Tim can be found flying his own plane, diving in the Caribbean, or whitewater kayaking. At other times, he likes to disassemble his network of 30 PC and UNIX workstations and reassemble them, always finding a few bits left over that can't really have mattered much. Tim can be reached at tparker@tpci.com.

Howard M. Swope III wrote his first computer program at the age of 10. Since that time, the study of computers has been a pursuit of love and fascination. Howard studied computers and information technologies throughout his school years. He has been working commercially for the last eight years, doing everything from running mainframe cable, to programming, to network administration. In October of 1994, Howard founded HMS Designs, a company specializing in software design and microcomputer services. Presently, he spends most of his time as CIO of the Wellness Web, an award-winning patient care site on the Internet. Howard has been an advocate and student of Windows NT since its release.

Viktor Toth, 33, is a Hungarian-born author and self-employed software developer. In 1979, he wrote the first Hungarian-language book on Erno Rubik's Magic Cube. Before moving to Canada in 1987, he wrote a professional reference on the Commodore 16 home computer. In the meantime, he worked on a variety of software development projects in the areas of scientific computing, real-time processing, and database applications for clients in Hungary, Austria, Germany, and the United Kingdom. In Canada, Viktor participated in consulting projects for the Canadian government and other international assignments. He also continued his career as a software developer (which he enjoys the most), writing his first Windows application in 1990. Currently, he is working on a product catalog and project-planning application for a manufacturer of air conditioning equipment.

Viktor is the author of *Visual C++ 4 Unleashed* and the co-author of *Windows 95 Programming Unleashed*, both from Sams Publishing. He lives with his wife in Canada's beautiful but cold capital, Ottawa, surrounded by several hundred pounds of computing equipment (his), knitting yarn (hers), and books. All they need is some cats added to the family inventory.

Thomas Wölfer was born some years ago. Not much has happened since, but he currently plans to get a life. If possible, this would not include software development for civil engineers, which is what some people think is his current job. Thomas can be contacted at woelfer@muc.de.

Tell Us What You Think!

As a reader, you are the most important critic and commentator of our books. We value your opinion and want to know what we're doing right, what we could do better, what areas you'd like to see us publish in, and any other words of wisdom you're willing to pass our way. You can help us make strong books that meet your needs and give you the computer guidance you require.

Do you have access to CompuServe or the World Wide Web? Then check out our CompuServe forum by typing GO SAMS at any prompt. If you prefer the World Wide Web, check out our site at http://www.mcp.com.

> **NOTE**
>
> If you have a technical question about this book, call the technical support line at (800) 571-5840, ext. 3668.

As the team leader of the group that created this book, I welcome your comments. You can fax, e-mail, or write me directly to let me know what you did or didn't like about this book—as well as what we can do to make our books stronger. Here's the information:

FAX: 317/581-4669
E-mail: opsys_mgr@sams.mcp.com
Mail: Dean Miller
        Comments Department
        Sams Publishing
        201 W. 103rd Street
        Indianapolis, IN 46290

Introduction

Windows, Windows everywhere! Unless you are new to this planet, you have probably heard of the Microsoft operating environment, *Windows*. Windows was a revolutionary improvement in the way PC users interacted with their computer systems. Historically, there was MS-DOS (and still is, much more than you might realize), which was implemented as a command-line interface. Using MS-DOS, you could give your computer instructions by typing them in one at time. This could be very archaic and time-consuming, and most potential computer users were reluctant to use this operating system due to its complexity.

The initial solution (or at least an attempt at a solution) was a new product called Microsoft Windows. It was supposed to change the lives of computer users and bring about an end to computing complexities, making computers more usable for the novice and the inexperienced.

To some degree, Windows' goal of easing the use of computers and shielding users from the DOS command prompt was achieved. However, through the succession of Windows versions, many problems associated with DOS remained, in addition to some problems that were entirely new to Windows. Keep in mind that Windows 3.*x* was only an operating environment that ran as an application on top of MS-DOS; it was not an operating system in itself. Although this was a vast improvement over DOS, the problems of memory usage and multitasking associated with DOS remained. MS-DOS is a single-tasking operating system, despite what you might have heard, which means that no more than one program can actually be running at a given time. If you are running Windows, that is the one program you can run. Within Windows it seems to be possible to run multiple programs at once, but looks can be deceiving. The reality is that at any given time, a single program is using the computer's resources and executing. You will notice that performance degrades significantly and proportionally to the number of programs you run (or try to run).

Another problem with MS-DOS was the use of memory. MS-DOS could not effectively address more than 16MB of RAM. When it was developed, this was not an issue because most systems did not have a hard drive that big! Over time, as computer hardware improved, this limitation became quite an obstacle, and it remained through MS-DOS 6.22.

Along with these problems, a more subtle problem arose. As the new Windows operating environment eased the use of computers, users began to see the potential for an even better and more robust system. Soon the users complained about the shortcomings of Windows and demanded more. In a relatively short time, Windows 3.1 was pushed beyond its limits with software applications that required a good portion of system resources and weren't always written to get along well with the other applications. Then came the introduction of the *General Protection Fault* and countless hours of lost work and productivity. Even the best of the best could not provide a consistent solution or explanation for these errors and system crashes.

As a result of all of these problems, after two years of shouting users and media hype, the fateful day came: August 24, 1995. This was the second coming of Windows—in the form of *Windows 95*, the solution to all of our problems. We were told again that this product would revolutionize how we use computers and that all of the problems would be a thing of the past. (Oh, and it would also bring peace to the world!)

Well, the second coming of Windows came and went, and the Earth did not open and reveal herself to us. But things did get somewhat better. No matter how you look at it, Windows 95 is considerably better than Windows 3.*x*. Yet, it still was not the answer we were looking for. Many of the historical problems with Windows 3.*x* were gone or masked, but limitations still existed. Despite what the media has said, Windows 95 is not a multitasking operating system; in fact, it is debatable whether it is an operating system at all. Underneath all of the bells and whistles lies MS-DOS 7.0. That aside, Windows 95 has greatly improved support for multimedia, networking, and a new thing called the Internet, along with a host of other features.

Now we must back up a little. During the course of Windows 3.1, another operating system was developed and released: Windows New Technology (NT) 3.1. It was delivered with far less fanfare than other Windows versions for some reason. Windows NT would be the foundation for the true answer users were looking for—robustness, stability, multitasking, excellent network support, and open systems architecture. Although the architecture was relatively sound and this was a good foundation, the problem with this new *operating system* (which uses no underlying DOS) was in its hardware requirements and speed. Consequently, Windows NT received little support or fanfare. So it was back to the drawing board.

Then, in the fall of 1994, Windows NT 3.5 was released. This was a remarkable improvement over version 3.1. The hardware requirements were basically the same, but after the period of time needed to develop the new version, they were no longer so incredible to consider. This version was markedly faster and much more stable, and it looked to be a viable solution in the business computing environment. Approximately six months later, Windows NT 3.51 was released, which provided support for the Power PC (NT already supported Intel, Alpha, and MIPS architectures) and a few other enhancements such as file compression.

Now let's return to the time when Windows 95 was released, in the fall of 1995, touting a new and more usable interface. Users were intrigued by this new environment, but too many shortcomings still existed to keep most businesses from being comfortable. The question of the hour was, "Should we use Windows 95 or Windows NT Workstation?" Windows NT had been building quite a name for itself over the course of 1995, and people were considering it as a viable option in the business world. Then, with the option of Windows 95 or Windows NT Workstation on the desktop, people had to stop and consider the dilemma of which one to use. The hardware requirements for Windows NT were only marginally greater than those of Windows 95, so why not go all the way and get the real deal? However, the new interface of Windows 95 was appealing to users, as were the new wizards and the relative ease with which the system could be configured.

Now we arrive at the present day—the fall of 1996. Users are closer than ever before to having their needs met. Microsoft has heard the cries of the masses. This is the dawn of Windows NT 4 Workstation targeting a corporate desktop near you. The new version of Windows NT incorporates the Windows 95 interface for ease of use, as well as many of the multimedia and networking features. The two operating systems look and feel so similar now that you might have to look at the Start menu to differentiate the two! Additionally, in the wake of Windows 95 comes a plethora of 32-bit applications that run on Windows NT as well. This opens the field to many new choices.

It is my opinion, based on extensive experience with Windows NT and countless users (and their problems), that Windows NT 4 Workstation is the right choice and the right solution for business computing. I further believe that many people out there feel the same way and are ready to deploy Windows NT 4 Workstation in their business environment, but they lack the knowledge and expertise to effectively deploy and support this new technology themselves. That is why this book has been written. Many small companies, or departments within large companies, do not have the luxury or the budget to have one or several full-time Windows NT engineers on staff to service and support the client population.

This book is intended to serve as a concise and comprehensive desktop resource and reference for power users and systems administrators alike. In this volume, we explore almost every aspect of Windows NT Workstation, we differentiate it from Windows 95, and we relate it to previous versions of Windows NT Workstation. I believe that this book is an indispensable resource for Windows NT users everywhere. Enjoy!

Windows NT 101

PART

I

What Is Windows New Technology?

by Sean Mathias

IN THIS CHAPTER

CHAPTER

1

A Brief History of Windows NT

In the beginning, Bill produced QDOS. And it was good. Over time, the computer evolved into a more powerful and useful tool, and with it DOS evolved. Gradually, DOS has improved and become the most popular and widely used operating system on personal computers. However, the major failing of DOS was that it required many steps to perform simple operations and was intimidating to many potential computer users.

Then, Bill made Windows, and we had a new beginning. Windows sought to hide DOS from the users and provide a graphical, easy-to-use method of navigating the computer and issuing commands with little or no knowledge of DOS. This opened the door of personal computing to the world at large. (Although some extremists claim the Macintosh already provided this functionality, I have never researched it myself and it remains unsubstantiated in my mind. Actually, Windows looks uncannily similar to the Mac OS, and much of its success in surpassing the Macintosh as the OS of choice is due to the application and marketing support of Microsoft.)

As with DOS and most other software programs, Windows went through a succession of revisions and improvements aimed at providing users with a better, more productive working environment. Windows evolved into a very functional and useful environment, but there were problems. The foremost of these was the simple fact that Windows was just a shell that ran on top of DOS and, as such, was subject to the limitations of DOS.

One of the more major issues was the inability of DOS and Windows to fully exploit more than 16MB of random access memory. As business applications were enhanced and given added features, this limitation became significant. Another issue was Windows' use of *heaps*, which are limited segments of memory used for the core system functions. Each of the three core Windows components—user, kernel, and GDI—was restricted to a 64KB heap that was shared by all running applications. It became quite common to receive Out of Memory errors due to exhausting a given heap, or General Protection Faults because one application attempted to use a portion of memory that another application was using, thus corrupting the data and crashing the application. The final problem was how Windows handled multiple applications running simultaneously. It didn't—at least not the way one would expect or desire. Windows was incapable of concurrently running multiple applications, so it utilized *cooperative multitasking*, meaning all applications shared one queue. If one application hung or misbehaved, it affected the entire system, often resulting in a system crash.

Then, Bill had a vision. He contacted Dave Cutler of Digital Equipment Corporation, who was the primary creator and developer of Digital's VMS operating system. He told Dave of his idea to create from the ground up a powerful, scalable, and reliable operating system for the next generation of computing. It had to be secure and integrate well into a networked environment, as well as meet a host of other requirements. And Dave came to Redmond.

In 1991, Windows NT 3.1 was born. And it was so-so. The concept and the ambitions were extraordinary, but it operated slowly. Very slowly. It required what was considered at the time an obscene amount of hardware. The Intel 486 chip had only recently begun shipping in quantity, and systems were much more limited in resources. Not to be entirely discounted, this was a major step in the right direction. Windows NT 3.1 eliminated the issue of heaps and applications crashing the system by utilizing a flat memory model and preemptive multitasking (in a sense, processes being segregated and protected from each other). But it lacked the performance and application support necessary for wide-scale acceptance and deployment in the corporate environment.

Some time later came *Daytona*, the project name for Windows NT 3.5. Between the time of the release of Windows NT 3.1 and Daytona, computer hardware improved significantly. Building large and powerful systems with abundant resources was now feasible and affordable for many companies. After much refinement and rewriting of the original system, as well as adding some exceptional new features, Windows NT 3.5 was produced. This was it. The original design goals had been adhered to, and some were improved upon, producing a true 32-bit operating system that was secure, reliable, and scalable. That, along with its native networking and preemptive multitasking, made it an attractive solution as a network server and ultimately fostered the ever-growing acceptance of Windows NT in the corporate environment, giving long-standing leaders such as Novell and UNIX (of most flavors) a serious new competitor.

Windows NT 3.5 supported three architectures: Intel *x*86, MIPS, and Alpha processors. With the release of NT 3.51, support for the Power PC architecture was added and the cumulative service packs and fixes from version 3.5 were integrated into the OS, as well as some additional features such as file compression on NTFS volumes and limited support for PC Cards.

Windows NT 3.5*x* has quickly proven itself to be a force to be reckoned with. Whether it is used as a network server or on a user's desktop, it is growing in popularity as the OS of choice for demanding users and mission-critical systems. The hardware requirements are still greater than Windows 3.*x* or 95, but the performance and reliability gained far outweigh the cost of the additional hardware. To users, this means that the loss of critical data at the worst possible moment due to system problems will no longer be a standard aspect of computing. To the administrator, it provides a common Network Operating System (NOS) that can be administered and maintained remotely, reducing site visits and user support.

This brings us to the present day. Windows 95 has been released to the public for nine months now, and administrators everywhere find themselves debating which OS to deploy. In terms of computing power, reliability, and room for future growth, the clear choice for the corporate desktop is Windows NT Workstation. That is what this book is about: Windows NT 4 Workstation and how to set up, administer, support, and use it. For end users and administrators alike, the goal of this book is to help you better use and understand this remarkable new solution called Windows NT 4 Workstation.

Improvements and Changes from Windows 95

Windows 95 and Windows NT 4 Workstation share many common characteristics. Some of the concepts and technologies for Windows 95 were borrowed directly from Windows NT 3.5*x*; likewise, some of the aspects of Windows 95 have been incorporated into Windows NT 4. The following section describes the similarities between the two—and, more importantly, what differentiates them.

The User Interface

At first glance, Windows NT 4.0 looks identical to Windows 95. Looks can be deceiving. Beyond the interface and some navigational similarities, these two operating systems are worlds apart.

First, the similarities. The obvious likeness is the desktop itself. As you can see in Figure 1.1, Windows NT 4 has taken on the Windows 95 user interface. The initial layout is identical: My Computer, Network Neighborhood, Inbox, Recycle Bin, and the Briefcase, along with the taskbar and the familiar Start button. Architecturally there are many more similarities, due mostly to the fact that much of the Windows 95 core architecture was borrowed and adapted from Windows NT 3.5*x* and *Cairo* (the next major release of Windows NT). Windows NT 4 Workstation has also included some other useful features of Windows 95, namely Wordpad (an enhanced version of Write), Internet Explorer 2.0, Autorun (automatically plays autorun-enabled CD-ROMs when inserted into the drive), 3-D Pinball, and the capability to dynamically change screen resolution without restarting the system.

FIGURE 1.1.

The new desktop look in Windows NT 4 Workstation.

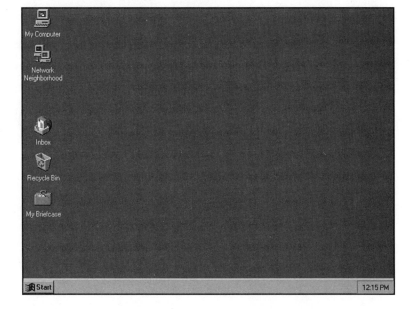

A Brief Tour of Windows NT

As with the Windows 95 desktop, My Computer is the container of storage devices, printers, and access to the Control Panel.

Network Neighborhood provides graphical browsing of your network (Microsoft, Novell, and others) and the capability to attach to various resources located on the network. The Inbox is the Microsoft Exchange e-mail client. This provides an inbox for various electronic-mail systems including MS Mail, MS Exchange, and Internet (SMTP) Mail. Third-party MAPI drivers can be added for other services such as CompuServe as they are made available.

The Recycle Bin is a welcome addition to Windows NT. This can provide some degree of safety against accidentally deleted files. If you have ever mistakenly deleted important files, you will appreciate this.

NOTE

Many administrators choose to disable the use of the Recycle Bin due to disk space or security issues.

WARNING

Files deleted through the File Manager or from a DOS command prompt do not go to the Recycle Bin; they are immediately deleted.

Another welcome feature of Windows NT 4 is My Briefcase. This optional component is extremely useful in synchronizing files between two computers. I have had extensive experience dealing with Windows NT 3.5x on laptops and, although it can be done, it is by no means clean or easy. My Briefcase is a helpful tool to synchronize files and/or directories on a mobile PC and another system such as a network server or docking station with a hard drive. This is an example of a well-received feature of Windows 95 that has made its way to Windows NT 4.

The Start button on the taskbar is just that—the place to start. This produces a pop-up menu identical to that found in Windows 95. The Shut Down option is used to initiate a system shutdown or allow the user to log off of the system. The Run command facilitates starting a program from a command-line prompt. The Help option provides access to system help files with full-text search capabilities. The Find option provides searching capabilities (locally and over the network) for files, folders, and computers. Settings provides access to the common configuration mechanisms such as Control Panel, printer installation and configuration, and the taskbar. The taskbar option enables customization of the taskbar and its behavior, the appearance of the Programs menu, and the option of clearing the Documents folder. The Documents folder provides quick access to the most recently used files for the logged-on user. This can be files such as Word documents, Excel files, or Internet locations, depending on which file types are registered with the system.

When you select the Programs folder, you see many familiar items. Here you find three more folders: Accessories, Administrative Tools, and the Startup folder. There is also an item for Windows NT Books Online, a good old-fashioned DOS prompt, and the Windows NT Explorer.

> **NOTE**
>
> What is the Explorer? That is a good question if you are not familiar with Windows 95. The Explorer, in the most fundamental explanation, is a replacement for File Manager. This can get confusing because you can still use the old File Manager. And whereas in Windows 3.x your operating shell was Program Manager (progman.exe), in Windows NT 4 and Windows 95 the operating shell is Explorer (explorer.exe).

Opening the Accessories folder produces more subfolders and programs. There is the familiar productivity killer, the Games folder, which has the ever present Solitaire and Minesweeper and a game called Freecell (a much more addicting variation of Solitaire). New to Windows NT is the Multimedia folder. This is another feature found in Windows 95 and brought over to NT 4. Here you will find a built-in CD Player, Media Player, and Sound Recorder, as well as a Volume Control—certainly nothing critical or earth-shattering, but useful nonetheless. Down the list, you find many familiar items:

> Calculator
>
> Character Map
>
> Chat (From WfW 3.11)
>
> Clipbook Viewer (From WfW 3.11)
>
> Clock
>
> Notepad
>
> Object Packager
>
> Paint (An improved version of Paintbrush)
>
> Print Manager
>
> Write

Several items were excluded from the preceding list because they merit further explanation. Included from Windows 95 is HyperTerminal, an improved version of the old Terminal program found in Windows 3.x. This is a long overdue and welcome upgrade, adding support for the more popular transfer protocols (namely Zmodem). There is also a Phone Dialer, one of the first telephony applications. This is basically a speed-dial program that enables you to dial out using your modem. It's not particularly useful or practical for most people, but I am sure there are some who will appreciate it. Finally, if your computer has TCP/IP installed, there is a Telnet item. This is a terminal emulation program for use over TCP/IP networks such as the Internet. It is a bare-bones version that is limited to the most basic functionality, but in the absence of another version it does the job.

Chapter 8, "The Administrative Tools," briefly covers the contents of the Administrative Tools folder and further discusses its applications. This folder contains the system maintenance and administration applications. Here you can do system backups, configure disk drives, manage users on the system, get specific information about the system, monitor performance, and view error logs. These applications are largely unchanged from previous versions but, as with Windows NT 3.5*x*, are often underutilized and not exploited to their full potential. These can be invaluable utilities to systems administrators and should not be discounted.

The Startup folder is identical to the group by the same name in previous versions of Windows. Anything placed in this folder will be run when a user logs on. Please note that items put in the Startup folder do not start when the system starts, but when a user logs on. If the user does not have sufficient rights to execute the application, it will fail. If you would like a program to start when the system starts, you must install it as a service and configure it appropriately. This is discussed in Chapter 11, "Windows NT Services."

Next is the *Books Online* item, used for browsing through the Windows NT 4 documentation on CD. If desired, these files can be copied to the hard drive for faster access or to a network drive for a shared copy available to all users. At the time of this writing the documentation files were approximately 5.5MB in size. The Command Prompt item is used to start a VDM (Virtual DOS Machine), which provides access to a DOS-style command prompt. Make no mistake—unlike other previous Windows versions, there is no DOS underlying Windows NT. A VDM is a 32-bit emulation of the DOS environment, provided by the Win32 subsystem, which is user-configurable as desired. This can be extremely useful in many situations, specifically for troubleshooting network problems. Finally, there is the Windows NT Explorer as mentioned previously.

The New Control Panel

The Windows NT Control Panel is very similar to that of Windows 95, as you can see in Figure 1.2. They do, in fact, share many common elements. Windows NT, however, has some applets that are absent in Windows 95. The following is a listing of the various Control Panel applets, each with a brief description of function:

■ **Accessibility Options**: Provides usability features and enhancements for people with disabilities. Support has greatly improved over version 3.5*x*.

- **Add/Remove Programs**: Provides the ability to uninstall applications cleanly and completely, provided the application vendor included an uninstall script with the application. This applet also provides access to Windows NT Setup (not the same as the setup to change mouse/keyboard as described previously). Here you can add, remove, and reconfigure components of Windows NT.

- **Console**: Used to customize the look, feel, and behavior of the Windows NT DOS-style command prompt.

- **Date/Time**: This is the standard applet to set the system date and time. A notable feature of NT available since version 3.5*x* is the capability to have the system automatically adjust for daylight savings time, if applicable to your locale.

- **Display**: Used to customize the desktop: color, wallpaper, pattern, screen saver, and font. It also has options to customize icon display and change the default system icons. Specify, configure, and change video display options such as resolution, color depth, and display adapter. This option is also available by right mouse clicking the desktop and selecting Properties.

- **Fonts**: View which fonts are currently installed on the system and add or remove fonts.

- **Internet**: Enable the system to be configured to access the Internet through a proxy server.

- **Keyboard**: Enable configuration of repeat key delay and rate and cursor-blink rate. Additional locales may be added here also.

- **Modems**: A modem wizard to assist in the installation and configuration of modems.

- **Mouse**: Configuration of double-click speed, swapping buttons, mouse speed, and animated cursors are configured here.

- **Multimedia**: All audio and video configuration is done here. This is discussed further in Chapter 10, "Advanced System Configuration."

- **Network**: Network installation and configuration is performed here. This option is also available by right mouse clicking the Network Neighborhood icon and selecting Properties. For further information, see Chapter 16, "Installing Windows NT Networking."

- **PC Card**: Used to add, remove, and configure many different PC cards for use in laptops, as well as to configure the PC card controller.

- **Ports**: An applet to configure communications ports.

- **Printers**: This applet greatly simplifies the installation and configuration of printers. Included is an Add New Printer wizard to assist in the installation of both local and network printers.

- **Sounds**: Applet to associate sounds with system events.

- **Telephony**: This is an applet from Windows 95, ported to NT. Microsoft is adamant about promoting the use of telephony (pronounced *tel-ef-any*). Here you configure the properties for your location and phone system and add or remove telephony drivers.

FIGURE 1.2.

The Windows NT 4 Control Panel.

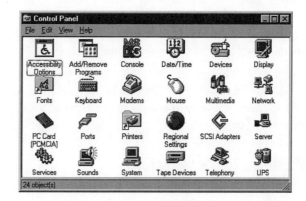

Most of these applets are directly adopted from either Windows 3.*x* or 95. The majority act identically or very closely to their counterparts, but Windows NT has an ever growing list of Control Panel applets that are specific to it. I will briefly mention them here and explore them further in later chapters.

- **Devices**: This lists all available and installed device drivers, their current status, and startup options. Devices can be stopped and started from here. Also, device startup options and hardware profiles can be configured here.

- **Regional Settings**: Locale configuration information is changed here. Windows NT natively supports wide character sets (Unicode), thereby making it possible to support virtually every country in the world natively. Language, number format, currency, time, and date can be set according to global region.

- **SCSI Adapters**: This utility has been moved from Windows NT Setup in version 3.5*x* to its own applet in version 4. This lists all installed SCSI adapters as well as ATAPI (IDE) CD-ROM devices and their respective drivers.

- **Server**: This is used to view currently connected users, shares available on the system, and files in use. Shares can be created or removed, users disconnected from resources, and administrative alerts configured here as well as directory replication service configuration.

- **Services**: This is a key applet in Windows NT, listing the services installed on the system and their state and startup options. See Chapter 11, for additional information.

- **System**: System and user environment variables are configured here as well as advanced options for virtual memory allocation, recovery options, and tasking. Further information is provided in Chapter 10, "Advanced System Configuration."

■ **Tape Devices**: Unique to Windows NT, this applet will scan for known tape devices, enable the addition or removal of drivers, and provide the properties for a selected device.

■ **UPS**: Windows NT provides native support for uninterruptible power supply devices, an integral piece of Windows NT's fault tolerance. This provides basic communication between the operating system and the UPS device, which facilitates sending alerts to appropriate individuals in the event of a power failure and shutting down the system cleanly prior to the battery failing.

Quite a list, isn't it? This goes to show just how extensive and well thought out this operating system is. Microsoft has designed Windows NT to meet the most critical and demanding needs of computing today and leave room for future growth. This is the operating system for the next generation of computing.

The Windows NT Architecture

Windows NT truly does have a remarkable architecture. Figure 1.3 illustrates its basic structure and workings, so that you can better understand just how extensible and robust this architecture model is.

FIGURE 1.3.

The Windows NT architecture model.

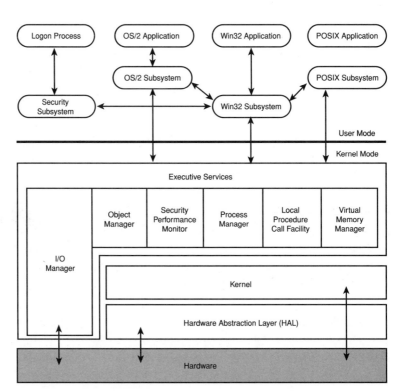

Windows NT is built in a modular design, which yields many benefits. This design enables third-party developers to write additional subsystems to further extend the capabilities of Windows NT. An example of this is OpenNT (Softway Systems), an add-on subsystem for NT that provides a true POSIX.1 and POSIX.2 environment, effectively providing a native UNIX subsystem to Windows NT. The exact reverse of this can also be beneficial. Subsystems that are not needed can be removed (except the Win32 subsystem), thus freeing resources and eliminating potential security issues or application problems. Another benefit is that replacement of a particular subsystem for a needed fix or enhancement can be achieved independently and transparently to the other subsystems. Due to the component model, the rest of the system will effectively be unaware that anything has changed.

I will touch briefly on the subsystems and their functions but not delve into the kernel mode systems except to give an explanation of the HAL. The Win32 subsystem is at the core of the user mode systems. It is responsible for handling all of the user input via keyboard, mouse, or other input device, as well as output to the display or printer. It also handles DOS-based applications through a 32-bit Virtual DOS Machine (VDM). Due to its preemptive multitasking, it is almost impossible for an application to hang the entire system. Provisions are made to kill a given process without affecting the rest of the system if an application stops responding.

Win16 applications are handled by the Win16 subsystem. Most Win16 applications operate normally under Windows NT, with the exception of those applications requiring low-level access to hardware, which is not allowed under Windows NT. Most hardware requests must be processed by the Hardware Abstraction Layer (HAL). This is the reason many communications programs (specifically fax programs) that were written for Windows 3.*x* do not function properly under NT.

The OS/2 and POSIX subsystems are for their respective application environments under NT. OS/2 support is limited to version 1.3 or earlier character-based applications. The security subsystem is fairly straightforward in its function. It interacts with the Win32 subsystem for initial logon and for security context checks when the user attempts to access an object or initiate a process.

> **NOTE**
>
> Windows NT 4 has a 486 emulator for RISC-based systems, allowing them to run Win16-
> and Win32-based applications not specifically designed for RISC systems. This was not
> possible prior to NT 4 because there was only a 286 emulator.

For most intents and purposes, a low-level understanding of the NT architecture is unnecessary. A fundamental understanding of the modular architecture and function of the subsystems is all that is required to successfully use and administer Windows NT.

File Systems and Security

Windows NT currently supports three file systems: FAT, NTFS, and CDFS. This feature, too, is modular and extensible. If a new file system is developed or a current file system is changed significantly, all that is required to support it is a new file-system driver for Windows NT. The following sections review the currently supported file systems, with a brief description of each and their advantages and disadvantages.

FAT (File Allocation Table)

This is the traditional DOS-file format. It has proven to be fairly stable and reliable, and developers are accustomed to working with this model, but it is very limited given today's storage and user requirements. The FAT file system does not accommodate large files too well. Also, Windows NT fault-tolerance features are not supported on FAT partitions. Additionally, FAT provides no support for Windows NT security. To support a dual-boot configuration (more than one operating system on a single computer), at least one FAT partition must be used for the boot loader and the second operating system. Also, RISC-based Windows NT systems must use FAT for the boot partition.

CDFS (CD-ROM File System)

CDFS is the file system used by Windows NT to read and access CD-ROM drives. This is the same file system that was implemented in Windows NT 3.5x for accessing CD-ROM volumes. In addition to standard CD-ROM format, Windows NT CDFS also provides support for bootable CD-ROM volumes, provided the system BIOS supports it also.

NTFS (New Technology File System)

If you delve into what makes up NTFS, it is truly a remarkable file system. It is extensible, as is the NT architecture. It was designed to support additional attributes in the future if necessary. It is modeled more like a database than a traditional file system, in order to facilitate and enhance the fault tolerance of Windows NT. Suppose, for instance, that a server with NTFS partitions is turned off in the middle of servicing several network requests. NTFS maintains something similar to a state table in a database; so when power is restored, it runs the chkdsk utility to verify the drive integrity and then checks its file structure and restores to their last known good state any files that were open when it went down.

NTFS also has native support for Windows NT security attributes and auditing of file access. NTFS is optimized for drives larger than 400 megabytes and will natively support DOS and Windows applications. The down side, if it can be considered that, is that in a dual-boot configuration the alternate operating system will not be able to access the NTFS partition. This is not an issue over a network because the translation is handled by the network redirector; this applies only to foreign operating systems on the same machine.

NOTE

Windows NT no longer supports the OS/2 file system HPFS. Windows NT 4 cannot access a drive formatted with HPFS; if you have a previous version of Windows NT installed on an HPFS partition, setup will not be able to upgrade it.

You can use the convert program from previous Windows NT versions to convert the partition to NTFS, but the convert program included with Windows NT 4 does not provide this functionality. Additionally, convert will work only on HPFS 1.*x* drive partitions smaller than 4GB. It cannot convert HPFS 2.*x* partitions.

An understanding of the Windows NT security model and system is essential. As before, however, low-level knowledge of it is not. This section presents an overview of the Windows NT security model and the authentication process.

The first thing a user new to Windows NT will notice when the system starts is the welcome dialog box, which says Press Ctrl+Alt+Delete to log on. This can be very disconcerting to a new user. The purpose of this key sequence is to defeat "Trojan Horse" crack programs. These are programs that simulate the log-on screen to capture a username and password when entered and pass that information down the network or write it to a file that could later be obtained to retrieve usernames and passwords. This process can be disabled, but it is not recommended or discussed in this book.

Windows NT 4 now supports log-on validation via dial-up networking. After pressing Ctrl+Alt+Delete, the user is prompted for a username, password, and domain. Typically, the user supplies this information and presses OK. Now there is a check box labeled Logon using Dial-up Networking. If this is selected, the system prompts the user for a Dial-up Networking account and profile to use, and validation is obtained from a remote server.

When a user account is created, it is assigned specific rights and a security level. This can be done explicitly, or by using the defaults for the type of user created. This information is stored in a unique security profile called an SID (Security Identifier). When the user logs on to the system and is validated, the appropriate SID is assigned to that user and will be used to check for appropriate rights and permissions each time the user attempts to access a file or network resource or to carry out some action. Virtually every action the user performs goes through a security-validation sequence.

NOTE

If a user's account is deleted, the SID associated with that user is permanently destroyed. No SID is ever reused on a given system. Even if the user is re-created using exactly the same properties, all of the user's file and directory permissions have to be reassigned as well as any network and system permissions. Unless you are absolutely positive that the user will not be returning in the future, it is a better idea to disable the user account for a set period of time and then delete it. This way, if the user returns in the future, it will not be necessary to re-create the user's security context and permissions.

This security behavior applies all the way down to the process and thread level. Each thread of each process associated with the user and/or an action on the user's behalf is executed in the security context of that user, unless configured to run under another account's context. It is quite an accomplishment to have developed such a comprehensive security model, and even more of an accomplishment that it has been optimized to have minimal impact on system performance.

NOTE

It is true that Windows NT is entirely capable of being configured to meet C2 security requirements, but it is not very practical. Because part of the requirements are that no networking software be installed, it is unrealistic to configure a system this way. C2 security, by the letter, almost dictates that a system be standalone, no network, locked in a closet. This certification serves more to illustrate just how secure the operating system is.

Multitasking

Windows NT is a true 32-bit multitasking operating system. It is true that on a single-processor system only one instruction can be completed at a time. However, given today's Pentium-based systems, which process upwards of 200 million instructions per second (MIPS), and RISC chips such as the R10000, which have demonstrated speeds of up to 1700 MIPS, this argument is no longer relevant. Multitasking in Windows NT refers primarily to the method in which the operating system handles multiple applications running at one time.

First, it is helpful to understand a little bit about how Windows applications work. Windows applications are not event-driven applications; they are message-driven. Windows applications generate messages and respond to messages. To facilitate this, the operating system maintains what is called a *message queue*—basically a stream of messages waiting for system resources and processing cycles, a response from another application, or the operating system. First, let's look at how Windows 3.*x* handled multitasking, then at Windows 95, and finally at Windows NT. This will help to demonstrate the progress Windows has made and will show how Windows NT surpasses the others in this area.

Windows 3.*x* is absolutely not a multitasking environment, despite opinions to the contrary. Because Windows 3.*x* is really just a shell sitting on top of DOS, and DOS is a single-tasking environment, it stands to reason that Windows cannot very well be multitasking. Although it is possible to have multiple applications open at once and even assign a priority to background applications, it is still a single-tasking environment. Anyone who has ever spooled a print job in the background has noticed a significant performance degradation. This is due to the print job dominating the message queue while processing, rendering, spooling, and finally printing the job. Windows 3.*x* uses a single message queue and one shared memory pool. Because of this, if one application hangs or crashes, usually the rest of the system follows shortly thereafter. If the application is hung, it basically jams the message queue and no other applications can process their messages, usually resulting in the user having to violently reboot the system with the three fingered salute, Ctrl+Alt+Del. The other aspect is the shared memory pool. Because all applications share the same memory pool, it is very common for one application to try to use memory that is already allocated to another application or even the operating system, generally resulting in a General Protection Fault (GPF). Sometimes these are recoverable, but most often the system is unstable after this and needs to be rebooted.

Windows 95 has done a lot to alleviate the majority of these problems but still suffers some of the same shortcomings. As mentioned earlier, Windows 95 has mostly overcome the heap limits of Windows 3.*x*. Thus, it is uncommon to receive Out of Memory errors. Although it is still possible to receive these errors, it is usually due to a problem with the application and not Windows 95. Windows 95 falls between Windows 3.*x* and Windows NT in the way it multitasks.

Although not a true 32-bit multitasking environment, Windows 95 is a move in the right direction. In Windows 95, Win32 applications each have their own message queue, but Win16 applications still share a common message queue. This means that the Win32 applications preemptively multitask among themselves. Likewise, VDMs preemptively multitask with the Win32 applications. The Win16 applications cooperatively multitask among themselves, with all Win16 applications sharing a common queue.

Suppose there are three Win32 applications, two Win16 applications, and two VDMs running. In a conceptually clockwise fashion (see Figure 1.4), each Win32 application and VDM has the opportunity to process a message, and one Win16 application has the opportunity to process a message (whichever application is next in the queue).

Referring to Figure 1.4, the message processing sequence would be as follows: 1, 2, 3, 4, 5, 1, 2, 3, 4, 6. This is how it works when everything is running smoothly and each process is running with the same priority. If needed, the system can increase or decrease a process's priority and allocate more processing time to another process, preempting the others (thus the name). In the event that a Win16 application will not release control of the Win16 queue, two scenarios are probable. Either that application will continue to process every time the Win16 queue has the opportunity for system resources, or the queue will hang, potentially crashing the Win16 applications. If a Win32 application hangs, the remaining applications continue to function properly because each has its own queue, as do the VDMs. The benefit here is that if a single application hangs or misbehaves, it should not affect the rest of the system too drastically. Windows 95 also provides a feature of Windows NT, the Task Manager. By pressing the Ctrl+Alt+Del key sequence, a task list is brought up that enables you to terminate an application no longer responding to the system.

FIGURE 1.4.

An illustration of the Windows NT multitasking model.

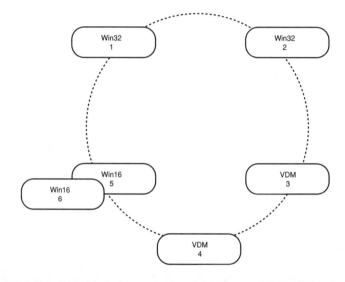

> **NOTE**
>
> Each Win16 application has one thread, each VDM has two threads, and each Win32 application has at least one thread (and possibly more, depending on the application).

In Windows 95, as with NT, each process can address up to 4GB of virtual memory, thus alleviating the Out of Memory errors for the most part. Of this 4GB of virtual memory, 2GB is system-addressable memory and 2GB is application-addressable memory. Obviously, most systems do not have this much memory. This is the theoretical limit that each process can map to. The Virtual Memory Manager (VMM) in Windows 95 uses demand paging to page memory to and from disk as needed, optimizing system performance.

As with Windows 95, Windows NT provides each application process with a 4GB virtual-memory address space and utilizes demand paging in the same fashion (demand paging was adopted from Windows NT into Windows 95). Being a true 32-bit environment, Windows NT uses a single Virtual Machine (VM) to run Win16 applications, just as it runs an emulator for OS/2 and POSIX applications. If you recall, the Win32 subsystem is at the core of the user-mode environment. The Win16 subsystem is coordinated and scheduled by the Win32 sub-system. As with Windows 95, Windows NT preemptively multitasks Win32 applications. The key difference is in how it handles Win16 applications.

Win16 applications are multitasked in the same fashion as in Windows 95, all being queued in a single VM and cooperatively multitasking among themselves. However, Windows NT offers an option of running a Win16 application in a separate memory space. This allows Win16 applications to have their own virtual address space, eliminating the possibility of one application violating another application's address space and corrupting it. The primary reason for the limitation on Win16 applications and multitasking is to have backward compatibility. This will be less of an issue in the future, because most popular applications now have 32-bit versions available. As with Windows 95, applications can be forcibly terminated if necessary by using the task list. The task list in NT 4 is brought up either by right-clicking the task bar and choosing Task Manager or by using the Ctrl+Alt+Del key sequence and selecting Task Manager. You can then select the application and choose End Task.

Overview of Windows NT's Advanced Features

This section briefly describes some of the advanced features of Windows NT 4. This is to serve as an outline of the functionality that Windows NT offers. These features are explored in more detail in Chapter 11 and Chapters 15 through 22.

Windows NT Networking

A major feature of Windows NT is its native networking support. Being one of the original design goals, network support is built into the operating system itself, providing a high degree of integration.

Natively, Windows NT Workstation supports many protocols and services for seamless network integration, even in heterogeneous environments. The following are the standard supported protocols:

- AppleTalk
- DLC
- NetBEUI
- NWLink IPX/SPX
- TCP/IP

Additionally, Windows NT 4 Workstation provides a host of different network services:

- Client Service for NetWare (NDS aware)
- FTP server
- Microsoft TCP/IP printing support

- Network monitor agent
- Remote access service
- RPC configuration (and RPC support for Banyan)
- SAP agent
- SNMP service
- PPTP client (point-to-point tunneling protocol)
- Peer Web Services

Clearly, Windows NT Workstation is capable of being integrated into almost any existing network.

> **NOTE**
>
> The client service for NetWare provides file and print support for NetWare 3.x and 4.x servers, and it allows for security authentication by NetWare servers and the execution of logon scripts. It does not, however, support NetAdmin or NWAdmin at the time of this writing. The Client Service for NetWare is discussed in Chapter 17.

The Network Monitor agent allows a remote server computer running Microsoft's Network Monitor to attach to the system running the agent and monitor another portion of the network. The RPC support has been improved to provide support for RPC on Banyan networks in addition to TCP/IP-based networks. The SAP agent is for use with NetWare networks to broadcast available services and resources, and the SNMP service is for use on TCP/IP networks with monitoring applications that can respond to or monitor SNMP traps.

Windows NT 4 Workstation supports up to 10 inbound network connections and unlimited outbound connections (up to the limitations of the physical hardware of the network). The Remote Access component in NT Workstation 4 supports a single inbound dial-up connection, which can be useful for attaching to the network from a remote site. The RAS component can also be configured to dial out and serves very well as a dial-up PPP connector to an Internet service provider.

Windows NT 4 Workstation can operate in either a domain or workgroup environment. If it is on a network with Windows NT Server computers, it can be configured to participate in a domain to use centralized security accounts. It can also operate in a workgroup capacity for peer-to-peer networking, although this becomes fairly complicated if there are several NT Workstation computers—each will have its own set of user accounts and security database. Windows NT 4 Workstation can also use a NetWare server for centralized security and validation.

Fault Tolerance

Windows NT 4 Workstation supports the creation of volume sets, the combination of multiple partitions into a single logical volume, stripe sets without parity for improved disk access, and mirrored partitions.

Volume sets and stripe sets without parity must be formatted using NTFS. Existing volume sets can be extended as needed to include up to 32 separate partitions. Stripe sets can also include up to 32 partitions. Advanced disk features will be revisited in Chapter 23, "Storage Devices."

Windows NT 4 Workstation also provides features to support system backups and UPS subsystems that can perform a clean system shutdown in the event of a power failure.

System Capacity

Out of the box, Windows NT 4 Workstation can support two processors, up to 4GB of physical memory, and, at last count, an obscene number of terabytes of disk storage (more than 2000TB). There is no question that Windows NT 4 Workstation can scale to meet the most demanding needs of users.

Summary

Windows NT 4 Workstation is the clear choice of operating systems for demanding users and critical environments, with the capacity to meet computing needs today and tomorrow. With features such as integrated networking and dial-up support, an intuitive user interface, an advanced file system and architecture, and fault-tolerant options, this truly is the operating system for the next generation of computing.

Touring the New Features

by Howard M. Swope III

IN THIS CHAPTER

CHAPTER 2

A Summary of the New Features

The previous release of Windows NT Workstation, 3.51, had few new features. It was, after all, an interim release stepping up from the 3.5 to the 3.51 designation. A utility was provided for the detection and fixing of the Intel Pentium floating-point error. Intel's late detection of an error in its Pentium processors was the hottest issue in the computing world at the time, and it was of the utmost importance to the end user. Support for the Windows 95 common controls was added to NT. This eased the burden of software designers developing software for both the NT and 95 platforms. File compression for NTFS, the native NT file system, was now available. Increased support for certain PCMCIA cards was also added.

Windows NT 4 Workstation is a major revision upgrade jumping from 3.51 all the way to the 4.0 designation. Although it is termed the Shell Update Release, release 4.0 brings with it a slew of new features in its user interface, underlying architecture, application programming interfaces, and provided applications. Many of the new features are included to bring the usability of Windows 95 to NT. Other features address key operating system architecture and programming issues. Several features expected to be released with NT 4 will be released just following the operating system release, and others will be held over until the next NT release (code-named Cairo) slated for 1997. The following is a list, by category, of new and deferred features with a brief summary of each. The remaining sections of this chapter focus on several of the key new features in NT 4 Workstation.

Interface Features

- Windows 95 User Interface

  Windows NT Workstation now has the 95-era user interface. New interface features follow an object-oriented approach stressing efficiency of motion. See the next section, "The Explorer User Interface," for a detailed discussion of the new interface.

- Plus! Companion for Windows 95 Features

  Many of the features from the Microsoft Plus! Pack for Windows 95 come standard with NT Workstation. Plus! provides visual, sound, and font enhancements as well as Internet automation.

- Hardware Profile Support

  Hardware profiling allows a user to choose a specific hardware profile at boot up. A hardware profile can designate different services, devices, and settings.

System Architecture and Operation Features

- Kernel-Mode User and GDI

  NT 4 now has the User and GDI components moved from the Win32 subsystem to the NT Kernel. This is transparent to the end user but increases performance in the area of graphics display. See the section "Kernel-Mode User and GDI" for a more detailed description of the move and its ramifications.

■ Network OLE

Network OLE and Distributed COM (component object model) allow software components to work with each other across a network. See the section "Network OLE: Distributed COM" for a more detailed description of OLE and the added network support.

■ Enhanced Metafile (EMF) Spooling

This feature increases network printing speeds by redistributing the work load of EMF rendering.

■ 486 Emulator for RISC Platforms

The 486 emulator for RISC platforms allows 386 enhanced mode, 16-bit applications to run on RISC machines.

■ Wins/DNS Integration

Wins/DNS integration allows for the resolving of naming differences between Windows NT domains and the Internet. This allows NT workstations to access NT servers over the Internet.

■ CDFS Enhancements

This new feature provides enhancements for CD-ROMs. It incorporates the autoplay feature and the CD-XA format.

■ NetWare 4 Client and Login Script Support

File/print capabilities and login script support have been added to the NDS client for NT Workstation. VLM support has been deferred until the 1997 release of NT.

■ Additional drivers

Many additional drivers have been added in the NT 4 release.

Provided Applications

■ Peer Web Services

Peer Web Services is a light version of the Internet Information Server provided with the NT 4 Server Product. Peer Web services provide basic Internet functionality for use in a peer environment.

■ Internet Explorer

The Internet Explorer, Microsoft's offering in the Web browser market, accompanies NT 4 Workstation. The latest release of Internet Explorer brings with it many avenues for interactivity and secure transactions over the Internet.

■ Microsoft Exchange Universal Inbox

The Universal Inbox is an application that lets the user do all of his or her correspondence from a single location. You can send and receive faxes and send or receive e-mail to or from several different types of networks—all from a single application.

- Windows 95 Compatible System Policies

  An administration tool providing for the management of NT 4 workstations.

- Windows 95 Nexus

  A set of administration tools to aid in the administration of NT Servers.

- Additional Applets

  Several other small applications are provided with NT 4. These applications include WordPad, a text editor; HyperTerminal, a small communications terminal; and Phone Dialer, a small application that dials your telephone.

API Features

- Direct Draw and Direct Sound Support

  Direct Draw and Direct Sound provide the ability to develop and run Windows 95 games and other applications that require direct access to sound and video hardware. It is implemented in a way that does not sacrifice NT's security.

- Telephony API (TAPI) and Unimodem

  TAPI provides the ability to develop and run applications that take advantage of certain telephony technologies such as fax and the exchange client.

- Cryptography API (CAPI)

  CAPI provides the ability to develop and run applications that require security in nonsecure environments such as the Internet.

Deferred Features

- FAX (will be delivered separately, following the release of Windows NT 4 Workstation)

  FAX refers to client software that facilitates the tasks encountered when sending faxes and cover pages, fax viewing, printing to fax, and so on. FAX utilizes exchange extensions allowing the fax client to coexist with other communications applications.

- MSN (will be delivered separately, following the release of Windows NT 4 Workstation)

  Support for The Microsoft Network.

- Plug and Play and Power Management (will be delivered in 1997 release of Windows NT Workstation)

  Plug and Play facilitates dynamic configuration of hardware devices. This does away with the need to set jumpers and settings manually for devices compliant with Plug and Play. Power management aids the user in managing and conserving machine power. This is of key importance to mobile computer users.

The Explorer User Interface

The most visible of the new features in Windows NT 4 Workstation is the user interface. So much importance was placed on the new shell that release 4 of NT has been termed the Shell Update Release (sometimes called SUR). Figure 2.1 shows the appearance of the Explorer interface.

FIGURE 2.1.

The appearance of the Explorer interface.

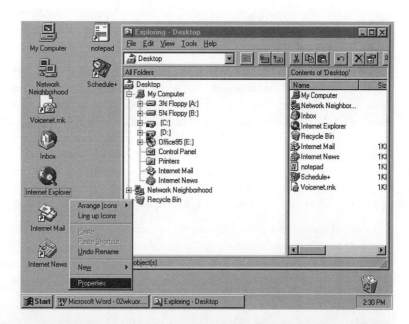

NOTE

The Program Manager shell is still available in Windows NT 4. However, its appearance and functionality have been altered. To change the shell of a particular machine, change the shell value in the registry under the following key:

```
HKEY_LOCAL_MACHINE
\Software
\Microsoft
\Windows NT
\CurrentVersion
\Winlogon
```

The value should reflect the shell that you want to use—explorer.exe for the explorer shell, or progman.exe for the Program Manager shell. (Theoretically, you could use any shell that meets NT's shell specifications.) Refer to Chapter 9 for information on the Registry.

The shell is called through `explorer.exe` and is therefore more properly referred to by the Explorer name. However, the interface connotes more than just the shell. It connotes a general appearance and style of use. This is why you hear the term *Windows 95 interface*. The *Windows 95* in this case doesn't refer to Microsoft's Windows 95 operating system, which premiered the interface; it refers to the 95-era windowing products from Microsoft.

The Explorer interface follows an object-oriented approach that stresses efficiency of motion and sight. It is much more user-oriented than its predecessor, the Program Manager. Despite its more elaborate and ornate appearance, the Explorer interface still has elegance and simplicity that make it very functional.

Object orientation is a concept that, like many of its uses, is abstract and has several levels of use. In the aforementioned instance, it is used in its most general form, meaning "of or relating to an object." Objects are defined as objects because they encompass several related issues of usefulness, which can be grouped under the idea of a single object and, therefore, are easier to work with. It is akin to words in a sentence. Individual words are not very useful except as explanatory entities, but words grouped together in a single sentence take on a complexity that is useful to the reader. The Explorer interface puts the focus on the object, whether it be a window, an icon, a file, a task, or any definable object. You can go to an object's representation on the screen and perform actions or retrieve properties for that specific object.

Efficiency of motion is a major factor in the new interface. Many actions that took several steps to perform under the old interface now take fewer steps or a single step. For example, you can close a window with a single click instead of a double click. This might seem like a minor factor, but when you consider the sheer number of times that this action and similar repetitive actions are performed, the importance of efficiency of motion is revealed.

Related to efficiency of motion is efficiency of sight. Efficiency of sight is also stressed in the Explorer interface. Icons, buttons, and menus have been shrunken, and much more can be seen in one glance at the screen than ever before. Because of this, you can open and close fewer windows, which saves time and movement. With more in sight at one time, you can see the bigger picture by viewing more objects and the way that they relate on the screen. All of this contributes to enabling you to deal with more complex tasks in one instance, which is why people invest so much money in these silly machines, after all.

Good software design dictates that a system should reflect to the user the real-world issues that it addresses, rather than the underlying computer science that allows the system to function. For example, assume that you are creating software to add two numbers inputted by a user. The two numbers that the user inputs will be stored in memory address A and memory address B until it is time for them to be added. This software should ask the user for two numbers to add, as opposed to asking for a value for memory addresses A and B.

The Program Manager interface dictates that only application windows or iconic application windows be open on the desktop window. If an application was running, it was running in an open window. If you wanted to run an application, you opened the Program Manager window. This was very simple and elegant if you were a computer (or someone who thought like one). However, most people work with items arranged on the desktop so that frequently used items can be reached quickly. Most people also tend to think more abstractly than the 1 or 0 mentality at the heart of the computer.

The Explorer interface follows a logic that is more complex and more intuitive to the user. The machine still receives the information and breaks it down to a few simple instructions for processing. The machine doesn't care how the information gets there; it only knows that it receives input, performs some action on the input, and returns a result. The user, however, works better if he or she can provide the information and get the information back in a meaningful way.

Personally, I have seen this in action. I was teaching a gentleman who was in his late forties to use a computer for the first time. He was not a computer professional and was not raised with computers. His relative lack of familiarity with computer logic makes him a perfect example. For the first month or so, he was using the Program Manager interface. Certain concepts just did not sink in. I told him that in order to accomplish task x, you must perform actions x, y, and z. No matter how many times we would go over performing a task, it just wouldn't sink in.

We eventually moved to the Explorer interface, and it was as if a light went on. Suddenly he was communicating with his machine in ways that were more natural to him. It made sense that in order to close a window he should press the X in the upper right corner instead of choosing Exit from the File menu. To him a file was information residing in a drawer in a cabinet and had nothing to do with closing a window on a computer screen. The letter X is always associated with negation, and he could see it on the window's title bar. He almost intuitively clicked on the X.

The improved communication between user and machine is best illustrated by a look at the main interface implementations. The next several sections of this chapter cover these items in a general sense. See Chapter 7, "The Explorer GUI," for a detailed discussion on usage.

Right Mouse Activation

The Explorer interface activates the right mouse button. Once impotent or used only rarely in specific applications, the right mouse button comes alive in the Explorer interface of Windows NT 4 Workstation.

NOTE

Usually, a left click on an item in Windows selects or activates that object. A right click usually provides further options for the object that was clicked. The additional options come in the form of a shortcut menu—a small popup menu with items specific to the object for which it was called. Figure 2.2 shows an example of a shortcut menu.

Figure 2.2.

A shortcut menu.

Right mouse activation is utilized in the object-oriented approach of the Explorer interface by tailoring the actions of the mouse click to the object on which it was clicked. Because you never have to leave the object in question, motion is conserved. The resulting shortcut menus are small and disappear after use, lending themselves to efficiency of sight. This approach is also intuitive because you expect options for a particular object to be available from that object, rather than from an obscure menu choice on a menu bar.

The Desktop

The desktop is considered the first open window of the system. Previously, in the Program Manager shell, only open application windows and iconic application windows resided within the desktop window. Under the Explorer interface, the desktop acts more like a folder. It can house files as well as two new additions: shortcuts and system folders. Figure 2.3 shows the new desktop.

Shortcuts such as the notepad shortcut in Figure 2.3 are program icons with advanced properties controlling program activation. The same properties and parameters can be set regardless of the executable that is activated by the shortcut.

System folders, such as the My Computer system folder in Figure 2.3, are also represented by program icons, but the actions that the system folders can initiate and the properties that they can have are dependent on the object they represent. The properties that are available for the My Computer system folder are properties relevant to my computer. If I were to view properties for Network Neighborhood, they would reflect network settings.

FIGURE 2.3.

The new desktop.

With files, shortcuts, and system folders residing on the desktop, it looks a bit more like an individual's desk. Items that are used frequently can be placed on the desktop for easy access. You can have a calculator, scheduler, and notepad out on the desktop. You can also place works in progress right on the desktop and then move them to a folder when they are finished. This method of organization is more akin to the way people are used to working. It is more complex and more intuitive than the old Program Manager interface.

The Task Bar

The task bar is a task management utility with running tasks appearing as buttons (see Figure 2.4). When you want to switch to a different task, you just click on the button representing the task and it is moved to the foreground. Under this system of task management, there is no more opening, closing, sizing, or hunting to find a particular window. If a task requires the constant switching of windows, the windows are only a single click away.

The task bar follows the principal of efficiency of motion. Task switching is done with only a single click, as opposed to the many actions that could be necessary under the Program Manager shell. The task bar also follows the efficiency of sight principle. It can be placed on any side of the screen, resized, and set to hide itself when not in use.

FIGURE 2.4.

The task bar.

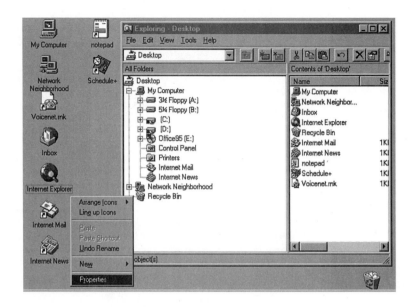

The Start Menu

The Start menu has received a lot hype in the media. It has been a focal point for a lot of advertising and is the subject of a popular Rolling Stones song. No. That can't be right. The Stones wrote that tune before the Start menu was in existence. Despite the hype, the Start menu, shown in Figure 2.5, typifies the user focus of the Explorer GUI.

FIGURE 2.5.

The Start menu.

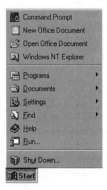

The Start menu itself is a popup menu and is out of sight when not in use. When open, the Start menu is a jumping off point for any activity. A user can activate a program, call up a document recently edited in any application, have access to all system settings, run a detailed search, or get help.

Never before in any interface has that kind of organization been brought to the end user. For those of us who are used to working with file managers, Program Managers, system utilities, and so on, this isn't that big a deal. We already know how to find these things. Imagine first-time users trying to initiate an action. Their first thought is not, "Hmmmmm, maybe I should double-click on a program item." A first-time user's first thought is probably more along the lines of, "How do I start this thing?"

The Explorer

The Explorer (not to be confused with the Explorer interface) is an application that provides management tools for an entire system. The Explorer uses a two-pane view, shown in Figure 2.6. In the left pane are icons representing your desktop, drives, system folders, and networked computers; in the right pane are the individual items contained within the selected object of the left pane.

FIGURE 2.6.

The Explorer.

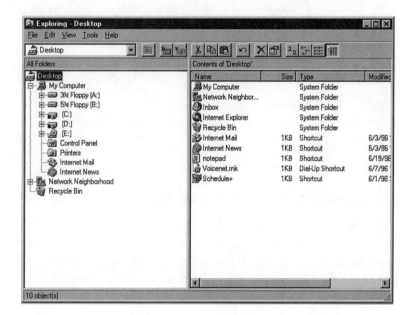

The two-pane view is quite popular and lends itself to efficiency of sight. The left pane holds a higher order of organization to give you the big picture; the right pane shows the lower order, or individual unit view. Applications such as the Explorer, which utilize this way of looking at things, are very efficient.

I have found that when working on a project, I need to listen to two voices within myself: the organizer and the doer. The organizer has to pay attention to the big picture and not focus on little details. Focusing on little details hurts the overall organization. The doer must focus on the task at hand and pay attention to detail. If the doer constantly focuses on organization, a job never gets done. The two-pane view within an application allows me to exploit both of those voices.

The Explorer has efficiency of motion, allowing you to navigate through the various objects of your system with a single click. A major advantage to this is being able to access a lower order of organization without leaving the selected object. For example, if you want to copy a file from the current directory into another directory that is not visible, you could navigate the Explorer to find the new directory in the left pane without losing sight of the file to be copied in the right pane.

The Explorer, like its namesake interface, follows an object-oriented approach. All available tools act on the object, selected with a left click. Properties are available for objects by right clicking.

> **TIP**
>
> Further options are available when moving objects if you right-click and drag the objects, as opposed to the traditional left mouse button drag.

Similar to the Start menu, the Explorer provides an organization to the end user. The end user gets a view of his or her entire system. The big picture is available to show how an object fits in with the rest of the system. At the same time, the individual, low-order object can be manipulated—and all from one location.

Kernel-Mode User and GDI

A major architectural change has been implemented in NT 4. The user and GDI components of the operating system have been moved from user-mode to kernel-mode. Except for noticeable performance gains, the change is transparent to the end user, systems administrator, and programmer alike. However, because of the magnitude of the change, the move warrants discussion.

As you see in Figure 2.7, the structure of NT can be divided into two sections: user-mode and kernel-mode. User-mode is made up of protected subsystems that run in separate processes, each with its own memory space. The protected subsystems provide the kernel-mode NT executive with user interfaces, programming interfaces, and execution environments. The executive provides lower-level operating system functionality. The two sections of the operating system communicate with each other through a uniform, complex message-passing schema.

FIGURE 2.7.

An NT component diagram from previous versions of NT.

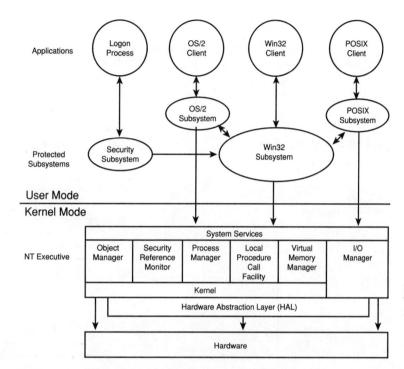

The exact nature of the communication system between the kernel and user modes isn't important for this discussion because it is of a fairly general nature. It is important to know that the communication, represented by the arrows in Figure 2.7, is implemented uniformly, and system resources are used in the implementation of the communications. The executive isn't concerned with which subsystem is sending a message as long it is using the proper protocol.

The idea of uniform communication is a constant theme throughout NT's internal communications. It provides for a high degree of security and modularity. Because processes can only communicate with the executive in a predefined fashion, the executive isn't subject to unexpected input or alteration, and it is therefore more secure. Also, because the communication is structured, the actual internal workings of the various components are not interdependent. One component could easily be switched with another as long as it follows the proper communication guidelines.

Although NT's internal messaging schema makes it easily changeable and secure, the level of abstraction that facilitates the messaging causes system overhead. An engine and data structures must exist to carry messages back and forth to the various NT subsystems. These structures take up memory and CPU time to perform their needed functions. Although they were highly optimized, the heavy traffic and shared nature of the user and GDI components under the old system made them ripe for performance degradation.

The user and GDI components of the operating system provide a large portion of NT's graphical capabilities. In previous versions of NT, these components were located in the Win32 subsystem, shown in Figure 2.8. Originally, the designers of NT planned to have the Win32 subsystem self-contained; but in order to reuse code and streamline performance, portions of the Win32 subsystem were used by other protected, user-mode subsystems. Refer to the arrows in Figure 2.7 for areas of communication with the Win32 subsystem. You can see that the heavy reliance on the Win32 subsystem, the increasing graphic intensity of modern applications, and the added overhead of a graphically intensive new shell can cause a great deal of traffic to this area to occur and is likely to eat up system resources.

FIGURE 2.8.
The Win32 subsystem in previous versions of NT.

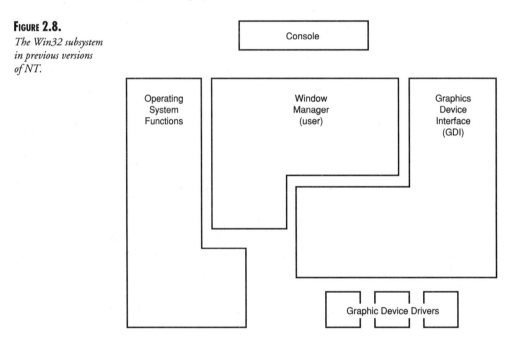

With the aforementioned concerns in mind, the NT design team moved the user, GDI, and related drivers to the NT executive. The result is improved graphics performance, smaller memory requirements, and a simplified Win32 subsystem. The new layout is shown in Figure 2.9.

Under the new design the user, GDI, and related drivers reside in the executive. The remaining portion of the Win32 subsystem is housed in the client/server subsystem. With the removal of the user and GDI, the client/server subsystem is much less complex, making it more efficient and closer to the intent of NT's original designers. The user and GDI—now in the kernel mode—do not create the vast system overhead that they would have if they used the complex message-passing schema required to maintain security in user mode.

2

TOURING THE
NEW FEATURES

FIGURE 2.9.

The NT component diagram from release 4.0.

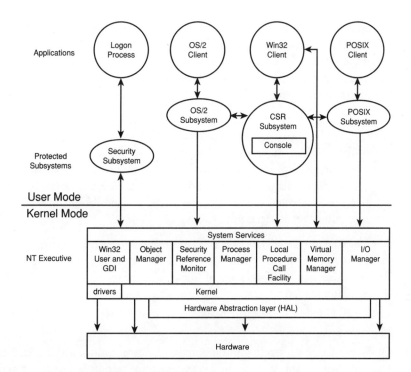

Network OLE: Distributed COM

Another major enhancement in NT 4 is the addition of Network OLE. OLE is a standard for communication between binary software components. OLE has not received the press that it deserves, but OLE has been evolving right along with the Windows operating systems. It is the technology at the heart of the evolution of windows into object-based operating systems. It allows for the integration of premade objects—regardless of creator, computer language, or version—into software and into end-user documents. Now, with the addition of network OLE, these integrated objects can reside on and be distributed across networks, including the Internet.

Originally, OLE (pronounced *O-L-E*) stood for object linking and embedding, which was the technology involved in making software that used compound documents. As the technology evolved to provide a set of interfaces and services through which components communicated, OLE began to be pronounced *o-lay*. Now it is common to hear OLE used interchangeably with COM (pronounced *kahm*), which stands for Component Object Model. COM encompasses the underlying technologies that allow OLE to function. With the recent addition of the technology allowing components to reside on and communicate over networks, you will often hear the terms Network OLE and Distributed COM.

OLE is a standard for communication between binary software components, which means that OLE provides a means for premade software components to interact. Neither of the communicating components is required to know the inner workings of the other. One component simply needs to have an interface to the other component so that it can request services or information from the other component. This interface is OLE.

OLE is likened to the technology that allows stereo components to work together. The turntable can be created by any manufacturer, and it can work any way that it wants. It outputs the appropriate signals to the receiver that, in turn, amplifies and sends the signal to the speakers. The speakers, too, could be made by any manufacturer and work in any fashion, as long as they receive the standard signal input and produce sound. Because of this, you can shop around and find the best sound system for your tastes. In a similar fashion, you can piece together a software solution that meets your needs.

Another scenario is to parallel OLE with current computer hardware standards. The hardware industry has many standards: for example, PCI bussing technology or VGA video technology. Because these standards are adhered to by manufacturers, you can use a VGA monitor made by any manufacturer with any video card that supports the VGA standard. If that particular VGA card applies PCI bussing technology, it can be placed in any machine that accepts PCI cards.

Similarly, if you are creating a hypothetical software solution to present company data on a series of global maps, you are unlikely to have the resources available to go out and map the world. You could easily purchase a map component that maps generic types of information. Because both the creator of the fictitious data mapping software and the creator of the map component adhered to the OLE standard, the map component could be used in the creation of the company data map software.

The learning curve, in this case, is relatively small because the software designers are familiar with the OLE standard and only the OLE specifics of the map component need to be learned. If you purchase a custom component (a component not adhering to a component standard), a unique interface must be learned. As the number of custom components increases, the learning curve increases over the life of the project.

The fictitious software could be written in any computer language that meets the needs of the project. The map component, because it is an OLE component, also could be written in the language best suited to the project of making an OLE map component. Because OLE facilitates communication on the binary level, the data map software and map component could work together even if one was written in C++, for example, and the other in Visual Basic.

Suppose that the developer of the map component came out with version 2 of its OLE map component software. The new version could be plugged into the existing version of the data mapping software without change. OLE requires backward compatibility. So now the existing software could have better, more colorful maps without any extra work. Then when version 2 of the data mapping software came out, the mapping software could take advantage of any new features added in version 2 of the map component.

2
TOURING THE
NEW FEATURES

The same power that OLE brings to the software designer can be wielded by the power user as well. A user can embed and edit from within an OLE application an object created by another OLE-enabled application. This object can, but is not required to be, linked to the original file housing the object.

For example, imagine that you are preparing a monthly financial synopsis. After typing a summary of the month's financial earnings in an OLE-enabled word processor, you can embed an OLE-capable spreadsheet containing the exact figures into the document. The spreadsheet can optionally be linked to the file housing the spreadsheet. If the spreadsheet object in the document is linked to the file housing the spreadsheet, any changes made to the figures in the spreadsheet are automatically updated in the document. Conversely, if you need to make last minute changes to the spreadsheet object, the object can activate its native application from within the document and make the necessary edits.

NT 4 adds Network OLE or Distributed COM. OLE has many such implementations, and with version 4 of NT comes the addition of Network OLE or Distributed COM. Network OLE brings with it the aforementioned characteristics of OLE, but now objects can be located anywhere on a network, including the Internet.

Suppose a software designer wants to create an application that uses up-to-the-minute stock data. The creator of this application could purchase an OLE component from an Internet stock service and use this component in the application. Whenever the application needs current stock information for whatever purpose, it navigates the OLE interface to retrieve the information necessary from wherever the stock service is located on the Internet. Figure 2.10 illustrates the layout of this fictitious system.

FIGURE 2.10.
The layout of a fictitious stock application.

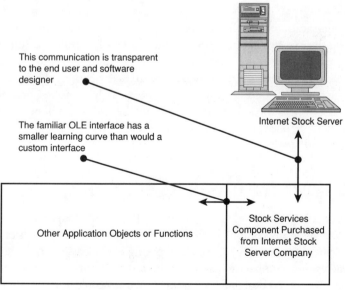

This communication is transparent to the end user and software designer

The familiar OLE interface has a smaller learning curve than would a custom interface

Internet Stock Server

Other Application Objects or Functions

Stock Services Component Purchased from Internet Stock Server Company

Stock Application Requiring Dated Stock Information

Similarly, OLE can be used by the power user. Imagine that you work in a financial institution that sends a lot of correspondence requiring up-to-the-minute stock information. You could create a document that embeds an object from software created by the aforementioned software designer. Each time the document is opened, a link to the stock software's object is updated, calling into the stock service to retrieve the timely data and updating the object in the document. Figure 2.11 illustrates the stock document scenario.

FIGURE 2.11.

*A document requiring
current stock
information.*

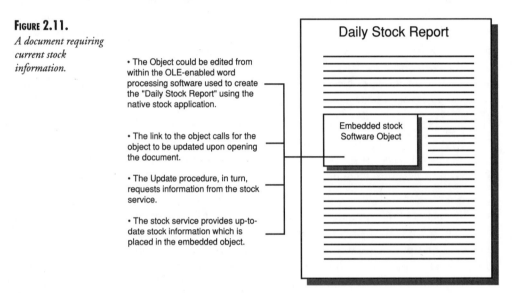

• The Object could be edited from within the OLE-enabled word processing software used to create the "Daily Stock Report" using the native stock application.

• The link to the object calls for the object to be updated upon opening the document.

• The Update procedure, in turn, requests information from the stock service.

• The stock service provides up-to-date stock information which is placed in the embedded object.

Daily Stock Report

Embedded stock
Software Object

The ramifications of OLE are many. This technology and technologies of this kind will be vital to take the next step in computing. Applications are becoming too complex to build from scratch. Too many resources are located in too many different places to manage. An object technology of this nature allows the multitude of resources to be codified and managed. OLE can provide for increasingly rapid development of increasingly complex applications, distributing their processes where needed. At the same time, the end user will be able to harness the power of complex applications in production-oriented tasks through compound documents and compound views.

Support for Mobile Computing

Release 4.0 of Windows NT Workstation adds increased support for mobile computing. Mobile computing is any computing that isn't done at a stationary workstation, or computing done on a portable computer. Mobile computing encompasses a wide range of implementations. Some users like to have a desktop at the office and bring work home on a notebook. People who spend a great deal of time traveling, such as people in sales, often have a notebook as their primary computer, and they rely on it for connectivity to the office when on the road. Other people use portable computers as data collection machines while visiting different locations, or they use them in the lab while working on various experiments. Often, users who use a notebook as their primary machine plug it into a docking station when at their primary location. Whatever the use, NT 4 has some handy features to help out the mobile user.

Dialup Networking

Dialup networking allows one computer to network with another computer remotely. The distinction between dialup networking and traditional remote computing is significant. In traditional remote computing, the end user often looks at a split screen, viewing remote and host data, respectively. Under dialup networking, communications between the host and remote computers are made as transparent as possible. Behind the scenes, various communications protocols handle the dialup-specific communications issues, while the remote user has the feeling that he or she is working in a traditional network environment.

Dialup networking can be used to connect to various types of machines and networks—for example, your office network or the Internet. The approach that dialup networking takes to remote computing is at the heart of the connectivity that has folks so excited about the Internet in recent times. The emphasis now rests with the information being communicated, as opposed to the engines or equipment that facilitate the communication.

Under the dialup networking scenario, remote connections to different types of networks are handled from a central location and handled in a uniform way. You could connect to the Internet or the office network over a phone line. The link can be initiated from one location or through the use of a shortcut. Figure 2.12 shows the methods for initiating a dialup networking session.

Different location profiles are available under dialup networking. You can set up different location profiles to use when dialing from different locations. You can specify the area code of a particular location and any dialing suffixes or prefixes. Dialup networking adds area code, suffix, or prefix to the number it dials, depending on the location from which the user is dialing.

Suppose a member of the sales team is on a tour of several countries to try to drum up business. The salesperson could dial in from a hotel to the office and conduct computing as if she were at the office. Obviously, the rate at which information is transferred is restricted by the medium on which that communication is taking place. At present, networking over a phone line is significantly slower than a standard network connection. Nevertheless, the salesperson could have access to her networked resources from anywhere with a phone.

To facilitate communications, the salesperson could set up different location profiles for each stop on her trip to reduce the overhead of changing calling numbers each time she arrived at a new location. If the salesperson is conducting business through electronic communications, she could connect to the Internet with dialup networking and send e-mail to her contacts at the other offices, informing them of timetables and related arrival times. At the same time, the salesperson could confirm travel plans or get information on the next location via the World Wide Web.

FIGURE 2.12.

You can initiate a dialup networking session from one central phone book or a shortcut.

Shortcut to Internet—
Service Provider

Central location for—
initiating dialup
networking sessions

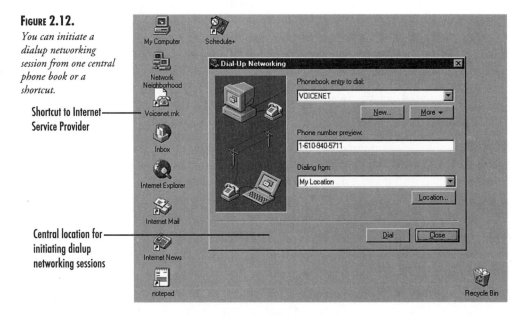

Briefcase

Briefcase coordinates the use of the same file on two machines. This is ideal for someone wanting to use both a notebook and a desktop machine. You can work on a file from your main desktop location, taking advantage of the niceties of the desktop such as a large monitor, keyboard, mouse, CD-ROM, and so on. Then, when the need arises to take that file on the road, you can drag it into the briefcase of a notebook computer for easy portability to different locations.

The briefcase requires that the two computers be connected via network or a cable to transfer the files. When connected, you can drag files from any location on the desktop computer to the briefcase on the portable computer. The notebook can then be detached and used on the road. The files in the briefcase will be altered with use. Upon returning to the desktop machine, the notebook computer needs to be reattached via network or cable. When it is connected, the original files on the desktop machine are updated with a click of the update files menu option. Figure 2.13 shows the process.

If you have to work overtime at home on a project from the office, you can drag the project-related files from the project folder on the desktop machine into the Briefcase on your notebook computer. Upon returning to work the next day, the original files from the project folder can be updated with the touch of a button. If you are collecting data on the road, you can drag your scheduler or contact management data files from any directory on the desktop machine into the Briefcase of the notebook to keep track of appointments or contacts on the road. Any alterations to these files will easily be updated upon your return. The data files from the data collection software, set up beforehand on the desktop machine, are dragged into the briefcase. The data is then collected and the data files are updated on the desktop computer for data collation.

FIGURE 2.13.

Briefcase facilitates the use of the same file when stationary and on the road.

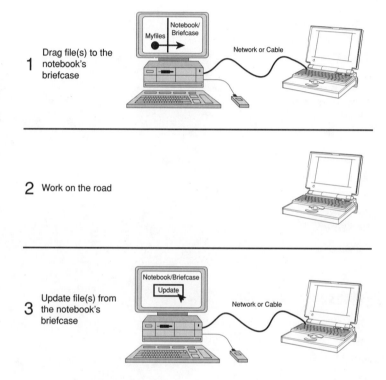

1 Drag file(s) to the notebook's briefcase

2 Work on the road

3 Update file(s) from the notebook's briefcase

With Briefcase, no copying or traditional file management is required. There is no need to find many files in many different directories in order to do updates, and the advantages of the desktop and notebook computers can be leveraged.

NOTE

The aforementioned file synchronization can also be accomplished by copying files to a local briefcase and copying the briefcase to a floppy disk for transport. However, in this scenario, briefcase size is limited by the size of the portable media.

Also, other cellular networking options are available that allow direct networked access to the files. These technologies are just beginning to be explored and are expensive. Cellular transmissions are presently not reliable and cellular modems are prohibited during commercial air travel.

Hardware Profiles and Docking Detection

NT 4 has the capability to set up different hardware profiles. Hardware profiles reflect installed devices and settings. Users can select a particular hardware profile at boot time, depending on what hardware is being used during the current session. NT 4 also has the capability to detect whether a notebook computer is docked and, if docking is detected, to select the appropriate hardware settings. Figures 2.14 and 2.15 show the dialog boxes used to facilitate hardware profiling and docking detection.

FIGURE 2.14.

The Hardware Profiles tab on the System Properties dialog is used to facilitate hardware profiling.

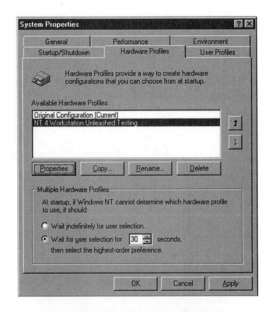

FIGURE 2.15.

Properties can be set for individual hardware profiles to facilitate docking detection and its appropriate hardware selection.

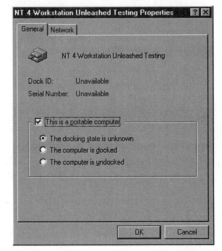

Suppose that you do a lot of work at the office and at home. Instead of using one of the briefcase scenarios from the "Briefcase" section of this chapter, you could use a notebook computer and docking station. At the office the notebook is plugged into the docking station. Attached to the docking station is a full-sized monitor, keyboard, mouse, and CD-ROM. NT 4 detects that the notebook is docked and chooses the appropriate settings to use the full-sized hardware components. Now the user has all the comforts of a desktop computer, but it's portable. When you leave for the evening, you detach the notebook from the docking station and easily transport the computer home. When the machine is used at home, NT detects an undocked state and chooses the appropriate hardware settings to use the notebook in the stand-alone state.

Another scenario in which you can take advantage of hardware profiling is when you use different hardware under different conditions. Perhaps you use a portable CD-ROM that plugs into a PCMCIA slot for various uses, but when not in use the PCMCIA slot is used for a modem. Under these circumstances, you could set up a hardware profile for both cases and select the appropriate one when needed.

The same example applies for lab-specific hardware. You might use a particular hardware device for chemical analysis but use a different type of hardware for monitoring temperature. You would set up a hardware profile for both cases. When chemical analysis was being done, you would select "my hardware profile—chemical," and when temperature-related experiments were being done, you would select "my hardware profile—temperature." There are as many scenarios as there are hardware devices and as many uses as there is imagination.

Internet Support Features

At present, society is in the middle of an Internet boom. Everywhere you turn (except perhaps the middle of a forest) you hear or see something about the Internet. But even the forests are affected by the Internet with its many animal rights and conservation areas. However, I doubt the creatures of the earth, except humans, care too much about the Internet. Nonetheless, if you are human and you watch TV, listen to the radio, read the newspaper, go to the movies, or read any computer literature, you will undoubtedly come into contact with the Internet.

Microsoft, sensing the growing importance of the Internet, has stopped on a dime and wholly embraced and extended the Internet. Microsoft has implemented plans to Internet-enable all its applications and operating systems. NT 4 Workstation is no exception. In the version 4 release of NT Workstation, several Internet support features are geared toward the workstation environment.

The growing Internet mania is bringing with it many new users and many new questions about the Internet, its use, and its ramifications. To dispel some confusion and provide further clarification, the next section of the chapter discusses the Internet in general, followed by an outline of the related features in NT 4 Workstation.

A Clarification of Networking Logic

Because of the sudden Internet boom, people are rushing to get onto the Net. They feel that if they are not connected, they are somehow being left behind. To a certain degree this is true. More and more services and information are being provided via the Internet, and there are no signs of this trend being halted. As folks are rushing onto the Internet, they are desiring instant knowledge and gratification. Because they want to know how to do something right away, their focus is task-oriented and they lose sight of what the Internet is at its root—a network of computers.

When more than one computer is connected and sharing information, the computers are networked. This concept is basic and sometimes overlooked; however, it is important not to lose sight of this fact. In order for two computers to be connected, a hardware connection must be established. In order for two computers to share information, a communications protocol must be in place to facilitate the passing of information over the hardware connection. After a connection and a protocol for passing information is established between two machines, work can be done.

At this point, the two computers have met each other and have decided on a medium for communication. Now the communication must move to the next level of complexity by deciding what subject the connected computers want to discuss and what language will be used to discuss this subject. Ideally, the subject discussed and the work done through the communication will fulfill some type of need, and the language used to discuss the subject will be appropriate to the subject at hand.

To facilitate performing some useful task with the now connected computers, a client/server model is common and is used on the Internet. In its simplest form, the client requests information and the server responds by returning the requested information. Suppose that I said to you, "Please give me a dollar." You then hand me a dollar. We both know the English language, and the dollar is a form of currency in many English-speaking countries; therefore, it is appropriate that we speak English. The need being fulfilled would be financial transactions. I would be the client requesting a dollar, and you would be the server fulfilling my request by handing me that dollar.

> **NOTE**
>
> More often than not, machines are dedicated for performing server tasks, while other machines are used as clients. This better distributes the workload involved in performing tasks. If you are performing many types of client tasks, you don't want to have your machine bogged down by servicing the requests of many other machines. Therefore, it is common to have unmanned computers dedicated to performing server tasks. This is why it is common to refer to a particular computer as *a server* or *the server*. Although many dedicated server machines are put together with hardware better suited for server tasks, it is a common misconception that the term *server* is somehow a hardware designation.

Now you have more than one computer connected, an established means of communication, an established language and engine to perform a useful task, and an efficient distribution of workload. Figure 2.16 illustrates this logic. Take this model and apply it on a global scale, and you have the Internet.

Figure 2.16.

The basic networking logic behind the Internet.

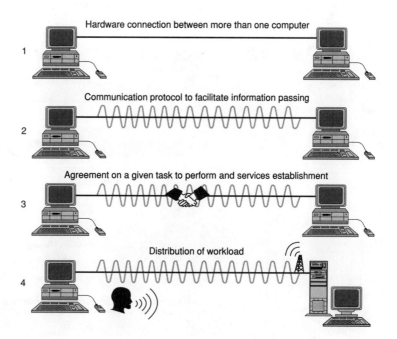

1   Hardware connection between more than one computer

2   Communication protocol to facilitate information passing

3   Agreement on a given task to perform and services establishment

4   Distribution of workload

The Features

NT 4 provides support for all steps of the networking logic model described in the previous section. The hardware connection to the Internet is made through NT's network adapter and modem support. NT includes Transmission Control Protocol/Internet Protocol (TCP/IP) to facilitate the passing of information over the communications medium. New to NT Workstation in version 4 are Internet Explorer and peer Web services, which provide Internet task-related services on both the client and server sides.

NT 4 supports, and previous versions of NT supported, a variety of network adapters and modems. You can add these devices through the control panel network and modem selections, respectively. Communications protocols can also be added through the control panel network option. The TCP/IP protocol used for Internet communications is included with NT 4.

The Internet Explorer is Microsoft's offering in the Web browser market. A Web browser and server use the http Internet protocol for implementing tasks related to the use of Web pages. The Web page gets its functionality through the use of Hypertext Markup Language (HTML)

files. These files, requested by the Web browser, present themselves as Web pages to the viewer. Web pages consist of text, graphics, sound bytes, and increasingly, multimedia implementations. One of the more versatile features of the Web page are hyperlinks, which provide jumping points to other pages on the Web. For example, if you are viewing information on cancer research, you might find a link to information specific to the prostate and have access to that information with a single click of the mouse. Figure 2.17 shows the Internet Explorer.

FIGURE 2.17.

The Internet Explorer is Microsoft's offering in the Web browser market.

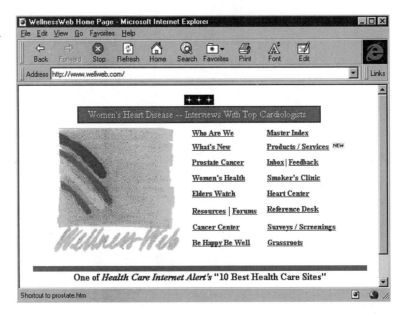

The latest version of the Internet Explorer, version 3, is a substantial improvement over previous versions. There is a new appearance, customization capabilities, speed enhancements, and a wide range of plug-in support applications and controls. This version brings with it ActiveX functionality. ActiveX is the name that is being used for some of the new technologies evolving at Microsoft for making the Internet more dynamic and interactive.

On the server side of Internet task-related applications, Windows NT 4 Workstation comes with Peer Web Services. Peer Web Services are a light version of the Internet Information Server provided with the NT Server product, and they provide server services for the three main Internet protocols: http, ftp, and gopher. These protocols facilitate Web page use, file transfers, and information search tasks, respectively. Figure 2.18 shows the Peer Web Services management utility.

Although Peer Web Services provide full Internet service functionality, they are geared toward working in the peer and intranet environment. Intranets are networks that are not connected to the Internet but implement services associated with the Internet. Because of some of the drawbacks to the Internet, such as poor bandwidth and security issues, many people are taking stock in intranets. The production, collaborative, and information-providing benefits of the Internet are being harnessed on company networks, which can provide better performance and improved security. Peer Web Services provide intranet capabilities on a workstation and workgroup level.

FIGURE 2.18.

The Internet Service Manager provides management features for the Peer Web Services provided with NT 4 Workstation.

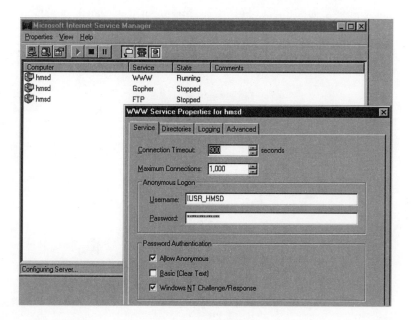

Summary

In this chapter, you got a quick glance at the new features in NT 4 Workstation, followed by a general discussion of the more important features and their underlying technologies. The later chapters of the book will provide detailed discussion on usage. Because this is a book geared toward a particular release, I tried to focus on issues and technologies that are important in general but also important as they relate to the present state of computing.

Release 4 is a significant upgrade. The new interface brought with it increased ease of use and an improved graphical model, an expected feature of Windows. NT's strong, adaptable core, seen in the relative ease with which the user and GDI move was made, heals the instability that was the major rallying cry of Windows detractors. Release 4 also brings with it an amazing amount of connectivity features that hold much promise.

OLE and Distributed COM give you impetus to take the next step in computing. In order to move forward, applications must be highly complex and connected, but created in a reasonable amount of time. As the divisions that communications boundaries hold break down and applications become more integrated, the strength of components will become increasingly important.

Similarly, we will have to strengthen the infrastructure on which communication takes place as we extend it. The embrace and extend strategy that Microsoft espouses is evident in the many Internet and intranet features provided in release 4.

NT is an operating system that puts design on an equal level of importance with feature count and cosmetic appearance. This is the reason for its elegance and stability. However, there is something to be said for a rich feature set and visually pleasing appearance. This release brought with it enhancements in core underlying technologies, which are the cornerstone of NT's strength, as well as beautification and functionality enhancements.

PART

IN THIS PART

Installation and Configuration

Preinstallation and System Analysis

by Sean Mathias

IN THIS CHAPTER

CHAPTER 3

For most users new to Windows NT, setting up Windows NT Workstation seems a strange and daunting task. Because Windows NT is an operating system in itself, there is no DOS from which you run the setup program and the setup routine can be very unforgiving (although this has improved greatly in version 4 over previous versions).

System Requirements

Before installing Windows NT 4 Workstation, it is advisable that you be somewhat familiar and comfortable with personal computers and, ideally, with the Microsoft Windows environment. It is not absolutely necessary, but it will significantly help if any problems arise.

Listed here is the recommended minimum system configuration for Windows NT 4 Workstation:

- Intel $x86$ or Pentium, Digital AXP, MIPS, or Power PC-based system
- VGA or compatible display adapter
- One or more hard disk drives with at least 117MB of free disk space on the partition that will contain Windows NT (124MB for RISC systems)
- For Intel $x86$-based systems, a high-density 3.5-inch floppy drive or a CD-ROM drive; for RISC-based systems, a CD-ROM drive
- For Intel $x86$-based systems, 12MB of RAM (16MB recommended); for RISC-based systems, 16MB of RAM
- Mouse or other pointing device (optional)
- Network interface card (optional)

That is the recommended minimum configuration as put forth by Microsoft. For most practical applications and usage, I recommend the following, more realistic minimum configuration:

- Intel Pentium or RISC-based system
- SVGA graphics adapter (2MB or more of memory)
- 2GB of disk storage space
- 4x or greater CD-ROM drive
- 32MB of RAM
- Mouse
- 32-bit network adapter

This configuration takes into account that you will probably want to run several applications concurrently and will expect good responsiveness from them. Considering the rapidly falling computer hardware prices of late, you should get the right system for the job. One thing to remember about Windows NT 4 Workstation is that it has high hardware requirements, but if you give it what it wants, you will not find a better working environment.

Ultimately, the hardware requirements vary by user depending on what the workstation is used for. My preceding recommendation is a good, general-purpose starting point. This can be augmented to accommodate the needs of a user after the initial configuration has been tested.

Preparing for Setup

Now that you have the hardware you need, you can move down the list and make sure that you are prepared. It is very disheartening and frustrating to be in a position where you are setting up a new operating system, about which you might know nothing, and have something go wrong. It is well worth the time to prepare for any possible glitches beforehand.

First, always read the release notes and the README.TXT file. I am terrible about doing this, and I have suffered the consequences more than once, so listen up—I'm giving pearls here.

Next, whenever possible, make a backup of at least all your data files (those you created with applications such as Word or Excel) or, ideally, the entire system. This is a precautionary measure in the event that something goes drastically wrong. Better safe than sorry! You can back up to a tape drive or a network drive. I don't recommend backing up to a floppy disk unless you have only a small amount of data files.

Just to be on the safe side, have available the *Windows NT Workstation Installation Guide*, a set of MS-DOS disks (for worst-case scenarios), a copy of your previous working environment (Windows 3.*x* or Windows 95), and finally, the number for technical support (found in the Windows NT Workstation documentation). As of this writing, users are given one free call for installation technical support. This information can be found in the documentation also.

Introducing the Hardware Compatibility List (HCL)

With Windows NT comes something called the Hardware Compatibility List. This is a list of hardware and devices that have been tested and certified by Microsoft to be compatible with Windows NT. The HCL is included on the Windows NT CD-ROM in the root directory (`monthyearHCL.hlp`), on the Microsoft Web site (`http://www.microsoft.com/hwtest/`), and as hard copy with Windows NT.

This list should by no means be considered exclusive. You should understand that this list gives only the components and systems that Microsoft has certified to be compatible with Windows NT. This also indicates that there are Windows NT drivers available for the device. Other hardware could very well be compatible, but it has not been tested yet or has not been placed on the HCL. The HCL is released approximately every three months, or with a new version of Windows NT.

Typically, Microsoft has over 2,000 systems and hardware components waiting to be tested for compatibility with Windows NT. This is very time consuming, which delays much of the new hardware from being certified and placed on the HCL.

As I said, this is not an exclusive list by any means. Basically, my advice is this: If you are buying new hardware, pick something off of the HCL so as to eliminate potential problems. Because you have not purchased the hardware yet, it is just as easy to buy something that is on the HCL, so here is an opportunity to save yourself a possible headache.

Microsoft writes an enormous number of hardware drivers for Windows NT and includes them with the product, greatly simplifying things. However, plenty of devices on the HCL are supported, but the drivers must be obtained from the manufacturer (usually they can be downloaded from the Internet). This is another nice feature of the HCL; if the drivers must be obtained from a third party, it will be indicated in a footnote. Also, if there are special configuration considerations, it will often be footnoted in the HCL.

> ## NOTE
>
> If you have cause to call Microsoft technical support for Windows NT Workstation, the staff will be very reluctant to troubleshoot problems that involve hardware not listed on the HCL.
>
> The reason behind all of the fuss involved with hardware support is due to the architecture of Windows NT. Unlike previous versions of DOS and Windows, Windows NT does not allow user-mode processes direct access to the hardware components. The reason for this design is portability and modularity, which is consistent with the rest of the Windows NT philosophy.
>
> By implementing a *Hardware Abstraction Layer (HAL)*, the underlying hardware is masked to the operating system. This allows a single device driver to be portable across all hardware platforms.
>
> All non-I/O hardware requests (accessing a network resource, for example) are passed from the appropriate subsystem to the Win32 subsystem, which then sends the request through security validation, to the Executive Services, and then to the Kernel, which passes the request to the HAL. The HAL "virtualizes" this request, interprets it, and makes the appropriate hardware call (sending a data stream over the network interface).
>
> This is a somewhat involved process; the preceding explanation is greatly simplified to illustrate the process involved. The end result is that the operating system is not restricted to a specific hardware architecture. This enables developers to port Windows NT to other hardware platforms much more easily than they could rewrite all of the hardware system calls. This also enables developers to write a single device driver for a specific piece of hardware.
>
> Due to this hardware abstraction architecture, most communications programs (such as fax and modem software) do not function properly under Windows NT. These programs require direct access to the hardware components. Initially this was a problem, but there are now a host of such applications for Windows NT — and support is growing.

Unsupported Hardware

As I mentioned earlier, the Hardware Compatibility List includes only those systems and devices that Microsoft has tested and certified to be compatible with Windows NT. Many hardware vendors make excellent quality products that, for whatever reason, are not on the HCL. Generally, they will include Windows NT drivers with the other accompanying drivers, or you might have to download them from the Internet.

The only problem with this approach is that you will have to turn to the manufacturer for troubleshooting and support of this device under Windows NT Workstation; typically, the hardware manufacturer's technical support team will not have the high degree of Windows NT knowledge that could be necessary.

What you should do to prepare for installation is to be sure you have Windows NT drivers for all of your hardware components prior to beginning the installation process. After you have all of the drivers, read the installation and release notes for the drivers to see if any special instructions or warnings are given (for example, compatibility problems with other hardware devices).

After you have obtained all of the driver support necessary for your hardware and are comfortable with their installation instructions, you are ready to begin the setup process.

The following list can be used as a quick reference to be certain that you are prepared to begin setup of Windows NT Workstation:

- The system meets the minimum hardware requirements.
- You have read the release notes for Windows NT Workstation.
- Your data files have been backed up.
- You have the Windows NT CD-ROM (or access to a network share).
- You have all necessary hardware drivers and support files.
- You know the system configuration. Have a list of hardware component configuration information such as what IRQ, memory, and network settings they are using.

If you are satisfied that you are prepared, it's time to begin the setup process.

Summary

Windows NT has many hardware restrictions that most DOS and Windows users will be unaccustomed to and probably consider unnecessarily cumbersome. It is not without cause. This provides easy portability to other hardware platforms.

Just think. If there were some major technological breakthrough and suddenly systems were 2,500 percent faster for the price of today's desktop system, it wouldn't be too difficult or take too long for Windows NT to be ported to that platform!

Whenever possible, use hardware that is on the HCL. Remember that if it is not on the HCL, it might not work; or, you might have to wait for driver support and, most likely, Microsoft technical support will not provide support for it.

Before buying any hardware not listed on the HCL, find out whether there are drivers available for Windows NT. Although this is a new concept, it does serve a good purpose. Save yourself headaches and buy supported hardware.

Installing Windows NT Workstation

by Sean Mathias

IN THIS CHAPTER

CHAPTER 4

Installing Windows NT Workstation is very different from installing DOS or previous versions of Windows. Remember that Windows NT is a true operating system in itself. Additionally, there are several methods for installing Windows NT Workstation depending on your system type (Intel *x*86 or RISC), current system configuration, and media type. The supported installation media are CD-ROM or network installation. Floppy-disk installation is no longer supported and disks are not provided, nor is there a utility to make installation disks.

Setup: Step By Step

Setup for Intel- and RISC-based systems differs slightly and therefore will be discussed separately where appropriate. Also note that if you are installing Windows NT on a portable system using PC Card devices that you want to configure during setup, the devices must be inserted prior to starting setup.

The following are the supported installation methods for Windows NT 4 Workstation:

- Using the three setup disks and CD-ROM drive (Intel)
- Booting from CD-ROM (RISC systems and supported Intel systems)
- Installing from a network share

> **NOTE**
>
> If you do not have the Windows NT Workstation setup disks or you need to re-create them, you can run the `winnt` or `winnt32` utility found on the Windows NT Workstation CD-ROM. From a DOS prompt or within Windows 3.*x*, run `winnt /o`; from Windows 95 or another version of Windows NT, run `winnt32 /o`. Another useful switch is the `/b` option. This option can be used from MS-DOS (`winnt /b`) or from an existing Windows NT installation (`winnt32 /b`). When you use this option, the install program copies all of the files necessary for setup to a directory on your local hard drive, eliminating the need for boot floppies and expediting the install process by using files from a hard disk rather than a CD-ROM.

To begin setup from the setup disks or CD-ROM, perform the following steps:

1. Turn off your computer.
2. Insert the disk labeled Windows NT Setup Boot Disk or, if your system BIOS supports bootable CD-ROMs, insert the Windows NT CD into the drive.
3. Turn on your computer.

For RISC-based systems, also perform these steps:

4. At the ARC screen, choose Run a Program from the menu.
5. At the command prompt, type `cd:\`*platform*`\setupldr` and press Enter.

To begin setup from a network share, perform the following steps:

1. Connect to the network share where the Windows NT 4 Workstation setup files are located.

2. If you are using a previous version of Windows NT, change to the appropriate directory for your hardware platform and run the `winnt32.exe` program; otherwise, run the `winnt.exe` program.

3. When the setup dialog shown in Figure 4.1 appears, choose Continue.

FIGURE 4.1.
The Windows NT 4 Workstation setup dialog.

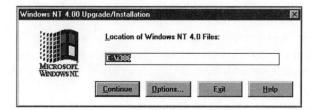

The setup program copies the necessary files to your local machine. Then, when the copying is finished, it prompts you to restart your computer and continue setting up Windows NT 4 Workstation.

> **NOTE**
>
> Previous versions of DOS, Windows 3.x, and OS/2 can be upgraded to Windows NT 4 Workstation or configured to dual-boot. Windows 95, however, cannot be upgraded. Windows NT 4 Workstation must be installed to a separate directory and configured to dual-boot.

Character Mode Setup

After you have finished copying files and restarted your computer, or you have begun setup from floppy disk or bootable CD-ROM, you are in the beginning phase of the character mode portion of Windows NT setup.

At this point, setup consists of a character-based blue screen similar to the old MS-DOS setup. In the bottom border of the screen is any pertinent information related to the current setup procedure—the current file being copied or loaded, for example, or various options that might be available at a given time.

The character-mode blue screen with Windows NT Setup in the top-left corner appears and initial system files are loaded, as shown in the status filed in the bottom border of the screen.

If this is the first time you have run Windows NT Workstation setup on this machine, press Enter to continue setup. If you have a another version of Windows NT or have had a failed installation attempt, you will see an option to repair a damaged Windows NT installation; this is discussed in Chapter 5, "Tips, Tricks, and Traps."

At any point in setup, you can press F1 for help on the current item, or you can press F3 to exit the setup program. If you exit setup, you need to rerun setup later to install Windows NT 4 Workstation. Typically, you do not want to end setup after it has begun unless there is a problem. If you do end setup, you probably can still boot to your previous OS, depending on how far the setup process went and how you chose to configure setup. Unless you reached the point of specifying where to install Windows NT and elected to upgrade your previous OS, you will be able to boot to your previous system when you restart the computer. If you chose to upgrade your current OS, the results will be unpredictable and you will probably have to successfully complete the installation of Windows NT or reinstall your previous OS.

Mass Storage Device Detection

After the initial process of loading the necessary device drivers and files needed for setup and making selections about your system type, Windows NT setup runs a mass storage device detection process to locate hard drives, CD-ROM drives, and SCSI or RAID controllers in your system. If you are using a controller or CD-ROM that is not on the Hardware Compatibility List (HCL), you need to have a driver disk for it available at this time. If you do not have the necessary drivers for your storage devices, Windows NT might not be able to find an appropriate location to install to.

First is the detection and specification of mass storage devices. CD-ROM drives (IDE and SCSI), hard disk drives, and SCSI and RAID controllers are detected here. Additional device controllers and storage devices can be explicitly specified here, as well as hardware for which you have an OEM-supplied driver disk. To specify additional drives, adapters, or controllers, press S. You are presented with a list of possible devices and given an option of Other (Requires disk provided by a hardware manufacturer).

If you have installed a device that is supported but is not detected, you can try to manually specify it, but you probably have a configuration problem that prevented Windows NT setup from detecting it.

To install support for a device for which you have a driver disk, select the Other option and provide the OEM-supplied disk when prompted. When a dialog is presented with the various devices supported by the supplied driver, select the appropriate device and press Enter. Windows NT setup will need to copy a few files from the disk at a later point in setup, so keep the disk available. It is also a good idea to keep all such device disks with your Windows NT setup boot disks and an emergency repair disk (discussed later in this chapter) in the event that you must reinstall Windows NT at a later time.

When you have finished specifying mass storage devices or all mass storage devices have been detected, press Enter to continue setup.

System Settings and Installation Location

Windows NT setup now examines all hard disks that have been found for content and available disk space, and then determines which file system is installed on the drive. If another version of Windows NT is found on any drive, you are prompted to decide whether to upgrade the existing installation or install a fresh copy of Windows NT Workstation. To upgrade the existing installation, press Enter; to install a fresh copy, press N.

Setup displays a list of hardware and software components of the current system as detected. This lists the computer type, display, keyboard and keyboard layout, and the pointing device. If you would like to change any items on the list, use the arrow keys to select the appropriate item, press Enter, and select the correct setting. When the settings are correct, press Enter.

You are now presented with a list of detected hard disks and partitions. Select the partition to which you want to install Windows NT 4 Workstation and press Enter. To create a partition on a drive with free space, use the arrow keys to select the partition, press C, specify the partition size, and press Enter.

To delete an existing partition, use the arrow keys to select the partition and press D. You are presented with a screen asking you to confirm that you want to delete the selected partition and warning you that all information contained will be lost. To delete the partition, press L. To go back and not delete the partition, press Esc.

When you are satisfied with the partition configuration and have selected a partition to install Windows NT Workstation to, press Enter.

Windows NT setup lists the partition to which you have chosen to install Windows NT 4 Workstation; its file system type, partition size, and space free; and disk ID. Select the file system that you want to use for this partition—NTFS or FAT—and press Enter. If security is an issue or you intend to use drives larger than 2GB, I recommend NTFS as the file system for its advanced security capabilities and its ability to efficiently manage large drive volumes. In a standalone configuration or on dual-boot systems, FAT would be the appropriate choice.

Provide the directory name to install Windows NT 4 Workstation to. Make your naming selection carefully, because you will be unable to change this name later without reinstalling.

You are now prompted to indicate whether you would like Windows NT setup to perform an exhaustive secondary examination of your hard disks. To allow the examination, press Enter (and go to lunch). To skip the exhaustive examination, press Esc. Basically, the exhaustive secondary examination is similar to a surface scan by the old Scandisk program in DOS. It thoroughly checks your drive for errors, but it is time-consuming. If this is a new drive or you believe it might be deteriorating in performance, you might want to use this option. However, if this drive has worked flawlessly in a previous OS, you can probably choose to skip this step.

Windows NT setup now builds a list of files that need to be copied and begins the copy process. The current file being copied is displayed in the bottom-right corner of the screen with a progress indicator in the center of the screen.

When the file copying is complete, Windows NT setup initializes your default configuration, and you are prompted to restart your computer to continue setup. Press Enter to restart your computer and continue.

Windows Portion of Setup

When your computer restarts, you are presented with the Windows NT boot menu. The installation reinitializes itself by default; do not choose another selection or you might have to begin setup all over again.

When Windows NT starts its Windows mode, setup continues and you are presented with a Software License Agreement (SLA). If, after reading this, you do not agree to the terms and choose No, setup closes. If you agree to the terms, select Yes.

Setup now reinitializes and continues copying files needed to complete setup. The rest of the setup process takes place using a setup wizard similar to that found in Windows 95. The initial screen advises you that the Wizard will guide you through the rest of the setup process. The next three steps in the setup process are as follows:

- Gathering information about your computer
- Installing Windows NT Networking
- Finishing setup

Gathering Information about Your Computer

When you are ready to continue, select Next. Setup now prepares your directory for Windows NT, displaying the progress in a progress bar. If at any time you want to go back and change a selection you have made, select the Back button.

You are now provided with a list of Setup options, listed here:

- Typical (recommended)
- Portable (includes mobile computing support)
- Compact (if there is little available disk space)
- Custom (to select components individually)

The Typical option installs Windows NT with a standard set of options for things such as wallpapers and migrating programs from a previous version of Windows, and it automatically begins network and printer installation. The Portable option is ideal for installing on laptop computers because it automatically adds support for mobile computing and minimizes the optional files installed to conserve disk space. Compact is similar to Portable, except it does not install mobile computing support; it installs only the minimum files necessary to run Windows NT. Lastly, Custom allows the user to make all selections about what components are installed. This is my preferred method because it provides much better control over the install process.

Make your selection and choose Next. Regardless of which selection you make, you can go back after installation is complete and use the Add/Remove programs applet in Control Panel to install additional Windows NT components.

You are now prompted to enter your name and organization for registration. After you have provided this information, select Next. You now need to provide a name for the computer. This name can be up to 15 characters and should not contain any spaces. If you are on a network, consult your system administrator; there might be a standard naming convention that you must follow. Also, it is advisable to use only letters and numbers (no additional characters such as asterisks or underscores).

You are then prompted to provide the password for the administrator account for this computer. Again, you might want to consult your system administrator if on a network because a standard administrator password might be in use. When you have entered your password and confirmed it, select Next.

> **NOTE**
>
> Be sure to use a password you will not forget or record and store it in a safe place, because you might need this in the future if you encounter problems or need to reconfigure your system. If you forget the administrator password and have no other administrator accounts, you need to reinstall Windows NT Workstation to re-create the administrator account and specify a new password.
>
> Also note that passwords in Windows NT are case-sensitive. This means that Password, password, and PASSWORD are not the same. You must enter your password exactly as you entered it when you created the account.

Next, you are prompted to decide whether you want to create an emergency repair disk. It is recommended that you do create one in the event that your installation becomes corrupted and you need to repair it. If your installation becomes corrupted and you do not have an emergency repair disk, you might have to reinstall from scratch. Note that having an emergency repair disk is still not a guarantee that a corrupted system can be recovered, but you stand a better chance. Various system and registry files are placed on this repair disk. In the event that the system becomes corrupted, you use the emergency repair process and provide this disk to give Windows NT a good starting point to recover from any corruption or misconfiguration.

If you selected the Custom Setup option earlier, you are now prompted to select the Windows NT components that you want to install. The component categories are listed as follows:

- **Accessibility Options**. Options to change keyboard, sound display, and mouse behavior for people with physical impairments. (See Chapter 10, "Advanced System Configuration," for more details.)

- **Accessories**. Optional applications such as calculator, Internet Jumpstart kit, and Imaging. These are some optional applets that are certainly not critical but are useful in many day-to-day functions.

- **Communications.** Communications utilities for online services. (See Chapter 10.)

- **Games**. The ever-present productivity killers.

- **Microsoft Exchange**. Electronic mail and messaging utilities. (See Chapter 7, "The Explorer GUI," for more details.)

- **Multimedia**. Programs for playing sound, video, and animation on multimedia-enabled systems. (See Chapter 10.)

To select an entire category, click on the corresponding check box. To select individual components of a category, highlight the category and select Details; check or clear the box next to each component as appropriate. When you are satisfied with the selections, select OK. The Reset button sets all categories back to their default selections. Information about the amount of space needed to install the components and available disk space free is listed in the bottom-left corner. When you have completed your selections, click Next.

Installing Windows NT Networking

After you make your selections for Windows NT components, you are presented with an informational dialog that shows Installing Windows NT Networking as the next phase of setup. Click Next to begin installing the networking components of Windows NT Workstation.

You are given the option to not install Windows NT Networking at this time or to participate in a network. If you choose to not install networking support now, you can install it at any time after setup has completed by running the Network applet in Control Panel.

If you choose to install Windows NT Networking support, you have the option of choosing how you are to be connected to the network—either physically wired to it using some form of network adapter and communications medium, or remotely connected through the use of a modem.

If you choose not to install Windows NT Networking at this time, you are presented with an informational dialog stating that the last step is Finishing Setup. Click Next to finish the setup process and skip to the next section.

To configure Windows NT Networking, use the following procedure:

1. Select Wired to the Network or Remote Access to the Network as appropriate, and then click Next.

2. Click the Start Search or Select from List button to install a network adapter.

3. When all network adapters have been installed, choose Next.

4. Select the network protocols you will use. The default protocol is TCP/IP or IPX/SPX, depending on any previous network software you might have had on your system. NetBEUI is also listed as an option, but it is no longer the default protocol for Microsoft networking. If the protocol you need is not listed, choose the Select from List button, which lists all available protocols. The only other communications protocol available is AppleTalk. Typically, most users will use one or more of the three defaults listed.

5. A default list of network services to be installed is displayed. If you require additional services, choose the Select from List button.

6. When all desired network services have been selected, choose Next.

7. You are informed that Windows NT is now ready to install the selected network components. Click Next to install Windows NT networking or Back to make changes.

8. Depending on the adapters, protocols, and services selected, you are prompted for configuration information. If you are unsure of the correct configurations, consult your system administrator.

9. After all adapters, protocols, and services have been installed and configured, you are given a bindings configuration dialog where you can enable or disable specific bindings. If this is necessary, consult your systems administrator.

10. A dialog informs you that Windows NT is ready to start the network. Click Next to continue.

11. If the network fails to start, go back and change your configuration settings where necessary. Usually this will be due to an improperly configured network adapter. At times, it might be necessary to exit setup and run the configuration disk for the network adapter to obtain the correct settings. If this is the case, I recommend completing setup without installing network support, because this step can be completed after setup is complete. This saves you from having to repeat the entire setup process again. To install Windows NT with no networking support, you need to click the Back button until you reach the screen described in step 1, and then deselect any network options.

12. Decide whether this computer will be a member of a workgroup or participate in a domain environment. If it is to participate in a domain environment, an account for the computer must be created in that domain. The system administrator can do this on a domain controller or can provide a username and password to use to create the account.

4

INSTALLING
WINDOWS NT
WORKSTATION

13. Provide the name of the workgroup or domain to which this computer will belong. If using a domain, check the Create Computer Account in the Domain box if necessary. Workgroups and Domains are discussed in Chapter 16, "Installing Windows NT Networking."

14. If needed, you are prompted for a username and password with the right to create computer accounts on the domain. Provide this information and click OK.

Provided everything goes smoothly, the networking components are now installed and configured properly. If you experience extensive problems, continue setup without installing Windows NT Networking and finish setup of Windows NT. After setup is complete, you can install Windows NT Networking by choosing the Network applet in Control Panel and following the same process as just described.

Finishing Setup

Several dialog boxes are displayed as Windows NT configures your computer and creates menus and groups. You are then prompted to specify date and time properties for this system. On the Time Zone tab, select the time zone appropriate for your locale. If applicable, select Automatically adjust clock for daylight savings changes. Now select the Date & Time tab and adjust the date and time as needed. When this is complete, choose Close.

Windows NT setup now attempts to detect your display adapter. The screen will blink black and come back with a dialog stating which display adapter the setup program has found. Select OK and begin configuring your display settings.

Provided the display adapter was detected properly, configure the adapter with the resolution, color depth, and refresh rate as desired (within the recommended settings of the manufacturer). When you have selected the desired settings, choose the Test button. You are informed that the new mode will be tested. Select OK. When the mode is tested, a bitmap of colors and patterns showing the screen size is displayed. After a few seconds, you are returned to the setup program. If the bitmap appeared correctly, select Yes and then choose OK. If it did not appear correctly, choose No and reconfigure your settings.

If the display adapter was incorrectly detected, accept the default setting for now. You can reconfigure it or specify another display adapter after setup completes by using the Display applet in Control Panel.

At this point, Windows NT Setup completes copying the necessary files to their permanent directory structure; updates all shortcuts, groups, and menus; removes temporary files; sets security information on files; and saves your configuration.

The process of saving the configuration consists of writing all configuration information to backup files located in systemroot\repair. Before completion of saving the configuration information, you are prompted to provide a high-density, formatted disk to create the emergency repair disk if you opted to create one earlier in setup. When this is complete, you are prompted to restart your computer. When you restart your computer, Windows NT will be installed and configured and you can begin using it or making modifications as necessary.

Summary

Now you can unball your fists and stop gritting your teeth. It really is not too difficult to install Windows NT Workstation. If you are able to install Windows 95 in three days or less, this should pose no problem to you at all.

This chapter has touched on almost every aspect of installing Windows NT and should be able to help you make your choices during installation. You should now be able to resolve any potential problems that you might encounter during the course of installation.

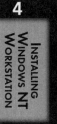

Tips, Tricks, and Traps

by Jefferson Mousseau

IN THIS CHAPTER

CHAPTER 5

All the documentation in the world won't be able to help you when you run into those little glitches. You know, those "undocumented features" that they fail to tell you about? One that springs to mind occurred when I attempted to install NT on a Hewlett Packard LS. After I selected the Adaptec 2940U+ SCSI controller during the install routine, an error appeared saying that NT could not find any storage devices even though the system had a Quantum 2.1GB hard drive.

Usually, when installing Microsoft Windows NT, you should do so on an extended NTFS partition. That way, if the workstation or server ever has startup problems, you can boot from a DOS disk and access the NTFS partition with a utility called DOS to NTFS, which is covered later in this chapter. Although it is possible to boot with a DOS diskette and run DOS2NTFS, formatting a small boot partition with FAT can speed the boot sequence and aid in troubleshooting.

The problem was that HP LS was meant to be a Web server and, as such, security was a primary concern. In order for the server to have met the C2 security specification, there could be no DOS partition.

I had completed all the basic troubleshooting on the HP LS and made attempts to install from the installation disks instead of the CD-ROM. I had created driver disks from the HP CD-ROM that came with the server and attempted more installs. I had tried manually copying the i386 subdirectory from DOS to the hard drive, coupled with copying the latest Adaptec SCSI driver and then installing NT from the hard disk. I checked the Adaptec Configuration Utility to make sure that "Enable Support for Drives Larger Than One Gigabyte" was enabled. Next, I double-checked the jumper settings on the hard disk and consulted the manual, hoping that it would yield the answer to the elusive problem. And finally I called technical support.

The chap on the other end of the phone was sympathetic, but after determining that I had already tried everything he recommended, he said it was a hard drive problem. However, there was one way, he added, that the problem could be overcome. He suggested trying a low-level format of the hard drive using the Adaptec Configuration Utility. Unfortunately, the HP Server requires an 8MB system partition in order to run the server utilities that HP bundles with the server. When I reminded him that by performing a low-level format, the 8MB system partition would be lost and thus the ability to run the system utilities also would be lost, he countered that the utilities could be run from the CD-ROM. Sensing that this solution was too good to be true, I continued my questions to him: "Will I be able to run all the system utilities as if they were installed on the hard drive?" Pausing for a moment, he conceded, "No, but you will be able to install NT!"

Only the experience of installing NT Workstation on a number of different platforms and under different circumstances can prepare you for the kinds of moments I've just described. This chapter covers some time-saving tips about installing Microsoft Windows Workstation 4.0, coupled with some traps that readers should be aware of.

Installation Switches

A number of extremely useful options are available to users when installing Windows NT 4 Workstation. For instance, the /U switch, when used with the optional /S switch, enables users to install Windows NT 4.0 unattended. So if you are in charge of installing NT Workstation on a number of computers, you might want to consider using this option because it can potentially save a lot of time.

By default, NT Workstation creates three installation disks when installing from the CD-ROM or from a network. This is when knowing about the /B switch can be very useful. This switch allows users to bypass the creation of the three Windows NT Workstation install disks. This is useful if you are installing NT from a CD-ROM or network connection and do not require the disks to initiate an install. On the other hand, if you need to create these disks without installing NT, typing winnt /o at the command prompt enables you to make three Windows NT 4 Workstation installation diskettes.

The following is a complete list of the switches available to you. You can also view this list by typing winnt /? ¦ more at the command prompt if you are installing from DOS, or type winnt32 /? ¦ more if you are installing from DOS or upgrading from a previous version of NT.

```
WINNT [/S[:]sourcepath] [/T[:]tempdrive] [/I[:]inffile] [/O[X]] [/X ¦ [/F]
[/C]] [/B] [/U[:scriptfile]] [/R[X]:directory]

/S[:]sourcepath
        Specifies the source location of Windows NT files.
        Must be a full path of the form x:\[path] or
        \\server\share[\path].
        The default is the current directory.
/T[:]tempdrive
        Specifies a drive to contain temporary setup files.
        If not specified, Setup will attempt to locate a drive for you.
/I[:]inffile
        Specifies the filename (no path) of the setup information file.
        The default is DOSNET.INF.
/O      Create boot floppies only.
/OX     Create boot floppies for CD-ROM or floppy-based installation.
/X      Do not create the Setup boot floppies.
/F      Do not verify files as they are copied to the Setup boot floppies.
/C      Skip free-space check on the Setup boot floppies you provide.
/B      Floppyless operation (requires /s).
/U      Unattended operation and optional script file (requires /s).
/R      Specifies optional directory to be installed.
/RX     Specifies optional directory to be copied.
```

Although NT Workstation can be installed on computers with different types of processors, users installing it from DOS can speed up the installation process. At the DOS command prompt, set Smart Drive to be equal to the amount of RAM in the computer. On a computer with an Intel system with 16MB of RAM, type smartdrv 16000 at the command prompt. When the installation of NT begins and files are being copied to the temporary directory on the hard drive of the computer, DOS will have more cache to store the information and users should notice an increase in the speed at which the NT installation occurs.

The Boot Process

As with other releases of Microsoft Windows NT Workstation, the boot process is often the area where the majority of troubleshooting occurs. Whether you are repairing corrupted boot files such as the BOOT.INI or NTLDR or tracking down conflicting IRQs, getting your hardware and NT to cooperate can sometimes be a time-consuming process. Ultimately, though, understanding NT's boot process helps increase your fundamental knowledge of the operating system and provides a good building block toward understanding its more complex functions and capabilities.

BOOT.INI

During some installations of Windows NT 4.0, it is possible for NT to incorrectly identify on what partition it has been placed. This information is contained in the BOOT.INI file, a hidden file located on the root of the boot or C:\> drive. You can use DOS's attrib command to change the attributes of this file in order to access it. If you've installed Windows NT 4.0 on an extended partition, your BOOT.INI file should look like this:

```
[boot loader]
timeout=30
default=multi(0)disk(0)rdisk(0)partition(2)\WINNT
[operating systems]
multi(0)disk(0)rdisk(0)partition(2)\WINNT="Windows NT Workstation Version 4.00"
multi(0)disk(0)rdisk(0)partition(2)\WINNT="Windows NT Workstation Version 4.00
[VGA mode]" /basevideo /sos
C:\="MS-DOS"
```

Terms of Reference

The terms of reference for BOOT.INI are as follows:

- multi or SCSI refers to which bus—whether it is an AT-bus or a SCSI-bus—the system uses to access the NT 4.0 partition.

- rdisk, disk specifies the disk that NT Workstation 4.0 was installed on. The r refers to rigit. In the previous example, NT Workstation was installed on the boot drive and as a result has a value of 0.

- disk specifies the disk controller with which NT Workstation 4.0 can be accessed. In the previous example, NT Workstation was installed to be accessed with the first disk controller and as a result has a value of 0.

- partition specifies which partition of the disk NT Workstation 4.0 has been installed on. In the previous example, NT is installed on an extended partition, and the value is 2.

If you can't boot Windows NT 4 Workstation after installing it, check to see that all the entries in the BOOT.INI have been set to the correct value. This is another reason that it is good to install NT on an extended partition. If you have trouble accessing NT, you can boot to the

DOS partition and then access the Windows NT 4.0 BOOT.INI file. Even if you specify to format the NT partition with NTFS, the system must reboot and run the convert utility to automatically convert the partition from FAT to NTFS for you. As a result, if you were unable to reboot, the partition should still be in FAT so that you can access it and check the partition.

If you have decided to install without a DOS partition and you were able to boot previously and make changes to the BOOT.INI, don't despair. There is help.

From the Internet, you can download a utility called NTFS File System Redirector for DOS/Windows V1.1, written by Mark Russinovich and Bryce Cogswell. This utility enables you to read files on an NTFS partition from DOS by booting the workstation with a DOS boot disk. Then from a floppy containing NTFS File System Redirector and DOS's COPY.EXE, type ntfsdos. You can now access the NTFS partition and copy the BOOT.INI to a floppy disk where you can make changes to it and then copy it back to the NTFS partition.

Troubleshooting Boot Errors

Like Windows NT Workstation 3.51, NT 4.0 uses the same type of boot process. So if you are familiar with troubleshooting NT boot problems, you will not have to jump through any hoops to feel comfortable here. Before restoring any of the following files, you should check the BOOT.INI file and make sure the values contained in it are set properly.

Boot NTLDR not found

If you receive the message Boot NTLDR not found, the NT's boot loader was either corrupted or deleted. You can restore the NTLDR.EXE file from the installation disks or the CD, and you should be able to boot your system.

NTDETECT failed

On Intel-based computers, NT 4.0 uses NTDETECT.COM to locate what type of hardware is installed on your system. If you receive the error NTDETECT.COM failed, you can restore from the installation disks or the CD, or you can copy from the install CD if NT was installed on a FAT partition.

Hardware Problems

Unlike Windows 95, Windows NT Workstation is not plug-and-play. So you cannot insert a sound card and have NT automatically detect it, prompt you for the driver disk, and automatically assign it an IRQ. This is true because NT does not allow hardware to directly access the hardware components of your system. As a result, with Windows NT 4.0, you will still find yourself troubleshooting those old problems such as configuring IRQs or interrupt requests.

Pentium Floating-Point Problem

Windows NT 4.0 setup is capable of automatically detecting the Intel Pentium floating-point division error. If you have a defective processor, setup asks you whether you want to disable the floating point processor. If you choose not to disable this during installation, you can disable it later from the command line by typing `pentnt`.

Network Interface Cards

One change from previous versions of NT is that Windows NT 4 Workstation now searches the DRVLIB subdirectory for network adapter drivers. This improves NT 4.0's capability to detect network adapter cards and install the proper drivers over previous releases.

If you encounter problems configuring a network adapter card, the problem probably lies in the IRQ settings of the card. First, check to verify that the network card is configured properly by checking the I/O address, interrupt setting, and jumper settings. This information should be contained in the documentation that came with your network adapter.

Interrupt or IRQ conflicts are generally the most common conflicts. They occur when a network card and another device are configured to use the same interrupt channel. Generally, a mouse is configured to use IRQ 3, and if a network card is configured to use the same IRQ, a conflict occurs.

It is always best to check the documentation that comes with the network card before you begin troubleshooting the problem. Open up the Event Viewer located in the Administrative Tools folder. If there are any errors, such as an IRQ conflict message, with the functionality of your PC's NIC, you can begin to take steps to fix the problem. First, shut down the system and remove the NIC. Turn the system on and then verify which IRQs are free by running the NT Workstation's Windows NT Diagnostics, located in the Administrative Tools folder. Click the IRQ/Port Status button and determine which IRQ is free. Then configure the network card by using the jumper settings or the software that comes with your card. If you set the IRQ with jumper settings, you can then reinsert the NIC and start NT.

If you have checked the Event Viewer for any messages and corrected the problem or still cannot achieve network connectivity, then—provided you have installed TCP/IP—you can use the TCP/IP Ping utility by pinging another host on the network. Open a DOS box and, at the prompt, type `ping` *n* where *n* is the address of the host. A sample output from a successful ping would look like this:

```
C:\>ping 10.1.4.1

Pinging 10.1.4.1 with 32 bytes of data:

Reply from 10.1.4.1: bytes=32 time=10ms TTL=255
Reply from 10.1.4.1: bytes=32 time<10ms TTL=255
Reply from 10.1.4.1: bytes=32 time<10ms TTL=255
Reply from 10.1.4.1: bytes=32 time<10ms TTL=255
```

Essentially, a successful ping response will tell you that both the NT Workstation and the host being pinged are able to communicate via the network. Therefore, their network cards are properly configured.

If TCP/IP was not installed but NetBEUI was installed, an alternative method to check connectivity is to use the net send command, as in the following example:

```
C:\>net send workstation2 Are you out there?
```

This message outputs on the screen of workstation2 a message saying Are you out there? and a message on the sending workstation saying The Message was Successfully Sent.

A number of other network commands are available to users to help troubleshoot network connectivity issues during install. When you type net help at the command line, you are provided with a comprehensive list, similar to the following list. For more information on network configuration, see Chapter 10, "Advanced System Configuration."

NET ACCOUNTS	NET HELP	NET SHARE
NET COMPUTER	NET HELPMSG	NET START
NET CONFIG	NET LOCALGROUP	NET STATISTICS
NET CONFIG SERVER	NET NAME	NET STOP
NET CONTINUE	NET PRINT	NET USE
NET FILE	NET SEND	NET USER
NET GROUP	NET SESSION	NET VIEW

NET HELP SERVICES (lists the network services you can start)

NET HELP SYNTAX (explains how to read NET HELP syntax lines)

NET HELP command¦MORE (displays Help one screen at a time)

Controller Cards

With the release of Windows NT version 4.0, the drivers for certain SCSI adapters have been moved from the base operating system to the Windows NT Driver Library DRVLIB subdirectory included on the Windows NT 4 Workstation CD. Check the following list to determine whether any of your adapters are affected by this change. If your computer has an adapter that appears on this list, you must create a driver disk before installing Windows NT version 4.0. Use this disk to install the appropriate drivers during setup, or you can install the driver later from the Control Panel after installation.

In order to create a driver disk, follow these steps:

1. Start with a blank, formatted 3.5-inch disk.

2. Copy all the files from the following directory to the disk:

   \drvlib\storage\retired*cpu_type*

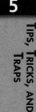

In this directory, *cpu_type* is the type of processor on which you are installing NT—for example, X86 if you have an x86-based processor, MIPS you have a MIPS RISC-based computer, or ALPHA if you have a Digital Alpha computer.

All popular SCSI controllers are supported by Windows NT 4 Workstation, but to be sure that the SCSI controller you have is supported, check the latest Hardware Compatibility List (HCL) available at Microsoft's Web site at www.microsoft.com.

File Format

Previous versions of Windows NT Workstation offered support for three file formats: FAT (File Allocation Table), NTFS (Microsoft's NT File System), and HPFS (IBM's High Performance File System). Windows NT Workstation version 4.0 offers support for only two file formats: FAT and NTFS.

If security is not an issue when installing NT, choosing FAT might be a viable choice. However, if enhanced security is required, you should format the partition or drive using NTFS. If you format a drive in FAT and later decide that you need the enhanced security features of NTFS, this section shows you how the partition or drive can be converted from FAT to NTFS without losing any data.

Compression

Windows NT 4 Workstation does not support any DOS-based file compression algorithm utilities such as Stacker, DoubleSpace, and DriveSpace. As a result, you will not be able to install NT on a workstation running any of these. If hard drive space is a consideration for you after installing NT and you have used the NTFS file format, you can compress the disks by double-clicking My Computer, selecting the drive you want to compress by clicking it, and then selecting Properties from the File menu. In the dialog box, click the Compress check box. Compressing the drives can also be done from the command prompt by typing compact *.* /s. The following is a complete list of switches. To view this list, type compact /? from the command prompt, like this:

```
COMPACT [/C ¦ /U] [/S[:dir]] [/A] [/I] [/F] [/Q] [filename [...]]
```

- /C compresses the specified files. Directories will be marked so that files added afterward will be compressed.

- /U uncompresses the specified files. Directories will be marked so that files added afterward will not be compressed.

- /S performs the specified operation on files in the given directory and all subdirectories. Default dir is the current directory.

- /A displays files with the hidden or system attributes. These files are omitted by default.

- ◼ /I continues performing the specified operation even after errors have occurred. By default, COMPACT stops when an error is encountered.
- ◼ /F forces the compress operation on all specified files, even those that are already compressed. Files that are already compressed are skipped by default.
- ◼ /Q reports only the most essential information.
- ◼ *filename* specifies a pattern, file, or directory.

Conversion

Changing the file format from DOS's FAT format to NTFS is easy with NT. Like compressing a drive, it can be done in the WINDOWS interface or from the command line. To perform this in the Windows NT WINDOWS interface, select Administrative Tools|Disk Administrator from the Start menu. Select the disk or partition you would like to change and then select Change format from the Tools menu.

> **CAUTION**
>
> Beware! If you format a drive or partition, or change the file format from the Windows interface, all data on the disk will be lost.

To perform a format conversion from DOS to NTFS from the command line, type convert *driveletter* /NTFS. A complete list of all switches has been included here. To view this list from the command line, type convert /?. The program will then inform you that the conversion will take place after you restart the computer. If you change your mind and want to perform this operation, you will have one more chance to stop. When the computer restarts, press the spacebar for the Last Known Good Menu option during the boot process. This bypasses the changes you have asked the computer to perform. This command can be extremely valuable under any circumstances when you have made changes to a system's configuration and found that it is no longer responding properly.

As mentioned earlier, if you install NT on a drive or partition formatted in FAT and then decide you want to take advantage of the security features of NTFS, NT contains a utility that converts the format without resulting in data loss. The command and accompanying switches are as follows:

```
CONVERT drive: /FS:NTFS [/V]
```

- ◼ *drive* specifies the drive to convert to NTFS. Note that you cannot convert the current drive.
- ◼ /FS:NTFS specifies to convert the volume to NTFS.
- ◼ /V specifies that Convert should be run in verbose mode.

> **WARNING**
>
> Although you can change the format of a drive or partition from FAT to NTFS without losing data from the command prompt, attempting to do so from the `WINDOWS INTERFACE` interface results in total data loss on the drive or partition. Changing formats from NTFS to FAT also results in complete data loss whether done from the `WINDOWS INTERFACE` or the command line. Therefore, only perform this function if you are sure that no data will be lost.

Summary

The topics covered in this chapter have hopefully provided you with the neccessities to navigate through the sometimes less than aesthetic qualities of NT Workstation. Plug-and-play–compatible devices are not workable under NT because such devices need to directly access the system hardware. As a result, the devices won't install as easily as they do on Windows 95. This should not cause users looking for a stable and secure operating environment to turn away from Windows NT 4 Workstation.

Many corporations are deciding to pass on the opportunity to upgrade to Windows 95 and are migrating instead to Windows NT 4 Workstation. They are making this decision based not just on the decreased licensing cost of upgrading from one operating system instead of two, but also based on the people hours involved in making two upgrades. In addition, commercial software and custom applications of a corporation, which ran predictably under Windows 3.*x* or Windows for Workgroups 3.11, need to be thoroughly tested and integrated. For many companies, such a move can't be taken lightly.

Windows NT 4 Workstation is improved over earlier releases, especially in the area of installation and detection. With these enhancements, users should find that troubleshooting, although not eradicated, is greatly reduced.

IN THIS PART

III

PART

Windows NT Basics

Control Panel Basics

by Thomas Lee

IN THIS CHAPTER

CHAPTER 6

Introduction to the Control Panel

To many people, the Control Panel is just one of those things you need, but only rarely. When I started writing this chapter, I agreed with this view. As I looked more closely, I saw that the Control Panel is, in many ways, a key component of Windows NT Workstation. To get the best out of Windows NT Workstation, you really do need to know how the Control Panel works. For the power user, some neat features are hidden away in the depths of the Control Panel.

Think of the Control Panel as a nice front end for setting the most important system and user preferences. Most users will use some of all the options, whereas the true power user will want to come to grips with his full potential.

I Know Windows NT 3.51—Is There Any Difference?

If you know how the Control Panel worked in either Windows 3.*x* or Windows NT 3.*x*, you'll understand the basics of the Control Panel in Windows NT Workstation. You're probably in for a bit of a culture shock; there have been some changes. Some people might even say that not all of these changes are for the better, but of course, I couldn't possibly comment. If you are a Windows 95 user, Windows NT's Control Panel will feel more familiar, but there are some important differences.

So What Is the Control Panel?

The Control Panel is a collection object—a collection of a number of smaller applications, or applets, each of which configure some part of your Windows NT Workstation environment. To configure a part of the system, you first invoke Control Panel and then invoke the applet.

Accessing the Control Panel

The two main ways of accessing the Control Panel are from My Computer and from the Start button (click Start, select Settings, and then select Control Panel) as shown in Figure 6.1.

FIGURE 6.1.

Two ways to invoke the Control Panel.

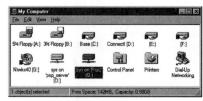

When you invoke Control Panel, Windows NT displays a folder containing a number of the icons, each one representing a Control Panel applet. As with all folders in Windows NT, you have the option of Large Icons, Small Icons, or Details view. My Control Panel, with Large Icons selected, is shown in Figure 6.2. Your Control Panel might look different, depending on what software you have loaded.

FIGURE 6.2.

The Control Panel.

What Are Control Panel Applets?

A Control Panel applet is a Windows NT dynamic link library (DLL) stored with the extension .CPL. Each applet is designed to configure one part of your Windows NT System, such as the mouse, the network, or the UPS.

Control Panel applets are found in the %SYSTEMROOT%\System32 directory. If you remove one or more of the applet files from the System32 directory, you will not see the applet's icon in the Control Panel the next time you invoke it. Likewise, you can add Control Panel applets simply by placing their files into the System32 directory.

A number of Control Panel applets are initially loaded with Windows NT. Adding extra features, such as dial-up networking, or other applications, such as Microsoft Office, results in additional Control Panel applets being installed. Installing Office 95, for example, will install the Find Fast applet, which automatically indexes Office documents.

If you don't see all the Control Panel applets shown in Figure 6.2, it might be because you haven't loaded all the related components of Windows NT Workstation.

System Settings Versus User Settings

In using the Control Panel, some settings such as network configuration are set up for the system as a whole, regardless of which user is logged in. Other settings are user-specific, and you can set them differently for each user with an account on the system.

All the settings controlled by Windows NT's Control Panel are stored in the Registry. The Registry is described more fully in Chapter 9, "What Is the Registry?"

Individual per-user settings are stored below the HKEY_CURRENT_USER\Control Panel key. The subkeys for the user settings match the names of the applets in most cases. The system settings are stored under the HKEY_LOCAL_MACHINE key and are not as easy to find.

WARNING

Throughout this chapter, I give details of where settings are stored in the Registry, as well as some settings you might want to play with. I've done my best to verify these, but mistakes can creep into any document! Be careful: Making changes to the Registry can damage your system. In such cases, reinstallation is the only option.

TIP

If you are a hacker and like viewing DLL files, you will note that, by default, you cannot select Quick View from the context menu to see a Control applet's Technical File Information as you can with other DLLs. To enable you to see this information, simply add the following two keys to the Registry:

\HKEY_CLASSES_ROOT\cplfile\shell\Quick View

\HKEY_CLASSES_ROOT\cplfile\shell\Quick View\Command

Next, edit the default value key for the Command Key to contain the following entry, adjusted for where you installed NT Workstation:

D:\Winnt40\system32\viewers\quikview %1

Then, you can view the SYSTEM32 directory and the technical details of the applet by selecting the default Quick View viewer. You have to select the default viewer, however.

The Common Control Panel Applets

Table 6.1 shows the most common Control Panel applets.

Table 6.1. Control Panel applets and their functions.

Icon	Control Panel Applet	Applet Function	System or User Setting
	Accessibility Options	Changes the accessibility options	User
	Add/Remove Programs	Installs and uninstalls certain applications and key NT components	System
	Console	Configures the console window	User
	CSNW	Configures client services for NetWare	User
	Date/Time	Sets the date, time, and time zone	System
	Devices	Starts/stops device drivers	System
	Dial-Up Monitor	Monitors the dial-up port(s)	System
	Display	Changes the Display settings	User/System
	Fonts	Displays, adds, or removes fonts	System
	Internet	Configures Internet Explorer Settings	System
	Keyboard	Configures your keyboard	User/System
	Mail	Manages Microsoft Exchange profiles	User
	Microsoft Mail Postoffice	Sets up and maintains a Microsoft Mail Workgroup post office	System

continues

Table 6.1. continued

Icon	Control Panel Applet	Applet Function	System or User Setting
	Modems	Installs and configures your modem	System
	Mouse	Configures the mouse	User
	Multimedia	Configures multimedia devices, including audio, video, and CD	System
	Network	Configures the network adapter, protocols, and services	System
	PC Card (PCMCIA)	Examines and configures PCMCIA cards	System
	Ports	Specifies the communications parameters for serial ports	System
	Printers	Installs and configures local and remote printers	System
	Regional Settings	Sets up local language settings (language, keyboard, currency, and so on)	User/System
	SCSI Adapters	Installs and configures SCSI adapters and IDE CD-ROMs	System
	Server	Reviews and manages the properties of the Server service	System
	Services	Controls NT system services	System
	Sounds	Associates sounds with events	User
	System	Reviews and manages system settings	System

Icon	Control Panel Applet	Applet Function	System or User Setting
	Tape Devices	Installs and configures tape backup devices	System
	Telephony	Controls and configures telephony functions	System
	UPS	Configures the Uninterruptible Power Supply	

Selecting any of the applets from Control Panel brings up a dialog box. Typically, these dialog boxes are tabbed and have additional buttons bringing up subdialog boxes. Some applets, such as The Network, are highly complex—with the options set on the various tab pages all interacting—whereas others are simpler. To help you get the most out of Windows NT Workstation, I describe each of these applets in more detail in the following sections. I probably provide more detail than the average user needs, but you never know when this sort of information will come in handy!

Security

Most of the Control Panel applets allow any user to invoke the applet and modify the related settings. Other applets, such as the Date/Time, are considered more secure and cannot be changed by normal users. In general, users cannot modify (change, add, or delete) any device drivers or system services. In order to use these applets, you must be a member of the Administrators local group on your workstation. This is all part of NT's normal security model, which is discussed in Chapter 1, "What Is Windows New Technology?"

The Control Panel applets that are not available to all users are Date/Time, Devices, Keyboard, Modems, Multimedia, Network, Ports, Printers, SCSI Adapters, Server, Services, System, Tape Devices, and UPS. The specific security restrictions for these applets are noted in the descriptions that follow.

What's Next?

In the sections that follow, I look at each applet in turn, show the key dialogs within each applet, and give some advice on how the applet might be used.

Accessibility Options

Microsoft is committed to making computers easier for everyone to use, including users with physical handicaps and disabilities. Windows NT 4 has a set of features known as the

Accessibility Options that let a disabled user use Windows NT more effectively. Although these functions were designed primarily for the disabled, they can be very helpful to the able-bodied, and I regularly utilize a number of them!

When you install Windows NT Workstation, you have the option to also install the accessibility options. If they were not installed when NT was first installed, they can be installed later using the Add/Remove Programs applet, which is described later in this chapter.

Accessibility settings are per-user settings stored in the Registry under the key `HKEY_CURRENT_USER\Accessibility`. Although most users will never need, or want, to use all these features, the Accessibility applet has a total of 10 separate and interrelated dialogs.

> **TIP**
>
> Most of the accessibility functions can be turned on and (optionally) off with keyboard shortcut keys. These are worth memorizing if you only want to use the features for short periods of time.

Selecting the Accessibility applet brings up the dialog box shown in Figure 6.3. This dialog box contains four separate tabbed dialogs, which control different aspects of the accessibility settings.

FIGURE 6.3.

Accessibility Properties.

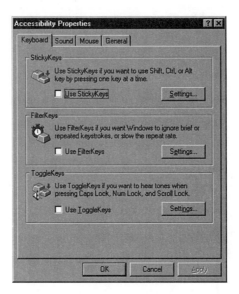

The keyboard functions, shown in Figure 6.3, allow you to modify the behavior of the keyboard, offering StickyKeys, FilterKeys, and ToggleKeys.

StickyKeys

Many Windows applications utilize one of the modifier keys (Shift, Alt, or Ctrl), pressed in conjunction with some other key. For example, you can press both the Alt and the F keys simultaneously to open the File menu in most Windows applications.

The StickyKeys function enables you to enter these modified keys by first pressing the modifier and then the key to be modified—that is, Alt followed by F. The StickyKey options are set in the dialog box shown in Figure 6.4.

FIGURE 6.4.

Settings for StickyKeys.

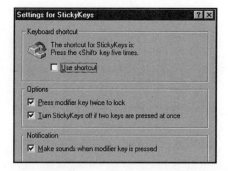

You can turn on the StickyKeys function either by selecting the StickyKeys function in the Keyboard dialog or (optionally) via the keyboard shortcut, pressing either the right or left Shift key five times. After StickyKeys is on, you can turn it off by pressing any modifier key and another key simultaneously (for example, Alt and F). This can be useful when you want to use the StickyKeys function only for a short time.

You can also lock the modifier by pressing it twice, which is very convenient for one-hand typing.

The Notification option specifies whether Windows NT should play a sound when the control keys governed by StickyKeys are pressed. The sound is a high-pitched beep when the option is turned on and a low-pitched beep when the option is turned off.

TIP

You can select StickyKeys for occasional use only if you enabled the shortcut keys in the StickyKeys Settings dialog. Don't forget that enabling the shortcut key to turn off StickyKeys is a separate option.

FilterKeys

The FilterKeys function directs NT to filter out keys typed too quickly. The FilterKeys functions are invoked by the dialog shown in Figure 6.5.

FIGURE 6.5.

Settings for FilterKeys.

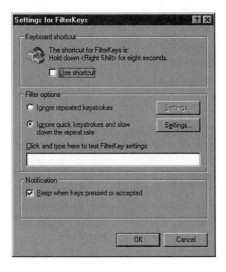

The Filter options directs NT to either ignore repeated keys or to ignore keys typed too quickly by slowing down the keyboard. Like the other accessibility options, FilterKeys can be invoked by a keyboard shortcut, holding down the right shift key for eight seconds.

Both Filter options have Settings buttons that allow the user to control how quickly or slowly the keyboard responds. Selecting the Settings button for the Ignore Repeated Keystrokes feature invokes the dialog box shown in Figure 6.6. This dialog enables the user to determine whether keystrokes typed within the range of a half a second to two seconds are ignored.

FIGURE 6.6.

Advanced FilterKeys settings—ignoring repeated keystrokes.

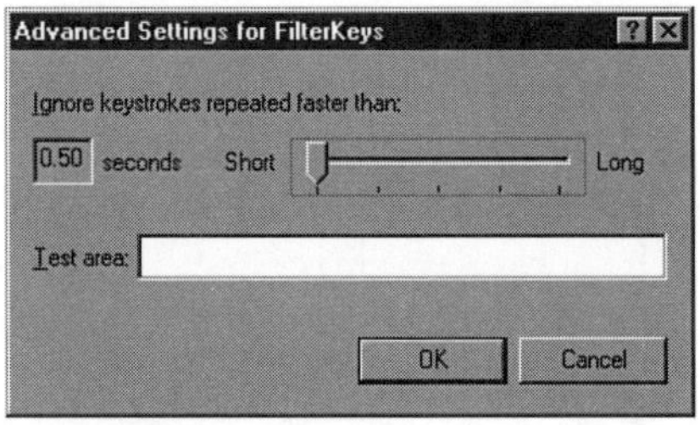

Selecting the Settings button for the Ignore Quick Keystrokes and Slow Down the Repeat Rate option invokes the dialog box shown in Figure 6.7. This enables the user to override the keyboard rate specified in the Keyboard Control Panel applet.

The user can direct NT to perform no keyboard repeats (that is, each key must be pressed and then released before the next keystroke is accepted) or to slow down the keyboard repeat rates. You set both the Repeat Delay and Repeat Rate within the range 0.3 to 2 seconds using the slider bars in Figure 6.7.

FIGURE 6.7.

Advanced FilterKeys settings—slowing down the keyboard repeat rate.

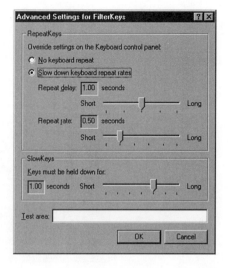

Both of the advanced settings dialogs and the main FilterKeys dialog offer a test area within the dialog box so that you can test the specific filter settings. You should probably test any changes to the settings before applying them.

ToggleKeys

The ToggleKeys function, shown in Figure 6.8, instructs your system to make a sound via the system speaker when the Caps Lock, Scroll Lock, or Num Lock keys are toggled. When you turn on ToggleKeys, the system makes a high-pitched sound whenever one of the modifier keys is turned on and a low sound when it is toggled off. The keyboard shortcut is enabled by checking the option as shown in Figure 6.8.

FIGURE 6.8.

Settings for ToggleKeys.

The ToggleKeys function is useful for those of us who touch type but not accurately. It gets so annoying hearing these sounds that after a while, your fingers stop hitting the keys by accident.

Sounds

The Sound functions, shown in Figure 6.9, allow you to control how Windows NT informs the user of common error events that are usually signaled by a sound (the beep). The two sound options are SoundSentry and ShowSounds.

FIGURE 6.9.

Accessibility sounds.

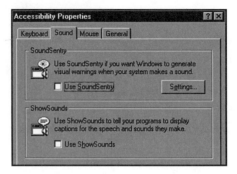

When Windows NT Workstation or a running application detects a user error, it usually indicates the error with a single beep of the system's speaker.

To assist users with impaired hearing, the SoundSentry function instructs Windows NT to flash part of the screen as an alternative to sounding the system speaker. With the Sounds applet, described in the section "Sounds" later in this chapter, you can make WAV files serve as these sounds.

You can choose to make no visual notification (the default), flash the active caption bar, flash the active window, or flash the entire desktop, as shown in Figure 6.10.

FIGURE 6.10.

Settings for SoundSentry.

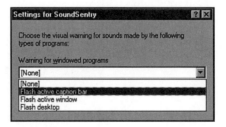

ShowSounds instructs programs that usually convey information only by sound to also provide all information visually, such as by displaying text captions or informative icons. Applications must be specifically written to utilize ShowSounds.

MouseKeys

Selecting the Mouse tab from the main Accessibility dialog invokes the MouseKeys functions, shown in Figure 6.11, which enable you to use the numeric keypad as an alternative to a mouse.

FIGURE 6.11.

MouseKeys settings.

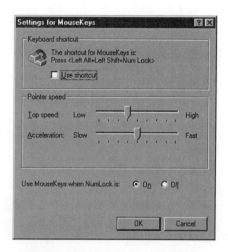

Like the other accessibility functions, the MouseKeys option has a keyboard shortcut, which is Left Alt+Left Shift+Num Lock. Selecting the function either by using the checkbox or the keyboard shortcut enables you to use the numeric keyboard on full-size keyboards as an alternative to using the mouse. This can be very handy for precision work where the mouse might be too crude or in situations where you have no mouse. The Pointer Speed slider bars let you inform Windows NT how fast to accelerate and move the mouse when you select the numeric keyboard keys.

TIP

You can use the MouseKeys on a laptop as long as the laptop implements an embedded numeric keypad. You should consult the manufacturer's documentation to determine whether your system supports an embedded keyboard and how to access it.

General Accessibility Features

The remaining accessibility functions are invoked from the General tab, as shown in Figure 6.12.

The Automatic Reset function causes NT to reset all accessibility options if they are not used within a certain time period, which can range from 5 to 30 minutes.

The Notification option shown in Figure 6.12 directs Windows NT to play a confirmation sound every time you use any shortcut key to turn an accessibility feature on or off. This is very useful as a way of alerting users who might turn on a feature accidentally.

FIGURE 6.12.

General accessibility properties.

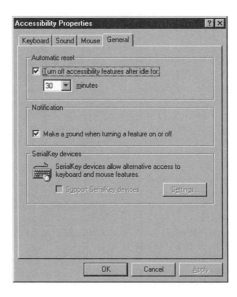

The SerialKeys feature allows you to attach an alternate input device (also called an augmentative communication device) to your computer's serial port. This feature is designed for people who are unable to use the computer's standard keyboard and mouse and have suitable hardware.

TIP

After you select a set of accessibility options, you can then apply them, which activates them for the current user. NT also allows you to invoke these settings as the default for all new users at the login stage before the current user is determined.

TIP

For additional information on Microsoft's products and services for people with disabilities, contact the Microsoft Sales Information Center in your local Microsoft subsidiary.

In the USA, contact

Microsoft Sales Information Center
One Microsoft Way
Redmond, Washington 98052-6393
Voice telephone: (800) 426 9400
Text telephone: (800) 892 5234
Fax: (206) 635 6100

Add/Remove Programs

The Add/Remove Programs applet, shown in Figure 6.13, provides a simple way to add or remove Windows applications as well as add or remove Windows NT options.

FIGURE 6.13.

*Properties for Add/
Remove Programs.*

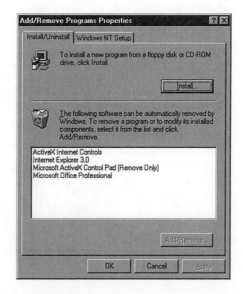

The Add/Remove dialog allows you to either install a new application or remove a previously installed application.

Installing or Removing Applications

You usually install most applications by running a vendor-supplied program, and because most application vendors utilize Microsoft's generic setup engine, the installation program is usually SETUP.EXE.

Although most users install applications by running the appropriate install program from the vendor-supplied CD or disk set, the Add/Remove Programs applet provides an alternative method. Selecting the Install button starts the Install Wizard, which first scans the floppy drive and CD. If the wizard is unable to find the setup program, another dialog enables the user to browse for the installation program.

The Add/Remove function also provides a consistent way to remove an application or run the setup to add new application components. This option is only available if the application's installation program was based on Microsoft's Install Shield functions. Because not all applications are installed this way, not every application can utilize the Uninstall feature of this dialog. If your application is not visible in the list and you need to update or remove it, consult the vendor's documentation to determine how best to do this.

Installing or Removing Windows NT Core Components

The Windows NT Setup dialog allows you to add or remove various components of Windows NT, as shown in Figure 6.14. When Windows NT was initially installed, some or all of the installable options were selected. The dialog box shown in Figure 6.14, which is similar to the one displayed by the Windows NT Install process, allows you to add or remove core Windows NT components.

FIGURE 6.14.

Add/Remove Windows NT components.

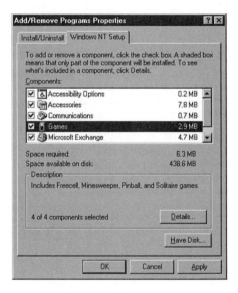

The components that you can install or remove by using this dialog are Accessibility Options, Accessories, Communications, Games, Microsoft Exchange, and Multimedia. With the exception of the Accessibility Options, all the components have subcomponents that you can select individually for installation or removal.

All the components, with the exception of the Accessories, have one or more associated Control Panel applets. If you don't see the related applet within Control Panel, the appropriate component probably was not installed. You should check the Windows NT Installation to ensure that the component was installed.

Console

Although most applications run from Windows NT are Windows applications, NT also provides good support for older DOS-based applications. Windows NT comes with a command interpreter, CMD.EXE, which looks and feels like DOS. The code for the command interpreter was based on DOS 5; as a result, CMD.EXE should be familiar to anyone who knows DOS. Command-line dinosaurs like me can even use EDLIN.COM to edit text files if they want!

Windows NT, like Windows 3.*x*, can display applications running under CMD.EXE either full screen or in a window, often referred to as a console window. A console window is a normal window that contains only the console prompt.

TIP

It might look like DOS and feel like DOS, but the command prompt is not DOS. The standard icon used to denote the command prompt program, the familiar C:\> prompt of CMD.EXE, might give you the impression that you're using DOS. Trust me—this is not DOS! To avoid confusion, consider changing the icon on any shortcuts to the command prompt to avoid confusion.

The Console Windows Properties applet, shown in Figure 6.15, enables you to configure the look and feel of the console windows.

FIGURE 6.15.

Console Windows Properties.

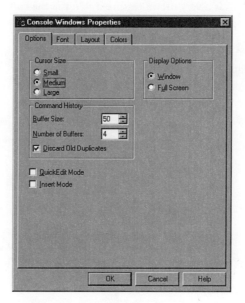

Console Options

The Options dialog, shown in Figure 6.15, enables you to specify the following:

- Cursor Size allows you to resize the cursor to be Small (the traditional underline cursor), Medium (a solid rectangle at half height), or Large (a solid, full-height rectangle).

- Display Options allows you to indicate whether to display the command prompt in a window or full screen, by default.

- With Command History, you can specify how large a command history buffer to keep, how many of the buffers to keep, and whether duplicate commands should be discarded from the buffer.

- QuickEdit Mode enables you to use a mouse to perform cut-and-paste operations without using the command window's Edit menu. If this option is selected, however, you cannot use the mouse to drive any DOS applications, such as EDIT.COM, started in the command prompt window.

- Insert Mode gives you the option to start the command prompt with insert enabled; as a result, the text you type is inserted at the cursor. If this is not checked, text typed at the cursor replaces any existing text. After the command prompt is started, you can easily toggle the insert mode off and on by pressing the Ins key.

The command interpreter CMD.EXE maintains a history of the commands entered and allows you to recall them in essentially the same way as the DOSKEY program that came with DOS 5. CMD.EXE automatically sets up this buffer based on the Command History settings noted previously. This is a very useful feature if you use the command prompt often.

Command Prompt Fonts

The Font dialog, shown in Figure 6.16, enables you to specify the font type and size to be used when a command prompt is displayed within a window.

FIGURE 6.16.

Console windows fonts.

The Font box lists all the fonts on your system that Windows NT uses within a windowed command prompt. The size of TrueType fonts is measured using normal point size; for raster

6

CONTROL PANEL
BASICS

fonts, the measurement in screen pixels indicates how wide and high the character should be generated.

The Window Preview window shows you how much of your physical screen will be taken up by the console window, and the Selected Font box at the bottom of the dialog shows what the selected font will look like when displayed in the window.

Command Prompt Layout

The Layout dialog, shown in Figure 6.17, allows you to configure how many rows and columns the command prompt screen buffer should contain, how many rows and columns to display, and where to place the window on the screen.

FIGURE 6.17.

Console Windows layout.

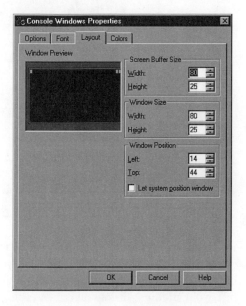

In the Layout dialog, the Screen Buffer Size represents the number of rows and columns Windows NT Workstation reserves for your console session, and the Window Size is how large the console window should be when it is first displayed. If the screen buffer size is greater than the initial display you configure, the window appears with the appropriate scroll bars. This dialog does not let you configure a window size smaller than the buffer. Also, if you increase the window size, Windows NT automatically reduces the size of the window font.

The Window Position option lets you specify where the upper-left corner of the console window should be. You can either specify the exact position by providing the offset relative to the upper-left hand corner of the screen, or let the system position it for you by checking the Let System Position Window checkbox.

Like the Font dialog, the Layout dialog has a Window Preview to let you see approximately how much of the physical screen will be taken up by the command prompt window.

Console Windows Colors

The Colors dialog, shown in Figure 6.18, allows you to set and review the foreground and background colors of text displayed at the command prompt.

FIGURE 6.18.

Console Windows colors.

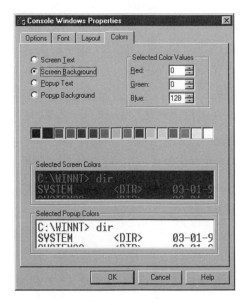

This dialog allows you to specify separately the colors used for the normal screen and any pop-up screens. For users with high-resolution video adapters, you can even mix the specific colors by indicating the precise mix of red, green, and blue. You can see any color selections made in this screen in the Layout and Font dialogs described earlier.

> **TIP**
>
> The values you specify in the Console applet decide the defaults for all console prompts. You can create multiple shortcuts to the CMD.EXE program and configure each one with a different combination of options, which may suit different applications. After you change any of options on any shortcut to the command prompt, however, changes made by the Console applet have no effect on those shortcuts.

Client Service for NetWare (CSNW)

Windows NT Workstation provides full client support for Novell NetWare 2.*x*, 3.*x*, and 4.*x* as a standard part of Windows NT Workstation. This client support is provided by loading the Client Service for NetWare in the Networks applet.

The CSNW dialog, shown in Figure 6.19, allows you to specify your default NDS tree and context (for 4.*x* servers using NDS) or your preferred server (non-NDS), as well as control key printing features.

FIGURE 6.19.

*Client Service for
NetWare configuration.*

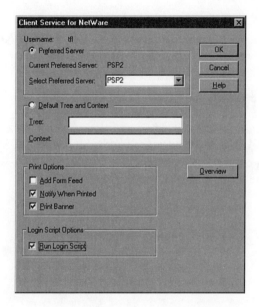

These settings are user specific but are stored in the Registry in HKEY_LOCAL_MACHINE\ SYSTEM\CurrentControlSet\Services\NWCWorkstation\Parameters\Options. If you look at this key, you see a subkey per user (identified by the Windows NT SID), below which you see the CSNW options. This does mean that these parameters are not transportable via roving profiles.

Configuring Client Services for NetWare

If you are using NetWare 3.*x* or 2.*x* (or 4.*x* with Bindery Emulation), you specify an initial server to log into as part of the NT login process. This server, the Preferred Server, is selected from the combo box, which initially contains all bindery-based NetWare servers that were discovered on the network. You also have the option of <None>, in which case no login is attempted until you try to access a NetWare server.

If you are using Novell NetWare 4.*x* and NDS, you can alternatively specify the NDS tree and context. As with the Preferred Server, when the Default tree and context are specified, Windows NT Workstation logs you into this context as part of the login process.

Under Print Options, you can configure the following:

- Add Form Feed causes the NetWare printer to add a form feed to the end of each document sent for printing.
- Notify When Printed provides notification messages when your documents have been printed.
- Print Banner generates a printer banner page for each document sent for printing.

You can find more details on interfacing with Novell NetWare in Chapter 17, "Windows NT Network Protocols."

Date/Time

NT uses the time and date held in your system's clock for a variety of purposes, such as time stamping files, checking for the latest version of files, and so on. It is important, therefore, that your system clock is set to the correct date and time. One way to do this is using the Date/Time Control Panel applet, shown in Figure 6.20.

FIGURE 6.20.

Date/Time properties.

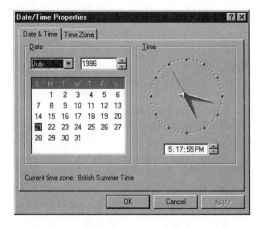

You must be a member of either the Power Users or Administrators group to change Date/Time settings.

Setting Date and Time

The Date/Time Properties dialog allows you to specify the current day, month, and year as well as the current time of day. This is done using a combination of a pull-down list, several spinner boxes, and a calendar.

Selecting Time Zones

In order to coordinate time around the world, which is vital in large global networks, Windows NT also needs to know your time zone, whether your time zone has a local summer time, and if so, the summer-time starting and ending dates. Time zones are selected using the dialog box shown in Figure 6.21.

FIGURE 6.21.

Selecting time zones.

The names and details of all time zones are held in the Registry under the `\HKEY_LOCAL_MACHINE\ Software\Microsoft\Windows NT\Current Version\Time Zones` key.

If the selected time zone information includes details of when local summer time starts and ends, Windows NT automatically adjusts your clock the first time you reboot after summer time starts or finishes. However, the definition of summer time start and finish has changed in some countries recently. NT's understanding of these dates currently appears to be correct, but you might need to edit your time zone information if these dates change.

> **TIP**
>
> The Windows NT Resource Kit has a utility `TZEDIT.EXE`, which allows you to modify the details of all time zones, as well as add new ones. Using this utility is probably easier and less error prone than modifying it manually, particularly because some of the time zone information is held in binary.

Devices

Windows NT supports a large number of hardware devices such as network cards, SCSI device drivers, and so on. In order for any device to be useable, it must have a device driver installed and running.

The Devices dialog, shown in Figure 6.22, allows you to manage the device drivers on your system if you are a member of the Administrators local group. With this dialog, you can start and stop individual device drivers, change the startup type for the devices, and include or exclude them from a hardware profile.

FIGURE 6.22.

The Devices dialog.

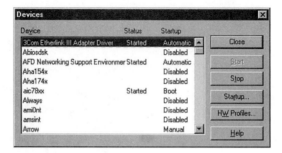

Windows NT automatically starts devices at different times during the loading of the system, depending on the device. The startup types include the following:

- Boot: The device drivers for boot types are loaded by the initial loader and initialized as part of the initialization of the NT Kernel. This class includes a SCSI disk controller.

- System: These devices, which are essential to the system's operation, start every time the system starts but after the boot devices. Such devices include the floppy disk, the system speaker, the CD-ROM, the disk unidriver, keyboard, and mouse.

- Automatic: These devices start after the boot and system devices. Generally, these devices are not critical to basic system operation and include devices such as the parallel port and network drivers.

- Manual: These devices are started either by the user or by a dependent device.

- Disabled: These devices cannot be started by the user (that is, using the Start button) as they usually relate to devices that you do not have on your system.

Selecting a device and clicking Startup in the Devices dialog invokes the Device dialog shown in Figure 6.23, which allows you to select the startup type.

FIGURE 6.23.

Configuring a device's startup type.

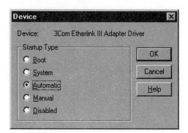

> **WARNING**
>
> For the most part, Windows NT configures all devices to start at the correct time. If you decide to change these options, you might render Windows NT unable to boot carefully. Be careful if you're messing around with device startup types!

Another important thing to remember is that to change a device driver's startup class or to start and stop a driver, you must be a member of the Administrators group.

Hardware Profiles and Device Drivers

Using the System applet, you can create hardware profiles. These profiles allow you to specify different hardware configurations that you can choose when Windows NT starts up. Hardware profiles are very useful, for example, for a laptop user who might have a docking station; the user can choose one profile when the laptop is docked and the other when the system is not docked.

After the profile is created, you can decide which devices you want to enable or disable for a given profile. You simply select the device and then click the HW Profiles button to invoke the dialog box shown in Figure 6.24. From this dialog box, you can enable or disable the device.

FIGURE 6.24.

Including devices in a hardware profile.

For more details on Windows NT device drivers, see Chapter 10, "Advanced System Configuration."

Dial-Up Monitor

Windows NT Workstation includes a powerful set of dial-up networking (DUN) facilities, described in more detail in Chapter 21, "Remote Access Service." Using DUN, you can connect to your corporate network or to the Internet via an Internet service provider. These connections are made using a modem, which you set up using the Modem Control Panel applet.

After you have a connection to a remote system, you can use the Dial-Up Monitor to monitor that connection. You also use the Dial-Up Monitor applet to set certain monitoring preferences, such as making a sound when a connection is made or dropped.

Dial-Up Networking Status

The Dial-Up Networking Monitor is shown in Figure 6.25. With this dialog, you see details about the active connection. The counters on this dialog are updated in real time as the data is transferred.

Figure 6.25.

Dial-Up Networking Monitor.

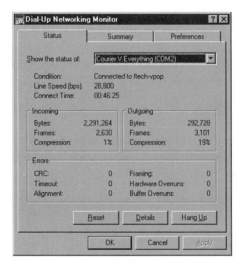

At the top of the dialog, you can select the connection to monitor and see a summary of that connection's current status, which shows the connection speed and how long the connection has been active.

In the lower portion of this dialog, you can see the current statistics for incoming and outgoing communications along with a summary of errors. For both incoming and outgoing data, the Dial-Up Networking Monitor displays the number of characters sent and received and how many network frames the data took, as well as the level of data compression achieved.

Depending on what data is transferred and what modem is used for the connection, the level of compression varies, possibly significantly. Downloading a binary file from a remote file server will probably not result in much, if any, data compression. Downloading a text file, particularly if you're using the right modem, is likely to result in much higher compression.

The Status dialog also displays a set of error counts. In general, any errors seen here are bad news, mainly because they degrade performance. This dialog box shows six types of errors: CRC, Timeout, Alignment, Framing, Hardware Overrun, and Buffer Overrun. These errors are caused by a number of factors, including noisy phone lines, poor modem connections, and badly be-having modems.

Windows NT always attempts to retransmit any data that was lost or transmitted in error. Although a few errors in a long connection are possibly acceptable, each error reduces your throughput. If you get more frequent errors, you should identify the cause and, if at all possible, eliminate it.

Connection Summary

The dialog box shown in Figure 6.26 displays a summary of any active connection, showing how long the connection has been active. With Windows NT Server, you can combine multiple physical connections for higher overall throughput. This facility, which you would monitor using this dialog box, is not available in Windows NT Workstation.

FIGURE 6.26.

Dial-Up Networking Monitor summary.

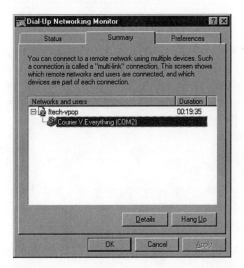

Monitoring Preferences

The Monitoring Preferences dialog, shown in Figure 6.27, provides you with a way of setting some monitoring features related to dial-up networking.

The Play a Sound group enables you to configure a sound to be played whenever a connection is made or dropped, whenever data is sent or received, or whenever a line error is detected. If you are experiencing connection errors, this might assist you in detecting and resolving these errors.

If you select the Include Dial-Up Networking Monitor in the Task List option, when you connect to your remote server, Windows NT starts up the Dial-Up Networking Monitor and includes it on the taskbar. After this is displayed in the taskbar, you can right-click the taskbar to perform certain administrative functions, such as disconnecting the connection.

FIGURE 6.27.

*Dial-up networking
preferences.*

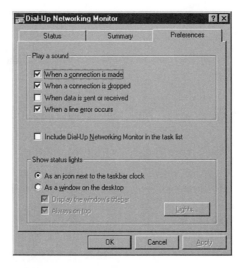

Dial-up networking can also give you a visual representation of data that is sent or received via the modem. The Show Status Lights section at the bottom of the dialog box enables you to choose whether the set of status lights is a separate icon on the desktop or a small icon on the taskbar next to the clock. Both representations provide a good method of determining how much data is sent and received.

Display

To many people, the display is the computer, and it is vital to the proper operation of their systems. The Display applet configures the properties for the Windows NT desktop, including the background, the screen saver, and so on.

You can select the Display Properties dialog, shown in Figure 6.28, either from the Control Panel or more directly by right-clicking anywhere on the desktop and selecting Properties from the shortcut menu.

Altering the Desktop Background

The Background dialog allows you to set a background pattern or wallpaper on the desktop. The top of the dialog box displays a thumbnail view of the currently chosen background.

Wallpaper is a bitmap, stored in a BMP file, that you can display on the desktop. My workstation has a wonderful picture of a tropical island—just right for those cold, rainy, winter days here in England! You can use one of the BMPs that come with Windows NT Workstation, download images from the Internet or use a graphics package to create your own. You can opt to show the bitmap at normal size or stretch it to fill the screen.

FIGURE 6.28.
Display properties.

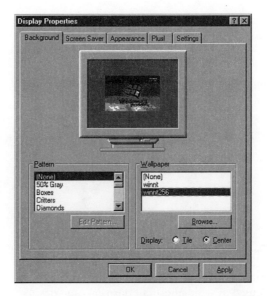

A desktop pattern is an 8 × 8–pixel pattern made up of either the desktop color set in the Appearance tab, or black. Each pixel can be either of these two colors. The 8 × 8 pattern is then tiled on the desktop.

You can choose to have either a pattern, the wallpaper, or both displayed on your desktop. If you choose to have both, the wallpaper appears on top of the pattern. If the wallpaper is stretched to fit the desktop (using the Plus! dialog shown in Figure 6.33) or the wallpaper is tiled to cover the entire screen, the pattern will not be visible.

TIP

Desktop patterns are stored in the Registry under HKEY_CURRENT_USER\Control Panel\Patterns.

Each pattern is stored in a string value as a set of 8 bytes, one for each column of the pattern. In each byte, each bit represents one pixel, the low order being the bottom row of the pattern and the high order being the top row. The pattern shown in Figure 6.29 is stored as 215 178 146 8 24 40 120 8.

You can add new patterns by first choosing an existing pattern and clicking the Edit Pattern button. This action invokes the Pattern Editor, shown in Figure 6.29, which you use to edit the pattern.

By left-clicking each pixel, you can toggle individual pixels, changing them to black or the desktop color. While you are editing the pattern, Windows NT shows what the pattern looks like at full size in the Sample window. If you type a new name in the Name text box, you can then add it to the list of patterns shown in Figure 6.28.

FIGURE 6.29.

Desktop Pattern Editor.

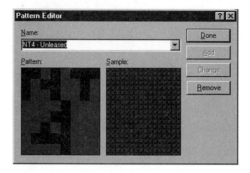

Screen Saver

A screen saver is a program that is set to run whenever the system is idle. Screen savers were traditionally used to avoid phosphor burn-in, caused when a single image is displayed for long periods of time. They also reduce the risk of someone viewing sensitive material when the screen is left unattended. Other screen savers are just plain fun!

The Screen Saver dialog, shown in Figure 6.30, allows you to designate and configure a screen saver. Windows NT Workstation comes with five 3-D and six 2-D screen savers. The 3-D screen savers are programmed using the OpenGL graphics library and are quite dramatic.

FIGURE 6.30.

Specifying a display screen saver.

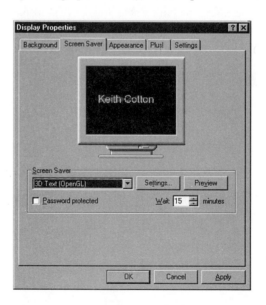

Each screen saver is stored in a file with an SCR extension. The screen savers are located in the %SYSTEMROOT%\System32 directory.

Although they are stored with the SCR extension, screen savers are executable programs. If you execute the file by running it from the command prompt, you see the configuration dialog. However, running the screen saver from the Start/Run dialog runs the screen saver itself. Who needs consistency when you have cool screen savers?

Most screen savers have configuration options that you can set by selecting the Settings box. If the screen saver can be configured, a dialog box appears (if not, you get an error message box). The configuration dialog for the 3D Text screen saver is shown in Figure 6.31.

FIGURE 6.31.

Configuring a screen saver.

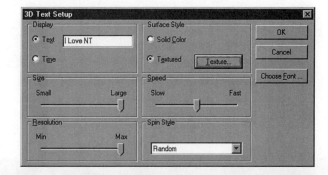

TIP

To display the list of NT developers, first select the 3D Text screen saver. Configure it to display the text I Love NT, and that's it. This trick worked in the beta versions of NT Workstation Version 4, but it doesn't work in the final version! With the final release version of NT Workstation Version 4, entering I love NT now produces the response good?. It's a puzzle. See if you can figure it out!

Appearance

The Appearance dialog, shown in Figure 6.32, allows you to configure the visual components of the Windows NT environment, such as the desktop color, menu font, icon spacing, and so on.

To configure an item, you first select it either by clicking the preview window or by selecting it from the Item pull-down list.

Windows NT comes with a set of predefined display schemes that you can select by using the Scheme pull-down list. If you change the setting on any element, you can then save the new scheme to a scheme name of your choice.

FIGURE 6.32.

Display appearance.

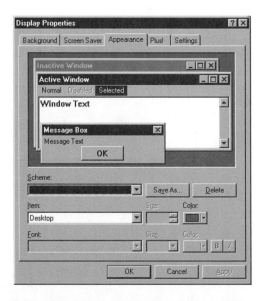

> **TIP**
>
> Although some display appearance schemes look seriously cool at first sight, they can be rather tiring on the eyes, particularly if you use your system for long periods of time. The default scheme is Windows Standard and seems to cause the least eye strain, even if it's not cool.

The display schemes are stored in the Registry under HKEY_CURRENT_USER\Control Panel\ Appearance\Schemes. The individual schemes are stored as long binary values and are probably best edited using the Display dialog.

Plus! Features

The Plus! pack is a set of add-on features for Windows 95, some of which are included as an integral part of Windows NT Version 4. The Plus! dialog, show in Figure 6.33, allows you to configure some elements of the display.

The Desktop Icons feature enables you to change the default icons for My Computer, the Network Neighborhood, and the full and empty recycle bin. By selecting one of the four icons in the preview windows and then clicking the Change Icon button, you can select an alternative icon to use. By selecting the icon and clicking the Default button, you can restore the default icons.

FIGURE 6.33.

Display Plus! features.

The Visual Settings feature allows you to affect the following aspects of the display:

■ Use Large Icons directs Windows NT Workstation to display larger icons in all displays involving icons (for example, the desktop, icon folder views, and so on), which can be a help to those with visual impairments or used for demonstration purposes.

■ Show Windows Contents While Dragging, known as Full Windows Drag in Windows NT Version 3.51, redraws any window that is dragged or resized as it moves, rather than just move or resize the window's outline and redraw when the window is finally dropped. This makes it easy to see how the window is affected by the drag. Because this function is very graphics intensive, you should probably use it only on more powerful systems.

■ Smooth Edges of Screen Fonts improves the appearance of screen fonts by smoothing the jagged edges, particularly with large fonts. To use this option, your video card and display monitor must support 256 colors, although support for high color (16-bit color) is recommended.

■ Show Icons Using All Possible Colors ensures that icons are displayed using the full color palette available, rather than a 16-color palette. Arguably, icons look better using the full palette, but this requires a graphics card and monitor capable of at least 256 colors. Changing this option requires a reboot before it takes effect.

■ Stretch Desktop Wallpaper to Fit Screen stretches the selected wallpaper so that it covers your entire screen. You must turn on the Center option in the Background dialog, noted previously, to use this option.

FIGURE 6.34.

Display settings.

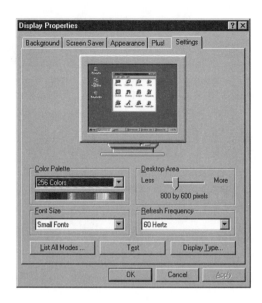

Display Settings

The Display Settings option enables you to specify the color palette depth, the desktop area, font size, and monitor refresh rate. The Settings dialog box is shown in Figure 6.34.

The specific settings available vary according to the video card and monitor in use. On my laptop, for example, I'm only able to get a maximum of 64 colors, a 640 × 480–pixel desktop area, and a refresh rate capable of only 60Hz—but my desktop system is capable of 16 million colors, 800 × 600 pixels, and a 72Hz refresh rate.

After you have selected settings, it is sensible to test them to ensure they work! Clicking on Test displays a simple test pattern using your new settings. After displaying the test pattern for five seconds, Windows NT reverts to the old settings and displays a dialog box asking whether you saw the pattern properly. If you saw the test pattern fully, the new settings are safe, and you can select them. If you didn't see the pattern, select No when prompted (which is the default) and you can try different combinations.

TIP

If you accidentally select display settings that result in a garbled display, you have two options to fix the problem. First, you need to reboot your system, which means powering it off and then back on. You can either select the VGA Mode option from the boot menu or select the Last Known Good control set by pressing space when prompted. To avoid this problem, always test your settings before selecting them!

For more details on configuring your display, see Chapter 10.

Fonts

The term *font* refers to the way in which characters are formed on an output device. Any given font has a number of specific features, including weight (how thick the font is), slant (whether it's an italic font or not), and so on.

With a large number of fonts available, you can literally find thousands. Microsoft Office loads a number of extra fonts, for example. CorelDraw! includes nearly 100 fonts (although I've yet to meet anyone who's found a use for more than a handful of these).

Fonts are important because they can reinforce the written message. A flowery, cursive font is probably better for writing poetry or thank-you letters than for a warning sign. Likewise, a bold sans serif font is more useful in a book for topic and chapter headings than for body text.

Windows NT supports a number of different types of fonts:

- ■ Printer fonts are built into the printer and vary by printer. Virtually all PostScript printers support a basic set of 35 printer fonts, whereas non-PostScript printers vary widely in what is supported.
- ■ Screen fonts govern how letters appear on the screen and generally come in predefined sizes that cannot be scaled.
- ■ TrueType fonts are fully scaleable fonts that can be used both as screen and printer fonts, thus enabling WYSIWYG (what you see is what you get). This is important if you want to proof something on the screen and know it will look like that on the printed page, something that is not always possible with screen and printer fonts.
- ■ Bitmap fonts consist of bitmaps for a particular size and weight and do not scale. Often referred to as soft fonts, these can be downloaded to the printer.
- ■ Vector fonts hold instructions about how they should be drawn, so they are scaleable. In general, they do not look as nice when scaled as TrueType fonts do.

With Windows NT Workstation, any fonts you install automatically become available from any Windows application, including Windows NT itself. DOS applications, however, are not able to take advantage of these fonts, and their fonts are loaded on a per-application basis.

After a font is loaded, you can use it in any Windows application that supports that font. You can also use it as an element of your desktop by using the Display applet's Appearance function.

NOTE

Some Windows applications do not recognize and use all the fonts loaded onto your system. The Console applet only works with fixed-width fonts. The HyperTerminal application also works with a limited range of fonts.

Fonts Folder

The Fonts folder, found in `%SYSTEMROOT%\Fonts`, holds all the fonts that applications running on Windows NT Workstation use. The Fonts option in the Control Panel is really just a shortcut to the Fonts folder. The Fonts folder on my system is shown in Figure 6.35.

FIGURE 6.35.

Fonts folder.

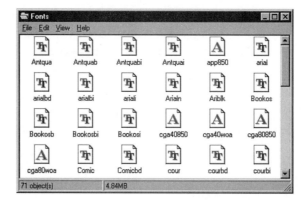

Font Sample Sheet

Selecting one of the fonts shown in Figure 6.35 and opening it brings up a Font sample sheet, as shown in Figure 6.36. This font sheet displays the font, any copyright information, and a sample of the font. At the bottom of the sample sheet, a sample sentence is displayed using the chosen font, repeated in different font sizes. This sample shows you what the font looks like in larger sizes, and you can print it to view the likely output.

FIGURE 6.36.

Font sample.

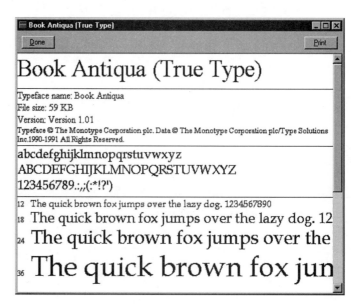

TIP

If you want to streamline your Windows NT Workstation, consider removing any unneeded fonts. Although fonts occupy memory when used, they do take up disk space. You might find some fonts are never used and only waste disk space.

Internet

Windows NT Workstation comes to you Internet-ready, which means that it has the essential components necessary for Internet connectivity. Of course, you need to install a modem, install and configure a dial-up networking connection, get an account with an Internet service provider (ISP), and wrestle through its login procedure. The basic software you need comes fully bundled with NT, and a seasoned hand can connect it all in a matter of five or ten minutes. Getting mail and news is only a little more tricky.

One nice feature of NT Workstation is the WWW browser that is built in. When Windows NT Workstation is shipped (and this sentence was written just minutes after I heard that NT 4 went gold), it will be shipped with Internet Explorer Version 2. This is a good, stable build, but the browser market is advancing at an awesome rate. By the time you read this book, Internet Explorer Version 3 will have been superseded by Version 4!

The Internet Control Panel applet, shown in Figure 6.37, configures the Internet Explorer, also know as IE. In the shipping version of NT Workstation, the Internet applet can only configure proxy servers for use with IE, as shown in the figure. Later versions of IE will make greater use of this applet.

FIGURE 6.37.
Configuring Internet Explorer.

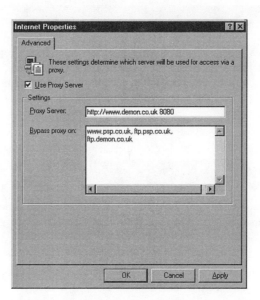

Proxy Servers

A proxy server can provide two general functions. First, it can provide a fire wall, enabling you to see outside your local area network without external users being able to see in. Although you tell IE to contact a remote server, say www.microsoft.com, IE sends your request to a proxy server that makes the request on your behalf. In such cases, the actual request appears, at least to the remote server, to come from the proxy server and not your system, thus providing an element of additional security.

The second function some proxy servers can provide is caching. If multiple users all try to get to http://www.microsoft.com/nt, the first person requesting that page causes the proxy to retrieve it, whereas subsequent calls to that page are satisfied from the proxy server's cache. This can significantly improve access time for commonly accessed Web pages or FTP files.

Configuring a Proxy Server

Using the Internet Control Panel applet, you can configure your proxy server. In the example shown in Figure 6.37, the proxy for my system is www.demon.co.uk, port 8080. The specific server and port number differs from company to company and from ISP to ISP, so be sure and ask your administrator or ISP for fuller details about proxy server names and port numbers to use. The example shown here is for Demon Internet Systems Limited, an ISP in the United Kingdom.

The Bypass Proxy On option allows you to bypass the proxy server whenever you are attempting to access certain servers. In the dialog box shown in Figure 6.37, accesses to ftp.psp.co.uk, www.psp.co.uk, and ftp.demon.co.uk all go directly to those servers. The first two are private servers not available on the Internet, and the second is my local provider's FTP server.

> **TIP**
>
> Keeping up to date with the latest on the Internet is a never-ending task. The technology is moving so fast! To keep up with Microsoft's Internet offerings, tune in to http://www.microsoft.com. By the time this book is published, you will be able to download a new version of Microsoft Internet Explorer, as well as a number of other new tools and toys. Happy surfing!

> **TIP**
>
> Most users connect to the Internet via an Internet service provider (ISP). Most ISPs offer one or more newsgroups that provide peer-to-peer support. You should ask your ISP about newsgroups.

For example, Demon Internet Systems Limited, the U.K.'s largest ISP, offers a number of peer-to-peer support groups, such as demon.ip.support. Most of the larger ISPs have something similar.

If you need more help configuring a proxy for your ISP, check your local newsgroups. Chances are someone has already worked out the best way to accomplish your task, which might save you considerable time and aggravation!

Keyboard

Like the display settings mentioned earlier, keyboard settings are a matter of personal taste. Some users might find some settings easier or more difficult to use. The Keyboard Control Panel applet, shown in Figure 6.38, allows you to configure your keyboard.

FIGURE 6.38.

Keyboard Properties.

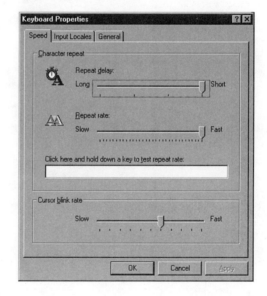

The Speed tab, shown in Figure 6.38, allows the following three adjustments:

■ Repeat Rate adjusts the wait before a character begins repeating when you hold down any key.

■ Repeat Delay adjusts how fast a character repeats when you hold down a key.

■ Cursor Blink Rate allows you to change the speed at which the cursor blinks.

You can also use the test box to check whether the repeat rate and delay settings you've just set are what you want. To the left of the slider in the Cursor Blink Rate setting is a blinking insert cursor that shows the currently selected blink setting. As with all settings, you should test the keyboard settings before accepting them.

If you are using the Accessibility options, the repeat rate set in the Keyboard Properties dialog can be overridden by the FilterKeys functions.

Input Locales

A locale effectively defines your keyboard language—that is, the language and keyboard layout on PCs generally used in your geographic area. Most PC users only ever set up one locale, such as English (US) or English (United Kingdom). Only a member of the Administrators local group can add or delete input locales.

By selecting the Input Locales tab, you can set up different keyboard configurations, as shown in Figure 6.39. This dialog is also a part of the Regional Settings applet.

FIGURE 6.39.

Input Locales.

The Input Locale dialog allows you to add or delete locales and configure which keyboard layout to use. The example shown in Figure 6.39 shows four locales that have been added, each with a different keyboard.

> **TIP**
>
> Setting up a locale is easy, but unless you have fonts installed that have the necessary characters, you might not see what you've typed. Not having the appropriate keyboard might make it difficult for a user in France to type Russian text, for example.
>
> One font that could help is Lucida Sans Unicode. This TrueType font has many, but by no means all, of the Unicode characters defined. It's worth a try!

Also remember that many keyboards outside your own country have what you might consider an odd layout. The French keyboard, for example, has the Q and A characters reversed. This can cause havoc for touch typists!

Keyboard Type

The General tab in the Keyboard applet allows you to define the type of keyboard you are using. This is distinct from the keyboard layout defined using locales, as described previously.

The Keyboard dialog allows you to select a list of keyboards, as shown in Figure 6.40. Most users probably use either the PC/AT Enhanced Keyboard (101/102 key) or the Standard 101/102-Key or Microsoft Natural Keyboard.

FIGURE 6.40.

Keyboard types.

Mail

To many users, e-mail is something they simply cannot live without. A key application for most Internet users is their e-mail, although opinions on what constitutes a good e-mail client are highly charged, to say the least.

Microsoft Exchange is a powerful messaging system and has two main components. The Exchange server runs on Windows NT Server, and holds and distributes the individual messages, e-mail items, to Exchange clients. Exchange clients are used to read and create messages sent to Exchange server. You can use Exchange in virtually any size organization from a small firm to a large multinational company.

Windows NT 4 has a basic Exchange client, a slimmed-down version of the full Exchange client that is part of the full Exchange product. The Exchange client is a basic mail reader and works in conjunction with Microsoft Mail.

More interestingly for many NT Workstation users, the Exchange client also works and interoperates with the Internet. Out of the box, it communicates with any POP3 Internet mail server, which makes it a good option for home users. If your Internet provider only uses SMTP, you have a variety of SMTP-to-POP3 gateways readily available.

The Mail applet is used to configure the Microsoft Exchange client shipped with Windows NT 4 Workstation. Selecting the Mail icon displays the dialog shown in Figure 6.41.

Figure 6.41.

*Configuring Exchange
e-mail.*

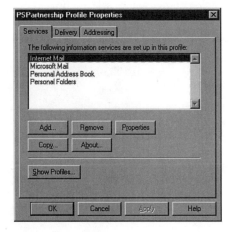

This dialog allows you to create different profiles and see the main components of a profile: Services, Delivery, and Addressing.

Complete details of configuring Microsoft Exchange, both client and server, could fill an entire book (and probably do). Basic instructions for configuring the Exchange client are found in Chapter 7, "The Explorer GUI."

Microsoft Mail Post Office

To assist users in smaller companies, Windows NT Workstation also supports a basic Microsoft Mail post office, which you can use in conjunction with the Exchange client. The Microsoft Mail Post Office applet allows you to configure or create a Microsoft Mail post office.

Chapter 7 provides full details on setting up a mail post office.

Modems

A modem is a small piece of electronics that enables your PC to call other systems and transfer data. It's hard to understand, at times, how such a small bit of kit can cause such problems. I regard anything to do with modem configuration to be a black art, best left to the high priest who mumbles the magic incantations of s54=129 and so on. The good news is that after you get your modem configured, you can pretty much forget about it until you upgrade it—then the fun begins all over again.

In order to utilize the dial-up networking features of Windows NT, you need to install and configure a modem. Only a member of the Administrators local group can add a modem. The Modem applet, shown in Figure 6.42, installs and configures a modem.

FIGURE 6.42.
Modem configuration.

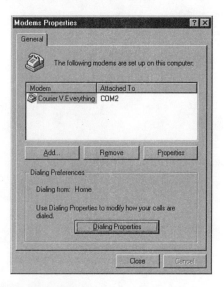

Selecting and Configuring a Modem

At the top of the dialog shown in Figure 6.42, you can see the currently installed modems. The Add button brings up a modem detection wizard that can detect your modem or allow you to specify the specific model and manufacturer.

> **NOTE**
>
> For the most part, automatic modem detection is another black art. The modem detection wizard does a good job of detecting most common modems, but it is not foolproof. In some cases, it either finds a modem that is not the one you have or simply finds a standard modem. Additionally, many models are sold in different countries, and the wizard
>
> *continues*

sometimes does not pick this up. If I were sarcastic, I might call this a feature! If you're installing a modem, you should know what type it is. As with all NT-related hardware, make sure it's on the hardware compatibility list.

TIP

If you plan to buy a modem for use with the Internet, do not simply buy the cheapest modem you can find. Some modems are decidedly better for Internet communications than others and can provide better throughput. Also, some modems work better with some ISPs than others. Ask your ISP for their recommendations, or ask other Internet users what modems they recommend.

After installing the modem, you might need to configure it. Selecting the Properties button shown in Figure 6.42 invokes the Modem Properties dialog, as shown in Figure 6.43.

FIGURE 6.43.

Configuring modem properties.

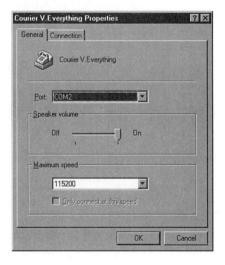

The modem properties include the communications port the modem is physically attached to, the modem speaker volume, and the maximum speed to run the modem.

Generally, your modem is attached to one of your serial ports, either COM1 or COM2, although on some systems you can use COM3 and COM4. Be careful if you use ports other than COM1 or COM2 because some hardware, particularly some graphics cards, can cause conflicts.

Some modems, notably internal modems, might not have a speaker, and as a result, the speaker volume slider might be grayed out. On some modems, the speaker might run at only two volumes: on or off. More sophisticated external modems (that is, the most expensive ones!) tend to have volume controls in the modem. The modem speaker can be highly useful during initial installation if you want to ensure that you dialed the right number and observe the progress of a call. It can also be useful if you use an ISP with less than perfect equipment. Some folks, on the other hand, find the noise quite irritating, particularly late at night!

The Maximum Speed list box refers to the maximum speed at which data is physically transferred between your modem and the computer, and not the speed that a data stream is transferred between the remote computer and yours. When transferring data between systems, most modems can compress the data being sent and decompress the data being received.

With data compression, the compressed data will travel between systems at the chosen rate (for example, 28.8Kbps), but the effective throughput is higher.

This assumes, of course, that compression of the data is possible—not all data is compressible. If you are downloading NNTP network news from the Internet, a modern 28.8K modem can achieve effective download speeds of 5000 to 6000 characters per second (cps) or higher at times. On the other hand, binary data top an effective 3000 cps. Note that these speeds assume you're using a 28.8K modem. If you are using a slower modem, you get correspondingly slower throughput figures. With modern PCs, you can usually select the fastest speed supported by your modem (and shown in the dialog box).

Run your modem as fast as you can, but check with the dial-up monitor to avoid running it too fast and generating overruns.

> **TIP**
>
> In general, run your modem as fast as NT lets you. Don't select the Only Connect at This Speed option. During the connection process (when all the funny noises come from the speakers), your modem attempts to connect with the remote system at the fastest speed set. If this is not possible, it works downward until it synchronizes with the remote system. If you selected the Only Connect at This Speed setting, your call is dropped if the initial connection fails to synchronize. If you have a bad line, you might be able to synchronize at a somewhat lower rate, and at least you'll get some data.

Dialing Preferences

Selecting the Dialing Properties from the main Modem Properties dialog displays the Dialing Properties dialog, which is a part of the Telephony facility, described in more detail later in this chapter.

The Dialing Properties, shown in Figure 6.44, allow you to specify how Windows NT should dial, including how to get an outside line, how to disable call waiting, and so on.

By setting up a location, you can define how Windows NT dials from one specific location. Mobile users often define a number of different locations for use on the road.

Before Windows NT dials a dial-up networking connection, it determines where in the world you are by reference to your currently selected location and where you're dialing. It can then put in the relevant country codes, international dialing access codes, and so on. This can be quite a time saver, but only if you have locations set up in advance.

FIGURE 6.44.

Dialing preferences.

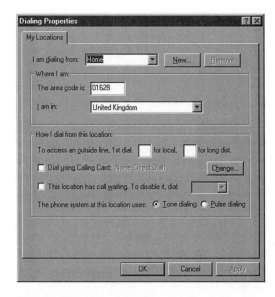

TIP

If you find yourself staying in hotels around the world, invest in a small tool kit (for dismantling phone sockets) and a set of phone adapters from TeleAdapt. In Europe, for example, each country has a different type of phone jack, none of which are compatible with the U.S. RJ-11. Also, get a line tester from TeleAdapt. Using an analog modem in a hotel with a digital switchboard can fry your modem (and in my case, it did). It is usually in the smaller hotels where you get the most problems, so be forewarned and forearmed.

You should also invest in some calling cards; hotel phone prices are often steep, particularly when you're dialing internationally. This can come as a very nasty shock, as I have recently discovered.

If all else fails, talk nicely to the hotel's manager or receptionist and ask to use the hotel's fax line—this often provides a connection when other methods fail. Naturally, you want to check your hotel bill carefully to ensure that they've charged you for any calls made this way.

You can find more details about modems in Chapter 10.

Mouse

For most users, using Windows NT means using a mouse or some other pointing and selecting device such as a trackball, glide pad, and so on. NT does a good job at detecting all supported pointing devices, but you might want to configure it to your own personal tastes.

Selecting the Mouse applet from the Control Panel brings up the Mouse Properties dialog,
shown in Figure 6.45, from which you can configure your mouse.

FIGURE 6.45.

Mouse properties.

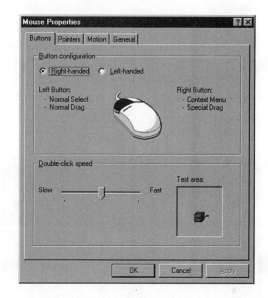

The mouse preferences are user specific and are stored in the Registry under the key
`HKEY_CURRENT_USER\Control Panel\Mouse`.

The Button configuration enables you to configure which button is the primary button (used
for selecting and dragging objects) and which is the secondary button (used to bring up context menus). Left-handed users might find this helpful, although many left-handed users I know
use the right-handed settings because many books and articles (including this chapter) simply
refer to right-clicking and left-clicking.

Double-clicking involves pressing one of the mouse buttons, usually the left or primary
button, twice quickly in succession. Windows NT interprets a double-click differently from
a single-click, and in many dialog boxes, a double-click has a specific action. For example,
double- (left-) clicking a folder on your NT Workstation desktop opens the folder, whereas
double-clicking a specific file in a standard File Open dialog selects that file. Double-clicks are
an important power-user technique.

The Double-Click Speed option allows you to adjust how sensitive Windows NT is to double-
clicking. If you click too slowly or the double-click speed is set too high, Windows NT

assumes you are just single-clicking the same object twice instead of double-clicking it. In general, less experienced users tend to be more comfortable with a slower double-click speed. If you make the speed too quick, double-clicking becomes almost impossible.

The test area allows you to move the mouse pointer into the area to see the effect of changing the double-click speed. Each time a double-click is detected by NT, the jack-in-the-box animation is triggered. Children of all ages love the animation!

Mouse Pointers

Applications running on Windows NT, including NT itself, can use one of 14 different standard pointer types to indicate the state of the current application. When the system or an application is busy and will not accept any user input, the mouse pointer is an hourglass, whereas when NT is busy in the background, you might get the pointer and hourglass combination pointer. The pointer shape provides useful and important feedback to the user.

Selecting the Pointers tab from the Mouse Properties dialog invokes the Pointers dialog, shown in Figure 6.46.

FIGURE 6.46.

Mouse pointers.

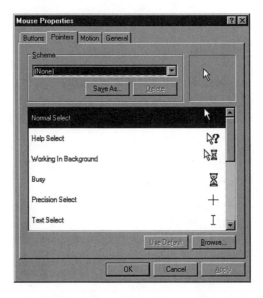

The shape of the mouse pointer is one of those desktop configuration issues that virtually no two users agree on. Some people just love the animated cursors, but others hate them. Personally, I intensely dislike the dinosaur cursors, but others feel quite different. To each his own!

Microsoft has grouped together sets of the 14 cursors into a cursor scheme, and 11 cursor schemes ship with Windows NT Workstation. Of course, you can choose different static or animated cursors for any of the 14 cursor types and save your choices as a new cursor scheme.

6

In addition to changing the entire cursor scheme, you can also change an individual cursor. Simply select the cursor to be changed and either double-click it or click the Browse button. This displays a common dialog to help you choose your cursor.

Cursors are stored, by default, in the SYSTEM32 directory (%SYSTEMROOT%\System32) with an extension of either CUR or ANI. The ANI cursors are animated and require more CPU power. These are not generally recommended for low-power systems.

> **TIP**
>
> If you go out to almost any large FTP site on the Internet, you can find hundreds of cursors to use with Windows NT Workstation. All the cursors used for Windows 95 will work on NT Workstation.
>
> You can find my personal cursor collection of over 900 cursors at http://www.demon.co.uk/pub/ibmpc/win95/cursors/tflcursors.zip. Enjoy!

> **TIP**
>
> The NT Resource Kit contains a utility called ANIEDIT.EXE that enables you to create your own animated cursors. With this tool, you create the individual frames that make up the animation and specify how long each of these frames should be displayed. This task is relatively straightforward but can be quite time consuming.

Motion

Selecting the Motion tab from the Mouse Properties dialog invokes the dialog shown in Figure 6.47. This dialog allows you to set the pointer speed as well as activate the Snap to Default feature.

By moving the slider bar in the dialog, you affect the relationship between how far you move the actual mouse and how far the mouse pointer moves on the screen. Moving the slider to the right makes the mouse pointer on the screen move further for any given movement of the actual mouse. As with the cursors settings, the setting here is a highly individual choice.

The Snap to Default feature is another thing you'll either hate or love—there seems to be no middle ground. When you select this option, any time a Windows NT message box is displayed, the mouse automatically moves over the default button (for example, OK, Cancel, and so on). For users with large screens, this can save a lot of mouse movement.

FIGURE 6.47.

Mouse properties—
motion.

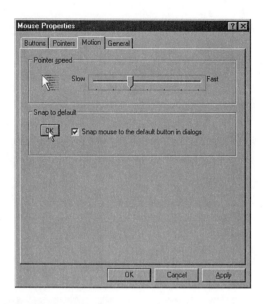

Selecting the Correct Mouse Hardware

Selecting the General tab in the Mouse Properties dialog brings up the General dialog, shown in Figure 6.48, which displays the type of mouse hardware you currently have installed.

FIGURE 6.48.

Selecting the mouse.

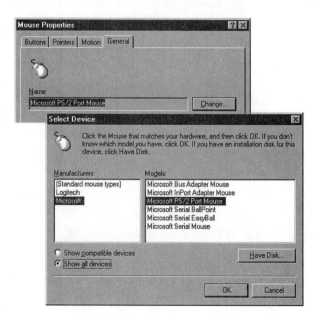

When you click the Change button, you get another dialog in which you can see all the different mice supported, out of the box, by Windows NT. If you have a mouse that is not supported as standard, you can select the Have Disk button and install the driver from a floppy disk.

> **TIP**
>
> I recently installed Windows NT on a number of machines that had mice, but during installation, they were not properly recognized. We had to use NT without a mouse to reconfigure those systems. This is not difficult if you know how to do it, and it is definitely something worth learning, preferably before it's necessary. For you technical support folks, driving the Windows NT interface without a mouse can impress the users!

Multimedia

The multimedia capabilities of personal computers have improved dramatically over the past decade, and what was once considered highly sophisticated features are now becoming almost commonplace. Windows NT Workstation does come with a good level of multimedia capability, but Windows 95 and the Macintosh are possibly more appropriate for more sophisticated multimedia applications.

The Multimedia Control Panel shown in Figure 6.49 configures the multimedia functions and installs and configures the related hardware.

FIGURE 6.49.

Multimedia Control Panel.

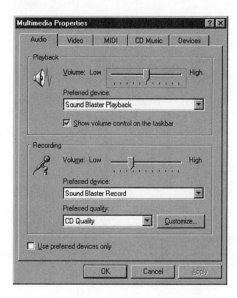

Audio Playback

The Audio tab, shown in Figure 6.49, controls playback and recording. Usually, playback is via a sound card and a pair of external speakers, whereas recording is via a microphone attached to the sound card. If you have multiple sound cards, you can select which one Windows NT should use.

The volume slider in the Playback section is a master volume control controlling the overall output levels. Many sound cards have additional volume controls, as do the speakers shipped with many computer systems. Selecting the right level on all three can take some time, but after they're set, you usually don't have to change them.

If you select the Show Volume Control on the Taskbar option, Windows NT places a small icon of a speaker on the right side of the taskbar. You can then use this control to change the master output level. Double-clicking this control displays a more comprehensive volume control dialog.

The Recording settings control the microphone input levels and the sampling rate. If the recording level is too high, the resulting sound quality is poor, so you need to perform some testing prior to doing any important recording.

All recording is done using digital sampling. When recording from a microphone, Windows NT samples the input port and records the result as digital data. The more samples taken, the better the quality of the resulting recording—but more data is needed to represent the recorded sound. The specific dialog is sound-card dependent.

Video

Windows NT Workstation includes Video for Windows, which means you can play back video clips on your PC. One small drawback to this otherwise splendid facility is that video clips take up considerable amounts of disk space. If you start collecting useful (that is, long) video clips, be prepared to invest in large amounts of storage space.

Video clips are played by the media player accessory, MPLAYER.EXE. You can also use this accessory to play audio clips, CDs, and MIDI clips, assuming you have the necessary hardware support (that is, a suitable sound card and a CD-ROM). By default, the media player accessory plays back video clips at the size they were recorded (which is usually quite small).

The Video tab in the Multimedia control applet invokes the dialog box shown in Figure 6.50.

The Video dialog allows you to control the size of the video playback, which can make video files easier to see. However, by increasing the size, you experience some loss of quality.

From this dialog, you can also select the Advanced button, which allows you to configure the media player to use some older, 16-bit code. Some older video clips might not work properly on Windows NT Workstation, and this option allows you to use 16-bit code that might work better.

FIGURE 6.50.
Multimedia video configuration.

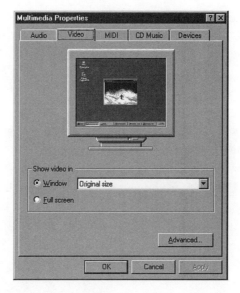

MIDI

MIDI (Musical Instrument Digital Interface) is an interface standard that allows you to use a large range of electronic musical instruments via a digital computer. Most modern electronic keyboards, for example, offer the capability of MIDI input and output, and many popular recording artists make significant use of this capability.

The MIDI configuration dialog, shown in Figure 6.51, allows you to select the specific instrument connected to your computer.

FIGURE 6.51.
MIDI configuration.

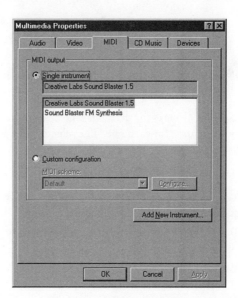

If you have multiple instruments connected, select the one you want to control. The custom settings allow you to configure various additional MIDI channels.

CD Music

By adding a CD-ROM drive to your computer, you can play normal music CDs by using the CD Player accessory (or using the media player described earlier). This makes it easy to listen while you work. If you work in a crowded office and your musical tastes are considered eclectic by co-workers, you might consider using a set of headphones (and preferably not the ones where everyone near you can hear just enough to be really annoying).

Choosing the CD Music tab brings up the dialog shown in Figure 6.52.

FIGURE 6.52.

Multimedia—CD music.

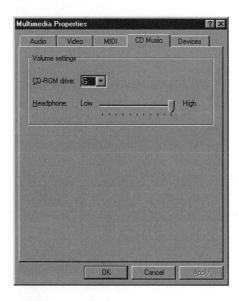

Most CD-ROMs come with a small headphone jack on the front that allows you to listen to music CDs.

The CD Audio dialog displays the detected CD-ROMs on your system and allows you to control the headphone volume for each one. The selected CD-ROM is then used as the default for any multimedia application that uses a CD-ROM.

Devices

The Devices dialog, shown in Figure 6.53, shows all the different multimedia drivers loaded on your system and allows you to specify their properties.

You must be a member of the Administrators local group to manage multimedia devices.

FIGURE 6.53.

Configuring multime-dia devices.

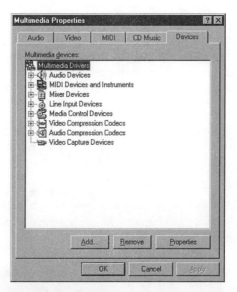

TIP

MIDI is generally pretty straightforward, but you have a lot of options. When configuring your multimedia devices, keep your device manuals handy. Also, don't forget most of the currently available devices have manuals based on Windows and, if you are lucky, Windows 95. Some of the configuration details might be upward-compatible.

TIP

NT is a great operating system, but its multimedia capabilities are not as good as, say, the Macintosh or Windows 95. Although Windows NT's capabilities are adequate for most business users, consider using another operating system if you want great multimedia. This could change by the time you read this, but for now, NT is not the multimedia enthusiast's first choice of operating system.

You can find more details on multimedia in Chapter 10.

Network

Networking was built into Windows NT since its first release, and the networking features have steadily improved ever since. Networking is a fundamental part of the design of NT and follows a very structured and layered model. Configuring networking on Windows NT is really pretty easy once you get past the jargon.

Although networking with Windows NT Workstation is pretty easy, before installing and configuring networking, you really do need a basic understanding of what networking is and the options you need to configure for any given network situation. Part V, "Networking Windows NT Workstation," discusses the networking aspects in great detail, and if you are a networking novice, read those chapters first.

The Network applet is where you do all network configuration. The Network applet is complex in that a lot of options are interrelated, and you need those options properly specified if networking is to be successful. When you understand the impact of the options and how to configure them, the dialogs are easy to use.

The Network Control Panel applet, which you can invoke by right-clicking the Network Neighborhood icon on the desktop and selecting the Properties menu, configures all networking. The applet is shown in Figure 6.54. Only a member of the Administrators local group can change the network settings.

FIGURE 6.54.

Network configuration.

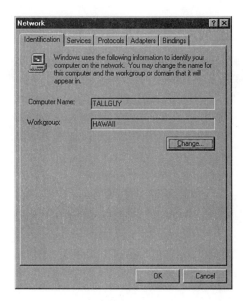

Identification

The Identification dialog, shown in Figure 6.54, allows you to view and change your machine and workgroup or domain name. If you change any of these items, you must reboot your system before they take effect.

Services

Network services sit above the network protocols and the adapters. Network services use lower-level components to implement various network-related functions. For example, the server service allows you to share files and directories with other users, whereas the Workstation enables you to connect to the server service on another system to access the shared resources on that system.

The Services dialog, shown in Figure 6.55, allows you to manage and control the network services loaded on your machine.

FIGURE 6.55.

Network services.

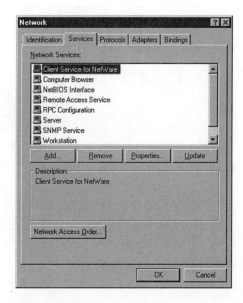

The Services dialog allows you to add and delete network services. In addition, some, but not all, services can be configured from this dialog.

Network services are discussed in more detail in Chapter 18, "Windows NT Network Services."

Protocols

The network transport protocols enable communication between two systems, possibly via other systems, using one or more of the configured network adapters. The network protocols sit below the network services and above the adapters. Examples include TCP/IP and IPX/SPX.

The network protocols loaded on your system are viewed in the Protocols dialog, as shown in Figure 6.56.

Full details of network protocols are given in Chapter 17.

Adapters

A network adapter is a hardware component that is either built into your computer's motherboard or implemented as an add-on card, which physically connects your computer to a network. To some degree, a modem is a network adapter, although the designers of Windows NT Workstation chose to treat it separately.

FIGURE 6.56.

Network protocols.

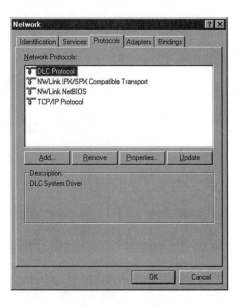

With the dialog shown in Figure 6.57, you add and view the network adapters in your system. Installing and configuring network adapters is discussed in Chapter 16, "Installing Windows NT Networking."

FIGURE 6.57.

Network adapters.

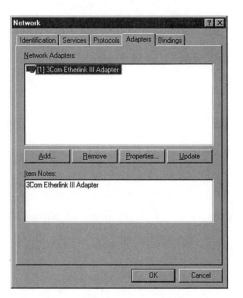

Bindings

A binding is a path that a given application request to the network might take from an application through the services and protocols and eventually down to the adapter layer. Although Windows NT Workstation generally configures all services bound to all protocols and adapters, the configuration might not be the best for performance because some possible bindings might not be useful. To maximize performance, you might need to remove or disable bindings.

For example, because all Novell-related traffic uses IPX and not TCP/IP, there is little point binding the client service for NetWare to TCP/IP. (In fact, the installation of the NetWare client knows this and is clever enough to set the binding.) If you have multiple cards, multiple transports, and multiple clients, adjusting your bindings can improve performance if you can eliminate unhelpful paths that can never be used in your environment. The Bindings dialog, shown in Figure 6.58, allows you to modify the binding paths.

FIGURE 6.58.
Network bindings.

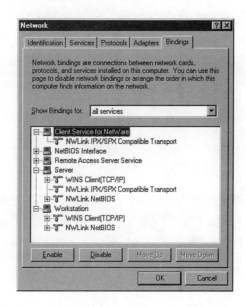

Chapter 16 discusses the network bindings in more detail.

PC Card (PCMCIA)

The growth in portable computing has been matched by the growth in the add-ons available for these systems. With a specification designed by a committee (the Personal Computer Memory Card International Association, or PCMCIA), a new type of interface card, the PC card, has become very popular. These cards were initially known as PCMCIA cards, but because most end users can't pronounce or spell it, they are now called PC cards.

PC cards are small credit-card sized hardware that are powered from the main system. The four physical types of PCMCIA cards are Type I, Type II, Type III, and Type IV. All these cards use the same 69-pin interface but vary in thickness and general usage.

Type I cards, which are 3.3mm thick, tend to be used for various types of memory such as RAM, Flash ROM, EEPROM, and so on. They are not very common today. Type II cards, which are 5mm thick, are very common and are used for a range of things, including network adapters. Type III cards, which are 11.5mm thick, are most often used for PCMCIA hard disks or radio communications devices that require more circuitry. Type IV cards, which have not been ratified by the PCMCIA consortium, will probably be used for higher capacity disk drives and are expected to be 18mm thick.

Most modern laptop computers support either two simultaneous Type II cards or one Type III card. Type I cards are rarely used these days, and Type IV cards are not yet supported.

The most popular uses for PC cards are for modems and network adapters, although a wide range of alternative uses include hard disks, SCSI adapters, Global Positioning by Satellite (GPS) radio receivers, ISDNs, external CDs, and sound cards.

> **TIP**
>
> Before buying a PC card for NT, make sure it's on the hardware compatibility list. You should also check with your system vendor to ensure the card works in your system. As I tell my clients, if it's not on the HCL and it doesn't work, it's your problem. Of course, if it is on the HCL and doesn't work, it is still your problem. In any event, *caveat emptor!*

> **TIP**
>
> One tip I give to people buying hardware in general—and this applies doubly to PCMCIA—is to order everything in writing, including words similar to "This equipment must work with Windows NT Workstation Version 4 in conjunction with my system." You should be as specific as possible (without going overboard).
>
> If the PC card fails to work when you get it, you might have some protection. Under U.K. law, for example, you have the legal right to get your money back in such circumstances, regardless of what the vendor might try to argue. If the firm you are buying from refuses to accept the order with that condition or says they're not sure or they don't know what NT is, you might want to think twice about that particular purchase.

NT Workstation supports PC cards, although the list of supported cards is not all that long. As you might expect, NT supports a large number of modems and a reasonable number of network cards, but not a lot else. However, the list is increasing all the time as notebooks become more popular. In summary, be careful before you buy a PC card for a Windows NT system.

Windows NT 4 Workstation does not fully support Plug and Play, which means, sadly, you cannot just remove or insert PC cards while the system is running as you can with Windows 95. Some folks think this is an oversight by Microsoft, but Plug and Play is promised for later versions of Windows NT.

Because Plug and Play is not fully supported, you must reboot your system to change the cards you use. If you do remove a card while NT is up and running, you run the risk of locking up your system, requiring a hardware reboot.

Despite all this gloom, supported PC cards do work with great ease. For the most part, you can just treat PC cards as any other card—that is, configuring a PC card network adapter with the Network applet or a modem with the Modem applet.

Invoking the PC Card (PCMCIA) Control Panel applet brings up the dialog shown in Figure 6.59. This has two subdialogs, Socket Status and Controller.

FIGURE 6.59.

PC Card (PCMCIA) configuration.

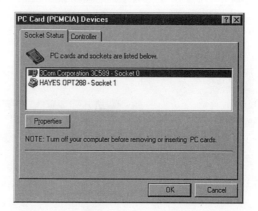

This dialog shows you the PC cards currently plugged into your computer. By selecting the Properties button, you can bring up a further dialog to enable you to configure the card, although as noted earlier, this is rarely necessary. The Configuration dialog is implemented by the card driver itself and thus will vary with the card. The Configuration dialog for a 3COM 3C589 PC Card Network adapter is shown in Figure 6.60.

TIP

If you are having trouble with a PC card, look at that card's configuration dialog under the General tab. If there is a problem with the device, NT displays more information and suggests a solution. The quality of the error information and suggested solutions vary, but hey—it's better than nothing! Sometimes, you might also see a problem code that can help the vendor's technical support folks help you.

FIGURE 6.60.

*Properties of a 3COM
PC card.*

Controller

The Controller dialog, shown in Figure 6.61, enables you to view the resources currently used by the PCMCIA controller. In general, you can't change the I/O port of conventional memory range on the controller because it is assigned automatically. In the unlikely event of a conflict with another device, you need to change the other device's resources to resolve the conflict.

FIGURE 6.61.

*PC card controller
status.*

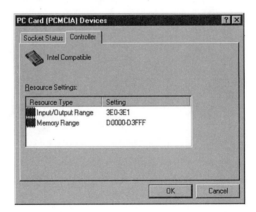

PC cards are discussed in more detail in Chapter 10.

Ports

Personal computers connect with the outside world using one or more ports. A port is simply a connection between the system and an external device. Two main ports supplied on all PCs are serial, or communications, ports and parallel, or printer, ports. Serial ports, as their name implies, transfer data serially, one bit at a time, whereas parallel ports can transfer data eight bits at a time.

Most PCs usually have two serial, or communications, ports that use either 9- or 25-pin serial connectors. You can connect a number of things to these serial I/O ports such as a modem, a mouse, or a printer. Historically, all modem communication happens via the serial port.

> **NOTE**
>
> Although the applet is called Ports and the dialog boxes are titled the same, you can only configure serial ports with the Ports applet. You can't configure parallel (printer) ports with this applet.

Windows NT Workstation supports up to 256 serial ports, although some substantial hardware is required if you want to support all 256! In my experience, all software that uses the serial ports is capable of configuring the serial port, so this applet is really not all that useful except to define additional ports.

The Ports Control Panel applet is shown in Figure 6.62.

FIGURE 6.62.

Ports applet.

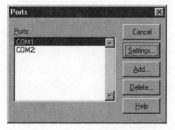

Selecting the dialog shows you the currently installed ports. Clicking the Settings button brings up a Settings dialog, shown in Figure 6.63, from which you can configure the key settings for your serial port. The specific settings required are usually defined either by the software connected to the serial port (for example, the modem, the printer, and so on) or by the software you use, so be sure to read the relevant manual.

FIGURE 6.63.

Configuring serial ports.

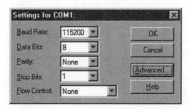

If you are installing more than the standard four serial ports, you need to configure the IRQ and I/O port. This is done using the Advanced Port Configuration dialog, shown in Figure 6.64. You must be a member of the Administrators local group to use the Advanced Port Configuration dialog.

FIGURE 6.64.
Advanced serial port
configuration.

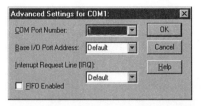

TIP

If you need to use more than four serial ports, you usually need to configure an I/O port
and IRQ for these extra ports, although some hardware can utilize shared IRQs. Read the
hardware and software very carefully. To find unused IRQs and I/O ports, use the Windows NT diagnostics, WINMSD.EXE.

You can find more details on ports in Chapter 10.

Printers

Printing in Windows NT has always been a mixture of good news and bad news. The bad news
is that the internal architecture is rather complex, but the good news is that printing works. In
my experience with Windows NT, virtually all the printing problems I've encountered are easy
ones: The hardware isn't plugged in, connected, or turned on, or I have the wrong drivers.

Printing Basics

Before I introduce the Printer applet, it's important that you understand the basics of printing
on NT and the following NT-specific definitions:

- The printing device is the chunk of hardware that actually puts the ink (or toner) onto
  the page.

- The printer is the software interface between the application and the printing device.
  That is, the application prints to a printer, and NT handles the transition to the
  printing device.

- The printer queue is simply the list of jobs waiting to print at a printer. The term
  queue has no actual significance (unlike in Novell).

- The print monitor is the software component that routes the final output from the
  printer to the printing device.

- The print server is the NT system on which the printer is defined and on which the
  print monitor runs.

- The port is where the print monitor sends the output. Usually, this is your system's
  parallel or serial port. However, this can also be a network port—for example, an HP
  printer with a Jet Direct card.

These definitions might be different from other systems you've used, particularly Novell NetWare, but they are the definitions used with NT, so you'll need to get used to them.

Before your application can do any printing, you first have to define a printer on your system, either by creating a printer on your machine or connecting to a printer somewhere on your network. After you have created or connected to the printer, your applications can then use the printer, although you might want to modify the printer's configuration.

The printer folder in Windows NT Workstation is the place where all printing-related configuration and management is carried out. You can access the printer folder in one of the following three ways:

- Opening the My Computer folder
- Using Start|Settings|Printers
- Selecting the Printers applet (or strictly speaking, shortcut) from the Control Panel

The printer folder is the same, no matter which method you choose to invoke it. The printer folder on my system is shown in Figure 6.65.

Figure 6.65.

Printer folder.

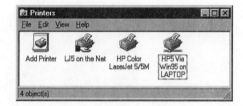

To set up a new printer on your system or connect to a printer on the network, you should use the Add Printer Wizard. This is a quick, easy, and almost foolproof way to define the printer.

Only a member of the Administrators local group can create a new local printer. The process of setting up a new local printer is illustrated in Figures 6.66 through 6.72 and involves the following steps:

- Specify whether the printing device is managed locally or is connected via the network, as shown in Figure 6.66.
- Specify the port the printing device is connected to. For a local printer, this is usually either a serial or parallel port, as illustrated in Figure 6.67.
- Choose the manufacturer and model of the printing device, as shown in Figure 6.68.
- Give the new printer a (local) name and specify whether this is the default printer for Windows applications running on this system, as shown in Figure 6.69.
- As shown in Figure 6.70, you next specify whether the printer is shared across the network and which printer drivers are loaded onto your system. If the printer is shared, you can also give it a share name used by others when they connect to this printer.

FIGURE 6.66.

Specifying local or remote printing.

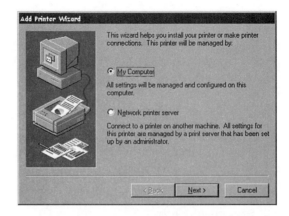

FIGURE 6.67.

Specifying the printer port.

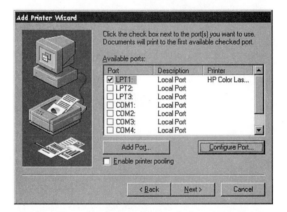

FIGURE 6.68.

Specifying the printer model.

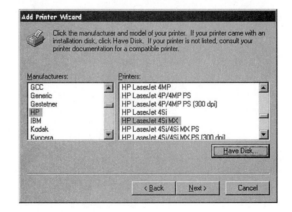

FIGURE 6.69.

Defining a printer name.

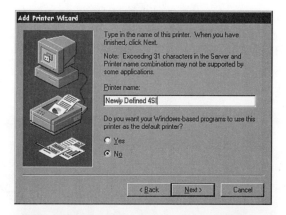

FIGURE 6.70.

Sharing a printer on the network.

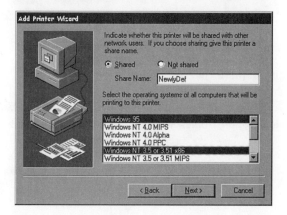

■ Finally, you get the opportunity to print a test page, as illustrated in Figure 6.71. You should always perform this useful test. After Windows NT has printed the test page as far as it can tell, you get a confirmation dialog, shown in Figure 6.72, where you can confirm the page has printed successfully.

FIGURE 6.71.

Printing a test page.

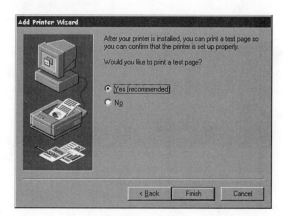

These steps are relatively simple and straightforward. In practice, they also tend to be idiot proof. The only problem you are likely to see at this stage relates to errors in selecting options presented by the New Printer Wizard. For example, if you have a PostScript printer and select a non-PostScript printer or if you tell NT that your printing device is a laser printer when it's really a daisy-wheel printer, unpredictable results occur.

FIGURE 6.72.

Confirming successful printing.

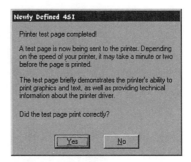

Other printer errors include the normal litany: The printer isn't turned on; the parallel, or serial, cable is not connected; the printer is out of paper; and so on. For the most part, these are very simple to troubleshoot. To simplify things even further, the Windows NT Help system comes with a Print Troubleshooter, which outlines all the most common printer errors, as shown in Figure 6.73.

FIGURE 6.73.

Print Troubleshooter.

TIP

If you are responsible for Windows NT Workstation support and users phone you with printer problems, tell them to try the Print Troubleshooter first and call you back only if that fails to resolve the problem. In my experience, printing problems have always been resolved using the troubleshooter, but of course, your mileage on this may vary!

Network Printing

Setting up network printing is almost as easy as setting up local printing. If you are going to share your printer on the network, the previous instructions are all you need. If you want to connect to an existing printer on the network, you also use the New Printer wizard. This process, illustrated in Figures 6.74 through 6.77, includes the following steps:

■ Select Network Printer Server (as shown in Figure 6.74).

FIGURE 6.74.

Selecting a network printer.

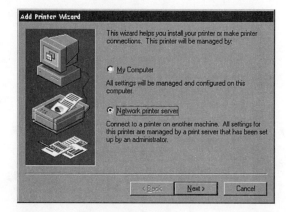

■ As shown in Figure 6.75, select the machine and printer you want to connect to.

FIGURE 6.75.

Connecting to a remote printer.

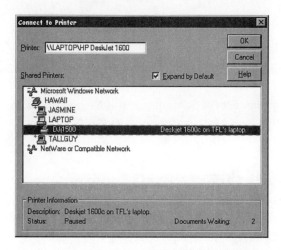

■ Specify whether this should be the default printer for Windows applications, as shown in Figure 6.76.

FIGURE 6.76.

Setting up a default printer.

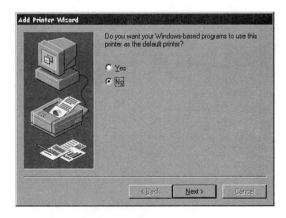

When these steps are completed, you get a final confirmation dialog, shown in Figure 6.77.

FIGURE 6.77.

Confirming a successful network printer setup.

If you have done a lot of printing (and troubleshooting) in the past, you might be forgiven for thinking that setting up a network printer is very easy. Well, it is; as I said earlier, printing is a no-brainer.

Networked Printer Drivers

As shown, setting up any printer is quick and easy. I hear you ask, "What about printer drivers?" You do need them, and the process of creating a printer asks you to load the printer drivers. These are typically on your Windows NT 4 Workstation CD-ROM. Alternatively, you might get them on disk with new printers, or you can download them from the Internet or the manufacturer's electronic bulletin board.

When you create a local printer, Windows NT loads the printer drivers for local printing. For network printing, NT gets clever; when you connect to a network printer, Windows NT simply downloads the printer driver for you from the machine where the printer was initially created. That's it!

NT achieves this by sharing the `%SYSTEMROOT%\System32\Spool\Drivers` folder as `PRINT$`. When a remote system wants to get print drivers from your system, it merely connects to `\\YOURSYSTEM\PRINT$` (where *yoursystem* is the NetBios machine name, defined in the Network applet). Directly below this, Windows NT creates one extra folder for each hardware platform for which drivers are held.

The only real issue to resolve is which printer drivers you should hold. A printer driver is an executable program, typically a DLL, designed to run on a particular operating system and hardware. If you define a printer for use by other users on the network, it is important that you hold all the printer drivers for all the various combinations of systems that are likely to access it. If Windows NT fails to find the correct drivers on the remote machine, it simply prompts for a location to find them, and when fed the appropriate disk, CD, or network share point, it can then load the drivers for this alternative location.

With NT Workstation Version 4, you can automatically load printer drivers for other NT systems as well as for Windows 95, as illustrated in Figure 6.70.

If you access the printer via Windows for Workgroups, Windows 3.*x*, or DOS, you have to load the printer manually on each of the client systems. Also, if you connect from your system to a printer defined on a non-Windows NT system (for example, Windows 95), you also must load printer drivers manually.

Printer Ports

Most printing is done via a system's parallel or serial port, and these are the ports usually specified for local printing (shown in Figure 6.67). Windows NT also supports other ports including the Digital Network port, HP Network port, Lexmark DLC Printer port, Lexmark TCP/IP port, and the LPD port (for printing to UNIX printers).

These ports enable you to directly connect a printer to the network for your Windows NT system to print directly to the printer. This requires a different print monitor, which is loaded automatically when you define the appropriate network. To print to a UNIX printer, you must load the TCP/IP printing services.

Printing from DOS Applications

If you are using DOS applications, printing becomes slightly more difficult. First, DOS applications each require their own printer drivers; sadly, they cannot use the Windows NT drivers. DOS Printer drivers are usually application-specific and must be obtained from the application vendor. This can be an issue for very old programs.

DOS applications also have no concept of networking and tend to open a configured LPT or COM port and dump their output, which is not much help when the printer is remote. To enable DOS applications to print successfully, you need to use the NET command from the command line on the client system. Go to the command line and use the following syntax:

```
NET USE LPT2: \\server\remoteprinter
```

LPT2 is the port your DOS application uses, and *server* is the machine on which the printer shared as *remoteprinter* is located.

After you have done this, you must configure your DOS application to use the port you just used. Printing across the network should now work!

You can view the printers you are currently using by typing NET USE from the command line.

Managing and Reconfiguring Printers

After the printer is defined, you might want to either update the printer properties or manage the printing process. Both of these operations are carried out from the Printer folder.

To modify a printer's parameters, you either select the printer and bring up the File|Properties menu or right-click the printer and select Properties. This brings up a dialog box that is specific to the printer being managed, which allows you to review and amend the printer's properties. The Properties dialog for my installed LaserJet 5M printer is shown in Figure 6.78.

Figure 6.78.

Printer properties.

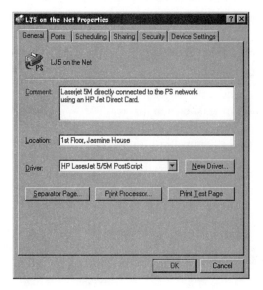

Advanced Configuration Options

Windows NT Workstation has a number of additional advanced printing features you might want to use. These features, which are set from the printer's property sheet, are as follows:

- Separator page: Whenever Windows NT sends a job to be printed, you can print an optional separator page at the beginning of the print job.

- Device scheduling: Because a printer is the interface between the system and the printing device, it is possible to make a printer available only during certain times of the day. Also, you can actually define two printers to print to a single print device and give one printer a higher priority. This is done using the printer's Scheduling tab as defined later in this chapter.

- Printer pools: A printer pool is where you have multiple printing devices attached to a single printer. This is ideal for situations where a single printing device is unable to print all the documents sent to the related printer, which could happen in a word processing department, for example.

- Printer device settings: The printer drivers enable you to configure a wide range of printing features. The Device Settings tab under the printer properties enables you to configure features of your specific printer.

Printer separator pages are very useful for highly used printers shared by many users, although the feature is rather wasteful of paper and toner. The three separator pages loaded by default are PCL.SEP, PSCRIPT.SEP, and SYSPRINT.SEP. PCL.SEP is used for HP LaserJet Printers and switches the printer into PCL mode. PSCRIPT.SEP switches the printer into PostScript mode but does not actually print a separator page. SYSPRINT.SEP simply prints a page before each document. If you have an HP printer, use PCL.SEP.

Printer pools are simple and easy to set up. About the only drawback is that they must either be the same actual model or be able to emulate the same model. If you have a LaserJet II and a LaserJet 5Si, you have to either create separate printers for these two devices or run a printer pool with both systems acting like a LaserJet II (so you wouldn't get the extra fonts and other features available in the LaserJet 5Si).

Security

Chapter 1 discussed the general security model for NT. In summary, all NT resources are owned, and the owner of the resource can enable other people to use that resource at his discretion. Additionally, any resource can be audited so that the use of the resource is logged to NT's event log. Printers are just another resource that you can secure. All security settings are configured from the printer's Security menu, part of the printer's properties, as shown in Figure 6.79.

The first security hurdle relates to who can create a printer. Only members of the Administrator or Power Users groups can create a local printer. Any user has the right to connect to a remote printer, which is subject to the printer's access controls.

FIGURE 6.79.

Setting printer security.

After a printer is created, it is owned by the person who created it. The owner has full control of the printer and can set the rights for every other user (including denying them access).

Printer ownership, as in files and directories, can be taken by a user who has sufficient privileges (for example, the administrator or a member of the Administrators group) or by any user with the full control permission on that printer.

The owner of a printer can give any other group or user defined on the system access to the group by using the printer's Permissions dialog, shown in Figure 6.80.

FIGURE 6.80.

Setting printer permissions.

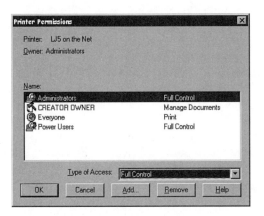

You can give four different permissions to a printer: Full Control, Manage Documents, Print, and No Access. When applied to a group or user, these permissions define what the user can or cannot do with the printer. Table 6.2 summarizes the printer permissions.

Table 6.2. Printer permissions.

Permission	Full Control	Manage Documents	Print	No Access
Chance document settings	X	X		
Change printer permissions	X			
Change printer properties	X			
Change printer settings	X			
Delete printer	X			
Pause/resume, restart, delete documents	X	X		
Pause/resume printer	X			
Print documents	X		X	
Purge printer	X			
Take ownership of a printer	X			

As you can see from the table, although you can print to a printer, you can't do much else unless you have the full control permission.

Printer Auditing

As with any other secure object, Windows NT allows you to audit a printer, which means you can tell who did what to the printer and when. You set up auditing from the printer properties Security menu by clicking the Auditing button (shown in Figure 6.79). This brings up the Printer Auditing dialog, shown in Figure 6.81.

With auditing, you first have to decide who to audit and then what to audit. You can audit any or all users or groups defined on your system by selecting the Add button. You can also remove users or groups using the Remove button.

After you decide who to audit, you have to decide which events to audit. When it audits a printer, Windows NT is, in effect, recording the use of the rights summarized in Table 6.2.

Printer Summary

Printing is extremely easy to set up and get working. Properly securing the printer takes a bit more work, but all the permissions are consistent with NT's overall security model.

Happy printing!

FIGURE 6.81.

Auditing a printer.

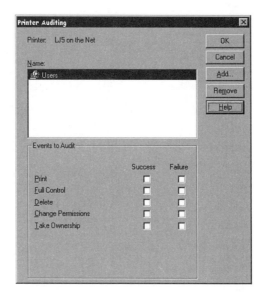

Regional Settings

As with earlier versions of Windows, Windows 95, and Windows NT, Windows NT Workstation Version 4 was designed as an international product. This means that it should be easy for anyone to customize it, taking normal national preferences into account. The Regional Settings applet configures Windows NT's international settings. Your applications, if properly programmed, can use these settings to make your version of Windows NT Workstation work properly in different geographical areas.

> **NOTE**
>
> Any well-behaved Windows application can take advantage of any regional settings, but some do not. Excel 95, for example, takes no notice of regional settings, although Explorer does. Interestingly, the command prompt uses some, but not all, of the settings. In general, only Win32 or 16-bit applications can use these settings; Posix, OS/2, and true DOS applications do not.

The Regional Settings dialog is shown in Figure 6.82. This dialog allows you to select a specific region. Based on the chosen region, Windows NT can then automatically modify all the related settings, including the formats of numbers, currency, time, dates, and keyboard.

FIGURE 6.82.
Regional settings.

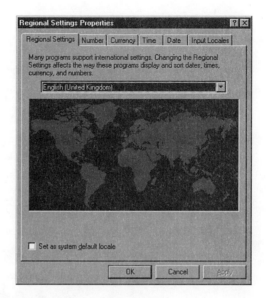

The following additional tabs in the dialog shown in Figure 6.82 allow you to override the defaults based on the chosen region:

■ The Number dialog, shown in Figure 6.83, allows you to select the ways numeric values are displayed.

FIGURE 6.83.
Number format.

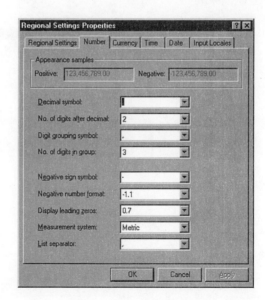

■ The Currency dialog, shown in Figure 6.84, enables you to change the way currency values are displayed.

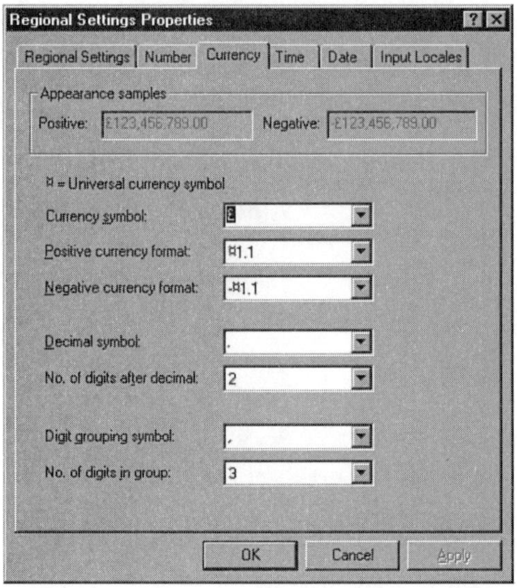

FIGURE 6.84.

Currency format.

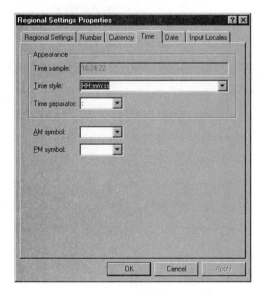

■ Using the Time dialog, shown in Figure 6.85, you can change the way time of day values are displayed.

FIGURE 6.85.

Time format.

■ With the Date dialog, shown in Figure 6.86, you can change the way dates are displayed.

FIGURE 6.86.
Date format.

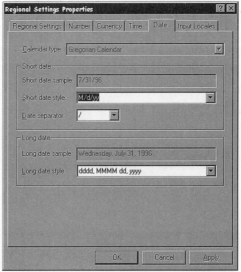

■ The Input Locales dialog, shown in Figure 6.87, enables you to change the keyboard layout. Only a member of the Administrators local group can use this dialog.

FIGURE 6.87.
Input Locales.

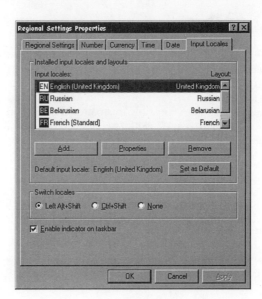

Most users do not need, or want, to modify these settings because the most obvious application (Excel 95) takes no notice of them. Don't forget that choosing the region also modifies all the related settings.

Some users, however, might want to make some specific changes, including the following:

- Adding digits after the decimal: Choose the Number tab and select the No of Digits After Decimal. To do this for currency values, change this setting in the Currency dialog.

- Changing the default measurement system: (This is particularly useful in the U.K., where we use both the Imperial and Metric measurements.) Choose the Number tab and select Measurement System.

- Changing the thousands and decimal separators: Some countries, such as France, use the . (period) as the thousands separator and the , (comma) as the decimal, so the number 1,234,345.33 is written as 1.234.345,33. To change this, modify the Decimal Symbol and the Digit Grouping Symbol in either the Number or Currency tabs (or both!).

- Changing the date and time displayed: Like many settings, this is another choice that is often quite personal. Use the Time and Date tabs to select time and date displays for your personal preference.

The individual settings for numbers, currency, and so on are user-specific and are stored in the Registry under `HKEY_LOCAL_USER\Control_Panel\International`.

SCSI Adapters

SCSI, Small Computer Systems Interface, is one of two principal ways of connecting disk drives and other peripherals to a Windows NT system. Chapter 10 provides more details on SCSI features and facilities.

The SCSI Adapters applet is possibly misnamed. In the initial version of Windows NT, this applet, which was then part of the Windows NT Setup program, only handled true SCSI adapters. In later versions, and now in Windows NT Workstation Version 4, this applet is also used to install certain supported but non-SCSI CD-ROMs.

For the most part, this dialog is rarely used because the devices handled by this applet are automatically detected at the time the system is loaded. You will most often use this applet when you are upgrading your system, adding new hardware, or updating your SCSI disk device drivers.

Selecting the SCSI Adapter applet from the Control Panel displays the dialog shown in Figure 6.88. This dialog shows all the installed SCSI controllers and the devices attached to each controller.

FIGURE 6.88.
SCSI adapters.

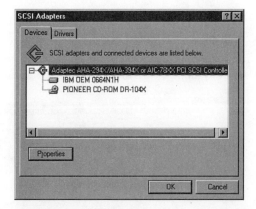

Devices

Selecting the controller, or a device, and clicking the Properties button brings up additional information about the drive or controller, as shown in Figures 6.89 and 6.90.

FIGURE 6.89.
SCSI adapter properties.

FIGURE 6.90.
SCSI peripheral properties.

Drivers

Clicking the Drivers tab in the SCSI Adapters applet brings up the dialog box shown in Figure 6.91. This dialog shows all the SCSI adapters loaded in your system and whether they have been started. In the example shown in 6.91, one driver was started, but the other failed to start.

FIGURE 6.91.

SCSI driver properties.

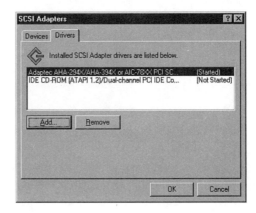

From the Drivers dialog, you can add and remove SCSI device drivers.

Because changing SCSI controllers and drivers is considered a relatively secure event, you must be a member of the Administrators local group on your machine before you can use the Device properties.

Server

A great feature of Windows NT Workstation is the built-in, peer-to-peer networking. As described in more detail in Part V, "Networking Windows NT Workstation," installing the file and printer sharing features is quick and easy.

At the core of the Windows networking are two key network services: the workstation service and the server service. The workstation service redirects I/O requests from your workstation to other systems on the network, whereas the server service accepts such remote requests from other systems, subject to the security you place on your system. These two software components work in conjunction with the I/O manager to allow you to share files and printers in an easy and secure fashion.

Both services sit on top of whatever networking infrastructure you have installed. At least in theory, you can run these on any installed transport protocol and with any installed networking adapter. Essentially, these two components are transport and hardware independent (although highly reliant on the proper functioning of the lower-level modules).

The Server Control Panel applet allows you to examine and manage the behavior of the server service. This is probably more important if you are managing a larger NT Server instead of an NT Workstation system, but it can still be useful, particularly if other users on your network are accessing files on your system.

Selecting the Server applet from the Control Panel invokes the dialog shown in Figure 6.92. You must be a member of the Administrators local group to use this applet. The applet, when it is invoked, summarizes the state of the Server service (as shown in Figure 6.92).

FIGURE 6.92.

Server dialog.

The Server applet offers five buttons that you can use to display and manage aspects of the server service:

- Clicking Users displays the dialog shown in Figure 6.93, which shows the users currently logged on to your system. By selecting a user, you can force a disconnection of that user or you can disconnect all users. This can result in data loss, so be careful.

FIGURE 6.93.

Active user sessions.

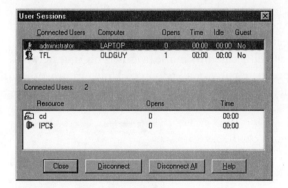

- As shown in Figure 6.94, the Shares dialog shows all the directories shared on your system and how many users are currently connected to that share. As with the Users option described previously, you can forcibly disconnect one specific user or all users. You cannot disconnect a single user from a single share, however.

FIGURE 6.94.

Shared resources.

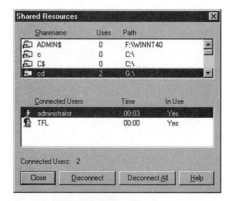

TIP

If you disconnect a user or all users from your system, you will probably notice that the disconnect didn't seem to work. You look again in a couple of minutes and the users are reconnected. In fact, the disconnected users probably didn't even notice the disconnection. That's because NT (and the other Windows family networking clients) sees the disconnected resource and simply reconnects. The clients assume the disconnection was a transient network error and do their best to fix the problem by reconnecting.

To really get rid of the user, you must first ensure that the about-to-be-disconnected user cannot get to the shared resource and then force the disconnect. A simple way to do this is to unshare the directory. When the user's system attempts to reconnect, it cannot get to the old shared drive because it no longer exists.

■ Selecting the In Use button invokes the dialog shown in Figure 6.95. This shows the specific files currently in use by others on your network. You have the option to close a specific resource or all resources. Unlike your work with the Shares and Users dialogs, you can refresh this view to display any changes to open resources.

FIGURE 6.95.

Open resources.

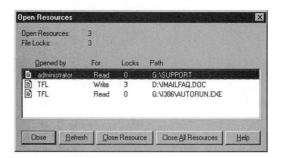

■   The Replication dialog in Figure 6.96 allows you to manage the Directory Replication service. Directory Replication allows Export servers (which must be Windows NT Servers) to export directories to Import servers (which can be other NT Server or Windows NT Workstation systems). Only administrators can configure replication.

FIGURE 6.96.
Directory replication.

The Export server exports one or more directories to specific, named systems. On the Import server, you first choose where the root of the imported directories is located in the To Path box in the dialog in Figure 6.96. Usually, the import path is `%SYSTEMROOT%\SYSTEM32\REPL\IMPORT`.

Using the Manage dialog, shown in Figure 6.97, you can choose which systems you want to accept imports from and which of the exported directories you want to import. When Directory Replication is fully working, this dialog displays the status of the imported directories.

FIGURE 6.97.
Managing imported directories.

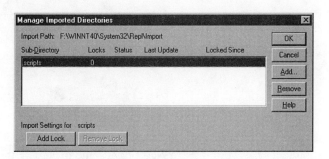

■   When a Windows NT Workstation system discovers a problem in the environment—for example, a UPS that has just lost power—it generates an administrative alert. Generally, these alerts are local to the system. By using the Alerts dialog, shown in Figure 6.98, you can redirect these alerts to other systems or users on the network. This is probably less useful on NT Workstation than on NT Server. Only Administrators can manage alerts.

FIGURE 6.98.

Administrative alerts.

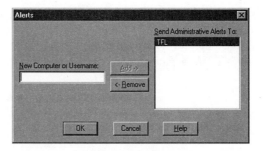

Most of these functions are straightforward, although Directory Replication can be more problematic. The error messages generated by the Directory Replicator service are often cryptic in the extreme and can often be downright mystifying.

Most problems with the replication process are caused because the Directory Replication service has not started or because of permission problems on the import directories. In the Services dialog (see the next section), you must select the Directory Replication service and ensure that you have specified a valid user for the service to log in, as shown in Figure 6.99. The chosen user must have the right to log in as a service and be a member of the Replicator local group on your system. Also, the user must have access to the import directories.

FIGURE 6.99.

Configuring the Directory Replicator service.

Another potential problem with directory replication is passwords. Make sure the directory replication user's password is set to Never Expire and make sure the User Must Change Password At Next Logon box is not checked.

Directory Replication is pretty simple, but it's also easy to get wrong, and the error messages could be improved. Have fun!

TIP

If you want to turn on administrative alerts, you must ensure that the alerter service is running. The easiest way to do this is to configure it to start automatically.

TIP

Directory replication is a nice facility when it's used wisely, but be careful in its use. Wherever possible, keep your export (and therefore import) directories flat with no subdirectories. If the replicated directories are flat, only changed files are transmitted. Also, do not edit files in the import directory. The Directory Replication service is very, very good at looking at your import directory, making it an exact copy of what's in the export directory, and wiping out all your changes.

Services

A service is a Windows NT process loaded by the operating system at boot time. NT services work in the background and perform useful functions, such as the server service, which responds to requests for access to files and printers on your system.

A service is a driver in the sense that it is part of the operating system, as described in the previous section. Chapter 11, "Windows NT Services," provides a good insight into the service architecture.

The Services Control Panel applet, shown in Figure 6.100, shows all the currently defined services, their status, and when the service is started. You can also stop, pause, or start a service from this dialog. You must be a member of the Administrators local group to start, stop, or configure services.

FIGURE 6.100.

Services dialog in the Control Panel.

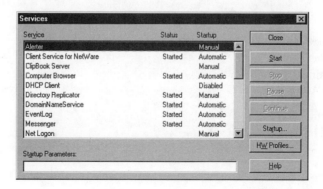

In this dialog, you see the service's common name, which is usually different from the filename of the executable file containing the service. The Windows NT service architecture enables a single executable file to contain one or more services.

TIP

To see the services that are running on your system, you should run the Resource Kit utility `TLIST.EXE`, using the `/t` switch. This generates a listing showing all the key processes, along with an indication of which processes started which other processes. The listing looks like the following:

```
System Process (0)
System (2)
  smss.exe (17)
    csrss.exe (22)
    winlogon.exe (31)
      services.exe (37)
        SPOOLSS.EXE (68)
        rpcss.exe (80)
        SNMP.EXE (83)
        tapisrv.exe (91)
        RASMAN.EXE (99)
        named.exe (133)
      lsass.exe (40)
      nddeagnt.exe (41)
explorer.exe (142) Program Manager
  systray.exe (153)
  internat.exe (155)
  clock.exe (157) Clock - 7/24/96
  FINDFAST.EXE (122)
  WINWORD.EXE (126) Microsoft Word - nt4 unleashed
  rundll32.exe (173)
    winhlp32.exe (169) Windows NT Help
  rundll32.exe (180)
  cmd.exe (186) F:\WINNT40\System32\cmd.exe - tlist /t
    tlist.exe (148)
rasmon.exe (171) Dial-Up Networking Monitor
```

In this list, you see the Service Control Manager, `services.exe`, and just below that, the service images that have been started.

> **TIP**
>
> Full details of all services are stored in the Registry. Look in `HKEY_LOCAL_MACHINE\` `SYSTEM\CurrentControlSet\Services` where you will see a large number of subkeys, each of which corresponding to a service. Note that most of these services are not enabled on your system.

In the Services Control Panel applet, you also see the network services, which are not shown in the task list (as noted in the previous tip). These are configured using the Network applet and should not need any additional configuration.

By selecting the Startup button, you bring up a subsidiary, as shown in Figure 6.101, which tells Windows NT when to start the service. This dialog also allows you to enter a user name under which the service should start. This can be useful to deny access to certain sensitive data to the service, thus increasing the security on your system. With the exception of the Directory Replication service, this security is rarely necessary.

FIGURE 6.101.

Configuring service startup.

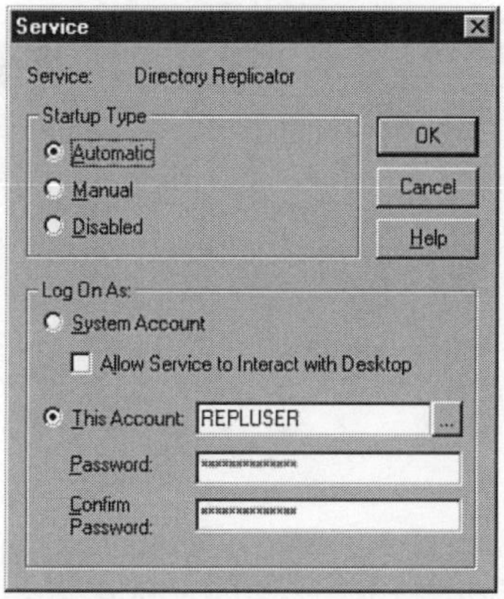

The service startup functions are described in more detail in Chapter 11.

> **WARNING**
>
> By experimenting with service startup types, you can get your system into a situation where it cannot start. Unless you understand the implications of changing startup types, this might be better left unchanged. Of course, if you do get it wrong, you should always be able to recover using the Last Known Good Control set. Being careful means never having to reinstall.

Hardware Profiles

As with devices, you can set up hardware profiles in which services can be enabled or disabled. Selecting a service and then clicking HW Profiles brings up a dialog box, as shown in Figure 6.102, which allows you to disable or enable the service in a profile. In Figure 6.102, I've disabled the Directory Replicator service because there is nothing to replicate if I'm starting with no network.

FIGURE 6.102.
Configuring a hardware profile.

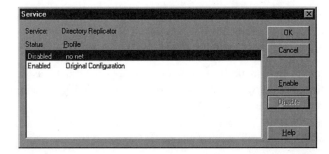

> **NOTE**
>
> Not all services can be disabled via hardware profiles. Neither the event log nor the Plug and Play services can be disabled.

Sounds

In Windows NT, a sound is a prerecorded digital representation of a sound. Sounds are usually played through the audio playback channel of a sound card and through speakers or headphones. Sounds can be recorded via your sound card and can come from a microphone or any other input media. Sounds are usually stored with the extension WAV.

The Sounds Control Panel applet allows you to assign specific sounds to various Windows events. Whenever the event occurs, such as when you empty the Recycle Bin, start Windows, or pop up a menu, the associated sound plays through your sound system.

Sounds were originally intended to assist the visually handicapped, and children generally love this feature, whereas adults generally hate it. Judicious use of sound can be fun—but overuse it and it can become annoying to everyone!

You can program any application to use the sounds setup with the Sounds applet. The application does this by first placing in the Registry a definition of the events that result in playing a sound. Then, each time the event occurs, the application reads the Registry and determines the sound to play. The sound player application is then invoked to play the relevant sound.

The sound event definitions are held in the Registry under the key HKEY_CURRENT_USER\
AppEvents\Schemes\Apps. Each application that uses sound places an additional key for the
application under this key with further subkeys for each sound-related event.

> **WARNING**
>
> If you are in an office, particularly if it's a crowded one, and you have sounds enabled with
> speakers turned on, you could discover that your co-workers are less than impressed. You
> might think it's seriously cool to have Clint Eastwood's voice saying, "Go ahead, sucker;
> make my day," each time an application starts up. You might even have some friends who
> agree. Trust me—after a while, you will find that your co-workers fail to share your enthusi-
> asm. Indeed, when they get annoyed enough, they might just make your day. I don't have
> sounds in the office—not anymore!

The Sounds dialog is shown in Figure 6.103. As you can see, you can associate each event with
a sound clip. Whenever that event occurs, Windows NT plays the associated sound.

FIGURE 6.103.

Sounds properties.

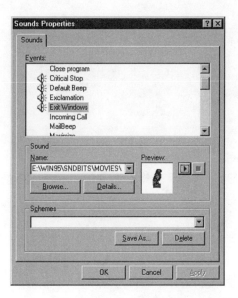

In the example shown in Figure 6.103, I've associated the Exit Windows event with Humphrey
Bogart's line from the *Maltese Falcon* where he says, "Now that'll be all. Just be sure to lock the
door behind you on your way out. Good night." Personally, I love it—but other people might
have different tastes.

Sound Schemes

You can collect a number of sound settings together in a single sound scheme. This is a good way to minimize the work needed to switch sound settings.

To create a sound scheme, set up the specific sounds you want to hear for each application event and then click the Save As button and enter your scheme name.

NOTE

Each new scheme creates an additional sound entry under each application event key. Although this makes for quick access, creating hundreds of schemes increases the size of your Registry and the amount of memory you need. In very tight memory situations, this can have a negative effect on performance.

Additionally, with sounds enabled, the system has to do more work for each event (opening menus, minimizing or maximizing windows, and so on). This work can also degrade your performance.

If you want to speed up your system, turn all sounds off by selecting the No Sounds sound scheme.

TIP

The Windows 95 Plus! Pack contains a number of desktop themes that include not only sounds, but also desktop icons, wallpaper, and so on. Something similar to this will be a part of the NT 4 Resource Kit (allegedly). In the meantime (if you are going to ignore my warning about sounds), do a Web search for Windows 95 themes using a good WWW search engine. Two Internet sites you might visit for more sounds are `ftp.cdrom.com` and `www.windows95.com`. Happy hunting!

System

The System Control Panel applet is shown in Figure 6.104. This applet displays general information about the system and allows you to configure a number of system-level settings. You can also invoke this dialog by right-clicking the My Computer icon on the desktop and choosing the Properties menu.

This applet has six tabs, each of which are described in the following sections in more detail.

FIGURE 6.104.

NT Workstation system properties.

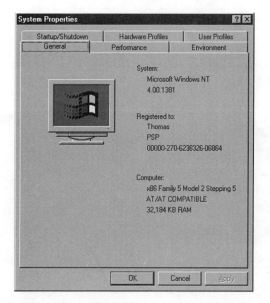

General

The General tab, which is shown in Figure 6.104, provides some basic information about the system, including the following:

■ System shows which version of Windows NT is installed on your system, along with the internal build number.

■ Registered To shows the registered owner and organization. Usually, this is the information entered at the time Windows NT Workstation was installed, but you can change it. (See the following tip.)

■ Computer gives a summary of the type of computer and how much physical memory NT detected in your system.

You might need this information if you make any support calls to Microsoft.

TIP

If you inadvertently enter an incorrect registered owner or organization when you install Windows NT Workstation, you can change it using the Registry Editor. Go to the key `HKEY_LOCAL_MACHINE\SOFTWARE\Microsoft\WindowsNT\CurrentVersion`, where there are two value entries, `RegisteredOrganization` and `RegisteredOwner`. You can change both of these by clicking the value name and entering the new value.

Performance

The Performance dialog, shown in Figure 6.105, enables you to view and modify how much of a performance boost applications in the foreground get and the details of where Windows NT should place its paging files.

FIGURE 6.105.

Configuring system performance.

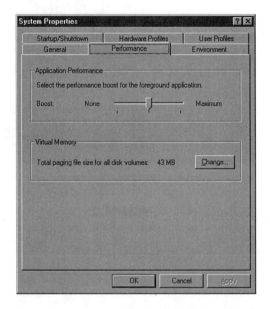

By default, applications that are running in the foreground get a scheduling boost over applications running in the background. For most Windows NT Workstation users, this is the correct behavior, but in certain circumstances, it might not be appropriate. If you are running a large FTP download or sending a large mail message, you want your FTP or mail application to get good performance, but you probably don't want to leave it in the foreground.

The application performance slider has three settings. Setting the boost to Maximum gives the foreground application the best response time. If you set the boost in the middle, the foreground application gets a "better" response time, whereas setting the boost to none means the foreground application gets no priority boost. A boost of None is probably the correct setting if you use communications programs or have multiple CPU intensive applications running concurrently.

Windows NT achieves this better performance by increasing the internal priority of all threads belonging to the foreground application. As a result, with appropriate settings of Application Priority, the foreground applications usually get priority over the background.

The other function of the Performance dialog is to configure your virtual memory settings. Windows NT Workstation uses virtual memory extensively to enable it to swap information between the hard disk and physical memory as described in Chapter 1. These settings can have a significant impact on performance.

The current amount of virtual memory defined is shown in the dialog box in Figure 6.105. Clicking the Change button invokes the Virtual Memory dialog, shown in Figure 6.106, which enables you to make changes to your virtual memory allocations.

FIGURE 6.106.

Virtual memory settings.

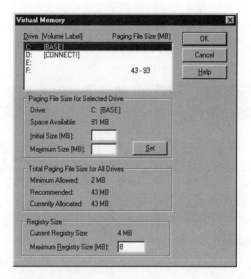

The Virtual Memory dialog lets you modify how much virtual memory is allocated on each disk partition in your system. You also use this dialog to change the maximum size of the Registry, which can be important if you load a large number of applications and other goodies onto your system. Only a member of the Administrators local group can manage page file settings.

The Virtual Memory page file is called PAGEFILE.SYS, and by using the Virtual Memory dialog, you can place a paging file on each partition of your system. You cannot put a paging file on a floppy or on the network.

The Virtual Memory dialog shows at the top each partition in your system and how big a paging file you have currently allocated on that drive. In Paging File Size for Selected Drive, you can review and modify how big your paging file is for each partition.

After making any changes to your Virtual Memory settings, you must click the Set button for your changes to be registered. Additionally, you need to reboot before these new settings can take effect.

Total Paging File Size for All Drives shows how much total paging file space was allocated. This section also gives a recommendation on the minimum amount of paging file space that you should allocate.

The Virtual Memory dialog also allows you to change the maximum size of your system's Registry. Most users do not need to change this. However, if you load a large number of applications, you might need to increase this size.

As noted previously, if you make any changes to the virtual memory settings, including changing the maximum size of your Registry, you need to reboot the system in order for the changes to take effect.

Unlike most of the Control Panel applets, the Virtual Memory dialog has a Help button and some good help information. If you're not a virtual memory whiz kid, you might find this information useful.

TIP

In general, it is best to have only one paging file per volume. Having multiple files might enable you to fit more information on a particular partition, but it can result in more paging.

If you have more than one physical disk in your system, you should try to put the paging file on the fastest disk.

Environment

Since the very early days of MS-DOS, application programs have used variables defined in the environment for extra control information. Although environment variables have been largely superseded by INI files and the Registry for holding key configuration information, Windows NT still uses environment variables for holding extra information.

NT makes heavy use of a few important environment variables. The variable SYSTEMROOT holds the full path of where Windows NT Workstation is installed, and USERPROFILE contains the path to the currently logged-in user's profile. You can see all the variables currently available to you by typing SET at the command prompt. You can also use these variables at the command prompt (CMD.EXE) and in batch files, although you must surround the variable name with %. At the command prompt, you can issue the command DIR %SYSTEMROOT% /S to get a full listing of all the files in the Windows NT installation directory (and all subdirectories).

Windows NT Workstation has two types of environment variables: system and user. System environment variables are set system wide, usually during the installation of an application or the operating system itself. User environment variables are set on a per-user basis. Both sets of variables are stored in the Registry. System environment variables are stored under the key HKEY_LOCAL_MACHINE\SYSTEM\CurrentControlSet\Control\Session Manager\Environment. User environment variables are stored in the key HKEY_CURRENT_USER\Environment.

Selecting the Environment tab brings up the Environment dialog, shown in Figure 6.107. This dialog shows all the currently set user and system environment variables.

FIGURE 6.107.

Setting environment variables.

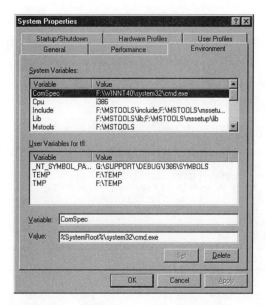

To set a user environment variable, just enter the variable name and value and click the Set button. To set a system environment variable, you must first click in the System Variables area and then enter the variable name and value. To delete any variable, just click it and then click the Delete button.

You can also set environment variables at the command prompt by using the SET command (for example, Set MYFILE=c:\myfile.dat). However, any environment variables set this way are lost when you exit the command prompt.

> **TIP**
>
> The DIR command in the command prompt uses the internal directory order by default when displaying files. To get a nicely formatted listing, you can use the /O switch (for example, /ogne to get a listing with directories grouped at the top and sorted by name and extension). To make this a permanent setting, create the variable DIRCMD and set it to /ogne. I've set this as a system environment variable so that every user automatically gets nicely sorted directories.

Startup/Shutdown

When Windows NT Workstation starts up, the NT System loader scans the file BOOT.INI, located in the root directory of your system disk, to build the boot selection menu. The

BOOT.INI file contains a list of NT versions to load and where to load them from. This file is initially given the file attributes system and read-only, which makes it more difficult to accidentally erase.

My BOOT.INI file resembles the following code segment:

```
[boot loader]
timeout=30
default=multi(0)disk(0)rdisk(0)partition(2)\WINNT40
[operating systems]
multi(0)disk(0)rdisk(0)partition(2)\WINNT40="Windows NT Workstation
➥Version 4.00" /sos
multi(0)disk(0)rdisk(0)partition(2)\WINNT40="Windows NT Workstation
➥Version 4.00 [VGA mode]" /basevideo /sos
multi(0)disk(0)rdisk(0)partition(2)\WINNT35="Windows NT Workstation
➥Version 3.51"
multi(0)disk(0)rdisk(0)partition(2)\WINNT35="Windows NT Workstation
➥Version 3.51 [VGA mode]" /basevideo /sos
multi(0)disk(0)rdisk(0)partition(3)\WINNT40="Windows NT Server
➥Version 4.00" /sos
multi(0)disk(0)rdisk(0)partition(3)\WINNT40="Windows NT Server
➥Version 4.00 [VGA mode]" /basevideo /sos
multi(0)disk(0)rdisk(0)partition(3)\WINNT35="Windows NT Server Version 3.51"
multi(0)disk(0)rdisk(0)partition(3)\WINNT35="Windows NT Server
➥Version 3.51 [VGA mode]" /basevideo /sos
C:\="Microsoft DOS 6/x and Windows 95"
```

As you can see, the BOOT.INI file has two sections:

■ Boot Loader tells the loader how long to wait for the user to make a selection before taking the default, which is also specified.

■ Operating Systems contains all the various copies of Windows NT, plus a reference to a DOS/Windows 95.

In both sections, each version of NT is shown using the ARC (Advanced RISC Computing) naming convention. This is followed by a string in quotes used to build the boot menu and some system startup options (for example, /sos to display the details of drivers loaded during the boot process).

After parsing the BOOT.INI file, the NT Loader displays a screen that is derived on the BOOT.INI file. Based on the BOOT.INI file shown previously, it might resemble the following segment:

```
OS Loader V4.00

Please select the Operating System to Start:

    Windows NT Workstation Version 4.00
    Windows NT Workstation Version 4.00 [VGA mode]
    Windows NT Workstation Version 3.51
    Windows NT Workstation Version 3.51
    Windows NT Server Version 4.00
    Windows NT Server Version 4.00 [VGA mode]
```

```
Windows NT Server Version 3.51
Windows NT Server Version 3.51 [VGA mode]
Microsoft DOS 6/x and Windows 95
```

```
Use ⬆ and ⬇ to move the highlight to your choice
Press Enter to Choose
```

```
Seconds until highlighted choice will be started automatically: 30
```

In this boot menu, the default, the first version of Windows NT 4 Workstation, will be highlighted. You can then use the up and down arrows to choose one of the other operating systems and select it by pressing the Enter key. Alternatively, you can wait the configured amount of time for the default to start. If you move the up and down arrows, the last line of the menu disappears, and for any system to get loaded, you must select the system and press the Enter key.

TIP

At first sight, these ARC names used in BOOT.INI look a little odd. Why couldn't Microsoft just have used the convention C: or D:? To Windows NT, the name C: is just an alias that you can change to point to any partition you like, including the CD-ROM. Until Windows NT is loaded, it is not possible to work out the meaning of C:. Using ARC names gets around this because ARC names are related to the hardware.

The ARC naming convention is pretty simple when you get used to it. Basically, you see one of two formats for names:

- multi(a)disk(b)rdisk(c)partition(d) is used with IDE or EIDE disks or with SCSI disks when using the SCSI boot BIOS.
- scsi(a)disk(b)rdisk(c)partition(d) is used for SCSI disks not using the controller's boot BIOS.

The value of a in these cases is the ordinal number of the hardware adapter/controller card, starting at 0 (that is, the first controller card is 0, the second is 1, and so on).

If the disk is a SCSI disk, b is the hardware unit number of the disk (or LUN, if the controller supports logical units), and c is always 0. If the disk is IDE, then b is always 0, and c is the ordinal number of the disk.

Finally, d is always the partition number on the chosen disk—confusingly, this starts at 1.

Think of it this way: The ARC name tells you which physical controller, which disk on that controller, and which partition of that disk to use. ARC names are just super disk labels.

Although these ARC names can be useful for Windows NT Workstation users, they are very important when implementing NT Server on large servers with multiple disks. My tip is to get used to them!

With this introduction to ARC names and the boot up process out of the way, the Startup/Shutdown dialog is shown in Figure 6.108.

FIGURE 6.108.

*Windows NT Startup/
Shutdown.*

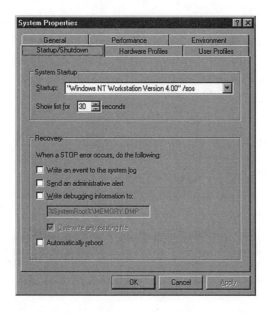

With the System Startup options, you can easily configure the [default] section of the BOOT.INI file, which is possibly the safest way for a beginner.

The Recovery options tell Windows NT what actions are taken in the unlikely event of a system crash. System crashes, which should be very rare, are also called the Blue Screen of Death because all you see is a blue screen containing details of the crash when Windows NT really crashes.

You have several options, and you can choose any or all (or none) of them:

- Write an Event to the System Log: When NT crashes, this option writes an event to NT's event log. You can view this later to determine the cause of the crash.

- Send an Administrative Alert: This option sends an alert to any user or system configured to get administrative alerts. A sample administrative alert is shown in Figure 6.109. The information saved in the event log and the information displayed by this dialog are identical.

- Write Debugging Information: This choice determines whether you generate a full memory dump when the system crashes and where to write the memory dump.

- Automatically Reboot: In the event of a system crash, this option causes NT to reboot.

For most users, these options are probably not all that useful. In practice, NT is so stable that the options are rarely ever used. The memory dump in particular is huge (it is the basically your entire swap file!) and tends to only be useful to highly trained technicians.

On my main desktop and laptop systems, I usually run with these options turned off. However, if you are a developer writing device drivers or other low-level code, these options are vital because they are often the only clue about why your code did not work as you intended.

FIGURE 6.109.
*Alert after a system
crash.*

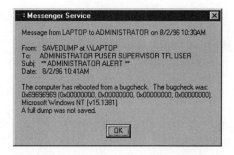

Hardware Profiles

Hardware profiles provide a good way to create different configurations that you can choose at
system startup. As noted in the sections "Devices" and "Services," you can disable almost any
device or driver in a profile. This can be very useful for laptop users on the run—simply turn
off all the services and drivers that are not actually needed.

By reducing services, you can reduce the system startup time and avoid running services that
are not much good. Disabling the Alerter service might be quite sensible if you are using your
laptop on an airplane—after all, who are you going to tell about administrative alerts when
you're 35,000 feet over the North Atlantic?

The Hardware Profiles dialog, shown in Figure 6.110, enables you to create, delete, and rename profiles and view and modify the property of a profile. You can also use this dialog to
configure how NT should behave at startup with respect to hardware profiles.

FIGURE 6.110.
*Managing hardware
profiles.*

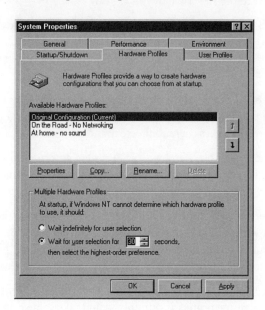

To create a new hardware profile, select an existing profile and click the Copy button. After a profile is created, you can rename it or delete it. The profile at the top of the Available Hardware Profiles list box is the default profile, and you can use the arrow buttons at the side of the dialog to adjust the order of the list.

When you define multiple hardware profiles, the section at the bottom of the Hardware Profiles dialog instructs Windows NT Workstation about its behavior at boot time. NT will either wait indefinitely for you to choose the profile or wait for some predefined time (the default is 30 seconds) and then choose the default hardware profile. Note that this menu appears in addition to the menu generated by the BOOT.INI file. You only see this menu if you have more than one hardware profile.

User Profiles

In Windows NT, all desktop and user-related settings are contained in a user profile and stored locally. These settings are set in the HKEY_CURRENT_USER tree in your system Registry. In addition, Windows NT creates a set of folders in the %SYSTEMROOT%\Profiles\userid directory, where userid is the user name you logged in with. This folder, which is also known as %USERPROFILE%, contains the contents of your desktop, your personal Start program menus, your favorite places, and your Send To menu.

If you use Windows NT Workstation on a computer that is a member of an NT Server domain, you can have a roaming profile. With roaming profiles, your profile is stored on a server and downloaded, if necessary, to your workstation each time you log in. Any changes are then uploaded back to the server when you log off.

Windows NT caches your profile locally and only downloads your profile when the locally cached profile is older than the profile on the server or when you have no profile currently cached on the system. Roaming profiles are very useful for users on the move, but they do have disadvantages.

Any file or folder stored on your desktop is automatically saved in the hidden directory %USERPROFILE%\Desktop. Dragging a couple of large files onto your desktop can dramatically increase the size of the Desktop subdirectory and the time it takes to download it from the server.

Each user who logs into a Windows NT 4 system automatically gets a new set of profile directories created on that system. If you are the sort of user who has a lot of stuff on your desktop and you log into a system, that desktop remains on that system until it's deleted.

The User Profiles dialog, shown in Figure 6.111, shows you the profiles defined on your system, the user who created each profile, and its current size. For users in an NT Server domain, the profile can be changed from a local profile to a roaming profile—if you are not in a domain, this option is grayed out.

As you can see in Figure 6.111, the user testu1 has a large profile, nearly 15MB on my system! If this were a roaming profile, it certainly would take some time to download. If you select the profile and click the Delete button, the profile is deleted from your system.

FIGURE 6.111.

User profiles.

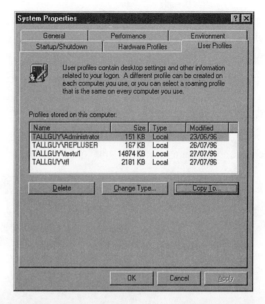

WARNING

If you delete a local profile, you could inadvertently lose data, programs, or both. In the example in Figure 6.111, the user testu1 created a lot of data on the desktop and copied some applications from the Internet. By deleting the profile, you delete all that data and the applications. Before deleting a profile, ensure it's really not needed!

Tape Devices

For many users, tape backup is the main method of backup. With CDR drives becoming affordable and new devices such as Iomega's ZIP and JAZ drives appearing on the market, the primacy of tape is, if not threatened, at least under review for the Windows NT Workstation user. With disk prices falling by the week, why bother backing up?

TIP

Disks were once expensive and unreliable—now they're cheap and unreliable. As I tell my clients, "Backup is that six-letter word beginning with 'back' and ending with 'up' that can prevent that other six-letter word that also ends in 'up.' Naturally, I mean 'foul-up!'" In summary, back up anything you don't want to lose (or you will be embarrassed when you do).

Windows NT comes with a built-in backup utility, NTBACKUP. This utility is discussed in more detail in Chapter 8, "The Administrative Tools." The important thing about this program is that it can back up, and later restore, your Registry.

NT Backup supports only a small range of tape devices, including QIC 40 and QIC 80 IDE-based devices and a wide range of 4MM DAT drives. For full details of the devices supported, you should refer to the hardware compatibility list.

To install, you first start the Tape Devices applet, shown in Figure 6.112. This simple applet lets you detect and install a tape drive and load and unload tape device drivers.

FIGURE 6.112.

Tape devices.

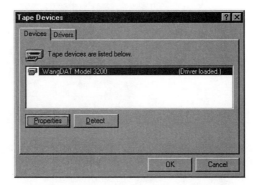

The first time you run this applet, the drive list will probably be empty. If so (and if you have a tape drive installed), simply click the Detect button, and the Tape Devices applet searches for a supported tape drive. If it finds one, it pops up a dialog box similar to Figure 6.113 from which you can install the necessary device driver. Be sure to have your installation CD-ROM available.

FIGURE 6.113.

Installing a tape device.

After the tape device is installed, you can use the Properties button in the Tape Devices applet to bring up the detailed properties, as shown in Figure 6.114 and Figure 6.115. This is probably extra information, but if you're installing the tape drive for the first time, it doesn't hurt to check that NT did pick up the right device.

As with SCSI adapters, you can install the tape device drivers independently of the tape device itself. This might be particularly useful if you use one or more external tape devices. You can

6

install the device driver and then configure the actual tape drive when necessary. To do this, select the Drivers tab from the Tape Device applet to display the dialog shown in Figure 6.116.

Only members of the Administrators local group can add or remove tape device drivers.

FIGURE 6.114.
Tape drive general properties.

FIGURE 6.115.
Tape device settings.

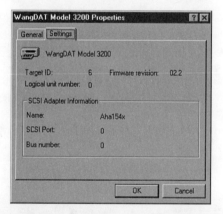

FIGURE 6.116.
Tape drivers.

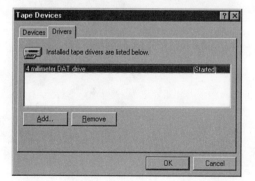

Telephony

As noted in the section "Modems" earlier in this chapter, Windows NT comes with some powerful telephony functions, often referred to as TAPI (Telephony API). The TAPI functions are used in Windows NT Workstation's Dial-Up Networking feature to dial the modem.

Central to TAPI is the concept of a location. A TAPI location is the place you are dialing from and includes the details of how you dial your phone. In a dial-up networking connection, you specify the details of the system you are dialing, including the country it's in and its dialing code and phone number. When TAPI dials this connection, it can work out where you're dialing from and to and add any necessary dialing codes (for area, country, and so on).

If you're moving around from place to place, country to country, this can be a major time saver. When you get to a new location, just start the Telephony Control Panel applet and define a new location, and you can then correctly dial any of the sites in your DUN phone book. If (or when) you return to a previously defined location, you just select the location before dialing. It couldn't be simpler.

The Telephony applet is shown in Figure 6.117. This allows you to select, remove, or modify a location or define an entirely new location. Unlike most of the other applets, the name of the applet (Telephony) is quite different from the name of dialog box (Dialing Properties). Don't let this throw you!

FIGURE 6.117.

Telephony (Dialing Properties).

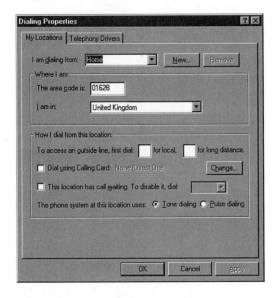

At the top of this dialog box, you can select an existing location with the pull-down combo box. If you type a new name into the combo box and click the New button, you can create a new location. If you have more than one location defined, you can select any of the locations and delete it.

To define a dialing location, you must first specify where the location is in terms of the country or area code. Note that some countries use different terms for what TAPI calls the area code. The United Kingdom, for example, uses the term dialing code or STD code instead of area code. As far as TAPI is concerned, these are the same.

The dialing codes should remain more or less constant, but they might not! TAPI country codes are stored in the Registry under the key `HKEY_LOCAL_MACHINE\SOFTWARE\Microsoft\Windows\CurrentVersion\Telephony\Providers`. The details of country names are stored using Unicode, so be careful when making any changes to these settings.

After defining your country and area codes, you need to define how you get an outside line. Generally, most offices use a 9 to get an outside line, regardless of whether it's local or long distance, but some offices use different codes.

TAPI assumes all calls are via an outside line and inserts the outside line code or long distance code for all calls. TAPI also uses the long distance code any time it needs to add the area code, which includes any international calls (that is, where it also has to add a country code).

The next configuration item is the Calling Card setup. You usually simply dial most calls and let the call charges fall on the owner of the phone connection you're using. If you are using a calling card or phone company credit card to pay for the call, select the Dial Using Calling Card box and then configure your calling card details by clicking the Change button. This displays the Change Calling Card dialog shown in Figure 6.118.

FIGURE 6.118.

Change calling card setup.

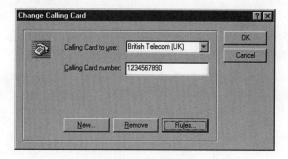

If your credit or phone calling card is not listed, you can select the New button on the Change Calling Card to define a new card. After entering the new card name, you are prompted to define the Dialing Rules, using the dialog box shown in Figure 6.119. This tells TAPI what tones to dial in order to invoke the new calling card.

Call waiting is a feature of most modern phone systems that tells you that someone else is trying to dial you when you're talking on the phone. This is neat because the second caller is unaware that you are busy. However, the call-waiting signal neatly disrupts modem traffic, usually killing the call. If you have this feature on your phone, click the This Location Has Call Waiting checkbox and enter the sequence of digits to disable it.

Figure 6.119.
Calling card dialing rules.

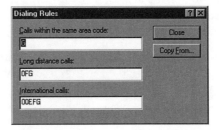

Most telephones and company switchboards these days use tone dialing, but there are still a lot of places where this is not available or the PABX does not support tone dialing. In these cases, you need to select Pulse dialing from the Dialing Properties dialog.

At first sight, this seems like a lot of effort to go through just to dial up a BBS or your Internet provider, but in practice, you can usually set up a new location in a matter of seconds. The tricky thing is getting the first location right!

UPS

Electricity to power a computer is something we take for granted. Generally, you just plug in your PC, turn it on, and it works. From time to time, the power to the socket you use for the system can disappear. This loss can be caused by something as simple as someone accidentally pulling the wrong fuse or a temporary loss of all main power. In today's crowded office where four-way power extensions are almost a normal occurrence, loss of power is all too common.

One solution to this possible loss of power is an Uninterruptible Power Supply, or UPS. A UPS is nothing more than a large, expensive, rechargeable battery, possibly with some intelligence built in. It's a simple concept, but when the power goes off, a UPS can be a life saver.

A modern UPS can also provide line filtering. This can prevent voltage spikes from damaging delicate computer equipment or prevent temporary voltage drops from affecting your system. Line spikes are all too common in older office blocks or houses that were probably not designed to handle today's modern power requirements.

The two types of UPS are intelligent and dumb. A dumb UPS just provides a simple battery capability: When main power is lost, the battery kicks in and provides the computer with power. Hopefully, the main power is restored before the battery runs down.

You can set up an intelligent UPS to communicate with Windows NT via a serial port. This allows the UPS to inform Windows NT that the power has been lost (or restored), which allows the UPS service to shut the system down gracefully. Before you can use this feature, you need to configure the UPS service using the UPS applet, shown in Figure 6.120. You must be a member of the Administrators local group to manage the UPS.

FIGURE 6.120.

Configuring the UPS.

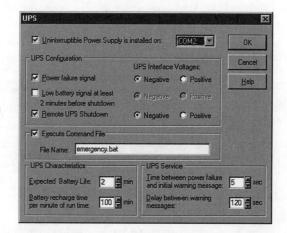

Because the UPS service can only support an intelligent UPS via a serial port, you must first tell Windows NT which port to monitor. This can be any configured serial port (as defined with the Ports applet).

Because a UPS has no automatic configuration, you must tell Windows NT the details about the UPS, including the following information (where appropriate):

- **Power Failure Signal:** If the UPS has this feature, power loss is communicated using the CTS cable signal. You need to tell the UPS service which voltage on the cable is set to indicate power loss (this information is in your UPS documentation).

- **Low Battery Signal:** If the UPS can tell Windows NT that the battery is low, you select this and define the voltage. The Low Battery condition is signaled using the DCD cable signal.

- **Remote UPS Shutdown:** If the UPS can accept a Remote Shutdown signal from the computer, this is signaled on the DTR cable signal. Even if you do not intend to use this facility, be sure to configure it.

If your UPS has a power failure signal but does not support the low battery facility, you must define the UPS characteristics in terms of Expected Battery Life and the Battery Recharge Time. You will find these figures in the documentation that accompanied your UPS.

If power is lost and NT determines that the battery is nearly exhausted because of the expected battery life or a low battery signal, it starts shutting down the system.

If you select the Execute Command File option and enter a filename, NT executes a command before shutting down the system. This command could attempt to gracefully close applications, for example, or send messages over the network indicating that shutdown is imminent. This command file must be either a batch or an executable file and must reside in the %SYSTEMROOT%\SYSTEM32 directory.

If the UPS implements a power failure signal, NT issues administrative alerts after the power failure is first detected and follows with alerts at regular intervals. You can configure the length of time the UPS service waits before issuing the first warning and the time between warnings using the two spin boxes in the UPS Service group.

> **TIP**
>
> If you have a UPS capable of issuing a power failure signal and power loss situations are not freak events, you might consider increasing the UPS service times.
>
> Where I live out in the country, short power drops are not uncommon, but they rarely last for more than 10–15 seconds. If the power is lost for longer than that, it's more serious. By making the time between power failure and the initial warning 30 seconds or longer, you avoid getting warnings for transient power losses.
>
> Likewise, if the warning messages are too frequent, a user attached to your system (with open resources that should be closed quickly) might get deluged with messages and not be able to get the files closed quickly enough.

Systems Management: Managing the System Using the Control Panel

The previous sections have introduced in some detail the various functions of the Control Panel. In this final section, I look at a few specific management tasks you might need to perform and which Control Panel applets would assist you.

Display

Some users tend to play around with their system settings and get their systems into a terrible state. Use the Display applet to fix display settings. If things get too bad, use the User Profiles dialog in the System applet to remove the profile altogether.

Modems

Configuring modems successfully is a bit of a black art. If you have trouble communicating with a remote site, try creating a modem log. This might assist in tracking down modem problems.

6

The default modem initialization strings set by Windows NT when you install the modem always enable all modems to reliably connect to all remote systems—sometimes, you must change or add specific settings. Use the Modem's Properties|Connections|Advanced to set these additional initialization settings.

Keyboard and Mouse

Use the Keyboard and Mouse applets to adjust the keyboard to your personal tastes. Remember that the Accessibility settings can override keyboard settings.

Troubleshooting Services and Devices

If devices or services fail to start during the boot process, you get a message suggesting that you look at the event viewer for more details. Sometimes, particularly if users are playing around, the system attempts to start drivers that do not exist or for which it does not have the appropriate hardware. Fix this with the Drivers applet by disabling the driver.

Although most services start with no user or password specified, some services do require that you specify a user ID. Use the Services applet to correctly specify the user name and password to start each service.

NT comes with the latest drivers for supported hardware. However, the drivers for most hardware are in a state of continuous improvement. If you have problems with a device, one possible solution is always new or updated drivers, which you can usually obtain from the hardware vendor's Internet or BBS site. Use the Control Panel to install new SCSI controllers and network and multimedia drivers.

Some motherboards do not allow Windows NT to use more than a certain amount of RAM, regardless of how many SIMM chips you add. Others might need BIOS settings changed before it can use the new RAM. If you add more RAM to your system, check the System applet to ensure that Windows NT is actually using the extra memory.

If you get regular Blue Screens of Death (that is, NT crashes), use the System applet to create a dump file. This might help the hardware vendor or Microsoft support track down the problem.

Sound

Turn sound schemes off unless you really need them.

Summary

If you've read this far, you now see that a good knowledge of Control Panel is important for effective management of Windows NT Workstation systems. This chapter has given you all the information you need so that you can use each of the Control Panel applets for best effect. Happy configuring.

CHAPTER 7

The Explorer GUI

by Sean Mathias

IN THIS CHAPTER

Navigation

Looking at Windows NT 4 Workstation, it is at once obvious that changes have been made. Windows NT 4 has adopted the Windows 95 Graphical User Interface (GUI). This interface differs greatly from the Program Manager of previous Windows versions.

No longer is the user's workspace restricted to a single, top-level container, as was the case with the Program Manager. Previously, users could create groups and items within groups, but that was as far as it could go without third-party utilities such as Norton Desktop for Windows. This certainly was not a critical shortcoming, but it was an inconvenience to the user. It is often desirable to have the ability to have groups within groups for organizational purposes (nesting), and with Program Manager this was not possible.

Another aspect of this problem was that all icons representing programs (program items) had to be contained within a group in the Program Manager. This required several steps to launch a program. This was partially alleviated by the introduction of "quick-launch" toolbars—the most common being the Microsoft Office toolbar, which allowed program items to be assigned to buttons on a toolbar residing on the desktop itself.

Since the introduction of Windows 95, and subsequently Windows NT 4, this has changed. Microsoft has moved to a "desktop-centric" model for the user shell in its current operating systems. The desktop is essentially the viewing screen of your monitor. Programs, shortcuts, and folders can be placed anywhere on the desktop to provide much easier access to programs and information. This enables the user to create a custom working environment that is best suited to his or her working habits and needs, utilizing the entire desktop. The Explorer GUI provides a taskbar and fully customizable desktop and Start menu.

The taskbar is a small border that can be placed on any side of the desktop and resized as you choose. This taskbar creates a button representing each running program for quick and easy access and ready visibility. The taskbar can be configured to always be visible or to "auto hide," disappearing when not in use. The Start menu is produced by clicking the Start button on the taskbar, and it displays a customizable menu of programs, folders, and shortcuts for quick access.

As mentioned earlier, the Explorer desktop is completely customizable by the user. Right-clicking on the desktop produces a context menu for customizing the desktop and display.

Through this context menu, the user can arrange the icons on the desktop by name, type, size, and date. There is also an Auto Arrange option, which lines up the icons on the desktop in a grid, as well as a Line up Icons option to straighten up the alignment of the desktop icons. From this context menu, the user has quick access to creating a variety of new objects. There are options to create new folders, shortcuts (described later in this chapter), briefcases (also discussed later in this chapter), bitmap Images, text files, and even new sounds.

The Properties option on the desktop context menu provides quick access to the Display properties page for configuring the desktop appearance, color scheme, screen size, and resolution and display adapter.

With these changes come other more subtle changes. The primary change to note is in how the Task Manager is accessed. In Windows NT 3.5*x*, it could be accessed by double-clicking on the desktop and pressing the Ctrl+Esc sequence, or through the Windows NT security dialog. Under Windows NT 4, it is now accessible either through the Windows NT Security dialog (accessed by the Ctrl+Alt+Del sequence) or by right-clicking the taskbar and selecting Task Manager.

The Task Manager is a popup screen that shows a list of running tasks (or programs) and their current state. This is very useful if an application hangs, because it provides a method of forcibly ending the task if necessary. The Task Manager also provides a run command from the menu to start a new task, and it has a tab for showing not only running tasks, but all running processes (foreground and background). Finally, a performance tab shows current system resource usage.

The next section takes a look at each new item of the Windows NT 4 Workstation desktop.

My Computer

The My Computer folder provides quick access to local resources such as storage devices (floppy, hard drive, and CD-ROM), printers (and an Add Printer Wizard), and the Control Panel, as well as network resources for which the user has established connections. The My Computer folder is shown in Figure 7.1.

FIGURE 7.1.
The My Computer folder.

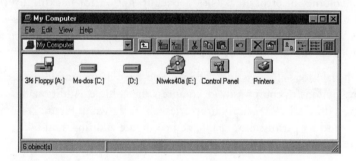

Storage Media

The File menu of My Computer provides a context-sensitive menu of options specific to the currently selected item. For storage media, the common options are to open the selected item or launch the Explorer application, giving a hierarchical view of the local computer, its resources, and the network, if any. Access is also available to the Find utility files, locally or on the network, and to the Format utility to format the storage media if necessary. The user can also create a shortcut to the item to be placed on the desktop.

By selecting the Properties tab for a storage device, a wealth of information is available. From the General Properties tab, the volume label can be changed. There is information about the type of media and the file system it uses. The total space and space used is displayed in a graphical pie chart, as shown in Figure 7.2.

FIGURE 7.2.

The General Properties tab for storage media in My Computer.

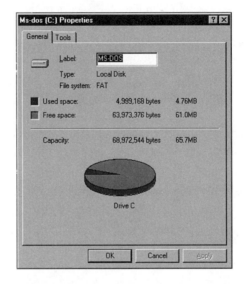

The Tools tab on the Properties sheet, shown in Figure 7.3, provides quick access to system tools relevant to the selected storage media. For hard drives, these include a tool for checking the volume for errors (chkdsk), a Backup option for backing up files and folders, and a Defragmentation option (which is grayed out because Microsoft has yet to provide this utility for Windows NT, although it is being offered by third parties such as Executive Software's Diskkeeper).

If the selected volume is an NTFS volume, the File menu and the General Properties tab will have options to compress or decompress the volume. Additionally, the Properties sheet will have a third tab—a Security Properties tab, as shown in Figure 7.4—from which the user can view and set permissions, enable and configure auditing, and take ownership of the selected item.

For CD-ROM devices, the File menu provides an option to Eject the media, provided this is supported by the CD-ROM drive. The Properties tab for a CD-ROM drive provides general information on the currently inserted CD, such as its label and volume size.

The My Computer folder, as with all folders, has a standard Edit menu with Undo, Cut, Copy, and Paste options, as well as an option to Select All or Invert the currently selected items.

FIGURE 7.3.
The Tools tab on the Properties sheet for storage media.

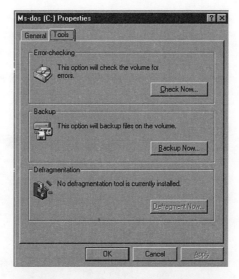

FIGURE 7.4.
The Security Properties tab for NTFS volumes.

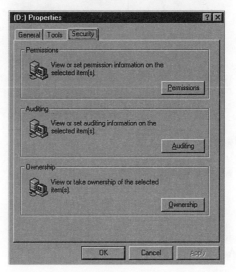

The View menu item provides options to display a toolbar and status bar, customizing the display of items within the folder as Large Icons, as Small Icons, or as a List or List with details. An option is also included for arranging and lining up icons, similar to that described earlier for the Desktop. There is a Refresh option, for refreshing the folder contents, and an Options selection.

The Options selection produces a sheet with three tabs, as shown in Figure 7.5. This Options sheet is a standard component for any item that is related to files and folders. Through this the user can customize how files and folders are displayed. The user can choose to browse folders using a separate window for each folder or using a single window that changes as new folders are opened.

Users can choose to display all files or hide files of specified types, as well as elect to not display file extensions. Through the File Types tab, the user can view the registered file types on this system and add, edit, or remove file types.

FIGURE 7.5.

The Folder Options sheet.

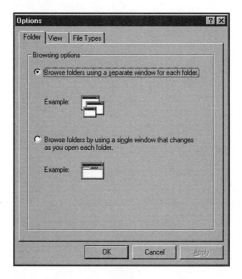

Last on the menu, as always, is a Help item, with access to Help Topics and the About Windows NT dialog box, which displays version information, the registered user and organization, and the amount of installed memory.

Printers

The Printers folder in My Computer produces another folder containing icons for installed printers and an Add Printer wizard, as shown in Figure 7.6.

FIGURE 7.6.

The Printers folder.

The Add Printer icon, when selected, launches a printer installation wizard, as shown in Figure 7.7. This is a new and welcome feature of Windows NT 4 that is sure to save much time and headaches for users and administrators alike by simplifying the process of printer installation and configuration by guiding the user through the process.

FIGURE 7.7.

*The Add Printer
Wizard in Windows
NT 4.*

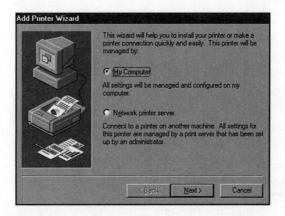

This wizard is straightforward and easy to use. It guides the user through the steps necessary to install and configure a local or remote printer, prompting where necessary for needed information.

Installing a Printer

To install a new printer, follow these steps:

1. From My Computer, open the Printers folder. (This can also be done through Start|Settings or Printers.)

2. Start the Add Printer Wizard. The user is prompted to install either a local or network printer.

3. Select My Computer (for a printer attached to the local system) or Network Printer Server (for a remote printer on the network), and then click Next.

If the printer you are installing is locally attached to your computer, see the following section, "Local Printer Installation Steps." If it is a printer shared on the network, skip to the section "Network Printer Installation."

Local Printer Installation Steps

The Add Printer Wizard initially asks whether you will be installing a locally attached printer or a network printer. Although they are similar, the processes for each have been separated in the following two sections based upon your situation. This section pertains to installing a locally attached printer.

1. The Add Printer Wizard now prompts you for the manufacturer and printer model. If your printer is not listed and you have a driver disk from the manufacturer, select the Have Disk option. If you do not have a driver disk from the manufacturer, cancel the printer installation, obtain the appropriate driver for your printer, and then run the Wizard again.

2. If you selected Have Disk, specify the location of the manufacturer-supplied driver disk and click OK. Then select the correct model of printer and select OK. The drivers for your printer are now installed. Click Next.

3. Specify which port the printer is connected to. If necessary, you can add a port (provided the necessary hardware is present) or configure an installed port. Click Next.

4. You are now prompted to supply a friendly name for the printer and decide whether it should be configured as the default printer for the system. Click Next.

5. Next you have the option of sharing the printer on the network and providing additional driver support for Windows 95 and the various versions and machine types of Windows NT. To share the printer on the network, provide a share name and select additional driver support as necessary. Click Next.

6. You are now given the option of printing a test page to verify that the printer is configured properly. Select Yes to print a test page (recommended) or select No. Then click Finish.

Network Printer Installation

Again, after starting the Add Printer Wizard, you are prompted to install a local or network printer. The steps for installing a network printer are as follows:

1. A browse box is displayed that enables the user to browse the network for shared printers. Either select a printer in the browse box or type in its Universal Naming Convention (UNC) share name (if known). Click OK.

2. If the appropriate driver for your system is installed on the print server, it is installed automatically to your system. If there is no suitable printer driver on the print server, the Wizard prompts you for the location of the printer driver. The default location is the Windows NT 4 setup directory. Provide either the setup CD-ROM or a manufacturer-supplied disk with the printer driver and click OK.

3. A message is displayed to inform you that the printer has been successfully installed. Click Finish.

The printer is now installed and ready for use from your system.

Configuring and Viewing Printer Properties

When an installed printer is selected, the File menu in the Printers folder provides options for opening the selected printer (displaying a window similar to the Print Manager in previous versions of Windows) with additional menu options.

From this window, the Printer menu option enables the user to pause, resume, and purge print jobs, as well as select the current printer as the default system printer and share the printer on the network. There are also options to refresh the display, select and configure properties for the printer (such as the driver and print processor used), and print a test page.

> **NOTE**
>
> The Properties page produced will vary according to the particular printer installed and selected. Not all printers provide the same configuration or device options.

The Properties page also has tabs for port configuration. This enables the user to add, remove, and configure ports for printer usage. There is a tab for Print Job Scheduling, which enables the following:

- Configuring times the printer will be available and allowed to print
- Specifying priority of print jobs
- Specifying the method used to spool the print job and send it to the printer

Network options for sharing the printer and setting security permissions are also accessible through the Printer Properties sheet.

The Document menu item in the selected printer folder enables the user to pause, resume, restart, and cancel specific print jobs, as well as display the properties of a specific print job. In this way, the job can be scheduled for a later time and assigned a priority other than the default. The paper size, source, page layout, and duplexing options are available through the Document Properties Page Setup tab.

Control Panel

My Computer also provides access to the Control Panel for configuration and customization of the system. See Chapter 6, "Control Panel Basics," and Chapter 10, "Advanced System Configuration," for detailed descriptions of the Control Panel applets and their respective functions and uses.

Network Neighborhood

Network Neighborhood in Windows NT 4, as in Windows 95, provides a graphical view of the attached network, the systems on the network, and any available resources. (See Figure 7.8.) This enables easy navigation of the network and finding available resources. By double-clicking on the Entire Network item, a top-level view of the network is displayed, listing the available networks; typically this will be Microsoft Windows Network and/or NetWare Compatible Network.

FIGURE 7.8.

Windows NT 4 Network Neighborhood.

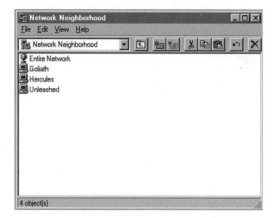

By double-clicking on one of these selections, the user is progressively taken one level deeper into the network. On a Microsoft Windows Network, this takes the user through Domains and Workgroups, then to servers and systems within that domain or workgroup, and ultimately to a list of any shared resources on the given system.

A similar sequence takes place with a NetWare Compatible Network. The difference is that the user is taken from the top level immediately to a list of NetWare servers. From there, it progresses downward through each server. With NetWare 4.*x* servers, volumes and printers available on that server (as well as the NDS tree structure for that server) can be traversed in the same manner. Effectively, they contain the same resources, but their appearance and how they are accessed depend on how the NetWare Client service has been configured. Configuring network client software is discussed in Chapter 18, "Windows NT Network Services."

To access a network resource, select the desired resource and right-click on it. This produces a context menu, as shown in Figure 7.9, enabling the user to open or explore the resource, map a network drive or create a shortcut to it, or view the item's properties.

After selecting the Printers folder, if present, in a server resource list, the user is presented with a list of installed printers on this server as well as an Add Printer option. The Add Printer item found here acts much the same as was described previously. The difference is that this wizard helps the user install a printer locally, which will be managed and configured remotely on the specified print server.

FIGURE 7.9.

Accessing network resources through Network Neighborhood.

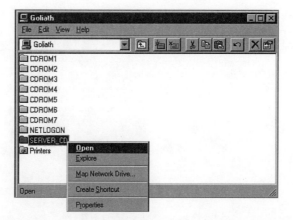

To install a printer that is shared from a remote system, right-click on the desired printer and select Install. This installs the driver to your local machine and configures your system to use the printer. (It will now appear in your local Printers folder as a connected network printer.)

When you highlight a system in Network Neighborhood and open the File menu, an Open and Explore option is available, as well as an option to create a shortcut or view the properties of the selected system. Choosing the Open option produces the same results as double-clicking the system, changing the display to show the available resources, if any, on that system. Choosing Explore launches the Explorer application, with the selected system expanded to show its available resources. The Create Shortcut option enables the user to create a shortcut to the system on the desktop. The Properties item displays general properties of the selected system, such as its name, any comment, the domain it belongs to (if any), and the type of system. There are also the standard Edit, View, and Help menus, as described previously.

Recycle Bin

A useful utility borrowed from Windows 95, the Recycle Bin is a temporary storage area for deleted items, providing functionality equivalent to the DOS utility undelete (though much safer). These can be programs, documents, shortcuts, or just about any type of file.

The Recycle Bin's behavior is controlled by its Properties settings. Right-clicking on the Recycle Bin icon produces—guess what?—a context menu. Select the Properties setting. A Properties sheet with several tabs appears. There is a Global tab and a tab for each installed hard drive, as shown in Figure 7.10.

On the Global tab, the user has the option of configuring drive space usage independently or by using one setting for all drives. The default setting is one setting for all drives, utilizing up to 10 percent of drive space for storing deleted files. The percent of disk space used for deleted files is configurable, using a slide bar to adjust the setting.

FIGURE 7.10.

Recycle Bin configuration settings.

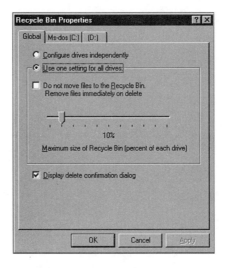

An option also exists to not move files to the Recycle Bin but instead delete them immediately, and another to display a delete confirmation dialog box when the Recycle Bin is emptied. The tabs for each installed hard drive are used to configure disk space usage when the user elects to configure drives independently. It is important to understand that when you delete a file or folder from Explorer or drag an item to the Recycle Bin, it is not deleted until you elect to empty the Recycle Bin, or until the recycle reaches its capacity and begins deleting items on a last in/first out basis. Technically, this does not affect the C2 security capability of Windows NT because objects are not "officially" deleted until they are explicitly emptied from the Recycle Bin or the Recycle Bin is disabled (an option from the Recycle Bin Properties sheet).

Double-clicking the Recycle Bin opens a window that displays the contents of the Recycle Bin. Users can highlight one, many, or all items contained, and then choose the File menu and the Restore option to restore the items to their original locations.

The File menu also contains commands to empty the Recycle Bin, permanently deleting all files contained therein. Selecting one, many, or all files and choosing Delete also permanently removes the selected files. There is also a Properties item that shows the properties for selected files.

Inbox

The Inbox is the new Microsoft Exchange e-mail client application. The Exchange client included with Windows NT 4 Workstation is not the full Microsoft Exchange Server client, but it is quite useful and functional all the same. The Windows NT version of the client is intended for use as a POP3 Internet mail client and should be replaced with the full Microsoft Exchange client provided with the Microsoft Exchange Server software.

Double-clicking on the Inbox icon on the desktop generates a dialog box asking users whether they want to install the Windows Messaging System (provided this component has not already been installed). The system prompts the user for the location of the Windows NT 4 installation directory (usually the Windows NT CD-ROM drive or network server share). It then copies the files necessary to run the Exchange client.

> **NOTE**
>
> After the Windows Messaging System is installed, another applet appears in the Control Panel—a Microsoft Mail Postoffice applet. This applet starts a Microsoft Workgroup Postoffice Admin Wizard. The user is prompted to decide whether to administer an existing postoffice or to create a new Workgroup Postoffice. It is recommended that there be only one Workgroup Postoffice on the network.

If you do not have a full-scale e-mail system in your company or you are new to messaging, Microsoft has been good enough to provide something called a Workgroup Postoffice (WGPO). A WGPO is a scaled-down but useful messaging system that is well-suited to provide minimal messaging services for communications for 20 or fewer users.

To create a new Workgroup Postoffice, follow these steps:

1. Start the Microsoft Workgroup Postoffice applet in the Control Panel.
2. Choose Create New Workgroup Postoffice, and then click Next.
3. Provide a location to create the new Workgroup Postoffice. This location must be accessible by all users who will use the postoffice. Click Next.
4. Click Next to confirm the location.
5. Provide the administrator information when prompted, and then click OK when done.

The new Workgroup Postoffice is now created and installed. To administer an existing Workgroup Postoffice, follow these steps:

1. Start the Microsoft Workgroup Postoffice applet in the Control Panel.
2. Provide the location of the existing postoffice (or browse for it), and then click Next.
3. Provide your mailbox name and password. Click Next.
4. A Postoffice Manager window is brought up, as shown in Figure 7.11.

From this screen, you can view and edit details such as name, mailbox, password, and contact information for users. You can also add and remove users and create shared folders for use with the Exchange client Inbox. When you are finished administering the Workgroup Postoffice, click Close.

FIGURE 7.11.

*The Workgroup
Postoffice Manager.*

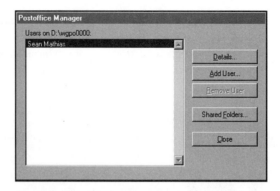

> **NOTE**
>
> This is not the full Microsoft Mail product but a functional subset of it similar to the Workgroup Postoffice available with the Microsoft Mail client included with Windows for Workgroups 3.11. This is for small workgroup/LAN messaging, such as a department or small company. There is no provision for connecting to other postoffices, utilizing gateways, or using remote mail capabilities. For this functionality, it is necessary to purchase the full Microsoft Mail Server or Microsoft Exchange Server product.

Double-clicking the Inbox icon again launches the Exchange client and prompts the user to create a service profile using a wizard. Depending on the system configuration, you have several installation options: Microsoft Mail, Internet Mail, Netscape Internet Transport, and possibly others, as more are developed for third-party mail systems.

To install Microsoft Mail services, follow these steps:

1. Start the Inbox wizard, as previously described.
2. Check the Microsoft Mail box in the information services selection, and then click Next.
3. Provide the location of the Microsoft Mail postoffice, and then click Next.
4. From the list of users, select your user account and click Next.
5. Provide the password for the user account and click Next.
6. Confirm or change the location of your Personal Address Book and Information Store files. Click Next.
7. Choose whether to add Microsoft Exchange to the Startup group and click Next.
8. Click Finish.

Microsoft Mail is now configured to run on your system.

Many users also have a need for a POP3 Internet mail client (usually for retrieving mail from an Internet Service Provider). The Microsoft Exchange client that ships with Windows NT 4 Workstation provides this functionality.

To install Internet Mail services, follow these steps:

1. Start the Inbox Wizard, as previously described.
2. Check the Internet Mail box in the Information services selection and click Next.
3. Select Modem or Network for how you will be accessing your Internet Mail server and click Next.
4. If you are using a network, skip to step 5. If you are using a modem, you will be prompted for the dial-up account to use and given the option of creating one, if necessary. Click Next.
5. Specify the IP address or name of your Internet Mail server and click Next. (This information is typically provided by your ISP.)
6. Select a mode for transferring messages—either Off-line or Automatic. Click Next.
7. Provide your Internet e-mail address and full name, and then click Next.
8. Provide your mailbox name (POP3 login name) and password, and then click Next.
9. Confirm or change the location of your Personal Address Book and Information Store files. Click Next.
10. Choose whether to add Microsoft Exchange to the Startup group and click Next.
11. Click Finish.

Internet Mail is now configured to run on your system.

One nice feature of the provided Exchange client is the Remote Mail capability (Remote Mail from the Tools menu in the Exchange client). This is especially useful for laptop users who often make long-distance calls from hotels to send and receive e-mail. The Remote Mail feature enables you to connect to your e-mail server (usually your ISP), download only the message headers (the From and Subject lines), and select only the messages you want to retrieve. This is very handy when someone sends you a large attachment with an e-mail and you do not want to retrieve it. You can read the mail you retrieve and compose mail to send while offline. Then you can send all of your mail at one time, minimizing the online telco costs.

Configuration of these two services is shown independently for illustrative purposes. They can be installed at the same time, combining several steps. Each account will be configured to use a Personal Address Book and a Personal Information Store for storing e-mail addresses and messages, respectively.

The Microsoft Exchange client is intuitive and easy to use. Refer to Figure 7.12, which shows the Exchange client Inbox. Notice storage folders on the left and folder contents to the right, with a mail toolbar along the top.

FIGURE 7.12.

The Exchange client Inbox.

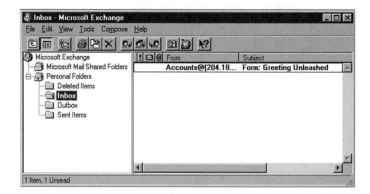

Depending on the services installed, more than one set of folders might be available. For Microsoft Mail, there is an item for Microsoft Mail Shared Folders: a Personal Folders item that contains the e-mail Inbox, Sent Items, Deleted Items, and Outbox, as well as any other folders the user creates. If connected to a Microsoft Exchange Server, additional Public Folders might be available.

NOTE

The Exchange client included with Windows NT 4 must be upgraded to operate with Microsoft's Exchange Server messaging system.

The toolbar includes items for moving up a level in the folder tree, hiding the folder list, and composing a new message. Items are also included to Reply to Sender, Reply to All, and Forward a selected message. The Address Book button brings up the local personal address book, enabling the user to add and remove e-mail addresses, view properties for addresses, and create distribution lists.

Shortcuts

Shortcuts are just that—shortcuts to programs. Shortcuts first made their appearance in Windows 95 and have come over as a part of the new user interface in Windows NT 4. To a developer, a shortcut can be likened to a pointer; it is a reference to another object in another location. Basically, it is an object that references the program or file you want.

Shortcuts can be created on the desktop and within folders. Almost any resource can have a shortcut pointing to it, including network resources, computers, drives, directories, and printers. Shortcuts are an item of convenience, allowing you to customize your environment to suit your needs.

To create a shortcut on the desktop, right-click on the desktop and select New and then Shortcut from the context menu. Enter the path to the resource for which you want to create a shortcut, or click the Browse button to locate it through the Explorer. Click Next. Provide a display name for the shortcut or accept the default (the resource name) and click Finish. To create a shortcut within a folder, select the File menu and New. The rest of the process from here is the same as previously described.

Notice that the New option in both the File menu and the context menu of the desktop provides many other options. The user can create a new briefcase container, as well as a variety of other objects, such as Word or Text documents, depending on the applications registered on the system.

Shortcuts are widely used throughout Windows NT 4 Workstation. Most program items in personal and common folders are actually shortcuts. Shortcuts are actually stored as files themselves. Typically, the majority of shortcuts are stored in the `%systemroot%\Desktop` and `%systemroot%\Profiles\` directories and subdirectories. Shortcuts are given the extension `*.lnk` (for *linkfile*). They range in size from 212 bytes up to approximately 2KB; so they do, in fact, require disk storage space, but it is minimal. Shortcuts are visually differentiated from actual target files by a small arrow placed in the bottom-left corner of the icon. This is useful in helping to avoid accidental deletion of target files by mistaking them for shortcuts.

The Taskbar

The taskbar (initially located at the bottom of the screen) is like the control center of the user environment. The Start button is located here, which is coincidentally the starting point for most actions in Windows NT 4 Workstation.

The Start button is the place the user goes to shut down or log off from the system; use the Run command line; access online help files; find files, folders, or computers; adjust system settings; and launch programs and documents. Figure 7.13 shows the Start button and menu.

The taskbar can be extensively customized by the user. By clicking the Start button and choosing the Settings|Taskbar option, or by right-clicking the taskbar itself and choosing Properties, the user is presented with the Taskbar Properties sheet (as shown in Figure 7.14) containing two tabs: Taskbar Options and Start Menu Programs.

The Taskbar Options tab enables the user to define some visual characteristics of the taskbar, such as forcing the taskbar to always remain on top and visible; an Auto Hide feature, which hides the taskbar while the user works on another task; small (rather than large) icons in the Start menu; and whether or not to show the clock in the System Tray (the 3-D panel on the far right end of the taskbar).

The Start Menu Programs tab provides options for configuring the Start menu. Here the user can add and remove items from the Start menu and its subfolders as well as clear the Documents folder on the Start menu. (This folder maintains a list of the most recently used files for quick access.) If desired, the user can configure the taskbar to "auto hide." Then when it's not in use, the taskbar disappears from the screen until the mouse passes over its location and it reappears. The size and position of the taskbar can also be customized by dragging it to any side of the desktop and sizing it as you would size a window.

FIGURE 7.13.

The Start button and menu.

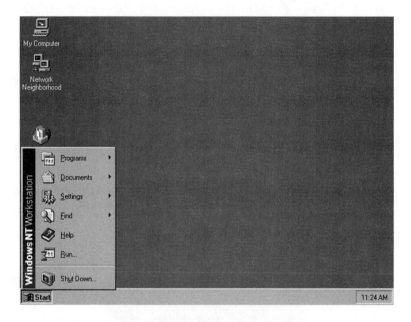

FIGURE 7.14.

The Taskbar Properties sheet.

To add or remove programs on the Start menu, the user clicks the appropriate tab—either Add, Remove, or Advanced. To add or remove programs from the Start menu, use the following step-by-step procedures.

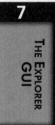

To add an item to the Start menu, follow these steps:

1. Click the Add button. This starts a wizard similar to that used to create a shortcut.

2. Provide the resource location and click Next.

3. Select where in the Start menu folder hierarchy you would like the item to appear, or create a new folder. Click Next.

4. Select a name for the item's shortcut (the display name), and then click Finish.

To remove an item from the Start menu, follow these steps:

1. Click the Remove button.

2. Select the item you want to remove and click Remove.

3. When you have removed all desired items, click Close.

The Advanced option gives the user a bit more control. This brings up the Explorer with the Start Menu Programs structure for the currently logged-on user. The user can move items and create and delete items, and folders themselves, without having to use the wizard.

In addition to providing access to the Taskbar Properties, the context menu for the taskbar provides the user with options to cascade windows or tile them horizontally or vertically, minimize all windows, and bring up the Task Manager (shown in Figure 7.15).

FIGURE 7.15.

The Windows NT 4 Workstation Task Manager.

As you can see, the Task Manager in Windows NT 4 is greatly enhanced from previous versions. The Applications tab lists all running applications and their status, and it gives the user the ability to switch to a selected task, end a task that has stopped responding, or create a new task using a Run command line. In the status bar at the bottom of the Task Manager are system statistics listing the number of processes currently running, the current CPU usage, and the current memory usage.

The Processes tab lists all currently running processes, their Process Identification Number (PID), their CPU utilization and time, and their memory usage. From here the user can end or kill a selected process using the End Process button.

The Performance tab is very useful and aesthetically pleasing, as shown in Figure 7.16. This shows a real-time graphing of CPU and memory usage, with a running history of each. Additional information is listed for total number of handles, processes, and threads—mostly irrelevant information, but at times it can be useful. There is much information on memory usage and where it is being used. Total physical memory is listed, with the amount available and amount allocated to file caching. Kernel memory (memory used by the OS kernel) is shown as a total, with paged and nonpaged broken down, as well as the size and usage of the paging files. Double-clicking on the Performance tab changes the view of the Task Manager window to a window-sized CPU Usage graph and histogram.

FIGURE 7.16.

*The Task Manager
Performance tab.*

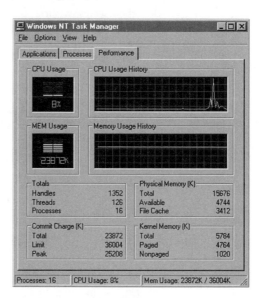

Windows NT Support for Mobile Computing

Microsoft has realized the need to make Windows NT viable for use on a laptop or portable computer. Microsoft has done much work in this area since version 3.5*x*, when it was possible but not too easy to successfully run Windows NT on a laptop. Many of the features included in Windows NT 4 Workstation for mobile computing were borrowed directly from Windows

95. With improved support for PC cards (formerly known as PCMCIA), hardware profiles, and My Briefcase, it is now practical and fairly easy to configure laptop computers to run Windows NT. Windows NT's only real shortcoming is in its inability to support laptop power-management utilities.

PC Card Support

Windows NT 4 Workstation now has native support for PC cards. A host of drivers is provided with the operating system itself, with many more being added all the time by OEMs and hardware vendors for their devices.

The majority of PC cards used today are modems and network cards, and, more recently, combination cards consisting of a modem and network card in one unit. In Windows NT 3.5*x*, a very limited number of PC cards were supported, and configuring them was difficult. A PC card applet for the Control Panel was available on the Windows NT Resource Kit utilities CD-ROM, which helped somewhat to determine the status of PC cards, the PC card controller, and drivers; but it lacked the depth and functionality of the same utility found in Windows 95 (not bad for a first effort, but it left much to be desired).

Windows NT 4 Workstation supports 58 portable computer systems and more than 190 PC card devices—and the list keeps growing.

The PC card Control Panel applet is very similar to its counterpart in Windows 95, as shown in Figure 7.17.

FIGURE 7.17.
The Windows NT 4 PC card Control Panel applet.

The PC card applet lists all recognized PC card devices. The dialog has two tabs: Socket Status and Controller. The Socket Status tab lists the devices currently in the system. The Controller tab lists the type of PC card controller installed and its resource settings, such as I/O Range and Memory Range.

> **NOTE**
>
> At the bottom of the PC card dialog a short note instructs the user to turn off the computer before inserting or removing PC cards. This is very important because damage to cards or the controller can result if inserted or removed while the system is running. This is different behavior from Windows 95, which allows "hot swapping" of PC card devices.

After selecting a PC card device from the list and choosing the Properties tab, the user is presented with another dialog having three tabs: General, Driver, and Resources. The General tab shows the device selected, device type, manufacturer, device map (if available), and the device status, shown in Figure 7.18.

FIGURE 7.18.

The PC card device Properties dialog.

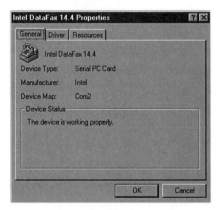

The Driver tab, shown in Figure 7.19, again shows the selected PC card device, the driver name and file used, and the driver status. If the driver is not currently installed, the Add button is enabled, allowing the user to install the necessary software driver for the device. If applicable, the Remove and Configure buttons are enabled, allowing the user to remove the driver (if it is no longer needed) or configure the device. Configuring the device is generally not necessary, because most PC cards are plug-and-play compatible.

Finally, the Resources tab lists the resources in use by the PC card device. This typically includes Interrupt Request (IRQ), I/O Range, and Memory Range.

Most PC cards supported by Windows 95 should work under Windows NT 4 Workstation, but as always, be sure to check the Hardware Compatibility List (HCL).

My Briefcase

My Briefcase is a tool to help users who need to be able to work on the same set of files at the office or home and on the road. The Briefcase is useful in its capability to synchronize the files and keep all copies up to date and consistent.

In order to keep your files synchronized using the Briefcase, you must first have a connection between the host computer and the portable computer (or whichever two computers are involved). This can be a network connection, a direct-cable connection, or even a modem (not recommended). To initialize the Briefcase, drag the files you plan to work on and keep synchronized from a shared folder on the host computer and drop them on the Briefcase of the target computer. When it is initialized, the Briefcase looks much the same as Explorer, but it includes only those files you want to keep synchronized, as shown in Figure 7.19.

Figure 7.19.

The initialized Briefcase view with files.

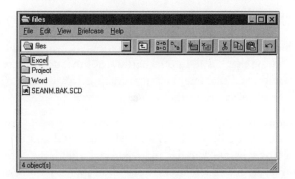

When you have finished working on the files and you want to update all copies, you must again have a connection between the two computers. When this is established, open the Briefcase on the system with the files you have been working on, select the Briefcase menu item, and choose Update All. This updates the files between the two computers.

Briefcase is straightforward in its usage. It is by no means complex, but nonetheless, it provides a great service for those of us who have need to travel and work and want to be certain that we keep our files consistent and up to date.

TIP

Two options available with the Briefcase component are not mentioned much. First, the Briefcase can be shared on the network, enabling collaborative use or synchronizing between computers on the network. Second, you can create a Briefcase on a floppy disk.

To create a Briefcase on floppy, you create the Briefcase as normal by right-clicking the desktop and then selecting New and Briefcase to create the object. Right-click on the new Briefcase and select Send To, 3-1/2 Floppy. Obviously the size is limited, but it is possible and can be helpful.

The Briefcase File menu provides many of the same options as does Explorer: Sharing, Send To, Open, Explore, Find, Create Shortcut, and so on. Again, there are the standard Edit and View menu items. The Briefcase menu item has only three options: Update All, Update Selection, and Split from Original.

As mentioned earlier, the Update All option synchronizes all files in the Briefcase. The Update Selection option synchronizes only the selected files, and the Split from Original option does just that—severs the relationship between the copy of the file in the Briefcase and the copy on the host system, creating what is called an *orphan*. When a file is orphaned, it can no longer be updated because it is not linked to any outside file.

Hardware Profiles

Hardware profiles were first introduced in Windows 95 and have subsequently made their way to Windows NT 4. This enables the user to select a specific hardware configuration at boot time. This is most useful with portable computers, which might sometimes be connected to a docking station that has additional hardware or that uses different PC cards. This is also useful for desktop systems that might use removable drives or need to select a configuration based on the peripheral devices currently in use.

At present, this feature proves useful for many users, but it leaves room for improvement. Configuring hardware profiles is somewhat involved and time-consuming, and it should be performed by someone familiar and comfortable with the Windows NT environment. Hardware Profiles are configured in three places, all applets in the Control Panel: the Devices applet, the Services applet, and the System applet's Hardware Profiles tab.

Creating Hardware Profiles

To create a hardware profile, open the Control Panel System icon and select the Hardware Profiles tab. The first time this is selected there should be only one entry—Original Configuration (Current). (See Figure 7.20.)

Selecting the Properties button produces another dialog with General and Network tabs. The General tab lists the selected hardware profile name and the Dock ID and Serial Number (for docking stations), if available, and it provides a check box to specify whether this is a portable computer. If this check box is selected, you can specify whether this hardware profile is to be used as the docked or undocked profile. The Network tab is simple. A single check box is used to specify whether this profile should be network enabled or disabled.

To create a new hardware profile, select an existing profile and click the Copy button. Provide a name for the new profile and choose OK. All profiles are created this way, using an existing profile as a template. All configured profiles are listed in the Available Hardware Profiles box. These are listed in order of preference, which is configured by selecting a profile and moving it up or down in preference by using the arrow buttons to the right of the list.

The additional options from this location are to Rename or Delete a particular profile and set startup options. The system can be configured to wait for the user to select a hardware profile to use at startup, or to wait for a specified number of seconds and choose the profile in the highest order of preference (similar to the boot menu).

FIGURE 7.20.
*The Hardware Profiles
configuration tab.*

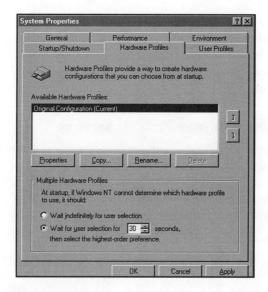

Configuring Hardware Profiles: Devices

After you have created a hardware profile, you need to customize and configure it. First you must configure the hardware-device aspect of the profile. To do this, go to Control Panel-Devices. This lists all hardware drivers installed in the system, their current status, and startup option (Boot, System, Automatic, Manual, or Disabled).

To configure a hardware profile, you must select each driver that you want to enable or disable for a given profile, and then select the HW Profiles button. This produces a Device dialog that lets you enable or disable the selected driver on a per profile basis, shown in Figure 7.21.

NOTE

Any driver that you do not explicitly configure will retain the settings from the configuration that was used as a template to create this profile.

FIGURE 7.21.
*The Hardware Profile
Device configuration
dialog.*

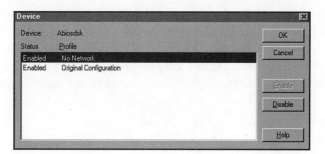

7

THE EXPLORER
GUI

Windows NT does not provide very friendly names for the drivers and devices listed, so this portion can be somewhat tricky. The best thing to do is to modify only those particular devices that are affected by adding or removing a given device and leaving the remaining drivers in their original configuration. If you are unsure about a particular driver, leave it in its current state or request help from your systems administrator.

Configuring Hardware Profiles: Services

Configuring Services for different hardware profiles is identical to the method of configuring Devices, except that the service names are a bit more understandable. The same principles apply; the new profile will inherit the configuration of the profile that was used as a template. Change only the services that you know will be affected by the different hardware configuration. And, when in doubt, leave the default setting.

For both Devices and Services, about the worst thing that will happen by leaving a setting with the default value is receiving an error message when Windows NT starts up. You can examine the Event Log to see which Device or Service failed and then correct the problem.

To initiate a particular profile at boot time, select the operating system environment you want (Windows NT 4 Workstation or Windows NT 4 Workstation [VGA Mode]). The next screen has a message instructing you to press the spacebar for the Hardware Profile/Last Known Good Configuration Menu. Press the spacebar and select the hardware profile you want to use during your session.

> **NOTE**
>
> Just as you should not remove a PC card while the system is running, you should not remove a portable computer from a docking station while it is running. To undock a portable computer and/or select another hardware profile, shut down and reboot the system. This saves you from frequently replacing your hardware.

Summary

You should now be comfortable with the Windows NT 4 Workstation operating environment and have a pretty good idea of how to navigate the system and perform most basic tasks. You now also have an understanding of the capabilities of Windows NT on a portable computer, its synchronization features and support for PC cards, and multiple hardware profiles. However, as with most other things, the best way to master something is to use and practice it.

IN THIS PART

IV

PART

Advanced Windows NT

The Administrative Tools

by Sean Mathias

IN THIS CHAPTER

Windows NT provides a group of tools and utilities, called *Administrative Tools*, for the configuration and management of various system components such as security and disk drives. These tools also provide a mechanism to monitor system performance, get detailed system information, and back up system files.

Disk Administrator

Windows NT provides a utility for the configuration and management of fixed disk drives and CD-ROM devices called *Disk Administrator* (shown in Figure 8.1). Disk Administrator is the tool that is used to create and delete partitions, create and manage *volume sets*, format drives and change drive letter assignments of both fixed drives and CD-ROM drives, and provide information about installed storage devices.

FIGURE 8.1.

The Disk Administrator utility.

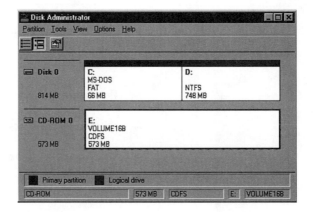

The first time Disk Administrator is run, or the first time it is run after adding a fixed disk drive, you will be prompted to write a signature to the drive. This happens so that Disk Administrator has a reference to the drive, and it is an entirely safe operation, meaning that no data will be affected. If you do not allow a signature to be written to the drive, it will be inaccessible to the Disk Administrator program.

Partitions

To create or delete a disk partition, or to mark a partition as active, you use Disk Administrator. Partitions are designated areas of hard disk space used for storing data and system files. For a disk drive to be usable, it must be configured with at least one partition. Because you must be in Windows NT to use Disk Administrator, you already have at least one primary partition that is active. If you have additional disk drives or you want to reconfigure disk drives, this is the tool you must use.

NOTE

Disk Administrator does not allow you to delete the active or current system partition. To do this, you need to either boot to an alternate operating system (if on a dual-boot system) and use FDISK, or boot from an MS-DOS floppy disk and use FDISK to delete the partition. If you are trying to delete an NTFS partition, it appears under the *non-DOS partition* section of the FDISK program.

To delete a partition, follow these steps:

1. Select the partition that you want to delete by clicking on it with the mouse.
2. Select Partition|Delete from the menu bar (or right-click on the partition and select Delete).
3. You are advised that all data on the drive will be lost. Confirm that you want to delete the selected partition.
4. When you have completed this operation, select Partition|Commit Changes Now to save the changes you have made.

NOTE

If any applications or services are using any of the resources on the drive that you are attempting to delete, you will be informed that the drive cannot be locked for exclusive use and the operation will fail. One of the most common causes of this failure is having a *pagefile* on the partition. To remove the pagefile, open Control Panel, choose the System applet, and select Virtual Memory. Set the pagefile for the appropriate disk to a starting and maximum size of zero. When you restart the system, you will be able to delete the partition.

To create a partition, follow these steps:

1. Select an area of free space on a disk drive (unpartitioned space on a drive) by clicking its graphical representation.
2. From the menu bar, select Partition|Create or Partition|Create Extended to create an extended partition. (This can also be accomplished by right-clicking on the area of free space and selecting Create or Create Extended.)
3. Specify the size of the partition to create (up to the maximum listed), and choose OK.
4. When this is completed, select Partition|Commit Changes Now from the menu bar to save the changes.

5. You can now format the partition by selecting it and choosing Tools|Format from the menu bar.

6. Select the file format to use, select an optional label, and, if desired, check the Quick Format option. Choose OK.

7. You are informed that all information on the drive will be lost. Click OK to confirm the operation.

8. The drive is formatted, and you are presented with a dialog showing the total disk space and available disk space. Choose OK.

Volume Sets

Volume sets are a collection of one to 32 areas of free space across one or more physical disk drives, which are combined to form a single logical partition. This very useful feature enables the user to combine multiple areas of disk space, which individually are of little use, into a larger volume that maximizes disk space utilization.

Here are a few important points that you should note about volume sets:

■ First, volume sets are not visible to other operating systems on the same computer. (They are visible across the network.) This means that if a system with a volume set is a dual-boot system, the volume set and its data will not be accessible to the alternate operating system.

■ Volume sets offer no fault-tolerance, which means that if any one disk or disk partition in the volume set is compromised, the entire volume set is lost.

■ Lastly, volume sets formatted using NTFS can be extended. Therefore, if you have a volume set consisting of three partitions for a total of 1150MB, and some time in the future you have another drive with 275MB of unused disk space, the 275MB can be added to extend the volume set.

As mentioned earlier, volume sets can be extended to include up to 32 areas of disk space. Volumes formatted using the FAT file system cannot be extended. Volume sets are not striped (as is RAID5), but they are written to sequentially, meaning that the first partition in the set is used first, followed by the second, the third, and so on. If you delete a volume set, all data on the set is lost; it is not accessible on a per partition basis.

> **TIP**
>
> Unlike stripe sets, volume sets provide no performance increase. Volume sets are strictly a method with which you can create large areas of storage or use several small partitions in a more practical manner.

To create a volume set, follow these steps:

1. Select one or more areas of free disk space by holding the Ctrl key down and clicking on each area of disk space.

2. When all areas have been selected, select Partition|Create Volume Set from the menu bar.

3. Choose the size of the volume set that you want to create (up to the maximum available), and click OK.

4. Choose Partition|Commit Changes Now, and confirm the action by clicking OK.

After the volume set has been created, you need to format it as you would a regular partition (described previously). Again, volume sets formatted with NTFS can be extended; those formatted with FAT cannot.

To extend an NTFS volume set, follow these steps:

1. Select the existing volume set by clicking on it, and select one or more additional areas of free space (up to a total of 32) by holding down the Ctrl key and clicking on the additional areas.

2. From the Partition menu, select Extend Volume Set.

3. Choose the size of the volume set that you want to create (up to the maximum available), and click OK.

4. Choose Partition|Commit Changes Now, and confirm the action by clicking OK.

The key thing to remember here is that volume sets provide a convenient method to make use of small disks or partitions, but they provide no fault-tolerance. If any member of a volume set is compromised, the entire set is lost!

Stripe Sets

Striping disks (or creating stripe sets) is a method to improve disk access time by creating a single logical volume across multiple physical drives. Unlike volume sets, stripe sets must be created across separate physical drives using partitions of approximately the same size. Similar to volume sets, stripe sets provide no fault-tolerance.

Stripe sets are created using from two to 32 partitions of approximately the same size on separate physical disk drives. If the partitions are of different sizes, the smallest partition is used as the common size; the remaining free space can be used individually or combined to create a volume set.

The advantage of this is twofold. First, you can create much larger volumes in this manner. Second, disk access time is improved because the data is written, or *striped*, across all members of the stripe set. In this way, the speed is increased because multiple I/O operations can be performed on the drives at the same time. Again, as with volume sets, if a member of a stripe set is compromised, all the data on the stripe set is lost. To overcome this limitation, you can use another form of striping—striping with parity (RAID 5). This is similar to disk striping, except that an additional stripe—a parity stripe—is interwoven into all disk writes, which provides a means of recovering if a disk drive fails. However, disk striping with parity is not available with Windows NT Workstation.

To create a stripe set, follow these steps:

1. Select one or more areas of free disk space (of approximately the same size and on separate physical drives) by holding the Ctrl key down and clicking on each area of disk space.

2. When all areas have been selected, select Partition|Create Stripe Set from the menu bar.

3. Choose the size of the stripe set that you want to create (up to the maximum available), and click OK.

4. Choose Partition|Commit Changes Now, and confirm the action by clicking OK.

Stripe sets are primarily a method to improve disk access speed, and like volume sets, they provide no fault-tolerance mechanism, nor can they be used as a system boot partition.

Disk Configuration Information

Disk Administrator provides a mechanism to save and restore a system's disk configuration information. This feature can be extremely useful in the event that the configuration information is lost or corrupted. This can also be used as a precautionary measure along with the Emergency Repair Disk in the event that Windows NT needs to be reinstalled.

If Windows NT is reinstalled on a system, it will recognize the file system and structure of hard disk drives, provided they are not volume sets or any level of RAID. If you use volume sets or software RAID through Windows NT, it is imperative that you save your disk configuration information. This is the only way you will be able to recover the information on the drives if you have a need to reinstall the operating system.

To save disk configuration information to disk, follow these steps:

1. Have a 1.44MB formatted floppy disk ready.

2. From the menu bar, choose Partition|Configuration and Save.

3. You are prompted to insert the floppy disk in the A: drive. Insert the disk and click OK.

4. When the operation is complete, place the configuration disk in a safe place.

Whenever you change the drive configuration, remember to update or re-create your disk configuration disk.

To restore configuration information from disk, follow these steps:

1. Insert your configuration information disk in the system's A: drive.

2. From the Partition menu, select Configuration|Restore.

3. You are informed that your current disk configuration information will be overwritten. Choose Yes to continue.

4. When the information disk is in the drive, confirm the operation by clicking OK.

5. When the operation is complete, you need to restart your system to effect the changes.

Again, if you are using volume sets or software RAID in Windows NT, you should always have a current copy of the system's disk configuration information in case you need to reinstall and recover your data.

Tools

The Tools menu item in Disk Administrator provides many management utilities for system disks. From the Tools menu, you can format a drive, change the existing file system format of a drive, check a drive for errors, label a drive, and view the properties of a drive.

Formatting

The Tools|Format command enables the user to format an unformatted disk partition using either the FAT file system or the NTFS file system. Also, if a disk partition that is formatted with the FAT file system is selected, this option is called Change Format and allows the user to convert the partition to NTFS. If you have made other changes to the disk configuration, the Format option will be unavailable until you select the Partition|Commit Changes Now option.

> **NOTE**
>
> A partition can be converted from the FAT file system to the NTFS file system, but a partition cannot be converted from NTFS to FAT.

To format a partition, follow these steps:

1. Select the partition to format by clicking it (or right-click it and choose Format from the context menu), and you are presented with a dialog, as shown in Figure 8.2.

2. Optionally, provide a volume label.

3. Select the format type for the file system to use (FAT or NTFS).

4. Optionally, select the Quick Format option.

5. Select OK.

6. When the operation has completed, you are shown a dialog with the total disk space available and disk space free. Select OK.

FIGURE 8.2.

The Format Drive dialog.

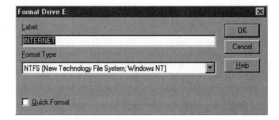

Changing the format of a drive from FAT to NTFS follows the same procedure just described, with the exception being step 3, in which the only option is to select NTFS.

> **NOTE**
>
> You cannot format or change the format of a drive containing Windows NT system files. These can be the boot partition, the partition containing the WINNT root directory, or a partition with a pagefile.

Checking a Drive for Errors

Disk Administrator provides a graphical version of *chkdsk*, the utility used to scan hard drives for errors and bad sectors and fix any problems that it can. When you select a drive and choose Check for Errors from the Tools menu (or right-click the drive and select Properties and Check Now from the Tools tab), you are presented with a dialog, as shown in Figure 8.3.

FIGURE 8.3.

The Check For Errors dialog in Disk Administrator.

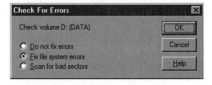

The user is presented with the following three choices:

1. Do not fix errors: This option scans the selected drive and only reports any errors found; it does not attempt to correct the errors. This option can be run against a volume that has open files or is in use.

2. Fix file system errors: This option scans the drive for file system errors and attempts to correct any that are found. If there are any open files or running processes on this drive that prevent the drive from being locked, the user receives the dialog and message informing him or her that the requested action cannot be completed at this time. The user is also asked whether he or she would like to schedule this process the next time the system reboots.

3. Scan for bad sectors: This option scans the drive for bad sectors and, if it finds any, attempts to map around them.

These utilities should be part of regular system maintenance and should be run at least once a month to verify disk and file system integrity so that you don't learn of a problem in some less practical manner (such as massive data loss).

Additional Utilities

In addition to the previously mentioned utilities, Disk Administrator provides a few additional utilities.

Set Volume Label

This is a very straightforward utility (found under the Tools menu). Selecting a drive and selecting this option produces a dialog through which the user can give the volume a descriptive label, as shown in Figure 8.4. This is also accessible by right-clicking the partition, selecting the Properties item, and then changing the label in the Label field.

FIGURE 8.4.

The Set Volume Label utility.

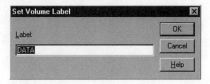

Assign Drive Letter

When you select a drive and click the Assign Drive Letter option under the Tools menu, the administrator can assign an alternate drive letter to a volume or specify that no letter should be assigned, as shown in Figure 8.5.

Drive letters are assigned sequentially, starting with c: for the system partition. Drive letters are then assigned sequentially by disk ID number (as enumerated by the system) for all installed drives. New drives—either fixed drives or CD-ROM drives—are assigned the next available drive letter.

FIGURE 8.5.

The Assign Drive Letter tool.

Properties

When you select a drive and choose Properties from the Tools menu (or right-click the drive and choose Properties), you are presented with a properties sheet that graphically depicts the size of the drive, used space, and free space (see Figure 8.6).

FIGURE 8.6.

The Volume Properties dialog.

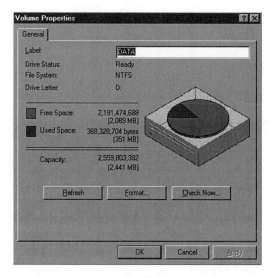

From this properties sheet, the user can perform most of the actions and run most of the utilities described earlier, such as checking a disk for errors or formatting a drive.

The remaining options contained in the View and the Options menu items are mostly user preferences of how volumes should be displayed and which colors and patterns to use to represent specific drive types and configurations.

Event Viewer

The Event Viewer in Windows NT is a user interface allowing the administrator access to the log files that the system records, as well as a method to customize how the logs are kept. Three separate logs are accessible through the Event Viewer: System logs, Security logs, and Application logs.

To select a particular log, select the Log menu item and choose from System, Security, or Application. Also available from the Log menu are options to open a previously saved log file and save the current log file, an option to clear out the current log, a Log Settings item that can be used to customize the logging parameters, and a Select Computer item to view the logs of another computer on the network.

Logs

As mentioned, there are three specific log types:

- System: This log represents various events, warnings, information, and errors reported by the operating system or a system component.
- Security: The Security log records events that are security related, as specified in the security auditing configuration found in User Manager.
- Application: The Application log records events as reported by system and user applications, and their informational, warning, and error messages.

Different events are represented by different icons in the Event Viewer, as shown in Figure 8.7.

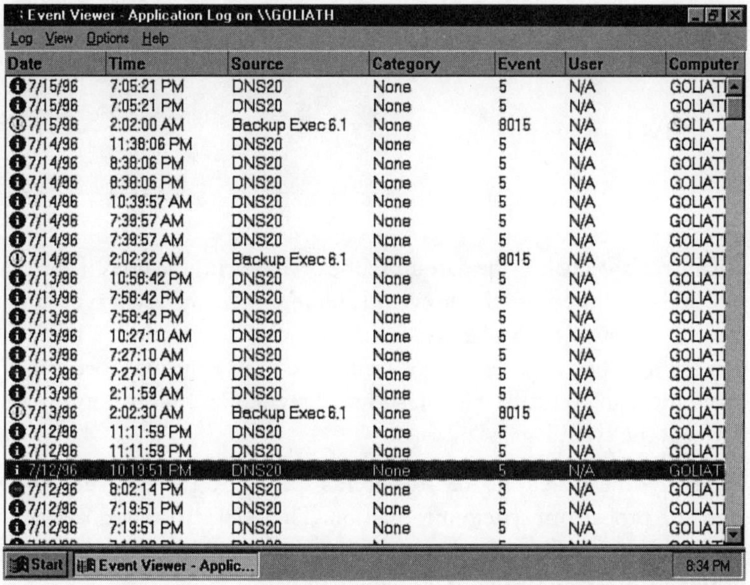

FIGURE 8.7.

The Event Viewer listing of the Application log.

Informational messages are depicted with a blue icon that has a white *i* in the center. Warnings or alerts are represented by a yellow icon with an exclamation point in the center. Errors are indicated by a stop sign icon. Specific to the Security log are two additional icons. A key icon represents some security event and is informational only. A padlock icon represents some type of security failure. This could be an unknown username or password or a user trying to exercise some action for which he has insufficient rights, depending on how the security auditing is configured.

When one of the logs is selected from the Logs menu, the log is presented in a row and column format with one row for each individual event and descriptive columns. When the user selects a particular event and double-clicks it or selects Detail from the View menu, an event detail is presented, as shown in Figure 8.8.

FIGURE 8.8.

The Event Detail dialog.

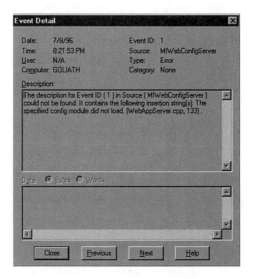

Each Event Detail lists the date and time of the event, the user (if applicable), the computer on which the event occurred, the event ID, the source, the event type, and the category. There is also a description box and a data box. Typically, the description box can be somewhat helpful, but the data box is generally not readable by mere mortals (because it's binary). To quickly scroll through events in the detail view, Previous and Next buttons are provided for moving through the event log.

Typically, the System log records events specific to the OS, such as device drivers failing to initialize properly or system information. The Security log audits a variety of events as defined by the security audit configuration. The Application log records application-specific events such as successfully completing backup operations.

The Event Logs should be examined periodically to determine whether any system problems have occurred and to test the general operating health of the system. For security purposes, Event Logs should be examined to determine whether there have been any unauthorized accesses or attempts at unauthorized access.

To clear the log settings, follow these steps:

1. Select the log that you want to clear by choosing the appropriate log from the Logs menu.

2. Select Clear All Events from the Logs menu.

3. A dialog box is presented asking whether you would like to save the log before clearing it. If you want to save it, choose Yes and provide a path and filename for the log file. If you do not want to save it, choose no.

4. A confirmation dialog is presented, which asks you to verify your action. If you want to clear the log, select Yes.

To configure log settings, follow these steps:

1. Select Log Settings from the Log menu.

2. A log settings dialog appears (see Figure 8.9).

FIGURE 8.9.

Event Viewer log settings configuration.

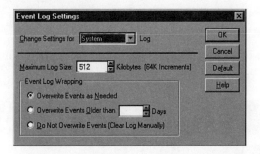

3. Select the log that you want to configure by using the Change Settings for list box.

4. Set a maximum log size in the Maximum Log Size text box (using 64KB increments).

5. In the Event Log Wrapping section, choose the method of log maintenance: Overwrite Events as Needed, Overwrite Events Older than *xxx* Days, or Do Not Overwrite Events (Clear Log Manually).

6. To reset the log settings to the system defaults (512KB maximum size, overwrite events older than 7 days), select the Default button and click Yes in the confirmation dialog box.

7. When you have the desired log settings, click OK.

I recommend the following configuration for all logs:

- Maximum Log Size: 8192KB.
- Event Log Wrapping: Do Not Overwrite Events (Clear Log Manually).

However, these are only suggestions. It is equally advisable to initially monitor the size and growth of the logs to best determine your specific needs.

The event log is an important system monitoring tool and should be checked daily for all systems in a network. This can be a tedious and time-consuming task, but it is one of the best methods to stay apprised of your system's health and activity and should be closely monitored.

> **NOTE**
>
> In the event that one of the logs becomes full and is not configured to overwrite events as needed, the system sends an error message to the console (and any other system or person that it has been configured to send alerts to) and stops logging. Some applications terminate or stop responding when a particular log is full, which makes it that much more important to monitor the event logs.

To view another computer's event logs, follow these steps:

1. Click Select Computer from the Logs menu.
2. Type in the computer name or select a computer from the browse list and choose OK.
3. Inspect the log as described earlier for a local system.

> **NOTE**
>
> You must have administrator rights on the remote system to view, change, or clear the event logs.

The user also has the option to save specific logs and later load them into the Event Viewer for review or historical auditing reasons. To save a log (System, Security, or Application), select Save As from the Log menu. Similarly, select Open from the Log menu to open a previously saved log file.

Performance Monitor

The Performance Monitor utility included with Windows NT is an extremely powerful and useful utility, and it is often overlooked or underutilized. Performance Monitor first and foremost provides a mechanism to monitor system performance in a general manner and provides the capability of isolating specific system components and monitoring them in minute detail to determine the root of a problem or cause of a bottleneck.

Performance Monitor has four separate components: Chart, Alert, Log, and Report. Each component monitors the performance of the specified components, but they handle the data in different manners.

- **Chart**: The Chart utility charts the specified components at user-configurable intervals and presents the data in the form of either a graph or a histogram.
- **Alert**: The Alert utility enables the user to specify components to monitor and can be configured to send an alert and/or execute a program if the counter on a specified component goes over or under a defined threshold.
- **Log**: The Log utility logs to file the value of specified counters for components at specified intervals.
- **Report**: The Report utility generates a report based upon the statistics of the specified counters.

Charting

The most common use of Performance Monitor, in my experience, has been to determine the cause of poor system performance. Unfortunately for most system administrator types, the time it takes to monitor system performance cannot be justified until a problem arises. If this is the case and a bottleneck exists in the system or the system just seems to be running poorly, the charting utility in Performance Monitor is the tool to use.

This utility charts the value of specified system components at any interval from 0 to 2,000,000 seconds as defined by the user, which can give a good indication (in real time) of where the bottleneck exists. Typically, system slowness will be in one of four areas: disk I/O, processor resources, memory resources, or the network component (if installed).

To monitor a given component, Performance Monitor uses what are called *counters*, which are a measurement unit as defined for a given component. Most Windows NT components have counters that can be monitored, although some must be installed manually. (To monitor TCP/IP performance, the SNMP feature of TCP/IP must be installed.)

To begin monitoring, you must specify the object that you want to monitor, the specific counters you want to monitor for that object (see Figure 8.10), and if applicable, an instance of the selected object. To add objects and counters to a graph, click the Add to Chart option from the Edit menu. Each object counter can be customized in color, scale, line width, and style through the Add to Chart dialog box.

FIGURE 8.10.

Adding objects and counters to a graph.

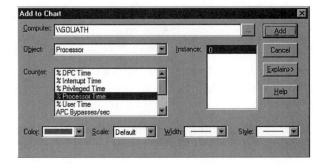

Typically, a good starting point for determining the area of the system causing the bottleneck is to use a general configuration such as Total Processor Time, Memory Page Faults, Memory Bytes Available, and Paging File Usage. This is illustrated in Figure 8.11.

FIGURE 8.11.

Performance Monitoring to determine which resources are overburdened.

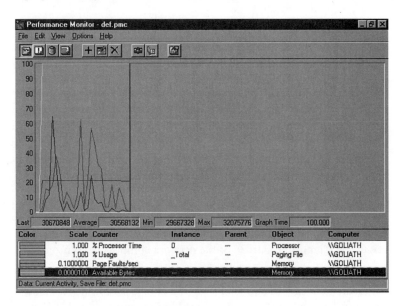

When you have determined which system component is the cause of the bottleneck, you can then customize your monitoring to drill down to the details of that subsystem and determine how to best relieve the bottleneck. This does not always require a hardware upgrade; sometimes it is as simple as reconfiguring a system component, changing the paging file size, or tuning the working environment.

Other options are available for customizing the chart that are also available for the Alert, Log, and Report functions. Here is a summary of the options:

■ **File Menu**

New Chart (Alert, Log, Report) begins a new instance of the utility with new counters.

Save Settings (As)… saves the current settings so that they can be reused at a later time without having to define the settings again.

Export exports the data to a delimited text file that can be imported to other applications and parsed as desired.

■ **Edit Menu**

Add to Chart… adds object counters.

Edit Chart Line… edits the selected object counter.

Clear Display clears the gathered statistics and starts counting fresh.

Delete From Chart removes the selected object counter from the display.

■ **Options Menu**

Chart (Alert, Log, Report) displays the options for the utility, such as whether to display the legend and value bar, how to display data, and the time interval to collect statistics.

Data From… allows the importing of previously collected data, and saved data can be loaded from a file to analyze.

Update Now causes the data to be updated immediately rather than waiting for the next specified interval.

Alerts

For those times when you are not actively trying to pinpoint a system performance problem, you can do other things to monitor ongoing system performance and be alerted to potential bottlenecks before they become critical, which gives you time to respond appropriately.

A very useful utility for this purpose is the Alert feature of Performance Monitor. Using this feature, you can specify object counters in the same way you did with the Chart previously. For each object counter that you want to monitor, you specify a threshold value for which an alert will be generated if that threshold is crossed.

When a threshold value is exceeded (or falls below the value), a record is written to the Alerts window in Performance Monitor (shown in Figure 8.12). Optionally, a program can be configured to run, an alert can be configured to be sent across the network to a specified individual or computer, and the occurrence can be written to the Windows NT Event Viewer Application Log.

This utility provides a good method for monitoring system performance over long periods of time while under normal usage, providing a clear picture of how the system holds up under real world usage over a period of time.

This can be helpful for situations such as monitoring a system throughout the course of a typical workday in order to determine when and why a specified object is pushed beyond its limits.

FIGURE 8.12.

The Alerts window in Performance Monitor.

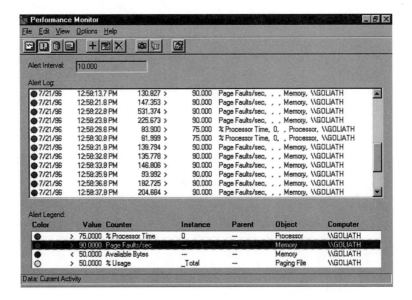

Logging

The logging utility in Performance Monitor is best used as a tool to gather system performance data over an extended period of time to export to another application for analysis.

Adding objects to the log is fairly similar to the other utilities, except specific counters cannot be specified; only objects can be specified. (By default, all counters for the selected objects will be logged.) Also, a log file must be specified (using the Options menu and Log item) to write the data to, and logging must be started manually by clicking the Start Log button.

As mentioned earlier, this utility is designed to monitor performance data over an extended period of time. It is recommended that the log interval not be set at less than 15-second intervals as the log file grows extremely fast and quickly becomes difficult to effectively parse and analyze.

When the log period is completed, the log file can be exported to a text delimited file for use in other applications such as Microsoft Excel, or it can be imported into the Performance Monitor chart utility for interpretation.

Reporting

The Report view window in Performance Monitor is a very straightforward view of selected objects and counters. The selected counters and statistics are displayed in a report format similar to a spreadsheet type report, providing a quick view of current activity and performance.

As you have seen here, Performance Monitor is a unique application that is very extensive and can provide invaluable information about system performance and ways to improve it. This tool should be well understood and utilized by any Windows NT system administrator or person responsible for supporting Windows NT. It can save much time and headache if it is understood and utilized on a regular basis.

Windows NT Backup

Windows NT provides a basic backup program for backing up data and system files to tape devices for archival and fault tolerance. This backup program works with all backup devices listed on the Hardware Compatibility List.

> **NOTE**
>
> When using a tape library or tape loader, Windows NT Backup is only able to use the device in single tape operation mode; it has no loader support built in. For tape loader support, it is necessary to use a third-party backup package.

This program is fairly basic, but it is useful nonetheless. There is no built-in software compression; any compression must be provided through the hardware device used. The user interface is simple and facilitates easy navigation and use, as shown in Figure 8.13.

FIGURE 8.13.
The Windows NT Backup program.

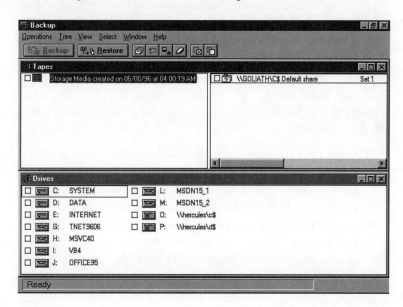

The Tapes window lists the currently inserted tape and its contents, as well as any other tapes for which it has a history. Double-clicking on the current tape brings up its catalog, and if none exists, a catalog operation is initiated to determine the contents of the tape. After a catalog is built, double-clicking the tape produces a File Manager type of file and directory listing, which allows the user to select files and directories for a restore operation.

The Drives window lists all local drives and CD-ROM devices as well as any mapped network drives. Double-clicking a drive produces a File Manager type of window that allows the user to browse the files and directories and make selections for a backup operation.

To use the Windows NT Backup program, you must first install a tape device using the Tape Devices applet in Control Panel. When the device has been installed, you are presented with a hardware dialog to select a default tape drive the first time you start Windows NT Backup. After you make this selection, you can begin using the Backup utility.

NOTE

If you have more than one tape drive installed, you can select the drive you want to use for a given session by selecting Hardware Setup from the Operations menu in NT Backup.

Backing Up Files and Directories

To back up files and directories, mark the files and directories that you want to back up using the Drives window. When selecting a checkbox, everything below that checkbox in the hierarchy is selected by default. When all desired selections have been made, click the Backup button or choose Backup from the Operations menu. This produces a backup configuration dialog, as shown in Figure 8.14.

By default, some information is filled in by the system, such as the tape label (unless a new tape is used), the tape creation date, and the owner of the tape. The options that are configurable by the user are as follows:

- Verify After Backup: This option indicates whether the backed up data should be verified against the system image after the backup operation has completed. This is a good practice, but it is not always practical because it effectively doubles the time needed for a backup operation.

- Backup Local Registry: If you have selected a Windows NT system partition, you have the option to back up the registry for the local system. Registries cannot be backed up across a network using Windows NT Backup.

- Restrict Access to Owner or Administrator: This option writes a header to the tape that will only allow the owner of the tape or an administrator to read or restore from it.

- Hardware Compression: This option enables hardware compression if it is available and supported by the current hardware device.

- Operation: This selection indicates whether the tape should be appended (added to while retaining previously backed up data) or overwritten (destroying previously backed up data).

- Description: This area is for a description of the tape. This information will appear in the Tapes window when this tape is loaded.

- Backup Type: This selection is the type of backup to perform. Options are Normal, Copy, Differential, Incremental, or Daily. These options are described later in this section.

- Log Information: This is a log file of the operation, which keeps a record of any skipped files or errors. Also, you have a choice of Full Detail, Summary Only, or None for Log Information.

FIGURE 8.14.

The Backup Information dialog.

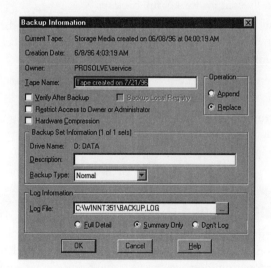

When the desired options are set, click OK to begin the backup operation. If this tape has data from a previous backup on it and you have selected the overwrite option, you will be asked to confirm that you want to overwrite the data. When the backup operation has begun, you will see a progress dialog indicating the number of directories, files, and bytes backed up; the elapsed time, number of corrupt and skipped files, and the current file and directory being backed up; as well as a view of the log file being recorded. (See Figure 8.15.)

FIGURE 8.15.

The Backup Status dialog.

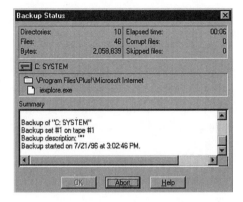

Backup Types

Several different backup methods or types are commonly used. The following is a list of the methods supported by Windows NT Workstation with a brief description of each.

- Normal: Backs up all selected files and directories and resets the archive bit. It is typically used for weekly full backups.

- Copy: Copies selected files to tape without resetting the archive bit. It is used to create a copy of the data without preventing the files from being backed up during the next incremental backup process.

- Differential: Backs up files that have the archive bit set but does not reset the archive bit.

- Incremental: Backs up files that have the archive bit set, indicating that they have been changed since the last backup cycle. This is typically run daily between Normal (or full) backup operations.

- Daily: Backs up files that have changed on the day that the backup is run.

Restoring Files and Directories

Restoring files and directories works in much the same way as a backup operation, except that the selections are made from a cataloged tape rather than the Drives window. If the tape you want to restore from does not have a catalog, you can either restore the entire tape blindly or you can catalog it first and make the desired restore selections.

To catalog a tape, follow these steps:

1. Insert the tape into the drive.
2. Highlight the currently inserted tape in the Tapes window.

3. From the Operations menu, select the Catalog item.

4. The tape is cataloged.

After the tape is cataloged, double-click on the inserted tape and select the files and directories that you want to restore. When you have made your selections, click the Restore button. As with the Backup option, the Restore option presents the user with a Restore dialog, which is shown in Figure 8.16.

FIGURE 8.16.
The Restore Information dialog.

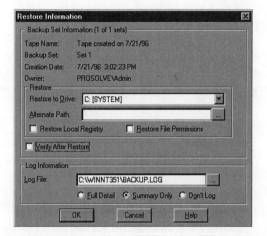

Similar to the Backup dialog, the Restore dialog provides information about the tape such as its name, creation date, and owner. The remaining restore options are fairly simple. The user can accept the default option of restoring to the original location or provide an alternate location in the Alternate Path box. If a registry backup is on the tape, an option is available to restore the local registry. There are also options to restore the original file permissions and verify the data after the restore (similar to verifying the data after a backup operation), as well as the same logging options used with the backup operation.

Tape Maintenance

Windows NT Backup provides several utilities for maintaining tapes. From the Operations menu, the remaining options are as follows:

- **Erase Tape:** This option erases the data on the tape in one of two ways. It uses a secure erase, which erases all data on the tape; or it uses a quick erase, which erases only the tape header.

- **Retension Tape:** Over a period of time, a tape can become loose on its spools, potentially causing problems. This option retensions the tape and is a good maintenance operation that should be performed occasionally.

■ Eject Tape: This option is for tape devices that require or support a software command to eject the tape from the drive.

■ Format Tape: This option formats the tape and prepares it for use.

As stated earlier, Windows NT Backup is a simple, functional backup program. For more advanced features such as software compression, scheduled backups, and tape loader support, it is necessary to purchase a third party backup solution.

Windows NT Diagnostics

Remember MSD.EXE from the good old MS-DOS days? Remember how useless it was? Well that is not the case with Windows NT Diagnostics. This looks strangely similar to the diagnostics utility found in Windows 95, but it provides a great service to Windows NT nonetheless.

From the Windows NT Diagnostics File menu, you will find a few options of interest:

■ Save Report: This option creates a report based upon three parameters that the user supplies, and it saves the report to a file.

■ Print Report: This option, similar to the Save Report option, prints a report based upon three parameters specified by the user. I highly recommend keeping a current hard copy printout of this report for your local machine because it can prove to be an invaluable resource for troubleshooting.

■ Select Computer: This option enables the user to run Windows NT Diagnostics to retrieve information from a remote Windows NT System. (Note that the Drives and Memory tabs are unavailable when running Windows NT Diagnostics against a remote system.)

■ Commands for Run and Find File are also available from the File menu of Windows NT Diagnostics.

Windows NT Diagnostics is a tabular dialog box with a wealth of information about the system on which it is run. It has nine tabs, and each one is described in the following sections.

Version

This screen is shown when the application is first started. It gives general information about the OS (Workstation or Server), the version and build numbers, the build architecture (x86 Uniprocessor Free, and so on), product ID, and the registered user and company name.

System

This tab provides system information such as the system type (clone, AT compatible, and so on), the HAL being used, BIOS information, and processor information listing each processor individually with a brief description.

Display

This tab provides information about the current display subsystem. Listed are a scrolling dialog box with the Display adapter BIOS information, an adapter section with the current resolution settings, and adapter information such as video memory and chip information as well as the drivers being used for the adapter.

Drives

The Drives tab, shown in Figure 8.17, lists all system drives (floppy, hard disk, and CD-ROM), as well as mapped network connections. Drives can be listed by type or by drive letter and can be selected by clicking the appropriate button at the bottom of the Drives tab.

FIGURE 8.17.

The Drives tab of Windows NT Diagnostics.

When you select a drive and click the Properties button, another dialog is presented with a General tab, which provides information about the drive such as the label and serial number, sector and cluster size, and total and available space. (See Figure 8.18.) There is also a File System tab that provides information about the drive's file system and configuration, such as maximum number of characters in a filename and whether case is preserved.

FIGURE 8.18.
*The Drive prop-
erties tab.*

FIGURE 8.18.
*The Drive prop-
erties tab.*

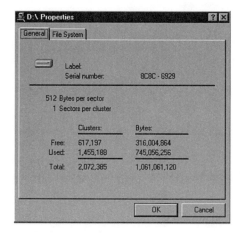

Memory

The Memory tab provides nearly information overkill. Five statistics sections provide information about Totals, Physical Memory, Commit Charge, Kernel Memory, and Pagefile Space. The Memory tab is shown in Figure 8.19.

FIGURE 8.19.
*The Windows NT
Diagnostics Mem-
ory tab.*

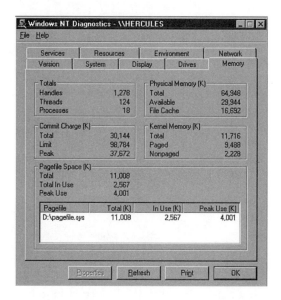

The Totals section provides information about the total number of handles, threads, and processes. The Physical Memory section provides memory information about the total physical memory installed, how much memory is available, and how much memory is in use for file cache.

The Commit Charge section provides information about the amount of data in memory and the threshold at which it will be written to disk. The Kernel Memory section lists the total memory in use by the kernel, how much is physical memory, and how much memory has been paged to disk (virtual memory). The Pagefile Space lists the size of the pagefile, the total amount of virtual memory in use, and the peak usage of virtual memory.

Services

The Services tab lists all installed system services and their current status. When you click the Devices button at the bottom of the page, a similar list is produced for the device drivers installed in the system and their status.

When you select a service or a device and click the Properties button, a dialog is produced with additional information about the selected service or device, as shown in Figure 8.20. The first tab, the General tab, lists information about the service or device, such as the start type, the service account name it uses, and various option flags. The other tab, the Dependencies tab, lists which services or devices (if any) the currently selected service or device is dependent upon.

FIGURE 8.20.
The Computer Browser Se Properties dialog.

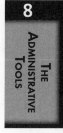

Resources

The Resources tab of Windows NT Diagnostics probably provides the most useful information. (See Figure 8.21.) This tab presents information about IRQ assignments, I/O Port addresses, DMA channels, reserved memory ranges, and running device drivers.

When you select the IRQ button, a list of IRQ assignments is displayed with the bus and device type listed. When you select a particular IRQ and click the Properties button, a dialog with information about the IRQ assignment is shown. (See Figure 8.22.)

FIGURE 8.21.

The Windows NT Diagnostics Resources tab.

FIGURE 8.22.

The IRQ assignment properties.

The I/O Port button changes the display to a list of memory I/O address assignments showing the assigned address range, device, and bus type. As with the IRQ list, selecting the Properties button produces a dialog with details specific to the selected I/O range.

The DMA button shows devices that have claimed or are assigned a DMA channel, the channel that they are assigned, and the bus and type on which they are located. The Memory button lists the extended memory ranges, which are exclusively mapped to devices that require dedicated memory, such as video cards and drivers.

The Devices button produces a list of device drivers that are loaded and using resources. When you select a device and click the Properties button, a dialog appears that lists all resources of all types in use by that device. (See Figure 8.23.)

FIGURE 8.23.

Device properties and resource usage.

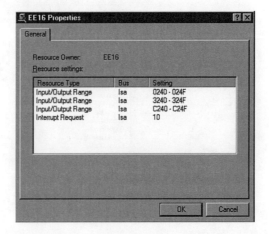

Environment

The Environment tab lists the current global environment variables for the local system, such as the ComSpec, CPU, and processor information; OS information; and the current path statement. Most of these environment variables are configurable through Control Panel's System applet.

A button called Local User at the bottom of the page displays the current user's environment variables and configurations specific to the user.

Network

The Network tab, shown in Figure 8.24, runs a close second to the Resources tab in terms of usefulness. A wealth of network related information is on this tab, which can be invaluable to systems administrators or support personnel. (Of course, this is of no use if you are not on a network.)

The General button (the default) of the Network tab lists some valuable information such as the current user's access level, the current Workgroup or Domain name, the network version, the number of logged on users, and information about the currently logged on users.

The Transports button produces a list of network transports (adapters or pathways) available to the local system, their hardware (MAC) address, the number of virtual circuits currently used, and whether the network is a WAN.

FIGURE **8.24.**

*The Windows NT
Diagnostics Net-
work tab.*

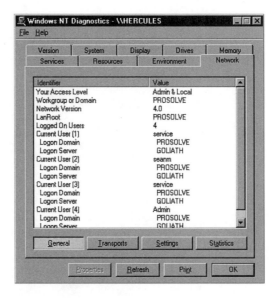

The Settings button provides an enormous amount of information about the network configuration and semantics. Here the user or administrator can see the connection and session
timeout values, various locking parameters, and caching and throughput values and options.

The Statistics button provides a summary of network activity broken down by various categories. This includes information about the total number of bytes received and transmitted, failed
operations, and server statistics related to the local system.

Summary

As you have seen in this chapter, Windows NT provides a host of extensive and intuitive applications for managing, administering, and maintaining the system, as well as for optimizing the
system and taking preventative and proactive measures to avoid potential problems. If you
understand and utilize them properly, these tools can provide you with a robust and stable
computing environment.

What Is the Registry?

by Thomas Wölfer

IN THIS CHAPTER

CHAPTER 9

One major difference between Windows NT and earlier (16-bit) versions of Windows is in the way configuration data is handled. This chapter will shed some light on the differences and tell you all you need to know about the new way to manage configuration data.

With 16-bit Windows 3.x, system and application configuration data was stored in .INI files, small human-readable files with bracketed headings and entries underneath these headings. Although some applications placed their .INI files in private directories, most of these files could be found in the \Windows\system directory. Because .INI files were to be easily accessed, they basically contained text; sometimes an application would store binary data in a hex format, but most did not.

The most important .INI files were WIN.INI and SYSTEM.INI, the central configuration files used by Windows. Some applications did store their configuration information in WIN.INI and SYSTEM.INI, which added to the confusion already created by the multitude of .INI files.

With the introduction of Windows NT and Windows 95, Microsoft replaced the .INI file mechanism with a more centralized way for storing configuration information: the Registry.

Basically, the Registry is a central database where all configuration data is stored. That is, everything that used to be stored in .INI files, information that could be found in AUTOEXEC.BAT and CONFIG.SYS as well as all application-specific data, is placed in the Registry.

Also, the Registry contains all available information about hardware installed in the system, as well as OLE-related information such as file type associations.

Although the Registry is a single database, the information within is not stored in a single file. Instead, several files located in the <winnt40>\system32\config directory, the file user.dat from the <winnt40>\profiles\<username> directory, and parts from other files (SAM and security, for example) make up the Registry. In fact, when NT Workstation is installed in a Windows NT domain and roving user accounts are enabled, it is even possible that parts of the Registry aren't stored on the local hard drive but on the server. (A *roving user account* is a user account that enables a Windows NT user to use the same configuration settings regardless of the machine she uses to log in.)

To the user, however, the contents of the Registry are displayed as a single database by using a single application: the Registry Editor. Because of this, it doesn't really matter where the information comes from. The Registry Editor takes care of pulling it from the appropriate places and makes sure changes are written back to the correct files. There is no user interaction needed, regardless of which file a piece of information is written to.

NT 4.0 Workstation comes with two versions of the Registry Editor. Both are located in <Winnt40>\System32, and none has a shortcut in the Start menu. The main reason Microsoft chooses to hide these tools is that manual changes to the Registry can render the computer unbootable. To remedy this, you either need to create a shortcut to the Registry Editors in your Start menu or run the editors by using the Run option from the Start menu. Figures 9.1 and 9.2 show the Registry Editor's windows.

CAUTION

Be extremely careful when editing the Registry. Mistakes in doing so can render your computer unbootable. If you aren't absolutely sure about what you are doing, don't mess with the Registry Editors.

FIGURE 9.1.

Regedt32.exe *is the Registry Editor with the Windows NT 3.1 user interface.*

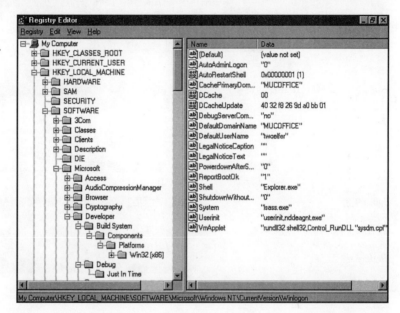

The two Registry Editors are regedt32.exe and regedit.exe. Regedt32 is the original Registry Editor; it has the Windows NT 3.1 look and feel. Regedit.exe, on the other hand, looks like the Windows 95 Registry Editor.

Although regedit might look better, it does not have all the functionality regedt32 has. For example, regedit completely hides the fact that NT Security is involved in each part of the Registry—which it is and which becomes obvious with the Security menu of regedt32. As with files on a NTFS partition, each and every key in the NT Registry has a security descriptor that handles ownership and access control. Also, access to the Registry can be audited, but all of this is only possible with the older editor. Figure 9.3 shows the Registry Key Permission dialog available in regedt32.

Because of the centralized way configuration information can be accessed using the Registry Editors, system configuration has become a lot easier than it was with 16-bit Windows. For example, it is possible to administer the Registry from a remote computer using the Registry Editor.

9

WHAT IS THE REGISTRY?

FIGURE 9.2.

Regedit.exe, *which is available only since Windows NT 4.0, has the Windows 95 look and feel.*

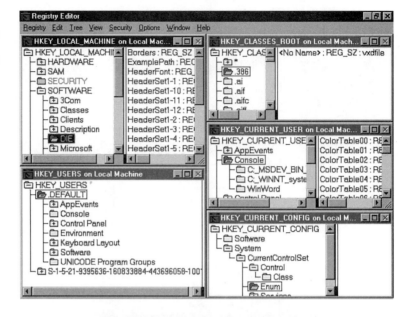

FIGURE 9.3.

Only regedt32 *provides an interface to NT security within the Registry.*

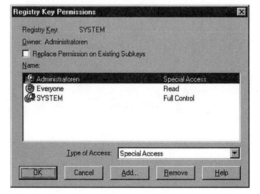

Nonetheless, the Registry Editor isn't supposed to be the standard mechanism for system maintenance and configuration. It is more like a last resort, when no other way to configure a certain aspect of the system is available. Under normal circumstances, Control Panel or an Options dialog supplied by an application should be used for setting up hardware and software or for changing options.

As soon as Control Panel isn't an option anymore and Registry Editor absolutely must be used, things turn out to be a little complicated: The amount of configuration settings exposed by the Registry Editor is overwhelming.

Information stored in the Registry isn't limited to human-readable text. Binary data, however, isn't exactly the type of information easily understood. The same goes for OLE identifiers. These are strings that look like {D3E34B21-9D75-101A-8C3D-00AA001A1652} and uniquely identify an application or a dll (paint, in this case).

> **CAUTION**
>
> Never change binary data or information such as OLE identifiers that obviously never were meant to be edited by a human in the first place. The one basic rule with editing the Registry is only change an entry when you know what you are doing.

The NT Registry is protected by NT security even if the Registry files aren't located on an NTFS partition. This means it is virtually impossible for a misbehaving application to destroy its contents; however, NT security does not protect the Registry from edits made by a user with administrative rights. Because such edits can be dangerous, it is always a good idea to have a backup copy or another way to get the NT installation back to a stable (running) state.

NT provides two mechanisms that fulfill that need. One, the Registry can be backed up to a tape using NT backup and two, NT itself does an automatic backup upon boot.

Backing up the Registry with NT backup is easy; however, actually using the backup can become quite a task. The bad scenario in this case is one in which the backup is needed because NT no longer boots due to changes to the Registry. If NT doesn't boot, how do you run the NT backup software to restore the backup? Well, you don't.

You can protect yourself against cases like this by having a second (working) installation of NT on the machine—but, in my opinion, this isn't really an option.

The automatic backup made by NT is more useful. Each time a user logs into the system, NT saves the Registry information used for that particular boot. The next time a boot fails, NT's fallback mechanism provides this saved configuration as the *last known good* one to boot with. If it is used, changes to the Registry during the last session are lost.

Of course this only works when the failure happens before the user logs in. If the system fails to start after the login, the *last known good* setup is already overwritten by the current one.

Neither a system backup nor the fallback mechanism are pleasant experiences, so be careful when editing the Registry.

> **CAUTION**
>
> Changes to the Registry can render Windows NT unbootable. It is vital to not change any entries without knowing their purposes.
>
> Also, if you rely on a tape backup and a second NT installation on your machine, it is always a good idea to test this backup at least once after a major change to your system.

9

WHAT IS THE REGISTRY?

When you use the Registry Editor, configuration data is displayed in a hierarchical order, just as when Explorer exposes the file system and other contents of the computer.

Data Types Found in the Registry

The hierarchy contains data as well as keys. *Keys* are equivalent to folders in the file system and build up the actual hierarchy. That is, keys might contain other keys as well as data. *Data* is what makes up the hierarchy's leaves. Each data item has a name that describes the item, a data type, and the actual value of the item. There are five data types exposed by `regedt32` and three data types exposed by `regedit`. Both editors know about string values, binary values, and dword values. Only `regedt32` knows about the data types `REG_EXPAND_SZ` and `REG_MULTI_SZ`.

String values are ordinary strings; that is, they might store information such as a username and street address. These values can easily be edited. *Binary values* contain data an application chooses to store in binary format and are thus hard to change or even read. *Dword values* basically are numbers. For example, they are used to store options where a 1 reflects the option being turned on and 0 means the option is turned off. `REG_EXPAND_SZ` is a special type of string that can contain environment variables. When an application requests such a data type from the Registry, the system replaces the embedded environment variable with the current setting from the system Control Panel applet. `REG_MULTI_SZ` is another type of string, where the data item can contain more than one string. (A string, in this context, is one from a programmer's point of view. That is, it is text that is terminated by a special symbol represented by the value zero. `REG_MULTI_SZ` can have more than one of these zero-terminated strings.)

In `regedit`, the Registry's root is split into six parts, whereas `regedt32` is split into five. However, the actual content of the Registry is split into four different roots. These are `HKEY_LOCAL_MACHINE`, `HKEY_CLASSES_ROOT`, `HKEY_CURRENT_USER`, and `HKEY_USERS`. `HKEY_CURRENT_CONFIG` and `HKEY_DYN_DATA` (the last one displayed by `regedit`) are not used to store configuration information but have other purposes that I will explain later in this chapter.

Just by looking at the cryptic names used by the Registry, you can see that it isn't actually intended as a tool for the end user; it is more a tool to be used by programmers.

HKEY_LOCAL_MACHINE

This part of the Registry contains configuration information relevant to the local computer. For example, the hardware configuration information collected by NT during boot-time is stored here. Also, installed drivers as well as their settings and configuration data used by applications on a systemwide base can be found here. The information from `HKEY_LOCAL_MACHINE` is used by the system regardless of the currently logged-in user.

HKEY_LOCAL_MACHINE is divided into five sections. These are HARDWARE, SAM, SECURITY, SOFTWARE, and SYSTEM.

- ■ The HARDWARE part is created each time the system boots and contains information about the installed hardware and resources used by that hardware.

- ■ SAM, which stands for Security Account Manager, contains security information about user and group accounts. In NT server, it also contains security information about NT domains.

- ■ SECURITY contains even more security information, but information from this section is used locally by the security subsystem only.

- ■ SOFTWARE contains system-wide software configuration data. For example, a vendor might choose to supply a default configuration that is used each time a new user starts an application. Also, a vendor might store path information about installed products on a system, which doesn't change when a new user logs on. This kind of information is also stored in the SOFTWARE section.

- ■ The SYSTEM section contains information about the way NT is configured to boot. For example, needed device drivers are listed here.

HKEY_CLASSES_ROOT

This part of the Registry is available only for compatibility reasons. It provides the same information as did the REG.DAT file in 16-bit Windows 3.x.

HKEY_CLASSES_ROOT contains the OLE file associations on the local computer. That is, when the Files Types dialog from Explorer's options is used to associate a file extension with an application, the association information is stored here.

32-bit Windows Applications do not use HKEY_CLASSES_ROOT but an identical copy of this section, which can be found under HKEY_LOCAL_MACHINE\Software\Classes. If you manually change an entry in either of these subkeys, Registry Editor ensures the other copy—the one you didn't change manually—does contain your changes.

HKEY_CURRENT_USER

This holds the currently logged-in users' profiles. A profile contains system settings as well as application-specific information. For example, the desktop's layout, available network resources and mapped drives, and the contents of the start menu as well as screen colors are stored here.

Most of the entries in HKEY_CURRENT_USER are created by installed applications and thus differ from system to system and from logged-in user to logged-in user.

However, there are some default subkeys created by the Windows NT that are always available. These are `Console`, `Control Panel`, `Environment`, `Keyboard Layout`, `Printers`, and `Software`:

- `Console` defines the look and feel of character-mode applications such as the Windows NT command prompt.
- `Control Panel` contains user-specific settings from, you guessed it, the Control Panel.
- `Environment` holds the user's environment variables that have been set via the System applet in the Control Panel.
- `Printers` contains a description of all printers available to the user.
- `Software` is the most interesting subkey because it holds all application settings for the current user. This includes system applications and Windows NT settings—for example, Task Manager preferences.

HKEY_USERS

`HKEY_USERS` contains all locally available user profiles, which basically look like the `HKEY_CURRENT_USER` profile and only differ in the actual values for the data items found within.

When a user logs in, her personal configuration is copied from her personal subkey under `HKEY_USERS` to `HKEY_CURRENT_USER`. During logout, information from `HKEY_CURRENT_USER` is copied back to the user's personal subkey in `HKEY_USERS`.

There are at least two subkeys in `HKEY_USERS`: one labeled `Default` and the one of the user currently logged in. When a user logs onto Windows NT for the first time, the system uses the `Default` subkey to create the initial user profile. In other words, the `Default` subkey can be used by the workstation's administrator to preconfigure settings for all new users of a machine. For example, a company logo could be used as the default background image for all new users.

All other subkeys apart from `Default` are security ID strings of the user they apply to. That is, the user's settings are not identified by username but by a string supplied by NT security. However, it is possible to resolve a username from this security ID string by looking into `HKEY_LOCAL_MACHINE\Software\Microsoft\WindowsNT\CurrentVersion\ProfileList`, where the usernames are listed below the security ID strings.

HKEY_CURRENT_CONFIG

This is not really a separate Registry section but a shortcut to the currently used hardware configuration from `HKEY_LOCAL_MACHINE\SYSTEM\CurrentControlSet\Hardware Profiles`. (Hardware configurations, also known as *hardware profiles*, are created with the System applet from Control Panel.)

Hardware configurations are most useful for laptop computers. For example, one configuration would be used while the laptop is docked to the docking station and the other configuration is used while the machine is undocked. When you do have several hardware configurations on your computer, you can select the one to use when the machine boots.

HKEY_DYN_DATA

Just like HKEY_CURRENT_CONFIG, HKEY_DYN_DATA isn't really a separate section in the Registry. Instead, as the name implies, it is a collection of dynamic data, meaning the data can change at any time. For example, the current state of plug-and-play devices can be found here.

Also, HKEY_DYN_DATA makes up the performance Registry. That is, measurement tools such as Performance Monitor use the data available in HKEY_DYN_DATA and the information needed for performance measurement is logged to this place.

However, because plug-and-play technology is not yet part of Windows NT and because performance data is available only via tools such as Performance Monitor, HKEY_DYN_DATA appears to be empty and uneditable. In fact, depending on your user rights, HKEY_DYN_DATA might not even be displayed in Registry Editor.

Working with the Registry Editors

Working with the Registry Editors is easy. Both editors provide menus that can be used to issue the available commands. For example, it is possible to create a new key and edit a data item. It is not really necessary to explain the Registry Editor command in full detail; all of them do exactly what their title implies.

Both Registry Editors provide a means to open a remote Registry via the Registry menu and print parts or all of the Registry branches. The editors differ in their search capabilities: regedit provides a way to search for data items (names and values) as well as keys, whereas regedt32 only provides a way to search for keys.

As already stated, only regedt32 provides an interface to NT security in the Registry, so if you need auditing capabilities for part or all of the Registry, you need to use the older tool.

WOW (Windows on Windows): 16-bit Applications and the Registry

For 32-bit Windows applications, the Registry is the standard database to store configuration information.

However, Windows NT also supports 16-bit Windows applications (by means of the WOW layer), and 16-bit Windows applications do not know how to access the Windows NT Registry. Because of that, Windows NT supplies a mechanism called *ini file mapping* for 16-bit applications. Also, NT provides a WIN.INI and a SYSTEM.INI—both essentially empty—for applications that might check for the availability of these files.

With ini file mapping, whenever a 16-bit Windows application attempts to read from an .INI file by using the appropriate 16-bit interface, the WOW layer provides the requested information from the Registry. If a 16-bit application attempts to write to an .INI file, the WOW layer places the information in the Registry instead of the .INI file.

Some applications fail to work correctly with mapped .INI files. For example, an application might employ other means of reading from or writing to an .INI file besides the correct 16-bit Windows interface. Because of this, not all .INI files are mapped automatically. Instead, mapping can be turned on for specific files by adding them to the list of mapped files under HKEY_LOCAL_MACHINE\Software\Microsoft\WindowsNT\CurrentVersion\IniFileMapping.

Some Tools for Working with the Registry

The Registry Editors are the most important tools for working with the Registry. However, some other tools are available for working with the Registry. The most important one—a document—is part of the Windows NT Resource Kit.

> **NOTE**
>
> At the time of this writing, the Windows NT Resource Kit for NT Workstation 4.0 has not been released. It is thus not possible to verify that it will contain all information and tools available in previous versions.

This document contains the complete documentation to all Registry entries known to the system, which includes entries for all device drivers delivered with NT as well as entries for software components like the login application or paint. In this documentation you can find information about topics such as automatic login or how to turn off parsing of the AUTOEXEC.BAT for a path statement.

The resource kit also contains various Registry tools. For example, it contains a tool to backup and restore the Registry without using a tape device and a tool to change the Registry using scripts. It also comes with a command-line utility to search the Registry and a tool to compare two Registry databases.

The resource kit is available as a separate package (in printed form) as well as a part of the Microsoft TechNet CD.

Another tool that should be mentioned is RDISK, the repair disk utility.

For unrecoverable system crashes, Windows NT keeps some repair information on your hard drive. This information can also be copied to a floppy disk known as the Windows NT Repair Disk. RDISK is the utility used to create this disk. RDISK can also be used to update the repair information on the hard drive.

However, as far as registry information goes, the repair disk only contains the information needed to boot the computer. It does not contain the complete registry information. (This is mostly due to the fact that the registry can grow quite large—up to several megabytes—and doesn't fit well onto a single floppy.)

Therefore, you should be aware that RDISK isn't the right tool to back up the registry. It is merely a very last resort to regain a bootable machine.

If you want to back up the registry without using NT Backup (for example, because you don't have a tape drive), you should use the REGBACK and REGREST tools from the NT Resource Kit.

Summary

This chapter taught you what the Registry is all about and how configuration data is stored in it. You also learned how to use the Registry Editors and identify their differences. Also, I told you about some other tools that might prove helpful when you are working with the Registry.

However, the most important thing that you should keep in mind is this: Never ever edit anything in the Registry when you are unsure about the possible results of your edit. The Registry Editors are extremely powerful tools and provide the means to poke around in every system setting available. They also provide a lot of rope to hang yourself.

Advanced System Configuration

by Eric D. Osborne

IN THIS CHAPTER

If you use your Windows NT system for more than the simplest tasks, you probably will eventually need to make some modifications to your configuration. The prospect of reconfiguring a workstation, particularly when it becomes necessary to add some new hardware component, is daunting to many users. That's understandable, particularly when a user has had prior experience with system reconfiguration under DOS.

Fortunately, the job of adding some new device to your system configuration or modifying an existing configuration is usually more straightforward under NT than it was under DOS or Windows 3.*x*.

One of the greatest problems that users face when reconfiguring DOS or Windows systems lies in their memory allocation models. The first 640KB of RAM (called *standard* memory) was a critical resource in high demand. The software used to control devices within a system always wanted to sit in that same lower 640KB of address space. This invariably resulted in memory allocation conflicts. It was quite common for a user to add a new device to a system and then discover that his or her application software no longer worked. Windows NT eliminates that issue, so the task of installing a driver is much less trying with NT than with older Microsoft operating systems.

Before delving into the specifics of advanced system configuration, it is probably wise to understand some of the basic concepts and terminology used when dealing with devices and the software that controls them.

A Short Tutorial on Device Drivers

There are probably thousands of existing option cards that you can put into personal computers. These cards come in a variety of styles, depending upon the bus and machine architecture that the card is designed to plug into. Both the number of available cards and the rapidity with which technology changes guarantees that it is impossible for Microsoft to build support into NT for every possible board.

Even if it were possible to support every known board, it wouldn't be desirable. Hardware manufacturers would be compelled to synchronize their product releases with new releases of NT itself. The situation would be a nightmare, both logistically and technically.

NT addresses the issue of supporting the nearly infinite variety of hardware options by using installable *device drivers*. A device driver, as its name implies, is a piece of software that drives (controls) a device. Windows NT provides a number of well-documented programmatic interfaces for device drivers, including routines for initializing, reading, and writing the device.

The device drivers let Microsoft separate Windows NT from the underlying hardware, which is good for Microsoft, device manufacturers, and end users. Microsoft gets to focus on developing new operating system features without the headaches of qualifying an unworkable number of device types. Device manufacturers can get their products to market more quickly, even if they supply niche market products that are impractical for Microsoft to qualify or support. End users, of course, get to enjoy the cost and availability advantages of a competitive and open aftermarket device industry. Everyone wins.

The downside to this model is the simple fact that device drivers are complex pieces of software. Most modern hardware interfaces are *interrupt driven*, which means that the device interrupts the system when it requires service. Interrupts provide an efficient means of causing the system to focus attention on a particular device only when needed. This provides operational efficiency but can result in complex data coherency or timing issues. Because drivers run as a privileged part of the operating system, drivers have full access to the memory of your system. That means that a bug in a device driver also has the potential to crash your system or corrupt your data.

The message to remember is this: If you have to install a driver, make sure you have some level of confidence in the supplier. Buggy drivers can render your system unstable or unusable. If that happens, you need vendor support to correct the problem.

Buses

Your system has a number of *slots*, or places where you can plug cards of different kinds. There are several types of slots, and the type and quantity of each are big factors in determining the kinds of choices that you have when adding cards to your system. Slots connect into a *bus*, so each slot in your system is associated with a specific type of bus.

Virtually all personal computers have some sort of support for the ISA bus. *ISA* means *Industry Standard Architecture*, which is the bus that the original IBM PC/AT used. The I/O mappings of the ISA bus are even used in most laptops, although laptops usually can't support ISA cards without the use of a docking bay.

The ISA bus, although ubiquitous, is well-known for being much too slow to support modern, high-speed I/O adapters. Display and disk adapters have long been too fast for the ISA bus. Newer 100MB/second fast Ethernet network adapters are also too fast to perform correctly on an ISA bus. Furthermore, the ISA bus was designed to support far too few interrupt and I/O base addresses. These limits continue to plague end users, and I discuss them at length later in the chapter.

IBM attempted to resolve the limitations of the ISA bus by introducing the proprietary Microchannel Architecture (MCA) bus. The MCA bus first appeared in IBM's PS/2 series of computers. MCA was complex to build, but more importantly, it was expensive to license. IBM required any company that built MCA-compatible systems or cards to pay fees to IBM. The industry at large rebelled against MCA, seeking an alternative approach.

Some vendors chose to create so-called *local buses*, or proprietary bus architectures designed for higher performance. Many of the original local buses were targeted toward memory expansion. Most were incompatible between system vendors.

A number of the largest system vendors, including Compaq, responded to the MCA licensing issues by defining a competing bus architecture called the *Extended Industry Standard Architecture* (*EISA*). The EISA bus was very fast and had the support of many system vendors. Unfortunately, EISA card designs were usually very complex, which tended to make them expensive. Furthermore, EISA systems required complex configuration utilities to install and manage installed EISA bus option cards.

The search for cheaper, faster, and simpler buses eventually led a number of vendors to create the VESA local bus (VLB) specification. VESA became very popular for systems that required high-performance video adapters and disk controllers, but VESA still didn't have industry-wide support. For one thing, most VLB systems had very few available VESA slots.

Finally, Intel and essentially all the major system vendors agreed on a new Intel-designed bus called *PCI*. PCI boards are much simpler to design than EISA cards, which means that they are usually cheaper. The PCI bus has better bandwidth (which means it's faster) than the other buses mentioned previously, and solves many of the issues relating to interrupts and I/O addresses. PCI was designed with the new plug-and-play standard in mind. Systems that support plug and play, such as Windows 95, automatically detect and configure installed hardware options. PCI originally supported only three slots per system, and many options simply weren't available in PCI cards. System vendors addressed this problem by putting both ISA and PCI slots into systems. This is the architecture used by most current Pentium class machines.

PCI is definitely the wave of the future, and it should be around for a long time. When you're buying a new system, the number of available PCI slots should be high on your list of decision criteria.

The setup of most PCI options requires little or no input from the user, and the selection of base addresses and interrupts is usually automatic. EISA configuration utilities are typically used when installing EISA devices. Although these utilities might require more input from the user than the installation of PCI devices, they are once again relatively automatic. The installation of ISA bus interfaces is a major headache for most computer users, so I include a detailed discussion of interrupt and address issues as they apply to ISA buses in the following section.

Interrupts

Whenever a system has a device that is intended to perform some input or output function, the system really has only two ways of knowing when the device needs service. First, the system can check the device at some set interval to see if it needs attention. This *polling* is a time-honored but relatively slow and inefficient method of I/O. The other method, mentioned earlier in this chapter, is for the device to notify (or *interrupt*) the processor whenever the device needs attention. Interrupts are often a source of problems when configuring your system.

Interrupts are implemented at the hardware level as a number of signals on the system bus that can be used to indicate to the processor that a device needs service. These signals are usually referred to as *Interrupt Request Lines,* or *IRQs.* The number of available interrupt lines is dependent upon the type of I/O bus that your system has and the number of devices that you have installed. Note that I/O cards are not the only things that use interrupts. Integrated devices such as COM ports, your mouse, and your keyboard also use interrupts.

The worst problems with interrupt availability occur on ISA bus systems or when you're installing ISA options in mixed-bus machines. ISA bus machines implement IRQs through a pair of cascaded interrupt controller chips. Each controller can nominally provide eight interrupt lines. Because the second controller connects to interrupt two of the first controller, a total of 14 interrupts are available for use. Many of these interrupts are taken by standard system functions. Table 10.1 shows the standard interrupt assignments. A blank in the device column indicates that the interrupt is usually available for use.

Table 10.1. Standard interrupt assignments.

Interrupt	Device
2	Connection to second interrupt controller
3	COM Ports 2 and 4
4	COM Ports 1 and 3
5	LPT2 (Printer port 2)
6	Floppy disk controller
7	LPT1 (Printer port 1)
8	Real-time clock
9	Connection from first interrupt controller
10	
11	
12	PS/2 style mouse
13	Math coprocessor
14	Hard disk controller
15	

Devices are not usually able to share interrupts, so it's important to make sure that any device you add to your system can be configured for an available interrupt.

10

ADVANCED
SYSTEM
CONFIGURATION

NOTE

You might have noticed that interrupts 3 and 4 are each assigned to support a pair of COM ports. In practice, using two COM ports on a single interrupt doesn't work well. If at all possible, avoid using more than one COM port on a single interrupt, especially at high baud rates, or you might see very erratic communications through the affected ports.

TIP

If you are using only one COM port on your system and your mouse is using interrupt 12, you can often configure a card to use the interrupt assigned to the unused COM port. You should disable the unused COM port before assigning its interrupt to another card.

I/O Addresses

Each of the cards in your system must be assigned a unique address that can be used to talk to the card's control and I/O chips or to any dedicated memory that the card might be equipped with. The system uses a set of special addresses called *port* addresses to talk to the control and I/O chips. These addresses are independent of memory addresses, and on PC systems, they always sit somewhere between 0x100 and 0x3ff HEX. The number of port addresses used by each card varies dramatically, so you have to be sure that you have enough address space available for any card that you intend to install. As with interrupts, many port addresses are assigned to built-in functions. Table 10.2 lists some of the most common of these.

WARNING

Most modern systems are capable of using port addresses above 0x3ff, but be very careful about configuring boards at these higher port addresses. The original 8-bit version of the ISA bus used only 10 address bits when decoding port addresses. That's where the maximum of 0x3ff comes from. 0x3ff is 1023, or 2^{10}-1. Unfortunately, many game controllers or simple I/O cards still use only 8-bit bus interfaces. These are normally so-called "short" cards, although some full-length ISA cards don't decode the full range of address bits. If you put such a card into your system, it shows at multiple address locations as "echoes" of itself. A card of this type installed at 0x250, for instance, would also be seen at 0x1250, 0x2250, and so on. If you have any other cards configured at those same upper-address locations, you will get address conflicts between the cards. This not only won't work, but it also might damage your system.

Table 10.2. Common port addresses.

Port Addresses	Device
200-20F	Game port
260-27F	LPT2 (second printer port)
2E8-2EF	COM 4
2F8-2FF	COM 2
360-37F	LPT1 (first printer port)
3C0-3CF	Video displays
3D0-3DF	Older CGA video displays
3E8-3EF	COM 3
3F8-3FF	COM 1

In addition to the addresses in Table 10.2, it is common for network cards to fall into the 300-31F range.

Some types of cards, particularly SCSI and network cards, have RAM on board that is used for buffering input data. This RAM shows up in the system memory map above the first 640KB of RAM but below the 1MB line that defines the start of extended memory. That region lies between addresses 0xA0000 and 0xFFFFF. Much of that region is occupied by standard system facilities. The BIOS ROMs sit between 0xF0000 and 0xFFFFF. Most of the region from 0xA0000 to BFFFF is dedicated for use by video adapters, so the area from 0xC0000 to 0xEFFFF is the only area that is usually available for I/O adapters.

This limit can be a big problem on DOS or Windows 3.*x* systems because memory managers such as emm386 or qemm need a 64KB area called a *page frame* to perform expanded memory simulation. The page frame often sits at 0xE0000-0xEFFFF, but you can move it with command-line options to your memory manager if necessary.

WARNING

You can sometimes get away with sharing interrupts between devices, but *never* try to share a port address or memory range between two cards. It almost certainly won't work.

Installing Drivers and Managing Devices

Now that you've had an introduction to the basics of hardware, you should be ready to install your new card and its associated driver. You also need to know how to manage the devices on your system.

10

ADVANCED
SYSTEM
CONFIGURATION

Unfortunately, there is no single answer to how to perform either task. Windows NT 4.0 still doesn't support the plug-and-play standard, so your devices probably need some kind of configuration. The installation of a driver and configuration of the associated device vary somewhat with the type of device or driver being installed. However, some general rules apply across the board. First, if your hardware vendor supplied you with a driver disk, you probably should use it. It's sometimes worthwhile to make sure that the drivers you have are the latest version because patches for drivers are released frequently on CompuServe, America Online, or the vendor's Web site.

The installation dialogs for all device types enable you to install a new driver. Configuration of the device is often specific to the device type and manufacturer, so make sure to read the device documentation thoroughly. Finally, when you install a driver, you always need to reboot Windows NT for the change to take effect. This is an area where NT is still lagging behind some other operating systems.

The remaining sections of this chapter detail the steps required to configure your system.

Communications: Ports, Modems, and Telephony

Computers usually interact with the rest of the world through *input/output* (*I/O*) ports. Unlike graphical displays or network interfaces, I/O ports have been a core feature of computers for decades.

Your computer has two types of ports. The first is the *parallel port*. Parallel ports are usually used to attach printers, but they are sometimes used to drive external tape devices or disks. Your system usually refers to parallel ports as *LPT1* or *LPT2*. External peripherals that attach to a parallel port are typically found on laptop computers that don't have any kind of expansion slot.

Parallel ports get their name from the way they transmit or receive data. Data is usually presented to the port one character at a time in 8-bit bytes. There is a separate signal on the port for each of the eight data bits, so all 8 bits are sent or received in parallel.

Parallel ports are simple to configure, mostly because they really don't have any options that you can set. They have no complex speed or flow control settings to worry about because the hardware itself takes care of all those things.

Your system's COM ports are a different matter. COM ports are called *serial* devices because they send or receive only one bit of data at a time. Each bit is pushed out onto the data signal at fixed time intervals. The speed at which the signals are pushed is called the *baud rate*. When serial interfaces were invented, they commonly connected to devices at 110 bits per second. Modern computers often connect to modems at speeds of 57,600 bits per second.

The hardware interface for serial connections requires far fewer signals than parallel ports do. A parallel cable requires a minimum of eight data signals, two or three handshaking signals, and a number of ground signals. In the simplest case, it is possible to establish a serial connection using only three signal wires. One of these sends data, one receives data, and the third acts as an electrical ground. Other signals are usually available on serial cables, but they are used for control purposes. The most important of these are Data Terminal Ready (DTR), Clear To Send (CTS), Request To Send (RTS), Data Set Ready (DSR), and Data Carrier Detect (DCD). DCD is sometimes referred to as simply Carrier Detect.

The CTS and RTS signals are often used as flow control signals between computers and high-speed modems. The modem and the computer set and clear these signals as a way of indicating when they are ready to receive data. The transmitting side of the connection stops and waits whenever the receiving side indicates that it is busy.

DTR is usually used to control the state of the modems or other connected devices. The computer sets the DTR signal when it is actively monitoring the COM port and clears it when the port isn't being used. You can set most modems to hang up the phone line when the DTR signal is cleared.

DSR and DCD can be used to indicate that the modem is online and ready. A RAS server, for instance, usually terminates a dial-up session if the DSR signal from a connected modem is cleared, because RAS assumes that the remote user has hung up the telephone.

Because the data transmissions of serial ports occur as a series of bits, the receiving side of the connection must synchronize to the incoming bit stream and determine where the individual bytes start and stop. This is usually done using *asynchronous* transmissions. The serial devices at each end of the connection are configured to some agreed-upon baud rate. When the transmitting side has data to send, it starts by sending a *start bit* that marks the beginning of the transmission. The receiver detects the state change represented by the start bit and starts a timer that indicates when the next bit will come through. The state of the signal—a binary 0 or 1—is sampled when the timer indicates that a bit change has occurred. That bit is collected by the receiver, and the process is repeated until all 8 bits of the byte have been sent and received. It is possible to send a *parity* bit, which is a primitive form of error correction. After the data and parity bits have been sent, one or more *stop bits* are sent at the end of the byte. The stop bits allow time between characters, which the hardware can use to resynchronize the clocking and shift register hardware.

The time-multiplexed nature of asynchronous serial transmissions makes them ideal for encoding onto telephone lines via the use of *modems*. The word modem is an acronym for *Modulator/Demodulator*, which describes the technique used to send data. Basically, the originating modem uses a modulated tone to represent the data that it is sending. The receiving modem uses a different frequency of tone to represent its transmissions. These tones are transmissible as audio through a standard telephone line, but the control signals associated with the port don't get encoded in this fashion. The software of your system must be set to match the communications parameters of a remote system in order to reliably communicate with it.

10

ADVANCED
SYSTEM
CONFIGURATION

COM Ports

COM ports are configured in Windows NT by using the Ports applet of the Control Panel. Figure 10.1 shows the Ports applet. Note the list of configured ports in the scrollable selection box.

FIGURE 10.1.

The Ports applet of the Control Panel.

> ## TIP
>
> Although you can set COM port parameters using the dialogs described here, you probably want to use the phone book settings described in Chapter 21, "Remote Access Service," to configure your port settings instead. Phone book settings allow you to define separate port settings for each service that you might contact with your modem.

To configure a port, highlight it in the selection box and click the Settings button. You see the dialog shown in Figure 10.2.

FIGURE 10.2.

Basic COM port settings.

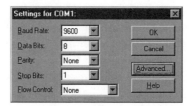

Use the Baud Rate box to set the speed for your port. If you are using a modem that supports data compression, you probably want to set the port to a speed that is higher than the line speed of the modem. If you have a modem that uses V.42 BIS at 28.8Kbps, for instance, you should set the port to 57,600 baud.

You can set the number of data bits sent in each character. For most practical purposes, this is set to 8. Some older systems might require 7 bits with a parity setting.

Because most modern modems use error-correcting techniques such as the MNP5 standard, parity bits are rarely required, so you usually set the parity to None. If necessary, you can set the parity to even, odd, mark, or space. A Stop Bit setting of 1 is almost always acceptable.

> **NOTE**
>
> The settings for parity, stop bits, and number of data bits must be consistent between your computer and the device on the other end of a connection. Check with your Internet service provider or the system manager of any remote systems to make sure that you have the correct settings for these communications parameters.

The Flow Control box allows you to choose None, Xon/Xoff, or Hardware. Choosing Hardware selects the CTS/RTS signal handshaking, described previously. This is the recommended setting for high-speed modems or other high-speed devices. Note that the use of hardware handshaking requires a cable containing modem control signals. You might want to use Xon/Xoff if you have a three-wire cable, if the device that you are connecting to doesn't support hardware handshaking, or if you are remotely connecting to a modem that doesn't support error correction. If all else fails, try setting Flow Control to None, but you should be aware that a setting of None will probably cause your system to drop characters at higher baud rates.

You can set more advanced options for the port by clicking the Advanced button. The dialog in Figure 10.3 shows the Advanced Settings options for COM ports.

FIGURE 10.3.
Advanced COM port settings.

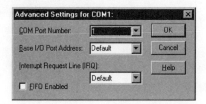

The COM Port Number box allows you to choose which of the COM ports on your system you want to configure. The Base I/O Port Address box sets the hexadecimal port address at which the COM port is located. You usually accept the default for this setting, but if you have more than two COM ports, you might need to reconfigure it. The Interrupt Request Line setting specifies the IRQ number for the port. Again, the defaults are usually best, and whatever you select for the IRQ and port address, it must match your hardware. Remember that although you can configure two ports on a single IRQ, it usually won't work well.

Some COM ports, especially in newer systems, have an on-board buffer called a FIFO. If your system has FIFO-capable COM ports, enabling this option improves performance of the COM port at higher speeds. Your system might lose input characters at high baud rates if your port doesn't have a FIFO or if the FIFO Enabled checkbox is cleared. Clicking the checkbox turns FIFO buffering on or off.

Modems

You configure the modems on your system by using the Modem applet of the Control Panel. You can invoke the Modem applet directly from the Control Panel, from the RAS setup tools (see Chapter 21) or from the Telephony setup described in the next section of this chapter. Figure 10.4 shows the Modem configuration applet.

FIGURE 10.4.

The Modem configuration applet.

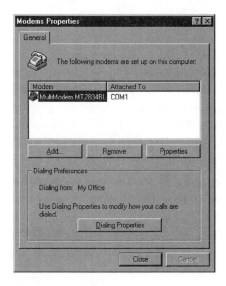

Adding Modems to Your System

As you can see, the Modem applet lists all the modems that have been configured on your system. You can add a new modem to your system by clicking the Add button. Clicking the Add button invokes the Install New Modem Wizard shown in Figure 10.5.

FIGURE 10.5.

The Install New Modem Wizard.

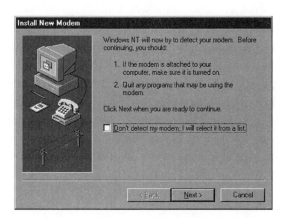

You can simply click Next, and the wizard attempts to figure out which port your modem is connected to and what kind of modem it is. This process might not work if the modem type is not known to Windows NT or if the modem is either turned off or disconnected from your system. You can select the Don't Detect My Modem checkbox in such cases and then configure the modem manually. After you've set the checkbox the way you want it, click Next.

Figure 10.6 shows the automatic detection of a modem in progress.

FIGURE 10.6.
Automatic modem detection.

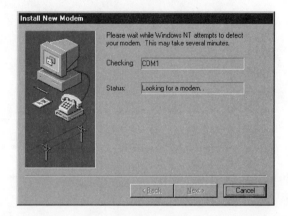

Figure 10.7 shows the manual selection of a modem from a list. Select the desired modem manufacturer and model number if it's listed. If your modem manufacturer has provided a disk, you can use the Have Disk button to load the modem driver. If you don't have a disk and your modem isn't listed, try using one of the Standard Modem Types.

FIGURE 10.7.
Selecting a modem from a list.

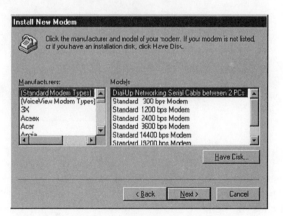

After you've selected the correct modem type, click the Next button. You see the dialog shown in Figure 10.8. Select the port or ports that are connected to the type of modem you have selected and then click Next.

FIGURE 10.8.
Modem COM port selection.

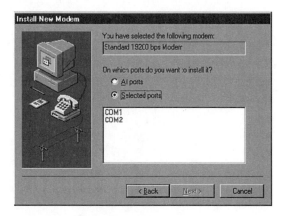

The modem setup wizard displays the dialog shown in Figure 10.9. Click Finish to complete the setup of your modem.

FIGURE 10.9.
Completing the addition of a new modem.

Deleting Modems from Your System

Deleting a modem from your system is a straightforward process. Invoke the Modem applet from the Control Panel, as shown in Figure 10.4. Highlight the modem you want to delete and then click the Remove button. You see a dialog similar to the one shown in Figure 10.10. Click Yes to remove the modem from the list.

FIGURE 10.10.

Removing a modem from your system.

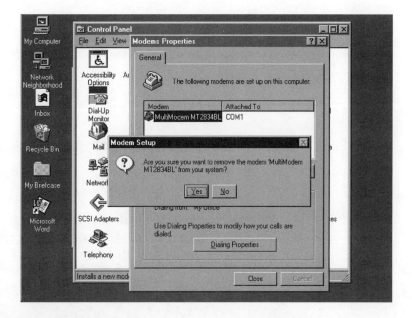

Configuring an Existing Modem

To change the configuration of a modem that was already set up on your system, invoke the Modem applet, shown in Figure 10.4. Highlight the modem to be configured and then click the Properties button. You see the dialog shown in Figure 10.11.

FIGURE 10.11.

Changing modem properties.

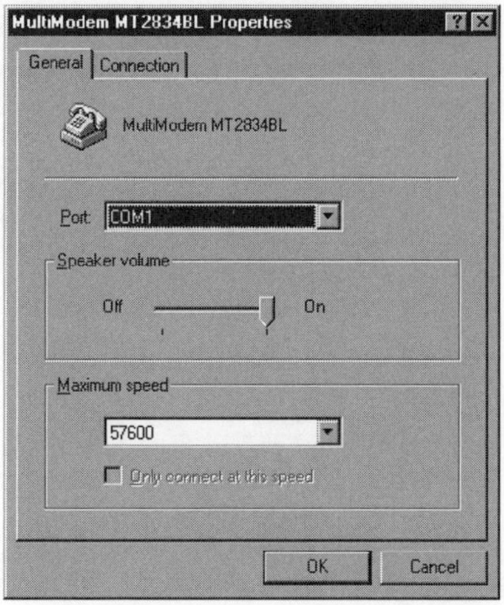

Use the Port selection box to change the COM port associated with the modem. You can use the Volume slide control to make the modem speaker louder or softer. Set the slide to Off to completely disable the modem speaker. Set the maximum baud rate using the Maximum Speed box.

Clicking the Connection tab shown in Figure 10.11 displays the Connection dialog shown in Figure 10.12.

FIGURE 10.12.

Changing modem connection preferences.

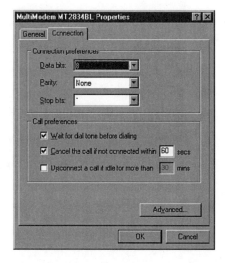

Set the communications parameters as described previously. You can check the Wait for Dial Tone Before Dialing box if your modem is connected to a standard phone line or clear it if you are dialing through a PBX or some other device that doesn't present a dial tone when the line goes off hook.

The Cancel the Call If Not Connected Within box specifies a time-out period for the call attempt. You can set the Disconnect a Call If Idle box to cause the modem to hang up idle sessions automatically. This prevents unnecessary charges from Internet service providers or telephone companies.

Clicking the Advanced button invokes the dialog shown in Figure 10.13. You use the upper-left side of the dialog to control modem error-correction features. Checking the Use Error Control box enables the modem's error-correction features. If you call a remote modem that also supports error correction, enabling this feature greatly improves the reliability of your connection, particularly across noisy telephone lines.

You can choose to connect *only* to modems that have error-correction features by checking the Required to Connect box. Selecting the Compress Data box enables your modem's data-compression features. Enabling data compression doesn't always improve throughput. If you connect to a RAS server that uses software compression, enabling the data-compression facilities of your modem might actually reduce your throughput.

FIGURE 10.13.
Changing advanced modem setup properties.

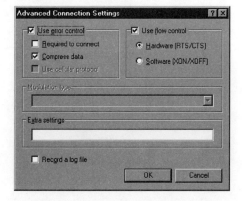

You use the upper-right side of Figure 10.13 to set modem flow-control options. You can either enable or disable flow control. If flow control is enabled, you can choose to use either hardware flow control or Xon/Xoff flow control.

You can use the Extra Settings box to specify modem configuration strings that you want sent to your modem when it is initialized. Make sure that you understand the implications of any string you put into this box because it could potentially override other settings that you made.

Configuring Telephony Options

It is possible to customize your system to the particulars of your local telephone system. Invoke the Telephony applet from the Control Panel to produce the dialog shown in Figure 10.14. If you use your computer from more than one location, use the My Locations tab to create a customized profile for each of the places that you dial out from.

The upper part of the dialog creates new location profiles. Set the location and area code parameters appropriately for the location that you want to define.

The lower part of the dialog defines the way the system calls from the defined location. Enter the digits, if any, required to get an outside line and initiate a long distance call. If your phone has call waiting, you might want to disable it to prevent your sessions from being interrupted. Check the box indicating that you have call waiting and then enter the digits that temporarily disable call waiting on your phone. If you have a rotary phone, select the appropriate button.

You might want to charge the call to a calling card. If so, you can check the Dial Using Calling Card box and then select the Change button. You see the dialog shown in Figure 10.15.

10

ADVANCED
SYSTEM
CONFIGURATION

FIGURE 10.14.

*Customizing telephony
properties.*

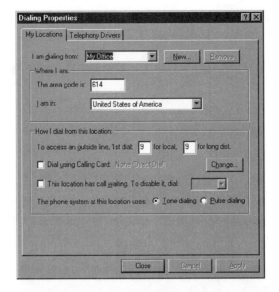

FIGURE 10.15.

*Using calling cards
when dialing.*

The Calling Card To Use combo box contains a list of predefined calling card names and rules
for most of the major telecommunications carriers. Figure 10.16 shows a partial list of
preconfigured calling card definitions. If your calling card type is listed, simply select it.

FIGURE 10.16.

*Selecting a calling
card type.*

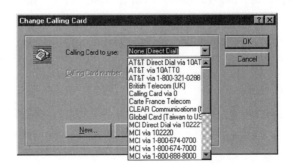

In the event that your card is not listed, you can create a custom type by clicking the Add button. After you have entered a name for the new card type, you must enter a set of rules for making calls using the new card type. Rules are entered as a set of characters. Table 10.3 lists the characters that you can use in defining rules and their meanings.

Table 10.3. Calling card rules.

Characters	Use
0-9	Digits to be dialed.
A-D	Digits to be dialed. These digits are available only on touch-tone systems and are used by some phone systems for control purposes.
E	Country code.
F	Area code (sometimes called a city code).
G	The local phone number.
H	Your calling card number.
*#	The * and # digits on your phone; digits to be dialed.
T	Dial the following digits using touch tones.
P	Dial the following digits using pulse dialing.
,	Inject a pause; useful for dialing through PBX systems.
!	*Flash* the hook. This is called *tapping* on some phone systems and activates features such as two-way calling or call waiting.
W	Wait for a second dial tone.
$	Wait for the "bong" tone indicating that you should enter a calling-card number.
?	Ask the user for input before continuing the dialing process.

After you have entered your rule set, click the Close button.

Adding SCSI Devices and Tape Drives

SCSI, the Small Computer System Interconnect, is a means of attaching disks, tape drives, CD-ROM drives, and other types of devices to a system. There are several types of SCSI interfaces. The most common variant of SCSI is called SCSI-2. SCSI-2 devices have a maximum transfer rate of 10MB/s. SCSI-2 uses a parallel data bus, performing I/O transactions in 8-bit bytes. Wide SCSI uses a 16-bit data path. SCSI adapters and devices are available in both single-ended and differential versions. Single-ended SCSI uses cheaper cables, but the cables can't exceed about six meters of total length, including the length of the adapter and any cabling internal to system or drive enclosures. Differential SCSI can use longer cable lengths.

SCSI devices are intelligent. The analogue read/write electronics of SCSI disks are embedded into the drives themselves. Data is transferred to the host using a completely digital format, so you can move SCSI disks between hosts without worrying about adapter incompatibility—at least between adapters of the same brand and model.

I/O requests are made to SCSI devices in a very high-level form. A command of the form "Send me three blocks of data starting at block 245" is issued. Commands are encoded as 6- or 10-byte packets. After a drive has received a command, it can disconnect from the SCSI bus until it has data available. At that point, it notifies the host that the data is available. This disconnection feature allows multiple parallel I/O seeks to occur on several drives connected to the same adapter.

Each SCSI device connected to an adapter has a unique ID. A single bit of the data path identifies each device during bus arbitration, so 8-bit SCSI can have a total of 8 devices, and wide SCSI can have 16 on a single bus. Because the host itself occupies one address, that means that an 8-bit SCSI-2 adapter can really connect up to 7 disks, tapes, or CD-ROMs. A wide SCSI bus can connect up to 15 devices, assuming that all the connected devices are capable of performing wide SCSI addressing and bus arbitration.

SCSI devices can be quite fast. The speed and flexibility of wide SCSI, combined with the high number of devices that can be supported, make it the interface of choice for most server-class systems. Increasing numbers of high-end workstations have SCSI adapters built into the motherboard.

Each SCSI bus must be terminated at both ends. You can usually configure your adapter board to terminate one end of the bus and then terminate the last device connected to the adapter. Note that if your adapter is connected to both internal and external devices, the adapter itself is probably *not* terminated. This means that both the last internal and the last external device must be terminated.

Make sure when adding SCSI devices that you don't configure the new device at an occupied target device address. Very unpredictable things can occur.

You can add SCSI adapters to your system by invoking the SCSI applet in the Control Panel. Invoking the SCSI applet produces a display similar to Figure 10.17.

Any SCSI adapters that are currently configured into your system appear in the list box. Double-clicking an adapter shows all the devices that are known to be connected to the selected adapter. The adapter shown in Figure 10.17 is connected to two hard disks and a CD-ROM drive.

Figure 10.17.

The Control Panel SCSI applet.

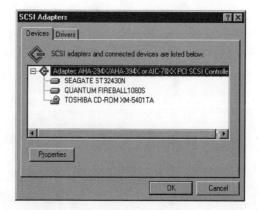

You can get information about any connected device by highlighting the device name and clicking the Properties button. You see information about the manufacturer of the device, the firmware revision number, and the SCSI target ID and LUN numbers.

SCSI devices connected to configured SCSI adapters generally require little or no configuration and are usually automatically detected at boot time.

You can add a SCSI adapter by clicking the Drivers tab, shown in Figure 10.17, and then clicking the Add button. You see a list of SCSI adapters that are known to Windows NT. If your adapter is listed, select it. If you have a driver disk from the SCSI manufacturer, you can select the Have Disk button to install it.

Multimedia and Display Settings

Multimedia has gone from a buzzword to a reality. The explosive growth of the Internet has helped to fuel the development of increasing numbers of multimedia-capable applications. Users have come to expect software that can talk to them, play music, or show them video clips in real time. Software companies continue to find newer and more innovative ways to exploit the interactive potential of multimedia.

This trend has caused multimedia hardware to become a *de facto* standard part of virtually every computer sold in recent history. Windows NT, like other software offerings, offers comprehensive support for this new and exciting capability.

Multimedia devices within Windows NT are added and configured from the Multimedia applet of the Control Panel. Figure 10.18 shows the Multimedia applet.

Note that the Multimedia applet is divided into a number of tabs across the top. The Audio, Video, MIDI, and CD Music categories each has a tab. The Devices tab installs and configures device drivers for new or existing multimedia devices. The other four tabs configure the user preferences for installed devices of the specified type.

FIGURE 10.18.

*The Control Panel
Multimedia applet.*

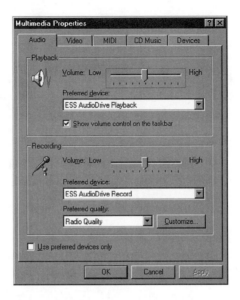

Using the Multimedia Applet Devices Tab

Figure 10.19 shows the Devices tab.

FIGURE 10.19.

*The Multimedia applet
Devices tab.*

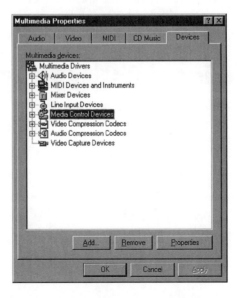

Note that there is a line for every category of multimedia device known to the system. Double-clicking any category or highlighting the category and then clicking Properties produces a list of devices of the selected type. Highlight a device and click Properties to see general information about the device. Figure 10.20 shows the properties for the ES1688 audio driver on the author's system.

FIGURE 10.20.

Sample multimedia device properties.

The type of information displayed varies somewhat, depending upon the device type. If the device has configurable settings, you can display or modify them by clicking the Settings button. Figure 10.21 shows the settings for my ES1688 audio device. Settings are device specific and dependent upon the hardware characteristics of the device. If your device can be software configured for different I/O addresses or IRQs, use the Settings button to display a configuration dialog. You cannot modify the settings for some devices, so the Settings button has no effect on them.

FIGURE 10.21.

Sample audio device settings.

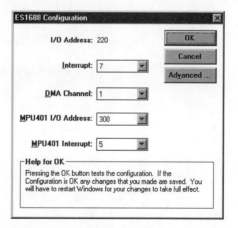

Using the Multimedia Applet Audio Tab

Windows 4.0 NT supports multimedia audio extensions. The Audio tab is shown in Figure 10.18. The upper part of the Audio tab controls audio playback characteristics. You can set the playback volume and the preferred playback device for audio output. The volume controls are unavailable if your audio device's volume can't be controlled by software.

The lower part of the Audio tab shown in Figure 10.18 controls audio recording functions. You can configure the volume, preferred audio recording device, and preferred recording quality. The setting of the Preferred Quality box has a very large impact on the way your system records sound and the size of the sound files that are produced. You can see the extremes with two of the built-in modes. The 8kHz, 8-bit monaural mode uses about 7KB of disk space per second of recording. That is about what telephony-grade recording requires. (Telephony actually uses slightly less.) A CD-quality sound track in 16-bit stereo at 44.1kHz uses a whopping 172KB per second. That is an increase of more than 2,400 percent in disk utilization.

Using the Multimedia Applet Video Tab

The Video tab of the Multimedia applet is shown in Figure 10.22. The Video tab configures characteristics of the display when it is used to play back AVI files or other video information.

FIGURE 10.22.

Configuring multi-media video options.

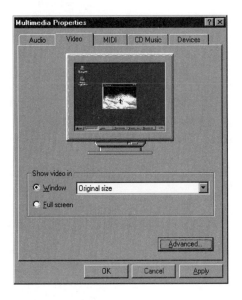

You can choose to display video clips either in full-screen mode or in a window. Video clips might be grainy when displayed in full-screen mode, so you might want to use a windowed mode to enhance readability. Selecting the Window button allows you to choose one of several zoom factors for your displayed video clips.

Selecting the Advanced button of the Video tab allows you to configure your video system to be compatible with the older 16-bit AVI standard. This is sometimes slower than using 32-bit AVI, but it helps to eliminate incompatibilities between NT 4.0 and older video applications.

Using the Multimedia Applet MIDI Tab

The *Musical Instrument Digital Interface (MIDI)* standard specifies electrical interconnections and communications configurations that allow you to use your computer to control and play digital musical instruments. Most popular keyboard manufacturers support the MIDI standard, sometimes even on lower-cost devices.

MIDI can allow you to control up to 16 instruments at once by assigning each instrument to a separate channel. For instance, you might have both a keyboard and a drum module attached to your system. Many MIDI devices are capable of producing very high-quality sound, particularly if you use external MIDI instruments instead of playing MIDI output directly through your sound card.

Figure 10.23 shows the MIDI tab on my system. Output is configured to use a single MIDI instrument—in this case, the integrated sound capabilities of the ESS AutoDrive hardware. You can change the output device by selecting the new device from the list box. If output is assigned to the MIDI port output, you see a list of configured MIDI devices. Selecting a configured device directs future MIDI output to the chosen instrument.

FIGURE 10.23.
Configuring multi-media MIDI options.

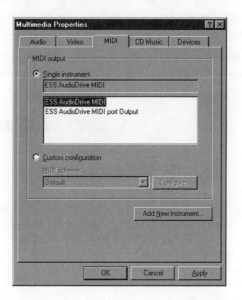

It is also possible to create a custom configuration for MIDI output. Custom configurations can use multiple concurrent instruments. Click the Custom Configuration button if you want to configure more than a single instrument for MIDI playback. Selecting Configure allows you to create your custom configuration. Figure 10.24 shows the MIDI configuration dialog.

10

ADVANCED
SYSTEM
CONFIGURATION

FIGURE 10.24.
MIDI playback scheme configuration dialog.

You use the top area of the dialog to select or create a MIDI configuration scheme for editing. You can enter the name of your scheme in the entry box. After you have configured all the instruments for this scheme, click Save As to record the scheme. You can delete an existing scheme by highlighting it and clicking the Delete key.

You use the lower part of the dialog shown in Figure 10.24 to select the channels and instruments for your new playback scheme. Highlight a channel that you want to configure and then click the Change button. You see a dialog like the one shown in Figure 10.25.

FIGURE 10.25.
Change MIDI instrument dialog.

Select the instrument that you want to assign to the channel using the combo box and then click OK. You are returned to the display in Figure 10.24. Repeat the instrument configuration procedure for each channel that you want to use in your scheme and then select OK.

Adding a MIDI Instrument

You can add a new MIDI instrument by clicking the Add New Instrument box shown in Figure 10.21. Clicking this button invokes the MIDI Instrument Installation Wizard shown in Figure 10.26.

FIGURE **10.26.**
*MIDI Instrument
Installation Wizard.*

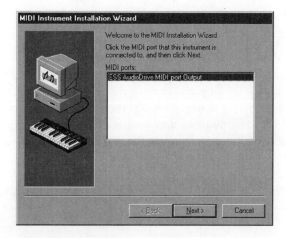

Select the MIDI interface that you want to attach your instrument to from the list box and
then click Next. You see the dialog shown in Figure 10.27.

FIGURE **10.27.**
*MIDI instrument
definition selection.*

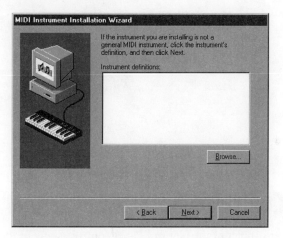

If the instrument that you are installing is a general MIDI instrument, you can ignore this step
and simply click Next. You might have a special instrument definition file that describes characteristics of the instrument. Such files are available from MIDI instrument manufacturers and
MIDI interface suppliers. If you have a MIDI instrument definition file for your instrument,
select it and click Next. Enter the name of the new instrument and then click Finish.

Using the Multimedia Applet CD Music Tab

You can usually use the same CD-ROM devices that are used for data devices for music playback as well. Many sound cards have a connector that allows the CD-ROM drive to play back

through the sound card amplifier. Most CD-ROM drives are also equipped with a jack that can directly drive headphones or a speaker.

The CD Music tab shown in Figure 10.28 controls the playback of music through a CD-ROM drive. If you have more than one CD-ROM drive connected to your system, select the drive that you want to use for playback using the combo box. You can use the slide control to set the volume of the output at the CD-ROM drive's headphone jack. Note that most drives are also equipped with a hardware volume control. The hardware control and dialog slide control can work against one another; so many times, it is easiest to set one to the maximum volume and always set the volume using the other.

FIGURE 10.28.

The Multimedia applet's CD Music tab.

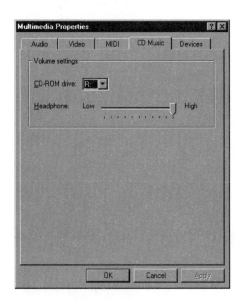

The Control Panel System Applet

The System applet of the Control Panel controls many of the tuning and configuration options that system administrators are charged with addressing. The System applet configures system startup and recovery options, executes performance tuning, and configures system and user profiles.

Using the System Applet Performance Tab

The Performance tab, shown in Figure 10.29, controls two significant parameters. The first of these is the Boost slider. The Windows NT Workstation installation process usually sets the slide control to the Maximum position. This setting optimizes the interactive response time but might leave your networking services or other background tasks with insufficient CPU resources. You can change the amount of preference given to running foreground applications by moving the slide bar. Be careful of setting the boost too low because your interactive performance might suffer.

FIGURE 10.29.

The System applet's Performance tab.

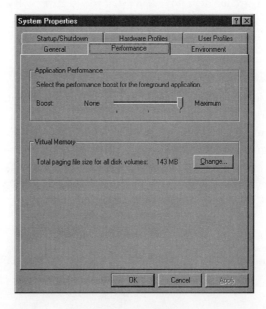

The lower part of the Performance tab sets the size of the paging files for your system. Clicking the Change button invokes the dialog in Figure 10.30. The list box at the top of the dialog displays a list of drives on your system and shows the amount of paging space available on each. You can change the size of a paging file by selecting the drive in the list box and entering the Initial and Maximum size values. Click the Set button after you have entered the new values.

FIGURE 10.30.

Setting system virtual memory.

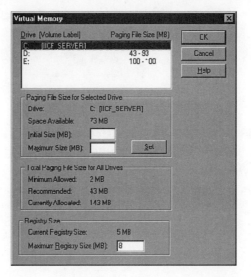

10

ADVANCED SYSTEM CONFIGURATION

The area at the bottom of the Virtual Memory dialog sets the maximum size of your system's Registry. The value you enter in the Maximum Registry Size box is not immediately allocated, and entering a value does not ensure that the Registry will have space available for expansion later. The value entered is used solely as a cap on the maximum size of the Registry. The system does not allow the Registry to grow past the indicated size.

Using the System Applet Environment Tab

The Environment tab sets environment variables. (See Figure 10.31.) Environment variables are maintained in the Registry. The system maintains both global and user-specific copies of environment variable settings. Users can modify their own environments using this dialog; only administrators can modify the system-wide variables. To enter a new variable, enter its name in the Variable box and then enter a value in the Value box. Click the Set button when you have entered both. To modify an existing variable, click it in one of the two list boxes. Edit the value in the Value box and click the Set button.

FIGURE 10.31.

Setting system-wide environment variables.

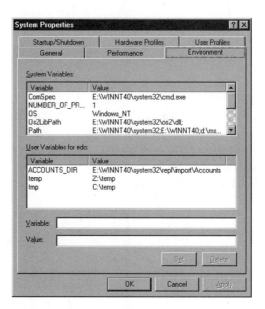

Using the System Applet Startup/Shutdown Tab

The Startup/Shutdown tab, shown in Figure 10.32, allows you to configure boot and recover options for your system. The top part of the dialog allows you to select the default configuration for booting. If you have more than one operating system (OS), you can change the default OS to boot with the Startup combo box. This has the effect of modifying the boot.ini file on your system drive.

FIGURE 10.32.

Setting system startup and recovery options.

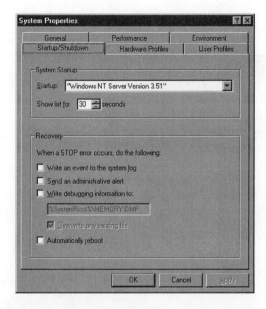

When Windows NT boots, it presents a list of known boot configurations. The default configuration to boot is highlighted. The user is given the option of changing the boot selection for the time-out period. That time-out period is controlled by the Show List For box.

The lower part of the Startup/Shutdown tab controls system recovery options. When a system STOP event is detected (producing the so-called "blue screen of death"), the system can

- Log the event to the system error logs.
- Send an alert about the error.
- Write debugging information to a file. You can select the checkbox to cause any existing log file to be overwritten. This facility is useful for debugging system failures.

Finally, clicking the Automatically Reboot checkbox causes the system to reboot itself after a STOP error.

Uninterruptible Power Supply Configuration

Uninterruptible power supplies (*UPS*) are basically batteries connected to a very fast switch and a charger. When system power fails, the UPS maintains power to your system for some fixed period of time. This gives your system time to shut down services in an orderly fashion and allows users to save any work that they might have open. A UPS is most useful when you have some sort of real-time transaction processing or database functionality on your system, but it can also be a lifesaver if you work in an area with unstable electrical power.

> **NOTE**
>
> I once worked in a heavy manufacturing plant that used massive welders and cranes. Until I installed a UPS, my system sometimes crashed several times *per* day. If you have dirty power, get a UPS. It quickly pays for itself.

The UPS Control Panel applet is shown in Figure 10.33. The typical UPS is equipped with an RS-232C control and communications interface that can be connected to your system via one of your COM ports. In the example shown in Figure 10.33, the UPS is connected to COM1.

Figure 10.33.

Configuring a UPS.

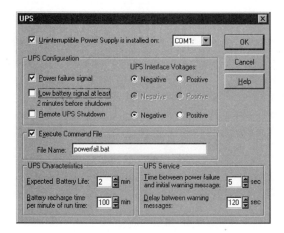

The UPS toggles a signal when the power has failed. This signal should be connected to the CTS signal of the selected COM port. You have to indicate whether your UPS makes the signal go high-to-low or low-to-high on power failure by selecting either the Positive or Negative button. Select the Power failure signal button if your UPS supports this feature.

If your UPS has a low battery output signal, it should be connected to the DCD line of your COM port. As with the Power Fail signal, you have to select the Positive or Negative button to indicate the polarity of the signal when the battery is low. Select the Low Battery Signal box if your UPS can send a low battery signal at least two minutes before your system must shut down.

The Remote UPS Shutdown indicates that your UPS can be turned off by the Windows NT UPS service. Connect the DTR line of your COM port to the remote shutdown signal of your UPS and then set the signal polarity to Positive or Negative as required.

The Execute Command File box specifies a command file that is run just before the system is shut down. You can put commands into the file that do things such as log messages, shut down databases, or perform other orderly shutdown procedures.

The UPS characteristics and UPS service areas at the bottom of the UPS applet tell NT about your UPS and how you want NT to behave during a power failure. The Expected Battery Life indicates how many minutes the batteries in your UPS last after the power fails. The Battery Recharge Time box tells NT how long it takes to recharge the battery for each minute of battery time that is used. This allows NT to estimate how much charge is left in the UPS batteries if more than one power failure occurs.

The first of the two settings on the right tell NT how long to wait after a power failure before warning users. The second setting tells NT how long to wait between messages. Note that although the battery life time values are expressed in minutes, the warning message values are rated in seconds.

> **NOTE**
>
> NT 4.0 provides good basic UPS handling mechanisms, but if you have more sophisticated needs, you might want to investigate third-party software. *PowerChute* from APC is probably the best of the third-party power management software. You can get more information on PowerChute on the World Wide Web at http://www.apcc.com.

Accessibility Options

Microsoft went to considerable lengths to make Windows NT 4.0 more accessible to physically challenged people. The Accessibility Options applet of the Control Panel allows the user to set a number of options that can improve system usability in several areas.

Setting Accessibility Keyboard Options

Figure 10.34 shows the Accessibility Properties applet. The Keyboard tab, also shown in Figure 10.34, allows users to set several options that can help physically challenged people better use the keyboard.

Some users might have difficulty with compound keystrokes, such as Shift, Control, Alt, or Control+Alt+Shift combinations. Selecting the StickyKeys box causes the system to let you press these keys sequentially. For example, pressing and releasing the Control key causes the system to view the Control key as active until a key other than Control, Alt, or Shift is pressed. Users can therefore press keys one at a time, in sequence, and build compound keystrokes.

FIGURE 10.34.

The Accessibility Properties keyboarding options.

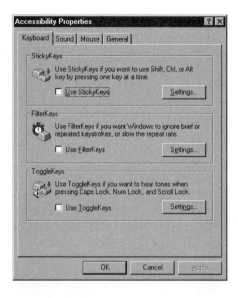

Setting Accessibility Sound Options

Figure 10.35 shows the Accessibility Sound tab. This tab sets options for hearing-impaired users. The upper part of this tab controls the SoundSentry feature. Checking the SoundSentry box causes Windows NT to display a visual warning whenever your system makes a sound.

FIGURE 10.35.

The Accessibility Properties sound options.

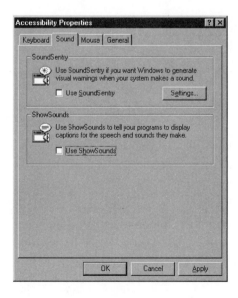

The lower part of the Sound tab controls the ShowSounds option. If ShowSounds is checked, Windows NT instructs your programs to issue visual information such as captions whenever the program usually issues sounds.

Setting Accessibility Mouse Options

The Mouse tab, shown in Figure 10.36, allows you to map mouse functions to your keyboard. Click the Use MouseKeys button to activate this feature.

FIGURE 10.36.

The Accessibility Properties mouse options.

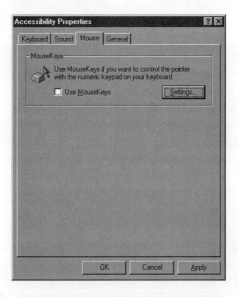

Click the Settings button to invoke the dialog shown in Figure 10.37. The upper part of this dialog allows you to set a shortcut key to activate and deactivate the MouseKeys feature. Click the checkbox to enable or disable the MouseKeys shortcut key (Left Alt+Left Shift+ Num Lock).

FIGURE 10.37.

The Accessibility MouseKey settings.

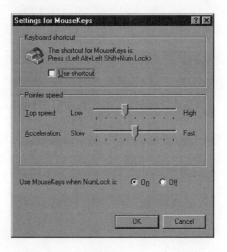

10

ADVANCED SYSTEM CONFIGURATION

The center part of the MouseKey Settings dialog configures the MouseKey pointer speed. The top slider sets the overall maximum speed for the pointer. The lower slider controls pointer acceleration.

The bottom of the MouseKeys dialog determines whether the MouseKeys feature is active with Num Lock on or off.

> **TIP**
>
> If you use MouseKeys, you might want to configure them to be active when Num Lock is off. That way, you can use the numeric keypad when Num Lock is on. Most keyboards have arrow keys and editing keys between the numeric keypad and the alphanumeric keys anyway, eliminating the need to use the numeric keypad for those functions when Num Lock is off.

Display Adapter Settings

One of the nicer features of Windows NT 4.0 is its capability to change the settings of the display adapter while the system is running. This is done using the Display Properties dialog, shown in Figure 10.38. You can invoke the Display Properties dialog by clicking the Display applet of the Control Panel or by right-clicking the screen background and selecting Properties from the menu.

FIGURE 10.38.

The Display Properties Settings dialog.

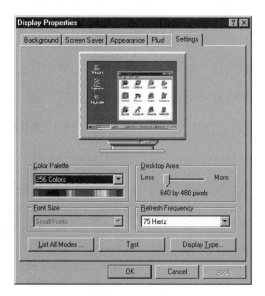

The Display Properties Settings dialog changes display characteristics such as refresh frequency, resolution, or number of available colors. Note that it is *not* a good idea to change any of these display properties unless you are very sure what you are doing because some combinations might not work or in some cases can even damage your monitor.

NT 4.0 does provide a relatively safe method for setting and testing display properties. Note the List All Modes button at the bottom of Figure 10.38. Clicking this button causes Windows NT to display a list of all the display modes that your display adapter supports. Figure 10.39 shows the available settings for my display adapter.

FIGURE 10.39.

The Detected Adapter dialog.

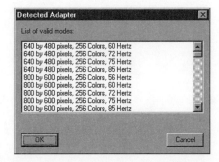

Note that the listed modes show legal combinations of resolution, refresh frequency, and number of colors for your installed video hardware. Choose the combination that you want to use and then click OK. You are returned to the dialog of Figure 10.38.

Click the Test button. You see the dialog shown in Figure 10.40.

FIGURE 10.40.

The Testing Mode dialog.

Click OK, and a test pattern appears on your display for five seconds. A dialog box asks if the pattern is displayed correctly. If the pattern displays correctly, click Yes. Click OK on the Settings dialog, and the system changes your display properties to match your new selection.

WARNING

Even if the five-second test seems to work correctly, make sure that your monitor is capable of supporting the refresh frequency that you choose. Driving a monitor at a refresh frequency above its rated maximum might make your monitor fail.

10

ADVANCED
SYSTEM
CONFIGURATION

Summary

The inclusion of UPS management software within Windows NT 4.0 Workstation is a testament to NT's constantly improving maturity and robustness. Many applications cannot withstand the impact of unscrolled shutdowns or interruptions. Configuring your system with an Uninterruptible Power Supply can greatly reduce the risk of unscheduled interruption and the associated loss of data. The capital expense of the UPS hardware can be offset many times over by one prevented data loss. If your system is used to process volatile data or if you run programs that don't recover well from an uncontrolled shutdown, buy a UPS. It's one of the better investments you'll ever make.

Windows NT Services

by Eric D. Osborne

IN THIS CHAPTER

There are many situations in which programs are not suitable for interactive control. Some programs, such as spoolers, might service repetitive requests. Others might have to respond very quickly to external events. Network server processes often fall into this category. Some programs must initiate specific events on certain days or at specific times. Many times, these types of programs must be active all the time, even when no user is logged in. The Remote Access facility described in Chapter 21, "Remote Access Service," is a perfect example of this. Remote Access Services can allow you to log into the workstation from a remote site. In order to accomplish this, the Remote Access server process must be running when the workstation is unattended.

In all of these cases, it is necessary for a program to be running without human interaction. Windows NT 4.0 comes with a number of such programs. Most start automatically and run quietly in the background, out of the sight and mind of users.

Background processes of this type are called *services* in Windows NT. UNIX users might view services as equivalent to UNIX *daemon* processes. In both cases, the process runs in the background and requires no interactive control on the part of a user. Many services are actually incapable of interacting with the user in any direct sense. Most of the services described in Chapter 18, "Windows NT Network Services," fall into this category. Services can be configured to allow desktop interaction when required. See the "Service Startup Options" section of this chapter for for information on configuring services for desktop interaction.

Understanding System Services

I mentioned previously that Microsoft Windows NT 4 Workstation incorporates a number of built-in services. The installation process configures many services to start automatically at system boot time. Other services must be started manually or configured for automatic startup by the user. Even if a process has been started automatically, it can still be stopped or paused by an authorized user. In general, it is possible to start, stop, or pause any service at any time. A user must usually have administrator privileges to stop system services, but most services can be started by ordinary users.

TIP

Services are special programs. It is usually not possible to use ordinary programs as services. If you need to use an ordinary program as a service, investigate the srvany.exe program supplied as part of the Microsoft Windows NT Resource Kit. The srvany.exe program allows you to run any program as a service. Another Resource Kit program, instsrv.exe, is used to actually install your service.

Services are installed, controlled, or examined by using the Services applet in the Control Panel. Figure 11.1 shows the resulting Services dialog box.

FIGURE 11.1.

The Services applet dialog box.

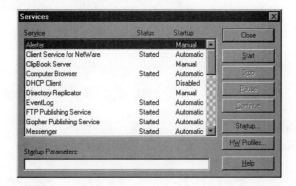

Although most services do not interact with the desktop, a few services do require human interaction. The Messenger service, which notifies selected users of critical system events, is one of the exceptions. Because the Messenger service sends messages to users, it has to be able to interact with the user's desktop.

Services must log onto the system before they are allowed to run. Each service is installed under an account that is used to log in the service. In general, the account specified is a special system account designated for use by services. It is possible, however, to install services to use nonsystem accounts.

Services and Hardware Profiles

Versions of Windows NT prior to 4.0 had a significant failing. Unlike DOS, which had the capability to boot under multiple configurations through the use of special commands in the config.sys and autoexec.bat files, NT always assumed the same hardware configuration. This meant that it was very difficult to address the issue of portable systems or systems that might not always be connected to a given network.

Microsoft has addressed this issue in Windows NT 4.0 with the addition of *Hardware Profiles*. These profiles allow the user to run with networking either enabled or disabled. Hardware Profiles can also be used to indicate the presence of a docking bay on portable computers. The creation and management of Hardware Profiles is discussed in detail in Chapter 10, "Advanced System Configuration."

It is possible to set individual services to be enabled or disabled depending upon the hardware profile selected at boot time. This is done by selecting the desired service and then clicking the HW Profiles button shown in Figure 11.1. Clicking this button opens a dialog that can be used to associate service states with specific hardware profiles. This dialog is shown in Figure 11.2.

FIGURE 11.2.

*Setting Service
hardware profiles.*

Click on the desired profile name in the selection box shown in Figure 11.2 and then select either Disable or Enable. Click OK to return to the Services configuration applet.

Starting, Stopping, and Pausing Services

The Windows NT installation process configures most important services to start automatically when your computer is booted. There are occasions when you must manually control a service. This can be necessary under any of the following circumstances:

- The service was installed to require manual startup.
- The service started automatically but terminated due to an error or some other condition.
- You want to temporarily disable a service for diagnostic reasons or for any other purpose.
- The service has become "confused."

> **TIP**
>
> The Spooler is an example of a service that sometimes terminates for a variety of reasons. This can have unexpected side effects. If the print manager is unable to add a new printer definition, for instance, it might be because the Spooler service has terminated.

The state of the system's services can be seen in the Status column of Figure 11.1. Running services will have the word Started or Paused in this column. The column is blank if the service is not running at all. Select the service that you want to control, and click the Start, Stop, Pause, or Continue button, as appropriate.

Please note that when starting a service manually, it is possible to specify optional startup parameters in the Startup Parameters box shown at the bottom of Figure 11.1.

WARNING

Be *extremely* careful when starting and stopping services. Stopping the Server service, for instance, causes any remote user to be immediately disconnected from your system. Make sure to give remote users time to properly save work before stopping any service that could impact a remote user.

Service Startup Options

To configure the startup options for a service, start up the Services applet as shown in Figure 11.1. Select the service that you want to configure and click the Startup... button. The dialog shown in Figure 11.3 appears. Select one of three Startup Type buttons. If the Automatic button is selected, the service is started by the system when your computer is booted.

FIGURE 11.3.

Setting Service startup options.

Note the selections at the bottom of the dialog under the Log On As heading. Most services, including the defaults, will operate under the special System Account. Select the This Account button only if your service *must* run under a specific, nonsystem account. This is required in certain situations. One thing to remember is that the System account is a strictly local account, and it does not have access to the network. Because of this, automatic network backup programs often must be run from an account that is a member of the Backup Operators group. In order to have such a program run automatically by the At command, the Schedule service would also have to log in using an account that was a member of the Backup Operators group.

> **WARNING**
>
> Services, like users, must issue a password to the system when logging on. Any account that is used by a service should have the Password Never Expires box checked in the User Manager. If the password on an account used by a service changes, the service will fail to start. In some cases, it is necessary to reinstall the service to correct the problem.

Selecting the Allow Service to Interact with Desktop box gives the service permission to display messages or receive input from the keyboard or mouse. Most services do not require such permission.

Select OK to record the desired settings for the service. You return to the dialog shown in Figure 11.1.

Service Security Contexts

It is important to understand the security implications of services. Services log onto the system under either the special System account or via a specified user account. The server process and any child processes that it might spawn take on the security context of the account that was used for the logon.

The security context of the running process determines its ability to access files, network resources, and other resources of your computer. It is critically important to ensure that each service is configured to run within a context that allows it to perform all intended tasks.

The special System account isn't likely to have many problems, although there are a few exceptions. The most notable failing of the System account lies in its inability to access network resources. If you need to have a service perform operations across the network, you should configure the service in question to use an account other than System. Be careful when choosing a logon account for your service, however; services installed to run under user accounts might have problems with file or share permissions. Be very careful to set correct access permissions on resources so that your service can get access to all the resources it needs.

> **WARNING**
>
> One very nasty implication of service security contexts lies in the potential danger of exposing your system to marauding hackers. If you create a service of your own—particularly if that service is accessible through the network—make very certain that you understand how or if your service can be used to gain unauthorized access to your system. Services installed under the special System account or an Administrator account are particularly dangerous, because they can get access to anything on your system.

Managing Services

This section gives you descriptions of Windows NT's default services. (See Table 11.1.) Additional information on the control and management of the Alerter and Directory Replicator services is also included.

> **NOTE**
>
> Network specific services are described in Chapter 18. Although the client/server nature of Windows NT often makes it difficult to distinguish network from non-network services, most of the services described in this section are either useful or required even on stand-alone systems. Services described in Chapter 18 are generally useful only in networked environments.

Table 11.1. Windows NT's default services.

Service	Description
Clipbook Server	Provides pages to the Clipbook Viewer. Because it is a client/server application, the Clipbook Server is capable of providing pages to Clipbooks on remote systems.
Computer Browser	Maintains a list of computers on your network. Applications such as the Network Neighborhood selection in the Explorer use this list to display known computers.
Event Log	Accepts event notifications from system processes or from user programs and records them in the system event logs.
Messenger	This service is the delivery agent for messages sent by the Alerter service described later in this chapter. It is also used to send and receive messages sent by Administrators.
Net Logon	The Net Logon service is used for user authentication when a workstation is part of a domain. The workstation uses the Net Logon service to verify user account and password information against a domain controller. On server systems, the Net Logon service performs the actual authentication. It also synchronizes local authentication information with the domain controller's authentication database.

continues

Table 11.1. continued

Service	Description
Network DDE	Provides Dynamic Data Exchange services to the network. This service acts as a network transport and security controller.
Network DDE DSDM	This service manages DDE conversations taking place across Network DDE.
NT LM Security Support	Many of the client/server facilities in Windows NT make use of distributed service requests called Remote Procedure Calls. Windows NT is capable of using several different transports to support these requests. Most use named pipes, but some must use a network transport such as TCP/IP. The NT LM Security Support Manager service provides security to RPC-based applications running across the various network transports.
RPC Locator	The list of available Remote Procedure Calls is dynamic. New RPC server applications can add new procedure calls to the list by registering their names with the RPC Locator service. Client applications can then query the RPC Locator service to find the desired RPC provider.
RPC Service	The RPC Service provides a number of miscellaneous control functions for the Windows NT RPC subsystem. One important task is endpoint mapping, which associates communications channels with new RPC requests. These endpoints can take the form of named pipes. In the case of TCP/IP connections, the endpoints are mapped to IP port numbers.
Schedule	Schedule services are the activation and completion agents for the AT command. The AT command is used to schedule events to run at some predetermined time and date. The commands scheduled with AT will never run if the Schedule service is not active.
Server	Provides additional RPC support, file, print, and other resource-sharing services. Note that users cannot attach to the resources of your system if the Server service is inactive. Stopping the Server service disconnects all attached users. Pausing it prevents new connections but maintains existing connections.

Service	Description
Spooler	Provides print spooling and print job notification.
UPS	The UPS service controls a connected Uninterruptible Power Supply. Responds to power failures with an orderly shutdown of the system.
Workstation	Provides the network and communications support required to connect an interactive user.

Default Services Requiring Additional Setup

Some of Windows NT's default services must be configured for your environment before they are actually useful. The setup of several such services is described in this section.

Alerter

The Alerter service allows your system to automatically send administrative messages to administrative accounts on your workstation or to other computers if you are connected to a network. The Alerter requires that the Messenger service be running in order to transmit its messages. Alerter receives messages from the Server service, among others.

After the Alerter service is running, it must be configured. This is done from the Server applet of the Control Panel, shown in Figure 11.4.

FIGURE 11.4.
The Server applet's dialog box.

Click the Alerts button to produce the dialog shown in Figure 11.5. Any user or computer listed in the Send Administrative Alerts To box will receive system-generated alert messages. To add a name to the list, type it in the New Computer or Username box and click the Add button. To remove a name, select the name and click the Remove button.

FIGURE 11.5.
Specifying alert recipients.

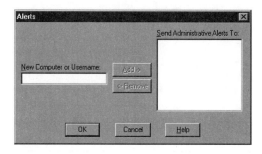

Directory Replicator

The Directory Replicator service, as its name implies, is used to copy directories and the files they contain from one place to another. The process is performed automatically at predetermined intervals. Windows NT 4.0 Advanced Server can both *export* (transmit) and *import* (receive) directories. Windows NT 4 Workstation can only import replicated directories.

Directory Replication is extremely useful for maintaining version control over pseudostatic information. Directory Replication is not suitable for highly volatile data for the following reasons:

- It does not update all copies of the data in real time.
- It copies at the file level. This means that if a single byte of a file changes, Directory Replicator will copy the entire file to the replication target.

Directory Replication is normally used in networked environments to distribute configuration information, logon scripts, and other types of nonvolatile data. A systems administrator needs only to update one copy of the data, and it will propagate to other systems on the network automatically.

The Server applet of the Control Panel is used to control Directory Replication. Invoke the Server applet as shown in Figure 11.4. Then click the Replication button to produce the dialog shown in Figure 11.6.

FIGURE 11.6.
Setting up directory replication.

Perform the following steps to allow remotely exported directories to be received and replicated by your workstation.

1. Enter the name of the domains or computers that you want to import directories and files from. Click on the Add button to display the dialog shown in Figure 11.7. Note that the captions on the entry fields in Figure 11.7 are somewhat deceptive. The box labeled Domain actually allows the entry of a domain or computer name. Computer names should be entered with a leading \\. You can get a list of the computers in a domain by double-clicking on the domain name in the Select Domain list. Click OK to return to the dialog shown in Figure 11.6.

FIGURE 11.7.

Selecting a replication source domain or computer.

2. Specify the To Path. The replicated directories are copied to a point underneath the specified path. By default, this is `%windir%\System32\Repl\Import`. If you change the default, make sure to change the logon script path as well.

3. Click the Manage button to further control your import settings. This produces the dialog shown in Figure 11.8. The most important controls in Figure 11.8 are the Add Lock and Remove Lock buttons. Setting a lock on any subdirectory effectively prevents that directory from receiving updates from the replication export server. You can use this to restrict updates that you don't want to receive.

FIGURE 11.8.

Managing imported directories.

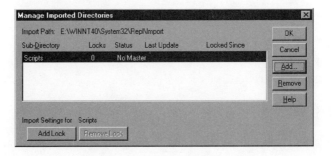

> **NOTE**
>
> The Add and Remove buttons shown in Figure 11.8 are of questionable utility, because any manual changes you make to the Sub-Directory list will be overridden by automatic updates from the Replication Export servers that you selected.

Summary

Not all computing needs can be adequately addressed by interactive programs. Such situations are relatively rare on single-user, single-tasking operating systems such as DOS or Windows 3.*x*. Mature operating systems such as Windows NT and UNIX provide sophisticated networking and spooling facilities that can only be met by detached, autonomous processes. These processes often must run when the system is unattended, and sometimes under an ID other than that of any currently logged on user. Windows NT Services provide a flexible and robust method for addressing such situations. Although they are sometimes less flexible than the UNIX daemon approach, tools such as srvany.exe in the Windows NT Resource Kit can allow essentially any program to run as a service, facilitating the user's ability to create unattended computing environments.

CHAPTER 12

System User Management

by Sean Mathias

IN THIS CHAPTER

User Manager is a powerful and integral tool of Windows NT that is used to create and manage users and groups for the local systems security database (SAM). User Manager also provides extended functionality to set system policies and auditing procedures and levels.

User Manager

As mentioned in Chapter 1, "What Is Windows New Technology?," Windows NT has an integrated security subsystem. Creating a security system that was an integral component of the operating system itself was one of the initial design goals of Windows NT, in order to provide the level of security needed in an environment containing sensitive data that must be protected.

The first evidence of this security system is the initial logon process that a user must complete to gain access to the system. The user is prompted to press the Ctrl+Alt+Delete key sequence and then provide a user name and password to gain access to the system.

The Ctrl+Alt+Delete key sequence is a precautionary measure to defeat Trojan Horse programs, which impersonate a logon screen and capture user names and passwords. The user name and password must be valid for the system that the user is attempting to log onto (or the domain that a user is trying to gain access to in a Windows NT Server domain environment). It was also a reasonable assumption on the part of Microsoft that no other applications would be using the key sequence because it had historically been used to reboot a Windows system.

> **NOTE**
>
> User names in Windows NT are not case-sensitive, but passwords are case-sensitive. This means that *PASSWORD*, *Password*, and *password* are interpreted as distinctly different passwords.

In order to be able to log onto a Windows NT Workstation computer, the user must have a valid user account on that computer. User accounts are created using a utility called *User Manager* (*User Manager for Domains* in a Windows NT Server environment). (See Figure 12.1.)

By default, two user accounts are automatically created during setup and installation: the *Administrator* account and the *Guest* account. Neither of these accounts can be deleted, but they can and should be renamed. If you are joining a domain, no individual user account will be created. However, if this is a stand-alone or workgroup configuration, an account will be created for the default user.

Renaming the default accounts provides an additional security measure. If they are left on the system, anyone familiar with Windows NT can use them and will need only the password to gain access to the system. When you rename these accounts, there is no logical starting point.

Additionally, the Guest account can be disabled, preventing its use entirely. Please note that the Administrator account cannot be disabled, and neither the Administrator nor the Guest account can be deleted. This is the default setting for Windows NT server, but it must be manually configured on a Windows NT Workstation.

FIGURE 12.1.

The Windows NT User Manager.

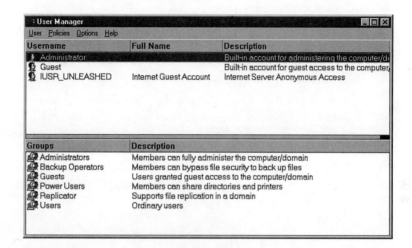

As you might guess, the Administrator account has full access and full control over the entire system and the Guest account has very limited rights and access. Typically, you should not use the Administrator account for normal logon, but only for explicit administrative needs. This allows for better auditing of system changes (which is discussed later in this chapter). It also helps to eliminate the chance of accidents such as permanently deleting the wrong files (something I speak of from experience).

User Management and Creation

User Manager is the tool used to create and manage system users as well as Local Groups. Windows NT uses an object called groups for grouping users in a logical manner, simplifying the administration and management of rights and permissions. Groups are also created and managed through User Manager. (Groups are discussed in the "Group Management" section, later in this chapter.)

When you select User and choose New User from the User Manager menu bar, a New User dialog is produced. (See Figure 12.2.)

To create a new user, use the following procedure:

1. From the User Manager menu bar, select User and then New User.
2. Provide a User name of up to 20 characters. (This is the name that the user enters to log onto the system.) It is a good idea to establish naming conventions such as first initial, last name for user names, for consistency and clarity.

3. Fill in the Full Name of the user.

4. Provide an optional description of the user (such as Accounting Manager).

5. You can optionally provide an initial password for the user or leave the field blank and the user will be prompted to change it when logging on for the first time. I suggest using a default password because this provides a safety net between the time the account is created and the time the user logs on and changes the password. Otherwise, anyone can provide this user name without a password and gain access to the system.

6. By default, the User Must Change Password at Next Logon box is checked. This forces the user to change the password the next time he or she logs onto the system.

7. If appropriate, there are check boxes for User Cannot Change Password (good for temporary employees), Password Never Expires (good for system service accounts), and Account Disabled (which prevents unauthorized users from using this account if a user will be gone or on vacation for an extended period).

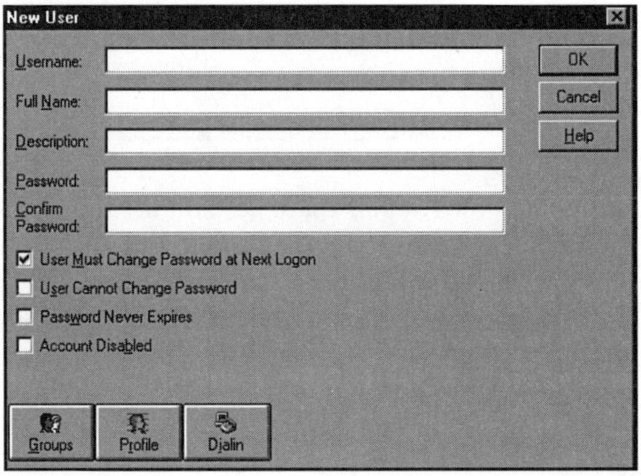

FIGURE 12.2.

The New User dialog.

Managing Group Membership

To specify which groups a user belongs to, select the Groups button, which produces the Group Memberships dialog shown in Figure 12.3. Each user, by default, is a member of the Users group. This dialog displays the currently selected user and has two lists for groups to which the user does and does not belong, with an Add button and a Remove button between the lists.

To add the user to a group, select the appropriate group from the Not member of: list and click the Add button. Similarly, to remove a user from a group, select the appropriate group from the Member of: list and click the Remove button.

User Environment Profiles

To configure a user's environment profile, select the Profile button. As you can see in Figure 12.4, this presents the administrator with a User Environment Profile dialog.

FIGURE 12.3.
The Group Memberships dialog.

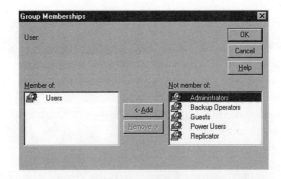

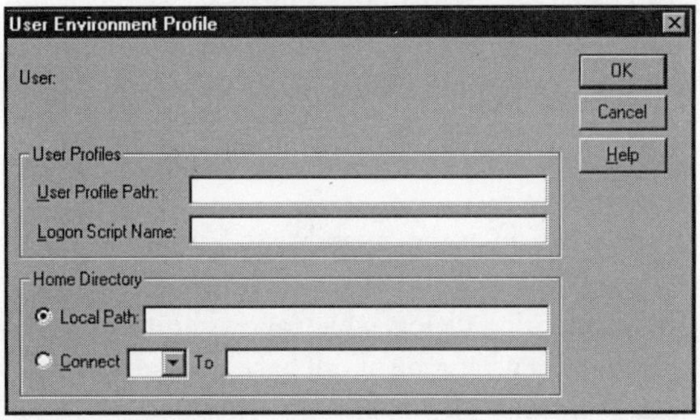

FIGURE 12.4.
The User Environment Profile dialog.

This dialog is used to specify a user profile and path (if any), an optional logon script, and the path to the user's home directory. The user profile is actually created using another utility, User Profile Editor, which is described later in this chapter. If user profiles are in use, this is where you must specify the path and filename for the appropriate profile.

A logon script is a command line batch file with either a .BAT or a .CMD filename extension. Typically, these files are used to synchronize system time with that of a network server, to map network drives and resources, and to specify environment variables using command line syntax. When a user logs onto the network, this script is downloaded to the user's local system and executed, carrying out the specified commands. Microsoft's System Management Server (SMS) is an application that makes extensive use of logon scripts for gathering information and managing client systems.

Lastly, a home directory can be specified for the user. This can be either a local directory on the user's system or a network directory on another system mapped to a network drive. To specify a home directory on the user's local system, select the Local Path button and specify the full path to the directory. To specify a network directory, select the Connect button and specify the drive letter to map the home directory to and the network path to that directory using the Universal Naming Convention (UNC) name (\\server\share).

> **NOTE**
>
> If your network has sufficient resources such as available disk space and bandwidth, it is advisable to use a network directory that can be backed up on a regular basis.
>
> Also, it is generally a good idea to avoid using the Z: drive letter for mapping home directories because the logon process temporarily uses this mapping for authentication and logon script processing.

The user's home directory, if specified, is the user's default working directory and will be the path displayed when the user chooses a File Save or File Open operation, unless the given application supports definition of an alternate working directory. This will also be the starting location in a command prompt window when a session is opened.

Dialin Information

New to Windows NT 4.0 is the capability to administer Remote Access Service (RAS) permissions through User Manager. When he selects the Dialin button, the administrator is presented with a Dialin Information dialog, which allows him to grant or revoke dialin access permission to the user and specify what type of call back features to implement. (See Figure 12.5.) This is different from Windows NT 3.*x*, in which RAS permissions had to be set through the Remote Access Service Administrator program, providing a more centralized administration of user privileges.

FIGURE 12.5.

The Dialin Informa-tion dialog.

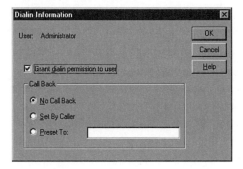

Group Management

As mentioned earlier, groups can be created to ease the management of users and permissions for users whose network needs are similar. Windows NT Workstation supports the use and creation of *local groups.*

By default, Windows NT creates several default groups with specific purposes and the necessary rights to perform specific tasks. The default groups created by Windows NT Workstation are as follows:

■ Administrators: Members of this group have full administrative rights over the local system and all of its resources. By default, the local Administrator account, which is created during Windows NT installation, is a member of this group.

■ Backup Operators: Members of this group are allowed special read and write access to all files and directories to perform backup and restore operations on the local system.

■ Guests: This group has minimal rights on the system and is available for users who might be visiting for a few hours or a day and have a need to print a document or use a spreadsheet program. By default, the local user account Guest is a member of this group.

■ Power Users: This group is for users who might need to perform more advanced operations such as system performance monitoring.

■ Replicator: This group is used for accounts that perform file replication in a domain environment.

■ Users: This is the default account for general users of the system. They have no special privileges.

These are the groups that are created by default on the local system. User rights can be modified on a per-user or group basis, providing more flexibility. Additionally, custom groups can be created by the administrator.

Each of the default groups provides specific functions for performing various tasks. The following list gives a brief summary of each group and the functionality provided:

■ Administrators: Membership in this group gives the user administrator rights and full control of the system.

■ Backup Operators: Members of this group are able to back up and restore all files on the system, even files for which they have no permission. It is important to understand that they have the ability to back up or restore these files using only Windows NT Backup or a third-party backup program. They cannot otherwise access files for which they are not authorized.

■ Guests: The Guests account is typically used for temporary access for users who would not normally be using this system. This group provides minimal rights on the system.

■ Power Users: This group provides additional rights that allow members to create shares (printer and disk) and manage printers.

■ Replicator: This group provides the ability to manage and facilitate file replication in a domain.

■ Users: This is the default account for ordinary users of the system.

To create a new group, use the following procedure:

1. Select User and then New Local Group from the User Manager menu bar.

2. A New Local Group dialog is presented, as shown in Figure 12.6. Provide a name for the group and, optionally, a description.

FIGURE 12.6.

The New Local Group dialog.

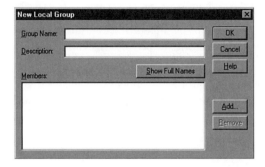

3. You can add users to the group at this time 6F selecting the Add button. You are presented with a user list for the local system. (See Figure 12.7.) Select the users that you want to add and click the Add button. When you are finished selecting users to add, click OK. (You can also add and remove users at a later time.)

FIGURE 12.7.

Adding users to a new local group.

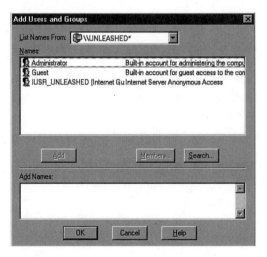

4. When you have given the group a name and description and (optionally) added users to it, click OK. The group is now created.

To modify an existing user or group, select the user or group that you want to modify and choose User and Properties from the User Manager menu bar. (You can make modifications to multiple users at the same time by selecting the range of users that you want to modify and choosing Properties.) Now make the modifications you choose.

The other available options from User Manager's User menu are as follows:

- Copy: Make an exact copy of a user or group.
- Delete: Permanently delete a user or group.
- Rename: Change the name of an existing user or group.

> **NOTE**
>
> If you delete a user's account, that user account information is forever removed from the system. Each user account is represented by a unique Security Identifier (SID), and no SID is ever reused on a given system. Therefore, even if you were to re-create the user account with identical properties, the user would not have his previous file permissions or network rights; the rights need to be reestablished.

12

SYSTEM USER MANAGEMENT

Policies

Each Windows NT Workstation computer has a set of local security policies that are configurable through User Manager. When you select the Policies menu item, you are presented with three distinct categories: Account, User Rights, and Audit.

Account Policies

Account policies set the configuration for various local authentication parameters. The Account Policy dialog is shown in Figure 12.8.

Using the Account Policy dialog, the administrator can configure the following options:

- Maximum Password Age: This can be set to Password Never Expires, which means that users are never required to change their passwords, or it can be configured to make users' passwords expire and require them to be changed after a certain number of days. I have found 45 or 60 days to be ideal because passwords have a tendency to become known in this period of time with many users.
- Minimum Password Age: This setting can be configured for Allow Changes Immediately, which allows users to change passwords anytime. (This is not recommended because users will consistently revert back to their old passwords, creating a security hole.) This setting can also be configured to require a certain number of days to pass before users can again change their passwords. This is partially contingent upon password uniqueness because users can alternate between two passwords, which undermines the point of changing passwords based upon age. Typically, users should not be able to change their password until one week prior to its expiration.

FIGURE 12.8.

The Account Policy dialog.

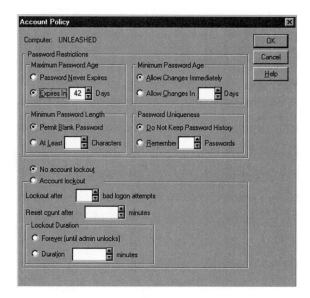

- ■ Minimum Password Length: This is the minimum number of characters that a password can consist of. The options are to Permit Blank Password (not recommended) or At Least *nn* Characters (the default is 6). I recommend 6 or more to make it more effective and to prevent users from using blank passwords.

- ■ Password Uniqueness: Users often switch back and forth between two familiar passwords, which presents a security issue. When you select Remember *nn* Passwords, Windows NT can keep a history of a user's last *nn* passwords, disallowing the use of a password that was used too recently.

The Account Policy dialog also has a configuration for Account Lockout. This can be set to No Account Lockout or Account Lockout. If the Account Lockout feature is selected, the administrator must set parameters for how many bad logon attempts a user can submit in a specified time period before that user account is disabled. This is highly recommended for security-conscious organizations. There is also a Reset count after *nn* minutes, which resets the number of bad logon attempts for a user to zero after *nn* minutes. Lastly, a Lockout Duration parameter specifies that the account should be locked out until an administrator unlocks it, or it should be unlocked automatically after *nn* minutes. For most instances, a setting of five bad logon attempts before lockout is appropriate. It is recommended that the account be configured to reset within 20 to 30 minutes in order to avoid Denial of Service (DoS) attacks by malicious individuals. Denial of Service attacks occur when an unauthorized user cannot gain access to a system but locks out all users by making bad logon attempts, another potentially damaging situation. (How much does it cost to have all of a system's users idle?)

User Rights

Windows NT provides a set of network user rights that can be assigned on a per-user or group basis. Some rights are assigned to specific users and groups by default. The User Rights Policy dialog is shown in Figure 12.9. Notice that at the bottom of the dialog there is a check box with an option to Show Advanced User Rights.

FIGURE 12.9.

The User Rights Policy dialog.

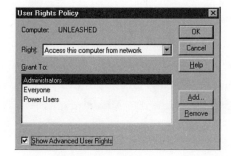

The standard user rights are as follows, along with a description and default assignments:

- Access this computer from the network: This allows the specified users the ability to make a connection with this computer across the network. Granted to Administrators, Everyone, and Power Users.

- Back up files and directories: This allows users special access to all files on a system to perform backup operations. Granted to Administrators and Backup Operators.

- Change the system time: This allows the user to change the system time. Granted to Administrators and Power Users.

- Force shutdown from a remote system: This allows the user to shut down the system remotely. Granted to Administrators and Power Users.

- Load and unload device drivers: This allows the user to add and remove hardware and components. Granted to Administrators.

- Log on locally: This allows the user to log onto the local system from the system console. Granted to Administrators, Backup Operators, Everyone, Guests, Power Users, and Users.

- Manage auditing and security log: This allows the user to view, delete, and change auditing settings and log settings, as well as examine the Event Log. Granted to Administrators.

- Restore files and directories: This allows users to restore from backup any files or directories. Granted to Administrators and Backup Operators.

- Shut down the system: This allows the user to shut down the system. Granted to Administrators, Backup Operators, Everyone, Power Users, and Users.

■ Take ownership of files or other objects: This allows the user to take ownership of objects and files on the system, which the user does not own and might not have permission for. Granted to Administrators. Some users can use this option if the owner of a file grants them permission to take ownership of that file.

To grant or revoke a specific right for a user, select the appropriate right and choose the Add or Remove button.

The advanced user rights are as follows:

■ Act as part of the operating system. Granted to None.

■ Add workstations to domain. Granted to None.

■ Bypass traverse checking. Granted to Everyone.

■ Create a pagefile. Granted to Administrators.

■ Create a token object. Granted to None.

■ Debug programs. Granted to Administrators.

■ Generate security audits. Granted to None.

■ Increase quotas. Granted to Administrators.

■ Increase scheduling priority. Granted to Administrators and Power Users.

■ Lock pages in memory. Granted to None.

■ Log on as a batch job. Granted to None.

■ Log on as a service. Granted to None.

■ Modify firmware environment variables. Granted to Administrators.

■ Profile single process. Granted to Administrators and Power Users.

■ Profile system performance. Granted to Administrators.

■ Replace a process level token. Granted to None.

Advanced user rights should be assigned carefully because they typically are not needed by users (even administrators) and can be disastrous if used improperly.

Audit Policy

Because the security component of Windows NT is integrated into the operating system itself, auditing capabilities are integrated into the security subsystem. There are three separate auditing configurations: auditing for file and directory access, which is configured through File Manager; auditing of printer usage, which is configured through Print Manager; and user activity logging, which is configured through User Manager.

This section covers the auditing of user activity. When you select Policies and Audit from the User Manager menu bar, you are presented with the dialog shown in Figure 12.10.

FIGURE 12.10.
*The Audit Policy
configuration dialog.*

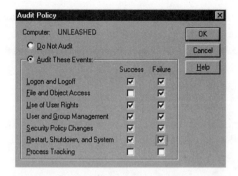

Initially, auditing is not enabled. To enable auditing features, select the Audit These Events button. It is then necessary to configure which events to audit and whether to audit successes, failures, or both. Keep in mind the level of security necessary for your particular organization and the fact that, for auditing to be effective, someone must monitor the logs and interpret them to look for problems.

Also, because the audited events are written to the security section of the Event Log, it is necessary to either closely monitor and maintain the log or modify its settings to accommodate the growth of the audit trail.

The following events can be audited for both success and failure:

- Logon and Logoff audits when a user logged on or off the workstation or made a network connection.

- File and Object Access audits when a user accessed a file or directory that has been configured for auditing or used a printer configured for auditing.

- Use of User Rights audits when the user exercised one of his user rights.

- User and Group Management audits when a change was made to the Security Account Manager database (add, remove, modify a user or group).

- Security Policy Changes audits when a change was made to the user rights or security policy.

- Restart, Shutdown, and System audits when the computer was shut down or restarted or a system event occurred.

- Process Tracking audits low-level process information such as duplicate handles or indirect object access.

It is generally a good idea to be sparing in your selections so that you have a manageable audit trail, but not at the expense of compromising security. Choose the events that are important to you and manage and track them closely, or this task can grow out of control or lose its value.

Also note that the more auditing features that are enabled, the higher the performance cost is on the system because the auditing process uses system resources.

Typically, I audit the failure of any of the events in the preceding list. But I also audit the success of User and Group Management, Security Policy Changes, and System Shutdown because it is a good idea to be able to track when these events occur and who initiated them.

Summary

User Manager is an extensive and integral tool of Windows NT. This tool controls and manages much of the security and policies for the system. The following are some of the functions of User Manager:

- Manage system users and groups.
- Manage the local system policies.
- Manage user rights.
- Manage security auditing of users.

Windows NT Subsystems and Application Support

by Sean Mathias

IN THIS CHAPTER

The Windows NT operating system, unlike many others, is comprised of various subsystems. This chapter covers the user mode or environment subsystems. In addition to these, there are various executive subsystems such as the Client-Server Runtime Subsystem (CSRSS.EXE) and the Local Security Authority Subsystem (LSASS.EXE).

The executive subsystems are kernel mode services used to facilitate the various operating system tasks and should not be directly tampered with by the user (using kill.exe or pviewer.exe) because this can cause unexpected and undesirable results. The user mode or environment subsystems are what the user interacts with and are used to facilitate things such as the GUI, I/O functions, and running applications. For a graphical model of the Windows NT architecture and subsystems, refer to Figure 1.3 in Chapter 1, "What Is Windows New Technology?"

Windows NT has a variety of environment subsystems and an open and well-defined interface for third party vendors to write additional environment subsystems. The reason for the plethora of executive and environment subsystems is to maintain Windows NT's modular architecture and provide support for the broadest range of applications and services possible. Environment subsystems are Windows NT processes that emulate various operating system environments.

One of the benefits of this modular architecture is that if one environment subsystem fails, the others continue to operate normally (unless the Win32 subsystem fails). Additionally, it is often possible and acceptable to reinitialize an environment subsystem without restarting the system. This is due to the fact that the environment subsystems are merely Windows NT processes.

All of the application environment subsystems (other than the Win32 subsystem) are optional and are dynamically loaded when needed. In fact, these subsystems can be removed from the system entirely if they will never be needed. I advise you to use caution and discretion removing subsystems because (from my own experience) it can cause headaches down the road if you have a need for a subsystem and it is no longer available.

Win32 Subsystem

The Win32 (Windows 32-bit) subsystem is the heart and soul of the user mode Windows NT environment. The Win32 subsystem is responsible for handling keyboard and mouse input and screen output for all of the environment subsystems, as well as running Win32 applications.

In its handling of user input, the Win32 subsystem is also responsible for initial message processing. Messages are the driving force that represent commands, events, or prompts to an application or process in a Windows environment. Messages in a Windows environment are passed to a queue where they wait for the appropriate application or process to retrieve and process them. In Windows 3.*x*, if an application or process stopped retrieving its messages, the system would stop responding because all applications and processes shared a common message queue.

In Windows NT, all messages are redirected by the Win32 subsystem to the appropriate environment subsystem queue. For each application environment, you have a single message processing queue. This means that if a Win16 or OS/2 1.*x* application quits checking for and processing messages, the queue, the environment subsystem, and all of its applications stop responding. For Win32 applications, each application has its own message queue. Therefore, if a Win32 application stops checking its message queue, only that application is affected; the other Win32 and other subsystem applications continue to function properly.

Win16 VDM

Windows NT uses a single Virtual DOS Machine (VDM) for running 16-bit Windows applications. A VDM is a Windows NT process that emulates an *x*86 computer running MS-DOS. The Win16 subsystem was primarily included to provide backward compatibility for the large number of 16-bit Windows applications in use. This is less of an issue today because most popular applications now have a 32-bit version available, but a large number of Win16 applications are and will remain in use.

This Win16 VDM is referred to as Windows16 on Windows32 (WOW) and is handled by the WOWEXEC.EXE Windows NT process. (You probably recognize the phrase "…has caused an application fault in module WOWEXEC….") Similar to Windows95, Windows NT preemptively multitasks all of the application subsystems and the various Win32 applications. This means that in regards to processing time, the application subsystems and the Win32 applications preemptively multitask among themselves. Each application in the Win16 subsystem cooperatively multitasks, meaning that a single Win16 application can dominate all of the resources made available to the Win16 subsystem, which prevents any other Win16 applications from processing but does not affect the other subsystems. For instance, suppose you have three Win16 applications and two Win32 applications running (for simplicity's sake). Picture it as a round-robin, in that each time the opportunity for processing resources comes around, each Win32 application gets the opportunity for resources and one of the Win16 applications has the opportunity for resources. Ideally, the Win16 applications will take turns at each opportunity. But if one hangs, it can stop all of the other Win16 applications.

Finally, the Win16 VDM is responsible for *thunking*. Thunking is the process of translating 16-bit Windows APIs and messages into Win32-compatible APIs and messages. The Win16 subsystem thunks all calls to the system to a form that the Win32 can quickly and easily process.

Because all interaction with the system hardware in Windows NT is processed by device drivers or calls to the Hardware Abstraction Layer (good ol' HAL), any Win16 application that attempts to directly access hardware resources will fail. Most common of these are fax and communication programs.

An additional measure of protection and prevention provided by Windows NT is the capability to run Win16 applications in a separate memory space. By default, all Win16 applications share a common pool of memory. This has the potential for disaster if an errant application violates or accesses memory space reserved by another program or process. To prevent this, you can check the "Run in a separate memory space" option of a Win16 program's Properties. However, this does consume more memory.

MS-DOS VDM

MS-DOS based applications also are run in a VDM (which is fairly obvious if you've been paying attention!). Unlike in the Win16 subsystem, each MS-DOS application is run in its own VDM with its own virtual address space, protecting each from the other if one chooses to misbehave. One point of note here is that prior to this release of Windows NT, the Win16 and DOS support for RISC-based Windows NT systems was much more limited than on *x*86 systems. Fortunately that has changed, as you will see in the last section of this chapter.

Character-based DOS applications can run in either a full screen or a window. Graphical applications automatically switch to a full window. The exception here is RISC-based systems. On RISC systems, all MS-DOS based applications run in a window.

The MS-DOS VDM and all VDMs emulate an *x*86 computer with 16MB of virtual memory and MS-DOS 5.0. When an MS-DOS application attempts to directly access hardware resources, it's all over. The application terminates, and you are given a less than friendly message informing you of this. All in all, there is pretty good support for MS-DOS based applications. Sadly, I find myself using the Windows NT command prompt more than I did in Windows 3.*x*, because it can be a very useful tool.

POSIX Subsystem

The POSIX (Portable Operating System Interface for Computing Environments) subsystem is an attempt to provide support for UNIX applications and utilities. This task was a serious undertaking, as any UNIX user can imagine. Most UNIX systems aren't too compatible with each other, and here you have a Windows-based system trying to provide support for UNIX applications!

POSIX is an IEEE standard that was developed to provide some commonality to the various flavors of UNIX. This is similar to an open API in Windows, a common standard for which UNIX system makers can build in support. Application developers can write their applications to POSIX specifications, and the applications can run on any UNIX system that has POSIX support.

Windows NT provides support for POSIX.1 applications (IEEE 1003.1). At the time Windows NT was developed, POSIX.1 was the only version of this standard effort that had made it to final form, so this was the extent of the support that could be provided. POSIX.1 only addresses programming and API issues and, therefore, does not provide any support for the type of application environment necessary for the execution and operation of applications. Clearly, the UNIX support in Windows NT leaves much to be desired.

Much of the functionality of the POSIX subsystem requires access to an NTFS file system. In the UNIX world, you find something called *hard links*, which are almost the same as shortcuts. Hard links are files with multiple names. Also, like Windows NT, UNIX filenames are case-sensitive, so they require a file system that is case-sensitive, such as NTFS. If an application does not require access to the file system, an NTFS partition is not necessary.

> **NOTE**
>
> As I have mentioned several times, Windows NT has a modular architecture designed to be open and extensible. One of the first vendors to really tap into this and use it to provide an excellent addition to Windows NT is OpenSystems. OpenSystems has produced a product called OpenNT, which is an installable application subsystem to replace the POSIX.1 subsystem of Windows NT with a POISX.1 and POSIX.2 compliant subsystem. This greatly enhances the available UNIX support for Windows NT. With this new subsystem, you have all of the previous support for UNIX applications provided by Windows NT, with the addition of support for command shells (Bourne, C, and so on) and tools.

OS/2 Subsystem

The OS/2 subsystem of Windows NT supports OS/2 1.*x* 16-bit character mode applications. The OS/2 subsystem is not supported on RISC-based systems. However, real mode OS/2 applications can be run in the MS-DOS environment on RISC systems. For applications that can be run in either the OS/2 or MS-DOS subsystem, the OS/2 subsystem is always used if it is available.

Probably the most common application run on Windows NT that requires support from the OS/2 subsystem is Microsoft Mail Server. I learned this from painful experience (a week with Priority Technical Support troubleshooting Microsoft Mail Server, when the problem was the OS/2 subsystem that I had removed!). But ultimately I understand why it is true. Microsoft Mail Server was originally developed for Microsoft LAN Manager, which was developed to run on OS/2, which was originally jointly developed by Microsoft and IBM. Given this background information, you can see how the dependency developed. Unfortunately, it was not resolved until the release of Microsoft Exchange Server.

Windows NT cannot run OS/2 2.*x* or later applications, Presentation Manager applications, or OS/2 applications on RISC systems (except as noted previously). An OS/2 1.*x* Presentation Manager subsystem add-on is available from Microsoft for those who are interested.

Again, take note of the fact that support for HPFS is being phased out, as is support for OS/2 as a whole. In its current implementation, the OS/2 subsystem is nearly useless because OS/2 has progressed two version numbers and continues to lack widespread user or application support. It is reasonable to assume that there is no compelling reason to dedicate the necessary resources to write a new OS/2 subsystem. With Windows NT version 4, it is no longer possible to install the system onto a partition formatted with HPFS or to convert it during the installation process. If the HPFS partition must be used, it must be deleted and reformatted with FAT before installing Windows NT.

486 Emulation for RISC Systems

One of the most requested and welcome new features of Windows NT 4.0 is the new 486 processor emulation in VDMs for RISC-based systems. In the past, there was only 286 emulation for RISC systems in Windows NT. This prevented the system from running any enhanced mode Windows 3.*x* applications—which, if you are familiar with Windows applications, is most of them.

Windows NT 4.0 now provides support for 486 emulation, which opens up an abundance of new doors and probably quadruples the available applications for Windows NT on RISC systems. Windows NT on RISC can now run virtually any Windows application that can be run on an Intel Windows NT machine, such as the Microsoft Office suite or Visual Basic.

Summary

Windows NT is a somewhat unique operating system by virtue of its support for a wide range of external applications through the use of subsystems. This is made possible through the open and extensible architecture of Windows NT. Through the strict and intuitive development efforts of Microsoft, third party vendors can develop new subsystems that will plug into the operating system and provide added functionality.

Windows NT in a Software Development Environment

by Viktor Toth

IN THIS CHAPTER

CHAPTER 14

The year was 1993. The place was Microsoft's developer support forum on CompuServe. The deed was unspeakable. It was then that Microsoft announced its plans concerning its popular Visual C++ development system. And the one item that this plan lacked, to the surprise (not to mention bitter disappointment) of many developers, was new and improved 16-bit versions of this product. Instead, we were told that, beginning with version 2.0, Visual C++ would only run under Windows NT and would only produce code for the Win32 platform. The 16-bit version of Visual C++ (version 1.5) would not be further developed by Microsoft.

We developers were completely taken aback by this news. Our collective howl of surprise reverberated throughout the forums. "What?" we asked indignantly. "Just when Windows is finally becoming really mainstream, when serious companies are beginning to accept it as an environment on which to base major development efforts, the preeminent development system will no longer be supported? Has Microsoft completely lost its market sense? Do we need to turn to other third-party development products whose makers—unlike Microsoft—have not decided to abandon us?"

In soothing comments, Microsoft's forum staff pointed out that 32-bit programming is the wave of the future; that Windows NT, Microsoft's only 32-bit operating system at the time, offered a much more stable development environment than Windows 3.1; and that the 16-bit platform can still be targeted using 32-bit development tools and the 32-bit extension of Windows 3.1 known as Win32s. Still, this was little consolation. At a time when Windows NT was barely out of beta and Windows 95 was not yet on the horizon, not even under its "Chicago" nickname, dreams of a glorious 32-bit future were a poor substitute for our present 16-bit programming needs.

Much has changed in the few years since then. True to its promise, Windows NT became the preeminent desktop development environment for programs targeting not only the NT platform, but Windows 95, Windows 3.1 through Win32s, and even the Macintosh. Hardware prices dropped, so even self-employed developers like myself can afford the once high-priced workstations that are needed to run Windows NT effectively. Windows 95 became a viable lower-cost alternative supporting most development systems. Also, 32-bit development tools have evolved so much that it is now a real chore to turn back to outdated 16-bit programs when an old project needs some maintenance work, for example.

In the rest of this chapter, the role of the Windows NT operating system in a development environment is reviewed. Obviously, tomes could be written about the subject; here, I would like to focus on tools and development information from Microsoft, the company that is the primary source of Windows-based development applications. The goal of the chapter is to answer questions that are likely to be asked by nonprogrammer professionals who are planning or managing a development exercise. In the end, this chapter will assist you in assessing your needs concerning hardware, software, and expertise; and it will help you estimate the technical difficulties and risks involved. This chapter will also help you weigh the pros and cons of Windows NT when you are evaluating it as a prospective platform for a programming project.

Windows NT as a Reliable Development Platform

In response to the concerns raised on CompuServe back in 1993, Microsoft's forum staff responded by pointing out the strengths of Windows NT as a stable development platform. The well-known "edit-compile-test" cycle was more like "edit-compile-test-restart Windows" under Windows 3.1, due to that operating system's complete lack of stability in the face of ill-behaved applications. (And what application isn't ill-behaved when it is still under development?) NT promised to speed up the development cycle through its stability, by eliminating the time-consuming and nerve-racking "restart Windows" part from the cycle.

How can Windows NT be so much more stable than its predecessor? What are the key differences between how Windows 3.1 and Windows NT respond to ill-behaved applications? The difference lies in how Windows NT manages the memory of individual applications, how it manages system resources, and how multitasking between these applications is performed.

Windows NT and 32-bit Memory Management

Windows NT makes use of a number of advanced memory management capabilities found in modern microprocessors. Through these capabilities, it can completely isolate individual applications from each other. Because memory addresses are mapped to different regions of physical memory by the processor's hardware, it becomes physically impossible for one application to mess up the contents of memory owned by another application. (See Figure 14.1.) A randomly generated address either refers to valid memory that the application owns or causes an error (generates an operating system exception) when used, which causes the application to terminate. But the rest of the system, including other applications, remains unaffected.

Another consequence of this kind of 32-bit memory management is that the dreaded "memory models," which made the life of 16-bit Windows programmers so miserable, are now a thing of the past. Application programmers no longer need to be concerned about tiny 64KB code and data segments, incompatible memory models, near and far pointers, huge arrays, and all the other paraphernalia of 16-bit programming on Intel processors.

Windows NT and System Resources

The About dialog in the Windows 3.1 Program Manager shows the amount of available memory and the percentage of free resources. This percentage value refers to several specific areas of memory used by Windows for storing information on windows an application created, fonts, pens, brushes, bitmap patterns, and other tools used (and shared) by applications. Unfortunately, Windows 3.1 did not do a very good job of managing these areas; in particular, when an application terminated abnormally, its allocated resources often remained allocated. The next time the application ran, it allocated a new set of resources. If it crashed again, those resources also remained allocated, taking up yet more of the areas reserved for these system resources. It takes little arithmetic to understand that if an application used up 20 percent of

14

A SOFTWARE
DEVELOPMENT
ENVIRONMENT

system resources, after crashing four or five times it quickly left the system in an unstable state from which the only way to recover was to restart Windows. Needless to say, the ones who experience application crashes the most often are the ones who deal routinely with incomplete, untested code: software developers.

FIGURE 14.1.

Mapping application addresses to physical memory.

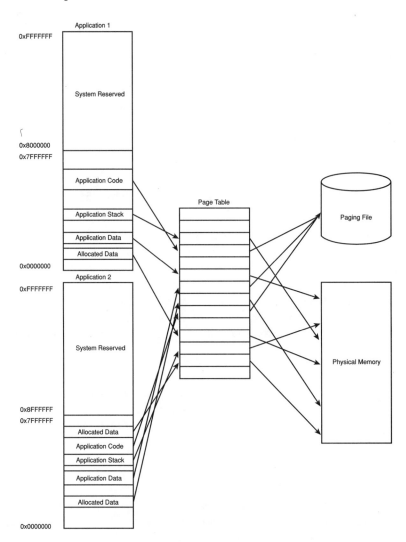

Windows NT does a much better job in the area of managing resources. Not only are much bigger (virtually unlimited) memory areas used for this purpose, but NT also tracks ownership of various system objects and is ready to delete them if the application that owns them terminates without freeing resources first. This does not relieve the programmer of the responsibility of properly freeing any allocated resources. (Otherwise, an application that runs for an extended period of time uses up an ever-growing amount of system memory.) However, this does alleviate the difficulties associated with program crashes.

Multitasking

Multitasking is another area addressed very differently by Windows 3.1 and Windows NT. With the exception of MS-DOS windows, Windows 3.1 relied exclusively on a cooperative multitasking scheme. This meant that applications had to regularly call specific system functions in order to yield control to other applications. This also meant that if an application failed to act this way, the entire system became frozen and unresponsive. The only way out was to perform the infamous "three finger salute"—that is, hitting Ctrl+Alt+Delete—and let Windows stop the failed program. However, for reasons explained earlier, Windows fails to clean up properly after forcibly removing the application and will likely become unstable afterward.

Windows NT, on the other hand, provides preemptive multitasking. In other words, Windows NT forcibly interrupts a running process to give way to other processes, even if that process fails to yield as 16-bit applications should. Applications must still regularly interact with Windows in order for their own user interface to remain responsive, but failing to do so no longer brings down the entire system.

Windows NT is also more reliable when it comes to shutting down misbehaving programs. To make a long story short, NT can terminate a running application while completely preserving the integrity of the operating system. (See Figure 14.2.) It is this stability that makes Windows NT a very desirable platform for software development work.

FIGURE 14.2.

Terminating Microsoft Word through the Windows NT Task Manager.

14

A SOFTWARE
DEVELOPMENT
ENVIRONMENT

Hardware Requirements for Developers

No developer on this planet will refuse an offer of a four-processor Pentium Pro system with 256 megabytes of memory, tens of gigabytes of disk space in a RAID array, and a 30-inch monitor as his personal workstation. Unfortunately, very few organizations can afford to equip their programmers with computers that carry five- or six-digit price tags. On the other hand, you cannot realistically use yesterday's 8MB 486SX25 computer and expect state-of-the-art development tools to function properly. Windows NT requires a considerable amount of horsepower, and most development tools are resource-hungry beasts in their own right. What, then, is a reasonable middle ground that is suitable as a platform for most development tools?

You could begin with the processor. Although a Pentium Pro might not be necessary, any programmer's workstation should contain at least a 100 MHz Pentium-compatible processor. Not only is Windows NT rather demanding in this regard, but so are the development tools themselves. Anything less than a Pentium and your C++ compiler, for example, will appear to crawl.

On the memory side, the smallest reasonable amount of memory for development purposes is 32MB. Although individual development tools might run in less memory (for example, the Visual C++ manual states 24MB as the product's minimum memory requirement under Windows NT), development work often consists of utilizing several tools at once. Also, keep in mind the fact that your potentially memory-hungry application will need to share available memory with the development tools used for debugging.

Development work can take a toll on disk space as well. Once "lean-and-mean" tools have become notorious for using prodigious amounts of disk space. Again, take Visual C++ as an example: Even simple projects can take 10MB to 15MB each, due to the large size of some intermediate files created during compilation (in particular, precompiled header files). These files can be safely deleted when a project is archived. However, while the project is under development (with potentially several versions on disk), these intermediate files are needed for fast recompilation. Therefore, a disk size of 2GB or more might be required.

One device that no development system can exist without is a CD-ROM drive. Most new development tools are only available on CD-ROM. Putting them on lower-density media would be completely impractical due to the large amount of data, such as help files and online documentation, that is packed on these disks. Although a CD-ROM drive is therefore essential, you don't necessarily need one of those new 10-speed wonders. The drives are not used for multimedia playback but as a depository of large amounts of searchable information; frequently accessed tools, such as compiler executables, are typically copied to the hard disk anyway. Because of this, I am still perfectly satisfied with the four-year-old, double-speed unit that I use in my everyday work.

A rather controversial issue concerns monitors. Does a programmer really require a high-priced, high-resolution display? Would such a device not be wasted on him, because it would be used mostly for viewing dirty pictures downloaded from the World Wide Web? (Or so your boss might think!) In answer to these questions, consider that most programmers spend at least eight hours a day, and usually more, in front of that monitor. And they do spend most of that time actually looking at the screen, unlike those in other professions who turn to their computers only part of the time during their working day. The work performed by programmers also involves some visual design; perhaps they are not graphic artists, but they still need to design the occasional dialog or report layout for an application. Furthermore, programmers more than anyone else tend to use a large number of windows simultaneously. Trying to arrange those on a screen that has little useful real estate to offer can be rather awkward. Last but not least, programmers must *test* their applications using a variety of screen resolutions that will likely be employed by users of their software. For these reasons, I would not recommend anything less than a 17-inch monitor, capable of a resolution of at least 1024×768 pixels, to be used on a programmer's desktop.

These specifications are merely guidelines for a minimal development system. Specific projects might impose specific requirements on the hardware used by the development team. More memory, more disk space, or better screen resolution could be required if the programmer's task is to develop and test memory-intensive, storage-intensive, or highly graphical applications.

Developing Windows NT Applications

The most obvious target for Windows NT–based application development is Windows NT itself. Creating Windows NT applications is accomplished through the Windows NT Software Development Kit (SDK). Creating hardware device drivers requires another tool—the Device Driver Kit (DDK). Both of these tools are distributed through the Microsoft Developer Network (MSDN) subscription service.

Neither the SDK nor the DDK is useful by itself. These kits contain software libraries, utility programs, and debugging tools; they do not contain development tools such as compilers. These tools must be acquired separately. On the other hand, many development tools are packaged with either the complete Win32 SDK or a reasonable subset of it. For example, for many development projects, it is sufficient to acquire the Visual C++ development system; there is no need to acquire the Win32 SDK separately.

The Win32 API and SDK

As with any other operating system, programming for Windows NT is accomplished through a series of operating system functions, organized into a collection often referred to as the API, or Applications Programming Interface. These functions are primarily intended to be called from the C or C++ programming languages, but they can easily be accessed from a variety of other languages, such as Visual Basic or FORTRAN.

The core API used for Windows NT programming is, in fact, a more generic collection of functions, which is commonly referred to as the Win32 API. In addition to Windows NT, Windows 95 and Win32s also provide a somewhat less complete implementation of this API. Furthermore, some Win32 implementations exist on other operating systems such as UNIX.

The Win32 API itself is subdivided into a number of programming areas. Those relate, for example, to managing windows, drawing to graphical devices such as the screen or printer, displaying dialogs, displaying menus, interacting with the Windows clipboard, or accepting keyboard and mouse input.

In addition to the Win32 API, a number of other, supplemental APIs and other components are part of the Win32 SDK. These include the programming interfaces to OLE (Object Linking and Embedding), Microsoft RPC (Remote Procedure Calls), the Messaging API (MAPI), the Telephony API (TAPI), OpenGL, and multimedia interfaces. From time to time, Microsoft adds new components to the Win32 SDK. Also, existing SDK components might not equally apply to all Win32 implementations; for example, OpenGL was implemented under Windows NT long before it was introduced under Windows 95, and it remains unavailable for Win32s programs running under Windows 3.1.

The Win32 SDK also includes a series of tools that are useful to the programmer. One such tool is the Pview utility that allows you to list all running applications (see Figure 14.3).

FIGURE 14.3.

Viewing processes with PView.

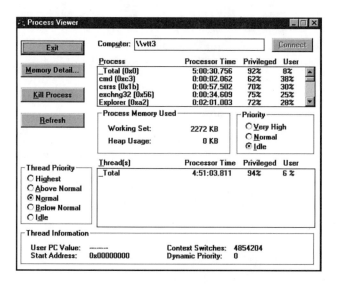

The Win32 SDK also contains the Microsoft Setup Toolkit, a toolkit for creating distribution disk sets and setup programs. However, this toolkit has largely been superseded by other, more powerful third-party utilities that offer benefits such as uninstall functionality in accordance with Windows 95 application compatibility requirements. The most widely used of these toolkits is the InstallShield utility from Stirling Technologies; a limited version of this utility is packaged with Microsoft's Visual C++ system.

Programmers might need to use additional SDKs from time to time—SDKs that are not, strictly speaking, part of the Win32 SDK. These include the ODBC SDK, the DAO SDK, or SDKs specific to other software packages, such as Microsoft's BackOffice SDK.

The Windows NT DDK

Under normal circumstances, Windows NT completely separates application programs from the underlying computer hardware. This separation is accomplished, in part, through a series of *drivers*. This separation also means that any new hardware requires driver software before it can be accessed from a Windows NT application. Such drivers can be developed using the Windows NT DDK.

Windows NT recognizes two types of drivers: *user-mode* drivers and *kernel-mode* drivers. The crucial difference between the two is that kernel-mode drivers operate as part of the Windows NT Executive—the core of the Windows NT operating system. As such, they have more unrestricted access to system resources and can operate at better performance, albeit at a risk: Bugs in kernel-mode drivers are much more likely to threaten the stability of the operating system overall. This is the reason behind the debate concerning Microsoft's recent decision to change video drivers into kernel-mode drivers for improved performance. As demonstrated by a recent BYTE magazine article, there are some fears that, because of this decision, Windows NT 4.0 might be faster but also less stable than its predecessors.

The language of choice for driver development is sometimes not C or C++ but assembly language, for reasons of performance. Microsoft's MASM macro assembler, version 6.11 is most often used for this purpose.

Development Tools

The number of development tools on the market that can be used to develop Windows NT applications is too numerous to count. But there is a relatively small set of "core" tools that are used in the development of a majority of applications. Although the core tools are based on technology developed by Microsoft, they contain an increasing number of components developed by third parties. This is due, in part, to the rapidly evolving concept of component-based programming that was first introduced to Windows programmers by Visual Basic and its VBXs (Visual Basic Custom Controls). VBXs are now largely a thing of the 16-bit past, replaced by the substantially more powerful technology of OCXs (OLE Custom Controls), now also referred to as ActiveX controls. All indications are that OCXs will play an increasingly important role in future development projects.

Rapid Application Prototyping with 32-bit Visual Basic

The story of Visual Basic is the story of a runaway success. Since the introduction of Windows, Windows programming has grown increasingly difficult over the years. Programmers had to master a variety of difficult-to-grasp concepts for event-driven programming in a message-based cooperative multitasking environment. Using the C programming language did not exactly help either; the shortest Windows example programs typically ran at several hundred lines of code, making them formidable objects of study for the beginner.

Visual Basic changed all that by providing an easy-to-use programming environment for the novice programmer. Many simple programming tasks did not require any programming skills at all; instead, all the programmer had to do was to manipulate objects (such as dialog elements) on the screen graphically.

To demonstrate this, it might be instructional to look at a very simple Visual Basic program. In the text-oriented world of C programming, a classic test program is a simple one that merely prints the message "Hello, World!" on the screen and then exits. This program's Visual Basic analog, shown in Figure 14.4, displays the same text in a dialog that can be dismissed by clicking on the OK button.

FIGURE 14.4.

A "Hello, World!" application in Visual Basic.

This dialog can be created, astonishingly enough, without writing more than a single line of Visual Basic code. All you need to do is place two controls—a static text and a button control—on a blank Visual Basic form and the application is almost complete. The one line of code that needs to be written controls the OK button's behavior. By double-clicking on this button while in form design mode, the procedure that belongs to the button, `Command1_Click`, can be opened. Into this procedure, a single line, containing a single Visual Basic command (the `End` command) needs to be inserted:

```
Private Sub Command1_Click()
End
End Sub
```

When this is done, the application can be run from Visual Basic or compiled into a stand-alone executable program.

In addition to its ease of use, Visual Basic's other main strength is its versatility that is accomplished through the use of custom controls. Like the simple button or static text controls in our example, custom controls representing complex functionality can often be simply dropped into a Visual Basic form. For example, Figure 14.5 shows a Visual Basic application that sports a custom Graph control. Creating this application was not any more difficult than creating the previous example. Controlling the graph's contents programmatically, perhaps by reading numerical data from a file, requires only a few additional lines of code.

FIGURE 14.5.

A simple Visual Basic charting application.

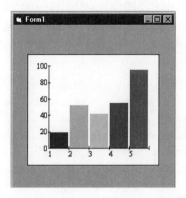

Visual Basic is now into its fourth incarnation, with version 5 expected soon. Version 4 was Visual Basic's first 32-bit implementation. Visual Basic 4.0 is also compatible with many versions of Microsoft's Visual Basic for Applications (VBA), the customization language of many Microsoft Office applications such as Microsoft Excel, Microsoft Access, and soon to come, Microsoft Word.

Visual Basic for Applications can also be added as the customization language for applications that you develop. Microsoft provides a variety of licensing options through third parties that allow you to incorporate the Visual Basic engine into your development project.

Visual Basic comes in three different editions. The Standard edition contains essential features; the Professional edition adds support for the development of 16-bit applications, OLE objects, and client/server solutions; and, finally, the Enterprise edition provides support for distributed workgroup applications. The Enterprise edition also includes a copy of Visual SourceSafe, Microsoft's version management system.

Visual Basic's ease of use makes it the language of choice for application prototyping. Even complex user interfaces can be modeled easily by putting together application dialogs graphically and adding the necessary few lines of code. Visual Basic can also serve you well as a system integration tool; it can be an excellent front-end development environment for many database servers that can be accessed through Microsoft's ODBC (Open Database Connectivity) or DAO (Data Access Objects).

The major drawback of Visual Basic is that it is an interpreted language. Programs written in interpreted languages are generally executed substantially more slowly than compiled programs. For this reason, writing performance-sensitive applications in Visual Basic is not recommended.

The one drawback that isn't really a drawback: A few years ago, most "serious" programmers would not have considered Basic as a serious programming language. Visual Basic has changed all that and become a preeminent Windows development tool.

Developing Professional Applications with Visual C++

Notwithstanding the success of Visual Basic, Microsoft's Visual C++ remains the company's flagship development environment and the development system of choice for most complex development projects.

My first professional encounter with Microsoft's C compiler was in 1989, when I worked on an MS-DOS–based software project for Canada Post Corporation. Back then, the entire compiler and development system fit on a handful of floppy disks. Although the compiler was recognized as high quality, Microsoft was remarkably late in producing a C++ compiler (and thus opened up the market for companies such as Borland). It was surmised that the company intended to wait until the C++ standard was finalized, in order to avoid the difficulties of coping with changes in a proposed standard. Whatever the reasons, eventually a C++ compiler was produced, soon to be followed by a Windows-based development workbench, the IDE (Integrated Development Environment) of Visual C++.

Present day, 32-bit versions of Visual C++ (at the time of this writing, the latest is version 4.2) are enormously complex 32-bit development powerhouses. The two most distinguishing features of Visual C++ are its AppWizards and its integration with the MFC (Microsoft Foundation Classes) library.

Back in the pre-C++ days of Windows development, many programs written in the C language were based on a simple application provided by Microsoft, the Generic application sample. This 600-odd line application did exactly nothing, but it did that in compliance with Windows user interface standards and recommendations. In other words, the program merely created a blank window with no functionality attached. However, it provided menu support, support for keyboard shortcuts, an About dialog, and some basic menu commands—that is, all the common user interface elements of Windows programs.

Visual C++ AppWizards carry this concept much further. Instead of a simple generic application skeleton, AppWizards can dynamically generate a customized skeleton that already provides support for many application features. For example, when you specify that you want to create an MDI (Multiple Document Interface) application, the AppWizard generates a skeleton application that already provides code managing multiple windows, a toolbar, a status bar, and partially functional code for loading and saving documents or printing. Or, if you request that AppWizard create an ODBC or DAO based database application, the generated skeleton will already include code that opens the database and browses its records. In short, AppWizards save you the burden of creating thousands of lines of code that is common to many applications.

Figure 14.6 illustrates the power of AppWizards. The application shown here was generated as an MDI application with OLE server and client capabilities and support for MAPI and context-sensitive help. The generated application was compiled as is, without adding any code. Yet, it already supports embedded OLE objects; in-place editing; and saving, loading, printing, and e-mailing files containing OLE objects.

FIGURE 14.6.

An AppWizard-generated OLE application skeleton.

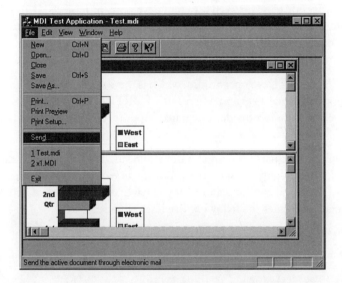

The power of AppWizards is due, in part, to the Microsoft Foundation Classes library. This library consists of a large number of C++ classes that encapsulate most areas of Windows functionality. At the heart of MFC is an application model based on the dual concepts of *documents* and *views*. A document, in this abstract sense, is the collection of data that an application would typically save in a file; views are visual representations of these documents that also provide the means for user interaction. A document can be associated with multiple views; for example, a word processor application can provide several child windows, each displaying different portions of the same document.

An AppWizard-generated skeleton application contains C++ classes derived from the base document and view classes, implementing specific functionality requested through AppWizard. For example, when an OLE container application is generated, the AppWizard creates a view class that already has rudimentary code for displaying embedded objects.

Other key MFC classes encapsulate such fundamental Windows programming concepts as windows, dialogs, tool bars, and control bars; device contexts, pens, brushes, bitmaps, fonts, and other drawing tools; OLE objects and containers; applications, threads, and system exceptions; and lower-level building blocks such as generalized objects, rectangles, points, or character strings.

14

A SOFTWARE
DEVELOPMENT
ENVIRONMENT

Not all Visual C++ projects do (or can) use the MFC "framework application" model. Visual C++ is also the development tool of choice when writing Windows NT service applications or 32-bit dynamic link libraries (DLLs). A special AppWizard assists in the development of OLE controls (OCXs), again enormously simplifying this task.

Another powerful new Visual C++ feature is the Component Gallery. This feature provides for efficient code reuse between different development projects. It also comes loaded with a number of goodies from Microsoft that can be used to enhance a skeleton application. These goodies include add-on components implementing clipboard commands, MAPI support, OLE automation, palette support, a variety of dialogs, and much more.

The Microsoft Developer Studio, which is the Visual C++ IDE, is also the IDE for Microsoft's Java tool (Visual J++) and Microsoft's FORTRAN Powerstation product. Furthermore, the Developer Studio provides integrated support for Microsoft's version management tool, Visual SourceSafe.

Finally, the Visual C++ compiler can also be used as a command line tool. Simple applications (typically text-only console applications) can easily be written and compiled from within an MS-DOS window. For example, if you have access to a system with Visual C++ installed, you might try to enter the following five lines of code:

```
#include <windows.h>

int WINAPI WinMain(HINSTANCE d1, HINSTANCE d2, LPSTR d3, int d4)
{
    MessageBox(NULL, "Hello, World!", "", MB_OK);
}
```

This is the simplest Windows equivalent of the infamous "Hello, World!" C application. Save this file as HELLO.C and type `cl hello.c user32.lib` at the Windows NT command line. The resulting file, HELLO.EXE, is a fully functional Windows NT program.

Developing for the Internet with Visual J++

Visual J++ is Microsoft's new development system for the Java language. It is a powerful development environment for Java scripts and applets. Visual J++ provides support (among other things) for Microsoft's ActiveX controls, and uses the same Developer Studio as Visual C++ and Fortran PowerStation. It also extends the power of AppWizards to the Java universe, automating the creation of simple Java application skeletons. Visual J++ works in conjunction with Internet Explorer 3.0, which provides the runtime and debugging environment for Java code.

The Microsoft Macro Assembler

The venerable old Microsoft Macro Assembler (MASM) is perhaps the oldest development tool in existence for MS-DOS and its distant relatives such as Windows NT. Version 6.11 is the latest 32-bit version of this distinguished macro assembler.

The importance of assembly language programming has diminished over the years. One obvious reason for this is that assembly language code is by definition processor-dependent; thus, any assembly language portions of an application would have to be completely rewritten if the application is ported to another hardware platform. Because of this and other reasons, most development projects nowadays contain no assembly language code at all. In many other cases, for the few assembly language instructions required, the inline assembler capability of languages such as C++ is sufficient. However, in the few cases when serious assembly language programming is needed, it is needed badly—and the tool of choice in these cases is MASM.

Compared with other graphical development environments, MASM is rather Spartan in appearance. The package consists of little more than a set of command-line tools for assembling and linking an assembly language program. However, these command-line tools can be invoked from within other tools. Therefore, it is possible, for example, to use the Visual C++ Developer Studio for editing and compiling MASM programs. Because most applications that use MASM code will nevertheless not be pure assembly language applications, this is often the preferred way for using MASM. By invoking it from the IDE of your development system, you can handle all your project's source files from within a single front-end tool.

Microsoft Office

Many development projects do not require the power and flexibility of dedicated development tools. Instead, these projects are implemented using the automation capabilities inherent to applications in the Microsoft Office suite.

Members of the Office 95 application family are all 32-bit applications. Despite the fact that their name implies versions for Windows 95, these applications also run under Windows NT 3.51 or later.

> **NOTE**
>
> There are known compatibility problems with Microsoft Access 95 and Microsoft Project 95 under Windows NT 4.0. Updated versions of these applications are available from Microsoft.

Two of the Office 95 applications, Excel and Access, use Visual Basic for Applications (VBA) as a macro or automation language. Microsoft Word still uses its own WordBasic language for the time being. These applications are all quite capable tools that can help solve many office automation problems.

For example, Word can be used for document automation. Through a combination of macros and form fields, many complex solutions are possible. Excel would be a powerful application even without a macro language capability, because it could still be used for automating tables; with the macro language, Excel becomes such a powerful platform that on many occasions it has been selected as a front-end for system integration projects. These applications also support a variety of methods for interoperability, such as OLE or DDE.

Microsoft Access, a relational database development system, is closer to being a "pure" development tool. Its visual interface makes it possible for nonprogrammers to create simple database solutions complete with customized forms and reports. More sophisticated solutions are possible through Visual Basic for Application code modules.

Two applications that are not part of the Microsoft Office suite should nevertheless be mentioned here. One is Project, Microsoft's project management application that, like Excel or Access, relies on Visual Basic for Applications to provide office automation capability. The other is Visual FoxPro, the latest in the FoxPro line of "Xbase" relational database development systems.

> **NOTE**
>
> Two Microsoft Office components, PowerPoint and Schedule+, do not offer macro language capabilities and are therefore not mentioned here. However, it is possible to develop extensions to Schedule+ using OLE Automation. The Microsoft Office Binder also exposes Binder objects through this interface.

Other Tools

A review of the tools provided by Microsoft would not be complete without mentioning Visual Test and Visual SourceSafe. (Yes, it seems that "Visual" is a mandatory adjective in new development product names.)

Visual Test is a test automation tool. This tool enables you to create testing scenarios and automate many repetitive testing tasks. Visual Test is another development application that uses the Developer Studio as its user interface.

Visual SourceSafe is a version management tool that is integrated with Visual Basic and the Developer Studio of Visual C++, Visual J++, and Fortran PowerStation. SourceSafe is particularly suited for projects that involve large development teams.

Third-Party Tools and Libraries

By this time, you are probably convinced that I am a paid agent of Microsoft, devoting so much of this chapter to development tools and utilities offered by the sometimes loved, often despised software giant. Regretfully, I am not that fortunate; my reasons for organizing the chapter in this fashion are not financial. Instead, the chapter reflects my preference to select development tools from the operating system's manufacturer if possible, and it also reflects the fact that Microsoft has by far the most extensive line of development products on the market.

Nevertheless, tools are available from other manufacturers, and it is sometimes necessary to work with them—for example, when maintaining a legacy application. At other times, heretical as it might sound, there are simply tools that are better than anything Microsoft offers.

For a long time, this was true of Borland's C++ compiler product. Long before Microsoft added C++ support to its C compiler, Borland already offered a high-quality C/C++ compiler for DOS and Windows development. Borland's current version is also a notable product with capabilities that in some areas even exceed those of Microsoft's Visual C++. In particular, I am of the opinion that Borland showed a greater commitment to continuing support of 16-bit development under Windows 3.1, an area Microsoft abandoned perhaps somewhat prematurely when the company stopped further development of its 16-bit C++ compiler, Visual C++ 1.52. Borland C++, in addition to supporting the company's own Object Windows Library (OWL), also provides full support for the Microsoft Foundation Classes (MFC). If you do not feel satisfied with Visual C++ or if you simply believe that Microsoft is big enough already without your financial contribution, Borland's C++ is definitely a compiler worth looking into.

Borland has another product that demands the attention of the serious developer. Of course, I am referring to Delphi, Borland's Rapid Application Development product. Calling Delphi Borland's "answer to Visual Basic" would be highly unfair, because Delphi is far from being yet another Basic interpreter. It is a unique product that combines the advantages of a compiled object-oriented programming language (Object Pascal), component-based programming through the Visual Component Library (VCL), and support for key Microsoft technologies such as OLE or ODBC. Delphi also offers support for Internet and Web development, ActiveX (OLE) controls, and the Microsoft Internet Information Server API, ISAPI.

Symantec is another company offering a high-quality C++ compiler. Symantec C++ also supports 32-bit development, the Microsoft Foundation Classes, and other core Windows technologies.

Another notable C++ compiler is Watcom C++, from Powersoft Corporation. The company's other popular product is PowerBuilder, which is for the development of client/server applications. Powersoft is also the manufacturer of the Watcom Fortran compiler.

This list is, of course, far from complete. Many other companies offer full-featured development products, code libraries, class libraries, testing and debugging tools, OLE controls, and other components. Information about these can often be found on the Internet. On other occasions, promotional versions offering varying degrees of functionality are distributed as special offers. For example, the version 4.1 Visual C++ subscription release contained such promotional editions of several third-party OLE controls that I found particularly useful for a project I was working on recently.

14

A SOFTWARE
DEVELOPMENT
ENVIRONMENT

Cross-Platform Development

So far, this chapter has concentrated on tools that help you develop Windows NT–based applications and automation solutions. However, Windows NT can also be effectively used for developing applications targeted for other platforms. These can include other Windows platforms as well as some non-Windows platforms such as UNIX or the Macintosh.

Developing for Windows 95

Because Windows NT 4.0 and Windows 95 share an almost identical API, most applications developed for one platform will run without modifications on the other. Exceptions include applications that utilize platform-specific features.

Most notably, Windows 95 does not support some of the advanced features of Windows NT in the areas of security, Unicode, the server side of client/server communications, and graphics. Applications that make use of these features must be modified before they can be run on Windows 95.

Many other differences between Windows 95 and Windows NT became a thing of the past with NT 3.51 and, now, with 4.0. Beginning with 3.51, Windows NT provides support for the new Windows 95 common controls; NT 4.0 adds support for shell extensions and other new Windows 95 features such as the DirectX API used for fast, arcade-quality video and sound in multimedia and entertainment software.

The tools used for Windows 95 development are the same as those used for developing NT applications. Windows 95 and Windows NT (Intel version) are binary code compatible.

32-bit Applications and Win32s

Although Windows 3.1 is a thing of the past, it has not been completely forgotten by Microsoft. Many new 32-bit applications can be run under Windows 3.1 using the Win32s extensions. Although the applications themselves run on that platform, the same is not true for development tools; the preferred development platform for Win32s applications is, in fact, Windows NT.

Most of the tools used for Windows NT programming can be used for developing Win32 applications. A notable exception is Visual C++: Beginning with version 4.2, Microsoft has discontinued support for Win32s development. The restrictions imposed on the developer by Win32s are severe. An application that must run under Win32s cannot use a variety of additional Windows NT features. But, through careful design and testing, it is easy to develop applications that run on all three platforms using a single binary executable.

Windows NT is also frequently used for remote debugging of Win32s programs. For example, Visual C++ 4.1 provides a remote debugging feature. The application under test would run on a Win32s workstation that is equipped with the Win32s debugging components of Visual C++.

The workstation would be connected to the developer's Windows NT machine using a serial cable, and the developer would use the Developer Studio's integrated debugger.

Developing 16-bit Windows Applications

Windows NT can also be used as the host for many 16-bit development tools. For example, it is possible to run Visual C++ 1.52 or 16-bit versions of Visual Basic on a Windows NT platform. However, only "well-behaved" Windows 3.1 applications can be developed this way. Any applications that attempt to directly access hardware, for instance, would fail under the 16-bit Windows on Windows (WOW) subsystem of Windows NT.

Tools for 16-bit Windows 3.1 development can also be used on the non-Intel versions of Windows NT through the Intel processor emulation available on these platforms.

Developing Applications for the Macintosh

Microsoft's Visual C++ provides a means for cross-platform development for the Macintosh computer. The primary benefit of this is portability; the same code base can be used for Windows and Macintosh versions of the same application, thereby providing very significant savings in terms of the development effort.

The Macintosh Cross-Platform Development Edition of Visual C++ must be purchased separately. It runs on Intel processors using Windows NT 3.51 or later.

Writing POSIX Applications

One Windows NT feature is the operating system's support for POSIX applications. POSIX is an acronym for Portable Operating System Interface and consists of a collection of ISO (International Standards Organization) standards or proposed standards. Windows NT provides POSIX.1 compatibility through a series of C header files and libraries. These are available as part of the Win32 SDK.

POSIX applications run under the Windows NT POSIX subsystem. This subsystem provides a series of POSIX-compatible services. For example, the subsystem provides access to file systems using POSIX naming conventions (for instance, `//C/subdir/execute.exe` instead of `C:\subdir\execute.exe`).

POSIX applications are compatible with source code across operating systems. A POSIX application that is strictly compliant (that is, an application that does not use libraries or operating system services beyond those specified in the standard) requires no modification prior to recompilation. Note that POSIX, on the other hand, does not provide binary code compatibility—not even on the same hardware platform. Thus, a POSIX application compiled under Windows NT, for example, would need to be recompiled under the Linux operating system.

14

A SOFTWARE
DEVELOPMENT
ENVIRONMENT

Porting Programs to Windows NT

So far, you have learned how to use Windows NT as a platform for developing new applications. Often, however, the problem involves moving an existing application to the Windows NT platform. Such a porting exercise most commonly involves 16-bit Windows 3.1 applications; less frequently, it becomes necessary to port applications from the UNIX or X Window System programming environments.

Porting 16-bit Windows Applications

Although 16-bit Windows applications can be run "as is" under Windows NT's Windows on Windows (WOW) 16-bit subsystem, this solution is often not sufficient. A true porting to the 32-bit environment is desirable for the ability to take advantage of Windows NT's "robustness features," improved 32-bit performance, or other services provided by the operating system. Because ported applications can also run better under Windows 95 (unless they utilize features specific to Windows NT), that can represent another incentive for porting.

Because of the similarities between the Windows 3.1 API and the Win32 API, porting is often an almost trivial exercise, at least in the case of simpler applications. The vast majority of Windows 3.1 API functions exist in identical or near identical form in the 32-bit environment. The few that are not implemented have functional equivalents, and replacing them in the source code is relatively easy.

One of the most notorious porting problems involves the difference in *word size* between the two environments. Under Windows 3.1, a *word* represents 2 bytes (or 16 bits) of storage; under Windows NT, a word is 4 bytes (or 32 bits). This difference is reflected in the C programming language in the int built-in type. An int under Windows 3.1 is 16 bits, and under Windows NT it is 32 bits. Although well-written programs should never rely on such operating system dependencies, the fact is that many real-life programs do. Bad programming habits, sloppy quality assurance, and the need to use legacy code can all be reasons why such dependencies creep into projects. Programs that are being ported must be carefully analyzed for dependencies like these, and those dependencies must be resolved before the ported program can be released as a robust Windows NT application.

The porting of C/C++ programs can also be made easier by using Microsoft's PORTTOOL.EXE utility. This utility can identify potential porting problems in your source code by finding references to API functions and Windows messages that changed or are no longer supported.

Porting UNIX Programs

Porting simple text-based UNIX utilities to Windows NT is often easier than it sounds—easier, in fact, than porting the same utilities to MS-DOS. The two main reasons for this are an identical word size and the ability to access many Win32 functions from a console program.

Like Windows NT, most UNIX implementations are 32-bit. For historical reasons, many UNIX C programs (especially older source code) implicitly assume an equivalence between the size of a pointer (that is, the address of a memory location) and the size of an integer. This makes porting some UNIX utilities to MS-DOS very difficult. However, under Windows NT the two types have the same size, so ported UNIX code will behave as expected.

Application programs running in MS-DOS windows under Windows 3.1 have no access to functions in the Windows 3.1 API. This is not so under Windows NT; console applications can access Win32 API functions. This makes these applications considerably more flexible because they can access operating system services that are hidden from MS-DOS applications. A good example for this is the WinSock socket library; Windows NT console applications can make most socket calls. This makes porting many UNIX applications easier; for example, text-based UNIX applications that use Berkeley-style sockets for communication over the Internet require very little change to run under Windows NT.

Accepting that, the difficulties associated with the porting of complex UNIX applications to Windows NT should not be underestimated. The NT multitasking model, the operation of the NT file system, and the Win32 API are all substantially different from anything found under UNIX. The porting of applications that use features (such as Sun RPC, System V shared memory) specific to a UNIX implementation can also present formidable porting obstacles.

Porting X Applications

The X Window System is a windowing system; Windows NT has a windowing subsystem. Here, the similarities end. The differences between the X Window System API and the Win32 API are so substantial that straightforward porting of X applications to Windows NT is not conceivable.

Consequently, unless you are prepared to spend a great deal of effort on what in essence would be the redevelopment of large chunks of your X code, alternative avenues might need to be explored. Fortunately, the situation is not entirely hopeless. It is possible to compile the X11R6 libraries under Windows NT and link your X code with it. On the server side, several companies provide X server implementations that run under Windows NT. My preference is an X server called Micro X-Win32 from StarNet Communications. This implementation can use Windows NT as its window manager, so that X Window applications run in their own top-level Windows NT windows. Using this server, I often have windows side by side belonging to applications that run on several different computers. (See Figure 14.7.)

Developer Resources

No discussion on Windows NT software development can be complete without mentioning some of the essential information resources available to developers. These resources fall into two basic categories: those distributed offline (for instance, on CD-ROM), and those available online, through the World Wide Web or through proprietary online services.

FIGURE 14.7.
X Window System applications running on a Windows NT X server.

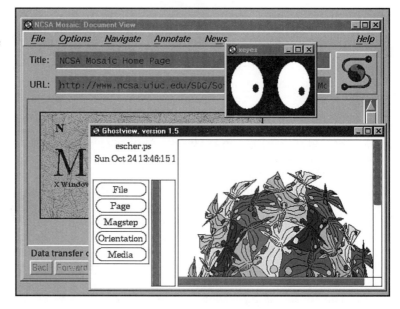

The Microsoft Developer Network

Perhaps the most useful CD-ROM collection on any Windows developer's desk is the Microsoft Developer Network's (MSDN) quarterly published CD-ROM set. The CDs include complete documentation in searchable electronic form on Microsoft's operating systems, development kits, and development tools; the Microsoft Knowledge Base of bug reports, resolutions, and other advice; other publications and books; and vast amounts of sample source code. Additionally, subscriptions are available that contain complete operating system and development tool releases.

Microsoft recently repackaged and restructured the Developer Network product. Currently, four subscription levels are available:

- The MSDN Library subscription currently consists of a pair of quarterly CDs that contain all product documentation, books and periodicals, sample code, and the Knowledge Base in a searchable electronic library form.

- The Professional subscription adds a series of CDs (typically 15 to 30 CDs quarterly) that contain all current Microsoft operating system releases (with the exception of Windows NT Server) and Software Development Kits (SDKs). Optionally, at no extra charge, DDKs (Device Driver Kits) and international operating system versions are also available to Professional level subscribers.

- The Enterprise subscription completes the set of operating system platforms by adding Windows NT server. It also includes all Microsoft BackOffice components (such as SQL Server and Exchange Server).

- The latest and most expensive member of the MSDN subscription family is the Universal subscription. To put it simply, this subscription includes everything. In addition to the contents of the Enterprise subscription, Universal subscribers receive most Microsoft development tools (including Visual Basic, Visual C++, and Visual SourceSafe) and all Microsoft Office components in US and international versions.

So which subscription do you need? Most, if not all, Windows programmers really should have access to at least the Library subscription, because it is a library of essential development information that often cannot be found elsewhere. The Professional subscription is also a must in many cases if proper testing of a new application is to be carried out. During my regular work, I often test code on Windows 3.1, Windows for Workgroups 3.11, Windows 95, and Windows NT Workstation; purchasing these platforms individually and keeping them current would be a nightmarish and expensive exercise.

The Enterprise subscription is only needed if you intend to develop server-side programs for Windows NT Server, or if you need to implement client-side applications that connect to a Windows NT Server. For example, a client-server database application can be developed using Visual Basic, Enterprise Edition, and Windows NT Server plus Microsoft SQL Server, obtained through an MSDN Enterprise subscription.

I view the Universal subscription as a great money-saving tool for developers who need access, from time to time, to all Microsoft development products. It represents a savings of several hundred dollars over the individual purchase price of the included products, and it also represents a guarantee that you will always have access to the latest product versions. Still, this subscription level is expensive, and it is obviously not for everyone.

Web and Online Resources

In these days of the global Internet, the worldwide network is becoming an ever more important resource for developers. It is often said that finding useful information on the Web is an increasingly difficult exercise. However, I found that by knowing the places where useful information is most likely to be located, and by being able to effectively utilize search engines, the Web can be used to quickly and accurately locate much needed information.

The most obvious place for any Windows NT developer to visit is the Microsoft Web page at http://www.microsoft.com. Here, Microsoft offers a complete, up-to-date, online version of the Microsoft Knowledge Base (http://www.microsoft.com/kb). Many Knowledge Base articles can be found here long before they appear on the Developer Network CDs. Another URL leads to the Developers Only area (http://www.microsoft.com/devonly). At this location, information about Microsoft's developer products can be found, as well as upgrades, patches, and occasionally free download offerings.

Support for Microsoft products is also available online. Until recently, the "official" location for product support was the CompuServe Information Service. Although Microsoft support forums still exist there, they are no longer maintained by Microsoft itself. Instead, Microsoft

14

A SOFTWARE
DEVELOPMENT
ENVIRONMENT

has established the Usenet newsgroup hierarchy of `microsoft.*` newsgroups. These newsgroups are available from the server `msnews.microsoft.com`.

Among other useful URLs are the URLs of companies such as Borland (`http://www.borland.com`), Symantec (`http://www.symantec.com`), and Powersoft (`http://www.powersoft.com`). Many useful downloadables, including development products, can be found at the Windows 95 shareware site at `http://www.windows95.com`.

In addition to Microsoft, other companies that provide development tools also often maintain a presence on online services such as CompuServe or America Online.

Summary

Since its introduction, Windows NT has become the platform of choice for the serious Windows developer. Windows NT is more robust than its predecessor, and it provides improved memory management, more robust management of Windows resources, and better multitasking.

A typical Windows NT development station runs Windows NT 4 Workstation on a 100 MHz or faster Pentium, 32MB of memory, at least 2GB of disk space, and a CD-ROM drive. A higher-resolution monitor (17-inch, 1024×768 pixels) is strongly recommended.

The primary tool of Windows NT application development is the Win32 Software Development Kit. This kit contains the necessary libraries, documentation, and tools for creating Windows NT programs. The SDK is available as part of the Microsoft Developer Network subscription; however, it is also often distributed as part of other development systems, and thus an MSDN subscription is not always necessary.

Windows NT drivers, necessary for directly accessing hardware devices, are created using the DDK. This kit is also available through MSDN.

The most popular Windows NT development tools are Visual Basic and Visual C++. Assembly language programming for Intel processors is possible through the Microsoft Macro Assembler. The Microsoft Office application suite offers extensive programmability, and it is frequently used as a system integration tool. Another recently released development product is Visual J++, Microsoft's new Java development environment. Other tools used during development include Visual Test (for extensive testing of applications) and Visual SourceSafe (for source code management).

Companies other than Microsoft also produce powerful development tools for Windows NT. Notable examples include Borland (Borland C++ and Delphi), Symantec (Symantec C++), and Powersoft (PowerBuilder, WatCOM C++, and WatCOM FORTRAN).

Windows NT can be used as the development platform for cross-platform development projects. The same tools used for developing Windows NT programs can also be used for developing Windows 95 and Windows 3.1 (through Win32s) applications. In addition, Windows NT can host 16-bit Windows development tools, and it can also run the Visual C++

cross-platform edition for Macintosh development. The Windows NT POSIX subsystem can facilitate the writing of POSIX-compliant applications that can run on many different operating system platforms after a simple recompilation.

The programmer's task is often to port existing applications to Windows NT. Porting Windows 3.1 applications is typically simple. Many applications that do not employ questionable programming practices (such as dependence on the 16-bit size of certain data types) require only a recompilation. For other applications, tools exist that identify potential porting problems in source code, easing the porting of more complex applications. Porting of UNIX applications can be simpler in some ways (similar size of data types) but more complex in other respects, due to the very significant differences between the Win32 API and typical UNIX APIs. Porting of programs from the X Window System can be a very complex task; for these applications, it is often better to use NT versions of the X11R6 libraries and an NT-based X server.

Developers can rely on a variety of sources for development-related information. The most significant of these sources is the Microsoft Developer Network that provides a quarterly subscription to development information, tools, and resources. Online, developers can access an up-to-the-minute version of the Microsoft Knowledge Base on the World Wide Web as well as other support and product information from Microsoft and other makers of development products.

CHAPTER 15

Windows NT as a Graphics Development Workstation

by Patrick L. Lujan

IN THIS CHAPTER

Introduction

Graphics development on Windows NT consists of the standard GDI graphics functions, `CreateDIBSection` (formerly known as WinG), the DirectX2 SDK, and OpenGL. Standard GDI functions and `CreateDIBSection` are used for normal 2-D graphics that don't require fast screen updates. Most multimedia applications use a combination of these two. DirectX has DirectDraw, which is used for very fast graphics and has the kind of speed that is required by games and real-time systems. OpenGL is a 3-D API, meaning it allows the programmer to create applications that give the end user gorgeous 3-D, rendered graphics. Because the standard GDI and `CreateDIBSection` are commonplace, this chapter focuses on DirectDraw and OpenGL. You first learn to create simple applications using both APIs, and then you create progressively more advanced applications.

I use Microsoft's Visual C++ 4.*x* development system throughout this chapter. Visual C++ contains all you need to develop DirectDraw and OpenGL applications. You might wonder why I chose to use Visual C++, and the reasons are that the DirectX2 SDK (which contains DirectDraw) is included with Visual C++, OpenGL is part of the regular Windows SDK for Windows NT, Visual C++ has MFC and ClassWizard, and most importantly, it is the only development environment I use. The DirectX2 SDK is also available for download on the Internet (34MB) from Microsoft's Web site and FTP site, `www.microsoft.com/gamesdev` and `ftp.microsoft.com/msdownload/directx2`.

The CD-ROM that accompanies this book provides two app wizards for use with this chapter: one for DirectDraw and one for OpenGL. They are in the `\source\chap15\DirectDraw` and `\source\chap15\OpenGL` directories. Copy the `*.awx` files to your Visual C++ directory, `...\msdev\template`. Replace `...` with the path to the location of the `msdev` directory. After you do this, you will have two new app wizards available for use inside Visual C++ when you create a new project.

One thing to note is that the DirectDraw app wizard does not use MFC; it uses the standard Windows SDK, but it is a C/C++ framework. It doesn't use MFC mostly because of performance and memory footprint reasons. Another consideration is that custom app wizards don't allow for a completely custom application. Two things that it does not support are linking in your library files and customizing precompiled headers. The library linking was handled with the `#pragma comment` definition, as can be seen in the `Std.cpp` file that the wizard creates, but the precompiled header information was not included. Currently, the wizard supports automatic precompiled headers. You can get the solution you want, which is similar to what every MFC app gets when created, by following these steps after you create the project:

1. Open the Project Settings dialog (Build | Settings on the menu).
2. Open the Settings For tree and select all the CPP files for both the release and debug versions. Deselect the `Std.cpp` file for both versions.

3. On the C++ tab, select the Precompiled Headers option from the Category list box. Select the radio button that says Use Precompiled Header File (.PCH). Type Std.h in the Through Header edit box. Figure 15.1 shows what your screen should look like.

FIGURE 15.1.

Using a precompiled header file.

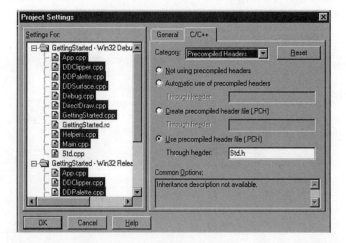

4. Now, back to the Settings For tree. Select only the Std.cpp file for both the release and debug versions. On the C++ tab, select the radio button that says Create Precompiled Header File (.PCH), and type Std.h in the Through Header edit box. Figure 15.2 shows what your screen should look like.

FIGURE 15.2.

Creating a precompiled header file.

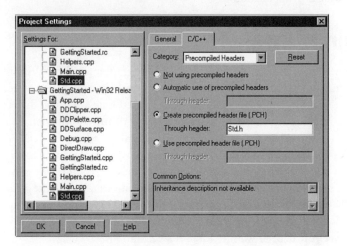

5. Click the OK button, and you are done.

15
A GRAPHICS
DEVELOPMENT
WORKSTATION

If you don't want to use the app wizard, you can copy the directory labeled Sams to a directory of your choice and use that project as your starting point. It is the same project that the app wizard would create with the fixes for the precompiled header information put in. You'll have to change the output filename from Sams.exe to whatever you choose by modifying the entry in the Project Settings | Link tab in the Output File Name edit box. Figure 15.3 shows what your screen should look like.

FIGURE 15.3.

Changing the output file name.

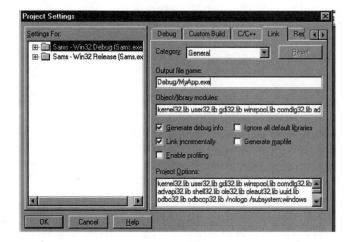

The OpenGL app wizard does not suffer from the aforementioned problem because it is a full-blown MFC application.

DirectDraw

DirectDraw, the very latest and very fastest graphics API for Windows, provides the methods required to make any 2-D multimedia and real-time graphics applications shine like never before. Among the benefits gained from DirectDraw are the ability to control the video mode and the color depth. You could not do this with any API previously on Windows, but now you can. If your video card and monitor can handle it, so can DirectDraw. Page-flipping, the process of drawing an image to one surface while displaying another surface, is also provided at no extra cost. Page-flipping allows your application to run between 30 and 100 frames per second, depending on what you are trying to accomplish. One of the greatest benefits of DirectDraw is that if your users have DirectDraw-supported video cards, your application runs even faster. Undoubtedly, if you want the fastest possible 2-D graphics for Windows, DirectDraw is the answer you've been waiting for. Let's get started.

What Is DirectDraw?

DirectDraw is part of the DirectX2 Software Development Kit (SDK) released by Microsoft. It was originally known as the Game SDK. The DirectX2 SDK is a set of dynamic link libraries (DLLs) for graphics acceleration, audio acceleration, advanced connectivity, joystick manipulation, and CD-ROM automation. The DirectX2 SDK also contains Direct3D, a set of real-time, 3-D graphics services that deliver fast, software-based rendering and transparent access to hardware acceleration.

You can use DirectDraw to develop very fast graphics applications. Currently, the majority of DirectDraw/DirectX-based applications are games for Windows 95 and Windows NT 4.0, but it is not limited to only that segment. You can create a drawing application with real-time updates, a kiosk system, or whatever you can imagine that would benefit from extremely fast screen updates. After you look at the demos included with the DirectX SDK, you can see just how fast it gets. Some demos run as fast as 82 frames per second on my development machine—now, that is fast!

How did DirectDraw come to exist, or why did Microsoft do it? The question is, "How many fast, exciting games were available for Windows before DirectDraw?" The answer is "Very few." Microsoft needed to develop an API so that it could attract the major game publishers to write games for Windows. The game companies wanted direct access to the video card, but Windows had no support for this. Microsoft knew that if they didn't provide this feature for Windows, the game companies might produce their own routines to achieve the results they needed. This might have caused serious problems with Windows itself; thus averting a potential disaster, Microsoft worked with game developing companies, video hardware companies, and others to produce a set of standards that would be part of Windows, and anyone who wants to use them can.

One of the best features of programming Windows applications is the common interface you have for achieving certain results, which contrasts with programming MS-DOS applications, where you are left to do everything on your own. In Windows, if you want to access the display, you do so by using certain API functions. These functions work on any computer, using whatever video card and whatever monitor the user has. Windows knows how to access the various video cards made by the numerous manufacturers. This transparent access is what makes Windows applications, versus DOS applications, a joy to create.

The most important thing about DirectDraw is that it gives you the same common interface to different manufacturers' display adapters at a level never before seen in Windows. DirectDraw, when initialized, collects data from your video card about its capabilities and puts in the hardware abstraction layer (HAL). (The HAL is supplied by the video card manufacturer.) This HAL is what provides a common interface between the many video card manufacturers and applications using DirectDraw.

In addition, DirectDraw is not limited to using the hardware available on the display adapter. If your application wants to use a specific type of display hardware, such as a hardware blitter (a highly specialized video card), but that hardware does not exist on the user's machine, your application uses the hardware emulation layer (HEL) included with DirectDraw. In this case, DirectDraw uses the built-in hardware emulation to emulate the missing hardware required by your program. Of course, your application runs slower when using emulation, but at least it runs.

Figure 15.4 shows DirectDraw and its association with other Windows display components. The regular Windows counterpart to the DirectDraw HAL is the Windows Device Driver Interface (DDI), which is the layer with which Windows talks to your video card. This interface is what makes it possible to write a Windows application without having to worry about what video card your user has.

FIGURE 15.4.
The DirectDraw universe.

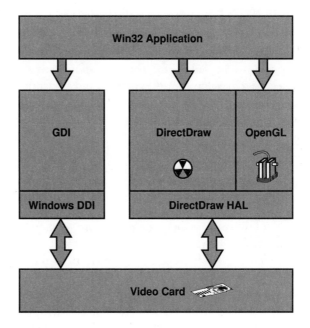

The DirectDraw Components

DirectDraw consists of the following components:

- ◼ `IDirectDraw`
- ◼ `IDirectDraw2`
- ◼ `IDirectDrawSurface`
- ◼ `IDirectDrawSurface2`

■ IDirectDrawPalette

■ IDirectDrawClipper

IDirectDraw and IDirectDraw2

IDirectDraw and IDirectDraw2 are the objects that do the majority of the work by controlling the display of images on the screen. The two objects are similar in functions, with two exceptions. Following are the methods common to both:

Compact	CreateClipper
CreatePalette	CreateSurface
DuplicateSurface	EnumDisplayModes
EnumSurfaces	FlipToGDISurface
GetCaps	GetDisplayMode
GetFourCCCodes	GetGDISurface
GetMonitorFrequency	GetScanLine
GetVerticalBlankStatus	Initialize
RestoreDisplayMode	SetCooperativeLevel
WaitForVerticalBlank	

One method, SetDisplayMode, exists in both classes, but it differs in the number of parameters it uses. The following line shows the syntax for the method on IDirectDraw:

```
HRESULT SetDisplayMode(DWORD dwWidth, DWORD dwHeight, DWORD dwBPP);
```

This method sets the mode of the display device hardware by allowing you to specify the width, height, and bits per pixel.

The following line shows the syntax for the method on IDirectDraw2:

```
HRESULT SetDisplayMode(DWORD dwWidth,DWORD dwHeight, DWORD dwBPP,
➥DWORD dwRefreshRate, DWORD dwFlags);
```

This method sets the mode of the display device hardware by allowing you to specify the width, height, bits per pixel, and monitor refresh rate. The dwFlags is not yet used by DirectDraw and must be 0. Future support for dwFlags will come in future versions of DirectDraw.

You should be aware of these differences between the two methods if you need to set the refresh rate of the monitor for your application. One other method, GetAvailableVidMem, is available only on IDirectDraw2.

15

A GRAPHICS
DEVELOPMENT
WORKSTATION

IDirectDrawSurface and IDirectDrawSurface2

IDirectDrawSurface and IDirectDrawSurface2 make up the surfaces that contain image information that is blitted or copied to and from the screen. These two objects are similar in function, with two exceptions. The following methods are common to both:

AddAttachedSurface	AddOverlayDirtyRect
Blt	BltBatch
BltFast	DeleteAttachedSurface
EnumAttachedSurfaces	EnumOverlayZOrders
Flip	GetAttachedSurface
GetBltStatus	GetCaps
GetClipper	GetColorKey
GetDC	GetFlipStatus
GetOverlayPosition	GetPalette
GetPixelFormat	GetSurfaceDesc
Initialize	IsLost
Lock	ReleaseDC
Restore	SetClipper
SetColorKey	SetOverlayPosition
SetPalette	Unlock
UpdateOverlay	UpdateOverlayDisplay
UpdateOverlayZOrder	

IDirectDrawSurface2 has three additional methods:

GetDDSurface

PageLock

PageUnlock

IDirectDrawPalette

IDirectDrawPalette controls the methods related to palettes for DirectDraw. It contains the following methods:

GetCaps

GetEntries

Initialize

SetEntries

IDirectDrawClipper

`IDirectDrawClipper` controls the methods related to clipping for DirectDraw. It contains the following methods:

GetClipList	GetHWnd
Initialize	IsClipListChanged
SetClipList	SetHWnd

Consult the DirectX2 Help file for complete information on all these functions and the rest of the DirectX2 SDK.

Using the DirectDraw App Wizard

Included with the source code for this chapter is a custom DirectDraw app wizard for Visual C++. It is in the `\source\chap15\DirectDraw` directory. Copy the file `DDWiz.awx` to your `msdev\template` directory. When you create a new project workspace, you can create a DirectDraw workspace for quickly getting up to speed with DirectDraw. The DirectDraw app wizard creates all the files you need to start working with DirectDraw. The framework I built for DirectDraw is included in the files. I use it for all the DirectDraw demos.

To get started, copy the app wizard as outlined previously. You are going to create your first DirectDraw application in less than five minutes when you create the Sams project that is on the CD-ROM. If you want to see the finished product, go to the `\source\chap15\DirectDraw\bin` directory on the CD-ROM and run `Sams.exe` to see what the DirectDraw app wizard creates by default. You can also run any of the other examples to see what you will be doing throughout this chapter.

Run Visual C++, create a new project workspace, select the DirectDraw app wizard, set the name of the project as `SamsDemo`, set the location for the project, and click the Create button. You'll see the New Project Information dialog box; click the OK button. You have a complete and ready-to-compile application. If you are interested in using the different precompiled header method discussed earlier, now is the time to do so. Compile and run the application. You should see a screen that looks like Figure 15.5. You now have a complete DirectDraw-based application. How's that for getting up to speed?

Take the time to look through the source code and learn how the framework works. In the upcoming demos and in the applications you write, you will see that you need to modify only three files: `main.cpp`, `yourapp.h`, and `yourapp.cpp`. These three files take care of your application-specific code, and unless you need to start the application a special way, you might not even have to modify `main.cpp`.

FIGURE 15.5.
The Samsdemo *output.*

As you can see, the Sams project is very basic. It does nothing but display the image and wait for you to exit the program. You must be thinking, "How boring," but you need to create a generic application to first learn from and then add to. The next few sections take a look at how to use the framework and the different DirectDraw capabilities, and then you get to the demos.

Using DirectDraw

To use DirectDraw in an application, you need to perform certain basic steps. The following steps take care of DirectDraw initialization.

You must first create a useable instance of DirectDraw. Use the DirectDrawCreate function to do this. In code, it looks like this:

```
HRESULT result = m_DirectDraw.Create();
```

In regular C or SDK style, the following code achieves the same result:

```
HRESULT result;
IDirectDraw* DirectDraw;
result = DirectDrawCreate(NULL, &DirectDraw, NULL);
```

The next step is to set up the display mode. This is a two-part process beginning with setting the cooperative level of DirectDraw, which determines the top-level behavior of the application and sets the low-level requirements for the mode. The SetCooperativeLevel method of IDirectDraw handles this part. There are numerous flags available for this method, but the majority of applications need only two; DDSCL_EXCLUSIVE and DDSCL_FULLSCREEN. DDSCL_EXCLUSIVE tells Windows that the application has exclusive control of the screen and can forget about the GDI. DDSCL_FULLSCREEN tells Windows that the application uses the entire screen surface. You must use these two parameters together. In code, it looks like this:

```
HRESULT result = m_DirectDraw.SetCooperativeLevel(m_window);
```

In regular C or SDK style, the following code achieves the same result:

```
HRESULT result;
// window is an HWND that points to the main window of our application
result = DirectDraw->SetCooperativeLevel( window,
  DDSCL_EXCLUSIVE ¦ DDSCL_FULLSCREEN);
```

The DDSCL_EXCLUSIVE and DDSCL_FULLSCREEN flags are the default for the framework, and you don't need to write them out.

The second part of the two-step process is to set the display mode. You do this by calling the IDirectDraw method SetDisplayMode with the width, height, and bits per pixel for the mode you want. The usual settings in most applications tend to be 640×480×8. This means 640 pixels across by 480 pixels down by 8 bits per pixel (256 colors). In code, it looks like this:

```
result = m_DirectDraw.SetDisplayMode();
```

In regular C or SDK style, the following code achieves the same result:

```
HRESULT  result;
result = DirectDraw->SetDisplayMode(640, 480, 8);
```

The 640×480×8 mode is the default for the framework, so you do not need to explicitly write it out. All the higher level functions in the framework are wrappers for the IDirectDraw interfaces that are meant to save time and add functionality. If you want to use different screen resolutions and color depths, you should call the IDirectDraw method EnumDisplayMode to give you a list of the available modes on the user's machine. Not following these rules could break your application on someone's machine.

So far, you have the three steps to start up DirectDraw: Create a DirectDraw object, set the cooperative level, and set the display mode. Your code for these steps should look like the following:

```
HRESULT result = m_DirectDraw.Create();
if (result == DD_OK)
{
  result = m_DirectDraw.SetCooperativeLevel(m_window);
  if (result == DD_OK)
  {
    result = m_DirectDraw.SetDisplayMode();
    if( result == ID _OK)
    {
      // rest of code goes here
    }
  }
}
```

Now what you need are some surfaces to write the graphics to. Create two surfaces, a primary surface and a back surface, with the following code:

```
// Create the primary surface with 1 back buffer
DDSURFACEDESC info;
info.dwSize = sizeof(DDSURFACEDESC);
info.dwFlags = DDSD_CAPS | DDSD_BACKBUFFERCOUNT;
info.ddsCaps.dwCaps = DDSCAPS_PRIMARYSURFACE | DDSCAPS_FLIP | DDSCAPS_COMPLEX;
info.dwBackBufferCount = 1;
result = m_DDSurface1.CreateSurface(&info);
if(result == DD_OK)
{
  // Get a pointer to the back buffer
  DDSCAPS DDSurfaceCaps;
  DDSurfaceCaps.dwCaps = DDSCAPS_BACKBUFFER;
  result = m_DDSurface2.GetAttachedSurface(&caps, &m_DDSurface1);
  if(result == DD_OK)
  {
    // the application is now ready for use
    return TRUE;
  }
}
```

This sets up two surfaces that allow you to display one on screen and draw to the other. This technique is called double-buffering and allows you to page-flip.

All the DirectDraw initialization code in the framework is in the StartDirectDraw method of the application class. You modify this method for your requirements and go from there. When the application runs and calls StartDirectDraw, it calls the InitApp method of your application class. This function initializes items after DirectDraw has started. In the Sams demo application, the code looks like the following:

```
BOOL CSamsDemo::InitApp(LPSTR CmdLine)
{
  RECT rect={0,0,640,480};
  HRESULT result = m_DDSurface1.BltFast( 0, 0, &m_DDOSurface1, &rect,
    DDBLTFAST_NOCOLORKEY);
  if(result == DD_OK)
  {
    TRACE("CDDTest.InitApp SUCCESS!\nApp is about to begin!\n");
    return TRUE;
  }
  TRACE("CDDTest.InitApp FAILURE!\nApp is exiting!\n");
  return FALSE;
}
```

Here, the code simply copies the bitmap from the second surface (m_DDOSurface1) to the first surface (m_DDSurface1). This ensures that when you run the application, the first surface has the bitmap on it so that the user sees the bitmap and not a blank screen.

All the code up to now sets up DirectDraw and the surfaces you need to develop killer graphics applications. Moving on in this introduction to DirectDraw, I now turn to the first example everyone starts with in learning to use DirectDraw, DDEX1. This is also an excellent time to talk a little more about the C/C++ DirectDraw framework. As stated earlier, the framework is mostly a wrapper for DirectDraw and provides an object-oriented view of DirectDraw. I first discuss the framework and then proceed with the example.

The class hierarchy for the framework is displayed in Figure 15.6.

FIGURE 15.6.

DirectDraw hierarchy.

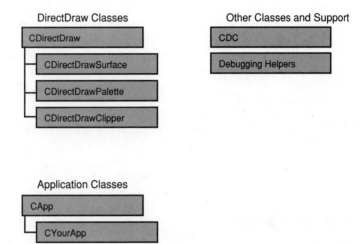

As you can see, the framework is very small, but it saves you the initial work to get an application started and provides a robust interface for your applications.

Your application class object is derived from CApp. Within this class is where the majority, if not all, of your specific code is located. To see this in better detail, load the GettingStarted demo from the CD-ROM (\source\chap15\DirectDraw\GettingStarted). Compile the project and run the demo. Take a look at it and then continue.

This is the most basic of DirectDraw demos and is identical in functionality to the DDEX1 demo included with the DirectX SDK. Take a closer look at the code to become better acquainted with the framework.

Open the GetttingStarted.cpp file, which is shown in Listing 15.1.

Listing 15.1. The GettingStarted.cpp file.

```
//////////////////////////////////////////////////////////////////
//
// GettingStarted.cpp : implementation file for CGettingStarted
//
//////////////////////////////////////////////////////////////////

#include "Std.h"
#include "GettingStarted.h"
```

15

A GRAPHICS
DEVELOPMENT
WORKSTATION

continues

Listing 15.1. continued

```
#ifdef _DEBUG
#define new DEBUG_NEW
#undef THIS_FILE
static char THIS_FILE[] = _FILE_;
#endif

CGettingStarted GettingStarted;

#define TIMER_ID    1
#define TIMER_RATE 50
#define RED         RGB(255,0,0)
#define BLUE        RGB(0,0,255)
#define BLACK       RGB(0,0,0)
#define YELLOW      RGB(255,255,0)

static char msg[] = "Page Flipping Test  :  Press ESCAPE to exit";
static char FrontMsg[] = "Front buffer";
static char BackMsg[]  = "Back buffer";

BOOL CGettingStarted::InitApp(LPSTR CmdLine)
{
  // clear out our surfaces
  m_DDSurface1.Fill(BLACK);
  m_DDSurface2.Fill(BLACK);

  HDC   hdc;
  RECT  rc;
  SIZE  size;

  GetClientRect(m_window, &rc);
  // draw some text.
  if (m_DDSurface1.GetDC(&hdc) == DD_OK)
  {
    CDC dc(hdc);
    dc.SetBkColor(BLACK);
    // write the front buffer message
    dc.SetTextColor(RED);
    dc.GetTextExtentPoint(FrontMsg, &size);
    dc.TextOut((rc.right - size.cx)/2, ((rc.bottom - size.cy)/2)-25, FrontMsg);
    // write the msg out
    dc.SetTextColor(YELLOW);
    dc.GetTextExtentPoint(msg, &size);
    dc.TextOut((rc.right - size.cx)/2, (rc.bottom - size.cy)/2, msg);
    m_DDSurface1.ReleaseDC(hdc);
  }
  if (m_DDSurface2.GetDC(&hdc) == DD_OK)
  {
    CDC dc(hdc);
    dc.SetBkColor(BLACK);
    // write the front buffer message
    dc.SetTextColor(BLUE);
    dc.GetTextExtentPoint(BackMsg, &size);
    dc.TextOut((rc.right - size.cx)/2, ((rc.bottom - size.cy)/2)+25, BackMsg);
    // write the msg out
    dc.SetTextColor(YELLOW);
    dc.GetTextExtentPoint(msg, &size);
```

```
      dc.TextOut((rc.right - size.cx)/2, (rc.bottom - size.cy)/2, msg);
      m_DDSurface2.ReleaseDC(hdc);
    }
    // Create a timer to flip the pages
    if((m_TimerId = SetTimer(m_window, TIMER_ID, TIMER_RATE, NULL)))
    {
      TRACE("CGettingStarted.InitApp SUCCESS!\nApp is about to begin!\n");
      return TRUE;
    }
    TRACE("CGettingStarted.InitApp FAILURE!\nApp is exiting!\n");
    return FALSE;
}

BOOL CGettingStarted::StartDirectDraw(void)
{
    // create the main DirectDraw object
    HRESULT result = m_DirectDraw.Create();
    if(result == DD_OK)
    {
      // Get exclusive mode
      result = m_DirectDraw.SetCooperativeLevel(m_window);
      if(result == DD_OK)
      {
        result = m_DirectDraw.SetDisplayMode();
        if(result == DD_OK)
        {
          // Create the primary surface with 1 back buffer
          DDSURFACEDESC DDSurfaceDesc;
          DDSurfaceDesc.dwSize = sizeof(DDSURFACEDESC);
          DDSurfaceDesc.dwFlags = DDSD_CAPS | DDSD_BACKBUFFERCOUNT;
          DDSurfaceDesc.ddsCaps.dwCaps =
            DDSCAPS_PRIMARYSURFACE | DDSCAPS_FLIP | DDSCAPS_COMPLEX;
          DDSurfaceDesc.dwBackBufferCount = 1;
          result = m_DDSurface1.CreateSurface(&DDSurfaceDesc);
          if(result == DD_OK)
          {
            // Get a pointer to the back buffer
            DDSCAPS DDSurfaceCaps;
            DDSurfaceCaps.dwCaps = DDSCAPS_BACKBUFFER;
            result = m_DDSurface2.GetAttachedSurface( &DDSurfaceCaps,
              &m_DDSurface1 );
            if(result == DD_OK)
            {
              TRACE("CGettingStarted.StartDirectDraw SUCCESS!\n");
              return TRUE;
            }
          }
        }
      }
    }
    TRACE("CGettingStarted.StartDirectDraw FAILURE!\n");
    char buf[256];
    wsprintf(buf, "Direct Draw Init Failed (%08lx)\n", result);
    MessageBox(m_window, buf, "ERROR", MB_OK | MB_ICONSTOP);

    return FALSE;
}
```

15

A GRAPHICS
DEVELOPMENT
WORKSTATION

continues

Listing 15.1. continued

```
long PASCAL CGettingStarted::WindowProc( HWND window, UINT message,
  WPARAM wParam, LPARAM lParam)
{
  switch(message)
  {
    case WM_ACTIVATEAPP : m_active = wParam; break;
    case WM_DESTROY     : OnDestroy(); break;
    case WM_KEYDOWN     : OnKeyDown(wParam); break;
    case WM_SETCURSOR   : SetCursor(NULL); return TRUE;
    case WM_TIMER       : OnTimer(); break;
    case WM_PAINT       : OnPaint(); break;
  }

  return DefWindowProc(window, message, wParam, lParam);
}

void CGettingStarted::OnKeyDown(WPARAM key)
{
  switch(key)
  {
    case VK_ESCAPE : PostMessage(m_window, WM_CLOSE, 0, 0); break;
  }
}

void CGettingStarted::OnDestroy(void)
{
  if (m_TimerId)
    KillTimer(m_window, m_TimerId);

  PostQuitMessage(0);
}

void CGettingStarted::OnTimer(void)
{
  // Flip surfaces
  if(m_active)
  {
    while(1)
    {
      HRESULT result = m_DDSurface1.Flip(NULL, 0);
      if(result == DD_OK)
        break;
      if(result == DDERR_SURFACELOST)
      {
        result = m_DDSurface1.Restore();
        if(result != DD_OK)
          break;
      }
      if(result != DDERR_WASSTILLDRAWING)
        break;
    }
  }
}
```

```
void CGettingStarted::OnPaint(void)
{
  PAINTSTRUCT ps;
  RECT        rc;
  SIZE        size;

  BeginPaint(m_window, &ps);
  GetClientRect(m_window, &rc);

  CDC dc(ps.hdc);
  dc.GetTextExtentPoint(msg, &size);
  dc.SetBkColor(BLACK);
  dc.SetTextColor(YELLOW);
  dc.TextOut((rc.right - size.cx)/2, (rc.bottom - size.cy)/2, msg);
  EndPaint(m_window, &ps);
}
```

Find the method called `StartDirectDraw`. Taking a close look at it, you'll recognize this as the DirectDraw startup code I talked about earlier. Now look at the `InitApp` method. Here, you do the initial work to set up the surfaces and create a timer. When the timer goes off, the application calls the `OnTimer` method and flips the surfaces. The other functions take care of a few other tasks that are self-explanatory.

If you take a look at the rest of the code, you'll see that nothing has changed from the Sams demo. That is the beauty of frameworks. Figure 15.7 shows an example of this demo. Now, you can move on to a more interesting demo.

FIGURE 15.7.
The GettingStarted *demo.*

Front buffer
Page Flipping Test : Press ESCAPE to exit

15

A GRAPHICS
DEVELOPMENT
WORKSTATION

Using DirectDraw Surfaces

Surfaces are pieces of memory that your application uses to transfer data back and forth. The memory that IDirectDrawSurfaces is made of is the memory on your video card. The more memory on your video card, the more surfaces you can create. IDirectDrawSurfaces can also use system memory to create surfaces, but they must eventually transfer the data to video memory, and system memory to video memory transfers are slow.

Most, if not all, of the time, you will create a DirectDraw application that must use flippable surfaces—that is, two or more surfaces to work with in the creation and display of graphics. One surface, usually called the primary buffer (m_DDSurface1 in the framework), is the surface that is displayed to the user on his monitor. The second surface, usually called the back buffer (m_DDSurface2 in the framework), is used for creating graphics. You create graphics or your scene on the back buffer and then flip the image to the primary buffer. I'll discuss how to do this in the framework. The discussion of events here centers around the code in the StartDirectDraw method.

The first step in creating flippable surfaces is to define the requirements for a surface. You do this using a DDSURFACEDESC structure. This is how it looks in the framework:

```
// Create the primary surface with 1 back buffer
DDSURFACEDESC info;
info.dwSize = sizeof(DDSURFACEDESC);
info.dwFlags = DDSD_CAPS | DDSD_BACKBUFFERCOUNT;
info.ddsCaps.dwCaps = DDSCAPS_PRIMARYSURFACE | DDSCAPS_FLIP | DDSCAPS_COMPLEX;
info.dwBackBufferCount = 1;
```

You must always remember to set the dwSize member of any DirectDraw structure. If you forget, the method you use with the structure fails with an invalid member error.

The dwFlags member determines which fields in the DDSURFACEDESC structure are filled with valid information. For the demo, you set dwFlags to DDSD_CAPS and DDSD_BACKBUFFERCOUNT, which specifies that you will use the DDSCAPS structure and that you want a back buffer.

Because you specified that you will use the DDSCAPS structure, you now tell the dwCaps member of ddsCaps the flags that you will use. You specify a primary surface, a flipping surface, and a complex surface. A complex surface is a surface that has more than one actual surface.

Finally, you specify one back buffer. Remember that this back buffer is where you do all the drawing.

As mentioned before, surface memory can be either display memory or system memory. DirectDraw uses system memory if the application runs out of display memory. You can also specify whether to use only system memory or only display memory by setting the dwCaps member in the DDSCAPS structure to DDSCAPS_SYSTEMMEMORY or DDSCAPS_VIDEOMEMORY. (If you specify DDSCAPS_VIDEOMEMORY, but not enough memory is available to create the surface, IDirectDraw::CreateSurface returns with a DDERR_OUTOFVIDEOMEMORY error.)

Now that you have the description of the surfaces you want, create them. This is how it looks in the code:

```
result = m_DDSurface1.CreateSurface(&info);
```

If this call succeeds, you then create the back buffer by calling the following method to get a pointer to the back buffer:

```
IDirectDrawSurface::GetAttachedSurface
```

This is how it looks in the code:

```
DDSCAPS caps;
caps.dwCaps = DDSCAPS_BACKBUFFER;
result = m_DDSurface2.GetAttachedSurface(&caps, &m_DDSurface1);
```

If this call succeeds, you are ready to start creating graphics on the back buffer. The application now proceeds out of the StartDirectDraw method and calls the InitApp method. Here, you display text on the surfaces and prepare them for flipping. This is what you have:

```
BOOL CGettingStarted::InitApp(LPSTR CmdLine)
{
  // clear out our surfaces
  m_DDSurface1.Fill(BLACK);
  m_DDSurface2.Fill(BLACK);

  HDC  hdc;
  RECT rc;
  SIZE size;

  GetClientRect(m_window, &rc);
  // draw some text.
  if (m_DDSurface1.GetDC(&hdc) == DD_OK)
  {
    CDC dc(hdc);
    dc.SetBkColor(BLACK);
    // write the front buffer message
    dc.SetTextColor(RED);
    dc.GetTextExtentPoint(FrontMsg, &size);
    dc.TextOut((rc.right - size.cx)/2, ((rc.bottom - size.cy)/2)-25, FrontMsg);
    // write the msg out
    dc.SetTextColor(YELLOW);
    dc.GetTextExtentPoint(msg, &size);
    dc.TextOut((rc.right - size.cx)/2, (rc.bottom - size.cy)/2, msg);
    m_DDSurface1.ReleaseDC(hdc);
  }
  if (m_DDSurface2.GetDC(&hdc) == DD_OK)
  {
    CDC dc(hdc);
    dc.SetBkColor(BLACK);
    // write the front buffer message
    dc.SetTextColor(BLUE);
    dc.GetTextExtentPoint(BackMsg, &size);
    dc.TextOut((rc.right - size.cx)/2, ((rc.bottom - size.cy)/2)+25, BackMsg);
    // write the msg out
    dc.SetTextColor(YELLOW);
    dc.GetTextExtentPoint(msg, &size);
```

15

**A GRAPHICS
DEVELOPMENT
WORKSTATION**

```
      dc.TextOut((rc.right - size.cx)/2, (rc.bottom - size.cy)/2, msg);
      m_DDSurface2.ReleaseDC(hdc);
    }
    // Create a timer to flip the pages
    if((m_TimerId = SetTimer(m_window, TIMER_ID, TIMER_RATE, NULL)))
    {
      TRACE("CGettingStarted.InitApp SUCCESS!\nApp is about to begin!\n");
      return TRUE;
    }
    TRACE("CGettingStarted.InitApp FAILURE!\nApp is exiting!\n");
    return FALSE;
}
```

Here, you clear out the surfaces by filling them with the color black, get the device context for each surface, write text onto the surfaces, and create a timer. The timer makes the application flip back and forth between surfaces.

Keep in mind that between the call to the IDirectDrawSurface::GetDC method and the IDirectDrawSurface::ReleaseDC method, your application, and the system blitter cannot access the memory of the surface. This gives you complete control of the surfaces and prevents errors from happening while you are writing to the surface.

If you're paying attention, you notice that you have written to the primary buffer. Usually, you don't want to do this. The only time you want to write to the primary buffer is during initialization of the buffer contents, as in the example. You might want to display a title page or something else while the rest of the application loads. Other than that, you don't want to place things on the primary buffer.

Having done all this, you let the application run and wait for the user to exit the application or for a timer event. You know what happens when the user exits the application, so look closely at what happens when you get a timer event. This is the code for the timer event in the OnTimer method:

```
void CGettingStarted::OnTimer(void)
{
  if(m_active)
  {
    while(1)
    {
      HRESULT result = m_DDSurface1.Flip(NULL, 0);
      if(result == DD_OK)
        break;
      if(result == DDERR_SURFACELOST)
      {
        result = m_DDSurface1.Restore();
        if(result != DD_OK)
          break;
      }
      if(result != DDERR_WASSTILLDRAWING)
        break;
    }
  }
}
```

Because you wrote separate information to each of the buffers, all you need to do is flip buffers. You simply don't need to write to the buffers again. This method has code to check whether a surface was lost—that is, whether the information in the surfaces was erased or corrupted somehow. If this happens, you need to replace the information and continue.

Also notice that this method does not return until the IDirectDrawSurface::Flip method returns with a code of DD_OK. If other events are happening that prevent the Flip method from completing successfully, the method keeps trying until it does the flip.

The demo SurfaceDemo1 showcases animation, as well as these important topics:

- Loading a bitmap and displaying it on the background
- Displaying sprites
- Triple buffering
- Using transparent images

You use a bitmap to display as the background, and it also contains the images for the sprite. Triple buffering is using three surfaces instead of two: one primary surface, one back surface, and one off-screen surface. DirectDraw surfaces can also do transparencies, and you'll see how to do this in the next demo. The code for this demo looks like the following:

```
///////////////////////////////////////////////////////////
//
// SurfaceDemo1.cpp : implementation file for CSurfaceDemo1
//
///////////////////////////////////////////////////////////

#include "Std.h"
#include "SurfaceDemo1.h"

#ifdef _DEBUG
#define new DEBUG_NEW
#undef THIS_FILE
static char THIS_FILE[] = __FILE__;
#endif

CSurfaceDemo1 SurfaceDemo1;
#define PaletteBmp "IMAGES"
```

You don't have to do anything special here, so you just say you're okay and continue:

```
BOOL CSurfaceDemo1::InitApp(LPSTR CmdLine)
{
  TRACE("CSurfaceDemo1.InitApp SUCCESS!\nApp is about to begin!\n");
  return TRUE;
}
```

This is where you create the primary and secondary surfaces and the palette:

```
BOOL CSurfaceDemo1::StartDirectDraw(void)
{
  // create the main DirectDraw object
  HRESULT result = m_DirectDraw.Create();
```

```
if(result == DD_OK)
{
  // Get exclusive mode
  result = m_DirectDraw.SetCooperativeLevel(m_window);
  if(result == DD_OK)
  {
    result = m_DirectDraw.SetDisplayMode();
    if(result == DD_OK)
    {
      // Create the primary surface with 1 back buffer
      DDSURFACEDESC info;
      info.dwSize = sizeof(DDSURFACEDESC);
      info.dwFlags = DDSD_CAPS | DDSD_BACKBUFFERCOUNT;
      info.ddsCaps.dwCaps =
        DDSCAPS_PRIMARYSURFACE | DDSCAPS_FLIP | DDSCAPS_COMPLEX;
      info.dwBackBufferCount = 1;
```

Here is the first surface:

```
      result = m_DDSurface1.CreateSurface(&info);
      if(result == DD_OK)
      {
        // Get a pointer to the back buffer
        DDSCAPS caps;
        caps.dwCaps = DDSCAPS_BACKBUFFER;
```

Here is the second surface:

```
        result = m_DDSurface2.GetAttachedSurface(&caps, &m_DDSurface1);
        if(result == DD_OK)
        {
```

Here is where you load the palette. Simply pass the filename of the bitmap, and `LoadPalette` loads the file and extracts the palette information. Note that this function works both with bitmaps in your application's resources and stand-alone files.

```
          result = m_DDPalette.LoadPalette(PaletteBmp);
          if(result == DD_OK)
          {
```

Here, you attach the palette to the primary surface. Doing this ensures that the image appears correctly.

```
            result = m_DDSurface1.SetPalette(&m_DDPalette);
            if(result == DD_OK)
            {
```

Here is the third surface. Load the bitmap into the third surface. This is where the background image and the sprite images are contained.

```
              result = m_DDOSurface1.LoadBitmap(PaletteBmp);
              if(result == DD_OK)
              {
```

Here is where the transparent image support comes in. You tell the off-screen surface that the color black (`RGB(0,0,0)`) is the color that you want as the transparent color. By giving the surface this information, any time a bitmap is blitted from this surface, the surface does not copy any pixels that are the color black, which gives you color transparency. You can specify a range of colors, not just one, to be used as transparent colors. Consult the DirectX2 Help file for more information on this topic.

```
                result = m_DDOSurface1.SetColorKey(RGB(0,0,0));
                if(result == DD_OK)
                {
                    TRACE("CSurfaceDemo1.StartDirectDraw SUCCESS!\n");
                    return TRUE;
                }
            }
        }
      }
     }
    }
   }
  }
 }
TRACE("CSurfaceDemo1.StartDirectDraw FAILURE!\n");
char buf[256];
wsprintf(buf, "Direct Draw Init Failed (%08lx)\n", result);
MessageBox(m_window, buf, "ERROR", MB_OK | MB_ICONSTOP);

return FALSE;
}
```

Here, you have a special (overridden) version of the Run method. What it does differently from the standard version is allow you to run without a timer. Timers are great for timed events, but when you want your application to run as fast as possible, this is the way to do it. If there are no more messages to process and the application is active, meaning it is the current application, then call the UpdateFrame method. With this method, it is possible to see your application running at 60 or more frames per second. You need only this special Run method when you want blazing speed.

```
int CSurfaceDemo1::Run(void)
{
  MSG msg;
  while(1)
  {
    if(PeekMessage(&msg, NULL, 0, 0, PM_NOREMOVE))
    {
      if(!GetMessage(&msg, NULL, 0, 0))
        return msg.wParam;
      TranslateMessage(&msg);
      DispatchMessage(&msg);
    }
    else if(m_active)
      UpdateFrame();
    else // make sure we go to sleep if we have nothing else to do
      WaitMessage();
  }
}

long PASCAL CSurfaceDemo1::WindowProc( HWND window, UINT message,
  WPARAM wParam, LPARAM lParam )
```

```
{
  switch(message)
  {
    case WM_ACTIVATEAPP : m_active = wParam; break;
    case WM_DESTROY     : OnDestroy(); break;
    case WM_KEYDOWN     : OnKeyDown(wParam); break;
    case WM_SETCURSOR   : SetCursor(NULL); return TRUE;
  }

  return DefWindowProc(window, message, wParam, lParam);
}

void CSurfaceDemo1::OnKeyDown(WPARAM key)
{
  switch(key)
  {
    case VK_ESCAPE : PostMessage(m_window, WM_CLOSE, 0, 0); break;
  }
}

void CSurfaceDemo1::OnDestroy(void)
{
  PostQuitMessage(0);
}

HRESULT CSurfaceDemo1::RestoreAll(void)
{
  HRESULT result = m_DDSurface1.Restore();
  if(result == DD_OK)
  {
    result = m_DDOSurface1.Restore();
    if(result == DD_OK)
      m_DDOSurface1.ReLoadBitmap(PaletteBmp);
  }
  return result;
}
```

This is the method that controls the application when there are no messages being processed:

```
// Decide what needs to be blitted next, wait for flip to complete,
// then flip the buffers.
void CSurfaceDemo1::UpdateFrame(void)
{
  static UINT lastTickCount[3] = {0,0,0};
  static int  currentFrame[3] = {0,0,0};
  UINT        thisTickCount;
  UINT        delay[3] = {50, 78, 13};
  int         i;
  int         xpos[3] = {288, 190, 416};
  int         ypos[3] = {128, 300, 256};
  HRESULT     result;

  // Decide which frame will be blitted next
  thisTickCount = GetTickCount();
```

```
for(i=0; i<3; i++)
{
  if((thisTickCount - lastTickCount[i]) > delay[i])
  {
    // Move to next frame;
    lastTickCount[i] = thisTickCount;
    currentFrame[i]++;
    if(currentFrame[i] > 59)
      currentFrame[i] = 0;
  }
}
// Blit the stuff for the next frame
RECT rcRect={0,0,640,480};
while(1)
{
```

Here is where you copy the background from the third surface onto the second surface. It also specifies that you are to use no color key or transparent color.

```
result = m_DDSurface2.BltFast( 0, 0, &m_DDOSurface1, &rcRect,
  DDBLTFAST_NOCOLORKEY );
if(result == DD_OK)
  break;
if(result == DDERR_SURFACELOST)
{
  result = RestoreAll();
  if(result != DD_OK)
    return;
}
if(result != DDERR_WASSTILLDRAWING)
  return;
}
if(result != DD_OK)
  return;
```

Because the images for the sprites are in the same bitmap the background is in, you need to figure out how to index them correctly.

```
for(i=0; i<3; i++)
{
  rcRect.left   = currentFrame[i]%10*64;
  rcRect.top    = currentFrame[i]/10*64 + 480;
  rcRect.right  = currentFrame[i]%10*64 + 64;
  rcRect.bottom = currentFrame[i]/10*64 + 64 + 480;
  while(1)
  {
```

Here, you copy the sprite image to a specified location from the third surface to the second surface. You are doing what is called building up the scene. Each of the three sprites on the screen must be accounted for. Notice here that you tell the surface to blit the images with color key information. This ensures that the sprites, which have holes, display correctly.

```
result = m_DDSurface2.BltFast(xpos[i], ypos[i], &m_DDOSurface1, &rcRect,
  DDBLTFAST_SRCCOLORKEY);
if(result == DD_OK)
  break;
```

```
      if(result == DDERR_SURFACELOST)
      {
        result = RestoreAll();
        if(result != DD_OK)
          return;
      }
      if(result != DDERR_WASSTILLDRAWING)
        return;
    }
  }
  // Flip the surfaces
  while(1)
  {
```

Here, you finally take the first and second surfaces and flip them. The second surface is flipped with the first surface because the second surface is attached to the first surface.

```
    result = m_DDSurface1.Flip(NULL, 0);
    if(result == DD_OK)
      break;
    if(result == DDERR_SURFACELOST)
    {
      result = RestoreAll();
      if(result != DD_OK)
        break;
    }
    if(result != DDERR_WASSTILLDRAWING)
      break;
  }
}
```

That is SurfaceDemo1. You added a few more features that make the demo more interesting to watch. Next, you're going to jump ahead a little and take a look at SurfaceDemo2. The one feature that it adds to SurfaceDemo1 is palette manipulation. Go ahead and run the application from the CD-ROM, and then I'll discuss it.

Using DirectDraw Palettes

In the source code file SurfaceDemo2.cpp, you'll see just a few more lines of code to support palette manipulation. You include the array of colors for the tori (the doughnut-shaped sprites) on the screen. Here is the added part in the StartDirectDraw method:

```
...
result = m_DDOSurface1.SetColorKey(RGB(0,0,0));
if(result == DD_OK)
{
  int i,x,y;
  // First, set all colors as unused
  for(i=0; i<256; i++)
    TorusColors[i] = 0;
  // lock the surface and scan the lower part (the torus area)
  // and remember all the indexes we find.
  info.dwSize = sizeof(DDSURFACEDESC);
  while (m_DDOSurface1.Lock(NULL, &info, 0, NULL) == DDERR_WASSTILLDRAWING) ;
  // Now search through the torus frames and mark used colors
```

```
  for(y=480; y<480+384; y++)
  {
    for(x=0; x<640; x++)
      TorusColors[((BYTE *)info.lpSurface)[y*info.lPitch+x]] = 1;
  }
  m_DDOSurface1.Unlock(NULL);
  TRACE("CSurfaceDemo2.StartDirectDraw SUCCESS!\n");
  return TRUE;
}
...
```

After setting the color key for the third surface, you build an array for the colors that the tori use. You lock the surface so that no one but you can access it, and you find the colors that the tori use so that later you can change the color of the tori without modifying the colors of the background.

The only other major change in the source code is in the UpdateFrame method. After you copy the background and the sprites (tori) onto the second surface, but before you flip the surfaces, you change the colors the tori use. There is no finite color you set for the tori; you simply randomize them for a greater visual effect. This is an advanced technique that could be used in many ways. Figure 15.8 shows a frame of SurfaceDemo2.

```
if((thisTickCount - lastTickCount[3]) > delay[3])
  {
    // Change the palette
    if(m_DDPalette.GetEntries(0, 0, 256, pe) != DD_OK)
      return;
    for(i=1; i<256; i++)
    {
      if(!TorusColors[i])
        continue;
      pe[i].peRed = (pe[i].peRed+2) % 256;
      pe[i].peGreen = (pe[i].peGreen+1) % 256;
      pe[i].peBlue = (pe[i].peBlue+3) % 256;
    }
    if(m_DDPalette.SetEntries(0, 0, 256, pe) != DD_OK)
      return;
    lastTickCount[3] = thisTickCount;
  }
```

Having gone through all that, slow down and learn more about palettes and DirectDraw palettes.

Palettes are tables that contain color information. You use them in concert with images so that they display correctly. In normal Windows, that is, 8-bit Windows, you only have 256 colors that can be displayed on the screen at any one time. Usually, when you want to create color-intensive applications, you quickly realize that you can use only 256 colors, and 20 of them have to be standard Windows colors. Having 236 colors is not inspiring in the least, and you must devise all sorts of tricks to give the illusion of more than 256 colors. When you're using DirectDraw and running it full-screen, you can use all 256 colors and forget about the Windows colors. This is better. The ideal solution is for everyone to buy cards that support 16-bit (65,536 colors) and higher modes, along with 4MB of memory. This is an expensive solution, but 1997 will see a solution from Intel that will enable you to use system memory as video memory. This will allow you to use high color modes and forget about palettes, but until then, you're stuck with them.

FIGURE 15.8.

A frame of SurfaceDemo2.

Using palettes is straightforward. PaletteDemo1 is a windowed DirectDraw application, which means that the application runs like any other Windows application. The main feature about PaletteDemo1 is that you can attach palettes with 256 colors and force Windows to display all of them. Obviously, this has a horrendous effect on other applications in terms of the display. Go ahead and run the PaletteDemo1 executable, play with it, and then read my discussion. Remember that if your Windows is running in anything higher than 8-bit mode, PaletteDemo1 does not work as intended. Run this demo in 8-bit mode because modes higher than 8-bit do not use palettes.

Some notable items in the source code are the different StartDirectDraw method, the list box for displaying results, and the palette-changing code. The version of the StartDirectDraw method here supports running the application in a window:

```
BOOL CPaletteDemo1::StartDirectDraw(void)
{
```

Here, you create a list box to display results to the user:

```
m_listbox.Create(m_window, 100);
// create the main DirectDraw object
HRESULT result = m_DirectDraw.Create();
```

```
m_listbox.PrintfDDRC( result, m_DirectDraw.GetDDErrorString(result),
  "DirectDrawCreate");
if(result == DD_OK)
{
```

Here, you set the cooperative mode to normal, which means it runs in a normal window.

```
result = m_DirectDraw.SetCooperativeLevel(m_window, DDSCL_NORMAL);
if(result == DD_OK)
{
  // create the primary surface
  DDSURFACEDESC info;
  info.dwSize = sizeof(DDSURFACEDESC);
  info.dwFlags = DDSD_CAPS;
  info.ddsCaps.dwCaps = DDSCAPS_PRIMARYSURFACE;
  result = m_DDSurface1.CreateSurface(&info);
  m_listbox.PrintfDDRC(result, m_DirectDraw.GetDDErrorString(result),
    "CreateSurface");
  if(result == DD_OK)
  {
```

Here, you create the palettes and set up to run:

```
    // set up palettes
    if(ResetExclusiveAndPalettes())
    {
      TRACE("CPaletteDemo1.StartDirectDraw SUCCESS!\n");
      return TRUE;
    }
  }
}
}
TRACE("CPaletteDemo1.StartDirectDraw FAILURE!\n");
char buf[256];
wsprintf(buf, "Direct Draw Init Failed (%08lx)\n", result);
MessageBox(m_window, buf, "ERROR", MB_OK | MB_ICONSTOP);

return FALSE;
}
```

The `ResetExclusiveAndPalettes` method creates the four palettes you use and also has code to switch the cooperative method from normal to exclusive:

```
BOOL CPaletteDemo1::ResetExclusiveAndPalettes(void)
{
  LPPALETTEENTRY ppe;
  HRESULT result;

  // create palette entries
  ppe = (LPPALETTEENTRY) LocalAlloc(LPTR, sizeof(PALETTEENTRY) * 256);
  if(ppe == NULL)
    return FALSE;
  // release existing palettes
  for(int i=0;i<MAX_PALETTES;i++)
  {
```

```
    if(m_OtherPalette[i].m_pPalette != NULL)
    {
      result = m_OtherPalette[i].Release();
      m_listbox.PrintfDDRC(result, m_DirectDraw.GetDDErrorString(result),
        "Release");
      m_OtherPalette[i].m_pPalette = NULL;
    }
  }
```

This section sets the cooperative level to either exclusive or normal. You need to run in exclusive mode if you want to change the palettes. If you run in normal mode, the palette attaching does not work. If you did not try this on the demo, go back now and see what happens.

```
if(m_IsExclusive)
  result = m_DirectDraw.SetCooperativeLevel(m_window,
    DDSCL_EXCLUSIVE | DDSCL_FULLSCREEN);
else
  result = m_DirectDraw.SetCooperativeLevel(m_window, DDSCL_NORMAL);

m_listbox.PrintfDDRC(result, m_DirectDraw.GetDDErrorString(result),
  "SetCooperativeLevel");

// set up 4 palettes
ppe[0].peRed = 0;
ppe[0].peGreen = 0;
ppe[0].peBlue = 0;
ppe[255].peRed = 255;
ppe[255].peGreen = 255;
ppe[255].peBlue = 255;

for(i=1;i<255;i++)
{
  ppe[i].peRed = 0;
  ppe[i].peGreen = 0;
  ppe[i].peBlue = 0;
}
result = m_OtherPalette[0].CreatePalette(DDPCAPS_8BIT, ppe);
m_listbox.PrintfDDRC(result, m_DirectDraw.GetDDErrorString(result),
  "CreatePalette");

for(i=1;i<255;i++)
{
  ppe[i].peRed = 0;
  ppe[i].peGreen = 255;
  ppe[i].peBlue = 255;
}
result = m_OtherPalette[1].CreatePalette(DDPCAPS_8BIT, ppe);
m_listbox.PrintfDDRC(result, m_DirectDraw.GetDDErrorString(result),
  "CreatePalette");

for(i=1;i<255;i++)
{
  ppe[i].peRed = 255;
  ppe[i].peGreen = 255;
  ppe[i].peBlue = 0;
}
```

```
result = m_OtherPalette[2].CreatePalette(DDPCAPS_8BIT, ppe);
m_listbox.PrintfDDRC(result, m_DirectDraw.GetDDErrorString(result),
  "CreatePalette");

for(i=1;i<255;i++)
{
  ppe[i].peRed = 255;
  ppe[i].peGreen = 0;
  ppe[i].peBlue = 255;
}
result = m_OtherPalette[3].CreatePalette(DDPCAPS_8BIT, ppe);
m_listbox.PrintfDDRC(result, m_DirectDraw.GetDDErrorString(result),
  "CreatePalette");
LocalFree(ppe);

for(i=0;i<MAX_PALETTES;i++)
  m_listbox.Printf("m_OtherPalette %d = %08lx", i+1, m_OtherPalette[i]);
return TRUE;
}
```

That discussion wraps up using DirectDraw palettes.

Using DirectDraw Clippers

You use DirectDraw clippers when you want to clip a certain area. In DirectDraw-based applications, you use clippers in applications running in a window. A clipper does the job of telling DirectDraw methods that they can write only to a certain area of the screen. In a window, this is very important, because you want to write only to the area of the screen that belongs to the application. If you didn't use a clipper, you would end up writing to parts of the screen that didn't belong to you and thereby cause visual havoc—not to mention that your software would be useless to everyone.

The last DirectDraw-based demo is ClipperDemo, shown in Figure 15.9. This demo runs in a window and uses a clipper to make sure you write only to the part of the screen that belongs to you. Creating and using a DirectDraw clipper is a straightforward process and is demonstrated in the StartDirectDraw method:

FIGURE 15.9.
The ClipperDemo.

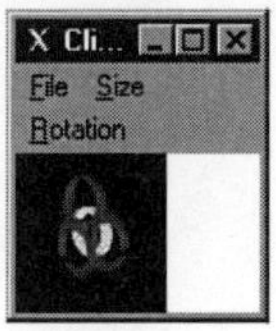

```
BOOL CClipperDemo::StartDirectDraw(void)
{
  // create the main DirectDraw object
  HRESULT result = m_DirectDraw.Create();
  if(result == DD_OK)
  {
```

15

A GRAPHICS
DEVELOPMENT
WORKSTATION

Here again, you set the cooperative level to normal, meaning the application runs as a normal window.

```
result = m_DirectDraw.SetCooperativeLevel(m_window, DDSCL_NORMAL);
if(result == DD_OK)
{
  // Create the primary surface with 1 back buffer
  DDSURFACEDESC info;
  info.dwSize = sizeof(DDSURFACEDESC);
  info.dwFlags = DDSD_CAPS;
  info.ddsCaps.dwCaps = DDSCAPS_PRIMARYSURFACE;
  result = m_DDSurface1.CreateSurface(&info);
  if(result == DD_OK)
  {
```

Here, you create a clipper. There is nothing to it—just call the `CreateClipper` method.

```
    result = m_DDClipper.CreateClipper();
    if (result == DD_OK)
    {
```

Here, you attach the application's window to the clipper so the clipper knows which coordinates to use when providing clipping information.

```
      result = m_DDClipper.SetHWnd(0, m_window);
      if (result == DD_OK)
      {
```

Attach the clipper to the primary surface. The process is completed with this line of code. After this, you don't need to worry about clipping because DirectDraw does it for you.

```
        result = m_DDSurface1.SetClipper(&m_DDClipper);
        if (result == DD_OK)
        {
          result = m_DDPalette.LoadPalette(bitmap);
          if (result == DD_OK)
          {
            result = m_DDSurface1.SetPalette(&m_DDPalette);
            if (result == DD_OK)
            {
              result = m_DDSurface2.LoadBitmap(bitmap);
              if (result == DD_OK)
              {
                TRACE("CClipperDemo.StartDirectDraw SUCCESS!\n");
                return TRUE;
              }
            }
          }
        }
      }
    }
  }
}
TRACE("CClipperDemo.StartDirectDraw FAILURE!\n");
char buf[256];
```

```
wsprintf(buf, "Direct Draw Init Failed (%08lx)\n", result);
MessageBox(m_window, buf, "ERROR", MB_OK | MB_ICONSTOP);

return FALSE;
}
```

You have taken a whirlwind tour of using DirectDraw and its related objects. This short introduction should get you up and running with DirectDraw. There is more, much more, that DirectDraw and DirectX can do, and if blazingly fast animation is what you're after, you've come to the right place.

Wrap-Up

One item I have not discussed is releasing the DirectDraw objects that you have created. You do not have to worry about forgetting to do this. The framework does this for you transparently. The CDirectDraw class's deconstructor calls the IDirectDraw::Release method. Any object created with this DirectDraw instance, meaning any IDirectDrawSurface, IDirectDrawPalette, or IDirectDrawClipper, is automatically released back to the system. This is just another advantage of having a framework.

The examples included on the DirectX SDK are invaluable for learning how to program DirectDraw and the rest of the API. You should take an extended look at these examples. Following are a few other resources that you can consult if you are interested in continuing your education and use of DirectX:

- *Windows 95 Game Developer's Guide Using the Game SDK*, Morrison and Weems, Sams, ISBN 0-672-30661-1.
- *DirectDraw Programming*, Bret Timmins, M&T Books, ISBN 1-55851-460-0.
- *Windows 95 Games Programming*, Stan Trujillo and Al Stevens, M&T Books, ISBN 1-55851-448-1.
- www.microsoft.com/gamesdev is the Web home for DirectX technologies and has tutorials.

The CD-ROM includes the shareware versions of Paint Shop Pro and Caligari trueSpace to give you some tools to develop graphics with. Have fun!

OpenGL

OpenGL is a 3-D API which helps you create applications that provide your users with a 3-D interface. It is used by companies that specialize in creating gorgeous 3-D applications. SGI machines usually use applications developed with OpenGL. It has been only recently that OpenGL made its way to Windows. Now that it is here for you to use, you can create applications that enable your users to manipulate 3-D objects and worlds. Microsoft has licensed OpenGL for use with Windows NT and Windows 95, which means you don't have to pay royalties for using OpenGL. If you are looking to write awesome 3-D applications, keep reading this section.

What Is OpenGL?

OpenGL is a graphics library for creating interactive 3-D graphical applications. It is a platform-independent library meant to work on various systems. Among the systems OpenGL works on are SGI machines, Windows NT machines, and other UNIX machines. OpenGL does not provide methods for using windows and user input. Although it would seem that you as a programmer and user of OpenGL are left to handle this task, an auxiliary library is usually provided to help out with these chores. The Windows implementation of OpenGL contains this library for your use. OpenGL works at such a low level that you have complete control of how and what your particular application does with OpenGL. To create models, you must build them up from a very small set of primitives—points, lines, and polygons. There are, of course, libraries that work on top of OpenGL that provide high-level methods for creating models, but a discussion of them is not within the focus of this chapter.

OpenGL does provide the means for generating images and interactive applications that use wireframe display, depth cueing, anti-aliasing, flat shading, smooth shading, shadows, texture mapping, motion blurring, and more.

The creation of OpenGL-based applications tends to follow these basic steps:

1. Construct shapes from geometric primitives such as points, lines, polygons, images, and bitmaps.
2. Compose a scene by arranging the objects in 3-D space and setting a vantage point for viewing the scene.
3. Calculate the colors of the objects. Colors for objects may be determined specifically by the application from specified lighting conditions or from textures applied to the objects.
4. Convert the mathematical description of objects and the color information to the screen.

This process is by no means the only way of programming OpenGL applications; you can add steps anywhere in the process to satisfy your needs, but you should follow the overall spirit of the process.

OpenGL types and commands are prefixed with GL and gl, respectively. Some examples are glVertex2i, GLfloat, GLshort, and glColor3f. This makes OpenGL types and commands stand out in your code and helps you to not confuse the regular system code with OpenGL code.

OpenGL is very much a C-based library. There is no object-oriented implementation of OpenGL, but there are libraries that have given OpenGL an object-oriented interface. Because

I am using MFC to write the demo applications, there is a mix of C and C++ in the applications.

OpenGL is a state machine, meaning you put OpenGL into various operating states. For example, the current color is a state. You can set the current color to any color you want—yellow, blue, red, and so on—and whatever object you draw after setting the color is drawn with that color. You can put OpenGL into many different states. For a complete list of all the states available, pick up a copy of the *OpenGL Programming Guide.* The information for this book is at the end of the section. This book is the best place to start learning OpenGL, because it was written by the people who made OpenGL.

Throughout this chapter, I develop an application tutorial style to show how you add functionality to the application and also so I can highlight a certain topic in the code. I start by creating the first version of the application, `gl`. All the source code for `gl` and the rest of the demo applications are on the CD-ROM in the `\source\chap15\OpenGL` directory.

Creating 3-D Objects

The DirectDraw section of this chapter has an app wizard, so it's only fair that OpenGL have a wizard also. The wizard is in the `\source\chap15\OpenGL` directory on the CD-ROM. You can copy it to your `msdev\template` library where you installed Visual C++. Installing this wizard is the same process as installing the DirectDraw wizard. Figure 15.10 shows what Visual C++ should look like if you installed the app wizard correctly. The OpenGL Wizard creates the demo application that you start with, `gl`.

FIGURE 15.10.

The first screen of the OpenGL app wizard.

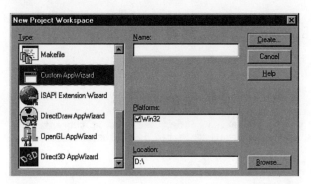

Among all the files generated for the application are two files that contain the bulk of the code that you need to make the application work. The rest of the code is there to provide the underlying base for the application to work. These two files are `GL1View.h` and `GL1View.cpp`. Throughout the demo applications, you only need to modify the class that is derived from `CGlView`. This saves time in getting an application up and running. Before you get to creating 3-D objects, take a look at how the code underneath works.

15

A GRAPHICS
DEVELOPMENT
WORKSTATION

All OpenGL applications use palettes, so you need to make sure that you are notified when palettes are changed or when you need to modify the system palette for use with the application. The palette-handling code is handled in `Mainframe.cpp`. You catch the palette messages by providing the methods `OnPaletteChanged` and `OnQueryNewPalette`. The two methods handle the work involved with the palettes. Because it is handled, you never need to worry about it.

The application demos use the MFC document/view architecture, but because you are not using files, the document class does nothing. It is only present to keep MFC happy and working. The view part of the document/view team is where the majority of the code happens. In this class is the code that sets up the initial view and provides helper methods for the derived class. All your application's code is in the class `C<yourapp>View` that is one level higher. This base view class provides your application with a device context and a palette for use by OpenGL, initializes OpenGL for use within your application, sets up the pixel format, creates an RGB palette, and provides simple error output.

Notice what happens when your application starts to get a better idea of what OpenGL is doing. `CGlView`'s life begins when its `OnCreate` member method is called. Take a look at what this looks like:

```
int CGlView::OnCreate(LPCREATESTRUCT lpCreateStruct)
{
  if (CView::OnCreate(lpCreateStruct) == -1)
    return -1;
  // start OpenGL
  StartOpenGL();
  return 0;
}
```

This is pretty straightforward—you let MFC create the view and then start OpenGL.

```
void CGlView::StartOpenGL(void)
{
  m_dc = new CClientDC(this);
  ASSERT(m_dc != NULL);
  if(!SetupPixelFormat())
    return;
  CreateRGBPalette();
  // create a rendering context and make it current
  HGLRC hrc = wglCreateContext(m_dc->GetSafeHdc());
}
```

Begin by creating a device context for use by that application that is based on the client area of the window. Keep this around until the application exits. Next, set the pixel format. When you set the pixel format, you are telling OpenGL what the environment wants to look like.

```
BOOL CGlView::SetupPixelFormat(void)
{
  static PIXELFORMATDESCRIPTOR pfd =
  {
    sizeof(PIXELFORMATDESCRIPTOR),  // size of this pfd
    1,                              // version number
    PFD_DRAW_TO_WINDOW |            // support window
      PFD_SUPPORT_OPENGL |          // support OpenGL
```

```
      PFD_DOUBLEBUFFER,              // double buffered
    PFD_TYPE_RGBA,                  // RGBA type
    24,                             // 24-bit color depth
    0, 0, 0, 0, 0, 0,               // color bits ignored
    0,                              // no alpha buffer
    0,                              // shift bit ignored
    0,                              // no accumulation buffer
    0, 0, 0, 0,                     // accum bits ignored
    32,                             // 32-bit z-buffer
    0,                              // no stencil buffer
    0,                              // no auxiliary buffer
    PFD_MAIN_PLANE,                 // main layer
    0,                              // reserved
    0, 0, 0                         // layer masks ignored
  };

  int pixelformat;
  if((pixelformat = ChoosePixelFormat(m_dc->GetSafeHdc(), &pfd)) == 0)
  {
    MessageBox("ChoosePixelFormat failed");
    return FALSE;
  }
  if(SetPixelFormat(m_dc->GetSafeHdc(), pixelformat, &pfd) == FALSE)
  {
    MessageBox("SetPixelFormat failed");
    return FALSE;
  }
  return TRUE;
}
```

After you set up the pixel format, you create the RGB palette:

```
void CGlView::CreateRGBPalette(void)
{
  int n = ::GetPixelFormat(m_pDC->GetSafeHdc());
  PIXELFORMATDESCRIPTOR pfd;
  ::DescribePixelFormat(m_pDC->GetSafeHdc(), n, sizeof(pfd), &pfd);

  if(pfd.dwFlags & PFD_NEED_PALETTE)
  {
    n = 1 << pfd.cColorBits;
    LOGPALETTE* pal =
      (PLOGPALETTE)new BYTE[sizeof(LOGPALETTE) + n * sizeof(PALETTEENTRY)];
    ASSERT(pal != NULL);
    pal->palVersion = 0x300;
    pal->palNumEntries = n;

    for (int i=0; i<n; i++)
    {
      pal->palPalEntry[i].peRed   =
        ComponentFromIndex(i, pfd.cRedBits, pfd.cRedShift);
      pal->palPalEntry[i].peGreen =
        ComponentFromIndex(i, pfd.cGreenBits, pfd.cGreenShift);
      pal->palPalEntry[i].peBlue  =
        ComponentFromIndex(i, pfd.cBlueBits, pfd.cBlueShift);
      pal->palPalEntry[i].peFlags = 0;
    }
    // fix up the palette to include the default GDI palette
```

```
  if ((pfd.cColorBits  == 8)                               &&
      (pfd.cRedBits    == 3) && (pfd.cRedShift   == 0) &&
      (pfd.cGreenBits  == 3) && (pfd.cGreenShift == 3) &&
      (pfd.cBlueBits   == 2) && (pfd.cBlueShift  == 6))
  {
    for (i = 1 ; i <= 12 ; i++)
      pal->palPalEntry[ defaultOverride[i] ] = defaultPalEntry[i];
  }
  if (m_pPalette)
    delete m_pPalette;
  m_pPalette = new CPalette;
  m_pPalette->CreatePalette(pal);
  delete pal;

  m_pDC->SelectPalette(m_pPalette, FALSE);
  m_pDC->RealizePalette();
  }
}
```

As you can see from the code, if you are in a video mode that requires a palette, you create a palette for OpenGL to use for any mode that is 8-bit (256 colors) or less; otherwise, you do nothing.

The last part of setting up OpenGL is to create a rendering context for OpenGL to draw on. The handle to the device context provides this for OpenGL.

After this is done, OpenGL is set up and ready to use. When the application is finished, the OnDestroy method is called to perform cleanup for OpenGL:

```
void CGlView::OnDestroy()
{
  wglMakeCurrent(NULL,NULL);
  if (m_hrc)
  {
    wglDeleteContext(m_hrc);
    m_hrc = NULL;
  }
  CPalette DefaultPalette;
  // Select our palette out of the dc
  DefaultPalette.CreateStockObject(DEFAULT_PALETTE);
  m_pDC->SelectPalette(&DefaultPalette, FALSE);
  if (m_pPalette)
    delete m_pPalette;
  if(m_pDC)
    delete m_pDC;

  CView::OnDestroy();
}
```

You first make the rendering context not current or turn it off. You don't want OpenGL drawing anything more. Do this with the call to wglMakeCurrent by specifying two NULL values as the required parameters. Next, delete the rendering context, reset the palette, delete the palette if you were using one, and delete the device context the application was using.

This is the basic, required functionality for OpenGL. With this code in hand, you are ready to start developing your own OpenGL/MFC-based applications.

Viewing 3-D Objects

Viewing an object with OpenGL is straightforward. In the gl demo, you create a box object and display it in the window. You also have to take care of a few chores to make sure the window always displays correctly. I discuss that before I talk about creating and displaying the box object.

The Gl1View.cpp file has all the important code for this demo. It is very short and very sweet. You need to take care of two chores so the applications always look correct, handling what happens when the window is resized and when the window needs to be repainted. The methods OnSize and OnPaint handle this functionality.

When your user sizes the window, you need to tell OpenGL that the viewport is resizing so it can reset itself for the new size.

```
void CGl1View::OnSize(UINT nType, int cx, int cy)
{
  CGlView::OnSize(nType, cx, cy);

  if ((cx <= 0) || (cy <= 0))
    return;
  //
  // Make the rendering context m_hrc current
  //
  BOOL bResult = wglMakeCurrent(m_pDC->m_hDC, m_hrc);
  if (!bResult)
  {
    TRACE("wglMakeCurrent Failed %x\r\n", GetLastError());
    return;
  }
  //
  // Set up the mapping of 3-D-space to screen space
  //
  GLdouble gldAspect = (GLdouble) cx/ (GLdouble) cy;
  glMatrixMode(GL_PROJECTION); OutputGlError("MatrixMode");
  glLoadIdentity();
  gluPerspective(30.0, gldAspect, 1.0, 10.0);
  glViewport(0, 0, cx, cy);
  //
  // No rendering context will be current.
  //
  wglMakeCurrent(NULL, NULL);
}
```

First, make sure you keep MFC happy and let the MFC view resize itself. Then, make sure the rendering context still works. If everything goes well, you then set up the 3-D space to 2-D space mapping. Here, you set the matrix mode and then replace the current matrix with an identity matrix. You then need to set the perspective of the view. Tell it the field of view angle, the aspect ratio, and the distances to the near and far clipping planes. Next, tell OpenGL the new size of the viewport and erase the current rendering context. All of this ensures that when the window is resized, OpenGL remains functional. You could have put this code in the base class, but your application might need to replace or modify some of the settings, so it's best to place it here so you can modify it to your liking.

The other order of business is to handle paint messages in `OnPaint` as follows:

```
void CGl1View::OnPaint()
{
  CPaintDC dc(this); // device context for painting
  // Select the palette.
  CPalette* OldPalette = NULL;
  if (m_pPalette)
  {
    OldPalette = dc.SelectPalette(m_pPalette, 0);
    dc.RealizePalette();
  }
  // Make the HGLRC current
  BOOL bResult = wglMakeCurrent(dc.m_hDC, m_hrc);
  if (!bResult)
    TRACE("wglMakeCurrent Failed %x\r\n", GetLastError());
  // Draw
  DrawScene();
  //Swap Buffers
  SwapBuffers(dc.m_hDC);
  // select old palette if we altered it
  if (OldPalette)
    dc.SelectPalette(OldPalette, 0);

  wglMakeCurrent(NULL, NULL);
  // Do not call CFrameWnd::OnPaint() for painting messages
}
```

Basically, just make sure the palette, if you are using one, is the current palette Windows is using. Make OpenGL use the rendering context, redraw the scene, and then erase the rendering context. This is straightforward because this demo really doesn't do much.

Now you get to the last part of this demo, which is the demo itself. You create and display a box:

```
void CGl1View::DrawScene()
{
```

Here, you create the color you use for the box:

```
  // Set up some colors
  static GLdouble yellow[3] = {1.0, 1.0, 0.0};
```

Set up the lights and depth color buffers:

```
  // Enable lighting calculations
  glEnable(GL_LIGHTING);
  OutputGlError("glEnable (GL_LIGHTING);");
  glEnable(GL_LIGHT0);
  OutputGlError("glEnable (GL_LIGHT0);");
  // Enable depth calculations
  glEnable(GL_DEPTH_TEST);
  OutputGlError("glEnable (GL_DEPTH_TEST);");
  // Clear the color and depth buffers
```

```
glClearColor(0.0f, 0.0f, 0.0f, 0.0f);
glClear(GL_COLOR_BUFFER_BIT | GL_DEPTH_BUFFER_BIT);
// Set the material color to follow the current color
glColorMaterial(GL_FRONT, GL_AMBIENT_AND_DIFFUSE);
glEnable(GL_COLOR_MATERIAL);
```

Here, you begin to draw the box. You set the matrix mode to model view (the box is a model) and then you load an identity matrix. Translate and rotate the box and set the box's color to yellow:

```
//
// Draw the box.
//
glMatrixMode(GL_MODELVIEW);
OutputGlError("MatrixMode");
// Translate and rotate the axis.
glLoadIdentity();
glTranslated(0.5, 0.0, -4.5);
glRotated(m_angle.cx, 1.0, 0.0, 0.0);
glRotated(m_angle.cy, 0.0, 1.0, 0.0);
glColor3dv(yellow); // Change the current color to yellow.
GLdouble size = 0.5;
```

Draw the six faces of the box: right, left, front, back, top, and bottom. Then, flush the drawing pipeline and you are done.

```
//
// Draw the six faces of the box.
//
glBegin(GL_POLYGON); // right
  glNormal3d( 0.0,  0.0,  size);
  glVertex3d(size,  size, size);
  glVertex3d(-size,  size, size);
  glVertex3d(-size, -size, size);
  glVertex3d(size, -size, size);
glEnd();

glBegin(GL_POLYGON); //left
  glNormal3d(0.0,  0.0, -size);
  glVertex3d(size,  size, -size);
  glVertex3d(size, -size, -size);
  glVertex3d(-size, -size, -size);
  glVertex3d(-size,  size, -size);
glEnd();

glBegin(GL_POLYGON); //Front
  glNormal3d(-size,  0.0,  0.0);
  glVertex3d(-size,  size,  size);
  glVertex3d(-size,  size, -size);
  glVertex3d(-size, -size, -size);
  glVertex3d(-size, -size,  size);
glEnd();

glBegin(GL_POLYGON);  //Back
  glNormal3d(size,  0.0,  0.0);
  glVertex3d(size,  size,  size);
```

```
      glVertex3d(size, -size,  size);
      glVertex3d(size, -size, -size);
      glVertex3d(size,  size, -size);
   glEnd();

   glBegin(GL_POLYGON);   //Top
      glNormal3d(0.0, size,  0.0);
      glVertex3d(-size, size, -size);
      glVertex3d(-size, size,  size);
      glVertex3d(size, size,  size);
      glVertex3d(size, size, -size);
   glEnd();

   glBegin(GL_POLYGON); //Bottom
      glNormal3d(0.0, -size,  0.0);
      glVertex3d(-size, -size, -size);
      glVertex3d(size, -size, -size);
      glVertex3d(size, -size,  size);
      glVertex3d(-size, -size,  size);
   glEnd();
   //
   // Flush the drawing pipeline.
   //
   glFlush();
}
```

That is a great deal of code just to draw a yellow box. The power behind OpenGL is that you have complete control to create objects in the scene as you see fit, and OpenGL gladly creates an image. This is also a disadvantage of OpenGL when you look at it from a high-level approach. You can't just call a method to create a box; you must create the method to create that box. The auxiliary library provides some of this high-level functionality, and I discuss that later.

Next, take a look at the second demo, gl2. gl2 builds from gl1 by creating an additional two objects, a pyramid and a dodecahedron. The only part of the code that changes is the DrawScene method, as follows:

```
void CGl1View::DrawScene()
{
```

Here, you set up the color yellow and two more colors, one for the pyramid and one for the dodecahedron.

```
   // Set up some colors
   static GLdouble yellow[3] = {1.0, 1.0, 0.0};
   static GLdouble blue[3]   = {0.0,0.0,1.0};
   static GLdouble orange[3] = {0.96,0.38,0.03};
```

Skipping down to the code for the pyramid, you see that creating the pyramid is similar to creating the box:

```
...
//
// Draw the pyramid.
//
glLoadIdentity();
glTranslated(-0.7, 0.0, -4.5);
glRotated(m_angle[Pyramid].cx, 1.0, 0.0, 0.0);
glRotated(m_angle[Pyramid].cy, 0.0, 1.0, 0.0);
glColor3dv(orange);
// Draw the pyramid
glBegin(GL_POLYGON);
  glNormal3d(-size,-size,-size);
  glVertex3d(size,-size,-size); //2
  glVertex3d(-size,-size, size); //3
  glVertex3d(-size, size,-size); //4
glEnd();

glBegin(GL_POLYGON);
  glNormal3d(-size, size, size);
  glVertex3d(size, size, size); //1
  glVertex3d(-size, size,-size); //4
  glVertex3d(-size,-size, size); //3
glEnd();

glBegin(GL_POLYGON);
  glNormal3d(size, size,-size);
  glVertex3d(size, size, size); //1
  glVertex3d(size,-size,-size); //2
  glVertex3d(-size, size,-size); //4
glEnd();

glBegin(GL_POLYGON);
  glNormal3d(size,-size, size);
  glVertex3d(size, size, size); //1
  glVertex3d(-size,-size, size); //3
  glVertex3d(size,-size,-size); //2
glEnd();
```

The code for drawing the dodecahedron is also in the same format.

```
//
// Draw the Dodecahedron.
//
glLoadIdentity();
glTranslated(0.0, 0.0, -2.5);
glRotated(m_angle[Dodec].cx, 1.0, 0.0, 0.0);
glRotated(m_angle[Dodec].cy, 0.0, 1.0, 0.0);
glColor3dv(blue);
GLdouble dsize = 0.35; // Size for Dodecadedron
GLdouble t = ((sqrt(5) - 1.0) / 2.0);
GLdouble tt = t*t;
t *= dsize;
tt *= dsize;
```

```
glBegin(GL_POLYGON); // Face 0
  glNormal3d(0, dsize, t);
  glVertex3d( t,     t,     t); // Vertex  0
  glVertex3d(tt,dsize,      0); // Vertex  7
  glVertex3d(-tt,dsize,     0); // Vertex  8
  glVertex3d(-t,     t,     t); // Vertex 15
  glVertex3d( 0,    tt,dsize); // Vertex  4
glEnd();
...
```

I skip the rest of the code because it just finishes creating the dodecahedron and flushing the pipeline.

If you continue to add objects to your scene, you quickly end up writing a great deal of code. Next, I take a look at how to make this process easier.

Using Display Lists for Performance

You need to be able to create objects and then store them so you can reuse them. You could break the code for creating the box, pyramid, and dodecahedron into their own methods. This would work, but if you create an object using this solution, you could still incur some performance penalties. For example, if you create a circle object this way, every time you call the method for drawing the circle, you still have to perform the trigonometry. A better solution is a display list. A display list is a group of commands that are stored for later use. You could create a display list for the circle. It figures the trigonometry once, so when you call it, you wouldn't waste time. The third demo, g13, shows how to create display lists for each of the three objects you've been using, the box, pyramid, and the dodecahedron, and then use them. Once again, the code for the application remains the same as before. This time, you only need to modify the DrawScene method and add a new method, PrepareScene. First, look at the new method, PrepareScene, and see how to create display lists.

```
void CGl1View::PrepareScene(void)
{
  // Faster than using glScale.
  GLdouble size = 0.5;
  GLdouble dsize = 0.35; // Size for Dodecadedron
  //
  // Attach the window dc to OpenGL.
  //
  BOOL result = wglMakeCurrent(m_pDC->m_hDC, m_hrc);
  if (!result)
    TRACE("wglMakeCurrent Failed %x\r\n", GetLastError());
```

Here is where you begin to build the display list for the cube.

```
  //
  // Build a display list for the cube.
  //
  glNewList(Box, GL_COMPILE);
  //
  // Draw the six faces of the cube.
```

```
//
glBegin(GL_POLYGON); // right
  glNormal3d( 0.0,  0.0,  size);
  glVertex3d(size,  size, size);
  glVertex3d(-size,  size, size);
  glVertex3d(-size, -size, size);
  glVertex3d(size, -size, size);
glEnd();
...

glBegin(GL_POLYGON); //Bottom
  glNormal3d(0.0, -size,  0.0);
  glVertex3d(-size, -size, -size);
  glVertex3d(size, -size, -size);
  glVertex3d(size, -size,  size);
  glVertex3d(-size, -size,  size);
glEnd();
glEndList();
```

As you can see, all you need to do is use the glNewList method, giving it a name for the object and telling it to compile the following commands. All the OpenGL commands that follow until the end of the cube description and the final call to glEndList are put in the display list.

The display lists for the other two objects follow the same procedure; you create a new display list using glNewList, do the commands, and then finish with a call to glEndList.

Now, take a look at the code for DrawScene.

```
void CGl1View::DrawScene()
{
  ...
```

The code in the draw scene has been cleaned up quite a bit. All you do now is perform operations on the box and then call the display list with glCallList. glCallList executes the commands that were compiled when you created the display list for the box.

```
//
// Draw the box.
//
// Translate and rotate the axis.
glLoadIdentity();
  glTranslated(0.5, 0.0, -4.5);
  glRotated(m_angle[Box].cx, 1.0, 0.0, 0.0);
  glRotated(m_angle[Box].cy, 0.0, 1.0, 0.0);
  glColor3dv(yellow); // Change the current color to green.
glCallList(Box); // Draw the box.
```

Here, you see the same process for the pyramid.

```
//
// Draw the pyramid.
//
glLoadIdentity();
  glTranslated(-0.7, 0.0, -4.5);
  glRotated(m_angle[Pyramid].cx, 1.0, 0.0, 0.0);
  glRotated(m_angle[Pyramid].cy, 0.0, 1.0, 0.0);
  glColor3dv(orange);
glCallList(Pyramid);
```

15

A GRAPHICS
DEVELOPMENT
WORKSTATION

Once more, you see the same process for the dodecahedron.

```
//
// Draw the Dodecahedron.
//
glLoadIdentity();
  glTranslated(0.0, 0.0, -2.5);
  glRotated(m_angle[Dodec].cx, 1.0, 0.0, 0.0);
  glRotated(m_angle[Dodec].cy, 0.0, 1.0, 0.0);
  glColor3dv(blue);
glCallList(Dodec);
//
// Flush the drawing pipeline.
//
glFlush();
}
```

This code is much faster than before, and you have cleaned up the main call for displaying the objects. Using display lists is the best way to get performance out of OpenGL, and you'll do yourself and your users a great service by using display lists whenever possible.

Animation

Now, take a look at how you can add animation to the demo. The demo g14 adds code to the demo g13 so that you can rotate one or all of the objects. Run the g14.exe application on the CD-ROM and see what the demo does; then, come back and step through the code to see how it's done.

To add animation for g14, you need to make modifications in the other files, not just in Gl1View.cpp. The biggest modification to the demo is in the gl.h and gl.cpp files. You need to use the idle functionality of the MFC application. Whenever the application is not processing messages, it enters an idle state waiting for a message. The application can take advantage of this, which is what you do for this demo.

The first change you make is to override the virtual method CWinApp::OnIdle. Whenever the application goes into the idle state, it calls this method, which provides the link for putting animation in the demo. You also add a method named SetIdleEvent to toggle between including animation and ignoring animation so the application supports both situations. You pass the main view class, CGl1View, to this method. The following code shows the new app class:

```
class CGlApp : public CWinApp
{
public:
  CGlApp();
  void SetIdleEvent(CGl1View* view) { m_pIdleView = view;}
  //{{AFX_VIRTUAL(CGlApp)
  public:
  virtual BOOL InitInstance();
  virtual BOOL OnIdle(LONG lCount);
  //}}AFX_VIRTUAL
```

```
  //{{AFX_MSG(CGlApp)
  afx_msg void OnAppAbout();
  //}}AFX_MSG
  DECLARE_MESSAGE_MAP()
protected:
  CGl1View* m_pIdleView;
};
```

gl.cpp has a new method, OnIdle:

```
BOOL CGlApp::OnIdle(LONG lCount)
{
  if (!m_pIdleView)
    return FALSE;
  m_pIdleView->Tick();
  return TRUE; // need more cycles
  //return CWinApp::OnIdle(lCount);
}
```

When the application goes idle, it calls OnIdle. Here, you check to see whether you want animation by checking m_pIdleView. If m_pIdleView points to the view class, the Tick method is called; otherwise, you don't do anything.

The Tick method in the CGl1View class in the file Gl1View.cpp looks like this:

```
void CGl1View::Tick()
{
```

If you do not rotate all the objects, you change the angle of rotation for the currently selected rotating object.

```
  if (m_RotatingObject != All)
  {
    m_angle[m_RotatingObject].cx += 10;
    m_angle[m_RotatingObject].cy += 10;
    if (m_angle[m_RotatingObject].cx >= 360)
      m_angle[m_RotatingObject].cx = 0;
    if (m_angle[m_RotatingObject].cy >= 360)
      m_angle[m_RotatingObject].cy = 0;
  }
```

If you rotate all the objects, you need to change the angle of rotation for all the objects.

```
  else
  {
    m_angle[Box].cx += 10;
    m_angle[Box].cy += 10;
    if (m_angle[Box].cx >= 360)
      m_angle[Box].cx = 0;
    if (m_angle[Box].cy >= 360)
      m_angle[Box].cy = 0;

    m_angle[Pyramid].cx += 10;
    m_angle[Pyramid].cy += 10;
    if (m_angle[Pyramid].cx >= 360)
      m_angle[Pyramid].cx = 0;
    if (m_angle[Pyramid].cy >= 360)
      m_angle[Pyramid].cy = 0;
```

15

A GRAPHICS
DEVELOPMENT
WORKSTATION

```
    m_angle[Dodec].cx += 10;
    m_angle[Dodec].cy += 10;
    if (m_angle[Dodec].cx >= 360)
      m_angle[Dodec].cx = 0;
    if (m_angle[Dodec].cy >= 360)
      m_angle[Dodec].cy = 0;
  }
  Invalidate(FALSE);
  UpdateWindow();
}
```

Finally, you invalidate the window area, forcing a repaint, which is how you provide animation support for this demo. Of course, you must add more code to fully support animation in the demo, but it is mostly code to tie in menu options, and you can look at it in `Gl1View.cpp` at your leisure.

Next, take a look at the two additional libraries that come with OpenGL, the utility and the auxiliary libraries.

The Utility Library

The OpenGL utility library provides methods for the following functionality:

- Manipulating images for use in texturing
- Transforming coordinates
- Polygon tessellation
- Rendering spheres, cylinders, and disks
- NURBS curves and surfaces
- Describing errors

Manipulating Images for Use in Texturing

Texture mapping, the process of applying a 2-D image onto a 3-D object, uses three methods. Although I have not covered texture mapping in this chapter, you can take a look at some of the examples included with Visual C++ in the ...\msdev\samples\sdk\opengl directory on the CD-ROM. Replace ... with the path to the location of the msdev directory. The methods are `gluScaleImage` for scaling images and `gluBuild1DMipMaps` and `gluBuild2DMipMaps` for generating sets of mipmaps, an advanced technique for storing images in different sizes so texture mapping is better.

Transforming Coordinates

The methods for transforming coordinates provide the capability to set the viewing mode for applications. `gluPerspective` allows you to set the viewing mode for a standard perspective.

gluOrtho2D provides for orthographic viewing. gluLookAt allows you to position the viewpoint at a point in space and look at another point in space. For example, in a scene using a camera and a model, you can have the camera look at the model. If the model moves, the camera could follow the object. gluLookAt does not provide all this functionality, but it does provide one step in the process. Remember that with OpenGL, you have to do the grunt work, but then you have complete control. gluPickMatrix allows you to handle picking objects in the scene, usually with a mouse or other pointing device. Two methods, gluProject and gluUnProject, allow you to convert between object coordinates and screen coordinates.

Polygon Tessellation

OpenGL is capable of displaying only simple, convex polygons, meaning the edges only intersect at vertices. There are no duplicate vertices, and only two edges meet at any vertex. When your application requires simple, nonconvex polygons or polygons with holes in them, you must perform tessellation on the polygons. Tessellation is the subdivision of nonconvex polygons into convex polygons. A discussion of tessellation is out of the scope of this chapter, but the *OpenGL Programming Guide* is an excellent source for more information. The following routines are provided:

gluNewTess	gluDeleteTess
gluTessBeginPolygon	gluTessBeginContour
gluTessVertex	gluTessEndContour
gluTessEndPolygon	gluTessProperty
gluTessNormal	gluTessCallback
gluGetTessProperty	

Rendering Spheres, Cylinders, and Disks

The utility library contains routines to draw various simple surfaces, such as spheres, cylinders, disks, and parts of disks, using different styles and orientations. The following routines are provided:

gluNewQuadric	gluQuadricNormals
gluQuadricTexture	gluQuadricOrientation
gluQuadricDrawStyle	gluCylinder
gluDisk	gluPartialDisk
gluSphere	gluQuadricCallback

15

NURBS Curves and Surfaces

NURBS are non-uniform, rational b-splines, which specify parametric curves and surfaces in two and three dimensions. They usually represent geometry in many computer-aided mechanical design systems. The following routines are provided:

gluNewNurbsRenderer	gluDeleteNurbsRenderer
gluBeginSurface	gluBeginCurve
gluEndCurve	gluEndSurface
gluBeginTrim	gluEndTrim
gluPwlCurve	gluNurbsCurve
gluNurbsSurface	gluLoadSamplingMatrices
gluNurbsProperty	gluGetNurbsProperty
gluNurbsCallback	

Describing Errors

The utility library provides one routine, gluErrorString, to help you debug your OpenGL applications. This routine turns an OpenGL error code into an understandable, descriptive string. Use this routine to minimize problems in your code.

For complete information on these and all the other utility routines, please consult the Visual C++ OpenGL SDK, the Visual C++ OpenGL samples, and the *OpenGL Programming Guide*.

The Auxiliary Library

You have seen and learned about the enormous potential of OpenGL applications and the amount of work involved in building scenes. You are also aware of the lack of functionality when it comes to creating simple objects quickly. This is where the auxiliary library comes in. The auxiliary library that is provided with OpenGL is simple. It is usually included to help you along in learning how to accomplish more complicated feats. The auxiliary library provides the following methods:

■ auxInitWindow opens a window on the screen for use with your applications. You use the Escape key to exit, and the background color of the window is set to black.

■ auxInitPosition tells auxInitWindow where to put the window on the screen.

■ auxInitDisplayMode specifies to auxInitWindow the attributes of the window, such as whether the window is RGBA or color-indexed and single- or double-buffered, and whether the window has an associated depth, stencil, or accumulation buffer.

■ auxReshapeFunc sets a callback function for actions to be taken when the window is resized, moved, or exposed. This is similar to the MFC methods OnSize and OnMove.

- ■ auxKeyFunc allows you to set a callback for an action to be taken when a user hits a specific key on the keyboard.

- ■ auxMouseFunc allows you to set a callback for an action to be taken when a user presses or releases a mouse button.

If you decide to use MFC, you can safely ignore most of these methods. The methods you want are the ones that draw objects. The following list outlines each method and what it does:

- ■ auxWireSphere renders a wireframe sphere.

- ■ auxSolidSphere renders a solid sphere.

- ■ auxWireCube renders a wireframe cube.

- ■ auxSolidCube renders a solid cube.

- ■ auxWireBox renders a wireframe box.

- ■ auxSolidBox renders a solid box.

- ■ auxWireTorus renders a wireframe torus. A torus is an object that looks like a doughnut.

- ■ auxSolidTorus renders a solid torus.

- ■ auxWireCylinder renders a wireframe cylinder.

- ■ auxSolidCylinder renders a solid cylinder.

- ■ auxWireIcosahedron renders a wireframe icosahedron. An icosahedron is an object with 20 faces.

- ■ auxSolidIcosahedron renders a solid icosahedron.

- ■ auxWireOctahedron renders a wireframe octahedron. An octahedron is an object with eight faces.

- ■ auxSolidOctahedron renders a solid octahedron.

- ■ auxWireTetrahedron renders a wireframe tetrahedron. A tetrahedron is an object with four faces. An example of a tetrahedron is a pyramid.

- ■ auxSolidTetrahedron renders a solid tetrahedron.

- ■ auxWireDodecahedron renders a wireframe dodecahedron. A dodecahedron is an object with twelve faces.

- ■ auxSolidDodecahedron renders a solid dodecahedron.

- ■ auxWireCone renders a wireframe cone.

- ■ auxSolidCone renders a solid cone.

- ■ auxWireTeapot renders a wireframe teapot.

- ■ auxSolidTeapot renders a solid teapot.

15

A GRAPHICS DEVELOPMENT WORKSTATION

The last demo, g15, is an MFC port of the auxdemo demo that comes with Visual C++. The demo g15 not only demonstrates using the auxiliary library, but also shows how to port SDK style demos to an MFC-based framework.

The three methods shown in Listing 15.2, excluding the create method, contain the code that makes this demo work. Figure 15.11 shows what this demo looks like.

Listing 15.2. The main methods of the g15 demo.

```
void CGlobeView::PolarView(GLdouble radius, GLdouble twist,
  GLdouble latitude, GLdouble longitude)
{
  glTranslated(0.0, 0.0, -radius);
  glRotated(-twist, 0.0, 0.0, 1.0);
  glRotated(-latitude, 1.0, 0.0, 0.0);
  glRotated(longitude, 0.0, 0.0, 1.0);
}

void CGlobeView::DrawLight(void)
{
  glPushAttrib(GL_LIGHTING_BIT);
    glDisable(GL_LIGHTING);
    glColor3f(1.0f, 1.0f, 1.0f);
    auxSolidDodecahedron(0.1);
  glPopAttrib();
}

void CGlobeView::DrawScene(void)
{
  static Glfloat whiteAmbient[] = {0.3f, 0.3f, 0.3f, 1.0f};
  static Glfloat redAmbient[] = {0.3f, 0.1f, 0.1f, 1.0f};
  static Glfloat greenAmbient[] = {0.1f, 0.3f, 0.1f, 1.0f};
  static Glfloat blueAmbient[] = {0.1f, 0.1f, 0.3f, 1.0f};
  static Glfloat whiteDiffuse[] = {1.0f, 1.0f, 1.0f, 1.0f};
  static Glfloat redDiffuse[] = {1.0f, 0.0f, 0.0f, 1.0f};
  static Glfloat greenDiffuse[] = {0.0f, 1.0f, 0.0f, 1.0f};
  static Glfloat blueDiffuse[] = {0.0f, 0.0f, 1.0f, 1.0f};
  static Glfloat whiteSpecular[] = {1.0f, 1.0f, 1.0f, 1.0f};
  static Glfloat redSpecular[] = {1.0f, 0.0f, 0.0f, 1.0f};
  static Glfloat greenSpecular[] = {0.0f, 1.0f, 0.0f, 1.0f};
  static Glfloat blueSpecular[] = {0.0f, 0.0f, 1.0f, 1.0f};

  static Glfloat lightPosition0[] = {1.0f, 1.0f, 1.0f, 1.0f};
  static Glfloat angle = 0.0f;

  static BOOL busy = FALSE;

  if(busy)
    return;
  busy = TRUE;

  glClear(GL_COLOR_BUFFER_BIT | GL_DEPTH_BUFFER_BIT);
```

```
glPushMatrix();
  m_latitude += 4.0f;
  m_longitude += 2.5f;
  PolarView(m_radius, 0, m_latitude, m_longitude);
  glPushMatrix();
    angle += 6.0f;
    glRotatef(angle, 1.0f, 0.0f, 1.0f);
    glTranslatef(0.0f, 1.5f, 0.0f);
    glLightfv(GL_LIGHT0, GL_POSITION, lightPosition0);
    DrawLight();
  glPopMatrix();
  glPushAttrib(GL_LIGHTING_BIT);
    glMaterialfv(GL_FRONT_AND_BACK, GL_AMBIENT, redAmbient);
    glMaterialfv(GL_FRONT_AND_BACK, GL_DIFFUSE, redDiffuse);
    glMaterialfv(GL_FRONT_AND_BACK, GL_SPECULAR, whiteSpecular);
    glMaterialf(GL_FRONT, GL_SHININESS, 100.0f);
    auxSolidCone(0.3f, 0.6f);
  glPopAttrib();
  auxWireSphere(1.5);
  glPushAttrib(GL_LIGHTING_BIT);
    glMaterialfv(GL_BACK, GL_AMBIENT, greenAmbient);
    glMaterialfv(GL_BACK, GL_DIFFUSE, greenDiffuse);
    glMaterialfv(GL_FRONT, GL_AMBIENT, blueAmbient);
    glMaterialfv(GL_FRONT, GL_DIFFUSE, blueDiffuse);
    glMaterialfv(GL_FRONT, GL_SPECULAR, blueSpecular);
    glMaterialf(GL_FRONT, GL_SHININESS, 50.0f);
    glPushMatrix();
      glTranslatef(0.8f, -0.65f, 0.0f);
      glRotatef(30.0f, 1.0f, 0.5f, 1.0f);
      auxSolidCylinder(0.3, 0.6);
    glPopMatrix();
  glPopAttrib();
glPopMatrix();

SwapBuffers(wglGetCurrentDC());

busy = FALSE;
}
```

As you look through the code, you can see where the auxiliary methods are used. A call to auxSolidDodecahedron draws a light attached to the wireframe sphere. A call to auxSolidCone draws a cone, and a call to auxSolidCylinder draws a cylinder inside the wireframe sphere. Then, the call to auxWireSphere draws the wireframe sphere.

This demo also shows another method to create animation in your applications by using a timer. The timer is created in the OnCreate method after all the other items are created. From then on, Windows calls the OnTimer method, and it calls the DrawScene method to fulfill the animation loop. This loop continues until the program is terminated.

The source code for the auxiliary library is provided with Visual C++, and you should take a look at it to increase your knowledge of OpenGL.

15

A GRAPHICS
DEVELOPMENT
WORKSTATION

FIGURE 15.11.

The gl5 *demo in action.*

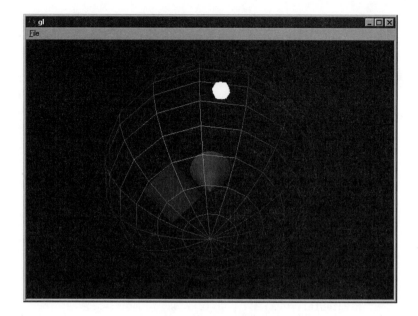

Wrap-Up

You should consult a few other resources if you want to continue your education and use of OpenGL:

- *OpenGL Programming Guide,* Neider, Davis, Woo; Addison-Wesley, ISBN 0-201-63274-8.

- *OpenGL Reference Manual,* OpenGL Architecture Review Board; Addison-Wesley, ISBN 0-201-63276-4.

- `www.sgi.com/Technology/openGL/opengl.html` is one of the best places on the Internet to get tons of information on OpenGL.

Visual C++ comes with OpenGL manuals in the online help and sample demos. You have a multitude of information waiting to be used.

Summary

As you can see, creating and using advanced graphics isn't hard. The only way you learn is to try and try again. With the information contained in this chapter, you should have a clearer understanding of what DirectDraw and OpenGL can do for your applications; the rest is up to you. Have fun.

V
PART

Networking Windows NT Workstation

Installing Windows NT Networking

by Sean Mathias

IN THIS CHAPTER

The installation of Windows NT Networking can be done during the initial installation of Windows NT itself, or it can be done at a later time. The fact that it can be delayed until after installation can be helpful when a problem arises with the networking portion of setup. The user can cancel the networking setup and finish installing the rest of the operating system rather than having to quit the setup of Windows NT and solve the networking issue.

In this chapter, you learn how to install Windows NT Networking after the initial Windows NT setup has completed, although the processes are identical for installing networking components during or after setup.

First, let me once again over-emphasize my point: Use a network card that is listed on the Hardware Compatibility List (HCL). Yes, you can use unlisted cards if you can get Windows NT drivers for them, but save yourself the headache and use a supported card. You will find that even the cards listed on the HCL can cause quite a headache and need a bit of work to get them functioning properly.

To begin installation of Windows NT Networking (assuming it has not already been installed), right-click the Network Neighborhood icon on the desktop and choose the Properties option. You are presented with a dialog, shown in Figure 16.1, informing you that Windows NT Networking has not been installed and asking if you would like to install it now. Click Yes. To be prepared for this process, be sure to know which network protocols are used at your location. Also, know the network protocol's appropriate configuration settings, the type of network adapter you are using and its settings, and the services you are to install. If you are in doubt, ask your IS group for the information.

FIGURE 16.1.

The Network Configuration dialog.

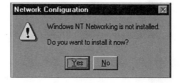

Clicking Yes starts the Network Setup Wizard. The Network Setup Wizard briefly analyzes and inspects your system, and you are then presented with a dialog asking how your computer should participate in the network—via local connection or using remote access. (See Figure 16.2.)

If you will be accessing the network through an ISDN adapter or network adapter, select the Wired to the network option. If you will be accessing the network remotely using a modem, select the Remote access to the network option, or select both if they are applicable to your situation. When you have made the necessary selections, click Next.

FIGURE 16.2.
The Network Setup Wizard configuration dialog.

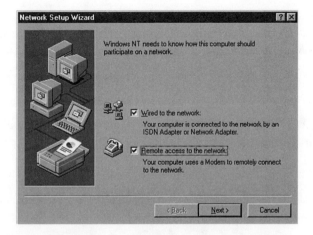

Installing and Configuring a Network Card

The next step is to install a network adapter. The Network Setup Wizard presents an adapter installation dialog that lists installed adapters in the system and provides two methods for installing network adapters. (See Figure 16.3.)

FIGURE 16.3.
The network adapter installation screen.

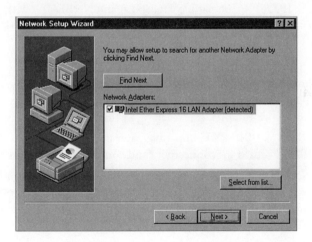

To let Windows NT search your system for a recognized network adapter, click the Find Next button. Windows NT searches your hardware for any recognized network adapters. When it finds a network adapter, it stops and lists it in the Network Adapters box. If you have more than one adapter installed in your system, click the Find Next button. Repeat this process until all installed adapters have been detected. If Windows NT does not find your adapter, you will have to use the Select from list option and manually specify your network adapter.

To manually select an adapter or specify an unsupported or unlisted adapter, click the Select from list button. Select the adapter that is installed in your system from the list; or, if you have a driver for an unlisted adapter or an updated driver, select the Have Disk button and provide the path to the network adapter driver files.

When all installed network adapters have been specified, click the Next button.

Choosing the Right Protocols

The next step in the Network Setup Wizard is to specify the protocols you want to use. This option depends on the protocols in use at your location, your networking needs, and your environment.

By default the Network Setup Wizard lists the three most common protocols—TCP/IP, NWLink IPX/SPX Compatible Transport, and NetBEUI—with TCP/IP being the only protocol selected (evidence again of Microsoft's focus on the Internet). This screen is shown in Figure 16.4.

■ TCP/IP: The Internet protocol suite. This is a suite of protocols originally designed to link diverse network and systems architectures over public and switched networks. This is a fairly efficient and flexible protocol, although given the explosion of the worldwide Internet, it is reaching its limits in its current version (IPv4).

■ NWLink IPX/SPX Compatible Transport: A NetBIOS-enabled implementation of IPX/SPX used for connectivity and communications with Novell NetWare servers.

■ NetBEUI: This is the long-standing protocol of choice for Microsoft networking. It is a very fast and efficient NetBIOS protocol, but it is not routable (except in rare circumstances of Token Ring networks with source-routing enabled). Therefore, NetBEUI is typically only used in small, nonrouted networks or departments.

To select or deselect a listed protocol, check or remove the check from the appropriate check boxes. To add additional protocol support, click the Select from list button. This produces a dialog of installable network protocols.

Installing Windows NT Networking

CHAPTER 16

421

16

INSTALLING
WINDOWS NT
NETWORKING

FIGURE 16.4.

The Network Setup Wizard protocol setup screen.

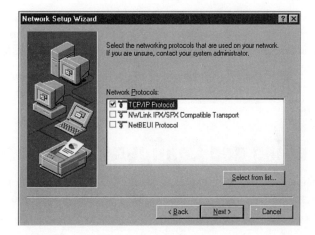

Windows NT offers the following additional protocol support:

- AppleTalk Protocol. This is for communications with Macintosh computers or on Macintosh networks.

- DLC Protocol. This protocol, used in a Windows NT environment, is primarily for communicating with and facilitating network printers using HP JetDirect cards.

- Point To Point Tunneling Protocol. This is a new protocol developed by an Internet Engineering Task Force (IETF) Working Group and implemented by Microsoft in Windows NT 4 to facilitate the use of the Internet as a secure medium of interconnecting systems or sites. This protocol establishes a secure virtual circuit (tunnel) between the interconnected systems and provides encryption at the protocol level for security.

- Streams Environment. An interface protocol used to provide network data stream support (similar to the STREAMS protocol in UNIX systems).

You can use a few general guidelines to determine which protocols to install and use. First, use as few protocols as necessary. This reduces network overhead and response time while increasing performance. To determine the protocols to use, take a look at the systems to be connected and the functionality needed.

If relatively few computers must be connected and they all use Microsoft operating systems (WfW, Win95, WinNT) and don't need to connect to other systems, the clear choice is NetBEUI. It will provide the best performance in this situation.

If you have need to communicate with systems on a Novell NetWare network, you need to install the NWLink IPX/SPX Compatible Transport. This allows communications with these systems provided the necessary application or gateway support is available.

If you will be in a large or routed network environment or will be connected to the Internet, you need to install and configure TCP/IP. Any one of these protocols can be used independently or any combination of them can be used together as needed.

After you have selected the necessary protocols, they must be configured to function properly. Configuring network protocols is discussed in detail in Chapter 17, "Windows NT Network Protocols."

Installing and Configuring Network Services

By default, during Windows NT Network installation, a group of standard services are selected for installation and cannot be deselected. These services are shown in Figure 16.5 and in the following list with a brief explanation:

■ Remote Access Service. This is the equivalent of Dial-up Networking in Windows 95. This service is installed by default when configuring a system with the Remote Access to the Network option in the Network Setup Wizard. If the system is not configured for this option, RAS is not installed by default but can be selected using the Select from list button.

■ RPC Configuration. This is the Windows NT networking method of communications between systems (similar to the Interprocess Communication, or IPC, service on local systems) and distributed applications.

■ NetBIOS Interface. The NetBIOS interface is another interprocess communication mechanism for use by distributed applications.

■ Workstation. This service allows Windows NT to act as a network client to other systems on the network and to access network resources.

■ Server. The Server service provides the opposite functionality of the Workstation service and enables Windows NT Workstation to share resources on a network.

FIGURE 16.5.

The Network Setup Wizard services installation dialog.

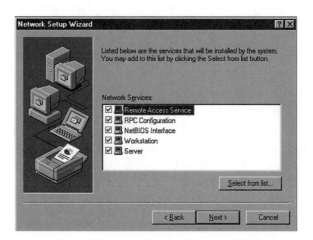

Consistent with previous experience, you add a service that is not listed by clicking the Select from list button. This produces a list of installable network services from which the user can select. (See Figure 16.6.) Again, consistent with other installation routines in Windows NT and Windows 95, the Have Disk button is helpful if the user has a third party network service to install.

FIGURE 16.6.

The installable network services list.

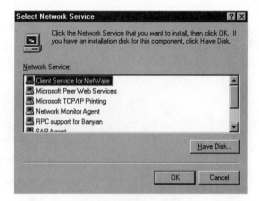

The installable network services provided by Windows NT Workstation are listed here with a brief description:

- Client Service for NetWare. This service provides access to file and printer resources on NetWare servers.

- Microsoft Peer Web Services. This service provides a platform for Web-based intranets or internets similar to Microsoft Internet Information Server. Microsoft Peer Web Services is described in detail in Chapter 19, "Integrating Windows NT into Heterogeneous Networks."

- Microsoft TCP/IP Printing. This service provides a TCP/IP-based print gateway. A shared printer can be created to provide Microsoft Networking clients access to a TCP/IP-enabled printer or, conversely, to provide UNIX clients access to a TCP/IP-enabled printer that is connected to a Windows NT system.

- Network Monitor Agent. This is a remote agent to support the Microsoft Network Monitor (or *Bloodhound*), which is bundled with Microsoft Systems Management Server (SMS) or the scaled-down version included with Windows NT Server.

- RPC Support for Banyan. This service provides RPC support for distributed applications located on Banyan VINES networks and servers.

- SAP Agent. This is a Service Access Protocol agent to make SAP-compatible broadcasts across the network.

- Simple TCP/IP Services. This is a collection of client software for services such as Character Generator, Daytime, Discard, Echo, and Quote of the Day.

- SNMP Service. This provides a mechanism for the system to be managed and monitored remotely using tools such as HP OpenView.

When the desired network services have been selected, click Next. When prompted with the informational dialog, click Next. You are prompted for the path of your Windows NT Workstation files. Provide the correct path and click Continue.

You are prompted for configuration information for your network card, protocols, and network services. Provide the correct settings and continue. Again, you are prompted for the path to your Windows NT files. Provide the correct path and click OK. After you provide the necessary configuration information for your network card, protocols, and services (described in greater detail in Chapters 17 and 18) and Windows NT has finished copying files, you are presented with a bindings dialog, shown in Figure 16.7.

FIGURE 16.7.

The wizard's bindings dialog.

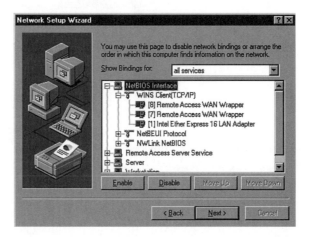

From the bindings dialog, the user can enable or disable specific network protocol and service bindings on a per-adapter card basis. This can be useful in some respects for security purposes. For instance, you can disable NetBIOS over an interface that is connected to the Internet to eliminate a potential intrusion point. Note, however, that you can impair or disable your network by arbitrarily disabling bindings. You should have a good understanding of networking and Windows NT before making these modifications.

When you have made all binding changes (if any), click Next. You are now instructed to click Next to start the network. After you do so, Windows NT attempts to start the network. If there are errors, you are informed and can go back to reconfigure the device, protocol, or service that caused the error.

Workgroups and Domains

You are now presented with the dialog shown in Figure 16.8. You are asked to specify a network name for the system and decide whether this system will participate in a workgroup or a domain. Computer names are limited to 15 alphanumeric characters, and I recommend not using spaces, underscores, or hyphens if possible (because they tend to present problems on the Internet and with various network applications).

FIGURE 16.8.

The computer name and network model dialog.

Workgroups and domains, while logically similar, serve two distinct purposes and are implemented in different fashions. The decision as to which model you choose largely depends on whether an existing network is in place at your location and which model it is using. The following sections describe workgroups and domains with their relevant characteristics, capabilities, and limitations.

Workgroups

Workgroups are really nothing more than a logical grouping of computers that belong to the same business unit, perform similar functions, or are somehow related in purpose or proximity. In a workgroup, each Windows NT computer maintains its own user and group account information and security policies.

Workgroups are best suited for small networks that do not require a dedicated server or central management of resources. Workgroups quickly become ineffective as the number of systems grows, because each system must have an account created for each user who needs access to its resources.

These accounts must be maintained on each individual system, which makes for quite an administrative task to keep accounts synchronized across multiple systems. Adding a single system to the workgroup can increase the administration factor exponentially.

Domains

Windows NT domains are very similar to workgroups in function and purpose, but they provide centralized management of users and resources on the network as well as advanced security features. Windows NT domains are created and controlled by a single, authoritative Windows NT Server, referred to as a Primary Domain Controller (PDC).

There can be one and only one PDC in a given domain, but there can be many Backup Domain Controllers (BDC) to distribute the load of user authentication and security across a domain. A PDC maintains a master list of user accounts, passwords, and security policies for a domain and replicates the list to the BDCs. This provides consistent security and user accounts across all systems in a domain and greatly reduces the amount of administrative overhead involved with maintaining user accounts.

Domains are the obvious choice for networks that consist of more than a handful of systems with users sharing resources. This allows for maximum flexibility and management.

If you choose to participate in a workgroup, specify the name of the workgroup. If the workgroup name you specify cannot be found on the network, it is created for you. There are no prerequisites to become a member of a workgroup.

If you choose to participate in a Windows NT domain, you must provide the name of the domain that you want to join. Windows NT computers, like users, must have an account on the domain to join. To create an account on the domain, either request that your domain administrator create one for you or check the Create computer account in domain box.

If you choose to create the computer account, you are prompted to provide a user name and password for an account in the domain that has administrative rights or sufficient rights to add workstation accounts to the domain.

Troubleshooting Network Services Installation

During the course of installing Windows NT Networking, it is possible that things won't go as expected. Believe it or not, even Windows NT is not a perfect operating system (although it is probably closer than most).

Windows NT Was Unable to Start the Network

The most common problem encountered during network installation is a misconfigured or incorrectly detected network interface card (NIC). If the network card is improperly configured or the wrong card is specified, you receive an error message stating that Windows NT was unable to start the network.

From this point, you are given the option to go back and reconfigure network settings or cancel network installation. If you choose to cancel network installation, networking components are removed and you are informed that you can install Windows NT Networking at a later time. If you choose to go back and reconfigure network settings, return to the settings that you think are incorrect, reconfigure them, and try to continue.

The DHCP Client Was Unable to Obtain an IP Address

Typically, this indicates a physical network connectivity problem. First, verify that there is a DHCP server on your network and that it has IP addresses available for use. Verify the TCP/IP settings and network card configuration.

A Domain Controller for Your Domain Could Not Be Contacted

This can indicate a physical connectivity problem with the network or a problem with the current configuration. Verify that the domain controller for your domain is up and functioning properly and that the workstation and domain controller are using compatible protocols.

The Domain Controller for This Domain Could Not Be Located

When trying to join a domain during network installation or trying to change domains at a later time, you might receive this message. Verify that a domain controller for the domain you are attempting to join is available and is reachable by your workstation.

The following is a general listing of the most common network error messages. As stated, most network errors are related to an improperly configured network card. The network card configuration should always be the first variable you look to when having network problems.

There certainly are many (hundreds) more network errors that you might encounter, but they all vary in cause, condition, and solution. Each should be addressed and solved based on its particular characteristics. The following is a general troubleshooting list that can be applied to most networking problems:

- Has the network ever worked?
- What, if anything, has recently changed on the system? This will solve most problems. Determine what has changed on the system that might be preventing it from operating properly.
- Is the physical connection to the network functioning properly? If you are using a twisted-pair network card (10Base-T), is the link light on the card lit and is there activity on the card? (Always check things such as making sure a cable is plugged into the network card before you get your protocol analyzer out; simple things are easy to forget and can be time-consuming if overlooked.)
- Is the domain controller for the domain up and available?
- Are the workstation and the domain controller using compatible protocols and are they configured properly?

Using this general troubleshooting checklist can solve the bulk of your network problems. It is also a good idea to keep a log of problems you have encountered and the solutions to them. This is especially helpful on larger networks where there is a good chance that a particular error could recur.

Summary

This chapter has demonstrated the process necessary to install Windows NT Networking and provided a general but useful outline and method for troubleshooting network-related problems. Remember to always look at the simple and basic things first. This will save you much time and headache in the long run.

Windows NT Network Protocols

by Sean Mathias

IN THIS CHAPTER

CHAPTER

17

This chapter examines the expanded network protocol support offered by Windows NT. In the beginning, Microsoft offered two protocol choices for its products: NetBEUI for Microsoft networks and NWLink IPX/SPX Compatible Transport for Novell networks.

Very quickly this became inadequate for growing networks. People wanted support for large, heterogeneous enterprise networks. NetBEUI was insufficient because it is not routable; the NWLink IPX/SPX Compatible Transport provided communications among Windows-based and Novell networks but still did not offer a solution.

Today, Windows NT 4 offers seven protocols and components for integration and communication in enterprise networks. This chapter discusses each of these components and their characteristics, strengths, and weaknesses.

NetBEUI and NWLink IPX/SPX Compatible Transport

As mentioned, NetBEUI and NWLink IPX/SPX Compatible Transport are the historical protocols associated with Microsoft Windows-based networking. Although each of these protocols has distinct advantages, neither is the appropriate choice for deploying a large-scale, diverse network.

NetBEUI

NetBEUI (NetBIOS Enhanced User Interface) is a protocol that was originally designed and developed by IBM Corporation to provide a fast and efficient communications transport between PC-based systems and host-based systems. This protocol really is an excellent transport, providing fast speed and very low overhead, but it suffers from a few key design and implementation limitations.

At the time NetBEUI was developed, most networks were Ethernet (10Base-5 or 10Base-2) and were connected using bridges. Routers were not nearly as common at this time. Because of this fact, NetBEUI was designed as a non-routable protocol (with one exception) to minimize its overhead and improve performance.

> **NOTE**
>
> The exception to NetBEUI's non-routable design is an IBM token-ring network with source routing enabled. This all ties in together because IBM developed NetBEUI and the token-ring technology—so it essentially designed a low overhead protocol for use on its token-ring topology.

NetBEUI, as stated, is an extremely efficient protocol with minimum overhead. Its limitations stem from the underlying architecture of NetBIOS (Network Basic Input/Output System). The most important limitations are that this protocol is not routable in mainstream network architectures (those without IBM token ring and source routing enabled) and that NetBIOS imposes a 15-character, name-space limitation.

With the growing concept of internetworking—whether it is the global Internet or a large, private corporate network—any given protocol must necessarily provide support for routing capabilities. Along these same lines, identification becomes an issue with ever-growing networks. NetBIOS's 15-character, name-space limits the capability to descriptively identify a large number of systems across an enterprise. This might seem to provide an adequate supply of names (36^{15} possibilities or 2.21^{23} using only alphanumeric characters); however, people typically prefer meaningful names rather than the alphanumeric combinations that machines prefer. This requirement dramatically reduces the number of practical possibilities, especially when you try to implement standardized or meaningful naming conventions.

In a small- or medium-sized company, NetBEUI is the appropriate choice for its simplicity and efficiency, as long as you do not want Internet or public network connectivity.

Even the installation and configuration of the protocol is simple and straightforward. To install NetBEUI, use the following steps:

1. Open the Control Panel and start the Network applet.
2. Choose the Protocols tab and select the Add button.
3. From the list of available protocols, choose NetBEUI and click OK.
4. Provide the path to your Windows NT installation files and click OK.
5. When you are done copying files, click OK.
6. Restart your computer when prompted.

This is a very simple procedure, and there is nothing to configure for NetBEUI other than providing a name for your computer that is unique on the network (which is done during the installation process).

NWLink IPX/SPX Compatible Transport

The NWLink IPX/SPX Compatible Transport was included initially with Windows for Workgroups 3.*x* to provide connectivity to Novell NetWare networks. It has subsequently been bundled with Windows 95, Windows NT 3.x, and now Windows NT 4.

The NWLink IPX/SPX Compatible Transport is a fairly good mainstream transport for private networks. This protocol is fully routable and does not incur any major transition overhead. The reason for its limited implementation is its lack of widespread public standardization. This transport is fully compatible with Novell NetWare IPX/SPX but never gained the acceptance of TCP/IP due to the fact that it was designed and developed by a private corporation (Novell) and thus was limited in function and flexibility by design.

If your organization wants to run its own private network and does not need a transport such as TCP/IP, NWLink IPX/SPX Compatible Transport is an excellent choice because it is routable and can be used to wrap or transport other protocols.

To install NWLink IPX/SPX Compatible Transport, use the following procedure:

1. Open Control Panel and start the Network applet.
2. Choose the Protocols tab and select the Add button.
3. From the list of available protocols, choose NWLink IPX/SPX Compatible Transport and click OK.
4. Provide the path to your Windows NT installation files and click OK.
5. When you are done copying files, click OK.
6. Restart your computer when prompted.

After the software is installed, you can opt to restart your computer later to configure the newly installed protocol. To configure the NWLink IPX/SPX Compatible Transport, perform the following steps:

1. Open Control Panel and start the Network applet.
2. Choose the Protocols tab and select the NWLink IPX/SPX Compatible Transport.
3. Click Configure.
4. You see a dialog similar to the one in Figure 17.1.

FIGURE 17.1.

NWLink IPX/SPX Compatible Transport configuration dialog.

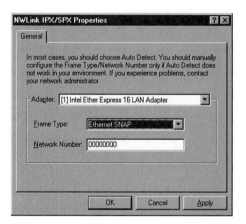

5. Select the adapter for which you want to configure the protocol, and select the Frame Type you want to use on the card. (The default, Auto Detect, does not always work well. If you experience problems, find out the correct frame type for your network and specify it explicitly.)

6. If you explicitly specify the Frame Type, you need to provide the Network Number for your network (see your system administrator).

7. When done, click OK and then click Close.

8. Restart your computer when prompted.

> **NOTE**
>
> You might notice that when you installed the NWLink IPX/SPX Compatible Transport, it also installed and listed the NWLink NetBIOS protocol. This is, effectively, NetBIOS over IPX. The difference is that it is installed by default and shows as a separate protocol. In previous versions, this was simply an option to be enabled or disabled in the NWLink IPX/SPX configuration.

Installing and Configuring TCP/IP

Transmission Control Protocol/Internet Protocol (TCP/IP) is fast becoming the enterprise network protocol of choice, due primarily to the rapid growth and use of the worldwide Internet. This certainly is not the only reason though. TCP/IP is a relatively efficient and flexible protocol that has been adapted to almost every network technology, such as Frame Relay and Asynchronous Transfer Mode (ATM), as well as applications such as video conferencing and multimedia.

The Microsoft implementation of TCP/IP has matured significantly since its introduction in Windows for Workgroups 3.11 (*Wolverine*, the 32-bit TCP/IP stack for WfW 3.11) and is getting closer to a standards-compliant stack. Windows NT 3.5*x* introduced an improved implementation of TCP/IP, providing much better compliance and integration as well as some Microsoft-specific features such as Dynamic Host Configuration Protocol (DHCP) and Windows Internet Naming Services (WINS).

With Windows NT 4.0, Microsoft has further extended its TCP/IP standardization and greatly enhanced its feature set to include native Domain Name System (DNS) name-resolution capabilities. Also new to the TCP/IP implementation is a security component that provides filtering capabilities (similar to a router access list or firewall) and Point To Point Tunneling (PPTP), facilitating the creation of Private Virtual Circuits (PVCs) over public switched networks such as the global Internet.

With the integration of WINS and DNS capabilities, Windows NT can now seamlessly resolve names such as *MYSERVER* or *www.myserver.com* from the command line or any interface, as long as the DNS resolution is configured properly. The obvious benefit is ease of use for the user. This means that a user can now map a drive to ftp.microsoft.com/data and access it through the Explorer rather than through a third-party application or the command line (shown in Figure 17.2).

FIGURE 17.2.
Mapping a TCP/IP-based volume to a network drive.

If you have not yet installed support for TCP/IP, use the following procedure to do so. If you have already installed the protocol, continue to the next section to configure TCP/IP for your network.

Installing TCP/IP Support

To install TCP/IP protocol support, use the following procedure:

1. From the Control Panel, open the Network applet or right-click the Network Neighborhood icon on the desktop and select Properties.

2. Select the Protocols tab and click the Add button.

3. Select the TCP/IP Protocol and click OK twice.

4. Restart your system when prompted.

Continue in the next section to configure TCP/IP for your network environment.

Configuring TCP/IP

Depending on your network environment and configuration, you have several ways to configure your TCP/IP support. The easiest, and preferred, method is to use a Dynamic Host Configuration Protocol (DHCP) server; the alternative is to statically configure your TCP/IP settings.

DHCP is the preferred method to use for TCP/IP administration and configuration because all IP addresses and configuration parameters are administered and maintained centrally. If a configuration change is necessary, you need to make the change only at the DHCP server rather than go around the network to each machine to affect the configuration change.

Not all networks have a DHCP server, nor do all clients support the DHCP service, and sometimes it is necessary to use a static configuration for TCP/IP, typically for hosts that offer Internet services.

To configure (or reconfigure) TCP/IP options, use the following process either during TCP/IP installation or any time after installation.

Open the Network properties page either using the Network applet in the Control Panel or by right-clicking the Network Neighborhood icon and selecting Properties. If using DHCP, select Obtain an IP Address from a DHCP Server and click OK; you need not configure anything else unless instructed by your network administrator. If you must use a static configuration, select Provide an IP Address and fill in the IP Address, Subnet Mask, and Default Gateway fields. Figure 17.3 shows the IP Address tab.

FIGURE 17.3.

The IP Address configuration tab of the TCP/IP protocol properties sheet.

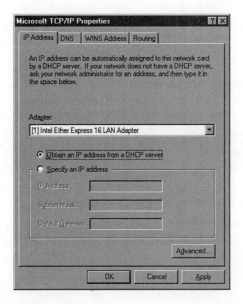

Next, select the DNS tab (shown in Figure 17.4). The host name, by default, is set to the computer name as defined during Windows NT installation; you should not need to change this. Provide the name of your TCP/IP domain name in the Domain field.

FIGURE 17.4.

The DNS configuration tab of the TCP/IP protocol properties sheet.

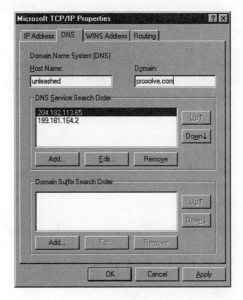

17

WINDOWS NT NETWORK PROTOCOLS

> **NOTE**
>
> A TCP/IP domain name is entirely independent of a Windows NT domain. TCP/IP domain names are names such as `isoc.org` or `microsoft.com`. If you are not on the Internet, you might not have a TCP/IP domain name. It is not necessary to have one, so if you're unsure, leave this field blank.

In the DNS Service Search Order section, click the Add button and add the IP addresses for as many as three of the DNS servers that your network uses. Use the Up and Down buttons to move the selected servers up or down in order of preference. In the Domain Suffix Search Order section, provide a list of TCP/IP domain names to append to host names to create Fully Qualified Domain Names (FQDN) for use when a host name is specified without a domain suffix. This parameter is optional, and you probably don't need it in most cases. You can specify up to six domain names to use, and as with the DNS servers, you can change the order of preference by using the Up and Down buttons.

Next select the WINS Address tab, shown in Figure 17.5, to configure Windows name resolution. In the Windows Internet Naming Services (WINS) section, select the adapter for which you are configuring WINS. Provide the addresses of a primary and secondary WINS server for your network. A WINS server maintains a database that maps computer (NetBIOS) names to IP addresses; this is different behavior from using a protocol such as NetBEUI where communications is facilitated by mapping computer names to hardware (MAC) addresses. When you use TCP/IP, a computer name is resolved to an IP address, which is then resolved to a hardware address, and then a session between the systems can be established. Not all networks use—nor are they required to use—WINS services. This is a Microsoft-specific implementation to further integrate Microsoft networking services with the TCP/IP protocol.

If appropriate, check Enable DNS for Windows Resolution. This is typically used in place of WINS services. If you check this option, the system attempts to resolve Windows names using DNS by getting the host name and applying the default TCP/IP domain name to generate a FQDN and then attempts to resolve that name to an address.

If systems on your network use LMHOSTS files, check Enable LMHOSTS Lookup. An LMHOSTS file is a text file with computer-name-to-IP-address mappings. This file can also include additional directives for specifying Windows NT domains and domain controllers. This is not an adequate method of name resolution because it is static and must be maintained on each system. If you choose to use LMHOSTS files and you have a default LMHOSTS file available to you, you can click the Import LMHOSTS button and provide the path to the default file to import it to your system.

If necessary, provide a scope ID for your computer. Scope IDs typically are not used anymore. Scope IDs are used to provide information for name resolution when a DNS server is not available. If you do specify a scope ID, you must be sure that it is the same on all the computers in your network that you want to communicate with because you cannot communicate with systems that have different scope IDs.

FIGURE 17.5.

The WINS Address configuration tab of the TCP/IP protocol properties sheet.

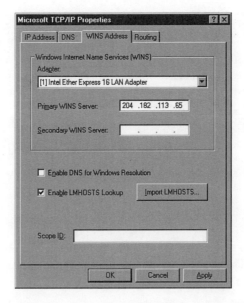

Lastly, select the Routing tab, shown in Figure 17.6. The one option is for multihomed systems that have more than one network interface card (NIC). If two or more network interfaces on a Windows NT computer belong to different IP networks or subnets, you can select this option to enable IP routing between the two interfaces, providing a path for systems on the two networks to traverse to the other networks. If you have only one NIC, leave this option unchecked. If you have more than one NIC and they belong to different networks, you can check this option to have your system act as a router.

FIGURE 17.6.

The Routing configuration tab of the TCP/IP protocol properties sheet.

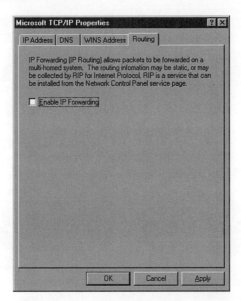

> **NOTE**
>
> Although you can use Windows NT systems as routers between different IP networks, you should consider a couple of issues. First, Windows NT (especially Workstation) is definitely not designed to act as a router, and consequently, the performance quickly diminishes as the size of the network increases and the routing function is utilized more. Second, there is a performance impact on the system acting as a router. The more route processing the system does, the less resources are available to the Workstation component, affecting the unfortunate user sitting at the console trying to get his work done. However, despite these issues, routing is a useful feature to have available. Windows NT is best suited to be used as a router for connecting and segmenting relatively small (less than 50) IP networks or as an Internet gateway for a small number of users.

After you have configured your TCP/IP parameters, you should not need to modify them often, if at all. The only time you need to modify the settings is when there is a change on the network or the system moves to another network.

Configuring TCP/IP Advanced Options

Windows NT Workstation also offers several advanced TCP/IP configuration options such as support for multihoming (multiple IP addresses), filtering, and Point To Point Tunneling.

To access the advanced TCP/IP configuration options, open the Network properties sheet and select TCP/IP Properties from the Protocol tab. From the IP Address tab, click the Advanced button to display the advanced configuration options page, shown in Figure 17.7.

FIGURE 17.7.

The advanced TCP/IP configuration dialog.

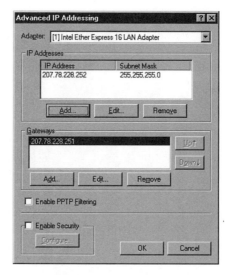

From the TCP/IP advanced configuration dialog, the user can configure settings on a per-adapter basis by selecting the appropriate adapter from the adapter list at the top of the sheet.

You can also add multiple IP addresses for a single card. This is often desirable to support TCP/IP domain name aliases, specifically for Microsoft Peer Web Services (discussed in Chapter 18, "Windows NT Network Services"). To add additional IP addresses, click the Add button in the IP Addresses section. For each IP address you want to add, provide the IP address and subnet mask for up to five addresses.

NOTE

To add support for more than five IP addresses, you must modify the Windows NT Registry directly. Modifying the Registry is not recommended or supported and should only be done by experienced Windows NT users.

To add more than five IP addresses, open the Registry Editor (`regedt32.exe`) and select the `HKEY_LOCAL_MACHINE` hive. From there, open the `\SYSTEM\CurrentControlSet\Services` branch. Next, find the key for your NIC. Usually, this is the driver name with an instance number such as `tc50481` for a Thomas-Conrad PCI 5048, adapter number one, or `EE161` for an Intel EtherExpress, adapter number one.

After you have found the correct key, open the sub-branch `\Parameters\Tcpip`. Select the `IPAddress:REG_MULTI_SZ` value and select Multi String from the Edit menu. For each IP address you want to add, enter it in dotted decimal notation (*xxx.xxx.xxx.xxx*), one per line. Also for each IP address, you must add a corresponding subnet mask. To do this, select the `SubnetMask:REG_MULTI_SZ` key and select Multi String from the Edit menu. Add the appropriate subnet mask for each IP address, in order, one per line.

Additionally, for networks with multiple routers or gateways, there is a configuration option to specify more than one gateway. To add an additional gateway, click the Add button in the Gateways section and provide the appropriate IP address for the gateway.

If this system will act as a PPTP gateway to the Internet, select the correct adapter from the adapter list and check the Enable PPTP Filtering box. Be aware that if this option is checked, only PPTP packets are allowed to traverse that interface; normal IP traffic is disallowed.

Finally, one of the welcome new features of Windows NT is TCP/IP security, accessed by checking the Enable Security box and then clicking the Configure button, which produces the TCP/IP Security configuration dialog shown in Figure 17.8.

FIGURE 17.8.

The TCP/IP Security configuration dialog.

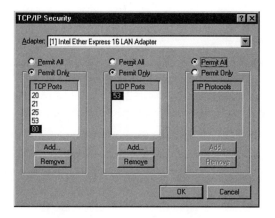

From this configuration dialog, you can configure a packet level filter (similar to a firewall). Using this configuration feature, the user can allow, or effectively disallow, specific IP protocols and TCP or UDP ports.

For each of the three configurable categories, TCP Ports, UDP Ports, and IP Protocols, the user has the option of permitting all port numbers or protocols or restricting the category to only specific ports or protocols.

The TCP and UDP Port categories are configured using port numbers as listed in the \SYSTEMROOT\SYSTEM32\Drivers\etc\services file. This file contains a listing of well-known services and their corresponding transport (TCP or UDP) with the assigned port number. Using this list, the user can determine which TCP and UPD ports to allow and configure TCP/IP security appropriately.

For the IP Protocol category, the access restrictions are based on the \SYSTEMROOT\ SYSTEM32\Drivers\etc\protocol file. This file contains a listing of protocols and their assigned numbers. Access can be restricted to specific protocols by defining them in the IP Protocol category of the TCP/IP security configuration.

To restrict access to a given subset, click the Add button for the appropriate category and add a protocol or port number to allow. Repeat this step until you have defined all desired ports and protocols. Do note, however, that if security is enabled on any of the three categories, that category exclusively permits the subset as defined by the user. There is no grace here; if security is enabled and a given port or protocol is not explicitly defined to have access, it will not be passed.

Testing the Configuration and Connectivity: the `ping` Utility

After the TCP/IP protocol has been installed and configured and you have restarted your system, you need to test its configuration and connectivity. Typically, I advise that you do this in a progressive fashion so that if the connectivity fails at some point, it is easier to pinpoint the error and resolve it.

First, open a command prompt window. At the command prompt, perform the following steps:

1. Type `ping` *xxx.xxx.xxx.xxx* where *xxx.xxx.xxx.xxx* represents your local IP address. You should receive a reply similar to the following:

   `Reply from xxx.xxx.xxx.xxx: bytes=32 time<10ms TTL=128`

2. Type `ping` *xxx.xxx.xxx.xxx* where *xxx.xxx.xxx.xxx* represents the address of your default gateway (router). You should receive a response similar to the previous response. These first two tests determine whether TCP/IP is configured properly and whether you can communicate on your local network.

3. Type `ping` *xxx.xxx.xxx.xxx* where *xxx.xxx.xxx.xxx* represents a DNS server for your network, preferably on a remote network. Again, the response should be similar to the previous response. This test determines whether you can communicate with the outside world.

4. Lastly, type `ping` *host.company.com* where *host.company.com* is something like `www.microsoft.com` or `www.atonce.com`. This is the final test that determines whether your name resolution is working properly and you are correctly configured.

If your system passes all these tests, everything is installed and configured properly and you can now use the resources available on your network and navigate the services of the Internet, if applicable. If one of these tests fails, something is configured improperly and you need to co-ordinate with your system administrator to resolve the issue.

Additional Protocol Support Offered by Windows NT Workstation

In addition to the protocols discussed so far, Windows NT offers support for several other less common or less popular protocols to offer better, more extensive network integration. Although some of these implementations are limited or restricted compared to their native counterparts, they are functional nonetheless and do offer some key features.

AppleTalk Protocol

The AppleTalk protocol, as its name implies, provides connectivity and communication between Windows NT systems and Macintosh systems. The protocol, as implemented in Windows NT Workstation, offers limited connectivity between the two types of systems. Using the AppleTalk protocol, a Windows NT system can use resources located on a Macintosh file server; however, a Macintosh system cannot access resources on a Windows NT Workstation system. To facilitate this functionality, you must have a Windows NT Server running Services for Macintosh and explicitly sharing resources for Macintosh systems.

To install support for the AppleTalk protocol, use the following procedure:

1. As always, to install additional protocol support, open the Network Control Panel applet or right-click the Network Neighborhood icon on the desktop and select the Properties item.

2. Select the Protocols tab and click Add.

3. From the list of available protocols, select the AppleTalk protocol and click OK twice.

After the files are copied to your system, you need to restart your system for the changes to take effect. After you have restarted your system, you need to configure the AppleTalk protocol. (You can also do this during the installation of AppleTalk support.)

To configure AppleTalk protocol support, perform the following steps:

1. Open the Network Control Panel applet or right-click the Network Neighborhood icon on the desktop and select the Properties item.

2. Select the Protocols tab, select the AppleTalk Protocol, and click the Properties button.

3. You see the AppleTalk properties sheet (shown in Figure 17.9).

FIGURE 17.9.

The AppleTalk configuration dialog.

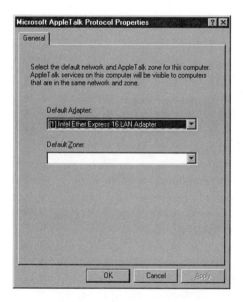

4. Select the adapter for which you want to configure AppleTalk support.

5. Select the default AppleTalk zone from the list of discovered zones.

6. When you're finished, click OK twice.

If you want to connect to a zone that is not listed, verify that it is physically accessible by your system and that the necessary server services on that zone are currently running. If the problem persists, contact your system administrator.

Data Link Control Protocol (DLC)

The Data Link Control protocol (DLC) was originally developed and introduced by IBM for connectivity between mainframe systems and terminals. In its implementation with Windows NT, it is primarily used for Hewlett-Packard network printing support (go figure…). Although you can still use it for host connectivity, much more practical and efficient alternatives are available for this purpose today.

For DLC, there is nothing to configure in the Network Protocols sheet. All configuration is done through Print Manager or the Printers folder when you are installing and configuring a Hewlett-Packard printer attached to the network with a JetDirect network print card.

Point To Point Tunneling Protocol (PPTP)

The latest and greatest (according to Redmond, WA) in Virtual Private Network (VPN) technology is the Point To Point Tunneling Protocol. This is an emerging technology used to establish secure connections between nodes across public switched networks such as the global Internet.

Through the use of PPTP, which is protocol independent (it carries or "tunnels" IP, IPX, or NetBEUI), remote users can connect to an Internet service provider's (ISP's) local point of presence (POP) and establish a secure VPN across the Internet, thus providing global, secure access to the corporate LAN (provided there is an available POP). For traveling or remote users, this also provides the benefit of saving on long distance charges.

PPTP is implemented as a RAS connection over the Internet. Users establish a connection to the Internet using a local ISP, and then, using the Internet strictly as a transport medium, they establish a PPTP session with a remote Windows NT PPTP system. After this connection is established, the remote user has a secure connection to the remote LAN. This is an important new feature with the increasing use of the Internet and the ever-present need of users for remote access to their home networks. This eliminates two of the fundamental implementation obstacles of remote access: security and cost.

To enable PPTP support on your Windows NT Workstation, perform the following steps:

1. Open the Network applet in Control Panel or right-click the Network Neighborhood icon on the desktop and select Properties.

2. Click the Protocols tab and then select TCP/IP Protocol and click the Properties button.

3. Click the Advanced tab.

4. Select the adapter for which you want to configure PPTP.

5. To enable PPTP, check the Enable PPTP Filtering box.

6. The changes take effect when you restart your computer.

Again, remember that if PPTP filtering is enabled for a given interface, no other traffic can cross that interface. That interface is effectively dedicated to PPTP traffic.

The implementation of PPTP in Windows NT Workstation is still a relatively new component, and as of yet, it is not fully mature. Performance and reliability are not guaranteed at this point. Chapter 18 discusses additional configuration and usage information relevant to PPTP.

Streams Environment

The Streams Environment is a multiprotocol wrapper that effectively provides an additional layer of abstraction between the device driver and the protocol driver. The Streams Environment helps to further the modularity of protocol stacks, providing easier access to interfaces and redesign of components.

The Streams Environment is installed in the same fashion as other protocols previously discussed. There is no additional configuration other than installing support for streams. Using the Streams Environment provides more flexibility and integration with other systems and moves the protocol stack closer to the ideal of the OSI model: a standardized, modular, and well-defined architecture.

Summary

Windows NT 4 Workstation has maintained the protocol support of previous versions of Windows NT and added or improved support for other protocols. Most notably is the improved TCP/IP protocol stack. There is now support for various filtering options and VPNs through the Point To Point Tunneling Protocol. Additionally, the improved implementation of the Windows NT TCP/IP stack provides for TCP/IP domain name resolution system-wide, allowing the user to seamlessly access and map remote TCP/IP shares as if they were Windows NT shares.

The enhanced network protocol support is well designed and moves us even closer to standardized integration with disparate systems. With the additional network service support and enhancements discussed in the next chapter, we are moving closer to a true enterprise platform.

Windows NT Network Services

by Sean Mathias

IN THIS CHAPTER

Windows NT network protocols provide a common language for computers to communicate, but this does not provide much in the way of functionality. The network functionality of Windows NT is provided through various network services. Windows NT network services are modular components that can be added or removed as needed (except for some core components) and can coexist with each other.

The implementation of network services is consistent with the network and architectural model of Windows NT—providing a modular design that allows for various components to be rewritten, upgraded, added, or removed, without rebuilding the entire subsystem or recompiling the kernel as with some other operating systems.

Following are detailed descriptions of each network service available in Windows NT 4 Workstation. Services that are installed by default and are necessary for basic network functionality are shown in the following list. In addition to these services, the modular architecture of the Windows NT networking subsystem and open API set allow for third-party vendors to write their own Windows NT compliant or compatible network services and integrate them seamlessly with the rest of the architecture.

Here are the default network services installed by Windows NT Network Setup:

- Computer Browser
- NetBIOS Interface
- RPC Configuration
- Server
- Workstation

Client Services for NetWare

Probably one of the most important services in the aspect of integration is the Client Services for NetWare. These services, along with the NWLink IPX/SPX Compatible Transport, provide access from a Windows NT Workstation computer to file and printer resources located on a Novell NetWare server.

Currently, the Client Services for NetWare are limited to accessing shared resources on a NetWare server. They provide no support for loading VLM-based applications such as the netadmin.exe utility for administering NetWare servers and no GUI-based tools to do so either, although Novell is rumored to be working on its own implementation of a Windows NT NetWare client service that bridges this gap.

To install the Client Services for NetWare, perform the following steps:

1. Open the Network applet in the Control Panel or select the Network Neighborhood properties by right-clicking the icon on the desktop.

2. Select the Services tab and click the Add button. You see a dialog of available services as shown in Figure 18.1.

FIGURE 18.1.
Adding additional network service support.

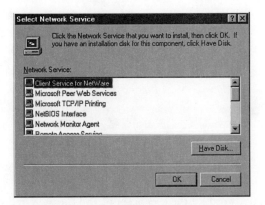

3. Select the Client Service for NetWare and click OK.

4. The necessary files are copied to your system, and if you have not yet installed the NWLink IPX/SPX Compatible Transport, you are prompted to do so. (See Chapter 17, "Windows NT Network Protocols.")

5. When prompted, restart your computer to effect the changes.

> **NOTE**
>
> The dialog of available network services has a button labeled Have Disk. This is how you install a third-party network service. Click the Have Disk button, provide the disk(s) when prompted, and proceed with the installation.

When your computer restarts and you log in, you see a secondary dialog prompting you for a username, password, and preferred server or default tree and context to log in to, as shown in Figure 18.2. Do note that you cannot change the username to log in, so that username must already exist on the NetWare network.

18

WINDOWS NT NETWORK SERVICES

Figure 18.2.

Specifying a preferred server or default tree and context to log in to.

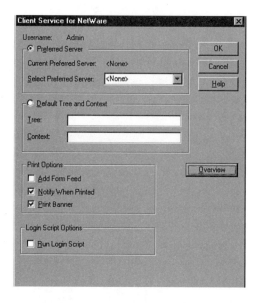

Provide the password for the user account and the preferred server or default tree and context to log in to; optionally, check the Run Login Script box to execute the NetWare login script. Be aware that not all login script commands are supported under Windows NT 4 Workstation—specifically, any commands that rely on VLMs being loaded.

Using the Client Service for NetWare (CSNW) applet in Control Panel, you can later modify these settings if necessary as well as specify print options such as adding a form feed, requesting print notification, and printing banner pages.

When you are logged in to a preferred server or to a default tree and context, you have access to file and print resources as well as any other resources. You can access them from the command line by mapping a drive, through Network Neighborhood or Explorer by browsing (see Figure 18.3), or in any other way that network resources are reachable.

As with previous versions of Windows NT, after you have connected to a resource and been authenticated, you can then share the resource on the network, providing access to it for other Microsoft networking clients by using a form of pass-through authentication.

Although the current implementation is somewhat limited, most prominently in their inability to provide access to NetWare management features for the administration of NetWare NDS trees, Client Services for NetWare provide the basic functionality and access to resources that most users need.

FIGURE 18.3.

Browsing NetWare resources through Network Neighborhood in Explorer.

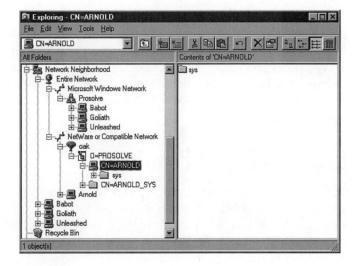

Computer Browser

The Computer Browser service is one of the default Windows NT networking services that is installed during the initial network configuration. This service provides two functions: a client-side function and a server-side function.

For the client-side function, the Computer Browser service maintains a local list of the current network, the computers on the network, and available resources. The service receives periodic updates from the domain master browser or a backup browser, systems responsible for discovering the available resources on the network and maintaining a current list. If you stop this service, the local system is unable to browse network resources in Network Neighborhood, Explorer, or a network-aware application.

The server side of this component enables the local system to act as a domain master browser or a backup browser if necessary. By default, all Windows NT systems are configured to act as master browser computers. Windows 95 systems are configured to act as browse masters if they have Microsoft File and Print services installed and enabled. To determine which system is the domain master browser, a computer sends out a broadcast when it comes online to determine whether a master browser currently exists. If it finds one, it passes this information to the client side to obtain and maintain its local list; if it does not find one, it attempts to become the master browser for the network. This is an imperfect process, and often, a system attempts to become the master browser when one already exists. In this situation, an election is forced to determine which system becomes the domain master browser.

Users familiar with Microsoft networking might notice (on a regular basis) while browsing the network that the system list is inaccurate; it lists systems that are no longer online, or it is missing systems that you know are online. This problem is due to the fact that there must be a

18

WINDOWS NT
NETWORK
SERVICES

balance between the accuracy of the browser and how much network bandwidth and system resources it uses to maintain the list. Maintaining a 100-percent accurate browse list at all times would put a burden on the master browser computer's resources and flood the network with discovery broadcasts, so you must settle on a less-than-perfect balance. Do note, however, that most network operating systems face this dilemma; with Novell NetWare, it is a common problem to have an overabundance of SAP broadcasts that serve basically the same purpose as the Computer Browser service.

Microsoft TCP/IP Printing

The Microsoft TCP/IP printing support service is yet another feature to further the enterprise integration of Windows NT. What this service provides is the capability to connect to and share printers that are directly connected to the network and TCP/IP enabled. You can also attach these printers directly to UNIX-based systems, thus providing the integration and access to disparate resources on a network. Note that Windows NT TCP/IP Printing supports only BSD style TCP/IP printing and does not provide support for System V style printing.

A computer that has TCP/IP Printing support installed and configured can print directly to the printers and act as a print gateway/server for other Microsoft networking clients on the network, thus extending the use of this resource to other computers on the network.

To install support for TCP/IP Printing, follow these steps:

1. Open the Network applet in the Control Panel or select the Network Neighborhood properties by right-clicking the icon on the desktop.
2. Select the Services tab and click the Add button. You see a dialog of available services.
3. Select Microsoft TCP/IP Printing and click OK. If you have not installed the TCP/IP protocol on your computer, you are prompted to do so. (See Chapter 17.)
4. The necessary files are copied to your system.
5. When prompted, restart your computer to effect the changes.

After you have installed Microsoft TCP/IP Printing support, you can create and configure TCP/IP network printers and share them on the network if desired. To do so, you must have the IP address of the network printer or the UNIX computer to which it is attached. (You can use the DNS name of the computer if you have configured support for DNS in the TCP/IP Protocol configuration.)

To create and configure a TCP/IP printer, perform the following steps:

1. Open the Printers folder in My Computer, select the Printers option from the Start Menu Settings item, or start the Printers applet in the Control Panel (so many choices!).
2. Start the Add Printer Wizard.
3. Select My Computer when asked where the printer will be managed; click Next.

4. For the port configuration, click the Add Port button.

5. You see a list of available ports; select the LPR Port and click OK.

6. You see the Add LPR Compatible Printer dialog, which prompts you for the name of the server the printer resides on or its IP address and the name of the printer. Provide this information, click OK, and then click Close.

7. The IP address and name of the TCP/IP printer is listed as a configurable port; check the corresponding box and click Next.

8. When presented with the list of printer manufacturers and printers, select the correct make and model of the printer you are connecting and click Next.

9. Provide a name for the printer and click Next.

10. If you want to share the printer on the network, select the Shared button and provide a share name for the printer. Select the appropriate operating systems that will use this printer so the necessary drivers can be installed. When you have finished, or if you are not going to share this printer, click Next.

11. Answer yes or no when prompted to print a test page and click Finish.

The necessary files are copied to your system, and if you elected to print a test page, you see a dialog asking whether the test page printed properly. If it printed correctly, click Yes; if it did not, click No. Clicking No launches the print trouble-shooting wizard, which helps resolve the problem. When this is completed, the Printer Properties page displays for you to configure the printer accordingly. (See the section "Installing a Printer" in Chapter 7, "The Explorer GUI.")

In addition to connecting, printing to, and sharing TCP/IP and UNIX-based printers, you can also provide TCP/IP print services to UNIX-based clients. For printers attached to or managed by your system, you can start the TCP/IP Print Server service and allow UNIX-based clients to print to your printer. To enable this function, type `net start lpdsvc` at the command prompt, or select the TCP/IP Print Server service in the Services applet of the Control Panel. If this is a service you intend to offer to UNIX clients, it is a good idea to configure the service to start automatically at startup. Also, keep in mind that this is a rudimentary implementation of the LPD service, and it might not behave as expected due to the vast assortment of UNIX varieties and their specific printing methods.

NetBIOS Interface

The NetBIOS interface is an often misunderstood network service. Most people seem to equate it with NetBEUI, which is understandable. However, you should understand why they are not the same and know how they differ.

The NetBIOS (Network Basic Input/Output System) interface is a session-level interface and interprocess communication mechanism, whereas NetBEUI (NetBIOS Enhanced User Interface) is an actual network transport protocol.

18

In its current implementation, NetBIOS is typically encapsulated in either the NWLink IPX/SPX Compatible Transport or TCP/IP to carry its traffic, providing NetBIOS over IPX or NetBIOS over IP (NBT). The Windows NT redirector is a NetBIOS-based application. The NetBIOS interface is responsible for establishing logical computer names on the network and for establishing sessions and providing reliable data-transport services for a given session.

Although the system allows you to remove this component, it is not recommended because removing it impairs interprocess communications and might result in unreliable or unpredictable network behavior. Some system services (such as the messenger service) rely on the NetBIOS interface.

Network Monitor Agent

The Network Monitor Agent is a component that gathers information and statistics from the local network interfaces. This agent is used by remote Windows NT Server systems running the Microsoft Network Monitor (also known as Bloodhound) or a Systems Management Server (SMS) system running the Network Monitor to gather information and monitor traffic on a remote interface or segment.

The Network Monitor Agent has no configuration options in Workstation.

Microsoft Peer Web Services

With the release of Windows NT 4 Workstation, Microsoft has furthered its move toward an Internet-centric environment not only by enhancing their TCP/IP Protocol suite and its integration, but also by bundling Internet services as installable operating system components.

Windows NT 4 Workstation includes Microsoft Peer Web Services, a suite of Internet or intranet services that are almost identical to the server version, Internet Information Server 2.0, which is included with Windows NT Server 4.

Microsoft Peer Web Services are aimed at providing the framework for an intranet within an organization or department. Included are components to facilitate World Wide Web (WWW) services, file transfer (FTP) services, and information search and retrieval services (Gopher).

To install Microsoft Peer Web Services, perform the following steps:

1. Open the Network applet in the Control Panel or select the Network Neighborhood properties by right-clicking the icon on the desktop.
2. Select the Services tab and click the Add button. You see a dialog of available services.
3. Select the Microsoft Peer Web Services and click OK.
4. Unlike the other services you have installed so far, Peer Web Services invokes its own external setup program. At the banner page, click OK to continue.

5. You see the Microsoft Peer Web Services Setup screen, shown in Figure 18.4. Select or deselect the various components based upon your specific needs, and accept or change the installation directory. When you are satisfied, click OK to begin the installation.

FIGURE 18.4.

Microsoft Peer Web Services Setup screen.

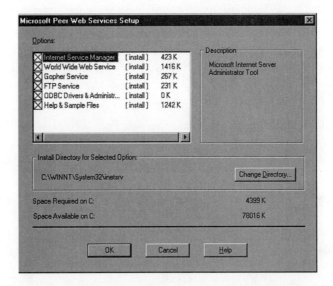

6. You are prompted to provide the location and directory root for each of the services you are installing, as shown in Figure 18.5. Provide the path to the desired location and click OK when you are satisfied with your selections.

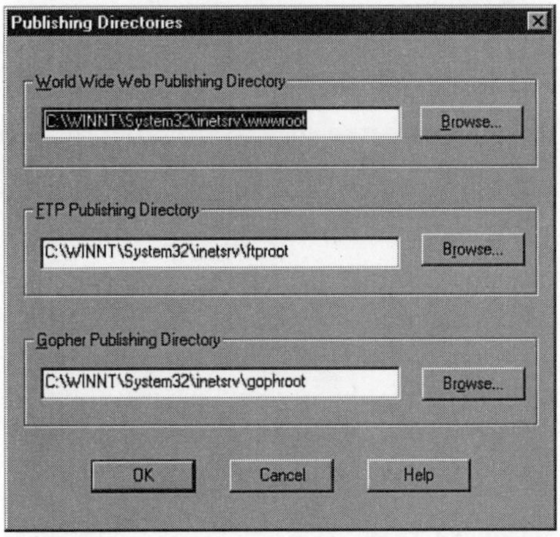

FIGURE 18.5.

The Peer Web Services directory path configuration dialog.

7. The necessary files are copied to your system.

8. If you chose to install ODBC driver support, you are prompted to select the drivers you want to install. Select the desired drivers and click OK.

9. You see a dialog informing you that the setup has completed successfully; click OK.

When the setup has finished, it is not necessary to restart the system. The services are installed and you can start them by selecting them in the Services applet of the Control Panel and clicking the Start button. You can point your Web browser to the IP address of the local machine and use the online documentation, information, and samples to get started (if you installed the World Wide Web Publishing service).

For additional information about Microsoft Peer Web Services, refer to Chapter 20, "Windows NT Workstation as an Internet Server." Because this is a fairly involved and extensive core component, we have dedicated an entire chapter to its use and configuration.

Remote Access Services

Another old service with a new look and added functionality is the Remote Access Services (RAS). Remote Access Services provides a mechanism with which the user can connect from a remote location (thus the name) to a system running Remote Access Server on the corporate LAN, for example. Additionally, RAS supports the use of NetBEUI, IPX/SPX, and TCP/IP as well as Point to Point (PPP) protocols, which makes this single client software component capable of connecting to another RAS server, a remote access device such as a Shiva LANRover, or an Internet Service Provider (ISP).

To install Remote Access Services, follow this procedure:

1. Open the Network applet in the Control Panel or select the Network Neighborhood properties by right-clicking the icon on the desktop.

2. Select the Services tab and click the Add button. You see a dialog of available services.

3. Select the Remote Access Service and click OK.

4. The necessary files are copied to your system.

5. If you have not yet installed a modem or other RAS-capable device, you are asked whether you want to invoke the modem installer to install one. Click Yes. For additional information about installing and configuring modems, consult Chapter 10, "Advanced System Configuration." After you have installed and configured a RAS-capable device, continue with the next step.

6. You see an Add RAS Device dialog (shown in Figure 18.6). Select the device you want to add and click OK.

FIGURE 18.6.

Add RAS Device dialog.

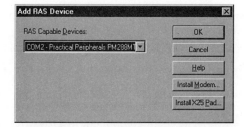

7. At the Remote Access Setup dialog (shown in Figure 18.7), click the Configure button to change the RAS port configuration to support dial out only, receive calls only, or both (the default is dial out only). When you are done, click OK.

FIGURE 18.7.

Remote Access Setup configuration screen.

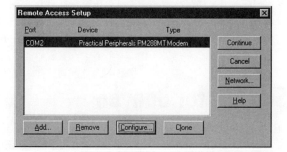

8. To configure network support, click the Network button.

9. Depending on your choice for port configuration, you have network configuration options for dial out, receive calls, or both. Check the boxes next to the protocols you want to support. For receiving calls, click the Configure button next to the protocol to make the necessary configurations.

10. When you're finished, click Continue and the service is installed. Click Close.

11. When prompted, restart your computer to effect the changes.

This process installs Remote Access with a basic configuration. For additional information and advanced configuration and usage as well as instructions on how to create and use dial-up networking connections, refer to Chapter 21, "Remote Access Service," which is dedicated entirely to this topic because it is a very versatile and extensive application.

RPC Configuration

The Remote Procedure Call (RPC) Configuration is another core network component used for interprocess communication (IPC) and locating services on the network. RPC is unique in its method of IPC in that it uses other IPC mediums to establish a session between the client and server services. For network connections, it uses either Named Pipes, Windows Sockets, or NetBIOS to communicate between the systems. If the client and server services are located on the same system, it uses the Local Procedure Call (LPC) facility. Because it is implemented in this fashion, RPC has the highest degree of flexibility of all the IPC mechanisms.

The server component of a distributed or network-enabled application registers its services with the RPC Locator service, which manages the RPC Name database (a database of services available on the network). The client component in a distributed or network-enabled application queries the RPC Locator service to find the necessary server applications on the network.

By implementing an IPC in this fashion, the system has much more latitude in the type of application it can support and the features of that application. By utilizing the other IPC transports, RPC can satisfy almost any IPC request. For instance, a given application may request a certain service from the IPC; when using RPC, it is able to request this from a much wider variety of services and applications due to its broad support of Named Pipes, WinSock, and NetBIOS. This provides a much more open and expansive foundation on which to build in the future.

RPC Support for Banyan

The RPC Support for Banyan service is a new offering in Windows NT 4 Workstation. What this service provides is an extension to the previous RPC Configuration mechanism, now incorporating support for Banyan systems IPC mechanisms and transports into the RPC subsystem. This addition allows an even more diverse horizon for network communications and incorporates those services available on Banyan Vines networks and servers into the RPC Locator service database.

SAP Agent

The SAP Agent is a NetWare-compatible Service Access Protocol agent that sends out broadcasts (SAP datagrams) announcing the services available on the local system for NetWare clients and servers. When you install this service, you are prompted to install the NWLink IPX/SPX Compatible Transport if it is not already installed. In some respects, this is similar to an RPC facility for NetWare networks.

Server

"What?," you ask. "A Server service? I thought this was Windows NT Workstation?" Well, right you are, this is Windows NT Workstation, version 4.0 to be precise; however, it has always included a Server service. It is the network service that makes it possible for remote systems on the network to connect to the local system and for the local system to share resources on the network. Again, by breaking down the core network services into individual components, Windows NT maintains the modular architecture that allows you to easily modify and upgrade individual network services rather than the entire network subsystem. Windows NT Workstation has no configuration options for the Server service.

Simple TCP/IP Service

The Simple TCP/IP Service provides functionality for some older and less common TCP/IP utilities, most of which are entirely irrelevant to the normal operation and usage of TCP/IP and TCP/IP applications. Provided with the Simple TCP/IP Service are the client software for the Character Generator, Daytime, Discard, Echo, and Quote of the Day services. If you install this service, the system can respond to requests from other systems that support these protocols. Probably the most common use of these services is using the Quote of the Day service to append a quotation to outgoing mail messages.

SNMP Services

The Simple Network Management Protocol (SNMP) component of Windows NT Workstation is an optional extension that you can install and configure to provide statistics, information, and alerts to a remote system running an SNMP management console application. In a limited fashion, this service also allows the system to be administered remotely by a system running an SNMP management console. If you install the SNMP service, performance counters for the TCP/IP protocol and services are also loaded and made available for use by the Performance Monitor.

To install the SNMP service, follow this procedure:

1. Open the Network applet in the Control Panel or select the Network Neighborhood properties by right-clicking the icon on the desktop.

2. Select the Services tab and click the Add button. You see a dialog of available services.

3. Select the SNMP Service and click OK. If you have not installed the TCP/IP protocol or the NWLink IPX/SPX Compatible Transport on your computer, you are prompted to do so.

4. The necessary files are copied to your system.

5. You then see the SNMP Properties configuration sheet. (See Figure 18.8.)

FIGURE 18.8.

*SNMP Properties
configuration sheet.*

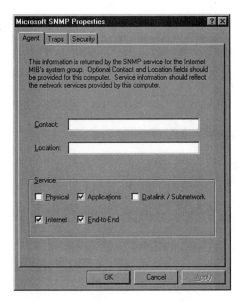

To configure the SNMP Service, perform the following steps:

1. In the SNMP Properties sheet on the Agent tab, provide the name of the primary user of the system and the location of the physical location of the system.

2. Select which services you want to enable SNMP monitoring and functions for. Your choices include the following:

   ■ Physical: Choose this option if this system manages any physical network devices such as a hub (OSI layer 1).

   ■ Applications: Choose this if this system uses any TCP/IP applications. You should select this for all systems (OSI layer 7).

   ■ Datalink/Subnetwork: Choose this option if this system manages any subnetworks or datalink devices such as a bridge (OSI layer 2).

   ■ Internet: Choose this option if this is a multihomed or gateway system (OSI layer 3).

   ■ End-to-End: Choose this option if this system is a TCP/IP host (you should select it for all systems) (OSI layer 5).

3. Select the Traps tab (shown in Figure 18.9). Here, you can remove and add community names for the SNMP service by selecting the community name and clicking the Remove button or typing the name in the community name field and clicking the Add button.

FIGURE 18.9.

*The SNMP Properties
Traps configuration
tab.*

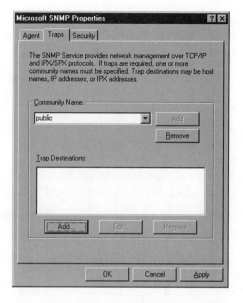

4. To add a trap destination, a host that is running an SNMP management console, click the Add button and provide the IP or IPX address of the trap destination. To change or remove a trap destination, select the trap destination and click the Edit or Remove buttons accordingly.

5. Select the Security tab (shown in Figure 18.10) to configure the SNMP service security.

FIGURE 18.10.

*SNMP Properties
Security tab.*

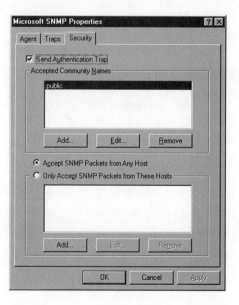

18

**WINDOWS NT
NETWORK
SERVICES**

6. To configure the system to send an SNMP authentication trap to authenticate a session request from an SNMP management console, check the Send Authentication Trap box.

7. Add to the list of Accepted Community Names all communities that are authorized to interact with the SNMP service and components. Edit or remove listed names as appropriate.

8. You can also configure the SNMP agent to accept SNMP packets from any host or from only explicitly specified hosts. To restrict access to defined hosts only, select the Only Accept SNMP Packets from These Hosts button. To add access for a host, click the Add button and provide the IP or IPX address of the host to allow. Repeat this for each host from which SNMP packets should be accepted.

9. When you have finished configuration, click OK and then click Close.

10. Restart your computer when prompted to effect the changes.

After you have installed and configured SNMP, you need some kind of management console or SNMP management application to use the SNMP service and remotely administer components of the SNMP-enabled system. Also note that to install and configure SNMP, you must be logged in as a member of the local Administrators group. This implementation of SNMP supports SNMP v.1 and Management Information Base (MIB) II.

Workstation

The Workstation service is another core network component, the counterpart to the Server service. This service provides the functionality necessary for Windows NT Workstation to act as a client on the network and to request and access network resources. The Workstation service has no configuration options and should not be removed.

Summary

The Windows NT Workstation network subsystem is broken down into modular components called services. This modularity provides for broad flexibility in implementation and allows you to add, remove, or update individual components without affecting other components or requiring the network core to be reconstructed.

Windows NT Workstation provides an open architecture that aids in integrating disparate network systems and allows for flexibility and coexistence with almost any network on the market today. Additionally, third-party vendors can write their own network services to further extend the functionality and increase the integration of Windows NT Workstation.

Integrating Windows NT into Heterogeneous Networks

by Timothy Parker

IN THIS CHAPTER

CHAPTER 19

Integrating your Windows NT Workstation machine with a network depends on you properly specifying the type of network and the network protocol in use. Before integrating your machine with an existing or new network, you should install the network interface card. (See Chapter 16, "Installing Windows NT Networking," for more information on installing and configuring network cards.)

Most network cards that you can purchase today support the most popular network protocols you will be using, but if your network uses a protocol from a much older networking system or one that is not widely distributed, you might experience problems. To avoid this, if you are not using a common protocol such as TCP/IP, NetBEUI, or IPX/SPX, make sure you check the network card's compatibility. Also, if you are using an older network card, make sure you can get drivers for your operating system. Many network cards from a couple of years ago did not include Windows NT drivers, for example. Therefore, you might have to track down the vendor's BBS or Web site and retrieve new drivers if Windows NT does not support the card directly.

After the network card has been properly recognized by your Windows NT Workstation machine, you need to specify the protocol in use on the network. You saw the most commonly used network protocols in Chapter 17, "Windows NT Network Protocols." The two most widely used protocols for networking are TCP/IP (Transmission Control Protocol/Internet Protocol) and IPX/SPX (Internet Packet Exchange/Sequenced Packet Exchange). IPX/SPX is usually found only on Novell NetWare-based networks, while TCP/IP is on a wide variety of networks (and is also supported on Novell NetWare). Less common networking protocols such as NetBIOS (Network Basic Input/Output System) and NetBEUI (NetBIOS Extended User Interface) are found on networks used by older Windows for Workgroups machines. There are several other network protocols in use, most based on minicomputer network protocols, but these are gradually being replaced by TCP/IP.

Setting up your Windows NT Workstation machine for the most popular networks is quite simple as long as you know which network protocol is in use. If you are not sure which network protocol to configure, ask the network administrator or check the configuration on another machine on the network.

Choosing Network Protocols

The network protocol to be used by Windows NT Workstation is specified through the Network icon of the Control Panel. Bring up the Control Panel and double-click the Network icon. This will display the Network dialog shown in Figure 19.1.

FIGURE 19.1.

The Windows NT Workstation Network dialog.

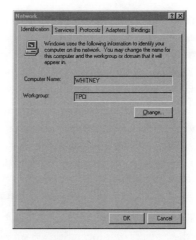

The Network dialog (which you have seen several times in the last few chapters) has five separate sections activated by clicking on the tabs at the top of the window. The five sections are

- Identification: Identifies the name of the workstation.
- Services: Lists the network services currently installed on your Windows NT workstation.
- Protocols: Lists the protocols that Windows NT uses to communicate on the network (or networks, if you have your workstation on more than one network).
- Adapters: Lists the network adapter cards currently configured on your workstation.
- Bindings: Shows the connections between network cards, protocols, and services that are configured on your workstation.

All five pages of information have to be properly filled in for your network communications to work without any problems. Let's look at each of the pages in a little more detail before configuring your workstation for a particular network.

The Identification Page

You should start your network configuration by examining the Identification page shown in Figure 19.1. This page has only two pieces of information, which will probably already be filled in based on data you supplied when you installed Windows NT Workstation. You can use this page to change this information at any time, which might be necessary if you skipped the data when installing, if you have a conflict with another machine on the network, or if you want to alter the name of the workstation for personal reasons.

19

INTEGRATING
WINDOWS NT

Each machine on a network is uniquely identified to every other machine by a number of pieces of information, some of which is transparent to you. The most common identification is through an IP address (used in TCP/IP networks). An IP address is unique to your network and your machine and can be used to route information over the network to or from your workstation. Some other network protocols rely on computer names or names that are mapped to numbers to identify your machine.

The Identification page of the Network window requests both a machine name and either a workgroup or domain name. The machine name is unique to your machine and should not be the same as any other machine on the network. The machine name can be anything that will help others associate your machine with you, such as your name. The workgroup or domain name is used by some networks to identify which network or subnetwork your machine belongs to.

Make sure both of these pieces of information are supplied and that no errors occur when you click the OK button to register your entries. Your workstation will try to communicate with a domain server to verify that the domain name you supply is valid.

Services

The Services page of the Network dialog shows a list of all the network services that are currently installed on your workstation, as shown in Figure 19.2. The list shows only those services that are installed and configured, not all the services that are available to you.

Figure 19.2.

The Services page shows all network services installed on the workstation.

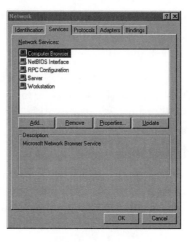

Your workstation will use several types of services. Some services let you share your directories and peripherals, and others provide automatic functionality such as backups and name lookups.

Most services have configuration details associated with them. You can usually see these details by highlighting the service name in the Services window and clicking the Properties button. This displays the Configuration dialog, such as the one shown in Figure 19.3 for the RPC (Remote Procedure Call) service.

FIGURE 19.3.

Most services have configuration information associated with them.

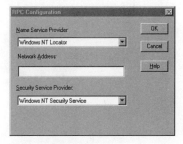

A few services do not have configuration information. These services display a message to this effect when you click the Properties button, as shown in Figure 19.4.

FIGURE 19.4.

If no configuration details are associated with a service, this message appears.

To add new services to your system, click the Add button below the Installed Services list. This compiles a list of all services that Windows NT Workstation has available to you. A dialog appears with the full list, as shown in Figure 19.5.

FIGURE 19.5.

This dialog shows all services available to the workstation.

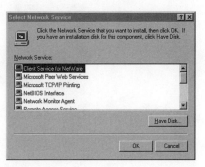

Selecting a service from this list starts the installation and configuration process, after which the service appears in the list of installed services. You will be adding some services later in this chapter to match the network requirements.

Protocols

The Protocols page shows the protocols that are currently installed on your workstation. Many protocols can be installed, although they don't all have to be used at the moment. An icon to the left of the protocol name shows that the protocol is used by the network. Figure 19.6 shows the Protocols page with a single protocol (TCP/IP) in use by the workstation.

FIGURE 19.6.

The Protocols page shows all the network protocols that are in use by the workstation.

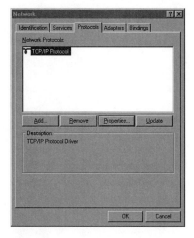

As with the Services page, a Property sheet is attached to each protocol. You can see the Property sheet and, hence, all the configuration information for each service by selecting a protocol in the list and then clicking the Properties button. Figure 19.7 shows the Properties page for the TCP/IP protocol shown in Figure 19.6.

FIGURE 19.7.

A Properties page is used for each protocol installed on the workstation to provide configuration information.

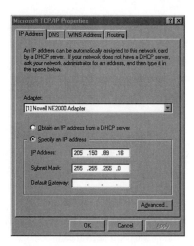

As you look at several network protocols later in this chapter, you will use the Property sheet to provide all the configuration information the workstation needs for using the network.

You can obtain a list of all protocols that the workstation knows about by clicking the Add button of the Protocols sheet. This generates a list of available protocols and displays them in a dialog box, as shown in Figure 19.8. You can install protocols other than the ones shown in this list, as long as you have the software drivers for the network. Some specialty networks have to be configured in this manner.

FIGURE 19.8.

The Select Network Protocol dialog lets you choose which network protocols to install on the workstation.

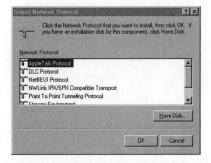

Adapters

As you might expect, the Adapters page lists all the network adapter cards that are configured and recognized by the Windows NT Workstation. You saw how to add and configure network adapters in Chapter 16, "Installing Windows NT Networking." This dialog is shown in Figure 19.9.

FIGURE 19.9.

The Adapters page lists all network adapters that are recognized by Windows NT Workstation.

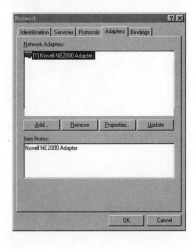

19

INTEGRATING
WINDOWS NT

This particular system is configured with a single network adapter, which is a Novell NE2000 type. Most TCP/IP and IPX/SPX network cards can be configured as this type of network card if the actual card description is not provided and you know that the card works with either or both network protocols.

As with Services and Protocols, a Properties sheet is associated with each network card that identifies the card's IRQ and memory address. For more information on configuring your network card, refer to Chapter 16.

Bindings

The Bindings page of the Network dialog is used to tie together adapters, protocols, and services. A selection list at the top of the page lets you see bindings for all services, adapters, or protocols. You can start with the services bindings, as shown in Figure 19.10. The list of bindings on this page shows the order in which the workstation tries to resolve requests for network services. By putting the most frequently used binding first, you can minimize the amount of time your workstation requires to accomplish network tasks. If you have several networks connected to your workstation or you use multiple protocols on your system, selecting the proper order for use is important because performance can be affected.

FIGURE 19.10.

The Bindings page lists connections between services, protocols, and network adapters.

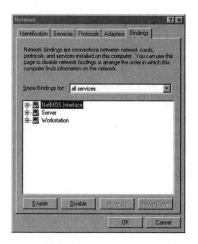

You can alter the order of bindings on this list, changing the way in which your computer deals with network services, by using the Move Up and Move Down buttons below the list. You can also disable or enable bindings by using the Enable and Disable buttons below the list. A disabled binding is ignored by the workstation when a network service is to be resolved.

The icon next to the name of each binding on the list visually shows you the status of the binding. A computer screen (such as the one shown in Figure 19.10) means that the binding is enabled and active. Disabled bindings have a red cross symbol next to them, as shown in

Figure 19.11, and have two bindings disabled. There are two disabled states. A red icon means the entire binding has been disabled, and a yellow icon means some of the bindings are disabled and some are enabled.

FIGURE 19.11.

A red or yellow cross icon next to a binding name means the binding is disabled completely or partly, respectively.

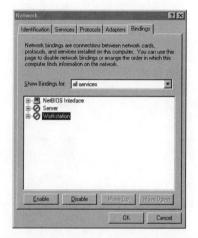

The left column of the Bindings list has a small box with either a plus sign or a hyphen in it. If there is a plus sign in the box, it means there are underlying levels of detail to the binding that can be shown by clicking either the box or the binding name. Figure 19.12 shows expansions of some of the bindings shown earlier. You can use this feature to expand or compress the Bindings list for better legibility or to provide details of all the services or protocols bound to each entry.

FIGURE 19.12.

Several levels of binding information can be available, depending on the icon to the left of the binding name.

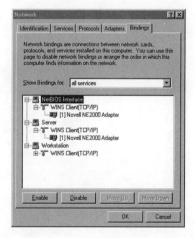

19

INTEGRATING
WINDOWS NT

Property sheets are not attached to each service, adapter, or protocol shown in the bindings page. The properties must be changed on the proper page in the Network dialog. For example, if you want to change your machine's IP address, you can't do it by clicking the TCP/IP Protocol entry on the Bindings page, so you must go through the Protocols page and select Properties there, as you saw earlier.

As mentioned, the Bindings page has a selection list that enables you to display the services or the bindings for each network adapter or network protocol. Changing the selection alters the Bindings list, as shown in Figures 19.13 and 19.14, which show the adapters and protocols bindings, respectively. In both of these figures, the lists have been expanded to show information below the top level.

FIGURE 19.13.

The adapter bindings show the protocols bound to each adapter card.

FIGURE 19.14.

The protocol bindings show the adapters to which each protocol or service is bound.

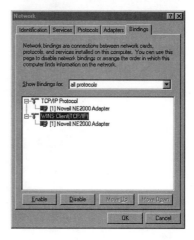

The three types of bindings lists let you see how the adapters, protocols, and services installed on your workstation interact. You will probably use all three bindings lists at one time or another to see how your workstation handles network functions.

You can now use the five pages of the Network dialog to configure your Windows NT Workstation machine for several different networks. In each case, as you already know, adding your workstation to a network is a matter of simply configuring the adapter, protocol, and service to work with the rest of the network. Usually, this is much easier to say than do, although a little experimentation usually sets things right quickly!

Configuring Windows NT for NetWare

Novell NetWare is widely used for PC-based networks. NetWare usually uses a network protocol called IPX/SPX, although it can be configured to use other protocols (most notably TCP/IP). Configuring your Windows NT Workstation machine to work on an existing NetWare IPX/SPX machine requires properly loading and configuring the NetWare services and protocols.

IPX/SPX doesn't have to be used with Novell NetWare machines; it is a stand-alone network protocol in its own right and can be used for networks of Windows NT machines with a NetWare system, for example. However, in most cases, you will be adding your workstation to an existing Novell NetWare-based network.

Windows NT Workstation uses a Microsoft implementation of IPX/SPX called NetWare Link IPX/SPX Compatible Transport (NWLink). NWLink is designed to allow Windows NT machines (both servers and workstations) to communicate with NetWare and NetWare-compatible systems using IPX/SPX. Included with Windows NT Workstation is the Client Service for NetWare, which is used to allow file and printer resources to be shared with NetWare servers. In addition, the Client Service included with Windows NT supports the Novell Directory Service (NDS).

Configuring the NetWare Services

After you have installed a network card that will work with IPX/SPX, you need to load the NetWare Client Service. This is done through the Network dialog's Services page. If this NetWare client was not loaded by default when you installed Windows NT, click the Add button to generate a list of all available services. From this list, click Client Services for NetWare (usually at the top of the list), as shown earlier in Figure 19.5.

When you have selected Client Services for NetWare, Windows NT loads drivers from the distribution media (usually the CD-ROM). After the proper drivers have been loaded and linked to the kernel, the Client Service should appear on the Services list, as shown in Figure 19.15.

FIGURE 19.15.

The Client Services for NetWare has been added to the Services list.

No Property sheet is associated with the Client Service for NetWare.

Configuring the IPX/SPX Protocol

After you add the Client Service for NetWare, move to the Protocols page of the Network dialog. Windows NT Workstation might have installed an entry in the protocol list labeled NWLink IPX/SPX Compatible Transport for you, as shown in Figure 19.16.

FIGURE 19.16.

The NWLink IPX/SPX protocol is added to the protocol list to provide NetWare compatibility.

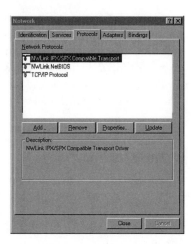

If the NWLink IPX/SPX entry does not appear on the protocol list, click the Add button to generate a list of all protocols available and choose that entry, as shown in Figure 19.17. Windows NT installs the proper drivers from your distribution media, and the NWLink entry is added to the protocol list.

FIGURE 19.17.

To add the NWLink IPX/SPX protocol to your system, choose it from the protocol list.

A Property sheet is associated with the NWLink protocol entry, as shown in Figure 19.18. To see the Property sheet, double-click the NWLink entry in the protocol list or highlight it and click the Properties button.

FIGURE 19.18.

The NWLink Properties dialog shows configuration information for the IPX/SPX protocol.

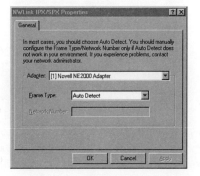

The Properties sheet provides a scrolling list of all network cards currently configured on your machine. If you have only a single network card configured on your machine, the NWLink IPX/SPX protocol will be associated with that card automatically. If you have more than one network card, you should choose the card that is to use NWLink IPX/SPX.

Below the network adapter card list is a field labeled Frame Types. By default, this is set to Auto Detect. This value should be left as Auto Detect for the vast majority of Novell NetWare and IPX/SPX-based networks, because it provides the most flexibility for your system. Change this value only if your network administrator instructs you to because incorrect values can prevent your machine from communicating with the network and, worse, might cause network problems for others. If you change the Auto Detect value to a specific frame type, you must provide a Network Number as well (from your network administrator).

19

INTEGRATING WINDOWS NT

Checking the Bindings

After you have configured the Client Service for Network and installed the NWLink IPX/SPX protocol on a network card, you can check the Bindings page of the Network dialog to ensure that everything is correctly set up. Figure 19.19 shows the bindings for a NetWare-based workstation.

FIGURE 19.19.

The bindings for using NWLink IPX/SPX and Client Services for NetWare are correct in this dialog.

If your Bindings page doesn't show the NWLink protocol bound to the Client Services for NetWare entry, an error has occured in configuration and you should check the other pages of the Network dialog again. The Protocol and Adapter bindings lists should show IPX/SPX bound to the proper network adapter card.

When you have all this information correct, you can click the OK button at the bottom of the Network dialog to update configuration information on your machine. Windows NT Workstation notifies you that the system must be rebooted to affect any changes. After a reboot, you should be able to use your machine to connect to other NetWare machines on the network.

Configuring Windows NT for TCP/IP

TCP/IP is the most widely used network protocol in the world. It is often used for networks that have UNIX-based machines on them because UNIX and TCP/IP are intimately tied together. (TCP/IP is the default network protocol of almost all UNIX systems.) The Internet uses TCP/IP, as well, so running a network with TCP/IP as the network protocol simplifies connections to other networks across the Internet. TCP/IP has a reputation for being difficult to configure and troubleshoot, but this is not correct. TCP/IP can be one of the easiest network protocols to install and configure, especially for GUI-based machines such as Windows NT Workstation.

You will need some information from your network administrator in order to configure your workstation properly. The information you need is an IP address (a unique number identifying your machine and network), a subnet mask, and a gateway address (if your network uses one).

The IP address is in dotted-quad notation, meaning there are four parts to the address, separated by periods. Each number is between 0 and 255, although there are some restrictions as to which numbers can actually be used. Your network administrator will tell you what your IP address should be, or at least tell you what other IP addresses are on your network and let you choose an unused number. You saw IP addresses in more detail in Chapter 17, "Windows NT Network Protocols."

The subnet mask allows one machine to send a message to all machines on the network by giving only part of the IP address, known as the network mask. The subnet mask essentially strips off the machine-specific part of the IP address and sends just the network address, so that all machines will pick up the message. The gateway address is required if your machine is to communicate with another machine for access out of your network or for specific services such as DNS (Domain Name Service). When you have all three pieces of information, you can configure your workstation for TCP/IP.

Configuring the TCP/IP Service

A number of TCP/IP-oriented services are supplied with Windows NT Workstation, although you do not need to install all of them. The most common TCP/IP-oriented services you might want to install are Simple TCP/IP Services (which include basic TCP/IP utilities) and Microsoft TCP/IP Printing (which enables you to send output to a printer connected by a network card directly to the network, not a local printer). You do not have to install either of these services for your workstation to run on TCP/IP, but they do not detract from your network performance, either.

To add either Simple TCP/IP Services or Microsoft TCP/IP Printing, select the service from the list produced when you click the Add button on the Services page. Windows NT installs the proper drivers from your distribution media, and then the service appears on your service list, as shown in Figure 19.20.

After any services you want to install have been added, you can install the TCP/IP protocol itself. You can add TCP/IP-oriented services to your workstation at any time, so you needn't worry about delaying the installation process. For example, you do not need to install Microsoft TCP/IP Printing until you need to print to a network printer. To add a service at any time in the future, just follow the procedure for adding new services.

FIGURE 19.20.

*Both Simple TCP/IP
Services and Microsoft
TCP/IP Printing have
been added as services
to this workstation.*

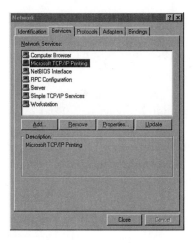

Configuring the TCP/IP Protocol

To add the TCP/IP protocol stack to your workstation, use the Protocols page of the Network dialog. If TCP/IP is not present in the protocol list, click the Add button to generate a list of supported protocols and then select TCP/IP. Windows NT reads the necessary drivers from the distribution media and adds TCP/IP to the list of installed protocols, as shown in Figure 19.21.

FIGURE 19.21.

*After TCP/IP has been
installed, the protocol
shows up on the
Protocol page.*

After the protocol has been added, you must provide details about your machine. Open the TCP/IP Properties page by double-clicking the TCP/IP entry in the protocol list or by highlighting TCP/IP and clicking the Properties button. The TCP/IP Properties dialog that appears has four pages. Usually, only the first page (labeled IP Address) has to be filled out for TCP/IP to work properly on your network. This dialog, shown in Figure 19.22, asks for the network adapter card that is to be used for TCP/IP and information about the IP address for your machine.

FIGURE 19.22.

The IP Address page specifies the network card and IP address.

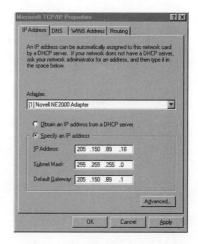

If your network has a Windows NT server, your network might be using the Dynamic Host Configuration Protocol (DHCP). DHCP allows a machine to connect with the DHCP server when it starts up and requests an IP address. The advantage of DHCP is that you don't need to specify any of the IP information in your configuration process. If you are using DHCP on your network, check the radio button that indicates this is the case, and you are mostly finished with your TCP/IP configuration. If you are not sure whether your network uses DHCP, check with your network administrator or assume you are not using it. (DHCP is often used on Windows NT Server-based networks, but it seldom is present on larger UNIX-based TCP/IP networks.)

If you are not using DHCP, you need to fill in two of the three pieces of information shown in the rest of the screen. The first is the IP address, which you know should be unique on your network. Make sure the address is entered correctly in the four windows. After the IP address is provided, fill in the Subnet Mask entry. This will usually be 255.0.0.0 for very large networks, 255.255.0.0 for medium-sized networks, or 255.255.255.0 for smaller networks. If you are not sure, check with your network administrator or examine the configuration of another machine on the network. Each machine on the network should have the same subnet mask.

If your network has a gateway machine that is used to access the Internet or another network or is used for some special services such as Domain Name Service (DNS), Network Information Service (NFS), or Network File System (NFS), you need to add the gateway IP address. This has the same format as your IP address, but the digits will be different. (In most cases, gateways have low-numbered IP addresses, but this is not a rule.) If you are not sure whether you have a gateway on your network, leave the entry blank.

The IP Address page has an Advanced button that displays the dialog shown in Figure 19.23. The information requested on this page is used to provide more flexibility and versatility to your workstation. The top of the screen lets you select the network adapter card that the configuration applies to. In most cases, this is the same as the IP Address page.

19

INTEGRATING WINDOWS NT

FIGURE 19.23.

*The Advanced IP
Addressing dialog lets
you add special network
routing and gateways
choices to your
workstation.*

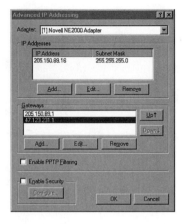

You can use the IP Address section in the middle of the Advanced page when you have a multihomed host, which means your workstation has more than one IP address. This might be because you have two or more networks connected to your machine and each has a different IP address. Alternatively, you might have different IP addresses to provide backward-compatibility with some older network systems or applications. In most cases, you will only have one IP address, but this section of the Advanced screen lets you add new IP addresses for your machine.

The lower section of the Advanced page lets you provide the IP address of more than one gate-way. If you are on a large network, your network might have several gateways to spread the load and to provide redundant pathways or services. You can add as many gateway IP addresses as you want using the Add, Edit, and Remove buttons below this section. The up and down buttons let you change the order of the gateways in the list. This is important because Windows NT tries the gateways in order, so put first the gateway IP address of the gateway you will use the most.

Below the gateway section is a button to enable PPTP filtering. PPTP is the Point-to-Point Tunneling Protocol, a new secure system that allows multiprotocol virtual private networks. If your network uses PPTP, select this option and only PPTP packets will be recognized by your machine. You should also load the PPTP service through the Services page so that your work-station can use PPTP. The PPTP service is part of the Windows NT Workstation distribution set. Most networks do not use PPTP, especially if they have been in operation for a year or more.

Finally, the Enable Security button at the bottom of the Advanced screen lets you activate TCP/IP security. This limits the types of packets that your machine will accept. Some network administrators prefer that all machines on the network employ this type of security, so check with the administrator before activating the option. Incorrectly setting the security can cause network reception and transmission problems.

If you select the Enable Security button, the dialog shown in Figure 19.24 appears. There are three lists on this dialog to enable you to select the packet types allowed through the TCP, UDP, and IP protocols. If security is active on your network, click the Permit Only button on the proper list and then the Add button. You are asked which port to allow traffic on. Because each protocol in TCP/IP has a unique port number, specifying the port tells the system which kinds of services to allow. For example, FTP uses ports 20 and 21. By preventing ports 20 and 21 from receiving packets, you effectively forbid FTP traffic to your machine. (There are other simpler ways to prevent FTP and similar service traffic, but packet security is sometimes used for this purpose.)

FIGURE 19.24.

The TCP/IP Security dialog lets you specify the types of packets to accept.

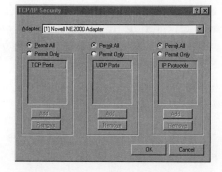

The second page of the TCP/IP Properties dialog is for DNS. DNS lets one machine access another by using its name instead of an IP address, which is a very useful feature on larger networks. DNS is often used on UNIX-based networks. If your network uses DNS, click the DNS page tab to display the DNS configuration screen, as shown in Figure 19.25.

FIGURE 19.25.

This dialog lets you provide DNS server information.

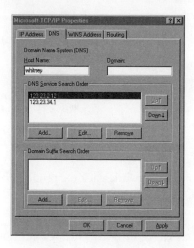

19

INTEGRATING WINDOWS NT

The DNS dialog includes your machine's name and domain at the top of the page, and a section beneath it for the IP addresses of each DNS server on your network. As with gateways, Windows NT connects to the DNS servers listed in order whenever it must resolve a name or address. You can add, edit, or remove entries from the list using the buttons beneath the list or by using the up and down buttons to change the order.

The lower part of the DNS page is for the Domain Suffix Search Order. The domain name is used to specify your network or company's address for others. This list is used to provide the DNS server names that your system should contact when it has to resolve a name. As with the DNS servers, you can manage the list by using buttons.

If your network does not use DNS, do not fill in any of the information on this page. Otherwise, your system will spend time fruitlessly trying to connect to servers that do not provide the service the machine wants, both slowing your machine and clogging the network with unwanted traffic.

The third page of the TCP/IP Properties dialog is for WINS, the Windows Internet Name Services, as shown in Figure 19.26. WINS allows a NetBIOS name to be resolved to an IP address, in much the same way DNS resolves IP names and IP addresses. If your network uses a WINS server, the IP addresses of the primary and secondary WINS servers should be provided in the proper spaces.

FIGURE 19.26.

If your network uses WINS to resolve NetBIOS names, fill in this page with WINS server addresses.

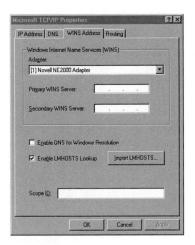

If WINS is used on your network, click the proper button to enable WINS lookups. You can also enable LMHOSTS lookup files, which are part of WINS. If your network does not use WINS, do not complete any information on this page.

The last page of the TCP/IP Properties dialog is for Routing, as shown in Figure 19.27. If you are on a multihomed machine (one with more than one IP address) and you want to have your workstation IP forward packets from one network to another, enable the forwarding button. For most networks, forwarding is not performed on workstations but on a router or server.

FIGURE 19.27.
If IP Forwarding is to be performed by your workstation, click the button on this page.

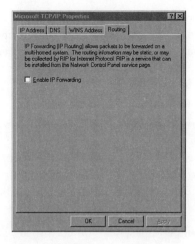

After all that, your TCP/IP service is configured. Close the Properties dialog by clicking OK, and you should be ready to check the bindings.

Checking the Bindings

The Bindings page of the Network dialog is used to check the proper configuration of your TCP/IP protocol stack. Click the Bindings page tab and examine the services list. You should see a TCP/IP protocol entry under one or more of the options when you expand them, as well as the network card to be used, as shown in Figure 19.28.

FIGURE 19.28.
Check to ensure that TCP/IP is bound to the services your system uses, and that the services are bound to a network card.

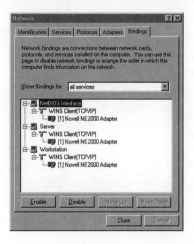

19

INTEGRATING WINDOWS NT

To check the protocol itself, use the Protocols option and examine the TCP/IP protocol for bindings to the network adapter. If all the bindings appear correct, exit the Network dialog by clicking the OK button, and Windows NT will probably ask for a machine reset to make the changes effective. After a reboot, you can test your network connection using TCP/IP utilities such as ping or Telnet.

Setting Up Other Network Protocols

If the network to which you are attaching your machine is not IPX/SPX- or TCP/IP-based, the process remains the same as for those two protocols: Make sure the network adapter card is configured, add the services for the network, add the protocol, configure the protocol parameters, check the bindings, reboot the machine, and test.

Some popular small network systems do not employ TCP/IP or IPX/SPX, instead relying on other protocols. Windows NT provides a rather complete list of protocols supported by the basic distribution set, but if your network protocol is not in the base set, you need a driver disk from the network manufacturer. These are usually available for a variety of network platforms, although when a new operating system version appears it can take a while for drivers to be readied.

Summary

As you have seen, setting up Windows NT Workstation to work with any network is a rather routine task. You use the Network Control Panel to specify the protocol and any services associated with that protocol. Make sure the bindings are correct and the configuration information is accurate, and let Windows NT do the rest. After you reboot the machine, the system should be able to access the network without a problem.

There are a lot of different network protocols in use today, although by far the majority of systems that use Windows NT workstations are IPX/SPX or TCP/IP. If you encounter a protocol you are not familiar with, a driver disk for Windows NT should be available from the network operating system (NOS) manufacturer. Most NOS manufacturers maintain bulletin boards or Web sites where you can obtain new drives.

As new services are added or made available through third parties, you can add even more functionality to your Windows NT system. The Network configuration process is simple, easy to understand, and as long as you have the necessary configuration information, very easy to work with. Windows NT 4.0 Workstation is a far cry from many of the configuration routines we had to work with years ago!

Windows NT Workstation as an Internet Server

by Sean Mathias

IN THIS CHAPTER

CHAPTER

20

With the power and flexibility of Windows NT Workstation comes yet another built-in feature—Microsoft Peer Web Services. This is basically Microsoft Internet Information Server by another name. I can find only minimal differences in the products, other than name and the fact that the Windows NT Workstation license agreement limits the number of simultaneous inbound connections to 10. Additionally, the Advanced configuration option for access control is not available in Peer Web Services as it is in IIS.

Microsoft Peer Web Services on Windows NT Workstation provides a complete package to support a small Internet presence or departmental intranet. Services for the World Wide Web, FTP, and Gopher come with this package, and all are easily installed, configured, and administered.

This chapter deals primarily with Microsoft's Peer Web Services and its configuration and usage, and it touches on some other Internet applications suitable for Windows NT. For information on the installation of Microsoft Peer Web Services, see Chapter 18, "Windows NT Network Services."

Microsoft Peer Web Services

Microsoft Peer Web Services is being touted as a scaled-down version of Microsoft Internet Information Server (IIS). As I mentioned, I can find no functional differences between the two products other than their names, the inbound connection limit, and the lack of an Advanced configuration option for access control.

The World Wide Web Publishing service (as it has been dubbed in Microsoft-speak) has become the preferred method of document browsing and information sharing and is rapidly becoming much more interactive through programmatic server extensions, database automation, and animation. The FTP Publishing service is still a very popular avenue for transferring files of all types, and the Gopher Publishing service is an information search and retrieval service, which is fast being replaced with Web-based counterparts.

In the following sections, you will learn about the configuration and administration of the Microsoft Peer Web Services components. This chapter assumes that Microsoft Peer Web Services has already been installed. You will also see some third-party Internet solutions for Windows NT Workstation.

Internet Service Manager

After you have installed the Microsoft Peer Web Services, it is necessary to configure the service to use the appropriate level of security, create and configure the necessary tree structures for your Web services, and set the logging options and other parameters. The primary interface for configuring Microsoft Peer Web Services is through the Internet Manager item in the Peer Web Services folder.

Using the Internet Manager shown in Figure 20.1, you can configure any Microsoft Internet Servers available on the network and their services, as long as you have sufficient permissions to do so.

FIGURE 20.1.

The Microsoft Peer Web Internet Service Manager.

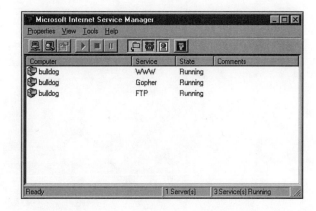

From the Internet Service Manager window, you can start, stop, pause, and configure service properties by right-clicking the desired service and selecting the appropriate item. On the Properties menu, you find options to connect to a specific server or search the network for all available servers and services.

Using the View menu, you can customize the look of the Internet Service Manager window to show only a specific type of service (WWW, FTP, Gopher) or sort the window by servers or services, and you can select from a Servers view, Services view, or a Report view (default). Many of these options are available from the toolbar as well. In typical Microsoft style, the look and customization of the display is very configurable by users to meet their personal preferences.

World Wide Web Publishing Service

First, let's look at the World Wide Web Publishing service properties and configuration. These services all share many common options for configuration, but each has options specific to its function. Open the WWW service properties by selecting the WWW service for the appropriate server in the Internet Service Manager. Double-click it, right-click it, and select Properties, or select Service Properties from the Properties menu. This produces the WWW Service Properties sheet, shown in Figure 20.2.

20

WORKSTATION AS
AN INTERNET
SERVER

FIGURE 20.2.

The WWW Service Properties sheet.

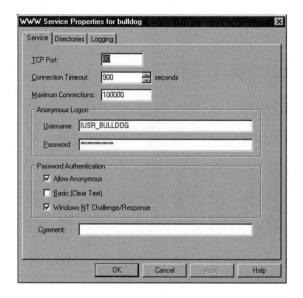

The Service Tab

The first tab on the WWW Service Property dialog is the Service tab. This tab has some basic configuration options that are consistent across all services. Here are the descriptions and explanations of these various options:

- Connection Timeout: This is the number of seconds that a WWW connection must be idle before the connection is closed. The default is 900 seconds (15 minutes). Depending on things such as your system resources, you might want to change this to a shorter timeout period.

- Maximum Connections: This is the maximum number of concurrent WWW connections allowed for this system. The default is 1000. This setting is very dependent on your available bandwidth and system resources.

- Anonymous Logon/Username: This is the Windows NT account that is used when a user connects anonymously. Anonymous logon is the most common method of accessing a WWW site. However, Windows NT requires all network connections to operate in a security context. This username is the security context that is assigned to anonymous logons.

- Anonymous Logon/Password: This is the password for the Anonymous Logon Username account just mentioned.

- Password Authentication/Allow Anonymous: This setting is used to permit anonymous connections to the WWW site. This is the default method of connecting to a site. If this is not enabled, users are prompted for a username and password to be permitted access.

■ Password Authentication/Basic (Clear Text): This option enables the use of advanced security, requiring users to provide an account name and password in order to be granted access to the site or restricted area of the site. Using this option, usernames and passwords are passed using clear text, unless some other form of encryption is employed (such as SSL).

■ Password Authentication/Windows NT Challenge/Response: This option utilizes the Windows NT Challenge/Response encryption scheme for encrypting usernames and passwords for transmission across the network.

■ Comment: This is a descriptive comment about this WWW server.

By default, when Microsoft Peer Web Services is installed, the setup program creates a user account (IUSR_computername), which it assigns a password and gives the rights of the guest account, with the exception that this account is granted permission to log on locally.

For security reasons, it is a good practice to explicitly grant access to the appropriate WWW directory structures and to explicitly deny access on all other drives and directories, which prevents anonymous users from gaining access to unauthorized areas of your system.

The security access control to specific pages or areas of a site is controlled by access permissions on files and directories in the wwwroot directory. If you are using the FAT file system, all users will have full access to the site. To restrict access and set permissions, you must be using NTFS and must set appropriate permissions on the relevant files and directories.

When you use Basic or Windows NT Challenge/Response password authentication, a user must have a valid Windows NT user account on the system running the WWW Publishing Service, in order to gain access to a site or restricted area of a site.

The Directories Tab

The Directories tab is where the actual structure of the WWW site is configured. Using this tab, shown in Figure 20.3, you configure the document root in a similar manner to a directory root. The document root is the starting point for a WWW site. Most sites (even those generated dynamically using a database) operate in a hierarchical fashion. Therefore, based on the user's navigation, sites traverse a tree moving up, down, and parallel, as well as "jumping" to entirely different locations or sites through a hypertext link (hence the name HyperText Transfer Protocol).

Looking at the Directory tab, you see two listings by default: the wwwroot and Scripts aliases. The wwwroot listing is the default document root and equates in this example to the c:\WINNT\system32\inetsrv\wwwroot directory on the local hard drive. Typically, the directory structure underlying this root acts as the WWW tree through which users navigate. The Scripts listing is the default location of any scripts such as CGI programs or IDC and HTX files for interacting with a database.

FIGURE 20.3.
The Directories tab.

Below this area, you see the Enable Default Document check box with a defined Default Document of `Default.htm`. This definition enables a user to move to a new location in a site using a link. If no specific document target is defined, the user is presented with the `Default.htm` page for that particular location. This can be disabled and the default document can be changed if needed.

At the very bottom, you see a Directory Browsing Allowed check box. When this option is enabled, the user sees the site in a directory tree fashion, similar to an FTP site or the old File Manager. The user can traverse and navigate the tree by selecting a directory or document to move to.

Microsoft Peer Web Services supports the use of Virtual Servers, as does Internet Information Server. Virtual Servers provide a means of supporting and operating more than one WWW site on a single system through the use of multiple IP addresses, which are each assigned a different document root.

To create a Virtual Server, click the Add button. You are then presented with a Directory Properties sheet (the same sheet used for editing the properties of an existing directory), as shown in Figure 20.4. To add another directory root, type the path in the Directory box or use the Browse button to establish the path.

Specify whether this is a Home Directory or a Virtual Directory. A Home Directory is just that—a document root for a WWW server. A Virtual Directory is a directory relative to the Home Directory, meaning that the path `c:\WINNT\System32\inetsrv\scripts` can be referenced in HTML simply as `../scripts` for a URL, rather than providing the entire path. If this is a Virtual Directory, provide an alias for the directory (such as Scripts).

FIGURE 20.4.

The Directory Properties sheet.

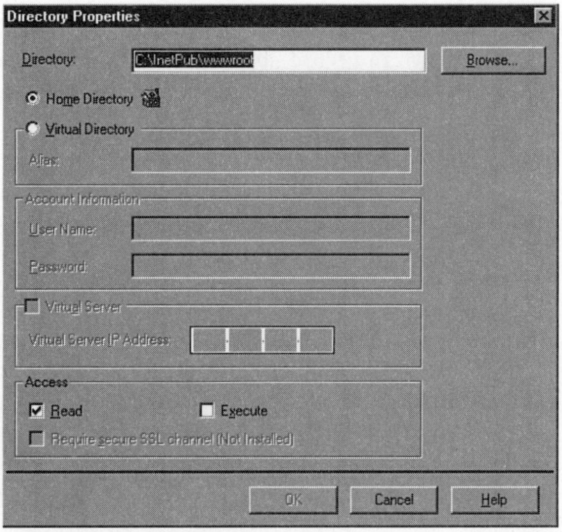

If the directory specified in the Directory path box is on a remote system (using UNC naming or a URL), you need to provide a User Name and Password with access to the remote system in the Account Information section, so that the directory will be accessible to users.

For a Virtual Server, which is an additional server on the same system, check the Virtual Server box and provide an IP address for the Virtual Server.

> **NOTE**
>
> To create Virtual Servers, you first need to assign additional IP addresses to the system using the Network applet in Control Panel. To do this, open the Network applet and select the Protocols tab. Select TCP/IP Protocol, click the Properties button, and then click the Advanced button. Click the Add button and provide an IP address and subnet mask. Repeat this process for each additional IP address, up to a total of five.
>
> To add support for more than five IP addresses, or for additional information, see the "TCP/IP Advanced Configuration" section of Chapter 17, "Windows NT Network Protocols."

For each directory root, Virtual Directory, or Virtual Server, it is necessary to configure the Access permission at the bottom of the Directory Properties sheet. For the default directory installed by Microsoft Peer Web Services, users have Read permission, and this is sufficient. For the default Virtual Directory /Scripts, users have Execute permission, which is all they need for scripts. If you have acquired and installed support for Secure Socket Layers (SSL), there is another option to require the user to use an SSL channel. When you have finished configuring the Directory Properties, click OK.

20

WORKSTATION AS AN INTERNET SERVER

The Logging Tab

The Logging tab, shown in Figure 20.5, provides two methods for logging activity on your WWW (and other services) site. To enable logging of site activity, check the Enable Logging box.

FIGURE 20.5.

The Logging tab.

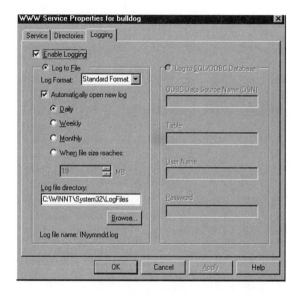

The two options available for logging activity are to log to a text file or to log through an ODBC data source to a database such as Microsoft Access or SQL Server. Select either the Log to File or Log to SQL/ODBC Database button to specify the type of logging desired.

If you choose to log to a text file, you have several configuration options. The first option is to automatically open a new log file at a specified interval: daily, weekly, monthly, or when the file reaches a specified size. For purposes of analysis, it is most common to configure this option to automatically open a new file daily. The frequency with which you choose to open a new log determines the name of the log file that is shown at the bottom of the Log to File section. A daily log file has the format In*yymmdd*.log, in which *yy* is the year, *mm* is the month, and *dd* is the day. In the Log file directory box, you can specify the directory to store log files in.

If you choose to log to a SQL/ODBC data source, things are somewhat more complicated, but ultimately the data is more flexible and useful than a large text file. The first step is to create the database and table that will be used to store the log data. Depending on which database you choose to use, this process will vary significantly. Fortunately, Microsoft includes a SQL script for creating a table in a SQL database, which can be used to create the table or to obtain the necessary filed names and types. The SQL script is called `logtemp.sql` and is installed to the `\server` subdirectory of the Peer Web Services installation directory (where `\server` is the directory in which Peer Web Services was installed).

The SQL script is as follows:

```
CREATE TABLE inetlog (
    ClientHost      varchar(255),
    username            varchar(255),
LogTime          datetime,
service          varchar(255),
machine          varchar(255),
serverip         varchar(50),
processingtime int,
bytesrecvd     int,
bytessent          int,
servicestatus     int,
win32status     int,
operation           varchar(255),
target           varchar(255),
parameters       varchar(255))
```

This script automatically creates the necessary table when run against an existing SQL Server database, provided the user has permission to create tables. An explanation of the various fields is provided in Appendix B, "Definitions for Peer Web Services Logging." If you will be using another database, such as Microsoft Access, this script is still useful because it provides the names of the necessary fields, their datatypes, and their sizes.

After you have created the database and table for storing log data, you need to create an ODBC System Data Source Name (System DSN). The database does not need to be on the local system; it can be on another system which can be accessed through an ODBC data source. To create an ODBC data source suitable for logging purposes, open the ODBC applet in Control Panel and click the System DSN button at the bottom of the Data Sources dialog. When the System Data Sources dialog opens, click Add. A list of installed ODBC drivers is displayed. Select the appropriate ODBC driver and click OK. If the necessary ODBC driver is not listed, you need to consult your ODBC package documentation or database documentation for information on installing ODBC support.

To create an ODBC Data Source for Microsoft SQL Server, follow these steps:

1. Open the ODBC applet in Control Panel and click the System DSN button.
2. Click the Add button, select the SQL Server ODBC driver, and click OK.
3. The ODBC SQL Server Setup dialog is displayed, as shown in Figure 20.6.

FIGURE 20.6.

Creating an ODBC System data source name.

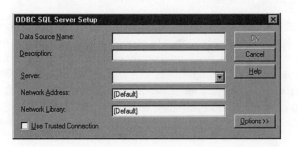

4. Provide a Data Source Name for this data source. (This is a name of your choosing.)

5. Provide an optional description for the data source.

6. Type or select from the drop-down list the name of the SQL Server machine.

7. The Network Address and Network Library fields can be left blank.

8. Click the Options button and provide the database name.

9. Click OK.

When the ODBC Data Source has been created, you can return to the logging tab to configure logging to a SQL/ODBC database. To configure logging to a SQL/ODBC database, follow these steps:

1. Provide the name of the ODBC DSN you created.

2. Provide the table name (`inetlog`).

3. Provide the user name and password for a user with permission to write to the database table.

When this is completed and the WWW Publishing service has been restarted, you are logging to a database.

FTP Publishing Service

The FTP Publishing Service provides an effective vehicle for transferring files of all types. The FTP Service is often used in conjunction with the WWW Publishing Service to provide information with links to additional information or relevant files.

The Service Tab

Opening the service tab, shown in Figure 20.7, you see an almost identical representation of the WWW Service tab. You see the FTP Port number, Connection Timeout and Maximum Connections parameters, similar to the WWW Publishing Service. Note that these settings are independent of their counterparts for the WWW Service. It is often desirable to set a much lower number for the maximum connections because FTP sessions usually involve much more network activity in transferring files than a WWW session, which passes relatively infrequent and small images and text.

Specific to the FTP Publishing Service are configuration options for anonymous connections. Historically, the standard method of accessing an FTP server is to use an anonymous connection. To enable anonymous connections, select the Allow Anonymous Connections check box. The Username and Password boxes—similar to those on the WWW Service tab—are used to provide a security context for anonymous FTP connections. By default, the username and password are the same as those used for the WWW Publishing Service.

FIGURE 20.7.

*The FTP Publishing
Service tab.*

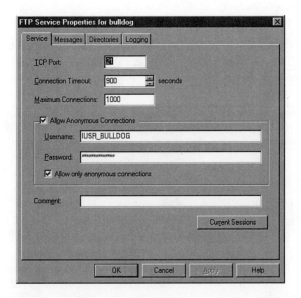

There is also an option to allow only anonymous connections. If this option is selected, only anonymous users are allowed to connect to this FTP server. If this option is not selected, users are allowed to log on to the server using a username and password of a user with additional rights on the server. Access to restricted areas of the server is controlled by setting the appropriate file permissions on the directory structure. FTP servers use anonymous logons primarily because when logging on to the system, the username and password are passed in clear text and can easily be intercepted by a third party.

Again, you have a Comment field where an optional description can be entered. Unique to the FTP Service tab is a Current Sessions button that, when clicked, displays a list of current connections, with the name used to log on, the client IP address, and the connection time. (See Figure 20.8.) The Refresh button refreshes the display of current sessions, the Disconnect button disconnects a selected user, and the Disconnect All button disconnects all current sessions (for days when you are feeling particularly mischievous).

FIGURE 20.8.

*The FTP User Sessions
dialog.*

The Messages Tab

The Messages tab, shown in Figure 20.9, provides an easy method of setting messages that will be displayed to users when they connect to your site, when they leave your site, and when too many users are already connected.

FIGURE 20.9.

The FTP Publishing Messages tab.

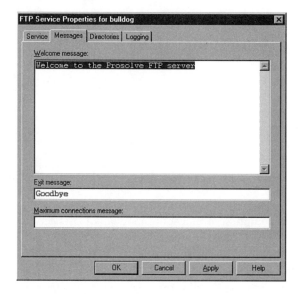

The Directories Tab

The Directories tab is similar in form and function to that of the WWW service. (See Figure 20.10.) One section lists the directories that have been defined for the FTP Publishing service; at the bottom of the page is a Directory Listing Style section. The two options for the Directory Listing Style are UNIX and MS-DOS. This option determines how files and directories are presented to users when they execute a `dir` or `ls` command to get a directory listing.

Looking at the Directory Properties, shown in Figure 20.11, you see a configuration dialog very similar to that of the WWW Publishing service. You have the option of both Home and Virtual directories. If you specify a directory on a remote system, you must again provide a user name and password to be used as a proxy so that FTP users can access the remote directory.

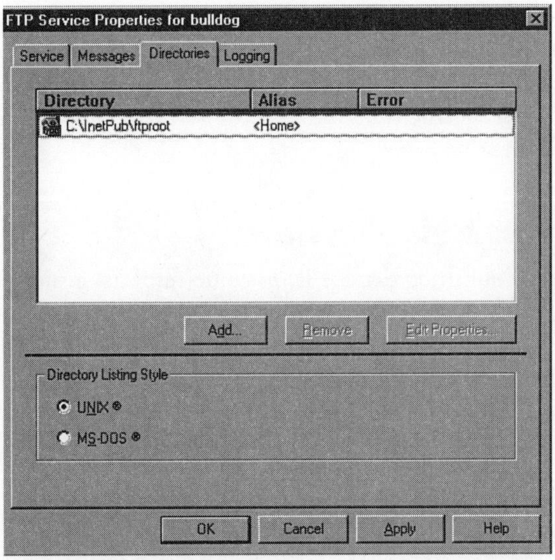

FIGURE 20.10.
The FTP Publishing Directories tab.

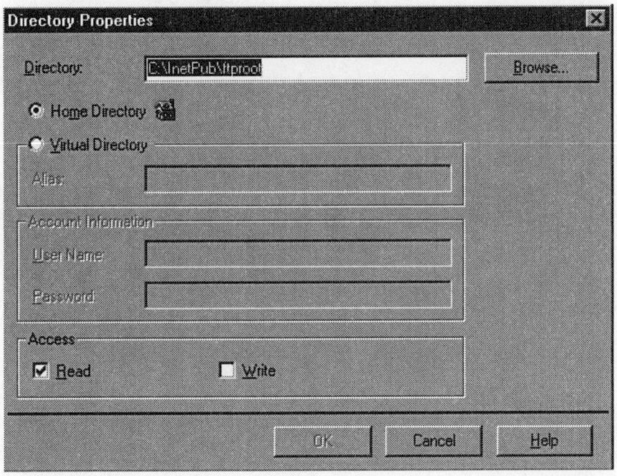

FIGURE 20.11.
The FTP Publishing Directory Properties dialog.

The access options at the bottom of the configuration dialog are unique to the FTP Publishing Service Directory Properties dialog. This is a point to note because it can cause undue stress. Not only must you grant users read and/or write permissions on the file system itself, but you must also specify here that users can read and/or write, or they will be unable to do so.

The Logging Tab

The Logging tab for the FTP Publishing Service is identical to that of the WWW Publishing Service. One point is important to remember here: If you are logging to a text file, FTP session activity is logged to the same file as WWW activity unless the logging frequency is different or you specify a different directory for FTP log files.

Also, you can specify the same ODBC Data Source and parameters to have all activity logged to the same database table. With a database, it can be advantageous to use a single table for logging, because you can very easily query the database to get information on only FTP or WWW activity or for a specific time frame. Database logs provide the most flexibility, and I highly recommend them.

Gopher Publishing Service

The Gopher Publishing Service is, in some respects, a mutated combination of the WWW Publishing Service and the FTP Publishing Service. The Gopher Publishing Service enables you to publish a file archive that looks similar to an FTP archive in how it is listed. However, Gopher allows you much more flexibility in linking to remote computers and annotating files and directories, as well as in its search capabilities.

The Service Tab

Are you seeing the consistency here yet? Microsoft has done a pretty good job of making the configuration of these services as similar as possible for ease of use and navigation. The Service tab for the Gopher Publishing Service offers the Connection Timeout and Maximum Connection options, as do the other services. (See Figure 20.12.) Also, the Anonymous Logon section is where you provide a Username and Password to be used for anonymous connections, as the other services do. And there is a Comment field in which you provide an optional description.

FIGURE 20.12.

The Gopher Publishing Service tab.

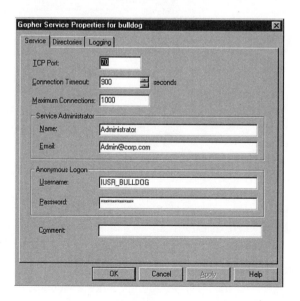

Specific to the Gopher Publishing Service tab is a Service Administrator section, where you are requested to provide a Service Administrator name and e-mail address for the site. Remote users can query the Gopher server for this information if needed.

The Directories Tab

The Gopher Publishing Directories tab is similar to the other Directories tabs, but it is certainly the most simple and concise. Here you are requested to provide a directory root for the Gopher Publishing Service, as you have done for the WWW and FTP services. The only options are to Add, Edit, or Remove directory entries.

When adding a new listing or editing a current entry, you are presented with the Directory Properties dialog, as you have seen previously with other services. You are prompted for a directory path—whether it is a Home directory or a Virtual directory—and, if it is a Virtual directory, you need an alias for the directory. Also, if this points to a directory on a remote system, you must provide a user name and password to be used for access to the remote system.

Again, the Logging and Advanced tabs are identical to their WWW and FTP counterparts. But let's not kick that dead horse again! They are identical in form and function, and you can reference the WWW or FTP section for information on them.

Key Manager

The Key Manager application interface, which is provided with Microsoft Peer Web Services, gives you an easy mechanism for enabling Secure Sockets Layer (SSL) security on your Internet server. (See Figure 20.13.)

FIGURE 20.13.

The Microsoft Peer Web Services Key Manager.

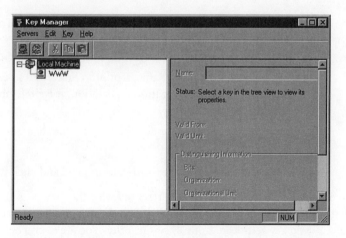

The process of enabling SSL on your Internet server involves several steps. First, you must generate a key pair; second, you must acquire an SSL certificate; third, you must install that certificate on your Internet server. After you install SSL on your Internet server and configure WWW services to use it, only SSL-enabled clients such as Microsoft Internet Explorer can access that server. You can specify which WWW Servers or Virtual Servers use SSL independently. Also, when the clients access an SSL location, they must use the notation https:// rather than http://.

20

WORKSTATION AS AN INTERNET SERVER

To generate a key pair using the Key Manager, follow these steps:

1. From the Key Manager Key menu, select Create New Key….

2. The Create New Key and Certificate Request dialog is presented, as shown in Figure 20.14.

FIGURE 20.14.

The Create New Key and Certificate Request form.

3. Provide a Key Name and Password and specify the number of bits to use for encryption. (The default is 1024.)

4. In the Distinguishing Information section, provide the requested information for your Organization, Unit, Common Name, Country, State, and Locality. If your organization has a top-level ISO Organization registration, it is preferable to use those conventions.

5. Specify the filename and location for the Request file that will be created.

6. Click OK.

7. When prompted, retype the password you supplied and click OK.

The new key is created, and you are presented with the New Key Information dialog telling you that the key has been created. However, the key will not be valid on the Internet until you receive a valid key certificate from a key authority. You are instructed to send your key request file, which you just created, to your default key authority to obtain a valid certificate. When you receive the certificate, select the key you created in the Key Manager and use the Install Key Certificate option from the Key menu.

When you send your key request file to a valid key authority such as VeriSign (`www.verisign.com`), you will receive a signed certificate similar to the following:

```
----BEGIN CERTIFICATE----

JIEBSDSCEXoCHQEwLQMJSoZILvoNVQECSQAwcSETMRkOAMUTBhMuVrM
mIoAnBdNVBAoTF1JTQSBEYXRhIFN1Y3VyaXR5LCBJbmMuMRwwGgYDVQ
QLExNQZXJzb25hIENlcnRpZmljYXRlMSQwIgYDVQQDExtPcGVuIE1hc
mtldCBUZXN0IFNlcnZlciAxMTAwHhcNOTUwNzE5MjAyNzMwWhcNOTYw
NTE0MjAyOTEwWjBzMQswCQYDVQQGEwJVUzEgMB4GA1UEChMXU1NBIER
hdGEgU2VjdXJpdHksIEluYy4xHDAaBgNVBAsTE1BlcnNvbmEgQ2VydG
lmaWNhdGUxJDAiBgNVBAMTGQ9wZW4gTWFya2V0IFRlc3QgU2VydmVyI
DExMDBcMA0GCSqGSIb3DQEBAQUAA0sAMEgCQQDU/7lrgR6vkVNX40BA
q1poGdSmGkD1iN3sEPfSTGxNJXY58XH3JoZ4nrF7mIfvpghNi1taYim
vhbBPNqYe4yLPAgMBAAEwDQYJKoZIhvcNAQECBQADQQBqyCpws9EaAj
KKAefuNP+z+8NY8khckgyHN2LLpfhv+iP8m+bF66HNDUlFz8ZrVOu3W
QapgLPV90kIskNKXX3a
------END CERTIFICATE----
```

Save this certificate to a text file, and then use the Key Manager to install the certificate. When you install your certificate, if you do not specify an IP address, the certificate will be used for all Virtual Servers on the system. To apply the certificate to only one Virtual Server, specify the IP address of the Virtual Server while installing the certificate.

Third-Party Internet Services

Although Microsoft Peer Web Services is quite good and the price is certainly right, it does not quite provide everything you need for an Internet presence. The two key services that are lacking are a DNS service for host name resolution and an SMTP/POP3 service for Internet mail.

Two companies in particular have stepped up to deliver these services and have done a commendable job, providing top-notch applications designed for Windows NT.

DNS Services

All of the services discussed so far are TCP/IP-based Internet services. Typically, we humans prefer to use names such as www.microsoft.com rather than a number (IP address) to locate a site or navigate the Internet. It is much easier for us to remember several names than it is to remember several numbers.

The product that I highly recommend and have had many good experiences with is MetaInfo's DNS for Windows NT (www.metainfo.com). This is a fully compatible Windows NT port of BIND (Berkeley Internet Naming Daemon). It is a reasonably priced product that runs on either Windows NT Workstation or Server as a native Windows NT service.

As much as is possible with DNS, MetaInfo's DNS is a fairly user-friendly implementation, complemented by clear help and sample configuration files—and excellent e-mail and phone support. MetaInfo also offers a free 30-day evaluation, and the product is available for all Windows NT hardware platforms.

20

WORKSTATION AS AN INTERNET SERVER

The other DNS package that I recommend is BIND for NT from Software.com (www.software.com). This is a fully functional BIND port for Windows NT (Workstation or Server). The product involves a bit more knowledge of DNS and is less user-friendly than MetaInfo's package. But the price is right, because it is a freeware package. Bear in mind that no support is offered for this package, and it can be difficult to install and configure properly.

SMTP/POP3 Services

Given the fact that you have installed Microsoft Peer Web Services (at least some components) and you are making the plunge into cyberspace, it is a reasonable assumption that you will want to communicate with others out in the great bit bucket called the Internet.

To facilitate this, you need some form of mail services. In the TCP/IP world of the Internet, this equates to an SMTP mail server for sending mail and a POP3 server for receiving mail. Most often, these two services are bundled in a single package.

Taking the lead in this arena is Post.Office from Software.com. This is an SMTP/POP3 mail server for Windows NT Workstation or Server, which runs as a native Windows NT service. Post.Office is configured through an intuitive WWW-based interface with context-sensitive help for almost every configuration option and parameter. This package was superb even 18 months ago when I first saw it in beta form, and it has continued to be improved and enhanced. Installation and configuration typically take less than an hour for small to medium sites. I have a long list of happy clients for which I have implemented this solution.

The other package I recommend is Sendmail from MetaInfo. (Yes, these two companies are going head to head and fostering the spirit of competition, which results in outstanding products for you and me.) This is MetaInfo's implementation of an SMTP/POP3 mail server for Windows NT (Workstation or Server), which also runs as a native Windows NT service.

I highly recommend any of the products covered in this section. They are all of excellent quality, from leading-edge companies that will do whatever is necessary to make the customer happy—a commendable and rare quality among businesses these days.

Summary

As you can see, everything you might need to make your Windows NT system a functional Internet server is available right now. Microsoft has done an excellent job with its Peer Web Services, providing the three major Internet information publishing services: World Wide Web, File Transfer Protocol, and Gopher.

The missing pieces—mail and name resolution services—have been provided remarkably by some bright new upstarts who saw a need in the Windows NT community and filled it. Both MetaInfo and Software.com provide excellent DNS and mail services solutions that operate as native Windows NT services.

Remote Access Service

by Eric D. Osborne

IN THIS CHAPTER

Today's computer users live in an increasingly interconnected world. The typical business user in today's environment works on a workstation attached to a LAN. Each of these desktops is in turn connected to the rest of the enterprise and, increasingly, to the Internet. The need for connectivity can often make it impossible for modern workers to effectively perform unless connected to networked resources. And, because many of today's workers are mobile, there is a corresponding need for networking technology capable of providing those mobile users with transparent and simple access to centralized facilities. Field engineers, sales personnel, and other travelers in today's competitive business environment require continual access to e-mail and corporate databases. The growing ranks of telecommuters require cost-effective and reliable access to corporate facilities. Even on the home front, the explosive popularity of the Internet and the World Wide Web all contribute to the need for connectivity.

Remote Access Service (RAS) is Microsoft's answer to this need. Microsoft has designed RAS to provide simple, effective, and reliable wide area networking. RAS is not new to Windows NT 4.0. It has been a part of Microsoft's operating system offerings since the introduction of Windows NT 3.1. Since that time, the technology focus of RAS has changed substantially.

The basic functionality provided by RAS essentially consists of an on-demand wide area networking transport and authentication service. Other facilities associated with RAS, such as file and print sharing, involve higher level protocols that layer on top of the RAS transport mechanism.

Microsoft has embedded RAS into all of its current windowing operating system offerings. Windows 95, and to a lesser extent Windows for Workgroups, are both capable of acting as RAS clients. Windows NT can act as both RAS client and server. Windows NT Server is capable of supporting many concurrent incoming RAS connections. Windows NT Workstation can provide the same RAS server functionality, but only for one incoming connection at any given time.

The RAS client can be viewed as software for turning your COM port and modem (or other supported device) into a network adapter. Establishing a RAS connection can be generalized to the following simple steps:

1. The user determines a need for some distant resource.
2. A connection, typically through a modem and telephone line, is established to a RAS server.
3. The user provides authentication (password) information to the server for verification.
4. Once authenticated, the user has access to server facilities and can then attach file shares or use Internet applications such as Netscape Navigator or Microsoft Internet Explorer.

It's important to note that client systems always initiate RAS sessions. This implies that the RAS server software must *always* be running and waiting on the server system. The RAS server can provide a myriad of services for a connected client, including the following:

- Providing access to disk or printer resources local to the server
- Providing access to disk or printer services on other servers within the server's domain
- Providing routing of TCP/IP or IPX/SPX packets to non-RAS resources on the server LAN
- Routing the user's packets to the Internet for access to Web or other services

Connection Technologies Supported by RAS

The connection technologies supported by the RAS client software include standard asynchronous modems, X.25 packet switched networks, and ISDN (Integrated Services Digital Network) adapters. All of these technologies provide the user with wide area networking capabilities through the telephone system.

Each has specific advantages. Modems, for instance, are relatively inexpensive and portable, and they can be used from essentially anywhere. Modern modems, supporting uncompressed data rates of up to 28,800 bits per second, provide sufficient throughput to support the needs of a very large percentage of users. The low cost, portability, compatibility with standard telephone lines, and ease of use of modems make them ideal for travelers or for low-cost home use.

ISDN provides much higher speeds than can be achieved through modems—up to 128 kilobits of uncompressed data per second—but it requires more costly equipment and higher fees. ISDN does not run across standard analog telephone circuits. ISDN circuits are available in Basic and Primary Rate variants. A Basic Rate ISDN connection is a digital interface, but it can be run across standard telephone wire. Basic Rate interfaces have a pair of 64 kilobit/second data channels and a 16 kilobits per second control channel. It is possible to aggregate the two 64 bit channels into a composite 128 kilobits per second channel. Primary rate connections are comprised of many channels and have a composite bandwidth of 1.44 megabits per second. Because ISDN connections require special connections to the telephone company, ISDN interfaces don't work for traveling users, but they are ideal for the professional programmer who telecommutes from home. Many locals within the United States still don't have telephone switches capable of supporting ISDN traffic. ISDN is extremely popular in certain European countries.

X.25 packet switching networks are available as a moderately priced wide area networking technology. X.25 networks predate the development of either TCP/IP or the ISDN standard. Most telephone switching networks are X.25 packet switching networks. Because of this, ISDN connections actually layer other protocols (such as PPP) on top of X.25 packet switching. This allows these higher level protocols to traverse the existing telephone network.

RAS connections over X.25 rely on devices called Packet Assembler/Disassemblers (PADs) to frame user data into X.25-compliant packets. It is possible to use X.25 across dial-up lines, but it is quite common for the end user to arrange for a dedicated telephone circuit to be installed.

The circuit is often permanently connected to a network service provider. Because the connection is commonly made through a dedicated circuit, it often seems like a LAN connection (but slower) to the end user. X.25 is not commonly used in the United States (except by telephone companies), but it is still very popular in Europe.

Like RAS client, RAS server supports all of the previously mentioned technologies. In addition to these, RAS server also supports connection via TCP/IP across a LAN. The reason that RAS server supports LAN connections is largely economic. A modem-attached RAS server intended to support a number of concurrent dial-up users would require some large number of COM ports and attached communications devices. Maintaining and administering these devices and their associated telephone lines can be too expensive or difficult for some organizations.

Microsoft has added a new protocol called Point to Point Tunneling Protocol (PPTP) to Windows NT 4.0 to address this problem. PPTP encapsulates and encrypts PPP packets from the client PC and transmits across a LAN or WAN to a server system. The effect is to create a private "tunnel" through a public network. The tunnel isolates the systems at each end of the connection, effectively establishing a private network contained within a larger network such as the Internet.

These kinds of private connections are sometimes called *Virtual Private Networks*, or *VPNs*. Both Windows NT 4.0 Server and Workstation support the PPTP protocol. PPTP allows a user to connect to an Internet Service Provider and then have a private, encrypted PPP session through the ISP to a remote RAS server. This eliminates the need for the RAS server to be equipped with a large pool of dedicated dial-in modems, because the remote RAS client can be assured of secure, encrypted connections even when connecting through an arbitrary Internet Service Provider.

I previously mentioned that Windows NT for Workstations supports RAS in both client and server modes. This means that the user can use RAS not only to dial out to a remote host, but also to provide a secure incoming interconnect to the workstation. This facility can be extremely helpful to users such as the telecommuting programmer described earlier. Consider the situation in which a user has traveled to a seminar or trade show, for instance. The telecommuter might have much of his or her work stored on the home system instead of the corporate RAS server. If the need arises, either the telecommuter or any other authorized user could dial into the telecommuter's workstation and copy files or access other information.

Installing Remote Access Service

Remote Access Service can be installed during a Custom installation of Windows NT, or at any later time from the Network Services dialog of the Network applet in the Control Panel. Figure 21.1 shows the Network applet. Clicking on the Services tab shows the list of currently installed network services. To install RAS, click Add.

Clicking the Add button produces a list of known but currently uninstalled network services.

FIGURE 21.1.
Examining installed network services.

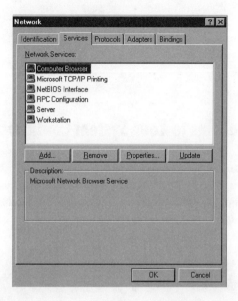

Scroll down and highlight the Remote Access Service selection, as shown in Figure 21.2. Then click OK.

FIGURE 21.2.
Adding the Remote Access Service.

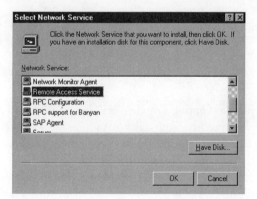

The Setup program displays a dialog requesting a path to the NT installation media (normally your CD-ROM drive). This is shown in Figure 21.3. Enter the correct path and click Continue. Remember to include the processor type as part of the pathname. The correct path would be *drive-letter*:\i386 for Pentium, i386, or i486 processors.

FIGURE 21.3.

*Installing RAS from the
Network applet.*

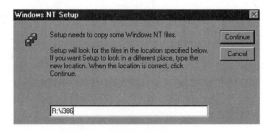

Adding Modems to Your System Configuration

After setup has installed files, the RAS installation process checks to see whether any RAS capable devices are installed on the system. Unless such a device has been previously installed for some other purpose, the RAS installation program displays the dialog shown in Figure 21.4. When this dialog is displayed, click on Yes to add a modem to your configuration. You can install additional modems or modify modem properties using the Modem applet of the Control Panel at any time in the future.

> **TIP**
>
> Depending upon the type of modem that you have, you might need manuals or other technical information about your modem to complete this step.

FIGURE 21.4.

*The RAS installation
modem setup dialog.*

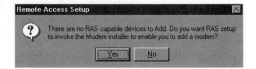

The next step in configuring a modem is shown in Figure 21.5. As you can see, it is possible to either select your modem from a list or to have Windows NT try to detect it automatically. The built-in list of modems in Windows NT covers most popular brands and models, so there is a very good chance that NT will correctly determine your modem type automatically. Simply click Next to have NT determine your modem type. You might need to click the check box labeled "Don't detect my modem; I will select it from a list" if any of the follow conditions apply to your system:

- The automatic detection process fails.
- Your modem is an external modem and is powered off.
- You simply want to manually configure the modem.

FIGURE 21.5.

*The modem detection
dialog.*

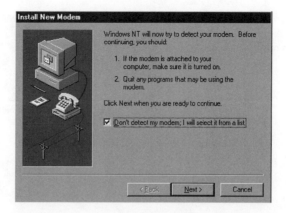

If you choose to manually select a modem type, the selection dialog shown in Figure 21.6 is
displayed. The selection box on the left is a scrollable list of modem manufacturers. The list on
the right is a list of modem models made by that manufacturer. Select the desired manufacturer and model of modem and select Next. If you have a driver disk from the modem manufacturer, click the Have Disk button.

FIGURE 21.6.

*The modem manual
selection list dialog.*

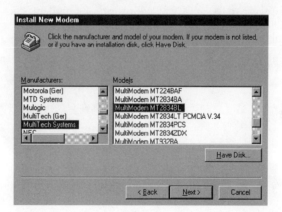

The automatic modem selection process, if successful, determines which port your modem is
connected to. If you have manually selected a modem type, the modem installation utility displays a list of available ports, as shown in Figure 21.7. Choose the correct port and select Next.
If you want to configure identical modems on all the available ports, click the All ports button
before selecting Next.

FIGURE 21.7.

The modem installation port selection dialog.

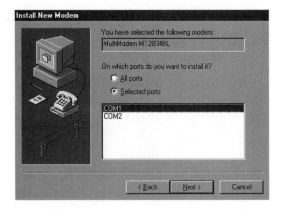

Selecting Communications Devices to Be Used by RAS

When you have chosen a port for your modem, you are returned to the RAS installation process. The dialog shown in Figure 21.8 allows the user to choose a RAS capable communications device. If you have configured a modem according to the preceding steps, it will be visible in the RAS Capable Devices scroll box. Select the desired modem and port information. If you want to use an X.25 Pad instead of a modem, click the Install X.25 Pad button.

FIGURE 21.8.

Selecting a RAS capable device.

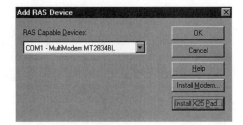

If you have opted to use an X.25 Pad instead of a modem, you are presented with the dialog shown in Figure 21.9. The dialog enables you to choose which port the Pad is connected to. It also enables you to choose an X.25 network provider from a scrollable list. This is required because X.25 network providers sometimes have subtle variations in protocols and authentication schemes.

FIGURE 21.9.

Configuring an X.25 Pad.

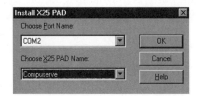

21

REMOTE ACCESS
SERVICE

After you've chosen a RAS device, you return to the window depicted in Figure 21.10. In the example shown, the user has installed a modem and chosen it as a device for RAS traffic. The user can configure connection type and protocol options at this point.

FIGURE 21.10.

The Remote Access Setup device configuration dialog.

Selecting the Configure button from the dialog in Figure 21.10 produces the configuration dialog shown in Figure 21.11. The user can configure the port to be used for incoming calls, outgoing calls, or both.

> **NOTE**
>
> A port must be configured for outgoing calls to use the RAS client software. A port must be configured for incoming calls to use the RAS server software (unless RAS is accessible through a LAN). If the same modem must be used for both RAS client and server functionality, make sure to configure the port to Dial out and Receive calls.

FIGURE 21.11.

The RAS options dialog for the selected port.

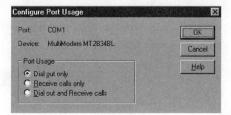

If you've configured a port for use by RAS, you are presented with a list of available dial-out protocols, as shown in Figure 21.12. Most people should select TCP/IP. TCP/IP is the most widely used network protocol suite in the world. The Internet runs across a TCP/IP backbone.

IPX/SPX is a protocol designed by Novell, and as such it is useful to most people only when connecting to corporate NetWare servers.

NetBEUI is Microsoft's NetBIOS Extended User Interface. Microsoft's NetBEUI protocols were designed long before Windows NT existed. The NetBEUI protocols were never intended to be used in wide area networks. NetBEUI relies heavily on broadcast packets for communication between hosts. These broadcast packets work well enough on a LAN but generally don't pass through routers. The fact that NetBEUI can't be routed restricts it to use on local LANs. NetBEUI was originally the only protocol supported by RAS. Older clients, such as Windows for Workgroups, still require NetBEUI by default.

Microsoft still supports NetBEUI on both the RAS client and server software, but TCP/IP is clearly the future of RAS.

> **NOTE**
>
> Although Windows for Workgroups must (by default) use NetBEUI to connect to a RAS server, it is possible to use third-party software to overcome this limitation. Packages such as TechSmith's *Foray PPP Client* allow Windows for Workgroups to attach to RAS servers through either a direct modem connection to an NT system or through an Internet Service Provider using TCP/IP.

FIGURE 21.12.
RAS dial-out protocol selection.

Additional Steps Required for Incoming RAS Connections

If you've configured a port to receive connections, the Setup program invokes the RAS Server TCP/IP Configuration dialog shown in Figure 21.13. This dialog is used to specify addressing and accessibility options for connecting clients.

FIGURE 21.13.
The RAS Server TCP/ IP Configuration dialog.

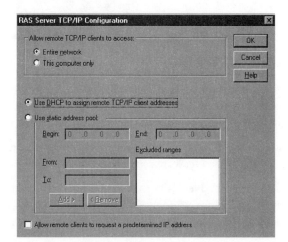

RAS Server Routing Options

TCP/IP is a routable protocol, which means that messages can find a path, or *route*, through interconnected LANs. This functionality is the basis of the Internet. If routing is disabled, a RAS client can use only those resources residing on the RAS server. When routing is enabled, the client can connect to any TCP/IP resource that the server is able to see.

Click on Entire Network if you want dial-up clients to be able to access any system on your network. Click "This computer only" if you don't want RAS to route packets through the current machine to the rest of your network.

> **NOTE**
>
> You must select Entire Network if you want dial-in users to be able to use Internet applications.

TCP/IP Address Allocation for Incoming RAS Clients

The RAS server allows three methods for defining the IP address of a connected client. These options are selected from the dialog shown in Figure 21.13. The first (and default) method uses the Dynamic Host Configuration Protocol (DHCP) to assign addresses. This implies that a DHCP server must be available on your network. It is important to note that a Windows NT 4.0 Workstation system cannot act as a DHCP server. That functionality is available only on Windows NT Server systems and some UNIX servers. If you are installing RAS in server mode on your NT 4.0 Workstation system, make sure that a DHCP server is available on your network before selecting the "Use DHCP to assign remote TCP/IP client addresses" button.

It is still possible to have the RAS server on your NT Workstation 4.0 Workstation system allocate client addresses, even if your workstation is not attached to a LAN with a DHCP server. Select the "Use static address pool" button to define a range of valid TCP/IP addresses for your incoming RAS connection. Enter the beginning address of the desired range in the Begin box. Enter the last address of the desired range in the End box. Make sure that the addresses entered are valid addresses within the subnet in which the Windows NT 4.0 Workstation host resides.

> **NOTE**
>
> If your Windows NT 4.0 Workstation is being installed at home, you almost certainly won't have a DHCP server available. Select the "Use static address pool" button. Even if your system can support only one incoming RAS connection, it is necessary to define a range of at least two addresses. This is because one of the addresses is allocated to the incoming port on your NT 4.0 Workstation system. The other address is allocated to the connecting RAS client system.

It is possible to exclude ranges of addresses from the static address pool. This allows RAS to accommodate address ranges that might have a few addresses that are occupied by hosts or network components. To exclude a range of addresses, enter the address of the first address to be excluded in the From box. Enter the address of the last address to be excluded in the To box. Then click Add. You can remove the excluded range by clicking on it in the Excluded ranges box and then clicking Remove.

If you choose, you can also allow the calling client to define its own IP address. Click the "Allow remote clients to request a predetermined IP address" check box to enable this functionality. The client must be configured (via the Dial-Up Networking facility) to use a static IP address within the correct subnet.

Configuring Remote Access Service Client (Dial-Up Networking)

The process of installing RAS performs most of the work of configuring the RAS server. The RAS client, however, requires substantially more information before it can be used.

NT 4.0 and Windows 95 refer to the RAS client as Dial-Up Networking. The Dial-Up Networking facility enables users to connect to NT servers, Windows for Workgroups servers, or Internet Service Providers. Dial-Up Networking allows users to define a list of known servers, maintaining separate configuration information for each. Configuration information is stored in a phonebook.

As an example of why a user might need separate configurations, consider the case of a professional programmer who is taking classes at a local university. This user might have separate accounts with an Internet Service Provider, on a UNIX server at the university where he or she is taking classes, and with an employer's corporate NT server. Separate configuration information, including telephone numbers, protocol specifications, and passwords would be necessary for each. Using the phonebook, this user could configure setups for all three servers and then connect to any of them by simply selecting a server from a menu.

To configure Dial-Up Networking, begin by clicking Start|Programs|Accessories|Dial-Up Networking. This is shown in Figure 21.14.

RAS maintains a list of servers that it knows, and configuration information about those servers, in a phonebook. Because the phonebook is empty until RAS has been configured, the first time the RAS client is invoked it asks whether you want to want to add an entry. See Figure 21.15.

FIGURE 21.14.
Invoking the Dial-Up Networking client program.

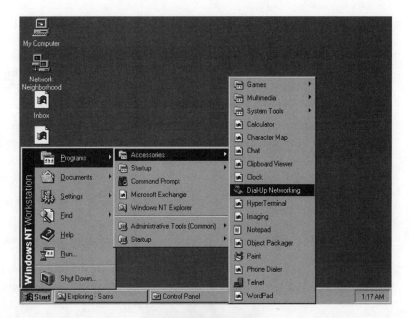

FIGURE 21.15.
The initial Dial-Up Networking dialog.

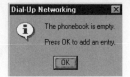

Creating Simple RAS Client Phonebook Entries

Selecting OK causes the system to begin the process of defining a phonebook entry. RAS presents the user with two options at this point, as shown in Figure 21.16. Novice users can enter a name for a new phonebook entry and allow RAS to step through a setup wizard. More experienced users can choose to directly edit the phonebook entries by clicking the check box shown in Figure 21.16. The default choices made by the New Phonebook Entry Wizard will work for most people, so let's use those to create an initial phonebook entry. Advanced editing of phonebook entries is discussed later in this chapter.

After entering the name of your phonebook entry, click the Next button. The dialog shown in Figure 21.17 appears. The Phonebook Entry Wizard uses the checked items to try to determine protocol and security characteristics of the server that you want to call. You should check as many of the boxes as apply to your server.

■ Check the first box if you are calling an Internet Service Provider or any non-NT system such as a UNIX server.

■ The second box defines the characteristics of the password that will be sent to the server. Most newer servers use encrypted passwords, meaning that the password will be encoded before being transmitted to the server. Some servers, however, only accept passwords in plain text. Plain text passwords can represent a security risk, because they can sometimes be detected by hackers that monitor the Internet. Check the second box if your server requires plain text passwords.

■ If you are connecting to a non-NT server or if you are connecting to an NT server through an Internet Service Provider, you might need to enter passwords or perform other tasks prior to starting RAS. You might also need to perform some special security process before you can dial, such as authorizing a long distance telephone call. Selecting the third box allows you to pop up a terminal window or run a script to address these issues.

FIGURE 21.16.

The New Phonebook Entry Wizard.

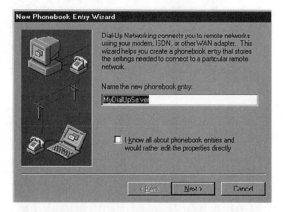

FIGURE 21.17.

Selecting server characteristics in the Phonebook Wizard.

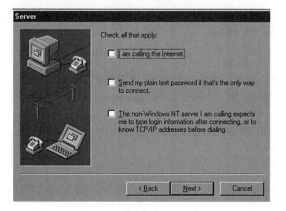

After selecting the desired buttons, clicking Next presents the dialog shown in Figure 21.18. Enter in the designated space the phone number for the server that you want to call.

FIGURE 21.18.

Entering phone numbers in the Phonebook Wizard.

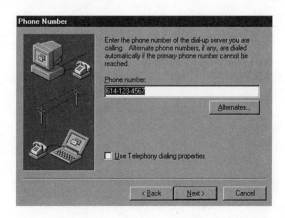

If you like, you can select the "Use Telephony dialing properties" check box, which changes the screen as shown in Figure 21.19. You can then enter in the indicated space the area code for the number you want to call.

FIGURE 21.19.

Selecting telephony dialing properties in the Phonebook Wizard.

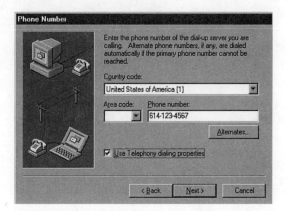

RAS allows you to enter multiple phone numbers for each server. If RAS fails to connect to the desired number because it is busy or otherwise unavailable, RAS automatically tries connecting to an alternate. Figure 21.20 shows the dialog for entering alternate telephone numbers. RAS dials the numbers in the order listed. You can use the Up and Down buttons to manually select the order for your list of phone numbers. If the check box at the bottom of the dialog in Figure 21.20 has been selected, RAS places the first successful number at the top of the list after dialing.

FIGURE 21.20.

Entering alternate phone numbers in the Phonebook Wizard.

Click OK and then select the Next button, as shown in Figure 21.20. This should take you to the final dialog in the New Phonebook Entry Wizard. Select Finish to complete your new entry. This is shown in Figure 21.21.

FIGURE 21.21.

Completing the phonebook entry.

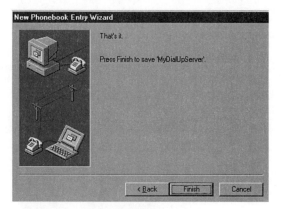

Advanced Editing of RAS Phonebook Entries

It is also possible to directly edit Dial-Up Networking phonebook entries. If you always want to directly edit phonebook entries, you can turn off the New Phonebook Entry Wizard. Invoke Dial-Up networking as shown in Figure 21.14. Click on the More button and select User Preferences from the menu. The User Preferences dialog appears. Select the Appearance tab. The dialog should now look like the one in Figure 21.22.

FIGURE 21.22.
*The Dial-Up
Networking User
Preferences dialog.*

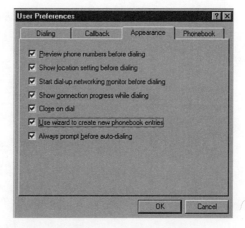

Make sure the check box labeled "Use wizard to create new phonebook entries" is not selected.
Click OK to return to the screen displayed in Figure 21.14.

Setting Phonebook Entry Basic Properties

You can now begin inputting your new entry. Click the New button to begin the process with
the New Phonebook Entry dialog shown in Figure 21.23. Note that there are several tabs on
this dialog. Make sure that the Basic tab is on top of the display; then enter the name of your
phonebook entry, enter a telephone number, and select a RAS device to dial out with.

FIGURE 21.23.
*Entering basic
information for a new
phonebook entry.*

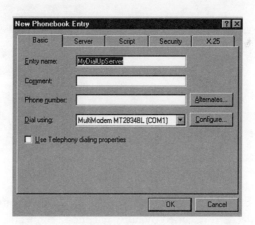

Clicking on "Use Telephony dialing properties" extends the dialog as shown in Figure 21.24.
You can now optionally enter the country code and area code for the new phonebook entry.

FIGURE 21.24.

Using Telephony dialing properties in a new phonebook entry.

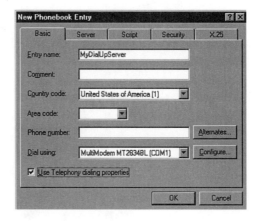

Setting Phonebook Entry Modem Properties

Manually editing phonebook entries allows you greater control in configuring your modem. Selecting the Configure box brings up the Modem Configuration dialog shown in Figure 21.25. Use the Initial speed selector to change the baud rate used by this phonebook entry. This can be useful if your system has problems keeping up with extremely fast connections. Some COM ports, for instance, do not have built-in buffering. If you don't have an extremely fast processor, your system might not be able to handle data at 57,600 bits per second. Use this setting to reduce the speed to 38,400 bits per second or 19,200 bits per second.

FIGURE 21.25.

Configuring modem properties for phonebook entries.

You should check the "Enable hardware flow control" box for fast modems. Most users should also check "Enable modem error control." This causes your modem to try to automatically correct any data errors caused by noisy telephone connections.

Surprisingly enough, you might not want to check the Enable modem compression box. RAS provides facilities for software compression of the data stream. Furthermore, PPP has built-in facilities for doing software compression of packet headers (often called VJ compression). Enabling the RAS software compression and disabling the modem compression usually results in better throughput than modem compression is able to provide.

Finally, you can use this dialog to disable the speaker on your modem. This might save some wear and tear on your ears, but it can make it somewhat more difficult to debug failed connections. Click OK when you have finished configuring your modem.

Setting Phonebook Entry Server Protocol Options

Selecting the Server tab of the New Phonebook Entry dialog allows you to configure protocol settings. The scroll box at the top of the dialog allows you to select the remote server type. Select "PPP: Windows NT, Windows 95 Plus, Internet" if the server you want to call is one of these types, or if you don't know what it is. PPP is the most widely used of the available protocols, so it is most likely to be correct.

SLIP, or *Serial Line Internet Protocol,* was the first protocol designed to allow TCP/IP connections over dial-up modems. SLIP is a relatively low-overhead protocol, but it is somewhat lacking in error correction and security facilities. SLIP has largely been replaced by PPP, but some older Internet sites still use SLIP. If you need to connect to one of these, select "SLIP:Internet" as your server type.

Select "Windows NT 3.1, Windows for Workgroups 3.11" if you are connecting to either of these older server types. You will have relatively limited functionality when compared to PPP connections.

Some PPP servers are capable of supporting IPX/SPX compatible connections. If the server you are connecting to is a Novell server, it might require that the IPX/SPC compatible box be clicked.

NetBEUI is a local-area protocol designed by Microsoft and IBM. It was the only protocol originally available for Windows for Workgroups clients and NT 3.1 servers. Unless you are connecting directly to a NetBEUI compatible server, you do not need to check the NetBEUI box.

The Enable software compression box should generally be checked. If you have trouble communicating with a server after the modem makes a connection, try turning this feature off. If you can leave it on, you will probably get better performance.

The Enable PPP LCP extensions box enables some of the newer protocol features of PPP. You should leave this feature enabled if possible. If you have trouble connecting to a server with this feature enabled, try turning it off.

If your server is using TCP/IP (using either SLIP or PPP), click on the TCP/IP Settings button to configure the TCP/IP protocol options. The PPP TCP/IP Settings dialog is shown in Figure 21.27. In most cases, the server assigns an IP network address to your client when you dial in. If you want to enter an address, select the Select an IP address button and type one into the appropriate space. Make sure that the address you enter is one that has been assigned by the network administrator at the site you want to call.

FIGURE 21.26.

Setting phonebook entry server protocol options.

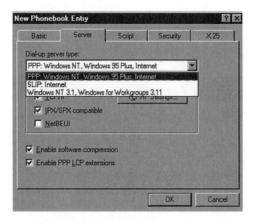

Setting Phonebook Entry Name Server Options

There are many systems on the Internet. Each of these systems has an individual network address number, but you don't have to know a system's network address in order to contact it. That's because system addresses are looked up using the Domain Name Service, more commonly known as DNS. DNS uses a hierarchical approach to translating system names to network addresses. Suppose, for instance, that in your Web browser you enter the address www.microsoft.com. The name consists of three parts. The first part, www, is the name of a specific system. The name www is used by convention as a default for an organization's Web server. The second part indicates that the system is part of Microsoft's corporate network. The third part indicates that the Microsoft network is part of a larger group of commercial enterprises. Government agencies within the USA have addresses ending with .gov, educational institutions have addresses ending with .edu, and so on.

Microsoft has created a variation of this model called Windows Internet Naming Service, or WINS. WINS serves the same functionality as DNS within NT domains by providing NetBEUI namespace to TCP/IP address translation. In a routed TCP/IP network, for instance, WINS can tell a client where to look for a domain controller in order to authenticate a domain logon. NT Dial-Up Networking resolves NetBIOS names through WINS. So if you intend to mount file or print shares through a RAS connection to an ISP, you need to either specify a WINS server address or build an LMHOSTS file for your NetBIOS hostnames.

You'll need access to a DNS server to perform name resolution when using programs such as Netscape, Internet Explorer, FTP, or Telnet. In most cases, the PPP protocols allow the server to specify the address of the DNS name server for you. In some cases, you might want to enter DNS or WINS server addresses yourself. If you want to enter the address of a DNS server, click "Specify name server addresses." Note that you can enter the addresses for both primary and secondary servers of both types. You probably do not need a WINS server address unless you are connecting to another NT system or domain through an intermediary ISP without using PPTP. If you are connecting through an Internet Service Provider solely to use Internet applications, the DNS server may or may not be needed. Ask your ISP to be sure.

Setting Phonebook Entry Gateway and Header Compression Options

Checking the "Use IP header compression" box enables the so-called VJ header compression on TCP/IP packets. This is used both on PPP and on a SLIP variant called CSLIP (Compressed SLIP). You will get better performance on your connections if this box is left selected, but if you have problems connecting to your RAS server, try turning it off.

Finally, connecting with any host other than the one you dial into requires that your network packets be routed through a gateway machine (either a host or a dedicated network router). If you click the "Use default router on remote network" box, your connections are automatically forwarded through the default router on the network that you dial into. You should normally leave this box selected.

Click OK to finish your TCP/IP protocol configuration.

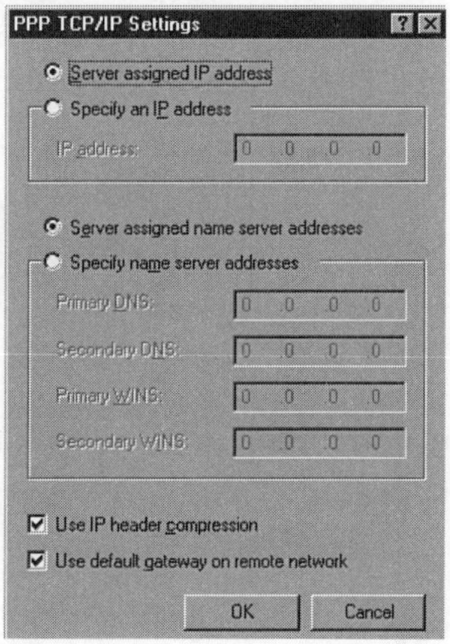

FIGURE 21.27.

Setting phonebook entry TCP/IP protocol options.

Using Scripts Within Phonebook Entries

The Script tab of the New Phonebook Entry dialog enables users to build customized programs for logging into remote servers. This can be required when the remote server requires special security provisions or when the telephone system has special requirements for dialing a number. As shown in Figure 21.28, the three basic options on this tab are as follows:

■ If the None button is selected, RAS dials the target telephone number and attempts to authenticate using the entered password. The authentication method is negotiated with the PPP server and can be either CHAP, MS-CHAP, or PAP. All of these encrypt the previously entered password and pass a secure encrypted token to the remote server for verification.

- If the "Pop up a terminal window" button is selected, RAS establishes a connection to the remote modem and then brings up a terminal window. The user can then manually type any commands required to complete authentication and connection.

- If the "Run this script" button is selected, RAS connects to the remote modem and then runs the script named in the box just below this button. Scripts can be used to wait for prompts from remote systems and to send complex responses. Several sample scripts are included with RAS.

FIGURE 21.28.

Configuring scripts within phonebook entries.

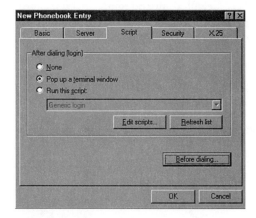

Selecting the Before Dialing button presents a list of options identical to those described in the previous section, but the options are applied before the modem has dialed the target number.

When you have finished setting script options, click OK to save the configuration changes.

RAS Security

Because RAS allows remote connections into the NT 4.0 system, security is an issue of some concern to most network and system administrators. RAS security is implemented at multiple levels. Remember that RAS on NT Workstation 4.0 has both server and client features. The RAS client always connects to the RAS server through a wide area networking technology such as a modem, an ISDN adapter, or an X.25 Pad. The RAS server can use any of these devices to accept the connection. If the client connects using the PPTP protocol, the server views the connection as a RAS client connection. Alternatively, the client can connect through an Internet Service Provider or other network agent using routed TCP/IP. In this case, the RAS server's view of the connection is essentially identical to that of local LAN connections.

RAS provides security facilities to address all of these connection schemes. Point to point devices such as ISDN adapters or modems attached to RAS servers should be configured to use the most secure authentication method possible. If the RAS clients can support it, require both MS-CHAP password encryption and data encryption. These options are set in the Network Configuration dialog of the Network control panel applet.

> **WARNING**
>
> If you allow remote users to connect to shares on your network via routed TCP/IP (without PPTP), you are probably opening up your network to outside incursions. If you must do this, set share permissions carefully. Share level protections are available for individual file and print shares that you make available from your NT system. Even if you don't intend to let users connect this way, be careful. If your system is connected to a TCP/IP LAN, which is in turn connected to the Internet, it is possible for arbitrary users on the Internet to connect to your file shares. Setting share permissions and diligently applying NT file level Access Control Lists protects your file shares from unauthorized access.

RAS client security options are set in the phonebook. Figure 21.29 shows the Security tab of the New Phonebook Entry dialog. The security options must be set to match the server being called. Again, if the targeted server is another NT system, select all of the Microsoft encryption options.

FIGURE 21.29.

Setting RAS security options on phonebook entries.

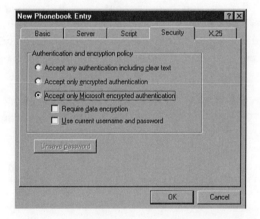

Callback options can be set to further enhance security. When callback is enabled, a user calls the RAS server from a remote site. Upon successfully authenticating the call, the RAS server notifies the caller that he or she will be called back. The server can either hang up immediately and call back at a predetermined number, or query the user for a phone number that the server can call back on.

If the server is set to call back to a predetermined number, the overall security of the system is greatly enhanced. Even if a user's password is stolen or broken, the intruder cannot get access to system resources without being physically present at the callback number.

Note that in some senses, callback schemes that allow users to enter a callback number are worse than no callback at all. This is because an intruder with a stolen password could call from a pay phone, hotel, or other temporary number, and then get your system to call back. Not only would this compromise your system, but it would potentially cause you to incur telephone charges in the bargain.

Callback security options are set from the User Manager or in the Users menu option of the Remote Access Administrator applet found in Administrative Tools.

RAS and the Internet

RAS gives your Windows NT system the capability to connect as a client to the vast resources of the Internet. All that is required to use your computer to access the Internet is the following:

1. A modem
2. A valid account with an Internet Service Provider or NT RAS server that is connected to the Internet
3. The RAS client software

Create a phonebook entry as described earlier. If you have properly configured your entry, you establish a PPP connection to your remote server. At that point you have effectively made yourself a part of a wide area TCP/IP network. Unless you are constrained by the network or server security facilities, you should be able to access essentially any other node on the Internet. Network browsers and other Internet capable utilities such as telnet and ftp will work across the RAS connection.

If you have connected through an Internet Service Provider, it is still possible to use file and print shares on other remote Windows NT systems. As long as you can reach the resource in question via TCP/IP, you have correctly configured your LMHOSTS file (or have access to a WINS server), and you have the proper passwords, you can reach out to NT systems anywhere on the Internet. This means that a single RAS dial-up connection from your home (or anywhere else) can be used to *simultaneously* access Web pages, file shares, and logons to remote systems.

The world is, indeed, an interconnected world, and it is shrinking all the time. Microsoft's inclusion of RAS into Windows NT has brought the power of wide area networking into the hands of the average person.

Summary

The Internet is fast becoming a part of everyday life. That is a trend that will continue and accelerate as time goes on. The ability to connect systems into global information networks is critical to any modern computing system. Windows NT 4.0 has risen to meet that challenge by providing robust and user-friendly tools for connecting to remote networked resources. Furthermore, Microsoft has taken significant steps toward improving the flexibility and security of Remote Access Services by incorporating support for the Point to Point Tunneling Protocol in both NT 4.0 Workstation and Server.

Maintenance and Administration

Backing Up Your System

by Eric D. Osborne

IN THIS CHAPTER

Simply put, backups are a computer user's best friend. Any professional system administrator or computer operator can spend hours recounting horror stories about disk crashes. If you are unprepared for a disk crash, it can be catastrophic—particularly if you are a professional user who is vulnerable to financial damage when a system is down.

Data is vulnerable to many other threats, as well. Viruses, marauding hackers, and natural disasters can all destroy precious data. Finally, there's the most dangerous threat of all—you and other users of your system. User error is easily the single most common cause for the deletion, loss, or modification of critical files. All of these threats to the security of your precious data can be overcome by implementing a regular and carefully followed schedule for backing up your system.

> **TIP**
>
> If your data is really important to you, simply making backups isn't sufficient. If your home or office burns down and your backup tapes are in the building, you might have a bit of a problem recovering data from melted tapes. Maintain a copy of your data offsite. For small installations, simply renting a safe deposit box might be adequate for the purpose. Larger installations might want to investigate data archiving services that can provide fireproof vaults for storing offsite copies of their backups.

Even if you have the time and skill to reload your operating system and all your application software from scratch, loss of your documents, spreadsheets, e-mail, and other personal data can be extremely painful—and completely unnecessary.

DOS and Microsoft Windows did a poor job of addressing the issue of backups. The base operating system had no direct support for tape devices, so many people routinely backed up their files onto diskettes. This was a slow and cumbersome process that few people were willing to undertake regularly. The problem was exacerbated by the ever growing size of hard disks and the size of software applications. It is now common for a desktop system to be configured with more than 1GB of disk space. Backing up that volume of data onto diskettes is simply not practical. Fortunately, the NT backup facilities provide an excellent solution to the problem.

The `ntbackup.exe` program supplied with Windows NT is designed to address the higher capacities of modern storage systems. The NT backup philosophy has turned 180 degrees away from the older DOS and Windows 3.1 models. NT requires tape devices to be used for backups. Tapes have the following advantages over other currently available storage media:

- Low media costs. Tapes provide by far the lowest cost per megabyte of the existing storage media. It is possible to buy 4- or 8-millimeter tapes for under $10 each.
- High capacity. The capacity of tape drives varies widely with the technology, but even extremely low cost cartridge drives can store several hundreds of megabytes. A 4- or 8-millimeter SCSI tape drive can provide capacities of 2.0 to 8 or more gigabytes, with

media costs sometimes falling below $10 per cartridge. That translates to storage at a cost of $1.50 to $5.00 per gigabyte. More exotic technologies such as SCSI-attached Digital Linear Tapes have capacities into the tens of gigabtyes. There are currently no other removable (or fixed) media devices that can provide that kind of capacity.

■ Speed. Although the speed of a tape drive is dependent upon the underlying technology, relatively inexpensive drives are capable of streaming at very high data rates. Further, the high capacity of tape drives means that media changes need not occur frequently. This also means that backups can occur quickly and efficiently, without human intervention. It is possible to configure a backup system that works completely automatically, operating at some off hour. This saves the most important resource of all—your time.

Supported Tape Technologies

The following paragraphs contain a brief overview of available tape technologies supported by Windows NT. Tape interface methods, media formats, and compatibility issues are discussed.

Tape Drive Interface Methods

Tape drives typically interface to PC systems via one of the following methods:

■ Dedicated interface cards are sometimes used to connect tape drives. This was particularly true with some older cartridge tape units. Dedicated interfaces are decreasing in popularity, so it might be difficult to obtain drivers for these types of units.

■ Many of the most popular low-end tape drives attach to the system floppy disk controller. Some tape drives of this type can also be driven by dedicated "accelerator" interfaces. Capacities and media formats vary for floppy controller based drives. Very inexpensive drives are available with capacities in the 800MB (compressed) range. Higher-end drives of this type can hold up to 3200MB on a single compressed tape.

■ Some tape drives can now be connected via EIDE disk interfaces. Again, these tend to be very reasonably priced drives with good speed and capacity.

■ Many "external" or "portable" tape units attach to the system via a parallel printer port. These drives have the advantage of easy portability, so they can be easily moved from one system to another. They are also compatible with laptop and notebook computers without the need for a docking bay or PCMCIA slot. External tape units that attach to the parallel port are usually QIC drives, although a few 4-millimeter DAT units are available with parallel interfaces. You should be very careful to ensure that any external tape drive you are considering is actually supported by Windows NT. The tape drive vendor might provide NT drivers for externally connected tape units.

■ Most of the higher-end tape drives on the market today use SCSI interfaces. It is normally possible to attach a mixture of tape, disk, and CD-ROM devices to a single SCSI adapter. SCSI tapes typically have much higher transfer rates than do floppy disk based or parallel port attached tape units. Some SCSI-attached units can be equipped with optional auto loader units capable of holding hundreds of gigabytes or even terabytes of tape storage.

Tape Media Formats

A wide variety of tape media is available. When choosing a tape subsystem, it is important to make sure that the selected device meets your requirements for reliability, capacity, and performance. Media cost is also important—particularly if you won't be able to reuse media on a regular basis. This typically happens when you have to provide long-term archival storage of your backups. The most popular tape formats are shown in Table 22.1.

Table 22.1. Popular tape formats.

Type	*Capacity*	*Comments*
DLT	40GB (compressed)	Digital Linear Tapes are among the highest-capacity, fastest, and most reliable tape drives on the market. They are normally available with SCSI interfaces. DLT tapes are excellent backup devices, but both the drives and the media are expensive. Media can also be difficult to find. (You probably won't find them at your local computer store.)
4mm DAT	4GB	Very reliable, fast, low media cost, small form factor. Usually requires a SCSI interface. The drives are relatively expensive when compared to TRAVAN type drives, but lower media costs can make up for that over time. You can connect multiple SCSI tape drives to a single SCSI adapter.
8mm	7GB	Very inexpensive media. Slower and less reliable than 4mm DAT, with higher soft error rates. Usually available as SCSI devices, these drives are losing popularity due to newer tape technologies. Therefore, if you don't already have one, you might not want one. The advantages of SCSI apply.

Type	Capacity	Comments
TRAVAN/QIC	3200 MB	Very low drive cost. Media costs are much higher than 4mm or 8mm tapes, but if you don't need a lot of media, the low drive cost makes the higher media cost worthwhile. These drives are available with SCSI, floppy, or parallel port interfaces.

Installing a Tape Device

Installing a tape device under Windows NT 4.0 is extremely simple. Invoking the Tape Drives applet of the Control Panel is usually sufficient to cause the system to detect the presence of the new tape drive. When the new tape drive is detected, it attempts to load the driver. This is shown in Figure 22.1.

FIGURE 22.1.
Installing a tape device.

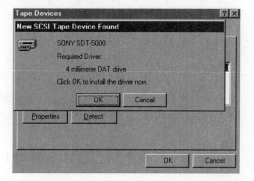

After your tape device is installed, you can begin using the `ntbackup` program included with Windows NT 4.0 Workstation. You invoke Backup by clicking Backup in the Administrative Tools taskbar menu. Upon entry, the display looks something like that shown in Figure 22.2.

Note that the display in Figure 22.2 has been split into two distinct regions, with the Tapes window on the left and the Drives window on the right. Your system might initially size these windows differently, or it might not show both windows. You can tile the Tapes and Drives windows by selecting the Tile option of the Windows menu.

Note that the Tapes window shows known tapes. It also shows the current status of the tape device. If the tape drive is busy or contains no tape, that information is reflected in the Tapes window.

FIGURE 22.2.

The NT Backup program's initial display.

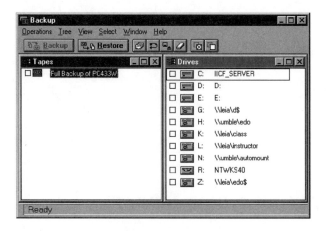

The general user interface of ntbackup is modeled somewhat after the File Manager supplied with older versions of Microsoft Windows and Windows NT. In simple terms, you select an item or items from one of the windows, and then you choose an appropriate operation. In Figure 22.3, for instance, you can see that the checkbox for drive C: has been selected. The Operations menu shows that you can back up the selected disk or perform any of several administrative functions.

The specifics of backing up the system are covered at length in the "Backing Up Files, Folders, and Drives" section of this chapter. Each of the other options is discussed in the following list:

- The Erase Tape option does exactly what its name implies. This option is necessary before using some types of tapes, or if you want to ensure that sensitive material is removed from a tape.

- Certain tape formats can get slack spots in the tape. This causes the tape to move at an inconsistent speed, which can result in tape errors. QIC cartridges are known to exhibit this behavior. The Retension Tape option causes the tape to fast forward to the end of the tape and then rewinds the tape in one continuous operation. This causes the entire tape to be wound at a consistent tension. Retensioning is not normally required with DAT or DLT tapes.

- After you have finished with a tape, use the Eject Tape option to remove it from your tape drive.

- NT tries to determine what tape devices are connected when the system boots, but if you have multiple tape devices it can make wrong choices. You can use the Hardware Setup option to select the tape device you want to use from the list of units available on your system.

FIGURE 22.3.
The Operations menu.

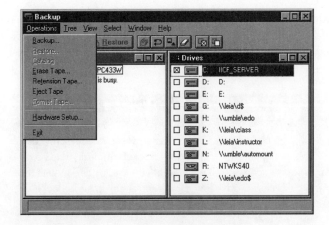

Backing Up Files, Folders, and Drives

Before you can start your backup, you have to choose the items that you want to preserve. Figure 22.4 shows an expanded view of the Drives window in Backup. As previously mentioned, it looks remarkably like the user interface of the Windows File Manager, with the addition of a small checkbox by the name of each object. The rule is simple: An object must be checked before it can be backed up.

FIGURE 22.4.
Selecting items for backup.

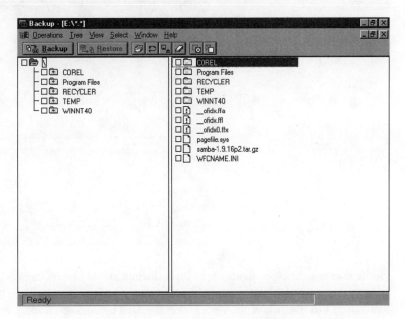

Selecting the top level of a tree selects objects below it. The Tree options of the menu bar can be used to expand and collapse trees. You can also check (or uncheck) many items at once by highlighting them with the mouse and then clicking on Check or Uncheck in the Select menu of the menu bar.

TIP

Selecting the checkbox of a drive letter doesn't necessarily select all the files contained in the drive or volume. This is because Backup normally skips over any file that you don't have permission to access. Make sure that you are logged in with the correct permissions. Then, after highlighting a drive letter, click on Check in the Select menu. That way, you will select all of the files on the drive.

Running the Backup

After you've selected the items that you want to back up, click either the Backup option of the Operations menu or the Backup button of the toolbar. You should see the Backup Information dialog shown in Figure 22.5.

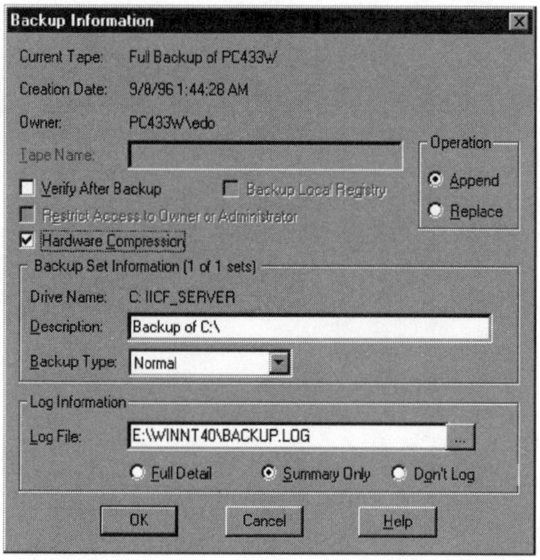

FIGURE 22.5.

The Backup Information dialog.

Notice that this dialog is divided into three distinct areas. The top area is used to set options relating to the tape itself. If the tape is a new one, you must enter a Tape Name in the designated entry box. If the tape has been previously used by Backup, Backup reads in the name of the tape and displays it in the Tape Name box. The tape name must be less than 32 characters in length.

> **WARNING**
>
> Be careful when you are backing up to a tape that already contains backup sets. Backup, by default, selects the Replace button. If the Replace button is selected when the backup begins, all data on the tape will be lost. If you want to keep the existing data, select the Append button. Backup will try to append the current data to the end of the tape.

The Verify After Backup option causes the Backup program to verify the tape contents against the original files. Selecting this option helps to ensure the integrity of your backups but slows the backup process considerably.

Backing Up the Registry

Select the Backup Local Registry option if you are backing up the local disk containing your Windows NT Registry data. Backup must take special actions when backing up the registry, because many of the files comprising the Registry are open all the time. These open files would normally be skipped. Note that you can't back up the Registry information of a network resource. That one limitation is the reason that ntbackup can't be used as a general-purpose backup solution for your entire network.

You can set the Restrict Access to Owner or Administrator option if you want to make sure that the tape can be read only by an authorized person. Note that the Restrict Access option is unavailable in the example shown in Figure 22.5. This is because the file system selected for backup is a FAT file system. Because FAT file systems have no security information, the Restrict Access to Owner option is not available for this backup.

Finally, if your tape device supports hardware compression, you can choose to make a compressed backup. This often greatly increases the capacity of the tape, but compressed backups are inherently less portable and sometimes less reliable than uncompressed backups. Use caution when selecting compression, particularly if you intend to use the tape on more than one computer.

The Backup Set

The middle of the Backup Information dialog contains information on what is being backed up. The number of backup sets is shown, as well as the Drive Name (read from the disk label). A description of the backup can be entered for informational purposes.

Types of Backups

Pay particular attention to the Backup Type selector. NT Backup supports five distinct types of backups, and the contents of your tape can vary dramatically, depending on which type you select.

In order to understand the types of backups, it is necessary to realize that NT maintains a special flag for each and every file on the system. This flag—called the *archive bit*—can be used to mark files as they are backed up. The flag is set if the file is later modified in any way.

NT uses the archive bit as a way of keeping track of which files have changed since the last backup. That way, it is possible to back up only the modified data. Although that might not seem particularly important if you have a 2GB tape drive and a 1GB disk, it can be extremely important if you have many gigabytes of disk space online.

The five types of backup supported by NT are as follows:

1. The *normal* backup copies all the selected files to tape, regardless of the state of the archive bit. As the files are copied, their archive bits are cleared. Normal backups are also referred to as *full* backups.

2. *Copy* backups, like normal backups, copy all the selected files to tape. Unlike normal backups, however, the archive bits of the selected files are not modified.

3. *Incremental* backups look at each file in the selected file set and copy only those with marked archive bits. This allows you to make a quick backup of only those files that have been modified since the last full or incremental backup. The archive bits are cleared as the files are copied to tape.

4. The *differential* backup is a variation on the incremental backup. Differential backups copy only the files that have marked archive bits, but they do not change the files as they are copied.

5. Finally, you can use a *daily* backup. The daily backup copies only the files from the selected file set that have been modified that same day. This can be useful for grabbing a quick copy of your most recent work for transport to a home system.

You should make full backups of your system at regular intervals. One common strategy is to make a full backup once each week. You can then make incremental backups on a daily basis (as described in item 3 of the preceding list). The full backup ensures that you have a snapshot of your system in some known state. The incremental backups give you a way of quickly picking up the changed components of your system.

If your system usage doesn't justify backups this frequently, you can adjust the backup intervals to be more appropriate for your usage patterns. Remember, though, that restoring your system will require you to restore the most recent full backup and then apply incremental restores for each incremental backup that has occurred since the full backup. It's important to make sure that the full backups occur frequently enough to make this process reasonable.

Differential backups and copy backups are useful when you want to create an image of your system without modifying it. You can sometimes use this technique to replicate a set of directories and files. In most cases, you won't routinely use copy or differential backups.

Logging Backup Results

The bottom of the Backup Information dialog is used to set the log options for your backup. It is generally a good idea to log your backups—especially if, like most people, you don't plan to sit and watch the entire backup run. Select the level of detail using the radio buttons at the bottom of the dialog. If you choose, you can also enter a path name for the log file in the Log File entry box.

Clicking the OK button of the Backup Information dialog initiates the actual backup process. At that point, a Backup Status dialog appears. The Backup Status dialog shows current information about backup operations. It also allows the user to abort the backup if so desired. As each backup set completes, you see information concerning the total number of files and the number of bytes that were backed up. You also see information about any files that were skipped. Files might be skipped if they are open for modification.

Recovery

If you're lucky, you won't need the recovery tools of Backup. If and when you do need to restore files, the operation of ntbackup is much the same as the operation described earlier for making backups.

Figure 22.6 shows an expanded view of the Tapes window of Backup. Note that it uses the same File Manager–like user interface that was described earlier. Select the desired tape, and then select the Catalog option of the Operations menu. A full catalog of the available backup sets will be presented.

FIGURE 22.6.

Selecting a backup set.

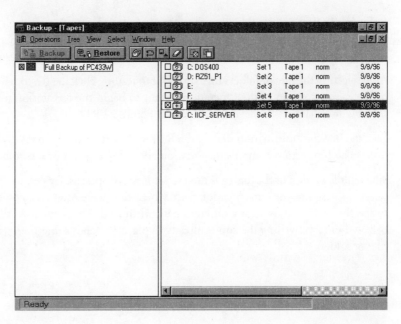

Double-clicking on Set 5, as shown in Figure 22.6, expands the Set 5 catalog to the display shown in Figure 22.7. It is now possible to select the files or folders that are to be restored. Again, just as when selecting files for backup, clicking the checkbox for a folder causes items contained within the folder to be equivalently checked. In Figure 22.7, all items have been left selected except the WINNT folder.

FIGURE 22.7.

Selecting folders to be restored.

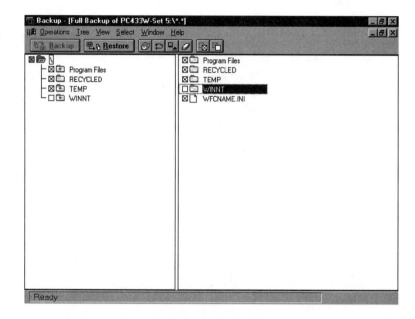

In Figure 22.8, the WINNT folder has been expanded to show its contents. The mouse has been used to highlight a set of files, and the Select option of the menu bar has been clicked. Clicking the Check option causes all of the highlighted items to be selected for restoration.

After selecting the files or folders that you want to restore, click the Restore button of the toolbar or the Restore option of the Operations menu to begin the restoration process. The Restore Information dialog is displayed, as shown in Figure 22.9.

Like the Backup Information dialog, the Restore Information dialog is divided into three sections. The top section contains information about the tape set or sets to be restored.

The middle section of the dialog is used to set Restore options. By default, Backup restores the selected file sets to the same location from which they were originally copied. You can choose to specify a different drive or a different path within a drive. This allows files to be restored to disk without overwriting the copies already in place, which is sometimes useful for comparing files or folders.

FIGURE 22.8.

Selecting files to be restored.

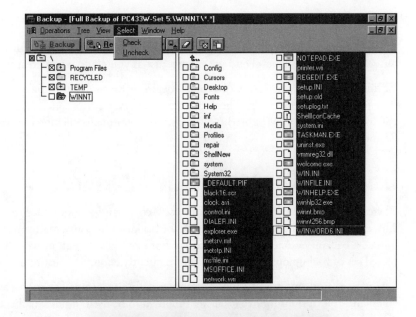

FIGURE 22.9.

The Restore Information dialog.

If the file set that you are restoring contains Registry information, you can choose to have that restored as well. You can also check the Restore File Permissions box if you want the files restored with the permissions that they show on the tape. If you don't set this box, the files will inherit the permissions of the directory to which you restore.

You can verify the integrity of the restore by checking the Verify After Restore box. If this box is selected, `ntbackup` first restores your data and then performs a verification pass that compares the restored files to the tape contents.

Restore Logging Options

Set any logging options using the Log Information area of the Restore Information dialog. You can select the log detail level and pathname, just as you could when creating the backup set.

Clicking OK causes the restore to actually begin. A Restore Status dialog appears, indicating the currently active operation. The dialog also displays statistics concerning the number of files and bytes that have been restored. You can stop the restore by clicking the Abort button of the Restore Status dialog.

Using the Command-Line Interface

There are times when you might want to use a command-line interface to run your backups. This can occur when you need to schedule the backup to run automatically, when you want to initiate a backup on one machine remotely from another system, or when you have some repeated set of backup options that you run frequently enough to justify using a script.

The `ntbackup` program provides a command-line interface for such cases. Most of the command-line options for `ntbackup` are intended to be used in potentially automated scripts, and they require no user input. The two exceptions to this rule are the `/nopoll` and `/missingtape` options.

Use the `/nopoll` option to force `ntbackup` to skip any cataloging actions and immediately erase the tape. This option is particularly useful when a tape has become corrupted, because the cataloging operations might otherwise produce errors or cause `ntbackup` to abort.

Use `/missingtape` if you want to read only one volume of a multitape set, or if you have a multitape set with a damaged or missing tape. Backup scans each tape in order to rebuild the catalog information.

The `ntbackup` command-line interface is used like this:

```
ntbackup operation path options
```

The *operation* is required and must be either `eject` or `backup`. `Path` is required for backup operations. Multiple paths can be specified.

Available options are shown in Table 22.2.

Table 22.2. The `ntbackup` options.

Option	Explanation
`/a`	Sets *append* mode. The backup sets will be appended to the end of the tape. If this option is not set, the existing contents of the tape will be overwritten.

Option	Explanation
/v	Causes all operations to be verified.
/r	Restricts access to saved information to administrators or to the actual owners of the saved files.
/d "description"	Enables you to enter a textual description of the backup. Use the quotation marks if the description text contains any spaces.
/b	If the drive being backed up contains Registry information, specifying the /b switch causes the registry information to be backed up as well.
/hc:{on¦off}	/hc:on turns hardware compression on. /hc:off turns compression off. Compression sometimes greatly increases tape capacity, but it can slow the backup down or make the tape less portable.
/t {option}	The /t switch is used to specify the type of the backup. Available types are normal, copy, incremental, differential, and daily. The types of backups are explained in the "Types of Backups" section of this chapter.
/l "filename"	This switch is used to specify a pathname for a log file.
/e	If the /e switch is set, the log file will contain only exception information.
/tape:{n}	Used to select the tape drive number, where *n* is a number from 0 to 9.

Any or all of the listed options can be specified. As an example, a full backup of the F: drive could be made on a compressed archive by using the following command:

```
ntbackup backup F:\ /d "F: Full Backup" /hc:on /t:normal
```

Scheduling Automatic Backups

The command-line interface to ntbackup makes it relatively simple to automate the process of backing up your system. You can use the NT At command to schedule tasks to be run at fixed times. If you place the ntbackup commands that you want to use into a script file, you can cause the script to be run by At during some off hour. In this way, you can get an automated backup every night at the same time. Consider the following simple batch script:

```
REM backit.cmd - An automated backup script
@echo off
ntbackup backup C: /d "C: Backup" /hc:on /t:incremental /r /a /b
net use x: \\server1\d$
ntbackup backup x: /d "Server1 D: Backup" /hc:on /t:incremental /a
net use x: /d
```

22

BACKING UP
YOUR SYSTEM

The preceding script runs an incremental backup of drive C: on the local system. It then connects the administrative share name \\server1\d$ to drive x: and runs an incremental backup of the remote drive. Finally, it disconnects the share from the local system.

Place the preceding commands into a file called `backit.cmd`, and then run the following command:

```
at 01:00 /every:m,t,w,th,f,s,su backit.cmd
```

Every morning at 1 a.m., an incremental backup of drive C: and \\server1\d$ will be run. You can expand the script by adding additional paths to the `ntbackup` command. You can also put conditional logic into the script to cause the script to perform different actions on the basis of environment variables or the output of other programs.

> **NOTE**
>
> The at command uses the Windows NT Scheduler service to run commands. In order for your backup to run correctly, you must be logged onto your workstation as an administrator or a member of the Backup Operators group.

Third-Party Backup Software

NT Backup is almost a complete backup solution. Its primary flaw lies in its inability to back up the registry information of remote systems. A number of quality backup programs are available from third-party software vendors to address that inability. Three of the most popular are Backup Exec from Arcada/Seagate Software, Networker from Legato Systems, and Cheyenne Software's ARCserve. Each has its own set of strengths and weaknesses, but any of these applications is an excellent choice for backing up networked NT systems.

Summary

The single most catastrophic mistake made by both novice and advanced computer users is the simple failure to make routine backups. It's a dull, unexciting task that many users rarely find time for. Avoid that pitfall. A little forethought can make backups an automatic and painless process that can save you endless hours of frustration or financial hardship. NT's integrated backup facilities are easy to use and robust for standalone workstations, so there's no real need to defer the task. Take time today—if you haven't already done so—to plan a backup strategy. Start by immediately making a full backup of your entire system. If you ever need it, you'll realize that it was time well spent.

Storage Devices

by Eric D. Osborne

IN THIS CHAPTER

Microsoft Windows NT 4.0 Workstation supports a wide variety of mass storage devices. IDE, EIDE disks, and SCSI drives are all supported as storage and/or boot devices. SCSI support has been somewhat improved over that provided in NT 3.51.

NT 4.0 allows the space on your disk drives to be used in a surprising number of ways. This chapter discusses some of the basic terminology and concepts relating to mass storage, and how those concepts apply to disk management under Windows NT.

Background

In the early days of MS-DOS, disk drives had extremely small capacities (by modern standards). The original IBM PC/XT, the first DOS machine with a hard disk, had only a 10MB drive. At the time, that seemed more than adequate to engineers, who didn't envision the huge storage capacities required to support modern applications under Windows NT or Windows 95. The MS-DOS file system was therefore designed with unfortunate limitations, much like the DOS restrictions that constrain conventional memory to the first 640KB of address space.

The net result of these file system restrictions has continued to haunt system designers and users until recent times. Disk technology has advanced rapidly over the last several years, bringing prices down at the same time that capacities continue to soar. The average Pentium system of today has at least 1GB of disk space. That is 100 times the capacity of the disk on the original IBM PC/XT. Unfortunately, the design of the MS-DOS file system couldn't easily keep pace with the improvements in the underlying hardware technology.

MS-DOS was originally designed around a floppy-disk–based environment. Each disk contained only a single directory (or *folder* in NT terminology). The use of space on the disk was controlled via a File Allocation Table (FAT). The basic MS-DOS file system is still referred to as the FAT file system.

Microsoft was quick to realize that a single folder per disk would be unworkable, particularly because the design of the FAT file system had a fixed limit on the number of files in the root directory of the drive. Microsoft extended the FAT file system to allow subdirectories. These extensions allowed the total number of files on a disk to be limited only by the available free space; but to this day, the FAT file system has a limit on the number of files that can be put into the root directory of each drive.

One other restriction that has remained is the size of individual file systems. The FAT file system originally restricted the size of a single file system to 32MB. That limit was extended to 512MB in MS-DOS 4.0. Many personal computers still assume that an individual FAT file system will not exceed 512MB. A number of third-party BIOS extensions and disk managers grew up over the years to allow DOS to use the full capacity of large disks within a single file system.

Partitioning

Microsoft's original solution for using large disks under MS-DOS was to logically segment the disks into a number of smaller, more manageable sections. These sections were called *partitions*. The MS-DOS partitioning scheme allowed each disk to be divided into as many as four sections. MS-DOS treated each of these partitions as if it were a separate disk.

This partitioning scheme is still used. Each disk contains a *partition table*, which is built on the disk when it is initialized. The same partition table format that was used by MS-DOS continues to be used by Windows 95 and Windows NT, largely so that hardware manufacturers can support all three operating systems with a single BIOS. The partition table contains partition-identifying information for each file system type. This implies that it is possible to support and boot multiple operating systems from a single disk. These kinds of multiboot systems are discussed in the section titled "The Boot Process," later in this chapter.

The partition table is used by the BIOS to determine where each partition is located on the disk. The size of each partition is also recorded in the partition table. Besides indicating the type and size of the partitions, there is also an indicator of which partition is active. The active partition is the partition from which the system boots.

It is important to realize that there are two types of partitions. *Primary* partitions are one of the four fixed sections of a disk, as described previously. One, and only one, of the partitions can be an *extended* partition. An extended partition can be logically subdivided into smaller logical partitions or have free space allocated to the advanced volume sets. One partition of your boot drive will be marked as *active*. This is the partition that the system will try to boot from, which is called the *system partition*. The *boot partition* is the partition from which NT itself is loaded. It might or might not be the same as the system partition.

The Boot Process

The boot process for a PC architecture system is conceptually simple. At boot time, the system firmware acquires information from the Master Boot Record on the drive. After the active partition is identified, its boot sector is read. The bootloader looks on the active partition for the NTLDR program, which in turn locates and runs NTDETECT.COM. NTDETECT.COM analyzes the hardware of your system so that the correct device drivers can be loaded. The BOOT.INI file is then read from the top directory of the boot device. This file contains information about where the actual NT kernel and operating system are on your computer. The operating system can reside on any of your mass storage devices. The following is a sample BOOT.INI file:

```
[boot loader]
timeout=30
default=scsi(0)disk(0)rdisk(0)partition(2)\WINNT35
[operating systems]
scsi(0)disk(0)rdisk(1)partition(1)\WINNT40="Windows NT Workstation Version 4.00"
```

```
scsi(0)disk(0)rdisk(1)partition(1)\WINNT40="Windows NT Workstation Version 4.00
    [VGA mode]" /basevideo /sos
scsi(0)disk(0)rdisk(0)partition(2)\WINNT35="Windows NT Server Version 3.51"
scsi(0)disk(0)rdisk(0)partition(2)\WINNT35="Windows NT Server Version 3.51
    [VGA mode]" /basevideo /sos
C:\="Microsoft Windows"
```

In this example, the system has both Windows NT Workstation Version 4.0 and Windows NT Advanced Server Version 3.51 installed. The system boots NT Workstation 4.0 from the first (and only) partition on SCSI disk ID 1 on the first SCSI bus of the first controller on the system. NT Advanced Server 3.51 is booted from SCSI ID 0, partition 2 of that same bus. Note that either can be booted using a choice of a configured video driver or in basic VGA mode. This allows the system to be booted to a known state if the video hardware is configured with incorrect settings.

You might have also noticed that the last line of the preceding BOOT.INI file specifies a location for booting Microsoft Windows. The Windows NT loader can be configured to boot many different operating systems by making changes to the BOOT.INI file. In general, you must install non-NT operating systems *before* you install NT if you want a multiboot system.

> **TIP**
>
> The boot files on your NT system might become corrupted or damaged. You can make an NT boot floppy that can sometimes be used to correct such problems, even if the emergency repair disk for your system fails. Just format the floppy from NT. (This is important. A floppy formatted from Windows, DOS, or Windows 95 will not work.) Copy the files NTLDER, NTDETECT.COM, and BOOT.INI to the new disk. If you use SCSI disks, also copy NTBOOTDD.SYS. You can then boot from the disk.

> **TIP**
>
> If you make a copy of your NT installation files on a second drive, you can edit the BOOT.INI file on your NT boot floppy to contain an entry for the copy. That way, if your primary system disk fails, you can still boot into NT and possibly recover your system. This is similar to the fault-tolerant boot disk used to boot from a drive mirror with NT Advanced Server. You can make a copy of the system area using NTBACKUP as described in Chapter 22.

Supported NT 4.0 File Systems

NT supports the older FAT file system and its own file system, called NTFS. Prior versions of NT supported the High Performance File System (HPFS) from OS/2, but support for HPFS has been dropped in NT 4.0 Workstation.

> **CAUTION**
>
> You can convert your FAT file systems to NTFS file systems at any time, but after they are converted, you cannot convert them back to FAT.

FAT File System

Many of the characteristics of the FAT file system were described previously in this chapter. Because FAT is an old and a simple file system, it has significant restrictions. One of the more annoying of these is the filename length restriction. The FAT file system is case-insensitive and restricts filenames to an eight-character name and a three-character extension. This constraint can make it very difficult to create meaningful names for your documents or other data files. Note that both Windows 95 and Windows NT support a variant of FAT called VFAT, which does not have the filename length restriction. Older DOS and Windows 3.*x* systems are still subject to this restriction.

It's also important to remember that the FAT file system was created well before PC networking protocols. It assumes that if you're using the computer, you are supposed to have access to the files. There is no concept of file ownership or access control. Anything that you put on a FAT file system can be read or modified by anyone who can get physical access to your system by booting DOS from a floppy disk.

If you use your workstation for gaming or to run operating systems other than Windows NT, you might need to put data on FAT file systems. The FAT file system is understood by most of the operating systems that run on PC architecture computers.

You should remember four things about FAT file systems when working with Windows NT:

1. If you have an ARC-compliant RISC computer using an ALPHA, MIPS, or another non-Intel processor, you must have the system partition formatted as a FAT file system. This means that you won't have any security on files stored on the system partition after your system has booted. You should, therefore, set the permissions on the partition itself to be accessible only to administrative users. This will prevent users from modifying critical system files such as BOOT.INI.

2. If you want to be able to boot your system under Windows 95, DOS, Linux, or SCO UNIX, you can use FAT file systems to contain files that you want to be accessible from operating systems other than NT.

3. FAT file systems have primitive error recovery and no security. Any data you put on a FAT volume is both more susceptible to crash damage and more vulnerable to illicit incursion than data on an NTFS volume. Make sure you understand the risks of leaving data on a FAT file system. See item 1 if you have a RISC computer.

4. Files that have been compressed with programs such as Stacker won't be readable from NT, and NT file and directory compression doesn't work on FAT volumes.

NTFS File System

The NTFS file system is the preferred file system for NT systems. NTFS has many significant advantages over the FAT file system, including the following:

- NTFS performs better than FAT. NTFS uses sophisticated disk caching algorithms to maintain significant amounts of data in RAM. It is also substantially less susceptible to fragmentation. The net result is much faster disk I/O than you typically get on FAT volumes.

- NTFS uses a technique called *journaling* to record changes being made to the state of the file systems. Journaling was a technique first developed for use by relational database vendors to safeguard data before it was permanently committed to the database. Whenever you write data to your disk, the operating system must update both your file and the file system *metadata*. Metadata tells the system where your data is on disk, what kind of access properties your file has, and other housekeeping information. If the system fails while the metadata is being updated, your file could potentially be lost.

  The basic effect of journaling reduces the volatility of your data, so that if your system crashes, NT can recover the file systems using the journals or logs. You are much less likely to experience data loss when using journaled file systems such as NTFS.

- There are sophisticated facilities for controlling file access properties. This is an area in which NTFS is not only superior to the DOS FAT file system but is superior to the standard file systems included with UNIX systems. NTFS supports a concept called Access Control Lists (ACLs). ACLs determine who can (or can't) access each file and what each individual can do with it.

- Both file- and directory-level compression are supported on NTFS volumes. If compression is set on a directory, any file that is copied there is automatically compressed.

- NTFS has integrated support for *volumes* and *stripe sets*. Both of these are file system extensions that allow you to span multiple disk drives or partitions with a single file system, although the effects are somewhat different. The next section discusses volumes and stripe sets in greater detail.

Disk Management

Windows NT includes a tool called Disk Administrator for managing your storage devices. Disk Administrator enables you to perform some extremely sophisticated tasks from a very user-friendly and easy-to-use interface. You can invoke the Disk Administrator by clicking the Disk Administrator command on the Taskbar's Start menu. You must be logged on under an account with administrator privileges in order to use the Disk Administrator. When you invoke Disk Administrator, you should see a display something like the one shown in Figure 23.1.

FIGURE 23.1.

The Disk Administrator (Disk Configuration view).

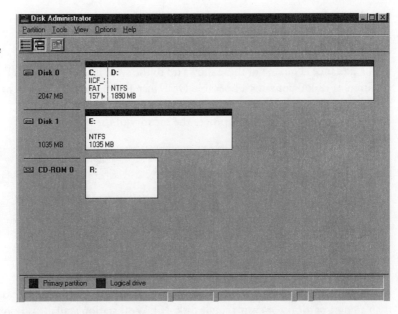

Disk Administrator always shows one of two views of your disks. The Disk Configuration view, shown in Figure 23.1, shows a view of the physical structure of the disks connected to your system. Each bar represents a physical device. The bars might be separated into partitions. Disk 0 in Figure 23.1 has been separated in this way. The Volumes view is shown in Figure 23.2.

FIGURE 23.2.

The Disk Administrator (Volumes view).

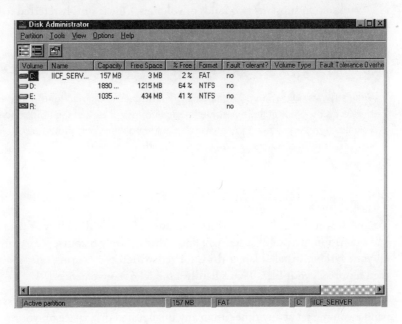

23

STORAGE DEVICES

Volumes

Refer to Figure 23.1 for a moment. As you can see, disk 0 contains two file systems, or *volumes* in NT parlance. The first of these shows up to the system as `c:`. It is a FAT file system. The `c:` partition of disk 0 contains a bootable DOS installation, so the file system has not been converted to NTFS. The other two disk partitions on this system are NTFS partitions, which increases the performance and improves the security of the system.

> **TIP**
>
> The `c:` partition could be made into an NTFS partition by running the Convert program:
>
> `Convert c: /fs:ntfs /v`
>
> Convert is smart enough to know when it can't lock a drive and will perform the conversion the next time your system reboots.

Although Disk Manager refers to the partitions in Figure 23.1 as volumes, volumes can be larger than a single partition or even a single disk. NT Workstation actually supports two much more sophisticated types of volumes. Both types allow you to bind a number of partitions or entire disk drives into a single large file system.

There are many reasons you might want to construct volumes. The mechanics of creating a volume differs somewhat depending upon what you want to do with it. That's why Windows NT Workstation supports two kinds of volumes. One is simply referred to as a *volume set*; the other is called a *stripe set*.

> **WARNING**
>
> Volume types can give you significant advantages in flexibility and performance, but you should be aware that there is some increase of risk. If any of the component disks of a volume fail, you will have to recover the entire volume. You should also remember that you can't boot from a volume, stripe set, or extended partition.

Volume Sets

Volume sets are intended to maximize the administrative flexibility of your system. If you ever had a partition run out of space, you know that the only recourse for expanding it was to back up your system, install a larger drive (or repartition the existing one, space permitting), and then restore all your files. That's hardly a model of convenience.

Volume sets provide a far more efficient model for expanding active file systems. You can expand a volume set at any time, using any unallocated disk space on your system. You can add space in essentially any increment. The component parts of volumes don't have to be the same size, so you can use a 1GB disk and a 500MB disk to create a volume and then expand it using an unallocated 100MB partition of a third drive.

> **WARNING**
>
> Although you can expand a volume set at any time, you can't reduce it again without destroying the entire volume. Make sure you really want to bind space into a volume set first.

Stripe Sets

Stripe sets are volumes that are optimized for high performance. Contrary to popular belief, very little of the time spent on typical disk I/O is spent doing data transfer. The real overhead in disk I/O comes from *seek time*, the time that is spent looking for the data on the disk. That's because most disk transactions actually involve relatively small amounts of data. The system is constantly shuttling the disk heads back and forth as it updates user data and the associated file system metadata. Any mechanism that can reduce seek time can result in very dramatic increases in disk performance.

The increased performance of stripe sets is realized by distributing operations across a number of disk drives. Each disk on your system is effectively a huge set of blocks. The file system metadata is grouped into relatively narrow regions of the disk, with user files making up the remainder. Most file accesses require I/O operations to at least three different regions of the disk media. Consider, for instance, a simple file read. When you open a file for read access, the file system first has to locate the directory entry for the file in question. That requires a seek to the directory entry and a read of the directory data. Information in the directory entry points to file system metadata that can be used to find the actual data blocks for the file. Locating and reading the metadata requires the disk to seek a second time. Reading the actual file data requires a minimum of a third seek. If a file write has occured, two to three additional seeks can be required as the system updates the file metadata and the free block list.

Now, here's the really interesting point. In an operation such as the one just described, you have a minimum of three seeks. With a good SCSI disk, those might take as little as 27 milliseconds. If your read then did a high speed transfer of 100 kilobytes of data at the rated SCSI-2 speed of 10 megabytes per second, it would take 10 milliseconds to transfer the data. That means that the seek time was 2.7 times as long as the data transfer time. Most real-world disk transactions involve less than 100 kilobytes of data, so the ratio of seek time to transfer time is even worse. Reducing seek times and head seek latencies is a primary goal of disk caches, because caches can't normally contain a significantly large percentage of the total blocks in use on a disk. Because the file system metadata is more active than the rest of the disk, it stays in cache. This reduces the number of disk seeks required to complete any given operation. However, note that although caching algorithms can reduce the effects of seek thrashing, seek time continues to be a major bottleneck on I/O through a file system.

Even in the best-case operation, where the system could read or write a huge amount of data at one time, the system would have to wait for the drive to complete each piece of the transaction before moving on to the next piece. This is where the effects of striping come into play. With a stripe set, the system allocates the first block of space on the first disk. The second block is on the second disk, and so on. When the last disk of the stripe set has been used, the next block goes back to the first disk.

This effectively allows the system to read or write to all the disks in the stripe set simultaneously. Instead of transmitting some data and then waiting a bit and transmitting more data, the system can queue multiple read and/or write operations to several drives at once. The drives perform these seeks at the same time, so the operation occurs in parallel. SCSI and EIDE disks release the bus during seeks, freeing the system to perform other I/O operations. The disks notify the system when data is ready to transfer. Note, however, that the EIDE or SCSI disk adapter can only transfer data to or from a single disk at a time. This means that even though the seeks occur in parallel, the data transfers still occur one at a time—unless you have multiple disk adapters. If you have multiple SCSI adapters or EIDE interfaces, the data transfers also occur in parallel across all the available I/O channels. The net effect is blazingly fast disk I/O.

Stripe sets do have some drawbacks when compared to volume sets. Stripe sets can't be dynamically extended, so make sure you create a stripe set that is big enough. You should also be aware that stripe sets always use the same number of blocks on each of the disks in the set. That means that if you mix small drives and large drives into a single stripe set, you will waste space on the larger drives. And, as with volume sets, if you lose any drive in a stripe set, you have to recover the entire volume.

Disk Administrator Volume Operations

You can perform most of the operations available within Disk Administrator from either the Disk Configuration or Volumes views. The Disk Configuration view is particularly useful when dealing with new disks or when reallocating space. Whenever you want to change your disk configuration, click the partition or volume icon you are interested in changing. You can then use the Disk Administrator 0 to select the operations to perform.

The Partition Menu

Figure 23.3 shows the options available under the Partition menu. You won't be able to select any options that are unavailable or not applicable to your system. The system shown in Figure 23.3, for instance, has no unallocated disk space, so any menu options that require free disk space cannot be selected.

FIGURE 23.3.

The Disk Administrator Partition menu option.

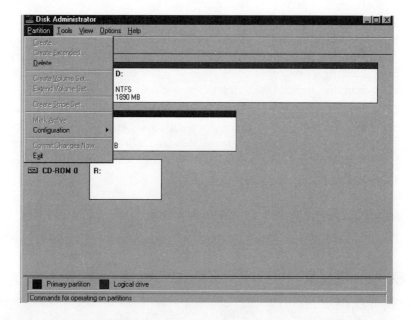

- Use Create and Create Extended to create new partitions from unallocated disk space. Select the targeted area of the disk, select Create to create a new primary partition, and then select Create Extended to create a new extended partition. You can specify the size of the new partition.

- Use the Delete option to remove a partition and mark the space it contains as unallocated. You can then use the unallocated space to create a new partition, or to construct or expand a volume. Select the partition you want to delete and click the Delete menu option.

- Use the Mark/Active option to set the active partition. Remember that the active partition is the one that the system will try to boot from. Make sure you know what you're doing before modifying the active partition.

- To create a new volume, select the first area to bind into the volume. Hold the Shift key and select additional areas. After you select the space you want to use, click the Create Volume Set option of the Partition menu.

- You can expand a volume in much the same way. Select an existing NTFS volume or volume set and hold Shift while selecting one or more areas of available space. Click the Extend Volume option. The space will be formatted and added to the volume when the system reboots.

23

STORAGE DEVICES

■ Pay close attention to the Configuration option. It saves or restores information about any volume or stripe sets that you have on your system. In the event of a system crash, you can use the emergency repair disk and the saved configuration information to reconstruct your volume or stripe sets. You should save configuration information to a floppy disk each time you modify your disk configuration.

■ The Commit Changes Now option causes changes that you've made to be committed to the disk. Many options are reversible until committed, so be absolutely sure that you want to make your changes permanent before selecting this option. If you've deleted a partition, you will have to commit the changes before you can use the freed space.

The Tools Menu

Use the Tools menu, shown in Figure 23.4, to do most of the normal housekeeping chores associated with disk drives. You can select a partition or volume and then select any of the available Tools options.

FIGURE 23.4.

The Disk Administrator Tools menu.

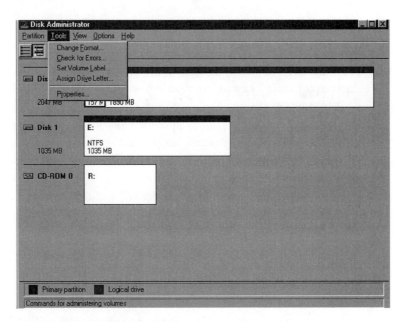

Here's a brief explanation of each Tools option:

■ Format is used to format partitions. If the partition is already formatted, this option will be relabeled to Change Format. You can't format any partition that has Windows NT system files on it. If you choose to reformat a partition, you will lose any information that it currently contains. Note that you can format the partition as either a FAT or an NTFS file system. There is no way to reformat a system partition from within Disk Administrator.

- Use Check for Errors to check the file system consistency. In the event that a volume can't be locked, the check can be scheduled to occur at the next system reboot.

- Use the Set Volume Label option to set or change the volume label of the partition or volume selected.

- One interesting (and useful) capability of Windows NT is that it can override the default drive letter assignments and assign any letter to any drive. The Assign Drive Letter button changes the letter for the selected drive. Note that the effect is immediate, so active programs might get confused when an associated path goes away after a drive letter is reassigned.

- The Properties option displays the dialog shown in Figure 23.5. The Properties dialog is really a concatenation of several of the other Tools options made available as a single integrated dialog.

FIGURE 23.5.

Disk Administrator: the Tools menu Properties dialog.

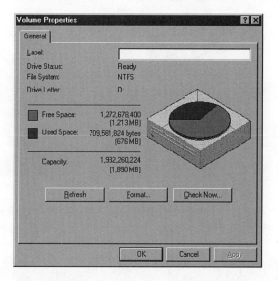

Note the Check selection of Figure 23.5. This option invokes the dialog shown in Figure 23.6 and can be used to check the integrity of your disk volumes. Again, if the volume cannot be checked immediately, you can schedule the system to run the check at boot time.

FIGURE 23.6.

Disk Administrator: the Properties Check dialog.

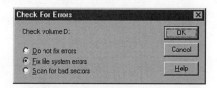

The Options Menu

Use the Options menu to configure various aspects of Disk Manager. As shown in Figure 23.7, you can use the first three selections of the Options menu to turn on and off the Tool Bar, Status Bar, and the Legend indicating the color and pattern combinations used for each type of partition or volume.

FIGURE 23.7.

The Disk Administrator Options menu.

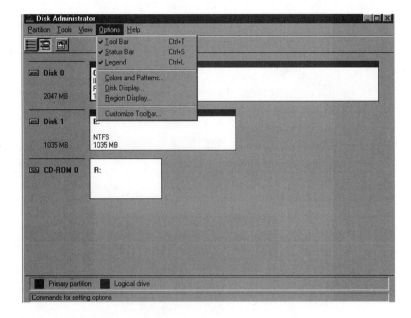

Use the Colors and Patterns dialog depicted in Figure 23.8 to set the color and fill pattern for each type of volume or partition supported by NT. The list in Figure 23.8 shows selections including Stripe with parity and Mirror set. These are advanced fault-tolerant technologies included with Windows NT Advanced Server, but neither is supported by Windows NT Workstation. Select an item from the list of Figure 23.8, and then select the color and fill pattern of your choice.

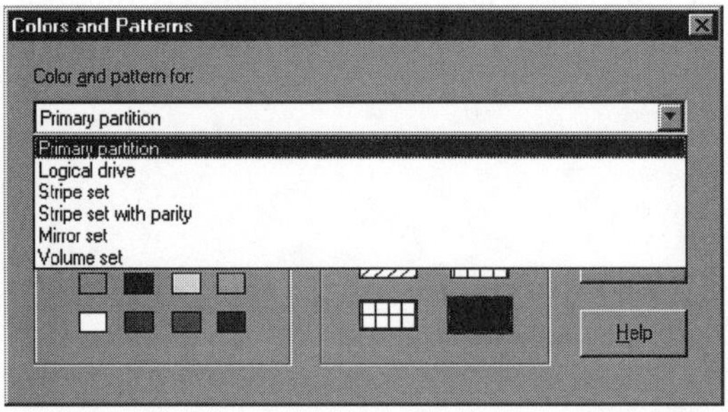

FIGURE 23.8.

Setting colors and patterns in Disk Administrator.

Use the Disk Display option to set the appearance of the bars in the Disk Configuration view. Selecting this option invokes the dialog shown in Figure 23.9. You can choose to have all disks shown in actual size or shown equally. If you choose to have the disk shown in actual size, each bar is scaled relative to the others. The effect is that larger disks have correspondingly larger bars.

Sometimes you might want to have the disks shown equally, particularly if some of your disks are disproportionately large compared to others. Be careful when using this display mode, however, because it can lull you into making incorrect assumptions when setting volume or stripe sets.

FIGURE 23.9.

Setting Disk Display options in Disk Administrator.

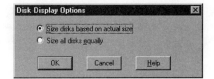

The Region Display selection of the Options menu performs a function similar to that performed by the Disk Display. The Region Display option sets the display attributes for individual partitions or regions of a disk drive. You can cause all regions to be sized equally or proportionally to their actual size, or you can let Disk Administrator choose how to display the regions. You can configure the region display attributes identically for all drives, or you can set individual characteristics for specific drives. Figure 23.10 shows the Region Display configuration dialog.

FIGURE 23.10.

Setting Region Display options in Disk Administrator.

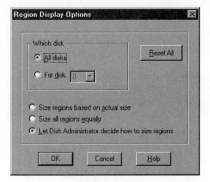

CD-ROMs

Because CD-ROM drives are normally read-only devices, you have limited options when dealing with them under Disk Administrator. Probably the single most useful option is the Assign Drive Letter option of the Tools menu shown in Figure 23.4. You can use that option to change the drive letter assigned to your CD-ROM drive. This is particularly useful for maintaining

23

STORAGE DEVICES

drive letter consistency when you have inconsistent numbers of hard drives on different systems. You can assign a uniform drive letter such as R: to the CD-ROM drive on each machine. That way, you always know where it is when trying to perform remote operations.

Summary

The I/O characteristics of different applications often require that physical disk I/O be handled in very different ways. Windows NT was designed with this point in mind. NT supports older FAT file systems for users who require backward compatibility with their DOS or Windows 3.*x* systems. The NTFS file system provides much needed enhancements for users who need file security, long filenames, or dynamic compression. And, finally, stripe sets and volumes allow system managers to build very large file systems that have been optimized for performance or easy scalability. NT Server provides some additional functionality targeted at fault tolerance.

The volume management facility of Windows NT isn't perfect quite yet. NT doesn't support the composite entities such as mirrored stripe sets that are available on some UNIX systems, marrying high performance to fault tolerance. Those kinds of capabilities don't come free, however, so the integrated storage features of Windows NT still represent an excellent value to the end user.

Event Viewer

by Thomas Lee

IN THIS CHAPTER

CHAPTER 24

Introduction to the Event Viewer

In Windows NT Workstation, an *event* occurs whenever anything significant happens that either NT Workstation or a running application feels you should know about.

The definition of "significant" is left up to the developers. Thus, the events that you are notified about can vary enormously—from fundamental system errors such as a network card not working or a fault-tolerant disk failure, to much less significant events such as a service starting or a print job completing.

When a software component detects an event to be reported, it uses the ReportEvent API to pass details about the event to Windows NT. The Event Log service then posts these details to one of three Event Logs:

- System Log: This log contains details about events that occur within the operating system, such as a driver failure.

- Security Log: Security-related Audit events—such as when someone attempts to log on without the proper password—are stored in this log.

- Application Log: This log contains details about events detected by applications running on your system. For example, a database application might record the failure to read a record.

The Event Log service is responsible for writing event details to the Event Logs, and it is one of the standard NT services that is started each time you load Windows NT Workstation.

TIP

When the Event Log service starts, it reports this to the System Event Log. The event logged is event 6005, which can be very useful in troubleshooting. By looking for this event, you can determine when the system last rebooted and thus see all the events that have occurred since then. These events also show you how often Windows NT Workstation has been rebooted.

To view the information that has been logged, you use the Event Viewer application. Event Viewer is automatically installed when you load Windows NT Workstation.

Event Viewer enables you to perform the following tasks:

- See a summary of the events that have occurred.

- See the details logged for each event.

- Save Event Logs away for future analysis and view saved logs.

- View the local Event Log and view Event Logs on remote systems (subject to security).

The Event Viewer is a powerful aid to troubleshooting and is usually a "first port of call" whenever a problem occurs on your system. Let's look at how you can use Event Viewer to diagnose problems in Windows NT Workstation. The Event Viewer is very straightforward to use. But getting the most out of it takes practice, because there is no overall consistency in what is logged when events occur.

Suppose that a driver fails to start when you boot Windows NT Workstation. If this happens, you receive a message box after you start up, as shown in Figure 24.1.

Service Control Manager
At least one service or driver failed during system startup. Use Event Viewer to examine the event log for details.
OK

FIGURE 24.1.
A driver startup failure.

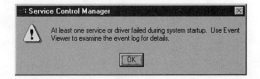

This message box tells you that something has gone wrong in the startup and that the Service Control Manager was not able to properly start one or more drivers. This message box, by itself, offers no indication as to what has happened; it only tells you that there has been a problem. If you've just changed or added a driver, this box alone might tell you what's wrong. But often this is just the first hint that there's a problem. To determine what went wrong, you need to run the Event Viewer.

Event Viewer to the Rescue

With the Event Viewer application, you examine and manage the three event logs. When you install Windows NT Workstation, the installation process installs the Event Viewer application as `%SystemRoot%\system32\eventvwr.exe` and sets up a shortcut under the Administrative Tools (Common) group in the Start|Programs menu.

Running this application brings up the window shown in Figure 24.2.

Event Viewer - System Log on \\LAPTOP
Log View Options Help
Date Time Source Category Event User
8/24/96 7:08:04 PM Service Control Mar None 7023 N/A
8/24/96 7:07:45 PM EventLog None 6005 N/A
8/24/96 7:07:52 PM Service Control Mar None 7000 N/A
8/24/96 6:58:14 PM Service Control Mar None 7023 N/A
8/24/96 6:57:56 PM EventLog None 6005 N/A
8/24/96 6:58:03 PM Service Control Mar None 7000 N/A
8/24/96 4:28:44 PM Rdr None 8003 N/A
8/24/96 4:28:44 PM Rdr None 8003 N/A
8/24/96 4:28:44 PM Rdr None 8003 N/A
8/24/96 3:55:46 PM BROWSER None 8021 N/A
8/24/96 3:55:46 PM BROWSER None 8021 N/A
8/24/96 2:55:41 PM Rdr None 8003 N/A
8/24/96 2:31:32 PM Rdr None 8005 N/A
8/24/96 2:31:32 PM Rdr None 8005 N/A
8/24/96 2:30:32 PM EventLog None 6005 N/A
8/24/96 2:31:32 PM Rdr None 8003 N/A

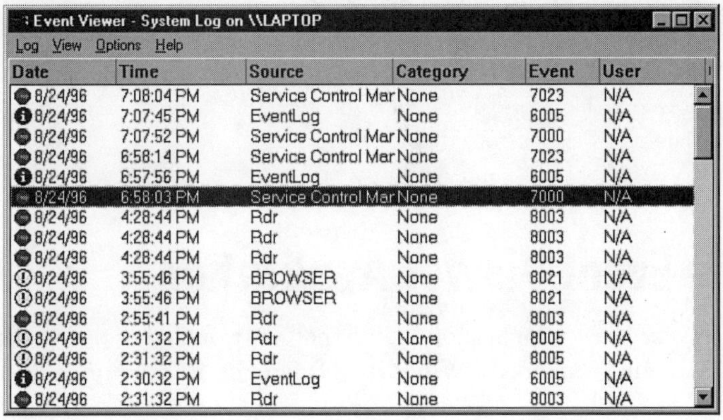

FIGURE 24.2.
The Event Viewer application.

If you look at the Event Log, you can see that there are a number of Error Events (the ones with the red stop sign to the left). Looking back chronologically, you can see the first event (since the last reboot). Selecting that event and pressing the Enter key brings up the Event Detail dialog, shown in Figure 24.3, which shows all the details that were logged.

FIGURE 24.3.

The Event Detail dialog.

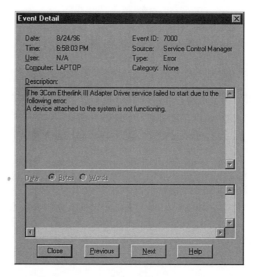

From this dialog, you can see that the network adapter is not functioning, at least as far as Windows NT Workstation is concerned. All you have to do then is work out why the network adapter is not functioning, fix it, reboot, and you're back in business. This is usually easier said than done! In this case, the problem was due to a PC Card that was not properly seated in the PC Card slot, but this could only be determined by looking at the PC Card, and not by looking at the Event Log entry.

> **NOTE**
>
> In the Event Detail dialog shown in Figure 24.3, the Service Control Manager is reporting that the device has failed to start and that it is not functioning. There could be an obvious reason and, therefore, an obvious solution. But the event details logged might not be all that helpful. Still, it's better than nothing!

The Event Viewer Application

The Event Viewer application is an important troubleshooting tool and is also very useful in administering networks of Windows NT Systems. By examining the Event Log, you can solve the problems that occur, and, more importantly, you can identify and correct problems before they become more serious.

As you saw in Figure 24.2, the Event Viewer application has four menu items:

- Log: This enables you to choose which log to view and to manage the log.
- View: This option helps you to view the logs and find events within the logs.
- Options: This option enables you to change the font used in the application, control saving settings, and set up a low-speed connection.
- Help: This option provides standard Help facilities.

The remainder of this chapter covers these features and how to use them best.

What Information Is Logged?

Each Event Log entry contains parameters, which are passed by the application to the RecordEvent API call. These are as follows:

- Source: This is the name of the software component that is reporting the event. The Source is either an application name or a component of a larger application.
- Event Identifier: This identifies the specific event and can be used by the support staff to aid them in determining the cause of the error. Event identifiers are unique to each Source.
- Type: Windows NT has five event types—Information, Warning, Error, Success Audit, and Failure Audit. Any event must be of only one of these event types.
- Category: To assist in organizing events (and to help users in reviewing the Event Log), a Source can define different categories. Although categories are not used much in the System or Application Logs, the security system uses several categories, including Logon/Logoff, File System Access, Privileged Actions, and Change in Security Policy.
- Description: This is a textual description of the event. The description is intended to provide you with the information needed to troubleshoot a problem, as opposed to programming details. The amount of helpful information included in the description varies significantly.
- Data: An event can have data associated with it. This could be a hardware error code, for example. Event data is not included for all events.

In addition to these parameters, each Event Log entry contains the time and date that the event was logged, as well as the system on which the event occurred. For security events, a userid is also provided.

> **NOTE**
>
> When you view events in Event Viewer, the time and date shown will be the time on the local computer. To enable you to correlate events that occur on different systems, it is important to have a consistent time on all machines on a network. Use the NET TIME command, possibly as part of a logon script, to synchronize the clocks on all systems. Although the synchronized time might still be wrong, at least it's wrong consistently!

When viewing events with Event Viewer, the summary view (which you saw in Figure 24.2) shows Date, Time, Source, Category, Event, User, and Computer. In order to see the description and any included data, you need to look at the Event Detail.

As noted earlier, each event is categorized into one of five basic event types:

- Information: Information events are ones that are infrequent but are successful. For example, the start of the Event Viewer is a useful event to note, because it is usually the first event to occur when you boot the system. Information events are noted with a white exclamation mark inside a blue circle. Information events are seen in the System and Application logs.

- Warning: Warning events can reflect problems in the making. These are events that indicate a problem that is not yet serious—for example, the browser being unable to retrieve a list of domains from the browse master. This should usually resolve itself, but if it continues, the administrator might want to investigate and resolve this. Warning events are noted with a black exclamation mark (!) inside a yellow circle. Warning events are seen in the System and Application logs.

- Error: Error events are events that usually represent a problem the user should be aware of, because these events usually indicate a loss of functionality. In the example in Figure 24.1, a network card failed to start; therefore, there will be no network functionality until the underlying cause is determined and rectified. Error events are noted by a red stop sign. Error events are seen in the System and Application logs.

- Success Audit: A success audit indicates that a successful audit event has occurred, such as a successful logon. A success audit event is noted with a key. Success audit events are seen only in the Security Log.

- Failure Audit: A failure audit indicates that an unsuccessful audit event has occurred, such as a failed logon. A failure audit event is noted by a small padlock. Failure audit events are seen only in the Security Log.

System and Application Logs

The System Event Log contains events detected by the Windows NT Workstation operating system. The Application Log is used mainly to log events detected by applications running on your system. If possible, you should look at the logs on a regular basis. This enables you to spot problems before they become serious.

Here are some events that you are likely to see in the Event Log:

- Event Log Startup: Each time the system restarts, the Event Log service logs an information event. This tells you when the system restarted.

- Driver Startup Failures: If a driver fails to start, an Error event is logged by the Service Control Manager to list the driver that failed. This can include error codes that can be very helpful to technical support staff but are not of much use to end users.

- Device Driver Errors: If a device driver encounters an error in operation, details of this error are written away to the System Log. If a particular device is constantly logging errors, you should try to determine the source of the error. In such cases, the details logged in the System Log might not be too much help in determining the error's cause.

- Browser Events: The Browser Services tend to log a lot of events. Although these can usually be ignored, if multiple systems are constantly forcing browser elections, some reconfiguration of the network's browsing might be in order.

- Service Startup: Some services, such as the SMNP service, log successful startups in the Event Log. You can usually ignore these events. But if they don't occur when they should, their absence might be worth investigating.

- Directory Replication: If your system is an Import Server, the Directory Replication service logs events in the System Log. The details logged, in this case, are cryptic at best!

- Printer Events: Whenever a new printer is added to your system or an existing printer driver is updated, Print Manager logs the event.

Most of these types of events result in clear and easy to understand System Event Log entries, although the Directory Replicator service is infamous for cryptic messages.

Security Log

The Security Event Log is used to report security-related events. These events can indicate attempted or actual breaches of your system's security.

> **NOTE**
>
> In order to view all three Event logs, you must be a member of the Administrator's local group. Without membership in this group, you can only view the System and Application logs.

Unlike the System and Application logs, you determine which events are to be included in the Security Log. This is done by setting the Audit Policy and selecting events to audit.

Before you can get any security-related events recorded, you must first set the Audit Policy in User Manager. First, bring up User Manager; then select the Audit item from the Policies menu to bring up the Audit Policy dialog, shown in Figure 24.4.

FIGURE 24.4.

The Audit Policy dialog.

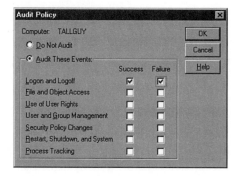

Before any security events can be logged, you must select the Audit These Events radio button. After you have set this option, you can select the specific security events to log and click on OK to accept these options. There are three main places where you can set up audit events to be logged in the Security Log:

- General security events are set up in User Manager (as you saw in Figure 24.4).
- Registry-related security events are set up in the Registry Editor.
- File-related events are set up by using the file or directory properties dialog.

General security events are selected in the Audit Policy dialog.

Selecting these events causes all occurrences of the event to be logged. Some events, such as the Use of User Rights or Process Tracking events, can log a large amount of data and might not be very useful unless you are developing and debugging an operating system component. The large amount of data that will be logged also will slow down your system.

Using the Windows NT Registry Editor (REGEDT32.EXE), you can log access to the system registry by a user or group of users. Using the Audit item from the Security menu in REGEDIT, you bring up the Registry Key Auditing dialog box, shown in Figure 24.5.

Unlike the general events, with Registry audit events you must select which users and/or groups should be audited. You do this by clicking the Add button and selecting the users and groups. Then you can select which Audit events should be logged.

Audit events can be set up on any key or keys in the Registry. If you select Replace Permissions on Existing Subkeys, you can replicate the auditing to all subkeys. Setting the auditing this way can take a lot of time, and if you set up very much auditing, you can generate many Audit events. There can also be a significant performance impact of having to log the data.

FIGURE 24.5.

Setting Audit events from the Registry Editor.

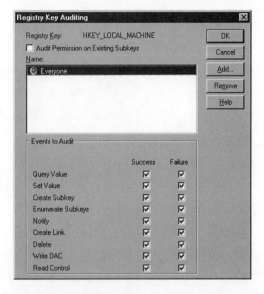

You can also log accesses by a user or group of users to any file or folder in your system. You set auditing by first selecting the folder or file to be audited and then right-clicking and bringing up the Properties dialog for the object. From the Properties dialog, you select the Security tab, which is shown in Figure 24.6.

FIGURE 24.6.

NTFS Security properties.

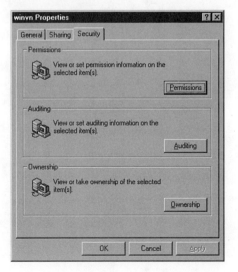

24

EVENT VIEWER

If you click on the Auditing tab in this dialog, you bring up the Directory Auditing dialog box (if you are examining the properties of a folder) or the File Auditing dialog box (if you are examining the properties of a file). These two dialog boxes, which are very similar, are shown in Figure 24.7 and Figure 24.8.

FIGURE 24.7.

The Directory Auditing dialog.

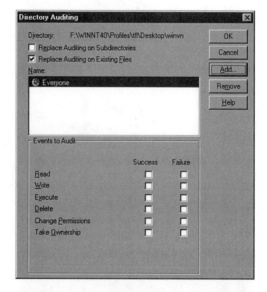

FIGURE 24.8.

The File Auditing dialog.

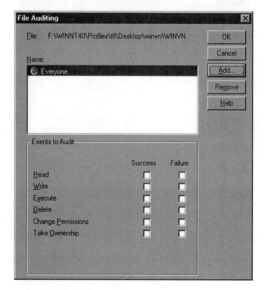

In both dialog boxes, you must first select the users whose access should be audited. Then you select which types of accesses you want to audit. It is not possible to log different Audit events for different users in a single file or directory.

In the Directory Auditing dialog, you can elect to replace the auditing information on all existing files within that folder, as well as to all the subdirectories.

> **WARNING**
>
> By default, the Directory Auditing dialog replaces all existing Audit events on all files in the chosen folder. If you have spent time setting up different levels of auditing on different files within a folder, clicking OK when viewing the Directory Audit dialog overwrites all the Audit events. This might not be what you want!

Viewing Logs Locally

When you start Event Viewer, it opens your local Event Log and displays whatever log was last being displayed (or the System Log, the first time you run the application). Depending on what logging you have chosen and how long it has been since you cleared the Event Logs, you might find the Event Logs rather big. The View Menu in Event Viewer has some options to assist you in finding events in the logs.

By default, all events logged are displayed. This can be a lot of data. Using the Filter Events item from the View menu brings up the Filter dialog, shown in Figure 24.9. From here, you can reduce the amount of data to wade through.

FIGURE 24.9.

Filtering events.

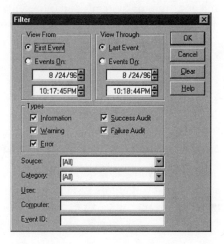

Using this dialog, you can select events that occurred between two times, as well as select which events to view. By selecting a specific source or user, you can see just the events generated by the related software component or by a specific user.

By default, Event Viewer displays the newest events at the top of the log and the oldest events at the bottom. You can change this order by selecting the Oldest First (or Newest First) option from the View menu. Personally, I find the Newest First option easiest, because the most recent events are typically the ones I want to see.

The Find item in the View menu can be used to find specific events. Selecting this option brings up the Find dialog, which is shown in Figure 24.10.

FIGURE 24.10.

Finding events.

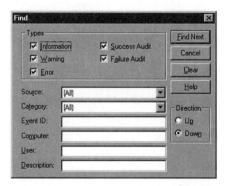

Using this dialog, you select which items you are interested in seeing. Clicking on the Find Next button finds the next occurrence of the event. If you are searching a large Event Log, you can hit the F3 key to find the next occurrence.

If you are looking at a running system's log and events occur, you might not see them. To refresh the log, you can use the Refresh option on the View menu. The F5 key is a shortcut to this function.

Viewing Event Logs Remotely

As a Windows NT Workstation user, you will probably only view the logs on your computer system. But in corporate networks, it might be useful to view remote Event Logs. Technical support staff, for example, might need to do this to diagnose problems remotely.

To view a remote system's Event Log, you use the Select Computer option from the Log menu. This brings up a browse list containing systems you can select, as shown in Figure 24.11. You can alternatively just type a machine name into the Computer name field.

FIGURE 24.11.

Selecting a remote system.

> **NOTE**
>
> Before you can view a remote system's Event Logs, you must be able to log on to that system over the network. If you do not have those rights or you are not logged on as a user known to the remote system (with the right password), you get an error dialog (`Access is Denied`).

After you select the remote system and get past the security, you can view the security logs on a remote system. Use the Log menu to choose which log to view and the View options to filter the log or find specific events.

Viewing the Event Logs on a remote system is as easy as viewing the logs on your own system.

If you are accessing a network via a slow connection (such as a modem), you might want to select the Low Speed Connection option. When this is selected, Windows NT will not enumerate all the computers on the network into the Select Computer dialog. This can save time if you are using a large network from a dial up modem connection.

Managing the Event Logs

The Event Log can get to be rather large, and on most systems the vast bulk of the information logged is of little use.

To clear the Event Log, use the Clear All Events item from the Log Menu. This clears the Event Log currently being viewed. Because the log might contain useful information, before Windows NT clears the log, it offers you the opportunity to save the log. Because clearing the Event Log is an irrevocable event, Windows NT also asks for further confirmation before actually clearing the log.

24

EVENT VIEWER

To keep the Event Logs from getting too large, you can use the Event Log settings to set a maximum size for each log. Selecting the Log Settings item from the Log menu brings up the Event Log Settings dialog, shown in Figure 24.12.

Figure 24.12.

The Event Log Settings dialog.

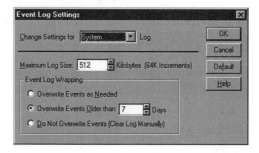

From this dialog you can select the maximum size of each of the three Event Logs. You can also use this dialog to tell Windows NT what to do when the log fills up. You have three choices:

■ Overwrite events as required.

■ Overwrite events over a certain number of days. (The range is from 1 to 365 days.)

■ Do not overwrite events.

If you choose not to overwrite events, you need to manually clear the log in order to get new events logged. Most sites do not need to set this option.

Some users feel that the default font used by Event Viewer to display the logs is unattractive. You can change this font by using the Font option in the Options menu. If you choose a new font, this only affects the main Event Log screen (which you saw in Figure 24.2). Event details are still formatted in the standard system font.

Saving and Restoring Logs

Because of the importance of the Event Logs, you can choose to save them, either when they get full or on a regular basis, rather than just clearing them, as discussed in the previous section.

To save a log, first select it from the Log menu. Then select the Save As item from the Log menu. This brings up the Save As common dialog box, where you supply the filename and the format to save the log.

> **NOTE**
>
> Event Log Filtering has no effect on the log entries saved. Saving a log saves all entries, regardless of any filtering.

You have three choices of how to save the log:

- Event Log format: This allows the saved log to be viewed by the Event Viewer application.
- Text: This saves the file as a simple text file.
- Comma Delimited Text: Similar to Text, this format puts a comma between each field in the saved log.

Saving the log as Comma Delimited Text enables you to consolidate the saved log into a spread sheet or database. Most spread sheet or database programs support importing data from a comma delimited file.

> **NOTE**
>
> If you are going to import a saved Event Log into a spread sheet or database, note that some description fields will contain commas. This might require extra work to ensure that all description fields are properly handled.

If you save an Event Log as an Event Log, you can later view the log using Event Viewer. If you use the Open item from the Log menu, you can open a saved Event Log and view it. A saved log can be filtered or searched in the same way as a live log.

Summary

The Event Viewer application is a great place to start most troubleshooting sessions or look for security violations. It is easy to use and can be very handy. Perhaps the biggest drawback is the quality of the messages that get posted—but this is not the Event Viewer's fault! All in all, this is a key application that any power user must be familiar and comfortable with.

24

EVENT VIEWER

Troubleshooting System Problems

by Pablo Geralnik

IN THIS CHAPTER

CHAPTER 25

Effective troubleshooting starts with preventive maintenance, regular backups, and good record keeping. Information is the key to troubleshooting, whether it's knowing what has changed since your system was last operating well, staying aware of known incompatibilities (software, hardware, or firmware), or staying abreast of the latest maintenance patches for both Windows NT (*Service Packs*, to use Microsoft's terminology) and your applications.

Before I start with the specific steps that you should take to troubleshoot your system, I'll take a step back and look at the whole picture—that is, what steps you can take ahead of time to make troubleshooting (and your life) easier.

Preventive Maintenance

A little preventive maintenance goes a long way. If you keep your system up to date, track any changes you make, and keep abreast of the latest patches, you'll be ahead of the game when it comes to troubleshooting. When a problem does pop up, you'll be prepared because you've heard about it already and know how to correct it. Or you'll know how to get back to a previously working setup. It all starts here.

Emergency Repair Disk

Usually, Windows NT creates the Emergency Repair Disk (ERD) at the end of its installation. If you chose not to create the ERD during installation, you should create it now. The ERD repairs system files and also helps repair the boot sector in case it becomes damaged or corrupted. You should update the ERD every time you make system changes, such as applying a Service Pack.

> **TIP**
>
> It's a good idea to keep two ERDs: one that is current before you update your system and one that you create immediately after updating your system. This helps you go back to a previously working setup if necessary.

To create or update the ERD, just run `rdisk` from the Start menu. You see the screen shown in Figure 25.1. Update Repair Info updates an emergency set of files that Windows NT keeps on your computer, which you can sometimes use for repair if you don't have an ERD. It's a good idea to run this option prior to running Create Repair Disk, which then creates the ERD for you.

FIGURE 25.1.

The Repair Disk Utility.

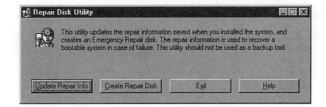

Service Packs

Microsoft periodically releases patches and updates, called Service Packs, for its operating systems. The Service Packs have two main purposes: patching defects in the operating system and adding functionality.

> **NOTE**
>
> Service Packs are cumulative. If you didn't install a previous Service Pack, you don't have to install it before installing the latest Service Pack. For example, you don't have to install Service Packs 1 and 2 before installing Service Pack 3. Installing Service Pack 3 effectively updates your computer.

It's important to be aware of the latest Service Pack, when it was released, what problems it solves, and occasionally what extra functionality it adds. Although Service Pack 1 is almost always a "must install," you don't necessarily have to install the ones that follow on the day of their release unless they solve a specific problem you're experiencing. Practice this discretion because Service Packs could introduce their own glitches to your system. The best way to keep abreast of this information is by monitoring a news source such as a CompuServe forum, an Internet newsgroup, or the appropriate Web site.

> **CAUTION**
>
> You might find that you need to back off from the latest Service Pack to the previous one. Although all that should be required is running the install/update program from the previous Service Pack, you should note a little twist that Microsoft introduced with Service Pack 4 for Windows NT 3.51 in case it applies to Windows NT 4.x as well: Even if you back off to a previous Service Pack, you have to use one of the system files from Service Pack 4 for Windows NT to run properly. Therefore, it's not a complete backoff, but it's still enough to have an almost complete previous configuration.

25

TROUBLESHOOTING SYSTEM PROBLEMS

chkdsk

You should run chkdsk on a monthly basis after completing a backup. Hard disks have a tendency to go bad, and files and directories get corrupted. Running chkdsk monthly keeps your files and directories clean, marks any bad sectors on your disk, and functions as an early warning system. Under Windows NT 4.0, you don't even have to shell out to a cmd window to run chkdsk. See the instructions that follow for two ways to run a graphical version of chkdsk, both of which wind up with the screen you see in Figure 25.2.

FIGURE 25.2.

The chkdsk *tool.*

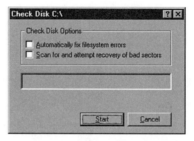

You should remember a couple of points before running chkdsk. First, if you have checked the options to "Automatically fix file system errors" and "Scan for and attempt recovery of bad sectors" (which you should for chkdsk to be effective), chkdsk needs exclusive access to the drive on which you've loaded Windows NT 4.0. In this instance, you are prompted to run chkdsk the next time you restart your computer. Choose Yes and restart your computer. You can run chkdsk on drives other than your system drive without rebooting. Second, running chkdsk can be a time-consuming process. The larger your hard drives, the more time chkdsk will take. The more problems that need to be fixed, the longer chkdsk will take. Keep this in mind so that you can schedule chkdsk during an "off-peak" period.

> **NOTE**
>
> You'll find that Windows NT 4.0, like Windows 95, gives you multiple ways to do the same thing. As you become more familiar with the new look of the operating system, you'll probably find your preferred method for most tasks.

The following lists show two ways to run the graphical version of chkdsk. Starting from My Computer, perform the following steps:

1. Double-click My Computer.
2. Single-click the disk you want to check.
3. From the File menu, choose Properties.

4. Select the Tools tab.

5. Select Check Now.

6. Select the options you want.

7. Select Start to run chkdsk.

Starting from the Start button, perform the following steps:

1. From the Start menu, choose Programs.

2. Choose Administrative Tools.

3. Select Disk Administrator.

4. Single-click the disk you want to check.

5. From the Tools menu, choose Properties.

6. Select the Tools tab.

7. Select Check Now.

8. Select the options you want.

9. Select Start to run chkdsk.

TIP

You can set up chkdsk to run automatically each month by using Windows NT's built-in scheduler, AT. Type AT /? in a cmd window to see how to use this potentially powerful tool, or look up AT in the Help menu and Windows NT Commands book.

Defragmentation

Defragmentation is included here because of the performance boost that a defragmented disk can give your system. As your disk becomes more fragmented, read and write actions to disk take longer to complete. The current version of Windows NT 4.0 does not have a built-in defragmentation utility, but third-party utilities are available.

Disk Space

Nowadays, disk drives are getting larger and cheaper, which is good, considering how huge applications and operating systems are becoming. The bad part is that most of us still have a tendency to save old programs, letters, recipes, and all sorts of junk on our hard disks. It's important to maintain as clean a system as possible. You should make monthly maintenance a regular procedure to clean out the old files. Filling a disk to capacity can result in loss of data, inability to save current work, and even (rarely) the inability to boot your computer.

Backup

Regular backups should not be a theory. Backups should be an important part of your everyday life. Murphy is waiting for that one day when you're too rushed to do a backup, and then, watch out! That said, you have a number of ways to approach backups. Optimally, you should back up your entire system (all hard drives, partitions, and so on). This can be a time-consuming process, but it enables you to restore your system in its entirety in case of a major problem.

When you're not doing a full backup, what should you back up? Back up data and your Windows NT setup (that is, whatever directory you have Windows NT installed in, such as `\Windows` or `\Winnt40`). As long as you have the original installation disks or CDs, you don't have as compelling a reason to back up all your programs and executables because you can easily reload them. Although you should back up all those important letters and reports you spent hours working on, you can get by without backing up Word or Excel on a daily basis. Although you can reinstall Windows NT, keeping backups of the Windows NT setup (and Registry) saves you from reconfiguring your setup as you like it. In addition, many applications copy additional files (for example, DLLs or INIs) to your Windows `system` or `system32` directories. If this directory isn't backed up, you might find yourself reinstalling many applications and resetting your preferences for how you like them to appear.

Record Keeping

Detailed record keeping helps you troubleshoot your system. It helps you with upgrades. It helps you in dealing with vendors. It helps you in dealing with insurance. Record keeping helps you. To that end, you should make and update a record of the computer's makeup, including a list of all major components (for example, the internal modem installed in your computer) as the computer is updated. You should note all pertinent information, such as the manufacturer's name, date purchased, BIOS and other revision, drivers installed, and so on.

Remember that troubleshooting is the act of narrowing down all possible causes of a problem to the actual cause of the particular problem you are experiencing. This means knowing (or discovering) all the possible causes of a particular problem and eliminating them one by one until you've solved your problem.

Don't forget the last integral part of troubleshooting: noting both the problem and its ultimate resolution. This can help you tremendously if you encounter future difficulties of a similar nature.

Your record keeping method doesn't have to be high-tech either. A simple three-ring binder will do. This enables you to add pages as necessary, plus rearrange your notes by type of problem or other categories. The other advantage to this low-tech solution is availability. If you are having trouble accessing your computer, any notes you keep on the computer will also be inaccessible. However, keeping a copy of your records on your computer is also a good idea. If you use almost any word processing program, doing a text search for a specific word or problem is that much easier.

Startup

Problems that occur upon startup can be the most irritating. After all, you haven't done anything yet and already you're having problems. Luckily, not every problem is major, and some can be solved with a simple reboot. Other problems might require more action on your part. Both are covered here.

General Issues

Problems that occur at startup range from the simple to the sublime. It's possible to spend hours troubleshooting what turns out to be a loose cable, or you might decide in minutes that the problem is best resolved by a reinstall of Windows NT. In this section, I mention the most common issues that occur. Two startup problems, the blue screen of death and networking issues, are covered in later sections of this chapter.

If you're having problems from the beginning, it's important to start with the basics:

- Is your computer plugged in?
- Is your computer turned on?
- Is the monitor turned on?
- Is the surge protector turned on?
- Are any peripherals turned on?

Yes, these are all simple and obvious items. Strangely enough, they continue to be overlooked, causing us to get gray hairs faster than necessary. If you haven't checked all of these areas, you're really not ready to move on yet.

NOTE

It's especially important to check these simple items when you share a computer with someone else. For example, when my computer is at the "safe to shutdown" screen, I power off the computer and monitor (and any attached peripherals such as my external modem), but I leave on the surge protector. The other person who uses my computer just shuts off the surge protector at this stage. Depending on who uses the computer last and next, we frequently fumble with on/off switches to power up. Kids, dogs, and vacuums also have a tendency to unplug equipment. You'd hate to open your computer only to discover that the surge protector is turned off.

When Windows NT first boots, you should see a menu that has at least two options: Windows NT 4 Workstation and Windows NT 4 Workstation [VGA]. If your system is multiboot, you see an MS-DOS option as well.

> **TIP**
>
> I recommend keeping at least a 200MB DOS partition. If everything else fails and you need to reinstall or partially reinstall Windows NT, having a DOS partition makes installation quite simple. It enables you to boot to DOS in order set up a new "temporary" Windows NT that can read your NTFS partitions. If your system was only NTFS, you wouldn't have this capability. The total of 200MB was simply derived from approximately 50MB for the installation files, 5MB for DOS, and approximately 122MB for Windows NT, which leaves you a little slack for diagnostic tools as well.

> **NOTE**
>
> You can change the menu titles of the startup screen to make them more meaningful by editing boot.ini, which is located on the root of your boot partition. This file's attributes are hidden and read-only. You must remove the read-only attribute in order to save any changes you make to the file. Don't forget to reset this attribute when you are done.

If you have a simple setup with no profiles defined and NT hangs on the blue startup screen (not the blue screen of death!), take the following steps to resolve the problem:

1. Shut down your computer.
2. Restart your computer.
3. When the menu appears, choose the Windows NT 4 Workstation [VGA] option.

Performing these steps boots Windows NT with the minimal drivers needed to get Windows NT up and running; it's not simply an option to use VGA mode to eliminate display driver problems. If Windows NT still refuses to finish booting, you probably have a more serious problem than you can resolve with a quick fix. Your options at this point are to do either a full install (to a new directory) or a partial reinstall (choose the Upgrade option and use the current directory) of Windows NT. If the partial install fails, try a full install. If both fail, you probably have hardware problems. If you're not using approved hardware, you must switch the inappropriate parts. If you're using approved hardware, you probably need to start by formatting your hard disk and proceed with a fresh install of Windows NT.

If you can log in from here, good. Your next step is to check Event Viewer (Start|Programs| Administrative Tools|Event Viewer) to see which error messages are listed. If you've recently added a new device to your computer or added a new program to your Startup folder, check whether any messages in Event Viewer reference these devices or programs. If so, you might want to disable the device or remove the program from your Startup folder, reboot, and try to log in under the regular Windows NT setup.

> **TIP**
>
> It's a good idea to clean out the Event Viewer every month. Save the log information if you continuously have trouble with your system. Otherwise, delete the log. If you let the log get too full and you start encountering difficulties, Windows NT cannot write the latest errors to the log, which makes troubleshooting that much more difficult.

> **TIP**
>
> I've never been a big fan of keeping anything in the Startup folder (or the Startup group in previous versions of Windows). Loading programs in the Startup folder (or group) takes more system resources than starting them manually. Additional problems occur when programs in the Startup folder (or group) depend on other services that haven't yet started. For some reason, there seems to be a greater chance of a "memory leak" when you load programs in the Startup folder (or group) as opposed to starting them manually.

If you've just changed your video driver, don't despair if your monitor goes blank after Windows NT displays the blue startup screen. Allow Windows NT to finish loading (wait a few minutes). Even though you can't see anything, you can run through the shutdown steps to cleanly reboot your system, choose the VGA startup mode, and change your video driver, as illustrated by the following instructions:

1. Press Enter to clear the Service failed to start message.

2. Press Ctrl+Alt+Del to bring up the login screen.

3. Press Alt+S to choose Shutdown.

4. Press Enter and wait a minute. If your computer doesn't reboot, press Enter again. (Alt+S displays the menu with the choices of Shutdown or Shutdown and Restart, and the default is whatever you chose the last time. If your last choice was Shutdown and Restart, pressing Enter forces a reboot. If your last choice was Shutdown, the first time you press Enter, Windows NT shuts down and displays the "It is now safe to turn off your computer" dialog, and Restart is the default choice if you press Enter.)

Hardware Profile

After you've successfully installed Windows NT, copy the Original Configuration profile and don't use it; that is, copy the Original Configuration, name it something such as everyday, and work with the everyday profile. (Right-click My Computer, select Properties, select the Hardware Profiles tab, and then choose the Copy button.) You should highlight your everyday profile and move it to the top of the list to use it by default. (See Figure 25.3.)

FIGURE 25.3.

The Hardware Profiles property sheet.

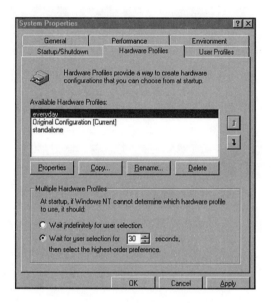

If your computer fails to start up properly, use the Original Configuration profile. If this works, edit your everyday profile to remove any new services or devices that you recently added. Then, boot with your everyday profile. You might have to reboot a number of times, going back and forth between the everyday and Original Configuration profiles until you've identified the service or device that is causing your problem. An easy way to disable devices for your everyday (or other) profile is to use Control Panel. Choose Devices. Then select the device you want to disable and choose HW Profiles…. You can then select whether to enable or disable the device for any of your profiles. (See Figure 25.4.)

TIP

Prior to adding a new device or service to your computer, especially one that requires a reboot, copy your current profile (which should be everyday if you follow the preceding advice) to something such as backoff. That way, if your computer fails to load Windows NT after a reboot, you can revert back to your original everyday configuration (now called backoff) and remove the offending device or service.

FIGURE 25.4.

The Device Profile dialog.

Last Known Good Configuration

Whenever you successfully log in to Windows NT, your configuration at the time of login is "remembered" by Windows NT. If you have trouble when you attempt to log in, especially after installing new drivers or software, press the spacebar at bootup and choose "Last known good configuration." This should restore your system to its state prior to the addition of the new drivers.

Personally, I don't like this method because I've never found it to be consistent. An earlier version of Windows NT had a bug: If you chose "Last known good configuration," it returned your system to its state at the time you originally installed Windows NT. That's a little too far back for my taste.

TIP

I recommend adding the /SOS switch to your boot.ini file for all your menu choices. Usually when Windows NT is loading, you see the blue screen, the top line of which reads Microsoft Windows NT and the build number. On the second line, you see a message about the number of processors and the amount of memory on your system. On the third line, as Windows NT is loading, you see a bunch of dots scrolling across the screen. Each of these dots represents a service that is loading. Using the /sos screen lists the services as they load, instead of representing them with a dot. If Windows NT fails to finish loading, you can sometimes spot at which service it is failing. You can then reboot and attempt to replace the "bad" file or DLL with the latest version.

25

TROUBLESHOOTING SYSTEM PROBLEMS

Networking

There are usually two immediate signs that networking isn't functioning: Either you get a message upon bootup that a service failed to start, or upon login you receive a message that a domain controller could not be contacted.

The first place to start with networking problems is the physical level:

1. Check the patch cable going into your network card at both the workstation and server.
2. Check the patch cable from your cable closet to the hub or concentrator being used.
3. Check that your network card is firmly seated.
4. Check the status of the link indicator light at your network hub and on your network card.

If these items are fine, it's time to move on to the next steps.

Open the Event Viewer (Start|Programs|Administrative Tools|Event Viewer). Press the F5 key to refresh the screen. Then, find the latest (time/date) blue information message that says EventLog, which should be near the top of the screen. This is the last time your computer booted and the Event Log was started. Work your way up from here and look for the first red STOP message. Double-click this message to open it. If the first problem listed is with your network card, try reseating it. If that doesn't help, try replacing it. If the network card has a problem, none of the other network services will start and you'll receive error messages for all of them.

One message that I've frequently encountered is `Elnk3` with an event code of `5012`. Double-clicking this message and reading the description box informs me `Elnk31 : The I/O base address supplied does not match the jumpers on the adapter.` (See Figure 25.5.) I receive this same message whether the network card has stopped working or whether a laptop computer I'm using is started when it's not docked. As you can see, the message description is merely a pointer to what area you should start checking first; it won't necessarily give you the exact cause of the problem.

If Event Viewer doesn't offer any help—that is, all systems started properly—check whether the domain server you tried to log in to is running. (You don't want to start changing all your settings just to discover that the network is down.) If the domain server is running, make sure you chose to log in to the domain and not to your local computer account. If the domain server is running and you attempted to log in to it and not to your local account, make sure you typed in your domain password correctly.

> **NOTE**
>
> Usernames are not case-sensitive, but passwords are. Although Pablo, pablo, and PABLO are all the same user to the domain, Password, password, and PASSWORD appear as three different passwords.

FIGURE 25.5.

The detailed screen for the Elnk31 *message.*

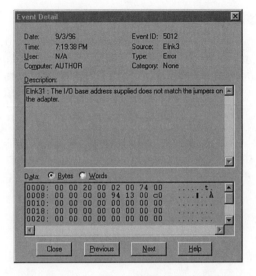

If you tried all the steps outlined so far in this section, it's time to check the network settings for your computer. You can find all the network settings information by right-clicking Network Neighborhood and choosing Properties. The five property tabs are Identification, Services, Protocols, Adapters, and Bindings. (See Figure 25.6.) I'll discuss all of these.

FIGURE 25.6.

The Network Neighborhood properties sheets.

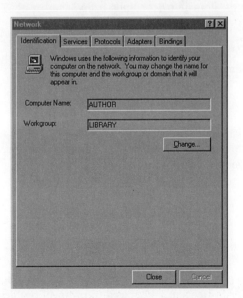

Identification

In order to have access to the selected domain, the administrator of the domain must add your computer name to the domain. If you've changed your computer name, your computer might not be recognized by the domain controller that is authenticating your login. You must select the Change button and rename your computer to its original name.

If you receive a message about a "trust" problem, the easiest way to resolve this is with the following procedure:

1. Have the network administrator delete your computer name from the domain.
2. From the Identification tab, select the Change button.
3. Make yourself a member of a workgroup (using any name) instead of the currently selected domain.
4. Reboot.
5. Have the network administrator add your computer name to the domain.
6. Log in to your local computer account.
7. Right-click Network Neighborhood and choose Properties.
8. Select the Identification tab.
9. Select the Change button.
10. Rejoin the domain by changing from Member of Workgroup to Member of Domain.
11. Choose OK.

If all network connections and properties are fine, you should receive a message welcoming you to the domain.

Services

On the Services tab (see Figure 25.7), check that you've got the Computer Browser, Server, and Workstation services installed. You need these if you'll be connecting to a Windows NT network. If you'll be connecting to a NetWare network, you should have the Client Services for NetWare service installed. These services are not configured from this tab.

Protocols

What protocols are listed? What protocols are being used? TCP/IP (used for most internetworking) or IPX (Novell default) are the most frequently used. Both can be running at the same time, although you generally need only one protocol to connect to a particular network. Networking problems can frequently be traced to protocol problems. The following sections outline some of these issues. (See Figure 25.8.)

FIGURE 25.7.

The Services tab.

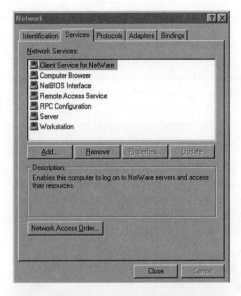

FIGURE 25.8.

The Protocols tab.

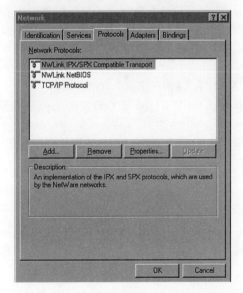

TCP/IP Protocol

If you highlight TCP/IP Protocol and select the Properties tab, you see a properties sheet with four more tabs. You can resolve most TCP/IP problems with either the IP Address tab or the WINS Address tab because many problems are caused by incorrectly entering IP address information.

25

TROUBLESHOOTING
SYSTEM PROBLEMS

On the IP Address tab, you can either specify an IP address or obtain an IP address from a DHCP server.

Select Obtain an IP Address from a DHCP Server, and then open a cmd window (Start|Run|cmd) and type ipconfig. This should list your currently assigned IP address, subnet mask, and default gateway. Regardless of whether any information is listed, type ipconfig /renew. This releases your current IP address (if you have one) and acquires an IP address. If you're IP address is released but no new address is obtained, you're not communicating with the DHCP server. If that's the case, follow the rest of the steps in this section.

If you select Specify an IP Address, you must ensure that all the addresses you specified for IP Address, Subnet Mask, and Default Gateway are correct. If you're off by one number or you transpose any numbers, you will experience networking problems. A simple way to test your connection is with the ping utility. In a cmd window (Start|Run|cmd), type ping 127.0.0.1. You should receive four replies to yourself with 32 bytes of information. Next, ping the address of the server you're trying to connect to. If a reply is received, this part of your networking is fine. If the ping times out, recheck the IP information you've entered and follow the rest of the steps in this section.

If the IP address information is correct, select the WINS Address tab. Check the information that's entered for Primary WINS Server and Secondary WINS Server. As with the IP Address tab, you want to make sure that all the information here is entered correctly.

NWLink IPX/SPX Compatible Transport

Selecting properties for NWLink IPX/SPX Compatible Transport displays a property sheet with only one tab. Although IPX/SPX is most frequently used for connecting to a Novell NetWare network, it's possible to run a Windows NT network on IPX/SPX as well. By default, the Frame Type is set to Auto Detect. If you have trouble connecting to an IPX/SPX network, ask the network administrator which frame type is used on the server or domain you want to connect to. Then, switch from Auto Detect to that frame type. Do not change the Network Number unless told to do so by the network administrator.

> **NOTE**
>
> Auto Detect does not work exactly as it sounds. If the network is running multiple frame types, Auto Detect selects the first frame type it finds. If you want to connect to a server running the 802.2 frame type, but Auto Detect first found an 802.3 frame from a different server on the network, it tries to use 802.3 for your connections.

Adapters

The Adapters tab lists the network cards installed in your computer. Selecting the tab and choosing Properties (see Figure 25.9) displays a screen that lists the I/O Port Address, Interrupt Number (IRQ), and Transceiver Type. Make sure the values listed match what you've set on your network card either by directly setting jumpers on the card or by running the software setup that most newer cards include.

FIGURE 25.9.

Properties for the network card from the Adapters tab.

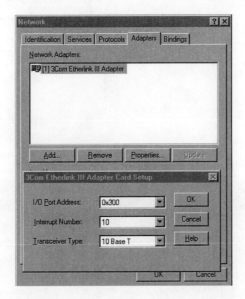

If you're using a plug-and-play card, try disabling plug-and-play and manually setting the values. Unfortunately, plug-and-play technology still hasn't matured to the point where plug-and-play devices won't conflict with each other or with other devices in the computer. Setting the values manually eliminates another possible area of conflict.

Bindings

The Bindings tab lists the relationships between the different network services for your computer. For example, if you choose to Show Bindings for All Adapters, you see all the protocols you've installed.

Your main objective is to make sure no service has a red circle through it, which marks it as disabled. (See Figure 25.10.) If any services are disabled, highlight them and choose the Enable button. Then, select OK and reboot your computer.

FIGURE 25.10.

The Bindings tab with Client Services for NetWare disabled.

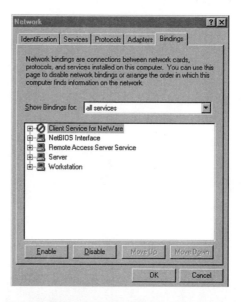

TIP

Having more protocols and services installed than you actually use slows down your computer. For example, if you're on a TCP/IP network, you have no reason to install IPX/SPX, which slows down your computer and uses more resources. However, if you connect at different times to different networks, you might want to install everything but only enable the services you use. This saves you time in installing and removing services and protocols.

Security and Access

It's important to create a copy of the administrative account to use in case of emergency. You never want to keep only one administrative account because if you can't use that account—for example, you forget the password—you cannot proceed without performing at least a partial reinstall of Windows NT. Creating a backup of the administrator account is a simple task. From the Start menu, choose Programs|Administrative Tools|User Manager. In User Manager, simply highlight Administrator and press F8. You are prompted for the username and associated information for this copy.

NOTE

If you are completely locked out of your system and unable to log in with any user name and password, partially reinstalling Windows NT creates a new administrative account and allows you to access your computer.

NOTE

On notebook computers, some of the letters double as numbers. If you're using a notebook, make sure you turn off the Num Lock. Otherwise, you might think that you're typing `hello` for your password while you're actually typing `he336`. The same applies to your Caps Lock key. Make sure it hasn't been turned on by default.

TIP

If you are the only person who uses your computer and you have absolutely no security concerns, the following trick automatically logs in to Windows NT without requiring you to enter a user name and password:

1. Start `REGEDT32.EXE`.
2. Choose the `HKEY_LOCAL_MACHINE` on the Local Machine window.
3. Work your way down the Registry tree to `HKEY_LOCAL_MACHINE\` `SOFTWARE\Microsoft\WindowsNT\CurrentVersion\Winlogon`.
4. You should see values for `DefaultDomainName` (your computer name) and `DefaultUserName` (your normal login account name). If the value for `DefaultUserName` is not the name you want to use for autologin, edit this value with the correct user name.
5. Next, you must add a key for the password. From the Edit menu, choose Add Value. In the Value Name field, type `DefaultPassword`.
6. The Data Type is `REG_SZ`.
7. Enter your password in the String field.
8. Next, you must add one more key to enable the automatic login. From the Edit menu, choose Add Value. For Value, enter `AutoAdminLogon`.
9. The Data Type is again `REG_SZ`.
10. In the string field, enter `1`.
11. Exit `REGEDT32`.
12. Exit Windows NT.

When you restart your computer, Windows NT automatically logs you in.

As an administrator, you have access to anything on your computer. Occasionally, your access to files or directories might be denied, or a program might tell you that you don't have sufficient rights. This is frequently a physical drive problem.

Another symptom of physical problems is a file or directory that is locked and does not allow you to copy, rename, move, or delete it. You can most easily fix these kinds of problems by running chkdsk on your hard drive. If the file or directory is important, you might want to run a backup first to try to salvage some information from this file. This might require third-party software if the file or directory is damaged.

If you have problems accessing a file or directory, right-click the problem directory or file, select Properties, and then choose the Security tab. (See Figure 25.11.) Click the Ownership button and take ownership of the problem directory or file.

FIGURE 25.11.

The Security tab for a directory.

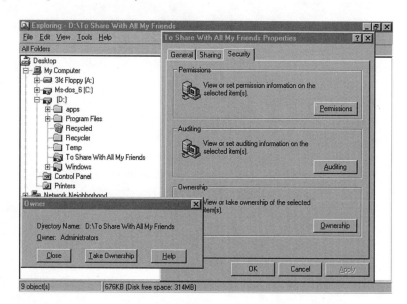

You can also select the Permissions tab and make sure you have all the appropriate rights. Sometimes, especially after a system crash, the rights to your files or directories might change. Checking permissions allows you to reset the rights as necessary.

Printing

As with all types of problems, it's important to start with the simple things and check the physical side first:

- Is the printer on?
- Are the cables attached?
- Is the printer online?
- Does the printer have paper?

Most printers allow you to print a diagnostic page. Read the instructions for your printer and print a diagnostic page to make sure everything is fine at the printer itself. Read the information the printer gives about itself. Check that the memory listed is correct; does it match what's set for the printer properties? Is the printer set to parallel (the way most home printers are usually set) or serial? After a power outage, one of my printers reset itself to serial instead of parallel. Printing a test page helped resolve this problem.

After you've checked all the physical settings and verified that the information on the test page matches what you've set under printer properties, you have one last step before you move on: Turn the printer off and then back on. It's amazing how many problems this simple step solves.

Choose Properties and select Print Test Page. (See Figure 25.12 for the Printer Properties sheet.) If this fails to work, Windows NT displays a printing troubleshooting wizard that is pretty thorough. I'm not going to outline its steps here. The only thing I would change is the order of one step. After you check the various settings, the troubleshooting wizard suggests removing and reinstalling the printer. I think you should reinstall the printer after you've checked all the physical settings and the initial printer properties. This gives you a fresh start and lets you make sure you know what values are set from the beginning.

FIGURE 25.12.

The Printer Properties page.

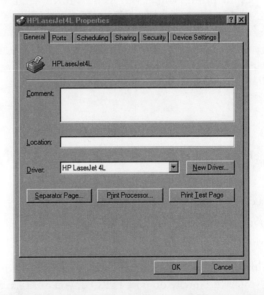

25

TROUBLESHOOTING SYSTEM PROBLEMS

NOTE

To install printers, simply double-click My Computer, double-click the Printers folder, and then double-click the Add Printer icon. An installation wizard guides you through the complete installation process.

After you've finished the preceding steps, you should at least be able to print a test page. If you still cannot do so, make sure that you are logged in as an administrator. Then, open Explorer, and check your rights to the spool directory and its subdirectories. This directory is located under your Windows NT install (usually either \Windows or \Winnt40) in the \system32 directory. Right-click the spool directory to display its properties. Select the Security tab. Click the Permissions button. As an administrator, your access should be set to Full Control. If it isn't, change the rights and make sure to select the Replace Permissions on Subdirectories checkbox. Then, select OK to apply these rights.

> **NOTE**
>
> While you're on the Security tab, check that the Everyone group has Read access, which is sufficient for regular access to the printer for all users.

If the test page printed correctly, try printing with your application. If printing works but you're getting a lot of garbage, the two main causes to check are the printer drivers and the printer memory. Does the printer come with its own drivers? For example, many Hewlett-Packard printers come with their own driver disks. If these disks are Windows NT compatible, they should be installed according to the manufacturer's instructions. If you've got the latest drivers available, try printing a small graphics file. If this works, you might simply be overflowing the printer's memory. If that's the case, your choice is to either get more memory for your printer or use smaller or less graphic- or code-intensive files.

RAS

As with other devices, the first step is to check the physical connections:

- Is the modem on?
- Is it securely attached?
- Is it connected to the right port?
- Do you have the right port set?

With Windows NT, you also have to check that you're not sharing interrupts (IRQs). For example, if you have a mouse on port 1 IRQ 4, you can't have your modem use IRQ 4 as well (even though earlier versions of Windows might have allowed this).

Installing RAS is a simple process, and just like installing a printer, you might be best off deleting the current setup and starting fresh. Running the RAS/Dial-Up Networking program is relatively painless, and it usually finds your modem, eliminating most problems from the start and ensuring that the connection you're establishing is valid.

If you've already tried deleting and reinstalling RAS, you have a few other items you can check.

First, make sure that any codes that you need to dial (area codes, codes to access outside lines, and so on) are correctly entered under Control Panel|Modems|Dialing Properties.

Next, make sure that the correct port is used. When you install RAS, it allows you to set up the modem with multiple ports. To narrow down any problems, remove modems on ports you are not using from Control Panel|Modems. The next step is to lower the Maximum (connection) speed by choosing the modem properties General tab, which is also found in Control Panel|Modems. The last item to check in this area is on the Connection tab by selecting the Advanced button. Under Use Flow Control are options to use either Hardware or Software. The default is to use Hardware flow control, but some older programs might require you to use Software flow control. (See Figure 25.13.)

FIGURE 25.13.

The Advanced Connection Settings screen.

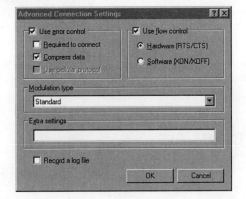

Next, move to the phonebook entries. Under the Phonebook Entry properties (My Computer|Dial Up Networking|More|Edit Entry and Modem Properties), check the Server tab. If you're using a PPP or SLIP connection with TCP/IP as the network protocol, it's important to check the TCP/IP Settings. (See Figure 25.14.) When dialing into most online services such as CompuServe or the Microsoft Network, you should have your PPC TCP/IP Settings set to Server Assigned IP Address. Whether you enter a name server address depends on the service you are using. Entering the wrong address gets you almost to the point of connection but continuously hangs up. Therefore, it's important to check any IP addresses for accuracy.

The Script tab gives you a number of options that are useful for troubleshooting. If you are consistently able to dial in but get disconnected without logging in, select Pop Up a Terminal Window After Dialing. When your connection is made, a terminal window pops up, allowing you to manually enter your name and password for the system you're trying to access. This enables you to check whether the problem is with the script or the name and password combination you are using.

FIGURE 25.14.

*The PPP TCP/IP
Settings screen.*

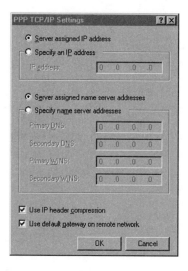

The last thing to check is the Security tab. Select Accept Any Authentication Including Clear Text. You should only use the other options when instructed by the administrator of the system you are calling.

Applications

Start this off with the simple stuff: If your application attempts to directly access hardware, it won't run under Windows NT. This is the problem that many DOS-based games experience. Your only solution in this case is to use a dual-boot system with at least one DOS partition to which you can boot and run these applications.

Applications that require *dongles* work with Windows NT, but you must get drivers specific to Windows NT. Dongles are devices that are physically attached to the computer, frequently via the parallel port, and are used for extra security. Your applications do not work with dongles that are using DOS, Windows 3.1, or Windows for Workgroup drivers. Contact the dongle manufacturer for Windows NT drivers and compatibility issues.

If your application appears to be hung, bring up Task Manager (press Ctrl+Alt+Del and select Task Manager), and choose the Applications tab to list the currently running applications and their status (Running or Not Responding). (See Figure 25.15.) If your application is listed as Not Responding, select it and choose End Task to terminate it.

Before attempting to run or install a new application, you should check that it is compatible with Windows NT. As mentioned previously, Windows NT does not allow applications that attempt to directly access the hardware to run. Installing incompatible applications might also overwrite newer DLLs, which can cause other programs to malfunction. If you're installing an application that you're unsure of, it's best to either take a snapshot of your Windows directories to note file dates and sizes or use an installer program that keeps track of changes made to your system by the program installation. In case of a problem, this allows you to restore your system to its previous configuration.

FIGURE 25.15.

The Task Manager screen.

Some applications require or look for specific settings in the `autoexec.bat` or `config.sys` files. Windows NT doesn't use these files but provides an `autoexec.nt` or `config.nt` for compatibility. (You can find these files in `\Windows_root\system32`.) For example, if your application requires a `files=100` statement in `config.sys`, you add this statement to `config.nt`. If you have multiple applications of this sort, you can set up each of them to run from a PIF file and specify an `autoexec.nt` and a `config.nt` for each. (Naturally, you use a different name for each `autoexec.nt` and `config.nt`.)

If you're still having trouble with older applications, you could try running them from a PIF file that specifies using `command.com` instead of the default `cmd.exe` that Windows NT uses.

The Blue Screen of Death

The Blue Screen of Death (BSOD) is what you see when Windows NT crashes. It's not pretty and it can be hard to decipher, but with a little luck you'll either avoid it entirely or see it so infrequently as to regard it as a novelty.

You can avoid seeing the BSOD (unless there are very major problems) by choosing to automatically reboot your computer when this occurs (Control Panel, System Properties, Startup/Shutdown, "Automatically reboot" check box), but I don't recommend this. Seeing the error, when it occurs, helps you troubleshoot more effectively. With some of the more minor BSODs, seeing the BSOD can be an early warning of a problem, which you might miss if you've set your computer to automatically reboot.

General Issues

When you get a BSOD, it's important to record some of the information listed. The first line of your screen has a STOP message and code, followed by four additional code parameters. The second line lists a STOP state and is followed by a short message that points to the cause of the problem. It's important to record both of these lines to help troubleshoot this problem now and keep track of problems for the future. You see one more line of "clear" text and code. Underneath this are two columns of memory address and driver information, some of which might be useful to you; and, lastly, you find a message from Windows NT letting you know that a crash has occurred. The Windows NT Resource Kit is a good source of information for what many of the error codes mean. Unfortunately, it's not as helpful in telling you what to do with the information (and being told to see the system administrator doesn't help much when you are the system administrator!).

How do you solve most BSODs? If it's an occasional problem or a fluke, a simple reboot will do. If the issue is more persistent, you need to track down what is causing the BSOD, whether it's a hardware or software issue.

> **NOTE**
>
> How can you tell whether a BSOD is persistent or a fluke? Check how frequently it's occurring. If a reboot brings back the BSOD, you've got a problem. If your computer crashes more than once a month, I'd be concerned. If the problem is less frequent than that, there's a chance that the error message, and what to do, is covered in section "The Most Frequent BSODs," later in this chapter.

Using hardware that's on the Hardware Compatibility List should help to keep BSODs down. Unfortunately, this is not a hard and fast rule. There are some computer manufacturers whose equipment I'd avoid, if at all possible, even though they are listed on the Hardware Compatibility List. Using unapproved hardware would seem to increase the possibility of problems. As I've mentioned, even with approved equipment, you're not out of the woods. For example, early BIOS revisions of the Adaptec 2940 controller cards had problems with Windows NT 3.5/3.51.

It was some time before a stable version of the software driver for the Adaptec 2940 controller was released. Of course, this makes the point that software drivers are another possible cause of BSODs. The code and message you receive when you get a BSOD helps you track this as a cause.

The Most Frequent BSODs

What are the most frequent causes of BSODs? My list is based on personal experience and not a scientifically conducted survey.

```
STOP:  0x0000007b (4 code parameters)
INACCESSIBLE_BOOT_DEVICE
```

Virus alert! If you see this message, get the latest virus-checking software (fast!) and run it against your computer. If you're using the FAT file system on your boot partition, boot from a write-protected DOS boot floppy disk and scan or clean your computer. If you are using the NTFS file system and are unable to boot into Windows NT, you also need to boot from a write-protected DOS boot floppy disk. You then have to run FDISK /MBR, which overwrites the boot record (and removes any boot sector virus). Naturally, because running FDISK /MBR overwrites the boot sector, Windows NT does not boot. You have to perform a partial reinstall of Windows NT, choosing repair instead of the full install and then choosing to repair the boot sector.

> **NOTE**
>
> As the resource kit states, this error can also be caused by repartitioning the system partition or by installing a new SCSI adapter or disk controller. If you've repartitioned the system partition, you must perform a partial install of Windows NT. If you've added a new SCSI adapter or disk controller, check that you have the latest Windows NT drivers for the new device. If you've installed a new driver for a current SCSI adapter or disk controller, you might actually have to return to a previous revision of the driver to get your system working again.

```
STOP:  0x0000007D (4 code parameters)
INSTALL_MORE_MEMORY
```

I've seen this message more often than I would expect, considering that our current base system has 36MB of RAM. Every instance where this message was received was resolved by either securing a loose memory chip or replacing a bad memory chip. Sometimes, Windows NT actually does give you a clear message.

```
STOP:  0x0000007F (4 code parameters)
UNEXPECTED_KERNEL_MODE_TRAP
```

Here's an error that I've been told should never happen because of how Windows NT handles memory. Nice theory. Bugs in applications can cause this to happen. The only thing I've found that you can do is write down what was occurring when this happened (the application that was running and other applications that were open and running in the background) and reboot. If you can reproduce this by following the same steps that first caused this crash, congratulations! You've got a winner to call Microsoft about. If you can't reproduce it, consider this a fluke in how Windows NT handled a problem.

```
STOP:  0x0000000A (4 code parameters)
IRQL_NOT_LESS_EQUAL
```

Here's an error that I've seen occur with some regularity on various systems. The Windows NT Resource Kit states that "This is usually caused by drivers using improper addresses." With this message, the four code parameters can be useful to you. If the second parameter is not `0x00000002`, you can compare the value of the fourth parameter with the list of codes and drivers that are listed on your screen. A matching code identifies the offending driver, which can be updated (if an update is available) or checked for corruption. If this message occurs frequently, the other step that works is backing up, reformatting the hard drive, and reinstalling Windows NT (and other applications) fresh. Reinstalling Windows NT over the existing setup did not seem to cure this problem.

```
STOP:  0x0000001E (4 code parameters)
KMODE_EXCEPTION_NOT_HANDLED
```

Here's another error that I've seen occur with some regularity on various systems. The four code parameters can also be useful to you with this message. Compare the value of the second parameter with the list of codes and drivers that are listed on your screen. A matching code identifies the offending driver, which can be updated (if an update is available) or checked for corruption.

```
STOP:  0x00000023 (4 code parameters)
FAT_FILE_SYSTEM
```

```
STOP:  0x00000024 (4 code parameters)
NTFS_FILE_SYSTEM
```

Both of these messages indicate problems with the file system. As long as your hard drive is not in horrible shape, you can usually resolve these messages by rebooting and running chkdsk. If chkdsk doesn't resolve this problem, you might be forced to reformat your hard disk and start over. If the format does not work, it's time to get a new hard disk. Don't despair; you'll probably be able to buy a much larger hard disk for less than you paid for your current one.

Summary

Unless you have the "Mr. Fixit" attitude, troubleshooting usually won't be a pleasant experience. Remember to keep a cool head. Hopefully, the steps outlined in this chapter will help you plan for problems before they occur, deal with them as they occur, and recover from them when you're done. Problems will never be avoided completely, but it is possible to minimize their impact on your daily routine.

VII
PART

The Future of
Windows NT

The Future of NT, Cairo, and Beyond

by Howard M. Swope III

IN THIS CHAPTER

With the release of Windows NT 4 comes much speculation about the future of NT. Cairo was the original code name for the next major revision of NT after 3.5 and was slated to ship in the first half of 1995. The key theme to the original Cairo vision was object orientation, and its key feature was to be an object-oriented file system. However, the industry's changing demands have altered the NT evolution, and Cairo was not released as a single product.

Several of the key Cairo technologies have come out in release 4, while others are being held over until release 5. The object-oriented file system was put on the back burner, while other pressing issues such as the new interface, mobile computing features, distributed component technologies, and Internet integration were pushed to the front by user demand. In fact, Cairo has become more of a vision, incorporating a set of technologies than an actual product. Now it appears that smaller releases of key enhancements will be seen over time, until the version 5 Cairo vision has been reached.

This is reflective of the annuity upgrade model that has been gaining favor among developers. In the annuity upgrade model, you pay a fee and then receive or download smaller upgrades, as opposed to purchasing a major revision release all at once. Microsoft has been offering these types of programs to its developers and through service pack upgrades for some time. The annuity model is more dynamic and better able to provide the end user with timely enhancements and fixes over a period of time.

The remaining sections of the chapter discuss technologies and features that will be released in NT as part of the evolving Cairo vision. The chapter also touches on some of the influences affecting the Cairo evolution and poses some thoughts as to the future of NT. Most of these enhancements are still on the drawing board, and nothing is set in stone. Also, given the close relationship between the NT Server and Workstation and the speculative nature of the chapter, some server issues are discussed.

Merging with Windows 95 Technologies

It has been interesting to watch the Windows 95 phenomenon. It has had a huge impact on the world and has received more press than any other industry enhancement. On one hand, the operating system has been built to accommodate older, less reliable technology. On the other hand, Windows 95 incorporates some interesting and innovative technologies. Although NT enthusiasts have forgone certain bells and whistles to work in a more stable, truly 32-bit environment, the media hype and flashiness of Windows 95 leave even the most ardent and patient NT advocate a bit green.

However, the relationship between NT and 95 is not parallel; it is symbiotic. Watching the two operating systems grow with each other over time has been fascinating. Fostering this joint evolution is quite a piece of genius on the part of Microsoft. Each operating system was designed with certain goals in mind, vastly different from each other. By taking cues from each other, the two systems have grown and continue to evolve with each other.

The Win32 Application Programming Interface (API) is the fundamental factor in the NT and 95 symbiosis. It provides the link that focuses the joint evolution. An API provides an interface for programmers to create applications that will run in a given environment. Because NT and 95 share a common API, they use the same calls to implement solutions. For example, to show a window on the screen in both NT and 95, an application would use the `ShowWindow()` function. However, the underlying implementation for `ShowWindow()` is different in the two operating systems. Both NT and 95 have different methods for making calls to the video driver and performing the function of painting the window's pixels on the screen, but still the application uses the `ShowWindow()` call to initiate the process on both systems. The result is software that runs on two different systems without having to implement some form of virtual machine or translation module.

From the beginning, certain NT implementations have not been mirrored within 95, and vice versa. Consequently, certain functions within the Win32 API apply only to NT or only to 95. Throughout the NT and 95 evolution, the differences in the feature sets and APIs have been reduced by merging and synchronizing various technologies, thus making the differences more transparent to both programmers and end users. The symbiosis has been occurring throughout the various iterations of NT and occurred throughout the massive Windows 95 beta testing.

Many of the Windows 95 implementations have ended up in version 4 of NT. It took more time to find ways to implement them in the secure NT environment, but slowly the systems are coming together in their feature sets. It will be interesting to see how long 95 remains a supported system as the older hardware is phased out. For a time, the two systems will grow together and promote growth in each other.

Some of the technologies in Windows 95 that have not been incorporated into release 4 of NT are planned for the future. Plug and play, dynamic PCMCIA, power saving features, and Microsoft fax are at the top of the list. The synchronization of the NT and Windows 95 Registry and device drivers is also in the works.

Plug and play is a technology that provides for the dynamic configuration of hardware through software means. With plug and play compliant devices, manual hardware configuration is not necessary. You don't need to set jumpers or use firmware configuration programs to assign interrupt, DMA, or other hardware settings. A centralized software program handles all configuration of plug and play compliant devices.

A particular device's driver is instrumental in the institution of plug and play. In order to institute plug and play within NT, the driver sets must be changed. At the same time, the drivers are synchronized with those in Windows 95. The synchronization removes the need to support two driver sets and cuts back on administrative overhead.

A related topic is the institution of dynamic PCMCIA and power-saving features, two features that will be instrumental for users of portable computers. Currently, PCMCIA devices must be present at boot time to function properly. With dynamic PCMCIA, often referred to as hot-swappable PCMCIA, PCMCIA cards can be removed and inserted while a machine is running. Portable computer users—because of the size restrictions and portability of their machines—often find the need to use several different PCMCIA cards. For example, you could use a network card while at the office, but a modem card on the road. Dynamic PCMCIA gives portable computer users the ability to change devices without having to reboot.

Portable computer users are also concerned with battery life. Future revisions to NT will contain advanced power saving features that will extend the battery life of a machine. With advanced power saving, a machine detects that certain devices are not in use and reduces the amount of power sent to them or cuts the power flow altogether. With extended battery life, the portable computer user will be able to work longer on a single charge and a computer, in general, will use less power resources.

Also planned is the synchronization of the 95 and NT Registries. The Registry is a repository for data. It stores system, user, application, and document configuration information. The Registry provides a common format and interface for configuration information that can be used in a variety of ways. (See Chapter 9, "What Is the Registry?," for more information on the Registry.)

Under the current system, there are variances in the way that the Registry is structured under Windows 95 and NT. Future releases of NT will have a registry that is synchronized with Windows 95's. This will lower administrative overhead and provide for common use of the two registries.

Another Windows 95 feature that is set to be released for NT is Microsoft Fax. Microsoft Fax is fax software that integrates particularly well with both Windows NT and Windows 95. It utilizes the exchange client and can share various address books and modems with other applications. Although it is much sought-after and a fine piece of software, MS Fax—like the medium that it facilitates—is a short term interim technology. There are much better electronic mediums for sending documents.

Traditionally, the fax machine has been used to send hard copy documents and is in paper form (at least on one end). Obviously, resources and trees can be saved by using a solely electronic medium. However, this does bring to mind an issue of which everyone should be cognizant. When should you use hard copy and when should you use an electronic medium? Surely resources can be saved by using the electronic medium, but consider how much information has been saved throughout the years and how many mysteries have been uncovered by reading a shred of paper that has been seemingly discarded.

Connectivity and the Internet/Intranet

Another major shaping force in the evolution of NT is connectivity, especially as it relates to the Internet. Although NT has always been concerned with connectivity issues as they relate to

WAN, LAN, peer-to-peer, dialup, and client/server, the past year has been the year of the Internet and the future will hold more of the same.

> **NOTE**
>
> An intranet is an application of traditional Internet technologies on a given network that is not connected to the Internet. Present security and bandwidth restrictions on the Internet make the intranet an appealing implementation of proven collaborative and information providing technologies. The majority of the issues that apply to the Internet apply to intranets as well. Distinctions will be made between the two when they are particularly relevant. This note is presented because of the timely importance of the intranet. Many people have been paying close attention to the possibilities of the intranet, as well as the Internet, in recent days.

When it became apparent that the Internet was going to play a dominant role in computing sooner rather than later, Microsoft stopped on a dime and turned the company around to embrace and extend the Internet. Microsoft has instituted or plans to institute Internet support in all its applications, to one degree or another. Initial offerings from Redmond didn't hold such promise.

The Internet has been around for close to 30 years. The ARPANET project, from which the Internet sprang, sent its first packets over the phone lines in 1969. The recent beginnings of Internet mania, whose key indicator is media coverage, didn't begin until a year or two ago. It was about this time that Internet support began to be seen in Microsoft's commercial products.

Initial Internet support was scarce. Earlier versions of NT and Windows 95 supported Internet connectivity through the operating system via dialup and TCP/IP support. The implementation was good. However, Microsoft was still backing its own commercial network venture, The Microsoft Network, as the commercial network of choice, and Microsoft Internet software was nonexistent. When early Internet software offerings appeared—for example, the remote mail that accompanied the exchange client—they were still very focused in the traditional Microsoft vision. The software didn't adhere to Internet standards and, frankly, was a slap in the face to Internet tradition.

Since this time, Microsoft has done a complete about-face, and embraced and extended the Internet in many ways. Microsoft's success in the endeavor has been nothing less than amazing. To take a company the size of Microsoft and change its focus to such a degree in such a short period of time and with such success is extraordinary. MS would probably tell you that it is still doing the same things it has always done, but a little differently, and they would be right. However, in modern business terms, it is nothing less than a miracle.

Lately Microsoft has been aggressively producing software that follows Internet guidelines. The Internet is an inclusive entity and, at its heart, calls for support of the lowest common denominator. Microsoft has been working closely with standards committees to ensure that everyone can use the technology that it is distributing. Microsoft has also taken great pains to ensure that if it customizes a solution, the traditional implementation is also supported.

On the Internet, if a technology is in place, it should be there for all people—not just people who can afford to spend hundreds of thousands of dollars on equipment, and not just those who use Microsoft operating systems. Many of the applications MS has introduced on the Internet have been free and have been released in many different languages. Microsoft has ported its applications to several platforms, and it works with others in the industry to see that its technologies can be utilized by all major platforms.

The strategy that Microsoft has employed should not come as a surprise. No other industry is as concerned with self-regulation as the computer industry. Because of Microsoft's huge market share and popularity, the industry has been watching the company with a careful eye. Even the slightest slipup in practices that might hinder competition in the industry is looked at with the utmost scrutiny. Consider what would happen if similar self-regulation was practiced in the beef or petroleum industries. We might have mothers whose milk isn't tainted with insecticides and hormones or energy sources that don't damage the environment. This is not to say that vigilance in self-regulation should not be employed. Perhaps industry vigilance played a big part in Microsoft's contribution to the Internet vision, or perhaps it was a shrewd business move motivated by financial interests.

Whatever the reason, Microsoft has dedicated itself to the carefully guarded Internet vision. Many of the technologies that NT employed before the "Internet mania" were not completely divergent from those employed on the Internet. Because of the recent enthusiasm over the Internet at Microsoft, the NT evolution has been shaped directly by adding Internet features and technologies, as well as indirectly by adding technologies that have been clearly influenced by the Internet vision. It is safe to say that NT and the Internet will be evolving closely together.

An HTML-based administration console employing ActiveX technologies is planned for NT. Hypertext Markup Language (HTML) is the dominant language of the World Wide Web and is the underlying code that makes up a Web page. ActiveX technologies are heavily OLE-influenced Microsoft protocols that make the Internet interactive. By combining the two into an administrative tool for NT, users can utilize the flexibility and multiplatform functionality of the Web and perform administrative functions on NT machines. At the time of this writing, the Web Administration Tool beta 1 is available.

The Web Administration Utility is predominantly a server and network administrator concern, but it is important to mention. It is reflective of the growing trend blurring the barriers between the Internet and the local machine. The evolution of NT and that of Microsoft's other products will be geared toward harnessing the power of the workstation while taking advantage of the connectivity provided by a highly distributed computing environment.

Along the same lines, an Internet file-sharing standard is being developed by Microsoft and others in the industry. The Common Internet File System protocol (CIFS) is based on similar technologies already utilized in the file-sharing systems of Windows 95 and Windows NT. The CIFS system is designed to provide remote access to files over the Internet and is compatible with existing systems. CIFS has multiplatform implementations and will allow users of different types of systems in different locations to collaborate and share files over the Internet through the traditional file access methods of their native applications. As of this writing, Microsoft has submitted the CIFS 1.0 protocol specification to the Internet Engineering Task Force (IETF) as an Internet-Draft document. The protocol is published and available for public inspection.

Because of the strong focus of the Internet as a dominant network medium in NT, the differences between the Internet and other network protocols will become less apparent. The differences in the ways the various network protocols are dealt with by the end user are becoming and will become more subtle.

Nashville and the Cairo Object Vision

Paralleling the increasing connectivity in hardware in NT is the integration of software and the blurring of the line (at least to the end user) where hardware ends and software begins. Perhaps it is more appropriate to liken the aforementioned blurring to subtle brush strokes on a canvas, because the Cairo object vision in NT's future focuses on the object at hand more than on the hardware medium and software infrastructure that allow it to function.

At the heart of the Cairo vision is the Nashville shell and universal browsing. The Nashville shell is a strongly Internet-influenced user interface, and will be available for both Windows 95 and Windows NT sometime next year. The Nashville shell was originally referred to as Sweeper or the Active Internet Platform (AIP). It is powered by OLE, ActiveX technologies that provide for a high degree of software integration. Nashville is a browsing type of interface similar to the Internet Explorer, and it enables you to browse any object that you have access to— whether it is a local, LAN, WAN, Internet, intranet, or application resource. Coupled with the long-awaited object file systems, NT Object Filing System (NTOFS) and NT Distributed Filing System (NTDFS), Nashville is a highly object-oriented interface. It provides the ability to navigate through and work with objects, while the location and method by which an object is stored is as transparent as the end user desires.

> **NOTE**
>
> As of this writing, there is speculation that the Nashville universal browsing system will evolve first as an Internet Explorer 4.0 release, rather than as a separate shell option.

The beginning implementations of Nashville are already at work in NT as the Internet Explorer 3.0. In the current version of Internet Explorer, you can browse a directory structure on an Internet FTP site or even on your local drives. Figure 26.1 shows the Internet Explorer version 3.0 browsing a hard disk.

FIGURE 26.1.

The Internet Explorer browses a directory on a hard disk.

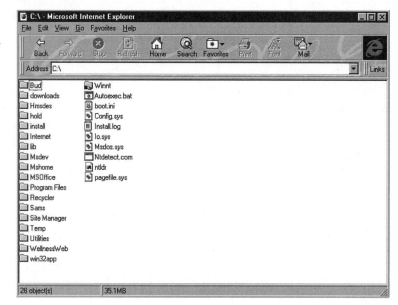

You can extend the scenario a little further to encompass the current OLE document container technologies. This too can be found in present implementations of the Internet Explorer. Figures 26.2 and 26.3 show a link to an MS Word document and the result when the link is navigated.

Notice in Figure 26.3 that all the standard buttons and menus from Microsoft Word have been integrated into the browser menu. From here, all editing can be done, just as if the native application is open in its own window. If changes to the document are made and you press the forward or backward browser button, you are prompted with a dialog box to save changes. This holds true for any application adhering to the OLE standards. Also, viewers are available for all Microsoft Office products for free download from http://www.microsoft.com. Therefore, if you want to disseminate information in a given format, the intended readers do not have to own the parent application. Most likely, the Nashville shell will come with a suite of viewers.

Although it is closely related but not strictly an NT issue, Microsoft Office 97 is under development, with enhancements that strongly reinforce the idea of universal browsing. Office 97 will have full HTML support and provide the capabilities for creating hyperlinks within native

Office documents. Also, in Office 97, Schedule Plus will be replaced with Outlook. Outlook helps to manage schedules and contact lists, and it performs many group and document management tasks. It will also have Nashville-like file navigation tools, as shown in Figure 26.4.

FIGURE 26.2.

A link to a Word document.

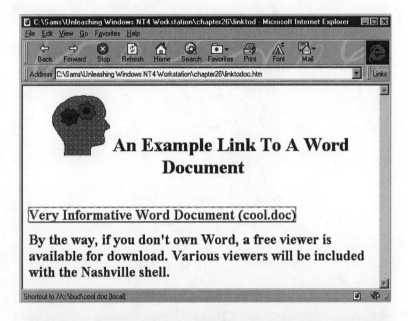

FIGURE 26.3.

A Word document open in a Web browser.

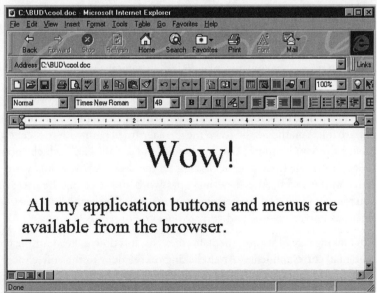

FIGURE 26.4.

The new Outlook for Office 97.

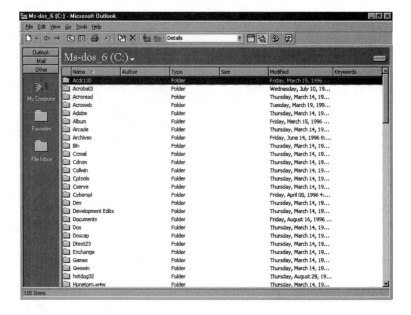

Nashville combines Internet Explorer, OLE, ActiveX enabled document containers and controls, an object-based file system, and a highly integrated office solution into a single universal browsing entity. The possibilities of what a system of this nature can bring to the desktop are intriguing. Imagine turning on your computer, logging on to your network or the Internet, and being taken immediately to your own personally designed home page. When the page is displayed, you hear a voice wishing you a good morning, afternoon, or evening, depending on the time of day. It then says, "Choose a direction."

You then see a screen of your own design, depicting a small three-dimensional Virtual Reality Markup Language (VRML) village covering the majority of the screen, with a network OLE, Internet-fed stock ticker and news feed scrolling along the bottom of the page. You notice that a stock you have been following has made a dramatic change and you must transfer some funds at the bank. You then walk down the virtual garden path with the scenery scrolling past you—leaving the My Computer icon and heading toward the bank, which you have so skillfully made to look like Fort Knox. Upon clicking on the door of Fort Knox, your financial software appears on the screen. After entering a password and selecting the necessary security protocols, you transfer funds to the necessary accounts. You choose the Back button on the browser, your financial software closes, and you are outside Fort Knox.

After taking care of your immediate concerns, it is time to head for the coffeehouse to catch up on e-mail correspondence. After clicking on the door to the coffeehouse, you slide the mouse forward and enter the coffeehouse, where you are presented with several paintings on the walls, which are the icons you have placed there as your coffeehouse tasks. You click on the e-mail painting and chuckle to yourself as you walk into the kitchen to get a cup of coffee while the e-mail is downloading. Returning with java in hand, you begin to do your e-mail routine, when a blinking window on the screen informs you that your project partner is attempting to contact you.

You accept the call. A voice comes over the computer's speaker, wishing you well and making a joke about why you are up so early. You both laugh because your business partner is an early riser on the West coast and you tend to rise late in the East. As you discuss the current project you are working on, a simulated chalkboard pops up with the new revisions to the project plan. You make a few checkmarks with the mouse, and your partner okays them, says goodbye, and leaves. You close the communication window and save a copy of the chalkboard for later review. After finishing with business correspondence—leaving the personal correspondence for after work hours, of course—you click on the painting of the newspaper on the coffeehouse wall. You are presented with a list of the trade publications and Usenet groups of your choice. After catching up on the latest breaking news in the trades, you click on the coffeehouse door to exit.

Once again, you find yourself in the village. You click on the overhead view button of the VRML add-in of your Web browser to get an overhead view of the village. You are on your way to work at the other end of town, so it is easier to fly than walk. Pushing the mouse forward over the village-scape, you see the rooftop of your office, which you have so cleverly denoted with the Internet smiley face emoticon. You chuckle, click on the rooftop, and go to work.

What Else Is in Store?

A few other issues warrant mentioning when discussing the future of NT. These issues aren't as colorful as the possibilities of universal browsing in 3-D, but they lend themselves to the power of functionality that makes NT a stable workhorse.

NT Server has come under much scrutiny because of its lack of directory services. Although it is a server issue, this is noteworthy because it has been the largest criticism in deploying NT. It was thought by many that, because of the lack of directory services, NT couldn't be deployed in large, multiplatform, multiuser, mission-critical environments. NT proponents argue that the domain/workgroup environment provides adequate structure for large operations, claiming that the Internet uses similar conventions and manages to function well in a multiuser environment.

In fact, NT has been instituted and deployed in larger environments with success, but regardless of the level of success, there is always room for improvement. As part of the Cairo evolution, NT Server will have comprehensive, integrated directory services. The new directory services will provide for a single point of administration for all resources—including files, peripheral devices, host connections, databases, Web access, and users. The directory server will have

Internet-compatible naming services, and it will support the lightweight directory access protocol (LDAP) as well as X.500 standards, including directory access protocol (DAP), directory system protocol (DSP), and directory information shadowing protocol (DISP). Some of the key features in the planned directory services are Internet universality, distributed security, multimaster replication, and scalability supporting up to 10 million objects per domain, with unlimited domains.

Another issue of importance for enterprise computing is the planned 64-bit addressing. The standard 32-bit addressing schema is adequate for most business applications. However, applications such as some large databases can benefit from a 64-bit addressing schema. The planned schema would allow for very large units of data to be mapped to a 64-bit addressed location.

Issues of this nature go hand in hand with the increased use of NT as an engineering platform. High-end engineering applications are beginning to be seen for NT, and the trend appears to be gaining speed. The engineering field continues to be dominated by UNIX-driven technologies, but the cost-effectiveness of being able to run NT on many platforms and on less expensive hardware, coupled with the powerful Windows desktop tools, makes NT an appealing alternative.

Summary

Whatever the use, NT has the power, combined with usability. This, along with connectivity, seems to be the pervading theme in release 4 of NT and will continue to be in the future. Traditionally, extreme power in computing meant that a solution probably wasn't much fun to use. Likewise, a solution that was user-friendly probably lacked the teeth to get any serious work done. NT shatters this illusion.

NT follows a principal of elegance in simplicity. It maintains a sound logic and stability while avoiding adding features for their own sake. At the same time, a pleasant and efficient graphical interface provides for ease of use and low overhead in administering the raw power of NT's multithreaded, multiprocessor capabilities. As NT grows—taking cues internally and from the multiplatform, multicultural environment of the Internet—it will take its logic, power, and elegance in simplicity to an increasingly connected, integrated, and therefore, object-focused computing world.

VIII
PART

IN THIS PART

Appendixes

Windows NT TCP/IP: Supported Standards

by Sean Mathias

Table A.1 gives a list of the Request for Comments (RFC) supported by the TCP/IP implementation in Windows NT 4 Workstation. RFCs are ongoing documentation efforts, proposals, and generally accepted standards in the TCP/IP community. Final versions of RFCs are approved and published by the Internet Engineering Task Force (IETF) but are always open for improvements, suggestions, and revisions. An index of current and past RFCs is available at this address:

```
http://ds.internic.net/ds/rfc-index.html
```

Table A.1. The supported standards and RFC compliance for Windows NT 4 Workstation.

RFC	Title
768	User Datagram Protocol (UDP)
783	Trivial File Transfer Protocol (TFTP)
791	Internet Protocol (IP)
792	Internet Control Message Protocol (ICMP)
793	Transmission Control Protocol (TCP)
816	Fault Isolation and Recovery
826	Address Resolution Protocol (ARP)
854	Telnet Protocol (TELNET)
862	Echo Protocol (ECHO)
863	Discard Protocol (DISCARD)
864	Character Generator Protocol (CHARGEN)
865	Quote of the Day Protocol (QUOTE)
867	Daytime Protocol (DAYTIME)
894	IP over Ethernet
919, 922	IP Broadcast Datagrams (broadcasting with subnets)
950	Internet Standard Subnetting Procedure
959	File Transfer Protocol (FTP)
1001, 1002	NetBIOS Service Protocols
1034, 1035	Domain Name System (DNS)
1042	IP over Token Ring
1055	Transmission of IP over Serial Lines (IP-SLIP)
1112	Internet Group Management Protocol (IGMP)
1122, 1123	Host Requirements (communications and applications)
1134	Point-to-Point Protocol (PPP)

RFC	Title
1144	Compressing TCP/IP Headers for Low-Speed Serial Links
1157	Simple Network Management Protocol (SNMP)
1179	Line Printer Daemon Protocol
1188	IP over FDDI
1191	Path MTU Discovery
1201	IP over ARCNET
1231	IEEE 802.5 Token Ring MIB (MIB-II)
1332	PPP Internet Protocol Control Protocol (IPCP)
1334	PPP Authentication Protocols
1518	An Architecture for IP Address Allocation with CIDR
1519	Classless Inter-Domain Routing (CIDR): An Address Assignment and Aggregation Strategy
1533	DHCP Options and BOOTP Vendor Extensions
1534	Interoperation Between DHCP and BOOTP
1541	Dynamic Host Configuration Protocol (DHCP)
1542	Clarifications and Extensions for the Bootstrap Protocol
1547	Requirements for Point-to-Point Protocol (PPP)
1548	Point-to-Point Protocol (PPP)
1549	PPP in High-level Data Link Control (HDLC) Framing
1552	PPP Internetwork Packet Exchange Control Protocol (IPXCP)
1553	IPX Header Compression
1570	Link Control Protocol (LCP) Extensions

A

WINDOWS NT
TCP/IP

Definitions for Peer Web Services Logging

by Sean Mathias

This appendix gives a listing of the various fields that comprise the `inetlog` table, which is used to log Peer Web Services activity in Windows NT 4 Workstation. Table B.1 lists each field in the table, the data type that is recorded for the field, and a description of what this field represents.

Table B.1. Field values and descriptions for the `inetlog` table.

Field Name	Data Type (Size)	Description
ClientHost	varchar(255)	This is the IP address of the remote client.
username	varchar(255)	This is the user name of the remote user (if provided). Most often this will be NULL or anonymous.
LogTime	datetime	The date and time the action or activity was executed.
service	varchar(255)	This is the service that the remote client was accessing: W3SVC, MSFTPSVC, or GopherSvc.
machine	varchar(255)	The machine name of the Internet server being accessed (local machine).
serverip	varchar(50)	The IP address of the server being accessed.
processingtime	int	The amount of time it took to process the request (in milliseconds).
bytesrecvd	int	The number of bytes received from the remote client for this operation.
bytessent	int	The number of bytes sent to the remote client for this operation.
servicestatus	int	An internal Windows NT status for the service.
win32status	int	The status of the Win32 subsystem.
operation	varchar(255)	The operation requested by the user or performed by the server.
target	varchar(255)	The target of the operation.
parameters	varchar(255)	The parameters passed with the requested operation.

I

INDEX

Symbols

2-D graphics
DirectDraw, 364-393
clippers, 391-393
components, 366-369
creating surfaces, 372
defined, 365-366
display mode setup,
370-371
GettingStarted demo,
373-378
hardware, 366
IDirectDraw object, 367
IDirectDraw2 object, 367
IDirectDrawClipper, 369
IDirectDrawPalette, 368
IDirectDrawSurface, 368
IDirectDrawSurface2, 368
initialization, 370-371
palettes, 386-391
SAMS demo application,
372
surfaces, 378-386
3-D graphics
Direct3D, 365
OpenGL, 393-414
animation, 406-408
auxilary library,
410-413
cleanup, 398
creating, 395-398
creating RGB palette,
397-399
defined, 394-395
display lists, 404-406
pixel format setup,
396-397
utility library, 408-410
viewing, 399-404
16-bit Windows applica-
tions, porting, 354
32-bit memory manage-
ment, 337

486 emulation for RISC
systems, 334
4mm DAT tape drives,
186, 530
64-bit addressing, 616
8mm tape drives, 530

A

/a option, 540
/A switch, 78
accessibility functions,
95-96
Accessibility Options
applet, 9, 87-96, 297-300
accessibility functions,
95-96
FilterKeys function, 91-93
MouseKeys functions,
94-95
setting keyboard
options, 297
setting mouse options,
299-300
setting sound options, 298
Sounds functions, 94
StickyKeys function, 91
ToggleKeys function, 93
turning functions
on/off, 90
accessing
Control Panel, 84-85
Printer folder, 147
Task Manager, 197
Accessories folder, 8
Account policies, 323-324
Account Policy dialog
box, 323
accounts
Administrator, 316-317
Guest, 316-317
active partitions, 553
Adapter dialog box,
139-140

adapters, network
configuring networks,
467-468
installing, 419-420
Adapters page (Network
dialog box), 467-468
Adapters tab, trouble-
shooting networking
problems, 591
Add Form Feed option, 104
Add Printer icon, 595
Add Printer Wizard,
147, 201
Add to Chart dialog
box, 237
Add/Remove dialog
box, 97
Add/Remove Programs
applet, 10, 87, 97-98
installing applications,
97-99
removing applications,
97-99
AddAttachedSurface
methods, 368
AddOverlayDirtyRect
methods, 368
addresses
Microsoft Sales Informa-
tion Center, 96
see also IP addresses
administering Remote
Access Service (RAS)
permissions, 320
administrative alerts
administrative, 167, 169
system crashes, 182
Administrative Tools,
224-252
Disk Administrator,
224-232
Event Viewer, 232-236
logs, 233-236

S

X-Z

GET CONNECTED
to the ultimate source of computer information!

The MCP Forum on CompuServe

Go online with the world's leading computer book publisher!
Macmillan Computer Publishing offers everything
you need for computer success!

Find the books that are right for you!
A complete online catalog, plus sample
chapters and tables of contents give
you an in-depth look at all our books.
The best way to shop or browse!

➤ Get fast answers and technical support for
MCP books and software

➤ Join discussion groups on major computer
subjects

➤ Interact with our expert authors via e-mail
and conferences

➤ Download software from our immense
library:

  ▷ Source code from books
  ▷ Demos of hot software
  ▷ The best shareware and freeware
  ▷ Graphics files

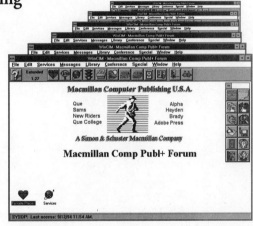

Join now and get a free CompuServe Starter Kit!

To receive your free CompuServe Intro-
ductory Membership, call **1-800-848-
8199** and ask for representative #597.

The Starter Kit includes:
➤ Personal ID number and password
➤ $15 credit on the system
➤ Subscription to *CompuServe Magazine*

Once on the CompuServe System, type:

GO MACMILLAN

for the most computer information anywhere!

MACMILLAN
COMPUTER
PUBLISHING

CompuServe

A VIACOM SERVICE

The Information SuperLibrary™

Bookstore	**Search**	**What's New**	**Reference**	**Software**	**Newsletter**	**Company Overviews**
Yellow Pages	**Internet Starter Kit**	**HTML Workshop**	**Win a Free T-Shirt!**	**Macmillan Computer Publishing**	**Site Map**	**Talk to Us**

CHECK OUT THE BOOKS IN THIS LIBRARY.

You'll find thousands of shareware files and over 1600 computer books designed for both technowizards and technophobes. You can browse through 700 sample chapters, get the latest news on the Net, and find just about anything using our massive search directories.

All Macmillan Computer Publishing books are available at your local bookstore.

We're open 24-hours a day, 365 days a year.

You don't need a card.

We don't charge fines.

And you can be as **LOUD** as you want.

The Information SuperLibrary
http://www.mcp.com/mcp/   ftp.mcp.com

Copyright © 1996, Macmillan Computer Publishing-USA, A Simon & Schuster Company

Peter Norton's Complete Guide to Windows NT 4 Workstation

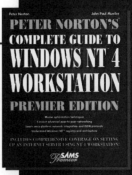

—Peter Norton

This book explores everything from interface issues to advanced topics such as client/server networking, building your own Internet server, and OLE. Readers will master complex memory management techniques. Explores peer-to-peer networking.

$39.99 USA/$56.95 CDN *User level: Casual — Accomplished*

ISBN: 0-672-30901-7 *936 pp.*

Windows NT 4 Server Unleashed

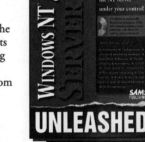

—Jason Garms

The Windows NT server has been gaining tremendous market share over Novell, and the new upgrade—which includes a Windows 95 interface—is sure to add momentum to its market drive. To that end, *Windows NT 4.0 Server Unleashed* is written for that growing market. It provides information on disk and file management, integrated networking, BackOffice integration, and TCP/IP protocols. The CD-ROM includes source code from the book and valuable utilities. Focuses on using Windows NT as an Internet server. Covers security issues and Macintosh support.

$59.99 USA/$84.95 CDN *User level: Accomplished — Expert*

ISBN: 0-672-30933-5 *1,100 pp.*

Windows NT 4 Web Development

—Sanjaya Hettihewa

Windows NT and Microsoft's newly developed Internet Information Server are making it easier and more cost-effective to set up, manage, and administer a good Web site. Because the Windows NT environment is relatively new, there are few books on the market that adequately discusses its full potential. *Windows NT 4 Web Development* addresses that potential by providing information on all key aspects of server setup, maintenance, design, and implementation. The CD-ROM contains valuable source code and powerful utilities. Teaches how to incorporate new technologies into your Web site. Covers Java, JavaScript, Internet Studio, and Visual Basic Script.

$59.99 USA/$84.95 CDN *User level: Accomplished — Expert*

ISBN: 1-57521-089-4 *744 pp.*

Programming Windows NT 4 Unleashed

—David Hamilton, Mickey Williams, and Griffith Kadnier

This book gives you a clear understanding of the modes of operation and architecture for Windows NT. Execution models, processes, threads, DLLs, memory, controls, security, and more are covered with precise detail. The CD-ROM contains source code and completed sample programs from the book. Teaches OLE, DDE, Drag and Drop, OCX development, and the component gallery. Explores Microsoft BackOffice programming.

$59.99 USA/$84.95 CDN *User level: Accomplished – Expert*

ISBN: 0-672-30905-X *1,200 pp.*

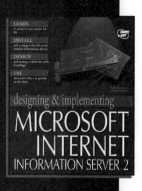

Designing and Implementing Microsoft Internet Information Server 2

—Arthur Knowles and Sanjaya Hettihewa

This book details the specific tasks involved in setting up and running a Microsoft Internet Information Server. Readers will learn troubleshooting, network design, security, and cross-platform integration procedures. Teaches security issues and how to maintain an efficient, secure network. Readers learn everything from planning to implementation.

$39.99 USA/$56.95 CDN   *User level: Casual – Expert*

ISBN: 1-57521-168-8   *336 pp.*

Microsoft Internet Information Server 2 Unleashed

—Arthur Knowles, et al.

The power of the Microsoft Internet Information Server 2 is meticulously detailed in this 800 page volume. Readers will learn how to create and maintain a Web server, integrate IIS with BackOffice, and create interactive databases that can be used on the Internet or a corporate intranet. Readers learn how to set up and run IIS. Teaches advanced security techniques and how to configure the server. CD-ROM includes source code from the book and powerful utilities.

$49.99 USA/$70.95 CDN   *User level: Accomplished – Expert*

ISBN: 1-57521-109-2   *800 pp.*

Microsoft Exchange Server Survival Guide

—Pete McPhedran—Aurora Communications Exchange

Readers will learn the difference between Exchange and other groupware such as Lotus Notes. This book also covers everything about the Exchange Server, including trouble-shooting, development, and how to interact with other BackOffice components. Includes everything operators need to run an Exchange server. Teaches how to prepare, plan, and install the Exchange server. Explores ways to migrate from other mail apps such as Microsoft Mail and CC:Mail.

$49.99 USA/$70.95 CDN   *User level: New – Advanced*

ISBN: 0-672-30890-8   *800 pp.*

Microsoft BackOffice 2 Administrator's Survival Guide, Second Edition

—Arthur Knowles

This all-in-one reference describes how to make the components of BackOffice version 2 work best together and with other networks. BackOffice is Microsoft's complete reference for networking, database, and system management products. Contains the fundamental concepts required for daily maintenance, troubleshooting, and problem solving. The CD-ROM includes product demos, commercial and shareware utilities, and technical notes from Microsoft vendor technical support personnel. Covers Version 2.0

$59.99 USA/$84.95 CDN   *User level: Accomplished*

ISBN: 0-672-30977-7   *1,200 pp.*

Add to Your Sams Library Today with the Best Books for Programming, Operating Systems, and New Technologies

The easiest way to order is to pick up the phone and call

1-800-428-5331

between 9:00 a.m. and 5:00 p.m. EST.
For faster service please have your credit card available.

ISBN	Quantity	Description of Item	Unit Cost	Total Cost
0-672-30901-7		Peter Norton's Complete Guide to Windows NT 4 Workstation (Book/CD-ROM)	$39.99	
0-672-30933-5		Windows NT 4 Server Unleashed (Book/CD-ROM)	$59.99	
1-57521-089-4		Windows NT 4 Web Development (Book/CD-ROM)	$59.99	
0-672-30905-X		Programming Windows NT 4 Unleashed (Book/CD-ROM)	$59.99	
1-57521-168-8		Designing and Implementing Microsoft Internet Information Server 2	$39.99	
1-57521-109-2		Microsoft Internet Information Server 2 Unleashed (Book/CD-ROM)	$49.99	
0-672-30890-8		Microsoft Exchange Server Survival Guide (Book/CD-ROM)	$49.99	
0-672-30977-7		Microsoft BackOffice 2 Administrator's Survival Guide, Second Edition (Book/CD-ROM)	$59.99	
		Shipping and Handling: See information below.		
		TOTAL		

❏ 3 ½" Disk

❏ 5 ¼" Disk

Shipping and Handling: $4.00 for the first book, and $1.75 for each additional book. Floppy disk: add $1.75 for shipping and handling. If you need to have it NOW, we can ship pro[...] to you in 24 hours for an additional charge of approximately $18.00, and you will receive your item overnight or in tw[...] [...] $8.00 for up to three disks. Prices subject to change. Call [...]

201 W. 103rd Street, [...]

1-800-428-5331 — Orders   1-800-835-32[...]

B38 907 297 9

What's on the CD-ROM

The companion CD-ROM contains software developed by the authors, plus an assortment of third-party tools and product demos. The disc is designed to be explored using a CD-ROM Menu program. Using the Menu program, you can view information concerning products and companies, and you can install programs with a single click of the mouse. To run the Menu program, follow these steps.

Windows 3.1 and Windows NT Installation Instructions

1. Insert the CD-ROM into your CD-ROM drive.
2. From File Manager or Program Manager, choose Run from the File menu.
3. Type *drive*\setup and press Enter, where *drive* corresponds to the drive letter of your CD-ROM. For example, if your CD-ROM is drive D:, type D:\SETUP and press Enter.

Windows 95 Installation Instructions

1. Insert the CD-ROM into your CD-ROM drive.
2. If Windows 95 is installed on your computer and you have the Autoplay feature enabled, the Menu program starts automatically whenever you insert the disc into your CD-ROM drive.
3. If Autoplay is not enabled, use Explorer to choose Setup from the CD drive.

NOTE

For best results, set your monitor to display between 256 and 64,000 colors. A screen resolution of 640×480 pixels is also recommended. If necessary, adjust your monitor settings before using the CD-ROM.